Volcano Instability on the Earth and Other Planets

Geological Society Special Publications
Series Editor A. J. FLEET

GEOLOGICAL SOCIETY SPECIAL PUBLICATION NO. 110

Volcano Instability on the Earth and Other Planets

EDITED BY

W. J. McGUIRE
Cheltenham & Gloucester College of Higher Education, UK
and University College London, UK

A. P. JONES
University College London, UK

AND

J. NEUBERG
University of Leeds, UK

1996

Published by

The Geological Society

London

THE GEOLOGICAL SOCIETY

The Society was founded in 1807 as The Geological Society of London and is the oldest geological society in the world. It received its Royal Charter in 1825 for the purpose of 'investigating the mineral structure of the Earth'. The Society is Britain's national society for geology with a membership of around 8000. It has countrywide coverage and approximately 1000 members reside overseas. The Society is responsible for all aspects of the geological sciences including professional matters. The Society has its own publishing house, which produces the Society's international journals, books and maps, and which acts as the European distributor for publications of the American Association of Petroleum Geologists, SEPM and the Geological Society of America.

Fellowship is open to those holding a recognized honours degree in geology or cognate subject and who have at least two years' relevant postgraduate experience, or who have not less than six years' relevant experience in geology or a cognate subject. A Fellow who has not less than five years' relevant postgraduate experience in the practice of geology may apply for validation and, subject to approval, may be able to use the designatory letters C Geol (Chartered Geologist).

Further information about the Society is available from the Membership Manager, The Geological Society, Burlington House, Piccadilly, London W1V 0JU, UK. The Society is a Registered Charity, No. 210161.

Published by The Geological Society from:
The Geological Society Publishing House
Unit 7
Brassmill Enterprise Centre
Brassmill Lane
Bath BA1 3JN
UK
(*Orders*: Tel. 01225 445046
          Fax 01225 442836)

First published 1996

The publishers make no representation, express or implied, with regard to the accuracy of the information contained in this book and cannot accept any legal responsibility for any error or omission that may be made.

British Library Cataloguing in Publication Data
A catalogue record for this book is available from the British Library.

ISBN 1-897799-60-8

Typeset by Aarontype Ltd, Unit 47, Easton Business Centre, Felix Road, Bristol BS5 0HE, UK

Printed in Great Britain by
The Alden Press, Osney Mead
Oxford, UK

Distributors

USA
  AAPG Bookstore
  PO Box 979
  Tulsa
  OK 74101-0979
  USA
  (*Orders*: Tel. (918) 584-2555
            Fax (918) 584-0469)

Australia
  Australian Mineral Foundation
  63 Conyngham Street
  Glenside
  South Australia 5065
  Australia
  (*Orders*: Tel. (08) 379-0444
            Fax (08) 379-4634)

India
  Affiliated East-West Press PVT Ltd
  G-1/16 Ansari Road
  New Delhi 110 002
  India
  (*Orders*: Tel. (11) 327-9113
            Fax (11) 326-0538)

Japan
  Kanda Book Trading Co.
  Tanikawa Building
  3-2 Kanda Surugadai
  Chiyoda-Ku
  Tokyo 101
  Japan
  (*Orders*: Tel. (03) 3255-3497
            Fax (03) 3255-3495)

Contents

Preface

This volume addresses the growing interest in destabilized and collapsing volcanoes which followed the spectacular landslide and climatic eruption at Mount St Helens in May 1980. Since this event, edifice collapse has been recognized at numerous volcanoes, both currently active and within the geological record, and the phenomenon is now recognized as constituting a normal occurrence within the life-cycles of all types of volcano.

The curiosity of the scientific community with regard to collapsing volcanoes is far from being purely academic, and is driven also by an awareness that such events constitute volcanogenic hazards of catastrophic potential. In this context, the Mount St Helens collapse can be viewed as a minor event three orders of magnitude smaller, for example, than the giant collapses which have occurred along the flanks of the Hawaiian Island volcanoes during the Quaternary and earlier. The threat posed by such events, both locally and regionally, and in some cases globally, require that a high level of research is maintained into volcano destabilization and structural failure.

This volume contains a collection of 26 papers, which together form a representative cross-section of contemporary research into volcano instability, both on Earth, and other 'terrestrial' bodies in the solar system. Papers have been broadly grouped, with the first two summarising contemporary issues and addressing the development of volcano instability in the Solar System. The following five papers focus upon the different ways in which a volcanic edifice may be destabilized and experience structural failure, while the succeeding four examine instability monitoring and hazard implications. The bulk of the volume (12 papers in all) is devoted to the description and discussion of instability-related processes and products at specific volcanoes or volcanic regions, both submarine, subaerial, and on Mars and Venus, while the final paper examines instabilities within the plumbing system of Stromboli volcano.

The volume stems from a conference that was held in May 1994 to debate and discuss the phenomenon of volcano instability. The conference was jointly convened by the Volcanic Studies Group of the Geological Society and the Joint Association for Geophysics of the Geological and Royal Astronomical Societies. The great success of the conference, and the compilation of this Special Publication reflect the help and support of many people. Specifically, I would like to acknowledge the conscientious contribution of numerous referees who ensured the high quality of the accepted papers, and the hard work of my co-editors Adrian Jones and Jurgen Neuberg. The staff of the Geological Society Publishing House and Burlington House are also sincerely thanked for their contributions. In particular, Sydney Barton is acknowledged for ensuring that the conference ran especially smoothly. Steve Saunders is thanked for demonstrating his projectionist skills, while the contributions of Jane Moss, Ashley Morrell, and Rachel Coninx on the registration desk are also greatly appreciated.

Bill McGuire
Cheltenham, December 1995

Volcano instability: a review of contemporary themes

W. J. McGUIRE

*Department of Geography & Geology, Cheltenham and Gloucester College of
Higher Education, Francis Close Hall, Swindon Road, Cheltenham GL50 4AZ
and Department of Geological Sciences, University College London, Gower Street,
London WC1E 6BT, UK*

Abstract: Active volcanoes are revealed to be dynamically evolving structures, the growth
and development of which are characteristically punctuated by episodes of instability and
subsequent structural failure. Edifice instability typically occurs in response to one or more
of a range of agencies, including magma emplacement, the overloading or oversteepening of
slopes, and peripheral erosion. Similarly, structural failure of a destabilized volcano may
occur in response to a number of triggers of which seismogenic (e.g tectonic or volcanic
earthquakes) or magmagenic (e.g. pore-pressure changes due to magma intrusion) are
common. Edifice failure and consequent debris avalanche formation appears to occur, on
average, at least four times a century, and similar behaviour is now known to have occurred
at volcanoes on Mars and Venus. Realization of the potential scale of structural failures and
associated eruptive activity has major implications for the development of monitoring and
hazard mitigation strategies at susceptible volcanoes, which must now address the possibility
of future collapse events which may be ten times greater than that which occurred at Mount
St Helens in 1980.

Since the spectacular landslide which triggered
the climactic eruption of Mount St Helens during
May 1980 (Lipman & Mullineaux 1981), considerable attention has been focused upon the
unstable nature of volcanic edifices, and their
tendency to experience structural failure. This
behaviour is now recognized as ubiquitous, with
evidence for edifice collapse identified both
within the geological record and at many
currently active volcanoes (Siebert 1984; Ui
1983). Francis (1994) notes, for example, that
75% of Andean volcanic cones with heights in
excess of 2500 m have experienced collapse, while
Inokuchi (1988) reports that over 100 debris
avalanche deposits have been identified around
Japanese Quaternary volcanoes. The potential
hazard presented by such behaviour is stressed
by Siebert (1992) who estimates that structural
failure of volcanic edifices has occurred four
times per century over the last 500 years. This
may in fact be an underestimate, with three
major sector collapses occurring this century in
the Kurile–Kamchatka region alone (Belousov
1994), and avalanche-produced cirques evident
on 22 Kamchatkan volcanoes (Leonov 1995).
Advanced submarine imaging techniques have
also shed light on the frequency of collapse at
island and coastal volcanoes, with extensive
debris avalanche and associated deposits identified on the sea floor adjacent to the Hawaiian
volcanoes (eg, Fornari & Campbell 1987; Moore
et al. 1994; Garcia this volume), Piton de la
Fournaise (Réunion Island) (Lénat *et al.* 1989;

Labazuy this volume), Martinique (Semet &
Boudon 1994), Stromboli (Kokelaar & Romagnoli 1995), Augustine Island (Begét & Kienle
1992), and the Canary Island volcanoes (Holcomb & Searle 1991; Carracedo 1994, this
volume; Weaver *et al.* 1994) amongst others.
Imagery gathered using the Viking, and more
recently Magellan, spacecraft, has also revealed
that volcano instability is not confined to the
Earth, with considerable evidence supporting
edifice failure in volcanic terrains accumulated
for both Mars (Cave *et al.* 1994; Robinson &
Rowland 1994; Crumpler *et al.* this volume;
Head this volume) and Venus (Guest *et al.* 1992;
Bulmer & Guest this volume; Head this volume).
Such phenomena are proving particularly significant in permitting the effects of such factors as
variations in gravity and atmospheric pressure
on the incidence of edifice failure and the
formation and transport of debris avalanches.

Volcano instability can be defined as the
condition within which a volcanic edifice has
been destabilized to a degree sufficient to increase the likelihood of the structural failure of
all or part of the edifice. Failure may occur in
response to active deformation or may result
over a long period of time due to oversteepening,
overloading, or peripheral erosion. Failure surfaces and post-failure mass transport may be
predominantly vertical, as in the formation of
collapse pits and calderas, or may incorporate a
significant horizontal vector as in dome disintegration, sector collapse, or lateral edifice

From McGuire, W. J., Jones, A. P. & Neuberg, J. (eds) 1996, *Volcano Instability on the Earth and Other Planets*,
Geological Society Special Publication No. 110, pp. 1–23.

spreading. These latter phenomena have constituted a particular focus for recent, 'post-Mount St Helens' research, and a review of these studies forms the basis of this paper, which seeks to address topical themes in the study of instability- and failure-related phenomena both on the Earth and other bodies in the solar system. No attempt is made here to address problems associated with collapse-caldera formation, which is largely driven by excess buoyancy of the magma in large reservoirs. Discussion of the structure and formation of collapse calderas and caldera-like structures is, however, included in a number of papers elsewhere in this volume (De Rita *et al.*; Marti *et al.*; Crumpler *et al.*) Here, emphasis is placed on the factors responsible for the development of edifice instability in active volcanic terrains, and the triggers which lead to destabilization and failure involving a significant lateral component. Consideration is also given to the hazards posed by volcano instability and collapse at all scales, and attention is paid to the problems involved both in forecasting failure events and mitigating their effects.

Generating structural instability and failure in volcanic terrains

Growing volcanoes may become unstable and experience failure at any scale (Fig. 1), from relatively minor rock falls, with volumes of a few hundred to a few thousand cubic metres, occurring along caldera rims and other steep slopes (e.g. Rowland & Munro 1992; McGuire *et al.* 1991, 1993; Munro & Rowland 1994), to

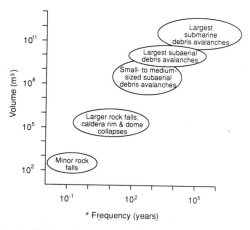

Fig. 1. Volume–frequency plot illustrating the range of scales and repeat-times displayed by collapse events in active volcanic terrains.

the giant megaslides involving volumes in excess of $5000 \, km^3$ generated around large ocean-island volcanoes (e.g. Moore *et al.* 1994; Carracedo 1994). Whereas low-volume collapse events probably occur at one active volcano or another every few weeks or less, the largest events have repeat times of tens to hundreds of thousands of years (Fig. 1). The causes of instability and failure are manifold (Fig. 2), with some volcanoes having a far greater potential for failure than others. Generally speaking, major structural failure is confined to the larger edifices, with small monogenetic cones and shields only experiencing small-scale slumping and sliding. Massive structural instability is only characteristic of major polygenetic volcanoes. These may be located on continental (e.g. Etna in Sicily, Rainier in the Cascade range, and Colima in Mexico) or oceanic (e.g. Mauna Loa and Kilauea on Hawaii, Piton de la Fournaise on Réunion Island, and Martinique in the Caribbean) crust, and on other planetary bodies (e.g. Olympus Mons on Mars). Instability and failure appear to be frequently induced in large, basaltic shield volcanoes, despite low slope angles and homogeneous structure. Here rifting, associated with persistent dyke emplacement constitutes a major contributory factor in the progressive development of instability, with local seismicity, changes in edifice pore pressures, and environmental factors, such as large, rapid changes in sea level, all constituting potential failure triggers. In marine settings, instability may be increased due to edifice spreading along weak horizons of oceanic sediment (Nakamura 1980) or in response to seaward-creeping masses of olivine cumulate (Clague & Denlinger 1994).

Large polygenetic edifices developed on continental crust are particularly prone to failure, although the scale of the collapse events in these environments rarely matches those recognized at their oceanic counterparts. Continental edifices are typically stratovolcanoes composed of mechanically unsound materials which are often superimposed in such a manner (e.g. alternating lava flows and weak pyroclastic layers), and weakened by hydrothermal alteration, so as to reduce the strength of the edifice as a whole. The potential for instability and structural failure is compounded by steep slopes and high precipitation rates commonly associated with elevated relief, which may contribute to changes in edifice pore pressures.

The development of instability and the potential for failure is enhanced at all types of volcano by the fact that actively growing edifices experience continuous changes in morphology, with the endogenetic (by intrusion) and

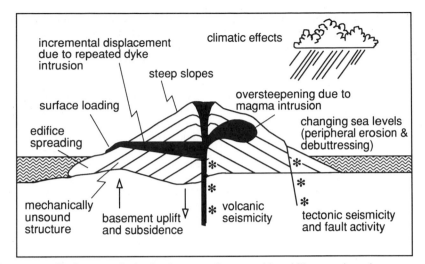

Fig. 2. Factors contributing towards the development of structural instability at active volcanoes.

exogenetic (by extrusion) addition of material leading, characteristically, to oversteepening and overloading at the surface. The behaviour of the sub-volcanic basement is also important, with both subsidence and uplift beneath the volcano having the potential to decrease edifice stability. Furthermore, the growth of a volcanic edifice on a sloping or weak (e.g. clay-rich) substrate, strongly favours the development of lateral spreading with all that this entails for the evolution of instability both within and below the edifice. Determination of the relative importance of the above factors, both in general terms, and for specific volcanoes, is crucial to any assessment of edifice instability and the potential for failure.

Although magma often has a role to play, the single, linking, contributory factor, in both the development of instability and in the initiation of structural failure, is gravity. Not only does this directly influence the edifice stress regime in such a manner as to favour increasing destabilization as edifices grow larger through time, and phenomena such as oversteepening and overloading become more prevalent, but it also provides the energy for the post-failure transport of the detached material. This applies equally well to edifice-growth driven lateral collapse events, due for example to persistent rifting, and to the creation of vertical collapse calderas in response to plumbing-system related instabilities such as magma-reservoir inflation, or eruption-related reservoir evacuation.

Destabilization of all or part of a volcanic edifice may be achieved over a period of weeks to months, or may develop over thousands or

tens of thousands of years. Rapid-onset instability is usually the result of a discrete event, such as the emplacement of the dacite cryptodome at Mount St Helens between March and May 1980, which generated over 100 m of lateral surface displacement in little over a month (Fig. 3a) (Christiansen & Peterson 1981). In contrast, slow, progressive destabilization is typically incremental, and often results from the cumulative effects of numerous small events. These may take the form of successive eruptions leading to the gradual loading of a steep slope by accumulating eruptive products (e.g. Murray & Voight this volume), or, as at Kilauea (Swanson et al. 1976) and Etna (McGuire et al. 1990, 1991) (Fig. 3b) may be represented by persistent dyke emplacement along rift systems causing increased flank destabilization due to progressive lateral displacement.

If the appropriate conditions are maintained, then slow, progressive destabilization may be cyclic. At Augustine volcano (Alaska) for example, edifice failure is followed by a period of reconstructive dome-growth which persists until oversteepening causes another failure and the cycle begins again. Begét & Kienle (1992) recognize at least eleven major debris avalanches at Augustine, separated by an average time interval of only 150–200 years. Such a short repeat time for edifice failure is unusual, and emphasises the very real threat to the local settlements around the Cook Inlet from volcanogenic tsunamis. Normally edifice-destabilization cycles are of much longer duration. At Colima (Mexico) for example, recurrent collapses appear to occur every few thousand years

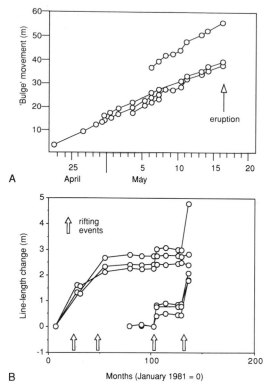

A

B

Months (January 1981 = 0)

Fig. 3. (**a**) Rapid-onset instability is illustrated with reference to the growth of a dacite cryptodome beneath the northern flank of Mount St Helens prior to structural failure and eruption on 18 May 1980. Between late April and this date, ground deformation monitoring revealed over 30 m of lateral growth of the surface bulge which developed above the cryptodome (from McClelland *et al.* 1989). (**b**) At Etna, a sector of the 1 km high cliff wall bordering the Valle del Bove flank collapse is being progressively displaced by repeated dyke-induced rifting. Since 1981, four rifting events have resulted in line-length increases totalling almost 5 m in a ground deformation network.

(Komorowski *et al.* 1994), while the giant flank collapses of the Hawaiian volcanoes have a repeat time of the order of 25–100 Ka (Lipman *et al.* 1988).

Triggering edifice failure

Structural failure – the common outcome of edifice instability – may, like the attainment of instability itself, take place over a range of time-scales, although it often takes the form of a near-instantaneous, catastrophic event. The eventual failure at Mount St Helens, for example,

occurred in a matter of seconds in response to the seismogenic ground accelerations which led to the detachment of the northern flank and the succeeding generation of a catastrophic debris avalanche. In some situations, however, deformation following structural failure may occur in a complex manner over a long period of time, and involve little in the way of rapid mass-movement. At Etna, for example, a large sector of the eastern flank has become detached from the remainder of the volcano, and has been sliding slowly seawards under gravity for at least tens of thousands of years (e.g. Kieffer 1985; Borgia *et al.* 1992; McGuire & Saunders 1993; Stewart *et al.* 1993; Firth *et al.* Montalto *et al.* Rasa *et al.* and Rust & Neri all this volume).

The slow, long-term, slumping under gravity of the eastern flank of Etna, and similar phenomena, do not require a discrete, instantaneous failure event to initiate movement, nor is any high velocity transportation of a large mass of material involved. Both phenomena do, however, occur during formation of debris avalanches, and the mechanisms involved are considered here. Once a block of volcanic terrain has become destabilised, due to one or other of the conditions outlined in the previous section, it becomes susceptible to failure in response to one or more of a number of 'internal' or 'external' triggers. The former are dominantly related to the extrusion or intrusion of fresh magma. Magma reservoir replenishment, the filling of open conduits, and dyke emplacement, all have the potential to trigger structural failure due to causing changes in pore pressure (Elsworth & Voight; Day; both this volume) or the over-steepening of surface slopes (Murray & Voight this volume), while extrusion of additional material onto an already heavily loaded slope may also initiate failure and collapse. Other internal triggers include strong volcanogenic earthquakes, and displacements associated with long-term edifice spreading. Many external triggers reflect the dynamic geological settings in which volcanoes are commonly located, and include basement fault movement and related tectonic seismicity. Environmental factors may also be important, with both precipitation (on a short time-scale) and changing sea levels (on a longer time-scale) having the potential to initiate structural failure by affecting pore pressures in the edifice.

As previously mentioned, the role of magma intrusion is typically paramount in triggering structural failure occurring during eruption. This may occur in response to a critical, destabilising change in edifice morphology, as in the Mount St Helens case, or may result from other less obvious effects. In particular, Voight & Elsworth (1992) and Elsworth & Voight (this volume) have drawn attention to the potential role of dykes in triggering structural failure as a consequence of their raising pore pressures by means of mechanical and/or thermal straining.

The role of water in structural failure

There is increasing evidence that water plays an important role in the destabilization and mechanical failure of volcanic edifices, and in determining the manner in which the failed mass behaves. Not only does hydrothermal alteration often play a major part in increasing susceptibility to failure (Siebert et al. 1987), but the common association of lateral collapse events with phreatic explosions (e.g. at Bandai-san, Japan, in 1888) supports a significant involvement by hydrothermal pore fluids in the failure process. Day (this volume) proposes that this results from a reduction in rock strength in response to the generation of pore pressures which are a large fraction of, or even higher, than contemporary confining pressures. As mentioned in the previous section, this situation may arise due to the heating effects associated with the intrusion of fresh bodies of magma (Voight & Elsworth 1992; Elsworth & Voight this volume). Additionally, Day proposes that similar conditions may result from intrusion degassing, the discharge of pressurised fluids from depth via clastic dykes, or by faulting-associated deformation and pore collapse.

Once structural failure has been initiated, water may also have a role to play in determining the behaviour of the collapsing mass, and in particular whether the event is aborted or proceeds to form a debris avalanche. The islands of La Palma and El Hierro (Carracedo 1994, this volume) in the Canary Islands, for example, provide excellent evidence for major, rift-related, flank failure, but also two examples of lateral collapse events which appear to have been aborted during the early stages of sliding. On the western side of the Cumbre Vieja ridge at La Palma, eruptive activity during 1949 was accompanied by the opening of a concave-downslope fracture system some 4 km in length. The vertical displacement on the fracture amounts to only a few metres, and testifies to a seaward-sliding event which was aborted immediately following initial failure.

On the neighbouring island of El Hierro, a similar event appears to have taken place, forming the San Andres fault system (J. C. Carracedo & S. J. Day pers. comm.) although

here over 300 m of vertical displacement occurred prior to cessation of deformation. The faults of this aborted collapse are well exposed and are characterised by dry fault breccias and ultra-cataclasites, rather than the extremely fluidised gouge muds and mud-rich breccias encountered in exhumed collapses elsewhere in the Canary islands (Day this volume and pers. comm.). It is possible that this lack of pressurised fluids on the faults, and a consequent lack of significant slip weakening (Rubey & Hubbert 1959; Rice 1992) or of brecciation of the collapsing slump blocks by gouge dykes (Day this volume) may have caused fault movement to cease without debris avalanche generation. This evidence from the Canaries permits the possibility of reinterpreting large flank slumps, such as those of Kilauea, as aborted collapse events which might have generated major debris avalanches if conditions had been more appropriate to the generation of high pore pressures, either in the fault zones or within the slump blocks as a whole, and thus to sustained slumping and slump-block disaggregation (Elsworth & Voight this volume; Day this volume).

Post-failure mass transport and emplacement

Structural failure in volcanic terrains inevitably involves the downslope, gravity-driven, mass-transfer of material from the source to an area of deposition. In cases of relatively minor rock-falls and slumps, the distances involved may amount to only a few tens or hundreds of metres, whereas at the other end of the scale, gigantic debris avalanches may be transported to distances of several hundred kilometres (Stoopes & Sheridan 1992; Moore et al. 1994). Table 1 summarizes the more important parameters of some of the longer, larger volume, volcanogenic debris avalanches. Depending upon a number of factors, including the nature of the failed material and the underlying terrain, and the precise failure mechanism, the transported mass may travel in a largely coherent manner or may become totally disrupted. Transport velocities may vary enormously, from over $100 \, m \, s^{-1}$ where failure has been catastrophic, to as little as $1–2 \, cm \, a^{-1}$ where displacement of the detached mass involves creep-like behaviour. Structural failure may be confined solely to the volcano, or may involve the underlying basement, with consequences, in the latter case, for the composition of the deposits formed.

Table 1. *Volumes and runout distances of selected subaerial volcanic debris avalanches*

Volcano	Deposit	Volume (km^3)	Runout (km)
Nevado di Colima		22–33	120
Socompa		17	35
Volcán de Colima		6–12	43
Shasta		26	50
Popocatapetl		28	33
Chimborazo	Riobamba	8.1	35
Mawenzi		7.1	60
Akagi	Nashikizawa	4	19
Galunggung		2.9	25
Mount St Helens	1980	2.5	24
Fuji	Gotenba	1.8	24
Shiveluch	1964	1.5	12
Bandai-san	1888	1.5	11
Egmont	Pungarehu	0.35	31
Unzen	1792	0.34	6.5
Asakusa	Migisawa	0.04	6.5

Data from Hayashi & Self (1992), Stoopes & Sheridan (1992), and Wadge *et al.* (in press).

Inevitably, the downslope removal of material during the failure process leaves voids in the source area. Where large-scale, catastrophic failure has take place, these commonly take the form of near parallel-sided amphitheatre-like depressions which open downslope (Siebert 1984) and which are typically surrounded, or partly bounded, by steep walls which may be in excess of a kilometre in height, although more complex forms also occur. Less spectacular events of an effectively instantaneous nature may leave small collapse scars, for example along the margins of actively growing domes or unstable caldera rims. Where failure-related transport is a slower, longer-term process, the area between the mobile, detached block and the remainder of the edifice is typically marked by incipient or open fractures or by active fault systems. Although the more impressive morphological features associated with catastrophic failure may remain extant and easily recognisable for a considerable period of time, those associated with less-rapidly operating mechanisms may be difficult to discern, and the recognition and nature of the displacement may require the use of ground deformation monitoring techniques.

Because catastrophic failure events are commonly associated with eruptive or intrusive activity, the deposits they produce often reveal a wide range of lithological and sedimentological characteristics (Ui 1989). The generation of 'dry' avalanches (Ui 1983), in the absence of accompanying volcanic activity, typically produces deposits made up of more or less disrupted volcanic material with or without a basement contribution. Where fresh magma is involved, either in triggering the collapse or due to post-failure unroofing and decompression of a shallow reservoir, juvenile material may be present in the form of chilled lava fragments which may show evidence of a plastic nature during transport. Such material is reported by Wadge *et al.* (in press) in the 7000 years BP Socompa debris avalanche deposit (Chile), where the occurrence of fresh, glassy lava blocks of dacitic composition is interpreted in terms of the extrusion of lava during the collapse event. Where structural failure triggers a major decompressive eruption, as during the May 1980 event at Mount St Helens (Fig. 4), base-surge and pyroclastic flow formation closely follows the generation of the debris avalanche, and deposits of these magma-rich events may be mixed with or overlie the more lithic-dominated avalanche material.

A volcanic 'dry' avalanche deposit has been defined by Ui (1983, p. 135) as a 'volcaniclastic deposit formed as a result of large-scale sector collapse of a volcanic cone associated with some form of volcanic activity'. This is, however, an unnecessarily restrictive definition as it implies that deposits formed by similar mass-removal events at volcanoes which are not associated with volcanic activity are somehow different. A more appropriate definition may be that

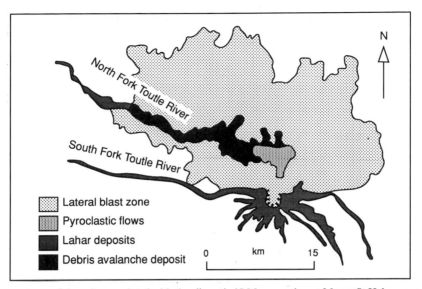

Fig. 4. The spectrum of deposits associated with the climactic 18 May eruption at Mount St Helens reveals how a major structural failure event can trigger a wide range of potentially hazardous eruption-related phenomena including pyroclastic flows, lahars, and atmospheric blast (after Lipman & Mullineaux, 1981).

proposed by McGuire (1995, p. 88), which defines volcanic 'dry' avalanche deposits as 'having been formed by the large-scale collapse of a volcanic edifice, or part thereof, in the absence of significant amounts of water'.

In many cases, however, the avalanches formed during catastrophic edifice failure are far from 'dry'. Available water from saturated volcaniclastic sequences, from snow and ice fields, or from surface water bodies commonly becomes entrained into the avalanching mass causing a progressive transition from dry debris avalanche to debris flow or debris-laden flood (broadly termed lahars when generated in volcanic environments) (Fig. 4). Large volumes of surface water are not, however, essential to transform a debris avalanche into a debris flow. According to Fairchild (1987), the water source for the North Fork lahars at Mount St Helens was finely comminuted ice incorporated within the avalanche deposit during collapse. Lahar formation here is attributed to liquefaction of the water saturated debris avalanche due to harmonic tremor associated with the post-collapse eruption.

Large debris avalanche deposits formed by structural failure display a number of common morphological and fabric-related features (Fig. 5). The surfaces of such deposits are typically hummocky in form, reflecting the underlying presence of relatively undisturbed megablocks and megablock 'nests' which may have dimensions in excess of a kilometre. The

topographic lows coincide with the more disrupted and finer-grained material, and succumb rapidly to post-depositional modification in which slumping and water channelling have a tendency to fill-in the lows and produce a planar surface from which the megablocks protrude. Marginal levées are a common morphological feature, and have been described from the 1792 avalanche deposits at Unzen volcano, Japan (Ui 1983), from Mount St Helens (Voight et al. 1981, 1983), and from Volcán Socompa in Chile (Wadge et al. in press).

Internally, dry, volcanic debris avalanche deposits typically have a bimodal fabric consisting of block and matrix facies (Crandell et al. 1984). Block dimensions may range from metres to hundreds of metres, and represent fragments of volcanic material together with entrained debris. Blocks are characteristically strongly fractured and broken, but individual pieces are often only in close proximity, resulting in the formation of an interlocking 'jig-saw' texture. This fabric argues against turbulent flow during emplacement, and for the transport of giant megablocks in a coherent manner. As might be expected, both the frequency and size of megablocks fall with increasing distance from the source, corresponding to a complementary rise in the matrix proportion (Mimura & Kawachi 1981). At both Mount St Helens (Glicken 1991) and Mount Shasta (Crandell 1989) in the United States, and at Nevado de Colima in Mexico (Stoopes & Sheridan 1992), debris-avalanche

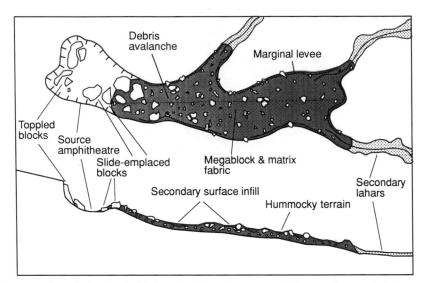

Fig. 5. Anatomy of a typical volcanic debris avalanche and source amphitheatre. Characteristic features include a region of relatively coherent blocks emplaced by toppling or sliding in the vicinity of the collapse source; a bimodal megablock and matrix facies; hummocky terrain commonly bounded by marginal levées; and the development of secondary lahars. Source amphitheatres may be in excess of 10 km across, while associated subaerial volcanogenic debris avalanche deposits may be over 100 km long. Megablocks may be over 1 km across and marginal levées may reach heights of over 100 m.

blocks are rare in distal locations, and the deposits are dominated by the poorly-sorted, pulverised matrix of angular clasts. Commonly, these clasts consist of centimetre- to decimetre-sized, lithic fragments of volcanic material, although soil and other components may have been entrained during transport. Evidence from the Socompa debris avalanche deposit in Chile (Francis & Self 1987), and from other volcanoes indicates that the spatial distribution of clast types reflects the original stratigraphy of the collapsing mass. This supports observations which reveal that debris avalanche emplacement involves laminar rather than turbulent flow.

As previously mentioned, where water is present, debris avalanche deposits often grade downslope into debris flows, the deposits of which may be distinguished on the basis of sedimentological differences. Such a transition is observed both at Mount St Helens and at Mount Shasta (Crandell 1989). Typically, megablocks are absent in debris flow deposits derived from debris avalanches, and the fabric is similar to that of the matrix facies of the latter. Reverse grading may be present, while stratification and cross-bedding may reflect hyperconcentrated flow during the waning stages of emplacement.

The role of persistent rifting

Siebert (1984), in his global review of the occurrence of volcanogenic debris avalanches, drew attention to the fact that structural collapse was more common at edifices characterised by the existence of parallel dyke swarms. This link, which supports the role of persistent, dyke-induced rifting as one of the major causes of edifice destabilization and failure, is clearly illustrated by the orientations of the long axes of flank collapse scars relative to adjacent dyke zones. At Stromboli (Tibaldi et al. 1994; Tibaldi this volume) and La Palma (Canary Islands) (Carracedo 1994, this volume) for example, these are oriented normal to a single dominant dyke zone (Fig. 6a and b), whereas at Etna (Fig. 6c) (McGuire & Pullen 1989; McGuire et al. 1993), Piton de la Fournaise (Réunion Island) (Duffield et al. 1982), and El Hierro (Canary Islands) (Fig. 6d) (Carracedo 1994, and this volume), sector collapses bisect the angles formed by two intersecting zones of persistent dyking. Where repeated dyke emplacement along a preferential path has taken place over a long period of time (e.g. 10^4 years or more), accumulated erupted and intruded products typically result in the growth of a pronounced topographic ridge overlying the rift zone. Due to

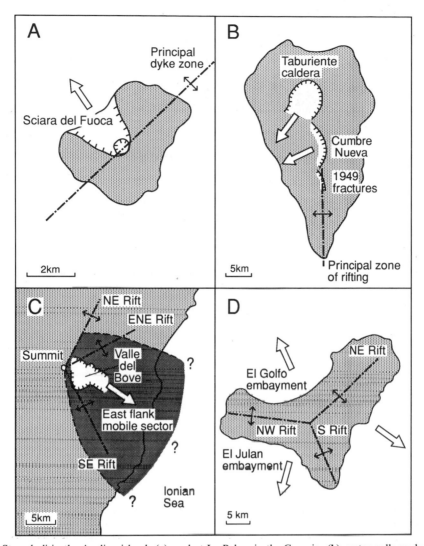

Fig. 6. At Stromboli in the Aeolian islands (**a**), and at La Palma in the Canaries (**b**), sector collapse has occurred in a direction normal to a single, principal zone of dyke emplacement. Contrastingly, at Etna in Sicily (**c**), and at El Hierro in the Canary Islands (**d**) sectors of flank mobility and collapse are bounded by two intersecting rift zones. In both scenarios, instability develops over a long period of time in response to incremental dyke-induced lateral displacements, and stresses are eventually relieved by edifice failure. Double-ended arrows show directions of dyke-related extension; larger single-ended arrows indicate directions of collapse.

oversteepening and loading effects, this structure tends to become less stable over time, and more susceptible to failure in response to single destabilizing events such as an earthquake (volcanogenic or otherwise), or dyking event. As previously mentioned, in the latter case a slope at the limit of its stability may be induced to slide by the mechanically, and especially, the thermally generated increases in pore-fluid pressure which accompany the emplacement of the magma (Voight & Elsworth 1992; Elsworth & Voight this volume). Pore-pressures generated in this way may reduce frictional resistance to failure by lowering the effective stresses on available basal failure planes, permitting failure and collapse even on the low angle flanks of shield volcanoes.

Due to the manner in which dyke orientations at shallow depths are controlled by a gravitational stress regime which is a reflection of the edifice morphology (McGuire & Pullen 1989), the existence of large sector collapse structures,

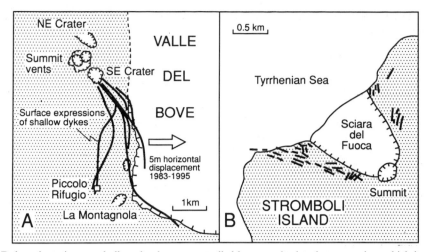

Fig. 7. Dyke orientations at shallow depths are controlled by a gravitational stress regime which is a reflection of the edifice morphology. The existence of large sector-collapse structures, which occurred in response to dyke-induced rifting, may in turn, therefore, control the disposition of post-collapse zones of persistent rifting. This behaviour is illustrated by the orientation of post-lateral collapse dykes at both Etna (**a**) and Stromboli (**b**) (after Tibaldi this volume). At Etna, dyke paths on the upper flanks are constrained to parallel the 1 km high western rim of the Valle del Bove sector collapse. This has the dual effect of channeling magma towards the major tourist base on the volcano, while at the same time laterally displacing (by almost 5 m in 12 years) a 2 km long block of the Valle del Bove rim.

which occurred in response to dyke-induced rifting, may in turn control the disposition of post-collapse zones of persistent rifting, and therefore the locations and directions of subsequent collapses. This behaviour is illustrated by the orientation of post-lateral collapse dykes at both Etna (Fig. 7a) (McGuire *et al.* 1990, 1991) and Stromboli (Fig. 7b) (Tibaldi *et al.* 1994; Tibaldi this volume). In the former case, dyke paths on the upper southern and eastern flanks of the volcano are constrained to follow a route which parallels the 1 km high western rim of the Valle del Bove sector collapse (Fig. 7a). Not only is this effect channeling magma towards the major tourist base on the volcano, but four dyke-induced rifting events over the past 12 years have led to the 5 m lateral displacement of a 2 km long block of the Valle del Bove rim (Fig. 3b), and a consequent increase in slope instability in this part of the volcano.

In addition to essentially vertical dykes, subhorizontal sheet intrusions (sills) have also been suggested to have a destabilising role. In particular, Adushkin *et al.* (1995) and Delemen (1995) have proposed that the emplacement of such a magma body at the unstable Klyuchevskoi volcano in Kamchatka may be sufficient to trigger future edifice failure resulting in a debris avalanche with a volume of 4–8 km^3.

Lateral edifice growth

Recent papers have highlighted a number of different ways in which volcanic edifices can become destabilized and experience failure during lateral edifice growth. Two contrasting mechanisms involve (i) relatively deep gravitational spreading along basal thrusts, due to their increasing mass, of volcanic structures such as those constituting the Hawaiian Islands (e.g. Nakamura 1980; Dieterich 1988; Borgia 1994; Clague & Denlinger 1994), and the Concepción and Maderas volcanoes in Nicaragua (van Wyk de Vries & Borgia, this volume), and (ii) shallow gravitational sliding of sectors of volcanoes due to oversteepening, peripheral erosion, basement slope or tilting, or a combination of these and other factors (e.g. Kieffer 1985; Lo Giudice & Rasa 1992; Stewart *et al.* 1993; Ancochea *et al.* 1994; Carracedo 1994; Tibaldi *et al.* 1994; Carracedo; Day; Firth *et al.*; Montalto *et al.*; Rasa *et al.*; Rust & Neri; Tibaldi; all this volume). Both mechanisms lead to lateral edifice growth which may contribute towards greater edifice instability. The manner in which the terms gravitational spreading and gravitational sliding are often used synonymously when applied to volcanic edifices, illustrates that the differences between the two mechanisms have not been clearly defined. Although, as the terminology indicates, gravity has a major role to play in both types of behaviour, this role is not identical and does not lead to the formation of the same phenomena.

Here, it is proposed that the term volcanic spreading should not be used in a genetic manner, and should be confined simply to describing the phenomenon of lateral edifice enlargement. Mechanisms by which spreading is accomplished can then be summarized as gravitational sliding, gravitational thrusting, or edifice collapse. Each mechanism may furthermore be described as being radial, where the entire circumferance of the edifice is involved, or sector, where spreading involves only part of the edifice. Using this classification, the form of spreading proposed for Kilauea would be described as sector thrusting, and that for Etna, as sector sliding. Other forms of spreading include radial thrusting at Mombacho (Nicaragua), radial collapse at Augustine Island (Alaska), and sector collapse at numerous volcanoes.

Within the proposed classification scheme, gravitational thrusting is reserved for the process whereby a volcanic edifice, and/or its substrate, spreads along basal thrusts entirely

due to the loading effect of the edifice itself. Manifestations of this type of behaviour are well summarized in Borgia (1994) and in van Wyk de Vries & Borgia (this volume), and include (Fig. 8a) peripheral compressive structures such as thrust-fault propagation folds, within the volcano and/or its substrate, together with tension-related features on the upper flanks. Characteristically, the substrate is depressed due to the volcanic load, and spreading is accomplished at least partly by means of outward and upward displacements along thrust faults. Effective gravitational thrusting requires either edifice growth directly on incompetent, deformable, sediments such as clays or evaporites, or at least that a similar weak layer be present within the sub-volcanic sequences although not immediately underlying the volcanic pile (van Wyk de Vries & Borgia this volume). Where such a substrate is not present, thrust-related deformation is either minimal or absent. Recently it has been suggested (Dieterich 1988) that for the Hawaiian volcanoes even a combination of a considerable volcanic load and a weak substrate is insufficient to maintain the observed thrusting behaviour and its associated geophysical phenomena. Clague & Denlinger

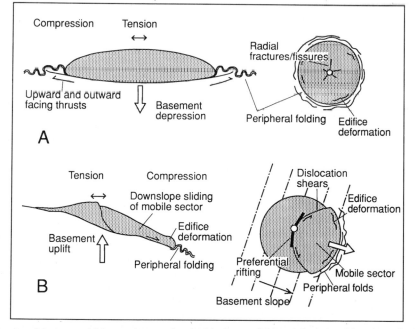

Fig. 8. Structural features which may be associated with the gravitational thrusting (**a**) and gravitational sliding (**b**) of volcanic edifices. The former occurs on an initially horizontal substrate and is characterized by basement depression and the formation of upward- and outward-facing thrusts. The latter requires a tilted basement and typically results in the detachment of a mobile sector of the edifice on the downslope side. Both phenomena are characterized by tensional conditions in the summit region and by peripheral deformation.

(1994) have, in response, proposed a new model in which thrusting is enforced by the seaward movement of dense masses of olivine cumulate material. This model highlights the potential importance of mineral rheology in generating and maintaining instability at active volcanoes. In addition to a role for olivine, weak, easily deformable layers of plagioclase-rich material may also potentially play a part in edifice spreading at some volcanoes by providing surfaces along which detachment and movement may occur.

Contrastingly, although the load of the volcanic edifice plays a part in the initiation of gravitational sliding, it is the form of the underlying substrate which provides the appropriate conditions. While the load-driven spreading mechanism is initiated on a flat substrate, which thereafter becomes downwarped, gravity-controlled sliding requires the development of an asymmetrical sloping surface beneath the edifice, which may, as at Etna, result from differential uplift beneath the volcanic pile (Fig. 8b). As with the thrusting mechanism, the sliding of large sectors of volcanic edifices along a sloping basement typically takes place at centimetric annual rates, but displacements occur along a decollement (or series thereof) which slopes downwards. Further similarities with gravitational thrusting involve the requirement for a ductile sub-volcanic horizon, the development of tensional conditions in the upper levels of the edifice and the potential for generating peripheral compressional features. In gravitational sliding, the long axis of the mobile sector of the volcano is typically oriented parallel to the slope of the underlying substrate, and is separated from the remainder of the edifice by faults or fault zones characterized by significant strike-slip components.

While convincing cases for the operation of gravitational thrusting have been made for the Hawaiian volcanoes, and a number of other smaller edifices (van Wyk de Vries & Borgia this volume), the mechanism has also been proposed, less credibly, to attempt to explain the unstable and mobile nature of the eastern flank of the Etna volcano (Borgia et al. 1992; Borgia 1994). Here, however, a combination of generally shallow seismicity (Lo Giudice & Rasa 1992; Montalto et al. this volume) and the common occurrence of creep-related surface ruptures (Rasa et al. this volume), argue strongly for gravitational sliding of the eastern sector of the edifice over a clay-smeared substrate which is downfaulted seaward and continues to be uplifted at an average annual rate of 0.8 to $1.4\,\text{mm}\,\text{a}^{-1}$ (Stewart et al. 1993; Firth et al. this volume).

Instability and failure at island and coastal volcanoes

Many of the largest landslides resulting from instability and structural failure are located adjacent to the margins of island and coastal volcanoes. All the Hawaiian volcanoes, for example, are surrounded by submarine aprons of allochthonous volcanic material emplaced by sliding or slumping (Moore et al. 1989, 1994), which may grade into volcanic turbidites (Garcia & Hull 1994; Garcia this volume). Similar deposits have been recognized around many marine volcanoes, using techniques such as sea-beam bathymetry and high-resolution side-scan sonar imaging, including Piton des Neiges and Piton de la Fournaise (Réunion Island) (Rousset et al. 1987; Lenat et al. 1989; Labazuy this volume), Piton du Carbet (Martinique) (Semet & Boudon 1994), the Marquesas volcanoes (Barsczus et al. 1992; Filmer et al. 1992), Tristan de Cunha (Holcomb & Searle 1991), the Galapagos Islands (Chadwick et al. 1992), the Canary Islands (Holcomb & Searle 1991; Weaver et al. 1994), Stromboli and Alicudi (Aeolian Islands) (Romagnoli & Tibaldi 1994), and at Augustine Island (Alaska) (Begét & Kienle 1992). The sizes of deposits are enormously variable although Holcomb & Searle (1991) report that many single landslides affecting oceanic volcanoes may have been sufficiently large as to involve the transport of up to 20% of the edifice volume. Some of the Hawaiian landslides have volumes greater than $5000\,\text{km}^3$ and lengths in excess of $200\,\text{km}$ making them the largest such structures recorded on Earth (Moore et al. 1994).

The common occurrence of aprons of destabilised material around marine volcanoes is to be expected for a number of reasons. Most significantly, the seaward-facing flank of any volcano located at the land–sea interface is inevitably the least buttressed. This applies both to coastal volcanoes such as Etna, where the topography becomes increasingly elevated inland, and to island volcanoes such as Hawaii where younger centres (such as Kilauea) are buttressed on the landward side by older edifices (e.g. Mauna Loa). The morphological asymmetry resulting from this effect leads to the preferential release of accumulated intra-edifice stresses, due for example to surface-overloading or to repeated dyke-emplacement, in a seaward direction (Fig. 9). This stress release may take the form of the slow displacement of large sectors of the edifice in the form of giant slumps, of co-seismic downfaulting, or of the episodic production of debris avalanches, or a combination of all three. The relatively unstable nature

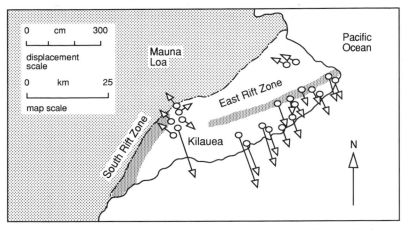

Fig. 9. Repeated dyke emplacement along the Southern and East Rift Zones of Kilauea leads to preferential and progressive seaward movement of the southern flank of the volcano. Horizontal surface displacements between 1958 and 1970 (after Swanson *et al.* 1976) total over 2 m at some locations.

of the seaward-facing flanks of any volcano is further enforced by the dynamic nature of the land–sea contact. Not only does marine erosion provide a constant destabilizing agent, but large changes in global sea levels of up to 130 m, occurring over periods as short as 18 000 years, with catastrophic rises recently identified of 11.5 m in <160 ± 50 years (Blanchon & Shaw 1995), offer the means of modifying internal stress regimes and water pore pressures in favour of edifice destabilization.

The Hawaiian Ridge, extending from near Midway Island to Hawaii, provides by far the most impressive evidence for volcano instability and collapse in the marine environment. Following a cooperative submarine survey by the United States Geological Survey and the UK Institute of Oceanographic Sciences, using the GLORIA side-scan sonar system, 68 landslides with lengths in excess of 20 km have been identified. In a comprehensive review of landslide generation along the Hawaiian Ridge, Moore *et al.* (1994) highlight a number of characteristic features which are likely to be generally applicable to the destabilization and collapse of marine volcanoes. Although occurring throughout the lifetimes of the volcanoes, the largest landslides occurred when the centres were young and unstable, were close to their maximum size, and when seismic activity was at a high level. The authors differentiate slumps from debris avalanches and report the existence of intermediate forms. Slumping and avalanching can therefore be viewed as end-members of a continuous sequence of emplacement mechanisms which is probably applicable to large-scale

mass-wasting processes at all volcanoes located in marine environments. The two mechanisms are not mutually exclusive, with debris avalanches often forming from the disaggregation of oversteepened or overpressured slumps, or from injection of pore fluids or gouge muds from the lower regions of slumps into the upper layers, which may then disintegrate (Day this volume).

Moore *et al.* (1994) draw attention to both the different characteristics and the alternative mechanisms responsible for the emplacement of the Hawaiian slumps and debris avalanches. While the former are typically both wide (sometimes over 100 km) and thick (up to 10 km), the latter are long (up to 230 km) and relatively thin (0.5–2 km). The authors explain that the slumps are deeply rooted in the edifice and may be bounded by rift zones on their landward side, and by the edifice-substrate interface at their base. Movement is typically slow and creep-like, although evidence for major co-seismic displacements are recorded on the active Hilina slump of Kilauea (Lipman *et al.* 1985). In contrast, the debris avalanche features reported by Moore *et al.* (1994) include well-defined amphitheatres in their source regions, hummocky terrain with megablocks up to 2 km across, and evidence for uphill transport on the Hawaiian Arch submarine ridge, implying high emplacement velocities. From the range of features described from the Hawaiian Ridge, it becomes apparent that the term 'landslide', which has common usage in describing the products of seaward mass-movement at coastal and island volcanoes, is not wholly appropriate. Strictly-speaking this term is best confined to describing the rapidly emplaced debris avalanche deposits, rather than the relatively slow-moving slump blocks.

The results of the extensive submarine surveys conducted around the Hawaiian volcanoes have highlighted the important role of large-scale edifice destabilization and collapse in constraining the morphological and structural evolution of marine volcanoes. Any chosen point in the lifecycle of such an edifice represents a 'snapshot' of a continuing conflict between constructive forces represented by endogenous and exogenous growth during, respectively, intrusive and extrusive activity, and destructive influences dominated by mass-wasting due to slumping, avalanching, and other erosive mechanisms. As suggested by Fornari & Campbell (1987), these latter phenomena may actually act in concert in the long term to restabilize the edifice by widening its base.

Although it is now apparent that many, if not all, coastal and island volcanoes are characterized by adjacent allochthonous materials deposited in the submarine environment, the source-region of the transported material often remains enigmatic. This is particularly the case in very active volcanic terrains or in areas of high sedimentation where collapse scars may be rapidly obscured. Determination of the source of collapse is important in order to resolve whether failure has occurred below sea level or subaerially. At Kilauea, the back-walls of at least some of the slump blocks are subaerial, as evidenced by the active fault scarps which mark the landward termination of the Hilina slump on the south flank of Kilauea (Swanson et al. 1976 Similarly, many of the Hawaiian debris avalanches appear to have at least a partly subaerial source, with morphological evidence supporting the existence of subaerial landslide amphitheatres associated with both the East Ka Lae (Moore & Clague 1992) and Alika (Moore & Mark 1992) debris avalanches. It is likely that in many cases, the scars left by such landslides extend below sea level, and many appear to be initiated immediately below sea level where some of the steepest slopes on the Hawaiian volcanoes (up to 19°) are encountered (Mark & Moore 1987). The apparent predominance of collapse events at the land-sea interface, for which there is also evidence from Stromboli hints once again at a role for changing sea levels in destabilising volcanic edifices, particularly when, as previously mentioned, these occur catastrophically (Blanchon & Shaw 1995).

Many of the features representative of volcano destabilization and collapse on the Hawaiian Ridge are mirrored around the shores of

Réunion Island in the Indian Ocean, in particular adjacent to the active Piton de la Fournaise volcano (Rousset et al. 1987) (Fig. 10). As at the Hawaiian volcanoes, both slumping and debris avalanche production appear to have been important in the seaward transport of large masses of volcanic material. Large, arcuate fault scarps have been interpreted (Duffield et al. 1982) as the back walls of giant seaward-slumping blocks analogous to the Hilina slump at Kilauea, while the cliff-bounded Grand Brûlé flank depression is evidence of the more rapid transport of material seaward. Lenat et al. (1989) report that this structure can be traced offshore for over 20 km and probably resulted partly due to landsliding and partly from seaward slumping of a relatively undisturbed block. Labazuy (this volume) reports that the total volume of allochthonous material derived from Piton de la Fournaise amounts to around 500 km^3, an order of magnitude smaller than the largest single slide on the Hawaiian Ridge but nevertheless evidence for the importance of gravity collapse at this relatively young volcano.

Comparisons of the terminologies used to define collapse structures and deposits at Piton de la Fournaise and the Hawaiian Ridge reveal discrepancies which need resolving in order to prevent confusion in the literature. In particular, large masses of allochthonous material transported for distances of tens of kilometres offshore are referred to as slump deposits (Rousset et al. 1987; Labazuy this volume). These features

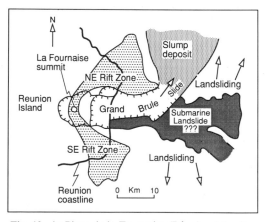

Fig. 10. At Piton de la Fournaise (Réunion Island), collapse of the eastern flank is related to repeated dyke emplacement along the NE and SE Rift Zones. On land, the Grand Brûlé represents the collapse scar, while offshore surveys have revealed the existence of large volume (totalling 500 km^3) debris avalanche deposits (after Rousset et al. 1987).

clearly do not have the same morphological and structural characteristics as the 'slumps' described by Moore et al. (1994) and others, from Hawaii, nor is the emplacement mechanism likely to be the same. The Piton de la Fournaise deposits appear to be rootless, and as such are likely to represent landslides in which the disruption of the collapsing mass has been minimal. The term 'slump' should be limited to masses of allochthonous material which satisfy all the following criteria; emplacement is slow and progressive, the structure is coherent and relatively undisturbed, and part of the mobile mass remains rooted in the source region. Structures such as the Hilina slump satisfy these criteria; at Piton de la Fournaise, however, these features are probably best exhibited by the subaerial, arcuate scarp-bounded blocks described by Duffield et al. (1982), rather than by the submarine deposits.

Many collapse scars such as the Grand Brûlé on Piton de la Fournaise, the Valle del Bove on Etna, and the Sciara del Fuoca on Stromboli were formed during the Holocene, and are only visible due to their youth. Older structures are, however, rapidly buried or covered, and may only be recognizable by unexplained variations in edifice morphology. At Mauna Loa, for example, anomalously steep slopes developed along the entire length of the west flank have been tentatively interpreted (Moore et al. 1994) in terms of young lava flows filling a sequence of older collapse amphitheatres. Similar anomalously steep slopes on the flanks of the Cumbre Vieja ridge on La Palma (Canaries), and other marine volcanoes may conceal structures generated by older collapse events, evidence for which may only be found in the submarine record.

The transport of volcanically derived debris into the marine environment due to catastrophic landsliding may be enhanced by the triggering of large-scale turbidite formation at the distal ends of the avalanches. Garcia & Hull (1994) and Garcia (this volume), report turbidite currents related to Hawaiian landslides, which travelled over 1000 km and flowed over sea-bed obstructions 500 m high. Similarly, Weaver et al. (1994), present evidence for turbidity currents over 600 km in length which appear to be related to slope failure on the flanks of the westernmost Canary Islands of La Palma and Hierro around 18 ka BP.

Further submarine surveys, using increasingly advanced imaging techniques, can be expected, over the next decade, to improve our knowledge of the morphologies and structures of volcanic landslides and associated deposits emplaced in the submarine environment. The numbers of landslides recognized are also certain to increase, as imagery is obtained for as yet relatively poorly studied volcanic island chains such as the Canaries and the Azores. Already, however, there is a sufficient body of data to indicate that repeated flank collapse is a ubiquitous occurrence in the normal lifecycle of marine volcanoes.

Evidence of volcanic edifice failure on other planetary bodies

High resolution imagery from the Moon, Mars, and Venus, has permitted comparisons to be made about the nature of volcanic edifice failure on a range of diverse planetary bodies with differing geological structures, gravitational fields and atmospheric pressures (Head this volume). Broadly speaking, both the Earth and Mars are characterized by the existence of large edifices which often show evidence of flank failure and sector collapse. In contrast on the Moon, where large volcanic structures are absent, and on Venus where volcano heights are lower, evidence for very large-scale collapse is absent.

Martian shield volcanoes display many of the features shown by those of Earth, including lithospheric loading effects, rift-zone development, summit caldera formation, and flank failure (Crumpler et al. this volume). As these edifices tend, however, to be volumetrically three orders of magnitude greater than their largest terrestrial counterparts the scale of edifice failure is equally increased. The gigantic sizes of the martian volcanoes are a reflection of a number of different factors, including the stability and thickness of the underlying lithosphere, which permits the accumulation of a huge volume of material at one site, and minimizes the degree of load-related height diminution due to lithospheric depression (Head this volume). As at Hawaii (Moore et al. 1989, 1994), both slumps and debris avalanches are observed on the large martian shield volcanoes. The latter, in the case of Olympus Mons, extend nearly a thousand kilometres beyond the basal scarp of the volcano, and have volumes of up to 170×10^3 km^3 (Head this volume); an order of magnitude greater than debris avalanches associated with the Hawaiian volcanoes. On an even larger scale, Crumpler et al. (this volume), report the possible existence of gravity sliding at Olympus Mons of the type evident at Etna, but with the entire edifice sliding down the regional slope of the substrate on a detachment horizon lubricated by water ice. Cave et al. (1994) draw attention to the link between water and instability and collapse in volcanic terrains on Mars. In particular, they point to the fact that many of the large fluvial outflow channels originate in areas of collapsed terrain and have a close association with volcanic centres such as in the Tharsis and Elysium regions.

In contrast to their martian counterparts, volcanic edifices on Venus have geometries characterized by greater height to width ratios, and reveal little evidence for the type of large-scale flank failure shown by the Tharsis volcanoes. The broader, flatter forms of large (c. 100 km) volcanic constructs on Venus are less susceptible to failure due to a number of factors outlined in Head (this volume). These include slower rates of vertical migration of magma, and the absence of liquid-lubricated slip zones due to the high surface temperatures. Smaller (c. tens of kilometres) volcanic constructs on Venus, particularly those of dome-like form, do, however, provide evidence for ubiquitous flank failure (eg, Guest et al. 1992; Bulmer & Guest this volume; Head this volume). Both collapse scars and associated debris avalanche deposits are visible, the latter of which tend to have longer runout distances, for a given drop, than those on Earth or Mars.

The hazard implications of volcano instability

As shown by collapse of the northern flank of Mount St Helens in 1980, the consequences of edifice failure can be both dramatic and catastrophically destructive. Failure to forecast such an event and/or to initiate the appropriate mitigation procedure – which can only involve evacuation of the entire population of the area at risk – will result in major loss of life. With velocities in excess of $100 \, \mathrm{m \, s^{-1}}$ ($360 \, \mathrm{km \, h^{-1}}$), and momentum sufficient to mount topographic barriers hundreds of metres high, no man-made structures can survive the impact of a major debris avalanche. The area affected is also likely to be large; the relatively small-scale debris avalanche at Mount St Helens travelled over 24 km from its source, but this is minimal compared with the 120 km long late Pleistocene debris avalanche at Nevado di Colima (Stoopes & Sheriden 1992), which covers an area of around 2200 km^2. A volcanic landslide on this scale has not been observed during historic times, and the problems involved in forecasting and mitigating the effects of such an event, particularly in a densely populated area, would be enormous. Nevertheless, such a scenario will

eventually occur and provision must be made for mitigating its impact.

Edifice failure at Mount St Helens was particularly important, from the hazard mitigation point of view, because it demonstrated clearly that volcanic landslides occurring in the presence of a shallow magma body can generate a whole spectrum of destructive phenomena in addition to the landslide itself, including lateral blast, lahars, pyroclastic flows, and extensive ash-fall. Furthermore, the speed with which these phenomena were unleashed following landslide initiation indicated that no mitigation procedures could be implemented once the sequence of events had started. The lesson being that such measures must be in place well in advance of the expected event.

Assessing the hazard posed by structural instability at a particular volcano should ideally adopt a two-pronged approach based upon mapping and surveillance. The former provides information on the nature, extent, and frequency of past collapse events, and identifies areas likely to fail at some point in the future, while the latter concentrates on detecting and monitoring the onset and development of instability using electronic distance measurement (EDM) and related techniques. Because edifice failure and debris avalanche formation is often an episodic event which constitutes part of the normal life-cycle of a volcano, considerable information about the behaviour of a future landslide can be gleaned from examining older deposits associated with similar events. Determining the extent of such deposits is particularly important in hazard zonation map preparation, as it provides an estimate of the area which might be affected by a future debris avalanche. The size-estimates and shapes of hazard zones determined on this basis must always, however, be regarded only as a guide to future behaviour. A volcano may not, for any one of a number of reasons, precisely replicate past activity, and destructive phenomena may affect larger or different parts of the surrounding terrain during a future collapse event. Furthermore, not all the effects associated with edifice failure may be sufficiently well-preserved in the geological record. At Mount St Helens, for example, the hazard zonation maps of Crandell & Mullineaux (1978) proved to be highly accurate for all phenomena except the lateral blast which accompanied the May 18 landslide. This extended three times further, and covered an area up to fifteen times greater than pre-dicted (Miller et al. 1981), probably reflecting the low preservation potential of the products of earlier, similar events. In assessing the potential for future instability and failure, detailed structural mapping also has an important role to play, particularly in identifying features which may provide clues as to the nature and locations of future collapse. These may include creeping/ episodically moving faults, peripheral thrust faults and folds, old collapses, active rift zones, and zones of alteration. Recognizing changes with time of fault geometries or dyke-zone orientations may also be important in terms of reflecting stress regime modifications prior to edifice destabilization.

As mentioned earlier, debris avalanche production in active volcanic terrains may be accompanied by other destructive phenomena. A particular threat lies in the transition, during transport, from debris avalanche to debris flow (lahar), due to the melting of snow and ice fields or to the entrainment of surface water during the collapse event. Such behaviour effectively increases the length of the runout, compared to dry avalanches, thereby enlarging the extent of damage and destruction. Debris avalanches may also provide conditions favouring lahar formation by damming water catchments and forming new lakes which may drain catastrophically (Costa & Shuster 1988). Additionally, lahars and mud-laden floods may be generated due to dewatering of the avalanche material (Janda et al. 1981), or may form by means of remobilization caused by heavy rainfall. In these ways, a major collapse event may provide a sufficient source of debris to feed numerous precipitation-related lahar/flood events over a period of years or decades. This is an extended-hazard problem which has become familiar to the inhabitants of towns in the vicinity of the Pinatubo volcano (Philippines) since the eruption in June 1991 (Pierson 1992). Although here the source of the lahars is a thick mantle of pyroclastic flow, rather than debris avalanche, material, a similar scenario could be expected to follow emplacement of a major volcanic landslide in an area of very high rainfall.

The Nevado del Ruiz (Colombia) catastrophe in 1985 (Herd et al. 1986; Voight 1990), in which close to 25 000 lives were lost, demonstrated graphically the devastating potential of lahars. Ironically, considering this was one of the worst volcanic disasters of the century, the detrimental effects of these phenomena are some of the easiest to mitigate. This is largely due to their being more topographically constrained than debris avalanches, tending to follow river valleys and pond in areas of low relief. It should be relatively easy, therefore, given the funding and political will, to effectively mitigate the lahar problem at any particular volcano. This may be accomplished by means of (i) a judicious construction policy which avoids susceptible areas, (ii) an effective monitoring system, based on alarmed trip-wires and seismometers, which is able to provide sufficient time for evacuation of the area, and (iii) having in place an effective plan for rapid evacuation. Damage to property can be minimised by the upstream installation of a sequence of sediment dams and baffles designed to reduce the sediment and boulder load thereby reducing the destructive power of the lahar.

The preference for destabilization and collapse on the seaward-facing flanks of volcanic edifices has already been discussed in terms of the buttressing effect of adjacent terrain on the landward side. From the hazard point of view, this effect has major implications, favouring as it does the formation of volcanogenic tsunamis. Some 5% of all tsunamis are estimated to have been formed by volcanic activity, and at least one fifth of these result from volcanic landslides (Smith & Shepherd this volume). One of the most recent occurred at Harimkotan (Severgina) volcano (Kurile Islands) during 1933, when a small (0.5 km^3) debris avalanche entered the sea and generated a 9 m high tsunami (Belousov 1994). As revealed by the Mount Unzen (Japan) collapse in 1792, even small landslides can generate highly destructive waves if they enter a large body of water. At Unzen, a collapsing volume of only about 0.34 km^3 (Hayashi & Self 1992), which was not connected with volcanic activity, entered Ariake Bay and triggered a tsunami which caused 14 500 deaths. Similar 'cold' collapses are probably relatively common events, particularly on steep-sided volcanoes in the marine environment. Kick 'em Jenny volcano in the Lesser Antilles, for example (Smith & Shepherd this volume), must be viewed as a volcanogenic tsunamis source. This submarine volcano has erupted 12 times in the last 53 years and possesses steep flanks bearing signs of previous collapse events. The steep-sided Stromboli volcano in the Aeolian Islands (Tibaldi et al. 1994; Kokelaar & Romagnoli 1995; Tibaldi this volume) might also be considered a prime candidate for flank collapse sufficient to generate a tsunamis capable of affecting the coastal regions of northern Sicily and western Calabria. Begét & Kienle (1992) also highlight the tsunami risk at Mount St Augustine volcano (Alaska). They report the formation of a 20 m high tsunami due to the emplacement of a small debris avalanche into the Cook Inlet during the 1883 eruption, and expect a similar event to occur sometime during the next century. Some of the largest volcanogenic tsunamis were undoubtedly associated with emplacement of the Hawaiian Island debris avalanches. A wave-train associated with a collapse on the flanks of Lanai volcano around 105 ka BP appears not only to have reached an elevation of around 375 m on the island itself (Moore & Moore 1984), but also to have crossed the Pacific and impinged energetically upon the coast of New South Wales in Australia. Here, Young & Bryant (1992) report the results of catastrophic wave erosion related to the tsunami, at heights of at least 15 m above present sea level. Both forecasting the onset of such a collapse and mitigating its effects are beyond current capabilities, and likely to remain so for some time.

It is worth noting that not all instability related hazards are associated with rapid-onset events such as debris avalanche formation. Slower-moving slumps, for example, can result in extensive damage to man-made structures due, as at Etna (Rasa *et al.* this volume), to continuous aseimic creep, or, as in the case of the 1975 Kilauea quake (Denlinger & Okubo, in press), to lower periodicity seismic activity related to episodic, but larger scale, downslope slump movement.

Monitoring and forecasting volcano instability and failure

Successfully forecasting collapse in active volcanic terrains remains strongly dependent upon the monitoring of ground deformation and displacement using geodetic and related methods. Such techniques are particularly important in identifying sites of increasing destabilization on the flanks of newly reactivated volcanoes, and in monitoring the development of instability with a view to defining progressively smaller predictive 'windows' in order to attempt to forecast the timing of eventual structural failure. Defining such windows relies upon observing an increasing acceleration in the rate of deformation or displacement, with failure becoming increasingly likely as the rate of deformation becomes greater.

This technique proved particularly effective, when combined with data gathered from other monitoring methods, in forecasting dome-destroying eruptions at Mount St Helens during the early 1980s (Swanson *et al.* 1983, 1985). Unfortunately, it was not so successful in predicting the major landslide event of May 1980. In this case, cumulative growth of the cryptodome-induced bulge demonstrated a constant displacement rate right up to the time when

structural failure and landslide inititation was triggered by a magnitude 5 earthquake (McClelland *et al.* 1989). It is a matter for conjecture whether or not an acceleration in the growth rate of the bulge would have been observed had it not been prematurely detached from the northern flank by seismogenic ground accelerations. The situation does, however, illustrate an important point, which is that external events – in this case seismic activity – may accelerate the onset of instability caused by a separate, although in this case related, phenomena (e.g. magma intrusion), and may initiate failure sooner than might otherwise be expected.

Monitoring edifice instability has also been shown to be a useful tool in predicting future eruptive activity at Etna, where geodetic monitoring has revealed a relationship between the rate of downslope creep on the upper eastern flanks of the volcano and the timing of future eruptions. Murray & Voight (this volume) propose that accelerating rates of downslope creep occur in response to increasing magma pressures. The creep behaviour eventually reduces the effective tensile strength of the rock to a level at which it is exceeded by magma pressure, thereby permitting eruption. On the basis of inverse-rate analysis of geodetic data accumulated during the 1980s, the authors also believe that this method permits good eruption predictions more than three months in advance.

A range of low- and high-tech ground deformation monitoring techniques are now in use for detecting and observing the surface displacements at active volcanoes which may signal increasing instability and presage forthcoming failure. At the low-tech end of the spectrum, simple steel tapes have been effectively used to measure displacements across basal thrust faults reflecting the progressive growth of the previously mentioned post- May 1980 lava dome at Mount St Helens, contributing invaluable data towards successful forecasts of future episodes of dome destruction (Swanson *et al.* 1983, 1985). More commonly used, less risky, but more expensive techniques involve using either infra-red or laser electro-optical distance meters (EDMs), which are capable of monitoring horizontal distance changes of only a few centimetres over distances of up to tens of kilometres (e.g. McGuire *et al.* 1990; 1991; Iwatsubo & Swanson 1992; Murray *et al.* 1995). Displacement data gathered in this way may also usefully be supplemented by tiltmeters and precise-levelling surveys (Dzurisin 1992; Murray *et al.* 1995; Toutain *et al.* 1995) to build a more comprehensive picture of the pattern of deformation associated with a destabilization event. Airborne (Garvin this volume), and space-based systems are also becoming more important, and the increasingly accessible and cost-effective global positioning system (GPS), in particular, can be viewed as an effective new tool in the armoury of geodetic hardware (Shimada *et al.* 1990; Nunnari & Puglisi 1995). Radar interferometry techniques using successive synthetic aperture radar (SAR) images from satellite platforms have also been shown recently (Massonet *et al.* 1993) to have enormous potential in measuring centimetric surface displacements associated with co-seismic deformation fields around active faults. This technique is now being applied in volcanology (Massonet *et al.* 1995) and offers the possibility of monitoring very precisely, and at one go, changes in the overall surface deformation pattern at a chosen volcano. On the ground, better prediction of the timing of landslide initiation may come from the seismic monitoring of seismogenic faults which have the potential to act as slide surfaces, the application of acoustic emission techniques, which may permit detection of very small-scale microfracturing preceding and presaging major structural failure, and ground penetrating radar (GPR) which may be suitable for mapping fracture patterns in unstable areas.

Summary

The development of instability and the conditions which favour structural failure of volcanic edifices will continue to form important foci of study into the next century. Accumulating evidence for the ubiquity of these phenomena has played an important role in redefining the frequency and scale of associated hazards, and has drawn attention to the potentially devastating consequences of a major structural failure event occurring at a volcano in a densely populated area. Both extant monitoring strategies and hazard mitigation blueprints at susceptible volcanoes must now be modified in order to plan for such a scenario.

Results presented in this paper relating to work on the Etna, Stromboli, and Canary Island volcanoes would not have been acquired without the support of the Commission of the European Communities, DG XII, Environment Programme, Climatology and Natural Hazards Unit, in the framework of the contract EV5V-CT92-0170.

References

ADUSHKIN, V. V., ZYKOV, N. YU. & FEDOTOV, S. A. 1995. Mechanism of volcanic slope failure. Assessment of potential collapse and debris avalanches at Klyuchevskoi volcano. *Volcanology and Seismology*, **16**, 667–684

ANCOCHEA, E., Hernan, F., Cendrero, A., CANTAGREL, J. M., FUSTER, J. M., IBARROLA, E. & COELLO, J. 1994. Constructive and destructive episodes in the building of a young oceanic island, La Palma, Canary Islands, and genesis of the Caldera de Taburiente. *Journal of Volcanology and Geothermal Research*, **60**, 243–262.

BARSCZUS, H. G., FILMER, P. E. & DESONIE, D. 1992. Cataclysmic collapses and mass masting processes in the Marquesas. *Eos, Transactions of the American Geophysical Union*, **73**, 313 (abstract).

BEGÉT, J. E. & KIENLE, J. 1992. Cyclic formation of debris avalanches at Mount St Augustine volcano. *Nature*, **356**, 701–704.

BELOUSOV, A. B. 1994. Large-scale sector collapses at Kurile-Kamchatka volcanoes in the 20th century. *In*: *Proceedings of International Conference on Volcano Instability on the Earth and Other Planets*. The Geological Society of London, 1994.

BLANCHON, P. & SHAW, J. 1995. Reef drowning during the last glaciation: evidence for catastrophic sea-level rise and ice-sheet collapse. *Geology*, **23**, 4–8.

BORGIA, A. 1994. Dynamic basis of volcanic spreading. *Journal of Geophysical Research*, **99**, B9, 17791–17804.

——, FERRARI, L., & PASQUARE, G. 1992. Importance of gravitational spreading in the tectonic and volcanic evolution of Mount Etna. *Nature*, **357**, 231–235.

BULMER, M. H. & GUEST, J. E. 1996. Modified volcanic domes and associated debris aprons on Venus. *This volume*.

CARRACEDO, J. C. 1994. The Canary Islands: an example of structural control on the growth of large oceanic-island volcanoes. *Journal of Volcanology and Geothermal Research*, **60**, 225–241.

——1996. A simple model for the genesis of large gravitational landslide hazards in the Canary Islands. *This volume*.

CAVE, J., GUEST, J. E. & BULMER, M. 1994. Slope instability on Elysium Mons & other martian volcanoes. *In*: *Proceedings of International Conference on Volcano Instability on the Earth and Other Planets*. The Geological Society of London, 1994

CHADWICK, W. W., MOORE, J. G., FOX, C. G. & CHRISTIE, D. M. 1992. Morphologic similarities of submarine slope failures: south flank of Kilauea, Hawaii, and the southern Galapagos platform. *Eos, Transactions of the American Geophysical Union*, **73**, 507 (abstract).

CHRISTIANSEN, R. I. & PETERSON, D. W. 1981 Chronology of the 1980 eruptive activity. *In*: LIPMAN, P. W. & MULLINEAUX, D. R. (eds) *The 1980 eruptions of Mount St Helens*. US Geological Survey Professional Paper **1250**, 17–30.

CLAGUE, D. A. & DENLINGER, R. P. 1994. Role of olivine cumulates in destabilizing the flanks of Hawaiian volcanoes. *Bulletin of Volcanology*, **56**, 425–434.

COSTA, J. E., SCHUSTER, R. L. 1988. The formation and failure of natural dams. *Geological Society of American Bulletin*, **100**, 1054–1068.

CRANDELL, D. R. 1989. *Gigantic debris-avalanche of Pleistocene age from ancestral Mount Shasta volcano, California, and debris avalanche hazard zonation*. Bulletin of the US Geological Survey, **1861**.

—— & MULLINEAUX, D. R. 1978. *Potential hazards from future eruptions of Mount St Helens, Washington*. Bulletin of the US Geological Survey, **1383-C**.

——, MILLER, C. D., GLICKEN, H. X., CHRISTIANSEN, R. L., NEWHALL, C. G. 1984. Catastrophic debris avalanche from ancestral Mount Shasta volcano, California. *Geology*, **12**, 143–146.

CRUMPLER, L. S., HEAD, J. W. & AUBELE, J. C. 1996. Calderas on Mars: characteristics, structure, and associated flank deformation. *This volume*.

DAY, S. J. 1996. Hydrothermal pore-fluid pressure & the stability of porous, permeable volcanoes. *This volume*.

DELEMEN, I. F. 1995 Gravitational instability mechanisms in volcanic cones (with reference to Klyuchevskoi volcano). *Volcanology and Seismology*, **16**, 649–666.

DENLINGER, R. P. & OKUBO, P. A huge landslide structure on Kilauea volcano, Hawaii. *Journal of Geophysical Research*, in press.

DE RITA, D., DI FILIPPO, M. & ROSA, C. 1996. Structural evolution of the Bracciano volcano-tectonic depression within the Sabatini volcanic district, Italy. *This volume*.

DIETERICH, J. H. 1988 Growth and persistence of Hawaiian volcanic rift zones. *Journal of Geophysical Research*, **93**, 4258–4270.

DUFFIELD, W. A., STIELTJES, L., & VARET, J. 1982 Huge landslide blocks in the growth of Piton de la Fournaise, La Rèunion, & Kilauea volcano, Hawaii. *Journal of Volcanology Geothermal Research*, **12**, 147–160.

DZURISIN, D. 1992. Electronic tiltmeters for volcano monitoring: lessons from Mount St Helens. *In*: EWERT, J. W. & SWANSON, D. A. (eds) *Monitoring Volcanoes: Techniques and Strategies used by the staff of the Cascades Volcano Observatory, 1980–90*. USGS Bulletin, **1966**, 69–84.

ELSWORTH, D. & VOIGHT, B. 1996. Evaluation of volcano flank instability triggered by dyke intrusion. *This volume*.

FAIRCHILD, L. H. 1987. The importance of lahar initiation processes. *Reviews in Engineering Geology*, **7**, 51–61.

FILMER, P. E., MCNUTT, M. K., WEBB, H. & DIXON, D. J. 1992. Volcanism and archipelagic aprons: a comparison of the Marquesan and Hawaiian islands. *Eos, Transactions of the American Geophysical Union*, **73**, 313 (abstract)

FIRTH, C., STEWART, I., MCGUIRE, W. J., KERSHAW, S. & VITA-FINZI, C. 1996. Coastal elevation changes in eastern Sicily: implications for volcano instability at Mount Etna. *This volume*.

FORNARI, D. J. & CAMPBELL, J. F. 1987. Submarine topography around the Hawaiian Islands. *In*: DECKER. R. W., WRIGHT, T. L. & STAUFFER, P. H. (eds) *Volcanism in Hawaii*. US Geological Survey Professional Paper, **1350**, 109–124.

FRANCIS, P. W. 1994. Large volcanic debris avalanches in the central Andes. *In: Proceedings of International Conference on Volcano Instability on the Earth and Other Planets*. The Geological Society of London, 1994.

—— & SELF, S. 1987. Collapsing volcanoes. *Scientific American*, **255**(6), 90–97.

GARCIA, M. O. 1996. Turbidites from slope failure on Hawaiian volcanoes. *This volume*.

—— & HULL, D. M. 1994. Turbidites from giant Hawaiian landslides: results from Ocean Drilling Program Site 842. *Geology*, **22**, 159–162.

GARVIN, J. B. 1996. Topographic characterization and monitoring of volcanoes via airborne laser altimetry. *This volume*.

GLICKEN, H. 1991. *Rockslide-debris avalanche of May 18th, 1980, Mount St Helens volcano, Washington*. US Geological Survey Professional Paper, **1488**.

GUEST, J. E., BULMER, M. H., BERATAN, K., MICHAELS, G. & SAUNDERS, S. 1992. Gravitational collapse of the margins of volcanic domes on Venus. *Lunar and Planetary Sciences*, **23**, 461–462 (abstract).

HAYASHI, J. N. & SELF, S. 1992. A comparison of pyroclastic flow and debris avalanche mobility. *Journal of Geophysical Research*, **97**, 9063–9071.

HEAD, J. W. 1996. Volcano instability development: a planetary perspective. *This volume*.

HERD, D. G. & THE COMITE DE ESTUDIOS VULCANOLOGICOS. 1986. The 1985 Ruiz volcano disaster. *Eos*, **67**, 457–460.

HOLCOMB, R. T. & SEARLE, R. C. 1991. Large landslides from oceanic volcanoes. *Marine Geotechnology*, **10**, 19–32.

INOKUCHI, T. 1988 Gigantic landslides and debris avalanches on volcanoes in Japan. *In: Proceedings of the Kagoshima International Conference on Volcanoes*. National Institute for Research Administration, Japan, 456–459

IWATSUBO, E. Y. & SWANSON, D. A. 1992 Trilateration and distance-measuring techniques used at Cascades and other volcanoes. *In*: EWERT, J. W. & SWANSON, D. A. (eds) *Monitoring Volcanoes: Techniques and Strategies used by the staff of the Casacades Volcano Observatory, 1980–90*. Bulletin of the US Geological Survey, **1966**, 95–102.

JANDA, R. J., SCOTT, K. M., NOLAN, R. M. & MARTINSON, H. A. 1981. Lahar movement, effects, and deposits. *In*: LIPMAN, P. W. & MULLINEAUX, D. R. (eds) *The 1980 eruptions of Mount St Helens, Washington*. US Geological Survey Professional Paper, **1250**, 461–478.

KIEFFER, G. 1985. *Evolution structurale et dynamique d'un grand volcan polygénetique: stades d'édification et activité actuelle de l'Etna.* Thèse Doct. Sci.; Univ. Clermont-Ferand.

KOKELAAR, P. & ROMAGNOLI, C. 1995 Sector collapse, sedimentation, and clast population evolution at an active island-arc volcano: Stromboli, Italy. *Bulletin of Volcanology*, **57**(4), 240–262.

KOMOROWSKI, J. C., NAVARRO, C., CORTES, A. & SIEBE, C. 1994. The unique tendency for recurrent collapse of Colima volcanoes (Mexico): the challenge of reconciling geologic evidence with C^{14} chronology, implications for hazard assessment. *In: Proceedings of International Conference on Volcano Instability on the Earth and Other Planets.* The Geological Society of London, 1994

LABAZUY, P. 1996. Recurrent landsliding events on the submarine flank of Piton de la Fournaise volcano (Réunion Island). *This volume.*

LENAT, J. F., VINCENT, P., & BACHELERY, P. 1989 The off-shore continuation of an active basaltic volcano: Piton de la Fournaise (Réunion Island, Indian Ocean); structural and geomorphological interpretation from sea beam mapping. *Journal of Volcanology and Geothermal Research*, **36**, 1–36.

LEONOV, V. L. 1995. Lineaments, tectonic fractures, and mechanical behaviour of Klyuchevskoi volcano. *Volcanology and Seismology*, **16**, 627–648.

LIPMAN, P. W. & MULLINEAUX, D. (EDS). 1981. *The 1980 eruptions of Mount St Helens.* US Geological Survey Professional Paper, **1250**.

——, LOCKWOOD, J. P., OKAMURA, R. T., SWANSON, D. A. & YAMASHITA, K. M. 1985. *Ground deformation associated with the 1975 magnitude 7.2 earthquake and resulting changes in activity of Kilauea volcano, Hawaii.* U.S. Geological Survey Professional Paper, **1276**,

——, NORMARK, W. R., MOORE, J. G., WILSON, J. B. & GUTMACHER, C. E. 1988. The giant submarine Alika debris slide, Mauna Loa, Hawaii. *Journal of Geophysical Research*, **93**, 4279–4299.

LO GIUDICE, E & RASA, R. 1992. Very shallow earthquakes and brittle deformation in active volcanic areas: the Etnean region as an example. *Tectonophysics*, **202**, 257–268.

MCCLELLAND, L., SIMKIN, T., SUMMERS, M., NIELSON, E. & STEIN, T. C. 1989. *Global Volcanism 1975–1985.* Prentice Hall, New Jersey.

MCGUIRE, W. J. 1995. Volcanic landslides and related phenomena. *In: Landslides Hazard Mitigation – with particular reference to developing countries.* The Royal Academy of Engineering, London, pp. 83–95.

—— & PULLEN, A. D. 1989. Location and orientation of eruptive fissures and feeder-dykes at Mount Etna; influence of gravitational and regional tectonic stress regimes. *Journal of Volcanology and Geothermal Research*, **38**, 325–344.

—— & SAUNDERS, S. J. 1993. Recent earth movements at active volcanoes: a review. *Quaternary Proceedings*, **3**, 33–46.

——, —— & PULLEN, A. D. 1993. Rifting at Mount Etna. *WOVO News*, **4**, 16–18.

——, PULLEN, A. D. & SAUNDERS, S. J. 1990. Recent dyke-induced large-scale block movement at Mount Etna and potential slope failure. *Nature*, **343**, 357–359.

——, MURRAY, J. B., PULLEN, A. D. & SAUNDERS, S. J. 1991. Ground deformation monitoring at Mount Etna; evidence for dyke emplacement and slope instability. *Journal of the Geological Society, London*, **148**, 577–583.

MARK, R. K. & MOORE, J. G. 1987. Slopes of the Hawaiian Ridge. *In: DECKER, R. W., WRIGHT, T. L. & STAUFFER, P. H. (eds) Volcanism in Hawaii.* US Geological Survey Professional Paper, **1350**, 101–107.

MARTI, J., VILA, J. & REY, J. 1996. Deception Island (Bransfield Strait, Antarctica): an example of volcanic caldera developed by extensional tectonics. *This volume.*

MASSONET, D., ROSSI, M., CARMONA, C., ADRAGNA, F., PELTZER, G., FEIGL, K. & RABAUTE, T. 1993. The displacement field of the Landers earthquake mapped by radar interferometry. *Nature*, **364**, 138–142.

——, BRIOLE, P. & ARNAUD, A. 1995. Deflation of Mount Etna monitored by spaceborne radar interferometry. *Nature*, **375**, 567–570.

MILLER, C. D., MULLINEAUX, D. R. & CRANDELL, D. R. 1981. Hazards assessments at Mount St Helens. *In: LIPMAN, P. W. & MULLINEAUX, D. R. (eds) The 1980 eruptions of Mount St Helens, Washington.* US Geological Survey Professional Paper, **1250**, 789–802.

MIMURA, K. & KAWACHI, S. 1981. Nirasaki debris avalanche, a catastrophic event at the Yatsugatake volcanic chain, central Japan (abstract). *Proceedings IAVCEI Symposium.* Tokyo and Hakone, 237.

MONTALTO, A., VINCIGUERRA, S., MENZA, S. & PATANE, G. 1996. Recent seismicity of Mount Etna: implications for flank instability. *This volume.*

MOORE, J. G. & CLAGUE, D. A. 1992. Volcano growth and evolution of the island of Hawaii. *Geological Society of America Bulletin*, **104**, 1471–1484

—— & MARK, R. K. 1992. Morphology of the island of Hawaii. *GSA Today*, **2**, 257–259

—— & MOORE, G. W. 1984 Deposit from a giant wave on the island of Lanai, Hawaii. *Science*, **226**, 1312–1315.

——, NORMARK, W. R. & HOLCOMB, R. T. 1994. Giant Hawaiian Landslides. *Annual Reviews of Earth and Planetary Science*, **22**, 119–144

——, CLAGUE, D. A., HOLCOMB, R. T., LIPMAN, P. W., NORMARK, W. R., & TORRESAN, M. E. 1989. Prodigious submarine landslides on the Hawaiian ridge. *Journal of Geophysical Research*, **94**, 17465–17484.

MUNRO, D. C. & ROWLAND, S. K. 1994. Implications of patterns of caldera instability in the western Galapagos Islands for mechanisms of caldera formation on the terrestrial planets. *In: Proceedings of International Conference on Volcano Instability on the Earth and Other Planets.* The Geological Society of London, 1994

MURRAY, J. B. & VOIGHT, B. 1996. Slope stability and eruption prediction on the eastern flank of Mount Etna. *This volume.*

——, PULLEN, A. D. & SAUNDERS, S. J. 1995. Ground deformation surveying of active volcanoes. *In*: McGUIRE, W. J., KILBURN, C. R. J. & MURRAY, J. B. (eds) *Monitoring Active Volcanoes: strategies, procedures, and techniques.* UCL Press, London, 113–150.

NAKAMURA, K. 1980. Why do long rift zones develop in Hawaiian volcanoes? – a possible role of thick oceanic sediments. *Bulletin of the Volcanological Society of Japan*, **25**, 255–269

NUNNARI, G. & PUGLISI, G. 1995. GPS – Monitoring volcanic deformation from space. *In*: McGUIRE, W. J., KILBURN, C. R. J. & MURRAY, J. B. (eds) *Monitoring Active Volcanoes: strategies, procedures, and techniques.* UCL Press, London, 151–183.

PIERSON, T. C. 1992. Rainfall-triggered lahars at Mt Pinatubo, Philippines, following the June 1991 eruption. *Landslide News*, **6**, 6–9.

RASA, A., AZZARO, R. & LEONARDI, O. 1996. Aseismic creep on faults and flank instability at Mount Etna volcano, Sicily. *This volume.*

RICE, J. R. 1992. Fault stress states, pore pressure distributions, and the weakness of the San Andreas Fault. *In*: EVANS, B. & WONG, T-F. (eds) *Fault mechanics and transport properties of rocks.* Academic Press, London, pp. 475–504.

ROBINSON, M. & ROWLAND, S. 1994. Evidence for large scale sector collapse at Tharsis Tholus, Mars. *In*: *Proceedings of International Conference on Volcano Instability on the Earth and Other Planets.* The Geological Society of London, 1994

ROMAGNOLI, C. & TIBALDI, A. 1994. Volcanic collapse in different tectonic settings: an example from the Aeolian Arc, Italy. *In*: *Proceedings of International Conference on Volcano Instability on the Earth and Other Planets.* The Geological Society of London, 1994

ROUSSET, D., BONNEVILLE, A., & LENAT, J-F. 1987. Detailed gravity study of the offshore structure of Piton de la Fournaise volcano, Réunion Island. *Bulletin of Volcanology*, **49**, 713–722.

ROWLAND, S. K. & MUNRO, D. C. 1992. The caldera of Volcan Fernandina: a remote sensing study of its structure & recent activity. *Bulletin of Volcanology*, **55**, 97–109.

RUBEY, W. M. & HUBBERT, M. K. 1959. Role of fluid pressure in the mechanics of overthrust faulting I: mechanics of fluid-filled porous solids and its application to overthrust faulting. *Geological Society of America Bulletin*, **70**, 115–166

RUST, D. & NERI, M. 1996. The boundaries of large-scale collapse on the flanks of Mount Etna, Sicily. *This volume.*

SEMET, M. P. & BOUDON, G. 1994. Large scale collapse structure at Piton du Carbet, Martinique: geological and petrological constraints. *In*: *Proceedings of International Conference on Volcano Instability on the Earth & Other Planets*, The Geological Society of London, 1994

SHIMADA, S., FUJINAWA, Y., SEKIGUCHI, S., OHMI, S., EGUCHI, T. & OKADA, Y. 1990. Detection of a volcanic fracture opening in Japan using Global Positioning System measurments. *Nature*, **343**, 631–633.

SIEBERT, L. 1984. Large volcanic debris avalanches: characteristics of source areas, deposits, and associated eruptions. *Journal of Volcanology and Geothermal Research*, **22**, 163–197.

——1992. Threats from debris avalanches. *Nature*, **356**, 658–659.

——, GLICKEN, H. X. & Ui, T. 1987. Volcanic hazards from Bezymianny- and Bandai-type eruptions. *Bulletin of Volcanology*, **49**, 435–459.

SMITH, M. S. & SHEPHERD, J. B. 1996. Tsunamigenic landslides at Kick 'em Jenny. *This volume.*

STOOPES, G. R. & SHERIDAN, M. F. 1992. Giant debris avalanches from the Colima Volcanic Complex, Mexico: implications for long runout landslides (>100 km) and hazard assessment. *Geology*, **20**, 299–302.

SWANSON, D. A., DUFFIELD, W. A., & FISKE, R. S. 1976. *Displacement of the south flank of Kilauea volcano: the result of forceful intrusion of magma into the rift zones.* US Geological Survey Professional Paper, **963**.

——, CASADEVALL, T. J., DZURISIN, D., MALONE, S. D., NEWHALL, C. G. & WEAVER, C. S. 1983. Predicting eruptions at Mount St Helens, June 1980 through December 1982. *Science*, **221**, 1369–1376.

——, ——, —— , HOLCOMB, R. T., NEWHALL, C. G., MALONE, S. D. & WEAVER, C. S. 1985. Forecasts and predictions of eruptive activity at Mount St Helens, USA: 1975–1984. *Journal of Geodynamics*, **3**, 397–423.

STEWART, I., McGUIRE, W. J., VITA-FINZI, C., FIRTH, C., HOLMES, R. & SAUNDERS, S. 1993. Active faulting and neotectonic deformation on the eastern flank of Mount Etna, Sicily. *Z. Geomorph.*, **94**, 73–94.

TIBALDI, A. 1996. Mutual influence of dyking and collapses, Stromboli volcano, Italy. *This volume.*

——, PASQUARE, G., FRANCALANCI, L. & GARDUNO, V. H. 1994. Collapse type and recurrence at Stromboli volcano, associated volcanic activity, and sea-level changes. *Atti dei Convegni Lincei, Roma*, **112**, 143–151.

TOUTAIN, J. P., BACHELERY, P., BLUM, P. A., DELORME, H. & KOWALSKI, P. 1995. Real-time ground deformation monitoring. *In*: McGUIRE, W. J., KILBURN, C. R. J. & MURRAY, J. B. (eds) *Monitoring Active Volcanoes: strategies, procedures, and techniques.* UCL Press, London, 93–112.

UI, T. 1983. Volcanic dry avalanche deposits – identification and comparison with non-volcanic debris stream deposits. *Journal of Volcanology and Geothermal Research*, **18**, 135–150.

—— 1989. Discrimination between debris avalanches and other volcaniclastic deposits. *In*: LATTER, J. H. (ed.) *Volcanic Hazards.* Springer-Verlag, Berlin, 201–209.

VOIGHT, B. 1990. The 1985 Nevado del Ruiz volcano catastrophe – anatomy and retrospection. *Journal of Volcanology and Geothermal Research*, **42**, 151–188.

—— & ELSWORTH, D. 1992. Resolution of mechanics problems for prodigious Hawaiian landslides: magmatic intrusions simultaneously increase driving force and reduce driving resistance by fluid pressure enhancement. *Eos, Transactions of the American Geophysical Union*, **73**, 506 (abstract).

——, GLICKEN, H., JANDA, R. J., & DOUGLASS, P. M. 1981. Catastrophic rockslide avalanche of May 18. *In*: LIPMAN, P. W. MULLINEAUX, D. R. (eds) *The 1980 eruption of Mount St Helens, Washington.* US Geological Survey Professional Paper, **1250**, 347–377.

——, JANDA, R. J., GLICKEN, H. & DOUGLASS, P. M. 1983. Nature and mechanics of the Mount St Helens rockslide-avalanche of 18 May 1980. *Geotechnique*, **33**, 224–273.

VAN WYK DE VRIES, B. & BORGIA, A. 1996. The role of basement in volcano deformation. *This volume*.

WADGE, G., FRANCIS, P. W., & RAMIREZ, C. F. 1995. The Socompa collapse and avalanche event. *Journal of Volcanology and Geothermal Research*, **66**, 309–336.

WEAVER, P. P. E., MASSON, D. G., & KIDD, R. B. 1994. Slumps, slides, and turbidity currents – sealevel change and sedimentation in the Canary Basin. *Geoscientist*, **4**(1), 14–16.

YOUNG, R. W. & BRYANT, E. A. 1992. Catastrophic wave erosion on the south-eastern coast of Australia: impact of the Lanai tsunami ca. 105 KA? *Geology*, **20**, 199–202.

Volcano instability development: a planetary perspective

JAMES W. HEAD III

Department of Geological Sciences, Brown University, Providence,
Rhode Island 02912, USA

Abstract: Analysis of the types and causes of volcano instability using the record seen on other planets, where volcanoes form in a wide variety of environments and are often better preserved, provides a perspective on the processes involved and deposits produced in edifices on Earth. The records on these bodies illustrate the potential significance of neutral buoyancy zones and rheological boundaries in relation to initial magma ascent and storage, related eruption styles, and subsequent edifice development and behaviour. On the Moon no Hawaii-like shield volcanoes are observed; the thick low-density anorthositic crust provided a density barrier to mantle plumes and the low frequency of dyke-emplacement events precluded development of shallow reservoirs and large shields. On Venus, the very high atmospheric pressure reduces volatile exsolution and fragmentation, inhibiting the formation of neutral buoyancy zones (NBZ) and shallow magma reservoirs near or below mean planetary radius; eruptions are predicted to be characterized by relatively high total volumes and effusion rates, and poorly developed edifices. Decrease in atmospheric pressure with elevation favours the development of NBZs and reservoirs at higher elevations. These and other factors result in low and broad volcanic edifices, with reservoirs predominantly in the substrate. Smaller loads, thicker lithospheres, and dry substrates combine to minimize large-scale vertical edifice growth and instability development. Exceptions include a wide array of collapse runout features associated with steep-sided domes. On Mars, low gravity and low surface atmospheric pressure cause density profile differences and flow length differences and massive volcanoes have been emplaced over long periods on a stable lithospheric plate and a volatile-containing upper crust. They exhibit a wide range of rift zone development, internal deformation related to lithospheric loading and flexure, flank and slope failure, and summit failure and caldera development. These planetary examples permit one to begin to isolate various factors in the development of volcano instabilities, including edifice geometry (height/width) and size, relation to lithospheric thickness as a function of time, potential role of neutral buoyancy zones and magma reservoir size and development, and the presence of fluids in the substrate. The extensive and well-preserved flank-failure deposits on Mars provide a significant areal perspective and analogue for the interpretation of less-well preserved deposits on Earth.

Volcano instability development describes a phenomenon that includes a host of processes and causes, focused on a particular landform. Instabilities may develop at many scales in different places on terrestrial volcanoes, and they may occur at different times in the evolution of an edifice. For example, instabilities may be related to relatively passive factors such as edifice loading, lithospheric flexure, and sector or flank collapse, or to more active factors such as dyke emplacement and rift zone formation, and magma reservoir evolution and caldera collapse. On Earth, the study of instabilities is aided by field access to recent volcanoes, the ability to monitor ongoing activity, and the preservation of eroded and dissected volcanoes. Study of terrestrial volcanoes is often limited, however, by erosional loss of key relationships, lack of preservation of or access to early stages, and the short historical time scales available.

Analysis of the types and causes of volcano instabilities using the record seen on other planets, where volcanoes form in a wide variety of environments, may help to increase our understanding of the processes involved in edifices on Earth. A comparison of the development of magma storage zones, eruption style, edifice formation and evolution, and resulting instabilities on the Moon, Venus, and Mars illustrates these points. A review of these planetary examples permits us to begin to isolate various factors in the development of volcano instabilities, including edifice geometry (height/width) and size, relation to lithospheric thickness as a function of time, influence of rift zone development, role of neutral buoyancy zones (NBZ) and magma reservoir size, supply rate, and development, and the presence of fluids in the substrate. In this paper, the characteristics of volcanic edifices on the Moon, Venus and Mars are reviewed, and the factors thought to influence their formation and evolution, and the development of instabilities and flank failure, are described for each body.

From McGuire, W. J., Jones, A. P. & Neuberg, J. (eds) 1996, *Volcano Instability on the Earth and Other Planets,* Geological Society Special Publication No. 110, pp. 25–43.

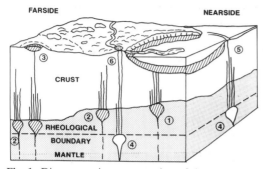

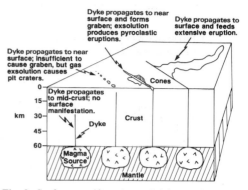

Fig. 1. Diagrammatic representation of the emplacement of lunar mare basalts. Early basaltic magmas rise diapirically to the density trap at the base of the crust (1 and 2). Post-stalling overpressurization results in propagation of dykes into the crust, most of which are confined to the lower and middle crust. Some events are of sufficient magnitude to propagate dykes to the surface to flood craters (3), form flows and sinuous rilles (6), or cause eruptions along the margins of basins (5, 6). With time, the lithosphere thickens and ascending diapirs stall at a rheological boundary (4), building up excess pressure to propagate dykes toward the surface. Eventually, source regions are so deep that surface eruptions are not favoured. From Head & Wilson (1992a).

Fig. 2. Surface manifestations of dyke emplacement on planetary crusts. From Head (1994).

Of course, in many cases the range of available information for specific aspects of different planets (e.g. the detailed crustal thickness and structure on Mars and Venus) is severely limited, resulting in uncertainty in the ultimate identification of causal factors. Nonetheless, the information provided by these specific examples and the perspective provided by considering different conditions on different planets, should prove to be a significant help in the overall consideration of volcano instability development. The purpose of this paper is to

provide an introduction to this perspective that will permit investigators to pursue those aspects of the problem most applicable to their terrestrial examples.

The Moon

On the Moon, basaltic volcanic deposits are concentrated in the lunar maria which cover about 17% of the surface, primarily on the near side. No large shield volcanoes, such as those seen on the Earth (e.g. Hawaii), Mars (e.g. Olympus Mons), or Venus (e.g. Sapas Mons), are observed on the Moon; large caldera-like features are also extremely rare. How can the lack of these features be accounted for?

The maria are superposed on the ancient globally continuous and thick low-density anorthositic highland crust derived primarily from global-scale melting associated with planetary accretion. This low density highlands crust

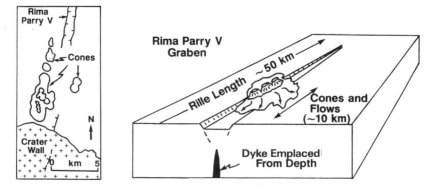

Fig. 3. Graben and eruptive cones at Rima Parry 5 the Moon. From Head & Wilson (1994).

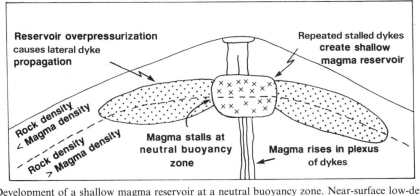

Fig. 4. Development of a shallow magma reservoir at a neutral buoyancy zone. Near-surface low-density rocks are due to vesiculation, presence of pyroclastics, and fracturing. This example portrays the general conditions interpreted to characterize Hawaii (Ryan 1987). From Head & Wilson (1992b).

provided a density barrier (Solomon 1975) to mantle plumes and basaltic melts ascending from the mantle. Rising diapirs and magma bodies thus tended to collect at the base of the 60–80 km thick crust. In addition, as the lithosphere thickened with time in early lunar history, it exceeded the thickness of the crust, resulting in the formation of a rheological barrier to rising plumes that deepened with time (Fig. 1). In both of these cases, following sufficient overpressurization of source regions, individual dykes propagated toward the surface. Thus, the thick highlands crust created a deep zone of neutral buoyancy for rising magma that could only be overcome by overpressurization events propagating dykes to the surface.

Whether there was intrusion or eruption was determined by variations in overpressurization and crustal thickness. Low levels of overpressurization resulted in intrusion into the lower crust, forming dykes which cooled and solidified. Dykes that were characterized by sufficient overpressurization to approach the surface could have several fates (Fig. 2). Intrusion close enough to the surface to produce a distinctive near-surface stress field often resulted in the production of linear graben-like features along the strike of the dyke and small associated effusions and eruptions. In the case of Rima Parry 5 (Fig. 3), small spatter cones are aligned along the central part of the linear graben (Head & Wilson 1994). Dykes propagating to slightly deeper levels may not create near-surface stress fields sufficient to form graben, but subsequent degassing may form chains of pit craters over the site of the dyke (Fig. 2) (e.g., Rima Hyginus or crater chains on the floor of the crater Mendeleev). Overpressurization events that are

large enough to propagate dykes to the surface are predicted to have very large volumes (Head & Wilson 1992a). Indeed, predicted volumes are comparable to those associated with many observed lava flows, such as the flows extending hundreds of kilometres into Mare Imbrium (Schaber 1973), and those associated with sinuous rilles, features which are thought to result from thermal erosion caused by individual high-volume, long-duration emplacement events (Carr 1974).

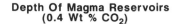

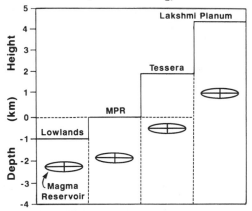

Fig. 5. Effect of different surface elevations on the depth of magma reservoirs for magma volatile content of 0.4 wt% CO_2. It is assumed that the entire crustal column was emplaced at the elevation where it presently outcrops. Modified after Head & Wilson (1992b).

The lunar maria were emplaced over a period of several billion years, but the total volume was relatively small (about 1×10^7 km^3, compared to the total present volume of the terrestrial oceanic crust, about 0.17×10^{10} km^3). Even at peak periods of mare emplacement (in the Imbrian Period, 3.8–3.2 Ga) the average global flux was low, about 10^{-2} km^3 a^{-1}, comparable to the present local output rates for such individual terrestrial volcanoes as Kilauea or Vesuvius. Output rates for individual eruptions could be extremely high, however. Several individual eruptions associated with sinuous rilles may have emplaced more than 10^3 km^3 of lava in about a year (Hulme 1973), a single event that would represent the equivalent of about 70 000 years of the average flux!

The relationship between magma source size and highland crustal thickness was such that the frequency of dykes propagating to the near-surface and surface to produce eruptions was relatively low (Figs 1, 2). This low frequency of dyke emplacement events meant that most dykes had sufficient time to cool before the next dyke was propagated. Thus, emplacement of a plexus of dykes at a sufficiently high frequency to create a shallow reservoir was very difficult on the Moon. The lack of Hawaii-like shield volcanoes on the Moon and the paucity of caldera-like features is thus attributed to the difficulty in producing shallow reservoirs which would then result in the emplacement of many individual flows to form an edifice and associated calderas (Head & Wilson 1991).

The lunar situation is analogous in many ways to basaltic magma bodies interacting with terrestrial continental crust. Here, zones of neutral buoyancy (Glazner & Ussler 1988)

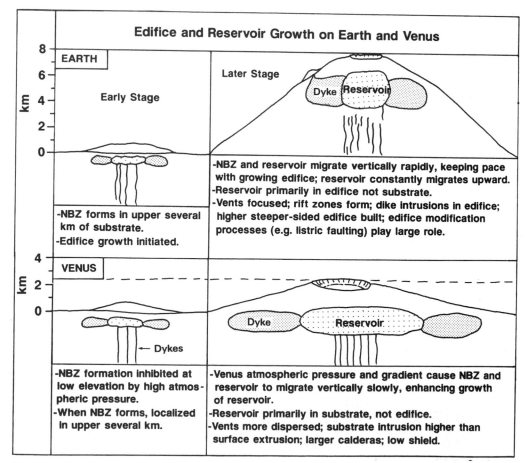

Fig. 6. Schematic diagrams showing factors in edifice and subsurface reservoir growth for volcanic edifices on Earth and Venus. From Head & Wilson (1992b).

cause buoyantly rising basaltic magma bodies to stall in the crust. Overpressurization events can cause the same array of features seen on the Moon (Fig. 2), as exemplified by many of the basaltic volcanic fields in the western United States (Lipman 1980), and indeed large-scale flood basalts can be emplaced that are comparable to the large lunar flows (Tolan *et al.* 1989). The low melting temperature of the continental crust relative to that of the more refractory lunar anorthositic crust means that stalled basaltic magma bodies in continental crust may cause associated and large-scale melting, resulting in a complexity not known to occur on the Moon. The continental crust and the lunar highlands illustrate the role of large-scale density barriers to the creation of significant shallow basaltic reservoirs, analogous to those on the ocean floor,

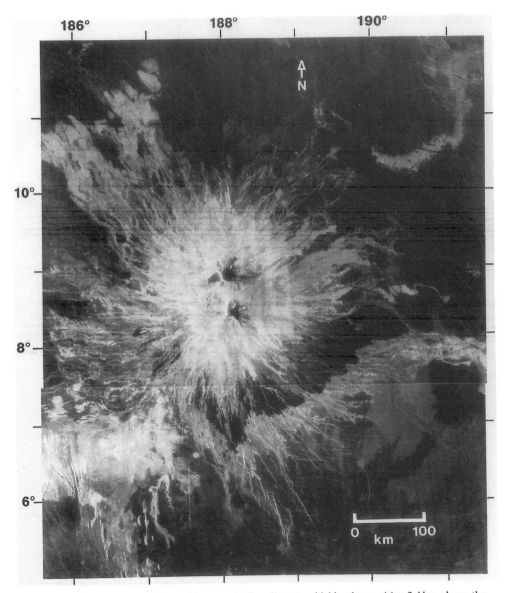

Fig. 7. Magellan image of Sapas Mons, Venus, a 600 km diameter shield volcano rising 2.4 km above the surrounding plains.

and the growth of large edifices with unstable flanks such as Hawaii. Complex shallow reservoirs do exist in continental crust, however, where local conditions of melt generation and, unlike the Moon, sustained supply rates, exist (as in continent margin subduction zones and central hot spot traces or rifting environments). In these cases, composite volcanoes with corresponding flank failure are common. No known analogue of these types of features exists on the Moon and Venus, but several possible examples may occur on Mars (e.g. Hecates Tholus; Mouginis-Mark *et al.* 1982; Wilson & Head 1994; Hodges & Moore 1994).

The lunar landscape illustrates another factor that is important in volcano instability. It is well known that earthquakes can be a significant factor in inducing instability and collapse in volcanoes and their associated deposits, and plate-margin earthquakes commonly precipitate instabilities many hundreds of kilometres from their epicentres. Less well appreciated is the tremendous amount of seismic energy associated with impact cratering events. Although only a small fraction of the total kinetic energy of the projectile goes into seismic energy, the total energy magnitudes are so great (Schultz & Gault 1975) that a crater the size of Copernicus on the Moon (diameter about 90 km) will produce the equivalent of a magnitude 10 earthquake with attendant seismic waves resulting in vertical oscillations of the surface at the antipodal point of the Moon of some tens to hundreds of metres! Thus, although the frequency of impacts is low in recent geological history, impact-induced instabilities should be considered in the past geologic record of the Earth and planets.

Venus

On Venus, the crust is largely basaltic and at least 80% of the surface consists of volcanic plains populated by more than 1500 edifices or volcanic sources in excess of 20 km diameter (Head *et al.* 1992). Over 150 of these edifices are major shield volcanoes, in excess of 100 km diameter. The heights of these shield volcanoes, however, are considerably less than those seen on the Earth and Mars, typically less than about 2 km above the surrounding plains (Schaber 1991; Keddie & Head 1994). In addition, there is little evidence on Venus of the large-scale flank instabilities and sector collapse structures seen on terrestrial and Martian volcanoes. How can this difference be accounted for?

As on the Earth (Ryan 1987), typical basaltic melts are positively buoyant and can stall at a neutral buoyancy zone caused by the production of a near-surface low-density horizon related to weathering and gas exsolution porosity (Fig. 4). The very high atmospheric pressure on Venus, however, reduces volatile exsolution and fragmentation, serving to inhibit the formation of NBZs and shallow magma reservoirs. For a range of common terrestrial magma volatile contents (<0.5 wt% H_2O, <0.35 wt% CO_2) magma ascending and erupting near or below mean planetary radius (MPR) should not stall at all to produce shallow magma reservoirs. In this case, magma would ascend directly from greater depth to the surface; such eruptions would be characterized by relatively high total volumes and effusion rates and poorly developed volcanic edifices (Head & Wilson 1992b). Intrusion to extrusion ratios would also be low.

Because there is a distinctive gradient in atmospheric pressure with elevation, the same range of volatile contents will result in the production of neutral buoyancy zones and magma reservoirs at elevations well above MPR. For the same range of volatile contents

Fig. 8. Steep-sided, scalloped margin dome (diameter about 30 km) on Venus showing associated slump and landslide deposits (F15S214).

at higher elevations (about 2 km above MPR) about half of the cases treated by Head & Wilson (1992*b*) result in direct ascent of magma to the surface and half in the production of neutral buoyancy zones. In general on Venus, neutral buoyancy zones and shallow magma reservoirs begin to appear as gas content increases and, because of the high atmospheric pressure, are nominally shallower on Venus than on Earth. The shallowest depths are about 1 km and depths increase slowly with increasing CO_2 content and rapidly with increasing H_2O content (especially above ~0.6 wt% H_2O). For a fixed volatile content, NBZs become deeper with

increasing elevation (Fig. 5). Over the range of elevations treated by Head & Wilson (1992*b*) depths differ by a factor of 2–4, which is about the same factor as that induced by variations in CO_2. NBZ reservoirs can become deeper than reservoirs on Earth produced with similar volatile contents if common terrestrial volatile content limits (0.5 wt% H_2O, 0.4 wt% CO_2) are exceeded. To a first order, the observations of the characteristics and global distribution of volcanic landforms that are largely extrusive (Keddie & Head 1994), and structures that reflect intrusive activity (Grosfils & Head 1995) support the predictions of the role of neutral

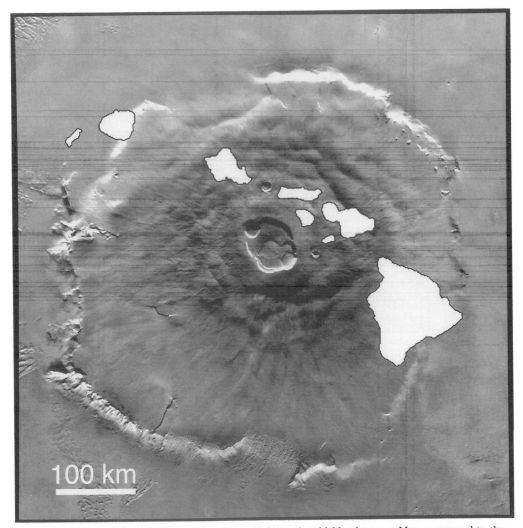

Fig. 9. Olympus Mons, the 600 km diameter, 25 km high massive shield volcano on Mars, compared to the Hawaiian island chain.

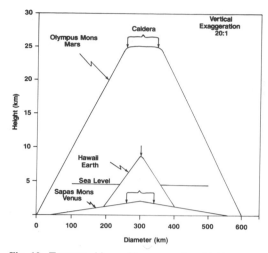

Fig. 10. Topographic profiles comparing shield volcanoes on the Moon (none), Venus, Earth, and Mars. Arrows show location of calderas or circumferential structures resembling calderas (Sapas Mons).

buoyancy in contributing to major aspects of volcano growth and development on Venus.

These considerations reveal several factors that may help to account for the low height of volcanoes on Venus. First, the Venus environment favours larger primary reservoirs which will cause the wide dispersal of conduits that build

edifices, resulting in broader, flatter structures. Secondly, models of the position of the shallow NBZ reservoir during edifice growth show that, for Earth, the magma chamber centre remains at a constant depth below the growing edifice summit, thus keeping pace with the increasing elevation (Fig. 6). In contrast, on Venus, because of the major change in atmospheric pressure as a function of altitude, the chamber centre becomes deeper relative to the summit of the growing edifice. Although the chamber becomes shallower with time in absolute terms, the rate of shallowing is low. Therefore, neutral buoyancy zones and magma reservoirs on Venus will remain in the pre-volcano substrate longer, and in many cases may not emerge into the edifice at all. In addition, the lower rate of vertical migration implies that, for a given magma supply rate, magma reservoirs would tend to stabilize, undergo greater lateral growth, and become larger on Venus than on Earth. In the first two cases the intrusion to extrusion ratio should be relatively high. Thus, the proportion of the available magma going into production of the edifice relative to that intruded into the substrate is smaller on Venus than on Earth. The resulting large reservoirs would encourage multiple and more widely dispersed source vents and large volumes for individual eruptions.

All of these factors result in volcanic edifices that are low and broad, with reservoirs predominantly in the substrate, rather than the

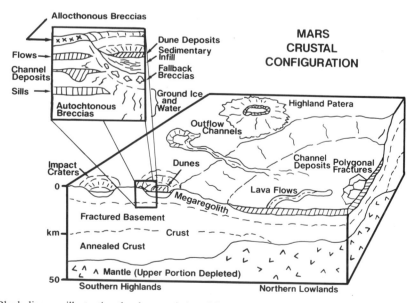

Fig. 11. Block diagram illustrating the characteristics of the crust on Mars. The presence of volatile-rich materials (groundwater and ground ice) in the substrate provide mechanisms to enhance instability development in volcanoes. From Wilson & Head (1994).

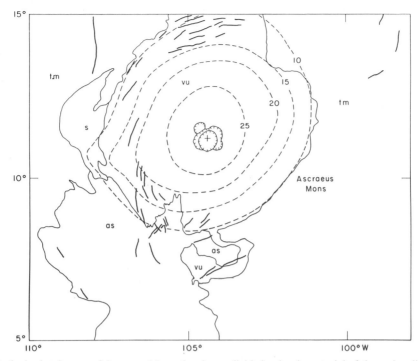

Fig. 12. Geologic sketch map of Ascraeus Mons showing undivided volcanic material of the main edifice (vu), intermediate age materials from other Tharsis volcanoes (tm), and young volcanic materials building out from a distinctive rift zone on the southwestern flank of the volcano (as). Also shown on the western flank is material (s) interpreted to be landslides and debris flows (Scott *et al.* 1981). From Comer *et al.* (1985).

edifice (Fig. 7). In addition, the very high surface temperatures on Venus mean that volatiles are not stable in the near-surface substrate, and that liquid-lubricated slip zones are not a likely source of instability. These factors combine to minimize large-scale edifice instabilities, such as those seen on the Earth and Mars.

In contrast to the major shield volcanoes, a class of smaller edifices known as steep-sided domes (Pavri *et al.* 1992) and scalloped-margin domes (Guest *et al.* 1992; Bulmer 1994) do show a wide range of flank collapse structures. These domes are up to several tens of kilometres in diameter and up to many hundreds of metres high. They occur in the plains and on top of edifices and display slumps and long-distance landslide-like aprons (Figs 7, 8) with mean runout distances of about 23 km and a maximum of about 82 km (Bulmer 1994). These landslides tend to travel further on Venus for a given vertical drop than those observed on the Earth, Moon, and Mars (Bulmer 1994). Extremely large runout distances for impact crater ejecta in the Venus environment (e.g. Schaber *et al.* 1992) suggests that the relatively dense atmosphere may play an important role. Further study of these numerous (>100), extremely well-preserved structures (Pavri *et al.* 1992) may provide insight into processes of dome collapse on other planets.

Mars

On Mars, in contrast to the Moon, large shield volcanoes have been emplaced that are at first glance similar in morphology to shield volcanoes on Venus and the Earth (Fig. 9). They exhibit a wide range of rift zone development, internal deformation related to lithospheric loading and flexure, flank and slope failure, and summit failure and caldera development (Carr 1973, 1981; Hodges & Moore 1994; Wilson & Head 1994). Their scales are quite different, however. Martian shields possess the breadth of many of the shields on Venus (compare Figs 9 and 7), but their heights are often a factor of three greater than Hawaii and a factor of 10–15 greater than those on Venus, such as Sapas Mons (Fig. 10). Volumes are so large as to be almost incomprehensible. Olympus Mons has a volume of about

$2 \times 10^6\,\mathrm{km}^3$, compared to $1 \times 10^5\,\mathrm{km}^3$ for the island of Hawaii and $1.1 \times 10^6\,\mathrm{km}^3$ for the whole Hawaiian-Emperor seamount chain (Barger & Jackson 1974). Martian caldera structures are much larger than those typical of Earth (Figs 9, 10) (Crumpler *et al.* this volume), and deformation and massive instabilities and gargantuan

landslides have occurred on edifice flanks. How do we account for these differences?

On Mars, low gravity and low surface atmospheric pressure cause differences in the crustal bulk density profile (Wilson & Head 1994), which means that magma reservoirs are expected to be deeper than on Earth by a factor of about

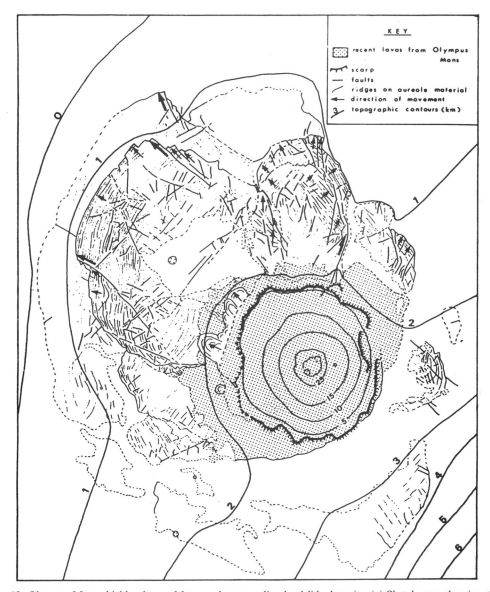

Fig. 13. Olympus Mons shield volcano, Mars, and surrounding landslide deposits. (**a**) Sketch map showing the main edifice and related flanking deposits, with approximate topographic contours superposed (from Lopes *et al.* 1982). (**b**) Mosaic showing aureole material to the northwest of Olympus Mons (Viking Orbiter-Quadrangle MC-8 NE). (**c**) Detail of the flanking scarp of Olympus Mons (Viking Orbiter frame 222A64; width is about 75 km). (**d**) Detail of the landslide deposit northwest of Olympus Mons (Viking Orbiter frame 512A30; width of the frame is about 220 km). (**e**) Detail of near-summit scarps interpreted to have originated by outward thrust faulting of the summit during loading-related deformation (Viking Orbiter frame 890A70; width of frame is about 185 km).

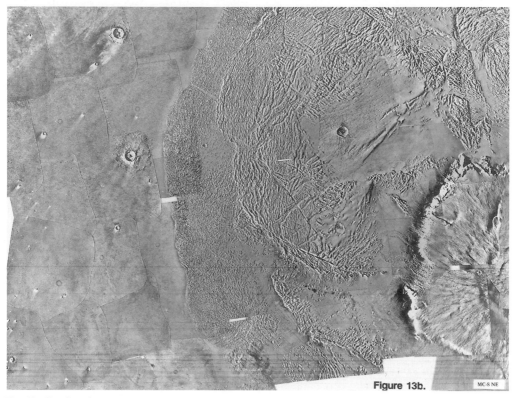

Figure 13b.   MC-8 NE

Fig. 13. Continued.

four. The lower gravity causes cooling-limited flows to be longer, and dykes to be wider and characterized by higher effusion rates, resulting in comparatively long flows (Wilson & Head 1994). Because the lithosphere has been stable and has not moved laterally over the majority of Martian history, regions of melting in the mantle (e.g. mantle plumes) concentrate their effusive products in a single area, rather than spreading them out in conveyor-belt like fashion, as in the case of the Hawaiian-Emperor seamount chain on the Pacific Ocean floor. Thus, melt products accrete vertically into huge accumulations (Carr 1973), loading the lithosphere and causing flexure, deformation, and flank failure. In addition, the volatile-containing upper crust of Mars (Fig. 11) provides conditions and environments conducive to instability development.

Although there is a wide range in the morphometric characteristics of volcanoes on Mars (Pike 1978), the Tharsis shield volcanoes provide good examples of the array of features related to volcanic instability observed on Mars. Comer *et al.* (1985) used the deformational structures surrounding several Tharsis volcanoes to assess lithospheric flexure caused by volcano loading and to estimate the thickness of the elastic lithosphere (Fig. 12). They found elastic lithosphere thicknesses in the range of 20–50 km for regions surrounding the majority of the Tharsis shields, and found it to be at least 150 km thick in the region of Olympus Mons. Thus, one factor contributing to the large height of the Martian volcanoes is the relatively thick elastic lithosphere during their formation; the volcanic load is not subsiding at a rate that would limit its height. In addition, variations in lithospheric thickness in space and time can also be very important in the construction and subsequent modification of volcanic edifices. For the volcanoes forming the Galapagos Archipelago, Feighner & Richards (1994) have shown that there is a relationship between lithospheric thickness and volcano size and structure across the archipelago between areas of effective elastic lithospheric thickness of 6 and 12 km.

McGovern & Solomon (1993) have modelled the details of lithospheric flexure and time-

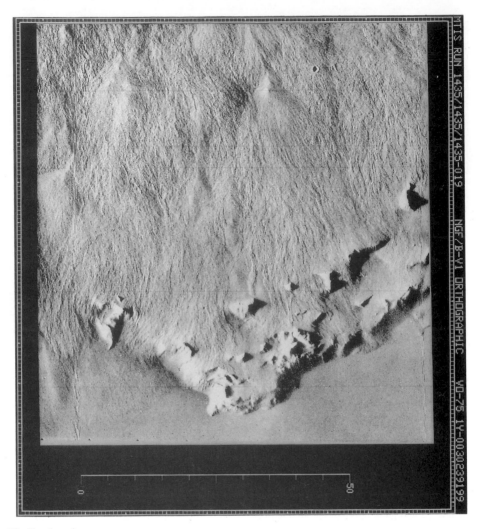

Fig. 13. Continued.

dependent stress and faulting on the Tharsis volcanoes and assessed the influence on magma transport. They show that there are three areas where stressess are sufficiently large due to flexure that failure by faulting results. These include (1) in the plains just outward of the base of the volcano where normal faulting is predicted, (2) near the base of the elastic lithosphere beneath the centre of the volcano where radially oriented normal faulting is predicted, and (3) on the upper flanks of the volcano early in the history of its growth, where circumferential thrust faulting is predicted near the summit and radial thrusting midway down the flanks. In addition, dyke intrusion can also serve as a trigger for instabilities such as large earthquakes which can contribute to catastrophic flank instability (Elsworth & Voight 1995).

Indeed, Olympus Mons shows evidence for most of these types of predicted behaviour (Fig. 13) (Morris & Tanaka 1994). On the upper flanks of the volcano are observed circumferential scarps that have been interpreted to be thrust faults (Thomas *et al.* 1990) (Fig. 13e). At the base of the edifice there is a massive escarpment up to 6 km in height which has been interpreted to be due to the normal faulting of the flanks of the edifice, and associated gravity sliding, perhaps aided by ice-lubrication in the substrate (Lopes *et al.* 1982; Francis & Wadge, 1983; Tanaka 1985) (Fig. 13c). Distal to

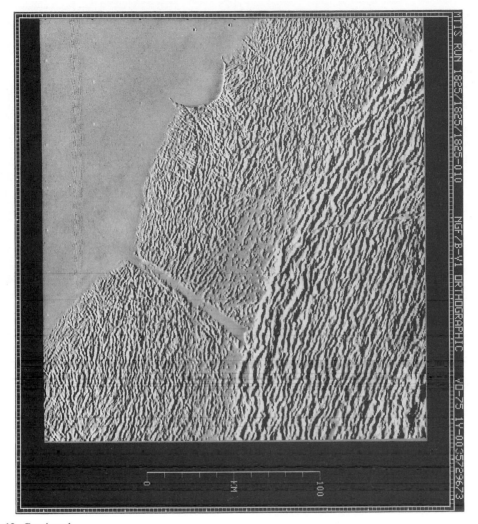

Fig 13. Continued.

this scarp is a wide range of massive landslide deposits that extend to distances from the basal scarp of greater than the diameter of the shield (up to 750 km) (Fig. 13d). These spectacularly developed and well-preserved deposits are asymmetrically developed around the volcano, superposed on one another, and are characterized by curvilinear ridges and troughs, graben structures, and some sinuous channels that may represent the release of groundwater or melted ground ice. Some lobes show clear evidence for lateral movement away from Olympus Mons and greater movement along lobe centres than flanks. Volumes of the most well-exposed main lobes range from 65×10^3 to 170×10^3 km³

(Lopes *et al.* 1982). Similar analyses of terrestrial volcanoes (e.g. Feighner & Richards 1994) should provide similar insights into these relationships.

Similar flanking features are observed around other major shield volcanoes on Mars (Zimbelman & Edgett 1992; Zimbelman 1993). Specifically, the Tharsis Montes, a series of three large shield volcanoes aligned along the Tharsis rise, show evidence for flank failure. These features, Arsia Mons, Pavonis Mons, and Ascraeus Mons, are 350–400 km in diameter and 10–15 km high from base to summit, and are separated from the adjacent volcano by about 750 km. All three volcanoes have large lobe-shaped features

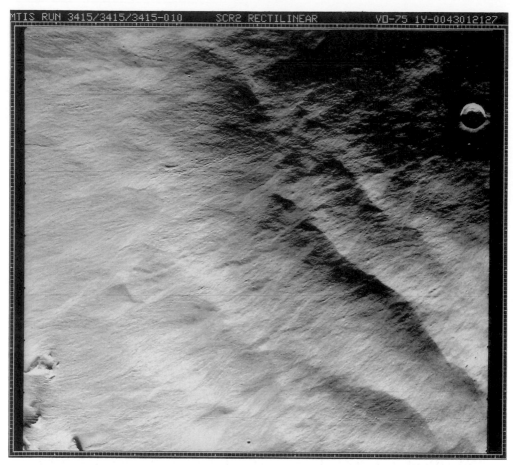

Fig. 13. Continued.

extending to the west-northwest from their base (see fig. 2 in Zimbelman & Edgett 1992). At Arsia Mons the lobe-shaped feature is about 350 km wide and extends 350 km from the base of the volcano, beginning at an elevation of 11 km on the flank and extending to an elevation of about 6 km at the distal margin. Terrain types within the deposit include a ridged unit along the margins of the lobe (Fig. 14), with ridges parallel to the distal portion of the lobe, and knobby terrain and lobate terrain composed of a fabric of features. At Pavonis Mons, the flanking deposit extends 250 km to the northwest and is almost 400 km wide, dropping from an elevation of 11 km to 6.5 km. The deposit is characterized by a marginal and distal ridge unit. Interior to the deposit are found the same units as seen in the Arsia Mons occurrence. Ascreaus Mons is characterized by the smallest flanking lobate deposit of the three volcanoes, extending about

90 km from the base of the shield from an elevation of about 7 to 5.5 km. Here again, ridged terrain encloses the deposit at the distal margins, and knobby and isolated mountainous terrain characterizes the interior.

The similarities in location and morphology of the three Tharsis Montes lobate deposits suggest a common origin. Interpretations must account for the tremendous size and lengths of the deposits, their morphology, and the lack of obvious source areas with sufficient volume on the flanks of the shields. Most workers have interpreted the Tharsis Montes features and the examples at Olympus Mons as being due to gravity-driven landslides (Carr *et al.* 1977; Lopes *et al.* 1982; Francis & Wadge 1983; Tanaka 1985; Scott & Tanaka 1986). Terrestrial land-slides are known that extend to distances of 40 km, such as one associated with Mt. Shasta (Crandell *et al.* 1984), and comparable isolated

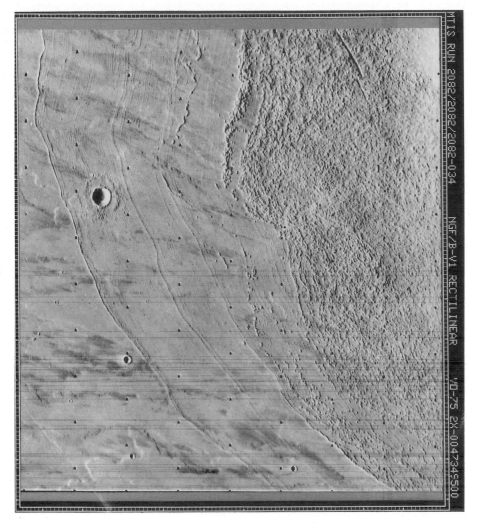

Fig. 14. Ridges at the distal end of the aureole deposit at the northwestern margin of Arsia Mons interpreted to be due to shear-induced folding. Viking Orbiter frame 42B35; width is approximately 200 km.

landslides on Mars are seen that attain runout lengths of up to 100 km within Valles Marineris and around the scarp of Olympus Mons (Sharp 1973; Carr *et al.* 1977; Lucchitta 1978, 1979; Zimbelman and Edgett 1992). Although the lobate deposits are much larger than these individual landslides, a gravity-driven catastrophic slide, possibly involving pore fluids to reduce friction, is the presently preferred mechanism of emplacement (Lopes *et al.* 1982; Francis & Wadge 1983; Tanaka 1985; Zimbelman & Edgett 1992). Anguita & Moreno (1992) have described and interpreted structures outward from the deformed aureole on the northwest flanks of Arsia Mons and interpreted them

as shear-induced folds forming at the distal end of the aureole deposits (Fig. 14). These are similar to many features surrounding terrestrial volcanoes (e.g. Borgia *et al.* 1994; Holroyd & Nicholson 1994) and may represent relatively uneroded examples of this phenomenon.

The lobate features observed on Mars are, to a first approximation, similar to those observed along the Hawaiian Ridge (Fig. 15). There, sonar images have revealed over 70 major landslides in excess of 20 km in length in an abundance sufficient to cover half the flanks of the ridge. The largest of the deposits exceed 200 km in length and 5×10^3 km^3 in volume (Moore *et al.* 1989, 1994). Two forms of landslides have been

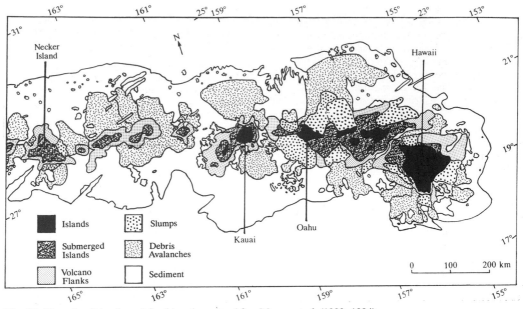

Fig. 15. Hawaiian Islands and flanking deposits. After Moore *et al.* (1989, 1994).

identified there: (1) slumps, which involve mass movement on flanks in excess of about 3° with minimal disruption of the structural coherence of the flanks, are deep-rooted in the volcano interior; (2) debris avalanches, on slopes generally less than 3°, which involve fragmentation, disruption, and dispersion of the original volcanic structures, are thinner, longer, and more surficial, and were likely emplaced catastrophically. Evidence for both of these types of features is seen on Mars (Fig. 13), but the scale of the Martian examples is much larger. Indeed, large-scale sector collapse is even noted on several of the Martian examples, e.g. Tharsis Tholus and Ceraunius Tholus (Crumpler *et al.* 1994, this volume; Robinson & Rowland 1994). In addition, many of the detailed facies within the Martian lobes, such as the hilly and hummocky terrain, may have analogues in the blocky sea-floor hills interpreted as gigantic slide blocks embedded in the larger landslide deposits on the flanks of Hawaii (Moore *et al.* 1995).

Formation of summit calderas represents another mode of instability associated with Martian volcanoes. Because of the large size of the Martian edifices, their calderas also achieve large sizes, with the Olympus Mons caldera approaching the size of Hawaii above sea level (Fig. 9). Two different types of calderas have been described (Crumpler *et al.* 1994, this volume). The Olympus type is characterized by short arcuate scarps or a nested sequence of depressions with

narrow inward-dipping slopes representing steep normal faults (Figs 9, 12, 13); this is most similar in morphology to features associated with Hawaiian volcanoes. The Arsia type has primarily concentric faults distributed over a broad region surrounding the summit depression and primarily forming graben. This type may be due to the larger reservoirs involved in these massive volcanoes and to subsidence and collapse of the broad summit related to this phenomenon.

Summary

Review of the planetary record of volcano growth and development, and associated features potentially related to volcano instabilitiy provides a perspective on terrestrial examples and their causes. Clearly edifice geometry (height/width) and size are significant. Venus volcanoes do not appear to obtain sufficient height to undergo gravitational failure typical of Earth and Mars volcanic edifices. Martian volcanoes grow to sufficient size to undergo flank failure which dwarfs that observed on the Hawaiian Ridge. Variations in lithospheric thickness are seen to be important in the subsidence of volcanoes and thus their maximum height, and in the location and abundance of related features. Thus it is clear that lithospheric thickness and its temporal change must be considered in assessing potential instabilities on Earth, both on the sea-floor and continents. Neutral buoyancy levels are a very significant factor in mapping out potential instabilities. The deep neutral buoyancy zones on the Moon preclude even the formation of significant shallow reservoirs and resulting major shield volcanoes. The lunar example highlights the difference on Earth between continental and oceanic crustal density structures, and reservoir and edifice formation and evolution. Lithospheric stability on Venus and Mars results in primarily vertical accretion of volcanic products; portions of the Earth's lithosphere that are relatively more stable with time (e.g. the African plate) may have a different history of vertical accumulation than the typical conveyor-belt mode of the Hawaiian-Emperor seamount chain. Magma reservoir size is much larger on Mars primarily because of the largely vertical accumulation of ascending products on a stable lithosphere. However, the high atmospheric pressure of the Venus environment is one of several factors that encourages lateral over vertical reservoir growth and this results in increased reservoir size, a factor that might also be important in the terrestrial submarine environment. The presence of groundwater and ice in the substrate on Mars appears to be required to explain the major flanking deposits there and this illustrates the importance of the nature of the substrate in determining potential instabilities associated with volcanic edifices. The widespread nature and excellent preservation of the Martian examples provides an analogue of wide areal extent which may be useful in interpreting the often eroded deposits of terrestrial volcanoes. Planetary examples can thus be utilized to provide perspective on related terrestrial processes.

Research for this paper was supported by grants from the National Aeronautics and Space Administration (NAGW-1873). Thanks are extended to Simon Day for a thorough, informative, and helpful review. Thanks are extended to Karen Plouff and Peter Neivert for help in preparation of the manuscript.

References

ANGUITA, F. & MORENO, F. 1992. Shear-induced folding in Arsia Mons aureole: Evidence for low-latitude martian glaciations. *Earth, Moon and Planets*, **59**, 11–22.

BARGER, K. & JACKSON, E. 1974. Calculated volumes of individual shield volcanoes along the Hawaiian-Emperor chain. *Journal of Research United States Geological Survey*, **2**, 545–550.

BORGIA, A., VAN WYK DE VRIES, B. & RYMER, H. 1994. Spreading at Concepcion volcano, Nicaragua. *Volcano Instability on the Earth and Other Planets*, Geological Society, London.

BULMER, M. 1994. Gravitational collapses on the margins of lava domes on Venus. *Volcano Instability on the Earth & Other Planets*, Geological Society, London.

CARR, M. H. 1973. Volcanism on Mars. *Journal of Geophysical Research*, **78**, 4049–4062.

——1974. The role of lava erosion in the formation of lunar rilles and martian channels. *Icarus*, **22**, 1–23.

——1981. *The Surface of Mars*. Yale University Press, New Haven and London.

——, GREELEY, R., BLASIUS, K. R., GUEST, J. E. & MURRAY, J. B. 1977. Some martian volcanic features as viewed from Viking Orbiters. *Journal of Geophysical Research*, **82**, 3985–4015.

COMER, R., SOLOMON, S. & HEAD, J. 1985. Mars: Thickness of the lithosphere from the tectonic response to volcanic loads. *Journal of Geophysical Research*, **23**, 61–92.

CRANDELL, D. R., MILLER, C. D., GLICKEN, H. X., CHRISTIANSEN, R. L. & NEWHALL, C. G. 1984. Catastrophic debris and avalanche from ancestral Mount Shasta Volcano, California. *Geology*, **12**, 143–146.

CRUMPLER, L., HEAD, J. & AUBELE, J. 1994. Calderas on Mars: Classification, characteristics, and processes related to mechanisms of formation. *Lunar and Planetary Science*, **25**, 305–306.

——, —— & ——1996. Calderas on Mars: Characteristics, structural evolution, and associated flank structures. *This volume*.

ELSWORTH, D. & VOIGHT, B. 1995. Dike intrusion as a trigger for large earthquakes and the failure of volcano flanks. *Journal of Geophysical Research*, **100**, 6005–6024.

FEIGHNER, M. & RICHARDS, M. 1994. Lithospheric structure and compensation mechanisms of the Galapagos Archipelago. *Journal of Geophysical Research*, **99**, 6711–6729.

FRANCIS, P. & WADGE, G. 1983. The Olympus Mons aureole: Formation by gravitational spreading. *Journal of Geophysical Research*, **88**, 8333–8344.

GLAZNER, A. & USSLER, W. 1988. Trapping of magma at midcrustal density discontinuities. *Geophysical Research Letters*, **15**, 673–675.

GROSFILS, E. B. & HEAD, J. W. 1995. Radiating dike swarms on Venus: Evidence for emplacement at zones of neutral buoyancy. *Planetary and Space Science*, **43**, 1555–1560.

GUEST, J., BULMER, M., AUBELE, J. ET AL. 1992. Small volcanic edifices and volcanism in the plains of Venus. *Journal of Geophysical Research*, **97**, 15 949–15 966.

HEAD, J. 1994. Lunar mare deposits: Mechanisms of emplacement, stratigraphy, and implications for the nature and evolution of source regions and secondary crusts. *Lunar and Planetary Science*, **25**, 523–524.

—— & WILSON, L. 1991. Absence of large shield volcanoes and calderas on the Moon: Consequence of magma transport phenomena? *Geophysical Research Letters*, **18**, 2121–2124.

—— & ——1992*a*. Lunar mare volcanism: Stratigraphy, eruption conditions, and the evolution of secondary crusts. *Geochimica Cosmochimica Acta*, **56**, 2155–2175.

—— & ——1992*b*. Magma reservoirs and neutral buoyancy zones on Venus: Implications for the formation and evolution of volcanic landforms. *Journal of Geophysical Research*, **97**, 3877–3903.

—— & ——1994. Lunar graben formation due to near-surface deformation accompanying dike emplacement. *Planetary Space Science*, **41**, 719–727.

——, CRUMPLER, L., AUBELE, J., GUEST, J. & SAUNDERS, S. 1992. Venus volcanism: Classification of volcanic features and structures, associations, and global distribution from Magellan data. *Journal of Geophysical Research*, **97**, 13 153–13 198.

HODGES, C. A. & MOORE, H. J. 1994. *Atlas of Volcanic Landforms on Mars*, US Geological Survey Professional Paper, **1534**.

HOLROYD, J. & NICHOLSON, R. 1994. Volcano instability and the problem of the origin of annular folds in the volcanic complexes of the British Tertiary igneous province. *Volcano Instability on the Earth and Other Planets*, Geological Society, London.

HULME, G. 1973. Turbulent lava flow and the formation of lunar sinuous rilles. *Modern Geology*, **4**, 107–117.

KEDDIE, S. & HEAD, J. 1994. Height and altitude distribution of large volcanoes on Venus. *Planetary Space Science*, **42**, 455–462.

LIPMAN, P. 1980. Cenozoic volcanism in the Western United States: Implications for continental tectonics. *In*: *Studies in Geophysics, Continental Tectonics*, National Academy of Science, Washington, DC, 161–174.

LOPES, R., GUEST, J., HILLER, K. & NEUKUM, G. 1982. Further evidence for a mass movement origin of the Olympus Mons aureole. *Journal of Geophysical Research*, **87**, 9917–9928.

LUCCHITTA, B. K. 1978. A large landslide on Mars. *Bulletin of the Geological Society of America*, **89**, 1601–1609.

——1979. Landslides in Valles Marineris, Mars. *Journal of Geophysical Research*, **84**, 8097–8113.

McGOVERN, P. & SOLOMON, S. 1993. State of stress, faulting, and eruption characteristics of large volcanoes on Mars. *Journal of Geophysical Research*, **98**, 23 553–23 579.

MOORE, J. G., BRYAN, W. B., BEESON, M. H. & NORMARK, W. R. 1995. Giant blocks in the South Kona landslide, Hawaii. *Geology*, **23**, 125–128.

——, CLAGUE, D., HOLCOMB, R., LIPMAN, P., NORMARK, W. & TORRESAN, M. 1989. Prodigious submarine landslides on the Hawaiian ridge. *Journal of Geophysical Research*, **94**, 17 465–17 484.

——, NORMARK, W. & HOLCOMB, R. 1994. Giant Hawaiian underwater landslides. *Science*, **264**, 46–47.

MORRIS, E. C. & TANAKA, K. L. 1994. Geologic maps of the Olympus Mons region of Mars, Atlas of Mars, scale 1 : 2 000 000 Geologic Series, *Map I-2327*, United States Geological Survey.

MOUGINIS-MARK, P. J., WILSON, L. & HEAD, J. W. 1982. Explosive volcanism at Hecates Tholus, Mars: Investigation of eruption conditions. *Journal of Geophysical Research*, **87**, 9890–9904.

PAVRI, B., HEAD, J., KLOSE, B. & WILSON, L. 1992. Steep-sided domes on Venus: Characteristics, geologic setting, and eruption conditions from Magellan data. *Journal of Geophysical Research*, **97**, 13 455–13 478.

PIKE, R. 1978. Volcanoes on the inner planets: Some preliminary comparisons of gross topography. *Proceedings of the Lunar and Planetary Science Conference*, **9**, 3239–3273.

ROBINSON, M. & ROWLAND, S. 1994. Evidence for large scale sector collapse at Tharsis Tholus, Mars. *Volcano Instability on the Earth and Other Planets*, Geological Society, London.

RYAN, M. 1987. Neutral buoyancy and the mechanical evolution of magmatic systems. *In*: MYSEN, B. O. (ed.) *Magmatic Processes: Physico-chemical Principles*. Special Publication **1**, Geochemical Society, 259–287

SCHABER, G. 1973. Lava flows in Mare Imbrium: Geologic evaluation from Apollo orbital photography. *Proceedings of the Lunar and Planetary Science Conference*, **4**, 73–92.

——1991. Volcanism on Venus as inferred from the morphometry of large shields. *Proceedings of the Lunar and Planetary Science Conference*, **21**, 3–11.

——, STROM, R. G., MOORE, H. J. ET AL. 1992. Geology and distribution of impact craters on Venus: What are they telling us? *Journal of Geophysical Research*, **97**, 13 257–13 302.

SCHULTZ, P. & GAULT, D. 1975. Seismic effects from major basin formations on the Moon and Mercury. *The Moon*, **12**, 159–177.

SCOTT, D. H. & TANAKA, K. L. 1986. Geologic map of the western equatorial region of Mars, scale 1 : 15 000 000, *Map I-1802A*, United States Geological Survey Miscellaneous Investigation Series.

——, SCHABER, G. & TANAKA, K. 1981. Map showing lava flows in the southeast part of the Tharsis quadrangle of Mars, *Map I-1269*, United States Geological Survey, Reston, VA.

SHARP, R. P. 1973. Mass movements on Mars. *In*: MORAN, D. E. (ed.) *Geology, Seismicity, and Environmental Impact*. Association of Engineering Geologists, University Publishers, Los Angeles, 115–122.

SOLOMON, S. 1975. Mare volcanism and lunar crustal structure. *Proceedings of the Lunar and Planetary Science Conference*, **6**, 1021–1042.

TANAKA, K. 1985. Ice-lubricated gravity spreading of Olympus Mons aureole deposits. *Icarus*, **62**, 191–206.

THOMAS., P, SQUYRES, S. & CARR, M. 1990. Flank tectonics of martian volcanoes. *Journal of Geophysical Research*, **95**, 14 345–14 355.

TOLAN, T., REIDEL, S., BEESON, M., ANDERSON, J., FECHT, K. & SWANSON, D. 1989. Revisions to the estimates of the areal extent and volume of the Columbia River Basalt Group. *In*: REIDEL, S. & HOOPER, P. (eds) *Volcanism and Tectonism in the Columbia River Flood-basalt Province*. Geological Society of America, Special Paper **239**.

WILSON, L. & HEAD, J. 1994. Mars: Review and analysis of volcanic eruption theory and relationships to observed landforms. *Reviews of Geophysics*, **32**, 221–263.

ZIMBELMAN, J. R. 1993. Comparison of flank modification on Ascraeus and Arsia Montes volcanoes, Mars. *Lunar and Planetary Science*, **24**, 1575–1576.

—— & EDGETT, K. S. 1992. The Tharsis Montes, Mars: Comparison of volcanic and modified landforms. *Proceedings of Lunar and Planetary Sciences*, **22**, 31–44.

Evaluation of volcano flank instability triggered by dyke intrusion

DEREK ELSWORTH[1] & BARRY VOIGHT[2]

[1] Department of Mineral Engineering, Pennsylvania State University, University Park, Pennsylvania 16802-5000, USA

[2] Department of Geosciences, Pennsylvania State University, University Park, Pennsylvania 16802-2712, USA

Abstract: Instability of volcano flanks may result from the mechanically and thermally generated pore fluid pressures that accompany dyke intrusion. These complementary methods of pore pressure generation act on potential basal failure planes, decreasing effective stresses and consequently decreasing frictional resistance to failure. The twin agents of pore pressure generation provide a rational and quantifiable means of initiating and sustaining flank instability, even as the driving forces provided by magma pressurization ultimately drop as flank displacement is initiated. Pore pressures developed by mechanical and thermal effects are readily evaluated using simple, but mechanistically rigorous, models. Mechanically induced pore fluid pressures are evaluated through an analogy with a moving line dislocation within a saturated porous-elastic medium. Thermally induced pore fluid pressures are evaluated from a one-dimensional advective–diffusive solution for low Peclet transport, representing behaviour around a plane feeder dyke of infinite extent. Induced pore pressure magnitudes condition stability through the parameters representing the geometry and dimensions of the flank and failing flank block, together with the parameters modulating volumetric magma intrusion rate and heat supply. Where appropriate parameter magnitudes are selected, the resulting mechanical and thermal pore fluid pressures are sufficient to initiate failure. Where the pervasive influence of thermally induced pore pressures is included, or where shear collapse of the saturated pore structure occurs, the disturbance is sufficient to sustain failure. This presents the possibility for long runout instabilities of extremely large volume.

Observational evidence exists at a number of oceanic-shield type volcanoes indicating massive landslides. These landslide deposits are now recognized as comprising products of the growth and ultimate destruction of shield volcanoes as part of an on-going cyclic process. At Mauna Loa, for instance, debris avalanche deposits more than 200 km long and 5000 km^3 in volume are apparent in the bathymetric record (Moore 1964; Moore *et al.* 1989). These debris avalanches are presumed to accompany all stages of cone building, continue long after dormancy, and develop in the form of both slow moving slumps and fast moving debris avalanches. Despite the clear evidence of these features in the bathymetric record, failure remains enigmatic for shallow inclination of these shield volcano flanks since estimated frictional resistance on basal failure planes appears insufficiently low to initiate and sustain failure (Iverson 1991). This inconsistency may be explained if all factors affecting shear strength are examined. Most importantly, the factors that affect shear strength may be considered in terms of effective stress analysis whereby both frictional resistance of the basal surface (a material parameter) and reduction of effective stresses through increased pore fluid pressures (an environmental factor) may be considered separately. Consequently, if pore fluid pressures can be increased sufficiently, then failure may be initiated (see also Day, this volume), even in the absence of an extensive underlying décollement.

Iverson (1992, 1995) considered several pore fluid pressurization mechanisms in the context of volcano flank failure, including gravity driven hydraulic gradients, sea-level changes, and gravitational consolidation due to a growing volcano edifice but concluded that these mechanisms were insufficient to cause large scale failure. Correspondingly, some alternative explanation is needed.

A process which has been shown to produce substantial pore fluid pressure increases is that of dyke injection (Voight & Elsworth 1992). Dyke injection may produce pore fluid pressures through the mechanisms of mechanical straining (Stefánsson 1981; Watanabe 1983; Elsworth & Voight 1992) and the complementary process of thermal straining (Björnsson *et al.* 1977). The anticipated magnitude of the pore fluid pressures developed by each of these processes is quantified in the following with specific regard to the potential to create flank instability in oceanic-shield type environments.

From McGuire, W. J., Jones, A. P. & Neuberg, J. (eds) 1996, *Volcano Instability on the Earth and Other Planets*, Geological Society Special Publication No. 110, pp. 45–53.

Mechanical pore fluid pressures

The pore fluid pressures, $p - p_s$, induced around a planar dyke of infinite extent and width, w, intruded at velocity, U, within a poroelastic medium may be readily evaluated (Elsworth & Voight 1992). The total uplift force, F_{pm}, applied to the block geometry of Fig. 1 may be evaluated by integrating this distribution over the basal extent of the block (for example see Fig. 2) as (Elsworth & Voight 1995),

$$F_{pm} = \int_{-\frac{1}{2}d}^{+\frac{1}{2}d} \int_0^{\bar{l}} (p - p_s) \, dl \, dx$$

$$= w_D U_D \gamma_w h_s^3 \int_{-\frac{1}{2}d_D}^{+\frac{1}{2}d_D} \int_0^{\bar{l}_D} P_D \, dl_D \, dx_D \quad (1)$$

where

$$P_D = K_0[U_D R_D] e^{U_D x_D} \quad (2)$$

and $k_0[x]$ is the modified Bessel function of the second kind of zero order, and dimensionless pressure, P_D, is controlled by the dimensionless intrusion velocity, U_D, and geometric variables R_D and x_D, illustrated in Fig. 1. For the planar dyke, these variables are defined as

$$P_D = \frac{2\pi(p - p_s)}{Uw} \frac{k}{\mu} \quad (3)$$

$$U_D = \frac{Uh_s}{2c} \quad (4)$$

$$w_D = \frac{\mu}{k} \frac{wc}{\pi \gamma_w h_s^2} \quad (5)$$

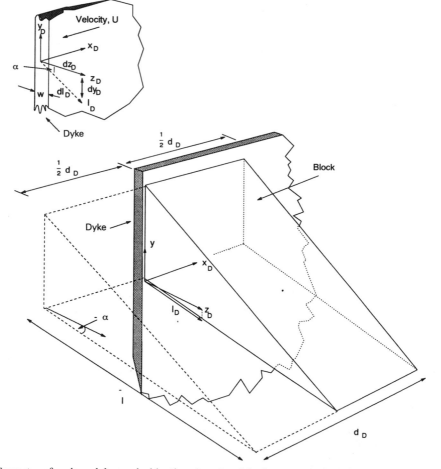

Fig. 1. Geometry of a plane dyke marked by the advancing dyke front at $x_D = 0$ and with a coordinate system that migrates with the moving dyke front. The dyke width is w and the front moves with dimensionless velocity U_D. Mechanically induced pressures are desired on a plane inclined at α degrees to the z-axis. The limits of integration are the extent of the plane, given as 0 to $\bar{l}_D$ and $-\frac{1}{2}d_D$ to $+\frac{1}{2}d_D$.

$$(x_D, y_D, z_D) = \frac{1}{h_s} (x, y, z) \qquad (6)$$

and

$$R_D^2 = x_D^2 + z_D^2. \qquad (7)$$

where permeability of the porous medium, k, dynamic viscosity of the saturating fluid, μ, and hydraulic diffusivity of the porous medium, c, are the material parameters controlling behaviour. An arbitrary length parameter, h_s, is incorporated to represent the diffusive length scale. In this particular case, h_s is selected as the height of the slope crest above sea level. $\bar{l}_D$ is the limit of integration measured along the basal trace and γ_w is the unit weight of water. The normalized width of integration along the x-axis, representing the path of dyke propagation, is $d_D = d/h_s$ with d representing the actual width.

The two primary factors influencing the magnitude of pore pressure generation are intrusion velocity and intrusion width. An increase in either of these quantities, given that all other parameters remain constant, results in increased uplift force acting on the free block. Increase in either velocity or width has the net effect of increasing the net volumetric intrusion rate, with a corresponding increase in the strain rate in the surrounding porous medium. It is this strain rate, manifest in the surrounding geologic material, that conditions pore pressure generation.

The assumptions of linear elastic behaviour and of invariant permeability are made in this feasibility analysis, despite processes of large deformation, fracture (Sleep 1988) and dilation (Rubin 1993) that may develop around the process zone at the dyke front. The linear analysis has already been shown adequate in representing real events (Elsworth & Voight 1992) where these non-ideal processes may be anticipated to operate, provided it is the mid- and far-field behaviour that is desired. This is especially true where the effects of local development of short-circuiting fluid pathways, crack tip dilation zones and concurrent thermal expansion and boiling effects will be masked by the gross response to a volumetric dislocation.

Thermal pore fluid pressures

Fluid pressures induced by thermal straining as a result of dyke intrusion may also be quantified (Delaney 1982). Various geometries are feasible in real volcanoes, but for purposes of illustration in this paper a geometry is assumed similar to that considered for the development of mechanical pore fluid pressures. The presence of a feeder dyke is assumed, to provide a nearly constant, moderately long-term (days to weeks) supply of thermal energy to the system. The idealized representation is similar to that shown in Fig. 1, with a planar dyke forming the rear scarp of a delineated failing block geometry. Again, uplift fluid pressures can be evaluated for the system where the time-dependent uplift force, F_{pt}, is given as (Elsworth & Voight 1995),

$$F_{pt} = \frac{d}{h_s} A_D \sqrt{\frac{t_D}{\pi}} \frac{1}{D \cos \alpha} \qquad (8)$$

with

$$A_D = \frac{A K_b D}{\gamma_w h_s} \qquad (9)$$

$$t_D = \frac{4\kappa t}{h_s^2} \qquad (10)$$

where the new dimensionless groupings represent the fluid volume generated by the temperature change, A_D, the ratio of thermal to hydraulic diffusivities, D, and dimensionless time, t_D. These controlling variable groupings are modulated by the additional component dimensional parameters of undrained bulk skeletal modulus of the solid, K_b, thermal strain, $A = \alpha_t \Delta T$ (where α_t is the coefficient of free thermal expansion and ΔT is temperature differential between the intruding magma and the host), thermal diffusivity, κ, and time, t.

Again the assumption is of linear behaviour where assumed thermal forcing, embodied through thermal strain (A), is sensibly constant for a variety of depths and magma temperatures (Delaney 1982). Other parameters may not be so conveniently constrained, such as the development of mechanical enhancement of permeabilities or consideration of free or forced convection. These processes represent mechanisms of increasing the rate of migration away from the intrusion with the consequence that the distribution of thermal pressures may be strongly affected but the integrated distribution will be much less influenced. It is this integrated distribution that is incorporated in the analysis.

Flank failure geometry

Flank failure may be considered in two specific geometries representing the potential for shallow failure and deep-seated rupture, respectively (cf. Dieterich 1988; Iverson 1995). These failure modes are represented in Fig. 2; the only difference between the two failure modes is the dip of the potential basal failure surface with

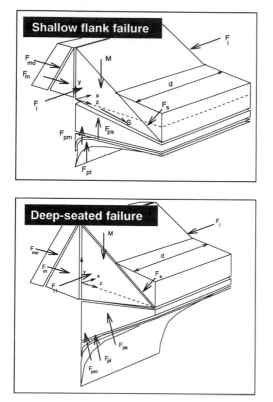

Fig. 2. Generalized geometry for limit equilibrium analysis of shallow and deep-seated flank failure. All quantities defined positive. α is positive for deep-seated failure and negative for long runout failure. Forces acting on the system are block weight, M, seawater pressure, F_s, lateral force, F_l, magma force, F_m, magma overpressure force, F_{mo}, static groundwater force, F_{ps}, and induced pore pressure forces that result from mechanical, F_{pm}, and thermal, F_{pt}, strains. Height of block crest above sea level, h_s, and block width, d, define block geometry.

The limit equilibrium behaviour of either of these shallow or deep geometries may be described using identical terminology. Delineating a block of width, d, enables a force balance to be performed on a system that includes the effects of block weight, M, magma force, F_m, magma overpressure force, F_{mo}, static groundwater force, F_{ps}, seawater force, F_s, lateral block force, F_l, and the two important environmental factors representing mechanically induced uplift force, F_{pm}, and thermally induced uplift force, F_{pt}.

Choosing a simple geometry with a flank slope of ten degrees, a crest of the failing block 1000 m above sea level, a basal failure plane inclination of six degrees, and a groundwater surface sloping up from sea-level at two degrees enables the stability of a simple geometry to be investigated. The static groundwater, seawater, and magma pressures remain relatively invariant under this choice of geometry where reasonable magnitudes of magma (28×10^{-3} MPa m^{-1}) and rock density (23×10^{-3} MPa m^{-1}) are selected. Correspondingly, the potential destabilizing influence of dyke intrusion through the development of mechanical and thermal pore pressures may be evaluated. This evaluation is most conveniently made using a normalized factor of safety, $F/\tan \phi$, to represent behaviour for a variety of undefined frictional resistance magnitudes, ϕ. The factor of safety, F, refers to the ratio of forces acting to resist failure to those destabilizing the block. Stabilizing forces are applied through the shear strength of the basal failure plane that may be reduced through available mechanically or thermally induced pore fluid pressures. Normalized factors of safety in the range 1–2 represent the limiting equilibrium condition for angles of frictional resistance in the range 45–27 degrees, respectively. The response of different materials to dyke intrusion through mechanical and thermal effects is detailed in the following sections. Ranges of these parameters are included in Table 1.

Mechanical pore fluid pressures

The anticipated stabilities of a volcano flank comprising volcaniclastic debris and fractured basaltic lava are illustrated in Figs 3 and 4 respectively. For the volcaniclastic material, an appropriate range of non-dimensional dyke widths, w_D, is of the order $10^0 - 10^6$. Apparent in the behaviour is the diminishing influence of lateral restraint acting to stabilize the failing wedge as width of the failing block increases. This effect is countered at very large magnitudes of block width where stability again increases as

respect to the slope of the volcano flank. For shallow flank failure, the dip of the basal failure surface is congruent with the dip of the flank and provides the potential for long run-out failure of the type observed in debris avalanches. In this the term *shallow* is relative since the rear scarp depth of these failures may be of the order of 1 km. This mode of failure is in contrast to deep-seated failure where run-out is not possible but where limited rupture close to the rear block scarp may result in the development of deep earthquakes which, in turn, may precipitate seismic destabilization of shallow failures as a result of both induced ground accelerations and the potential influence of liquefaction in weak materials.

Table 1. *Material parameters selected as representative of the mechanical and thermal properties of flanks of oceanic-island volcanoes (after Elsworth & Voight 1995)*

Parameter	Symbol	Magnitude	Units	Source(s)
Slope height above sea level	h_s	1000	m	
Shear modulus	G	3×10^3	MPa	Davis, cited by Rubin & Pollard (1987)
Poisson ratio	ν	0.22–0.28	–	Rubin & Pollard (1987)
Frictional resistance	ϕ	20–60	degrees	*
Coefficient of earth pressure at rest	k_0	0.5	–	Estimated from Dieterich (1988)
Unit weights				
water	γ_w	10×10^{-3}	MPa m^{-1}	
rock	γ_r	23–29×10^{-3}	MPa m^{-1}	Zucca & Hill (1980); Zucca *et al.* (1982); Rubin & Pollard (1987)
magma	γ_m	26–28×10^{-3}	MPa m^{-1}	Decker (1987)
Volcaniclastic debris				†
Permeability	k/μ	1–2×10^{-11}	m^2 Pa^{-1} s^{-1}	Sigurdsson (1982); Bodvarsson *et al.* (1984)
Hydraulic diffusivity	c	$770 - 1550$	m^2 s^{-1}	Sigurdsson (1982); Bodvarsson *et al.* (1984)
Intrusion width	w	$1(1 \times 10^{-3})$	m	Tryggvason (1980); Elsworth & Voight (1992)‡
Intrusion rate	U	$0.27 - 0.75$	m s^{-1}	Brandsdottir & Einarsson (1979); Elsworth & Voight (1992)
Fractured lava				†
Permeability	k/μ	1.65–7.2×10^{-6}	m^2 Pa^{-1} s^{-1}	Thomas (1987); Mink & Lau (1980)
Hydraulic diffusivity	c	1.5–6.5×10^{-6}	m^2 s^{-1}	§
Intrusion width	w	1	m	Delaney & Pollard (1981); Rubin & Pollard (1987)
Intrusion rate	U	0.1–0.5	m s^{-1}	Delaney & Pollard (1981)
Thermal parameters				
Thermal strain	A	0.9–1	–	Delaney (1982)
Skeletal modulus	K_b	0.4–1.2×10^3	MPa	Delaney (1982)
Thermal diffusivity	κ	10^{-6}	m^2 s^{-1}	Delaney (1982)
Intergranular porosity	n	0.05–0.2	–	Delaney (1982)

* Possibly ϕ may be close to, or lower than, the lower limit of the range where clays dominate the key stratigraphic horizon, but it is questionable whether these low values are appropriate for the entire basal failure plane, including subaerial and submarine parts. Lower range values representative of clays and mudstones. Upper range values representative of angular granular debris or weak rock, and include the effect of cohesion on apparent friction angle.

† Volcaniclastic data based on studies at Krafla volcano by authors cited; lava data based on studies in the Hawaiian Islands by authors cited.

‡ Unbracketed value represents observed thickness. Bracketed value represents thickness estimate consistent with parameters used in the evaluation of intrusion-induced fluid pressures.

§ Magnitude of hydraulic diffusivity is estimated from $c = 2(k/\mu)G(1 - \nu)/(1 - 2\nu)$ to give representative value for incompressible fluid and grains (Rice & Cleary 1976). Parameter range obtained through using $\nu = 0.25$, and shear modulus, G and permeability, k/μ, ranges defined in the table.

the size of the potential failing block increases beyond the extent of the pressure bulb induced by dyke injection. For the larger magnitudes of non-dimensional dyke widths anticipated, mechanically induced pore fluid pressures appear sufficient to result in destabilization. These block widths are relatively large representing real block widths of the order of 1 to 100 km ($d_D = 1 - 100$). For the fractured lavas, the appropriate range of non-dimensional dyke widths is of the order of 10^{-4} to 10^0 and the corresponding influence on stability is minimal, as illustrated in Fig. 4. Correspondingly, the potential destabilizing influence of mechanically induced pore fluid pressures appears closely related to the mechanical and fluid transmissive characteristics of the rock surrounding the intrusion.

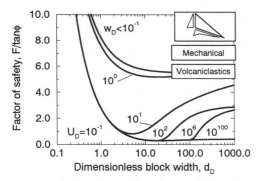

Fig. 3. Variation of normalized factor of safety for a long runout failure of a volcano flank with mechanically induced pressures resulting from dyke intrusion. Basal failure plane is inclined at $\alpha = -6°$. $h_m/h_s = 1$ with h_m given as the magma column height and $U_D = 10^{-1}$, representative of volcaniclastic debris. Dotted results represent behaviour for material parameters beyond anticipated range.

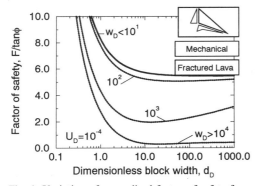

Fig. 4. Variation of normalized factor of safety for a long runout failure of a volcano flank with mechanically induced pressures resulting from dyke intrusion. Basal failure plane is inclined at $\alpha = -6°$. $h_m/h_s = 1$ with h_m given as the magma column height and $U_D = 10^{-4}$, representative of fractured lava. Dotted results represent behaviour for material parameters beyond anticipated range.

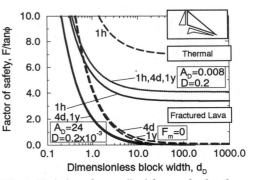

Fig. 5. Variation of normalized factor of safety for a long runout failure of a volcano flank with thermally induced pressures resulting from dyke intrusion. Analysis includes the disturbing influence of the magma column for both maximum (solid) and minimum (dotted) anticipated thermal effect. Results for the maximum thermal effect are illustrated (long dashed) where the driving influence of the magmastatic forces at the rear of the block are neglected (i.e. $F_m = 0$). Basal failure plane is inclined at $\alpha = -6°$.

Thermal pore fluid pressures

The influence of thermally induced pore fluid pressures is evaluated for the geometry described previously. The destabilizing influence of a feeder dyke present at the rear scarp of the block is identified in Fig. 5 where sets of thermal parameters having alternately the maximum and minimum influence on behaviour are included. For parameters representing the minimum influence, the thermal effect is not discernible over the normal static behaviour. Where the maximum effect is included, sustained thermal exposure over the period of a number of days, or more, is sufficient to drastically reduce stability. This effect is apparent in Fig. 5 and appears sufficient to induce failure of relatively wide and, therefore, voluminous rock monoliths.

To gauge the potential to sustain movement, once initiated, the influence of the maximum thermal effect is applied to the geometry where the magma drive at the rear scarp is removed ($F_m = 0$). This behaviour is also illustrated in Fig. 5 where stability both in the presence and absence of magma drive at the rear scarp is contrasted. This analysis may be used as a qualitative indicator of the potential for sustaining failure once initiated and therefore defines the potential of developing the debris avalanche modes evident in the bathymetric record. As apparent in Fig. 5 the development of long runout avalanches appears plausible for blocks of considerable magnitude, providing thermal disturbance is available for periods of the order of days and greater.

Earthquake loading

Behaviour with the additional destabilizing influence of earthquake loading may be gauged using a simple pseudo-static analysis. Pseudo-static accelerations in the range $\delta = 0.0$ to $0.2g$ may result from seismic activity spawned in the deep crust or through deep rupture (greater

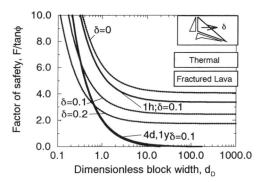

Fig. 6. Variation of normalized factor of safety for shallow failure of a volcano flank subject to lateral pseudostatic earthquake acceleration, δ, and with static groundwater and thermally induced pore fluid pressures applied. Magmastatic pressures are applied for all analyses. Basal failure plane is inclined at $\alpha = -6°$.

than 10 km) accompanying magma injection at depth. The influence of these pseudo-static accelerations is to uniformly reduce stability with increasing level of acceleration, as illustrated in Fig. 6. Consequently, where earthquake accelerations are applied to the system loaded only by static groundwater pressures, F_s, and rear scarp magma pressures, F_m, the seismic accelerations are sufficient to cause destabilization only for the largest accelerations. Where the seismic effect is superposed on an already apparent thermal signature, then again, the net result is one of destabilization capable of initiating and sustaining failure block widths of the order of 1 km or greater.

Conclusions

From the somewhat idealized geometry and characteristics described previously, the magnitude of induced pore fluid pressures that may accompany dyke intrusion appears sufficient, under some circumstances, to initiate failure in oceanic shield type volcanoes. The magnitude of uplift pressures is influenced by the mechanical, thermal and fluid transmissive characteristics of the cone material and is therefore controlled by the magnitude or severity of the intrusive event. For the ranges of material characteristics deemed applicable to these environments, the initiation of failure is certainly plausible.

To some degree, the impacts of mechanically and thermally induced pore fluid are additive, although the two processes operate on different timescales. Mechanically induced pore fluid pressures are the fastest acting and may be anticipated to operate over periods of hours to days. The development of significant thermal pore fluid pressures requires sustained supply of feeder dykes over periods of days to weeks, although the larger and more diffuse form of the pore fluid pressures developed by this mechanism appears to have a greater potential for destabilization than mechanical effects. In addition to the agents of mechanical and thermal pore pressure generation, deep-seated earthquakes may also trigger shallow failure through the development of horizontal ground acceleration. These three mechanisms may act in an additive manner to result in flank destabilization and produce failure only for an intrusional eruption of some critical severity. In this, the block size of the resulting failure is conditioned by a minimum size required to overcome the influence of lateral restraint and a maximum defined by the extent of the length of the intruding dyke. Theoretical critical block widths for oceanic shield type volcanoes appear in the range of kilometres to tens of kilometres, and this is consistent with the evidence from the Hawaiian Islands, and elsewhere.

Local complicated distributions of permeability could enable short-circuiting of pore fluid flow, with the result of less-than-critical pore fluid pressures over much of a potential failure plane. Under such circumstances, flank failure will not occur. This circumstance is not rare as most dyke and fire-fountain events simply do not produce flank failures. But some do, and that is the focus of this paper.

The purpose of this paper is to present the general idea of the potential for suprahydrostatic pore pressure generation, not to compare all variations in geometry and material variability. Correspondingly, constant parameter magnitudes are assumed for the purpose of mathematical tractability. More realistic models might consider parameter variation with environmental factors, such as temperature dependence of thermal expansion, or non-uniform and time-varying permeability, among others. These complications, which may be important in some circumstances, are beyond the scope of this feasibility analysis. In some cases, such as for Krafla, Iceland (Elsworth & Voight 1992), parameter variations with environmental factors appear to be of small importance. Similar processes may apply to hydrothermal systems, even in cases for which slope failure is not accompanied by volcanism.

Once initiated, the development of the instability into a debris avalanche requires that a critical disturbing force imbalance is sustained, even though the driving forces due to magma may drop. For instance, the pore fluid pressures induced by thermal strains appear sufficiently high and widespread that failure may be sustained even after the driving influence of the magma drops following the initiation of failure. Earthquake generated liquefaction in the area of the basal failure plane, pressure generation as result of pore collapse, frictional heating on the failure plane and undrained loading of sediments in the over-run area at the toe of the block may all contribute to maintaining movement of the slide once initiated.

These mechanisms of pore pressure generation offer plausible means of resolving the enigma of failure in low-inclination flanks of shield volcanoes. Although attention has been restricted to geometries representative of shield volcanoes, similar triggering mechanisms may be shown to act in strato volcanoes (Voight & Elsworth 1994). For strato cones, the initially steeper flank inclination requires that a smaller relative pore pressure change is required to bring the flank to limit equilibrium, and consequent failure. Correspondingly, the conclusions drawn above for shield-type volcanoes appear applicable for stratocones with even less constraints.

This work was supported,in part, by the National Science Foundation under grants EAR-9106134, EAR-91173396, MSS-9218547, and EAR-9316739. This support is gratefully acknowledged. The thoughtful reviews of Simon Day and Andy Pullen improved the final manuscript and W. Meyer assisted with technical data.

References

BJÖRNSSON, A., KRISTJÁNSON, L. & JOHNSON, H. 1977. Some observations of the Heimaey deep drill hole during the eruption of 1973. *Jökul*, **26**, 52–57.

BODVARSSON, G. S., BENSON, S. M. SIGURDSSON, O., STEFÁNSSON, V. & ELIASSON, E. T. 1984. The Krafla Geothermal Field, Iceland, 1, Analysis of well test data. *Water Resources Research*, **20**(11), 1515–1530.

BRANDSDÓTTIR, B. & EINARSSON, P. 1979. Seismic activity associated with the September 1977 deflation of the Krafla central volcano in northeastern Iceland. *Journal of Volcanology and Geothermal Research*, **6**, 197–212.

DAY, S. J. 1996. Hydrothermal pore fluid pressure and the stability of porous, permeable volcanoes. *This volume*.

DECKER, R. W. 1987. Dynamics of Hawaiian volcanoes *In*: DECKER, R. W., WRIGHT, T. L. & STAUFFER, P. H. (eds) *Volcanism in Hawaii*. US Geological Survey Professional Paper, **1350**, 997–1018.

DELANEY, P. T. 1982. Rapid intrusion of magma into wet rock: Groundwater flow due to pore pressure increases. *Journal of Geophysical Research*, **87**, 7739–7756.

—— & POLLARD, D. D. 1981. Deformation of host rocks and flow of magma during flow of minette dikes and breccia-bearing intrusions near Ship Rock, New Mexico. *US Geological Survey Professional Paper*, **1202**, 1–61.

DIETERICH, J. T. 1988. Growth and persistence of Hawaiian volcanic rift zones. *Journal of Geophysical Research*, **93**, 4258–4270.

ELSWORTH, D. & VOIGHT, B. 1992. Theory of dike intrusion in a saturated porous solid. *Journal of Geophysical Research*, **97**, 9105–9117.

—— & ——1995. Dike intrusion as a trigger for large earthquakes and failure of volcano flanks. *Journal of Geophysical Research*, **100(B4)**, 6005–6024.

IVERSON, R. M. 1991. Failure and runout of giant landslides on Hawaiian volcanoes: Cases of enigmatic mechanics? *Geological Society of America Abstracts Programs*, **47**, A125.

——1992. Rigid-wedge models for metastable flanks of Hawaiian volcanoes, (abstract). *Eos Transactions of AGU*, **73**(43), Fall Meeting suppl., 505.

——1995. Can magma-injection and groundwater forces cause massive landslides on Hawaiian volcanoes? *Journal of Volcanology and Geothermal Research*, in press.

MINK, J. F., & LAU, L. S. 1980. *Hawaiian Groundwater Geology and Hydrogeology, and Early Mathematical Models*. US Geological Survey Technical Memo Report, **62**.

MOORE, J. G. 1964. Giant submarine landslides on the Hawaiian Ridge. *US Geological Survey Professional Paper*, **501-D**, D95–D98.

——, CLAGUE, D. A., HOLCOMB, R. T., LIPMAN, P. W., NORMARK, W. R. & TORRESAN, M. E. 1989. Prodigious submarine landslides on the Hawaiian Ridge. *Journal of Geophysical Research*, **94**, 17465–17484.

RICE, J. R. & CLEARY, M. P. 1976. Some basic stress diffusion solutions for fluid-saturated elastic porous media with compressible constituents. *Reviews in Geophysics*, **14**(2), 227–241.

RUBIN, A. M. 1993. Tensile fracture of rock at high confining pressure: implications for dike propagation. *Journal of Geophysical Research*, **98**, 15919–15935.

—— & POLLARD, D. D. 1987. Origins of blade-like dikes in volcanic rift zones. *In*: DECKER, R. W., WRIGHT, T. L. & STAUFFER, P. H. (eds) *Volcanism in Hawaii*. US Geological Survey Professional Paper, **1350**, 1449–1470.

SIGURDSSON, O. 1982. *Analysis of Pressure Pulses Resulting from Volcanic Activity in the Vicinity of a Well*. MS thesis, University of Oklahoma, Norman.

SLEEP, N. H. 1988. Tapping of melt by veins and dykes, *Journal of Geophysical Research*, **98**, 10255–10272.

STEFÁNSSON, V. 1981. The Krafla geothermal field, northern Iceland. *In*: RYBACH, L. & MUFFLER, L. J. P. (eds) *Geothermal Systems; Principles and Case Histories*. John Wiley, New York, 273–294.

THOMAS, D. 1987. A geochemical model of the Kilauea east rift zone. *In*: DECKER, R. W., WRIGHT, T. L. & STAUFFER, P. H. (eds) *Volcanism in Hawaii*. US Geological Survey Professional Paper, **1350**, 1507–1525.

TRYGGVASON, E. 1980. Subsidence events in the Krafla area, north Iceland, 1975–1979. *Journal of Geophysics*, **47**, 141–153.

VOIGHT, B. & ELSWORTH, D. 1992. Resolution of mechanics problems for prodigious Hawaiian landslides: Magmatic intrusions simultaneously increase driving force and reduce driving resistance by fluid pressure enhancement (abstract). *Eos Transactions of AGU*, **73**(43), Fall Meeting suppl., 506.

—— & ——1994. Role of magma in volcano collapse mechanics. *Geotechnique*, in press.

WATANABE, H. 1983. Changes in water level and their implications to the 1977–1978 activity of Usu volcano. *In*: SHIMOZURU, D. & YOKOYAMA, J. (eds) *Arc Volcanism: Physics and Tectonics*. Terra Scientific, Tokyo, 81–93.

ZUCCA, J. J. & HILL, D. P. 1980. Crustal structure of the southeast flank of Kilauea Volcano, Hawaii, from seismic refraction measurements. *Bulletin of the Seismology Society of America*, **70**, 1149–1159.

——, —— & KOVACH, R. L. 1982. Crustal structure of Mauna Loa Volcano, Hawaii, from seismic refraction measurements and gravity data. *Geological Society of America Bulletin*, **72**, 1535–1550.

Mutual influence of dyking and collapses at Stromboli volcano, Italy

ALESSANDRO TIBALDI

Dipartimento di Scienze della Terra, Università di Milano, Via Mangiagalli 34, 20133-Milano, Italy

Abstract: The island of Stromboli represents the emergent part of a 2.6 km high composite volcano. The evolution of this summit zone is characterized by a complex dyke pattern and repeated collapses. Three summit collapses and one southeastward minor lateral collapse occurred between 85 and 21 ka BP. From 13 ka to a few thousand years ago, three large lateral collapses occurred northwestwards. During the last 100 ka of volcanic history, which is reconstructed on the basis of data derived from the emergent part of the cone, the majority of dykes have been injected along a NE–SW zone of weakness which cuts the summit of the volcano. In the southern part of the island a N–S dyke zone connected, for a short period, the main Stromboli conduit to an off-shore crater. Another dyke zone developed after 13 ka BP along the walls of the earliest lateral collapse which occurred towards the NW at around this time. Dykes are vertical, especially along the NE-trending weak zone, whereas the other more external dykes tend to parallel the cone slopes and the collapse depression. Cumulative dyke thicknesses have a NW–SE horizontal maximum. Dyking along the NE–SW weak zone may have exerted a geometric control and provided a trigger for the NW–SE lateral collapse event. In turn the more external dyking was extremely sensitive to the local $\sigma 3$ induced by debuttressing, in the case of injection planes parallel to the lateral collapse escarpments, and by the gross volcano morphology, in the case of dykes which parallel the cone slopes.

The island of Stromboli and two other volcanic centres constitute a large, 2.6 km high, volcanic complex at the NE tip of the Aeolian archipelago (Fig. 1). The Stromboli volcano constitutes the island of that name; Strombolicchio is a volcanic neck forming a small island to the north east; and Cavoni is a submerged centre identified on the basis of marine geophysical data (Gabbianelli *et al.* 1993) to the south. The internal structure of Stromboli volcano is complex because of the alternating constructive and destructive phases. The latter range from slow, slope-erosive processes to rapid slope failure, and have created several unconformities which enabled Rosi (1980), Francalanci (1987), Keller *et al.* (1993) and Pasquarè *et al.* (1993) to distinguish the main cycles of activity. The nature of the summit feeding system is revealed by a complex dyke pattern. Dyke swarms are well exposed all around the island because the host rocks, comprising breccia deposits and highly fractured lava flows, are more prone to erosion, and because of the continuous erosive activity of the sea. Dykes crop out from sea-level to about 900 m a.s.l., corresponding to two-fifths of the height of the edifice. As such, Stromboli constitutes an exceptional case study which permits analysis of the feeding system and the inner structure of the upper part of a composite volcano which has experienced multiple collapse.

Dykes and fractures are not arranged in a typical radial pattern as observed in the summit zones of other composite volcanoes (Chevallier & Verwoerd 1988; Manetti *et al.* 1989; Ferrari *et al.* 1991), but have developed preferentially along a rectilinear axial zone. Dyke arrangement is complicated by a N–S zone of injection in the southern flank of the volcano, and by E–W and WNW–ESE trending zones on the western flank (Fig. 2). Such features have been considered as reflecting zones of weakness by Zanchi & Francalanci (1989), and have never been dated or fully explained. Eruptive fissures and flank craters are also important volcano-tectonic characteristics of the island.

Several coaxial semicircular escarpments, which are partially associated with depressions, and an overall NE–SW trending elongation dominate the island morphology. The most obvious depression is the 'Sciara del Fuoco' (7 in Fig. 2), a large horseshoe-shaped depression which opens to the northwest, and which continues below sea-level (Romagnoli *et al.* 1993).

Here I present data on the orientation, dilation, and cross-cutting relationships of the Stromboli dykes, together with their stratigraphic relationships to dated geological units and associations with the geometries and ages of the various collapse events. For information on methodology and terminology relating to the measured geometric and kinematic dyke parameters, the reader is referred to Berger (1971), Pollard *et al.* (1975), Baer & Reches (1987), and Bussel (1989). The results show a strong

From McGuire, W. J., Jones, A. P. & Neuberg, J. (eds) 1996, *Volcano Instability on the Earth and Other Planets*, Geological Society Special Publication No. 110, pp. 55–63.

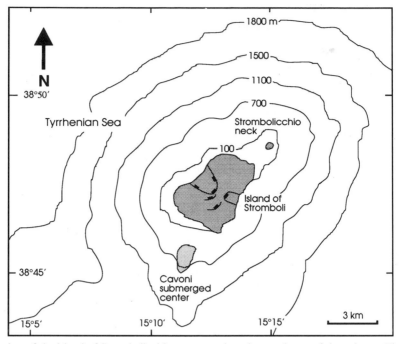

Fig. 1. Location of the island of Stromboli with respect to the submerged part of the volcano. The other two volcanic centres of Strombolicchio and Cavoni are also indicated. Bathymetry is taken from Gabbianelli *et al.* (1993).

correlation between age and geometry of dyking, and the formation of collapses, thus shedding some light on the possible influence of rapid changes in volcanic cone morphology on magma paths in the upper levels of volcanic edifices.

Geological background

The oldest lithological unit on the island of Stromboli crops out at La Petrazza along the eastern shore and is here named Paleostromboli 0 (Pst 0) (Fig. 3). An angular unconformity marks the contact with the oldest unit recognized by Keller *et al.* (1993) and termed Paleostromboli I (Pst I). At an altitude of about 400 m a.s.l., the Pst I deposits are interrupted by a major angular unconformity corresponding to the oldest collapse of the island (1 in Fig. 2), which was interpreted as a caldera by Pasquarè *et al.* (1993). Above this the volcanic succession was ascribed to the Paleostromboli II (Pst II) cycle by Keller *et al.* (1993).

Another major unconformity marks the passage to that part of the upper succession known as Paleostromboli III (Pst III), and is in turn followed by an unconformity separating Pst III from the overlying succession which

constitutes the Vancori cycle (Keller *et al.* 1993). The latter unconformity has been created by a second caldera collapse of the summit part of the volcano (3 in Fig. 2) and by a lateral collapse towards the SE in the eastern flank (2 in Fig. 2) (Pasquarè *et al.* 1993). Another escarpment, due to a pit crater, is close and sub-parallel to the previous summit collapse and cuts the Lower Vancori (LV) lava flows (4 in Fig. 2) (Tibaldi *et al.* 1994). This depression is infilled by deposits constituting the Middle (MV) and Upper (UV) Vancori units. The more recent Neostromboli (NS) deposits of Keller *et al.* (1993) partially cover a large area of the NW side of the volcano onlapping or hiding a depression escarpment cut into the UV deposits (5 in Fig. 2). This horseshoe-shaped rim represents the remnant of the earliest large sector collapse. The NS products end at an escarpment formed during another sector collapse (6 in Fig. 2).

The most recent unit is confined mainly to the northwest of the UV rim and is named Recent Stromboli (RS) by Keller *et al.* (1993). It shows several angular unconformities indicative of the onlap on the escarpments of UV (5 in Fig. 2) and of NS (6 in Fig. 2). The RS deposits were affected by the last collapse which formed the

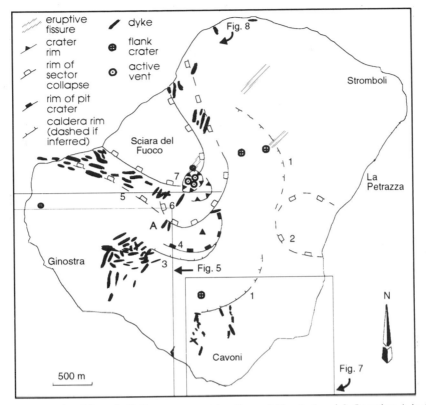

Fig. 2. Structural sketch of Stromboli. Boxes represent locations of Figs 5, 7 and 8. Location A is discussed in the text.

present-day Sciara del Fuoco (7 in Fig. 2). The active pyroclastic cones have been building up along the upper rim of this flank collapse, with other recent products being erupted along NE-trending fissures or vents located mainly in the NE part of the island (Fig. 2).

Dykes

General geometry and relative stratigraphy

Considering the entire population of dykes on the island, they strike, in decreasing order of frequency, ESE, NE, and SSE (Fig. 4), while cumulative dyke thickness has a NW–SE horizontal maximum. Most dykes have a sinuous shape both in plan view and in vertical section. In some cases the strike or dip of the dykes changes in the proximity of rheological variations of the host rocks, but in many other cases are independent.

Whereas dykes are lacking in the eastern part of the island where the oldest rocks crop out, dyke density is noticeably greater in the following

zones (Fig. 2): (1) along the NE-trending divide between the relatively old SE side of the island and the younger NW flank of the volcano, where the highest density dyke swarm is located; (2) in the southern part of the island, near Cavoni; (3) along the southern shoulder of the Sciara del Fuoco and; (4) along the northern shoulder of the Sciara del Fuoco where dykes are very scattered.

The dykes of zone (1) mainly intrude rocks up to the Pst III, and less commonly cut younger rocks (Fig. 5). An important cross-cutting relationship can be observed at locality A in Fig. 5A, where the widest dyke on the island crops out. This sub-vertical dyke is 8 m wide, strikes NE, and is truncated by a marked erosion surface inside the Paleostromboli succession (Fig. 6). Some 20–30 m E and W of this dyke, the same unconformity is cross-cut by dykes striking between NNE and ENE. In this zone a few ESE-striking dykes dislocate the NE set. This zone of weakness can be extrapolated north-eastwards towards the summit region on the basis of the following data (Fig. 2): (a) the presence of a further two large NE oriented and one N–S

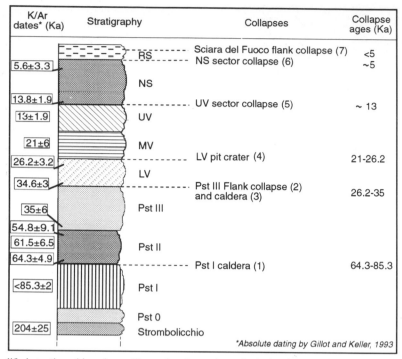

Fig. 3. Simplified stratigraphic column illustrating the main geological units cropping out on the island of Stromboli and at Strombolicchio, and the timing of collapse events. Stratigraphy from Keller *et al.* (1993) and Pasquarè *et al.* (1993); dates from Gillot and Keller (1993); collapse origin from Pasquarè *et al.* (1993) and Tibaldi *et al.* (1994).

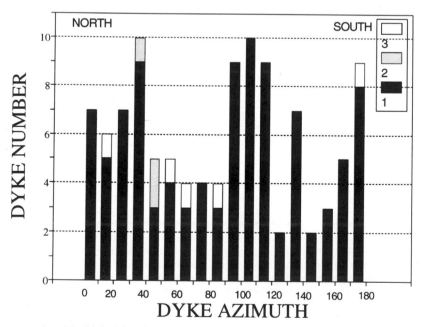

Fig. 4. Frequency (y-axis) of dyke (1) and eruptive fissure (2) strike, and of flank crater alignment with respect to the summit vent zone (3) of the island of Stromboli.

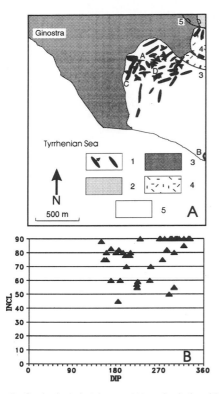

Fig. 5. Geological sketch map (**A**) and relationships between dyke inclination (y-axis) and dip (x-axis) (**B**) of the area around Ginostra. For location and collapse symbols see Fig. 2. (1) Vertical and inclined dykes, arrow shows dip, (2) Recent Stromboli, (3) Neostromboli, (4) Vancori, (5) Paleostromboli II and III. A B, C and D are locations referred to in the text.

aligned dykes; (b) the active crater is elongated in a NE direction; (c) the UV collapse rim (5 in Fig. 2) has its upper side elongated in a NE direction; and (d) the eruptive fissure opened in 1985 strikes NE (De Fino *et al.* 1987). On the NE flank of the volcano the NE-trending dyke swarm is expressed at the surface by both NE-striking fissure eruptions, and by some flank craters ascribed to the NS activity (Keller *et al.* 1993).

All these data are consistent with the previously proposed (Rosi 1980; Zanchi & Francalanci 1989; Gabbianelli *et al.* 1993; Pasquarè *et al.* 1993) existence of a NE-trending axial zone of weakness that cuts the Stromboli volcano and which can be linked to the Strombolicchio neck. It is possible that this NE weak zone has been active since the inception of the oldest volcanic activity currently exposed on the island and has persisted through to very recent times.

Dykes belonging to zone (2) intrude rocks of Pst I (Fig. 7) and only a very few cut the Pst I collapse rim. These dykes do not affect the Pst II and the youngest deposits apart from a single feeder dyke evidenced by a flank crater of the MV cycle.

The dykes of zones (3) and (4) intrude rocks as young as NS (Fig. 8), and on the whole, they define a zone which coincides with the UV sector collapse (5 in Fig. 2) and parallels the Sciara del Fuoco escarpment.

Dyke attitude and morphology

Dykes in the area of Ginostra mostly strike between NNE and ENE with a >80° inclination (Fig. 5B). A smaller number dip towards the SW, and are sub-parallel to the local cone slope. Dyke thickness ranges from a few decimetres to 8 m. In some dykes belonging to the NNE to ENE set, thickness increases asymmetrically upwards; the dyke plane facing towards the SE is vertical to sub-vertical, whereas the opposite plane dips towards the SE at a low angle. This is well represented in a NNE-striking dyke which passes upwards to an asymmetric plug (location C in Fig. 5A). The direction of magma flow is sub-horizontal but as reliable evidence is only visible in about 10% of dykes, the data are too limited to be representative. The best example is at site A of Fig. 2 where two NNE to NE-striking vertical dykes have uniformly oriented, sub-horizontal lineations, vesicles, and phenocrysts. Drop-vesicles and apophyses indicate magma flow towards the southeast (i.e. outwards from the volcano summit), while downward-terminating ('rootless') dykes also indicate horizontal flow (location D in Fig. 5A). In some cases horizontally propagated dykes reveal an inner zone of angular clasts with the same composition as the more massive external part of the dyke. No striations are present along dyke walls or in the breccia zone thus excluding tectonic reactivation.

The inner brecciation may have been induced by rapid gas escape near the topographic palaeosurface. Some particularly interesting features having a bearing on this are present in a sub-vertical NNW to NNE-striking dyke located at site B of Fig. 5A. Its external zones are 15 cm wide laminated tuffs, whereas the internal zone is an 80 cm wide heterogeneous breccia made of clasts of tuff and intrusive crystalline rock in a fine tuff matrix. Where the fine portion dominates, there are horizontal planar or locally folded laminations. Apophyses, uniformly oriented elongated clasts, asymmetric folds, and laminations indicate a

Fig. 6. The widest dyke at Stromboli, here shown in the centre of the frame (note man for scale), crops out at locality A of Fig. 5 and strikes NE. It is cut by a major unconformity surface (large arrow) which, in turn, is cut by NNE to ESE striking dykes (small arrows).

horizontal flow in a southerly direction. Given the location of the dyke at sea-level, these features could have resulted from water–magma interaction.

In the area of Cavoni (Fig. 7), most of the dykes strike NNW to NNE, with a subordinate number oriented SE. Inclinations range from 30° to vertical, with dominant southwestward dips sub-parallel to the local slope. Thickness ranges between 0.4 m and 3 m. No data on direction of magma flow have been obtained in this area.

In the vicinity of the Sciara del Fuoco (Fig. 8) dyke azimuths concentrate in three groups which, in decreasing order of frequency, are oriented ESE, NNE, and SSE. Most dykes dip towards the Sciara del Fuoco, and dyke thickness ranges from 0.5 m to 3 m. Although kinematic indicators are rare, those observed suggest sub-horizontal or sub-vertical magma flow.

Dyke ages

Ages of collapse events at Stromboli have already been established by Tibaldi *et al.* (1994) and are here summarized in Fig. 3. Dyke ages can be determined on the basis of their relationships with already temporally constrained stratigraphic units. Most dykes of the Cavoni area cut rocks dated up to 85.3 ± 2 ka BP, while a very few cut the Pst I caldera rim and younger deposits. These data indicate that the earliest visible caldera and most of the Cavoni dyke swarm developed between 64 and 85 ka BP (Figs 3 and 9B, C).

The NNE to ENE-trending intrusions partly crossing and partly limited by the surfaces of the Pst III and LV collapses in the area NE of Ginostra, indicate a continuation of magma emplacement with this geometry in the period 35–21 ka BP.

The first large lateral collapse of the island is dated at 13 ka BP (Fig. 9D), followed at 5.6 ± 3.3 ka BP by the NS sector collapse, and by the flank collapse of Sciara del Fuoco. The dykes striking from NNE to NE around the easternmost part of the Sciara del Fuoco (Figs 2 and 8) intrude rocks up to the RS, whereas several dykes parallel or sub-parallel to the northern and southern escarpment of UV sector collapse intruded the NS deposits (13.8 ± 1.9 ka to 5.6 ± 3.3 ka BP) (Figs 3 and 9E).

Discussion and summary

Five main volcano-tectonic features characterize the history of Stromboli island: (1) the persistence of the NE-trending zone of weakness;

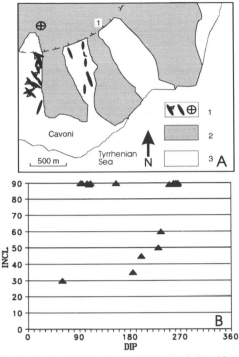

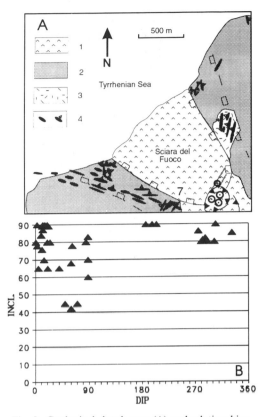

Fig. 7. Geological sketch map (**A**) and relationships between dyke inclination (y-axis) and dip (x-axis) (**B**) of the area near Cavoni. For location and collapse symbols see Fig. 2. (1) Vertical and inclined dykes, arrow shows dip, and pyroclastic cone, (2) Paleostromboli II and III, (3) Palaeostromboli 0 and I.

Fig. 8. Geological sketch map (**A**) and relationships between dyke inclination (y-axis) and dip (x-axis) (**B**) of the area around the Sciara del Fuoco. For location and collapse symbols see Fig. 2. (1) Recent Stromboli, (2) Neostromboli, (3) Vancori, (4) vertical and inclined dykes, arrow shows dip.

(2) the episode of dyke intrusion in the Cavoni area; (3) the preferential development of lateral collapses towards the NW since 13 ka BP; (4) the post-13 ka BP dyke injection also along the Upper Vancori collapse escarpment; and (5) the dominance of inclined dykes of an outward dip. Each of these features is discussed in more detail below.

(1) During the entire constructional history of the Stromboli volcano, the NE-trending zone of weakness has relieved the majority of the hydraulic pressure accumulated due to magma inflation, by fracture opening, propagation of fractures throughout the volcanic pile, and dilation resulting from magma intrusion (Fig. 9). For the older growth stages (Fig. 9A) the importance of this weak zone is revealed by the presence of marine abrasion platforms which are confined to the NE and SW sectors of the volcanic complex, and which contain sedimentary deposits which provide evidence for several cycles at least partly related to Late Pleistocene sea-level fluctuations (Gabbianelli

et al. 1993). These abrasion platforms have positive gravity anomalies which mark the locations of early formed, mainly basic magma bodies (Bonasia & Yokoyama 1972; Francalanci *et al.* 1988). Moreover, these platforms are aligned with the Strombolicchio neck dating back to 204 ka BP.

The volcano-tectonic data on the island of Stromboli itself, the exposed rocks of which date back to 100 ka BP, show that within the NE-trending zone of weakness many dykes are sinuous and distinct segments mostly strike between NNE and ENE. The origin of the weak zone may be tectonic because NE-trending regional lineaments are present around the volcano (Gabbianelli *et al.* 1993). Quaternary normal motions along NE-striking faults in the southeastern Tyrrhenian Sea and coast have also been reported by Pescatore & Ortolani (1973),

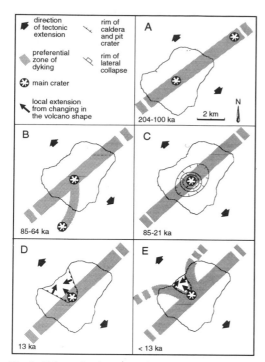

Fig. 9. Schematic plan view of the volcano-tectonic evolution of the island of Stromboli and surrounding

D'Argenio *et al.* (1975), Bartole *et al.* (1984) and Fusi *et al.* (1990). This suggests that a tectonic NW–SE least-principal stress ($\sigma 3$) affects the volcano at all altitudes up to the summit.

(2) Dyke intrusion in the southern flank of the volcano can be explained in terms of an episodic secondary magma path which linked the short-lived Cavoni volcanic centre to the main Stromboli eruptive zone (Fig. 9C). Over the last 64 ka this secondary weakness zone drained magma only once resulting in the formation of a small pyroclastic cone (Fig. 7).

(3) The preferential westward dyke dip and asymmetrical thickening of some plugs may be explained in terms of the sea-floor deepening towards the NW (Gabbianelli *et al.* 1993). In this context, dyke geometries may reflect an asymmetric distribution of buttressing forces with greater support on the SE side of the volcano where the sea-bed is shallower. The geometry of lateral collapses may also be related to a combination of asymmetric expansion of the volcano and sea-floor morphology. Expansion of the summit due to magma intrusion contributed to increasing the flank instability in a direction perpendicular to the NE–SW zone of weakness. This is consistent with the results obtained for various collapsed volcanoes by

Siebert (1984). At the same time, unbuttressing towards the NW, as a consequence of the rapid sea-floor deepening in the same direction, could explain the preferential northwestward development of lateral collapses.

Prior to 21 ka BP, the island of Stromboli suffered summit collapses (Fig. 9C), while in the following period, which commenced at 13 ka BP, only lateral collapses towards the NW are evident (Fig. 9D and E). This age coincides with the rapid 15–12 ka BP global sea-level increase, and supports a potential link between the behaviour of volcanoes and changing Quaternary sea-levels (Rampino *et al.* 1979; Nakada & Yokose 1992). Sea-level changes as large as 100 m can induce variations in the state of stress within coastal and island volcanoes (Wallmann *et al.* 1988). It is also not unreasonable to suggest that volcano flank erosion due to the sea-level increase may have been a triggering factor in the onset of preferential lateral collapse since 13 ka BP (Tibaldi *et al.* 1994; McGuire 1992; Weaver *et al.* 1994).

(4) The geometry of the post-13 ka BP dyke zones along the escarpment of the Upper Vancori sector collapse represents another important perturbation of the high-level magma feeding system dominated by the NE-trending dyke zone (Fig. 9E). It is here proposed that, notwithstanding their original orientation at depth, the deep dykes which were localized NW of the main weakness zone become reoriented near the summit, and adopt a geometry parallel to the unbuttressed depression of the sector collapses. As seen at Mount Etna (McGuire & Pullen 1989), these dykes are therefore 'attracted' to the unbuttressed walls of the collapses, as they propagate horizontally outwards at shallow depths from beneath the summit cone.

(5) The dominant outward dip in the inclined dykes testifies to their tendency to parallel the volcano slopes.

I gratefully acknowledge field co-operation of C. Lodigiani, G. Pasquarè and V. Ventricelli. I thank two anonymous reviewers for thoughtful comments on an early version of the manuscript. The work benefited from a fellowship from the Istituto Nazionale di Geofisica – Gruppo Nazionale per la Vulcanologia, a grant by the Commission of the European Communities, DGXII, Environment Programme, Climatology and Natural Hazard Unit, no. EV5V-CT92-0170, and a grant from CNR no. 91.02249.PF62.

References

BAER, G. & RECHES, Z. 1987. Flow patterns of magma in dykes, Maktesh Ramon, Israel. *Geology*, **15**, 569–572.

BARTOLE, R., SAVELLI, D., TRAMONTANA, M. & WEZEL, C. F. 1984. Structural and sedimentary features in the Tyrrhenian margin off Campania, Southern Italy. *Marine Geology*, **55**, 163–180.

BERGER, A. R. 1971. Dynamic analysis using dykes with oblique internal foliations. *Geological Society of American Bulletin*, **82**, 781–786.

BONASIA, V. & YOKOYAMA, Y. 1972. Rilevamento gravimetrico di Stromboli (Isole Eolie). *Rivista Italiana Geofisica*, **21**, 109–113.

BUSSEL, M. A. 1989. A simple method for the determination of the dilation direction of intrusive sheets. *Journal Structural Geology*, **11**(6), 679–687.

CHEVALLIER, L. & VERWOERD, W. J. 1988. A numerical model for the mechanical behaviour of intraplate volcanoes. *Journal of Geophysical Resarch*, **93**(B5), 4182–4198.

D'ARGENIO, B., PESCATORE, T. & SCANDONE, P. 1975. Structural pattern of the Campania-Lucania Apennines. *In: Structural Model of Italy*, Quaderni de la Ricerca Scientifica, **90**, 313–327.

DE FINO, M., FALSAPERLA, S., FRAZZETTA, G., LA VOLPE, L., NERI, G., ROSI, M. & SBRANA, A. 1987. L'eruzione dello Stromboli del 6 dicembre 1985–25 aprile 1986. *Bollettino Gruppo Nazionale Vulcanologia*, 273–284.

FERRARI, L., GARDUNO, V. H. & NERI, M. 1991. Distribuzione e caratteristiche geometriche dei dicchi della Valle del Bove, Etna. *Memorie Società Geologica Italiana*, **47**, 495–508.

FRANCALANCI, L. 1987. *Evoluzione Vulcanologica e Magmatologica dell'Isola di Stromboli (Isole Eolie): Relazioni tra Magmatismo Calc-alcalino e Shoshonitico*. Tesi di Dottorato, Dipartimento di Scienze della Terra, Firenze.

——, BARBIERI, M., MANETTI, P., PECCERILLO, A. & TOLOMEO, L. 1988. Sr isotopic systematic in volcanic rocks from the island of Stromboli (Aeolian Arc). *Chemical Geology*, **73**, 164–180.

FUSI, N., TIBALDI, A. & VEZZOLI, L. 1990. Vulcanismo, risorgenza calderica e relazioni con la tettonica regionale nell'Isola di Ischia. *Memorie Società Geologica Italiana*, **45**, 971–980.

GABBIANELLI, G., Romagnoli, C., Rossi, P. L. & CALANCHI, N. 1993. Marine geology of the Panarea-Stromboli area (Aeolian Archipelago, Southeastern Tyrrhenian sea). *Acta Vulcanologica*, **3**, 11–20.

GILLOT, P. Y. & KELLER, J. 1993. Radiochronological dating of Stromboli. *Acta Vulcanologica*, **3**, 11–20.

KELLER, J., HORNIG-KJARSGAARD, I., KOBERSKI, U., STADLBAUER, E., FRANCALANCI, L. & LENHART, R. 1993. Geology, stratigraphy, & volcanological evolution of the island of Stromboli, Aeolian Arc, Italy. *Acta Vulcanologica*, **3**, 21–68.

MANETTI, P., PASQUARÈ, G., TIBALDI, A. & TSEGAYE, A. 1989. Geologia dell'Isola di Alicudi (Arcipelago delle Eolie). *Bollettino Gruppo Nazionale Vulcanologia*, **2**, 903–916.

McGUIRE, W. J. 1992. Changing sea levels and erupting volcanoes: cause and effect? *Geology Today*, **8**(4), 141–144.

—— & PULLEN, A. D. 1989. Location and orientation of eruptive fissures and feeder-dykes at Mount Etna; influence of gravitational and regional tectonic stress regimes. *Journal of Volcanological and Geothermal Research*, **38**, 325–344.

NAKADA, M. & YOKOSE, H. 1992. Ice age as a trigger of active Quaternary volcanism and tectonism. *Tectonophysics*, **212**, 321–329.

PASQUARÈ, G., FRANCALANCI, L., GARDUNO, V. H. & TIBALDI, A. 1993. Structure and geological evolution of the Stromboli volcano, Aeolian islands, Italy. *Acta Volcanologica*, **3**, 79–89.

PESCATORE, T. & ORTOLANI, F. 1973. Schema tettonico dell'Appennino campano-lucano. *Bollettino Società Geologica Italiana*, **92**, 453–472.

POLLARD, D. D., Muller, O. H. & DOCKSTADER, D. R. 1975. The form and growth of fingered sheet intrusions. *Geological Society of American Bulletin*, **86**, 351–363.

RAMPINO, M. R., SELF, S. & FAIRBRIDGE, R. W. 1979. Can rapid climatic change cause volcanic eruptions? *Science*, **206**, 826–829.

ROMAGNOLI, C., KOKELAAR, P., ROSSI, P. L. SODI, A. 1993. The submarine extension of Sciara del Fuoco feature (Stromboli Is.): morphological characterization. *Acta Volcanologica*, **3**, 91–98.

ROSI, M. 1980. The island of Stromboli. *Rendiconti Società Italiana Mineralogia e Petrografia*, **36**, 345–368.

SIEBERT, L. 1984. Large volcanic debris avalanches: characteristics of source areas, deposits, and associated eruptions. *Journal of Volcanological and Geothermal Research*, **22**, 163–197.

TIBALDI, A., PASQUARÈ, G., FRANCALANCI, L. & GARDUNO, V. H. 1994. Collapse type & recurrence at Stromboli volcano, associated volcanic activity, and sea level changes. *Atti Accademia dei Lincei*, **112**, 143–151.

WALLMANN, P. C., MAHOOD, G. A. & POLLARD, D. D. 1988. Mechanical models for correlation of ring-fracture eruptions at Pantelleria, Strait of Sicily, with glacial sea-level drawdown. *Bulletin of Volcanology*, **50**, 327–339.

WEAVER, P. P. E., MASSON, D. G. & KIDD, R. B. 1994. Slumps, slides, and turbidity currents – sea-level change and sedimentation in the Canary Basin. *Geoscientist*, **4**(1), 14–16.

ZANCHI, A. & FRANCALANCI, L. 1989. Analisi geologico-strutturale dell'isola di Stromboli: alcune considerazioni preliminari. *Bollettino Gruppo Nazionale Vulcanologia*, **2**, 1027–1044.

The influence of regional stresses on the mechanical stability of volcanoes: Stromboli (Italy)

GUIDO RUSSO[1], GRAZIA GIBERTI[2] & GIOVANNI SARTORIS[2]

[1] Dipartimento di Geofisica e Vulcanologia, Universita di Napoli,
Largo S. Marcellino 10, 80138 Napoli, Italy
[2] Dipartimento di Scienze Fisiche, Universita di Napoli,
Mostra d'Oltremare pad. 19, 80125 Napoli, Italy

Abstract: An elastic model was developed to study the mechanical stability of a volcanic system that includes a volcanic edifice and a magmatic feeding system (conduits and reservoirs) with axial symmetry around a vertical axis. Stability depends critically on the horizontal regional stress which comes into the problem as a boundary condition imposed at large horizontal distance. We considered three types of boundary conditions: (1) zero horizontal displacement (NHD); (2) lithostatic regional stress (LITH); (3) non-axisymmetrical regional stress corresponding to a strike-slip regime (NAS). For the third case (NAS), we used a 3-D model. The stress distributions were calculated by a numerical finite element method. The development of tensile tangential stress in the elements adjacent to the walls of conduits and reservoirs is assumed to be a sufficient condition for the instability of the plumbing system. In compression, we have adopted the Navier–Coulomb criterion for failure. We apply this model to Stromboli volcano, which is characterized by a steep volcanic edifice and open conduits filled with magma. There is geochemical evidence for a deep reservoir ($c.$ 10 km depth) of unknown size and indirect evidence of a shallower reservoir (at the base of the edifice) with volume of the order of 1 km^3. The persistent explosive activity has been steady for the last 2000 years: this implies that the feeding system is mechanically stable. It is found that the deep reservoir has no influence on the stability of the edifice. With NHD boundary condition, implying that the horizontal regional stress is one-third of the vertical component, Stromboli's volcanic system is unstable. In general, any volcanic system with an open and magma-filled plumbing system, with NHD boundary conditions, is mechanically unstable. With lithostatic regional stresses (LITH), the magmatic feeding system is mechanically stable and the slopes of the subaerial edifice are unstable, being subject to landslides. Both NHD and LITH conditions imply that the regional horizontal stress is isotropic which is not appropriate for the Southern Tyrrhenian Sea. With the NAS boundary condition, the stability of the plumbing system of Stromboli volcano allows us to place an upper limit on the maximum shear stress $\Delta_0 = (|\sigma_h|_{max} - |\sigma_h|_{min})/2$. For $\Delta_0 = 10$ MPa, the magmatic feeding system is at the limit of mechanical instability. The subaerial edifice has steep slopes and it is at the limit of gravitative instability independent of the boundary conditions.

The rise of magma from a deep source or oversaturation of volatile species in a shallow magma reservoir implies an increase of pressure (from P to $P + \Delta P$; ΔP is called the over-pressure) on the wall of the feeding system of a volcano. In general, the deformation of the surrounding rocks can be interpreted in terms of stress changes caused by the overpressure ΔP. A knowledge of the actual state of stress in the volcano is instead required if we want to explain the distribution of seismicity, focal mechanisms, failure of the wall of the magmatic feeding system, emplacement of dykes, and the evolution of a volcanic (possibly eruptive) crisis. These latter phenomena concern the mechanical stability of the volcano and are related to failure of country rocks. Failure is caused by a change of stress and occurs only when the actual stress goes beyond the failure threshold. Even in recent literature there is some confusion on this subject, which was inherited from a tradition of exactly solvable models.

Since the classic papers of Anderson (1936, 1938), exactly solvable models were developed in order to calculate the distribution of stress around pressurized cavities, the development of fractures, and the emplacement of secondary intrusive systems fed from the reservoir (Odé 1957; Robson & Barr 1964; Roberts 1970; Pollard 1973a, b; Phillips 1974; Koide & Battacharji 1975; Blake 1981, 1984; Gudmundsson 1986; Sammis & Julian 1987; Tait et al. 1989; Parfitt et al. 1993). These analytical solutions were obtained by neglecting the influence of gravity and the non-uniformity of the far-field stresses, whereas these effects are very important for mechanical stability (Sartoris et al., 1990).

From McGuire, W. J., Jones, A. P. & Neuberg, J. (eds) 1996, *Volcano Instability on the Earth and Other Planets*, Geological Society Special Publication No. 110, pp. 65–75.

Recently, numerical models have been proposed. Ryan (1988) calculated only the stress changes associated with dyke intrusion. Chevallier & Verwoerd (1988) evaluated the actual stress in an axisymmetric volcano, but still assumed uniform regional stresses (which come into the problem as a boundary condition imposed at large horizontal distance). Sartoris *et al.* (1990) developed a numerical model to study the mechanical stability and evolution of a magma reservoir. Their model includes the effect of gravity and assumes regional stresses increasing with depth. These remote stresses were varied in a continuous range having as a lower limit a state of stress implying no horizontal displacement in the far field, and as upper limit a state corresponding roughly to a lithostatic state of stress. They reached the conclusion that mechanical stability of a reservoir depends critically on the regional stress.

In this paper we develop a numerical model to analyse more accurately the effects of regional stresses on the stability of a volcanic system, which depends on the actual state of stress in relation to the conditions for failure to occur. The actual stress is determined by: the geometry of the volcanic system; the physical properties of the magma and of the host rocks; the total pressure $(P + \Delta P)$ applied to the walls of conduits and reservoirs; the gravitational body force; and the regional stresses. We consider a model which includes a volcanic edifice and a magmatic feeding system (conduits and reservoirs). The geometry is axially symmetric around a vertical axis. We assume axisymmetric and non-axisymmetric regional stresses increasing with depth.

We apply this model to Stromboli volcano (Italy) which is characterized by a simple geometry and open conduits filled with magma (implying that the total pressure is known). The persistent explosive activity has been steady for the last 2000 years: this implies that the feeding system is mechanically stable.

The first objective of this paper, taking into account the stability of the plumbing system, is to put some constraints on the regional stresses. A second objective is to assess the stability of the volcanic edifice.

Structure of Stromboli volcano

Stromboli is characterized by a steep volcanic edifice, mostly submarine (conic shape; 3000 m high; summit at about 900 m above sea level; the subaerial part is about 2 km in radius at its base), and by open conduits filled with magma

up to a level which stays remarkably stable. Its persistent activity (2000 years at least) consists of mildly explosive activity (on average, five to seven events per hour), interspersed with more violent explosions and moderate lava flows (the last in 1985) occurring at intervals of several years (Chouet *et al.* 1974; Blackburn *et al.* 1976; Capaldi *et al.* 1978; De Fino *et al.* 1988; Ripepe *et al.* 1993). The average lava output rate is of the order of 1 kg s^{-1} (Ripepe *et al.* 1993; Capaldi *et al.* 1978; Wadge, 1982). In order to maintain this steady eruptive regime, magma must release both gas and heat. The explosive degassing is only a minor fraction of the total gas output; the quiescent degassing is predominant (Allard *et al.* 1994). The gas-to-lava mass ratio is exceedingly high (Chouet *et al.* 1974; Blackburn *et al.* 1976; Ripepe *et al.* 1993; Vergniolle, 1994, pers. comm.), showing that the magmatic gas derives almost entirely from unerupted magma which is degassing at low pressure (i.e. at shallow depth). The time-averaged gas flux in the explosive activity requires a minimum amount of degassing magma of 200 kg s^{-1} (Giberti *et al.* 1992). Considering also the quiescent degassing, this value reaches 800–1600 kg s^{-1} (Allard *et al.* 1994) which is two or three orders of magnitude larger than the lava flux, and comparable to the value inferred at Kilauea volcano, Hawaii (about 1000 kg s^{-1} (Swanson, 1972)). This magma cannot sustain further explosive activity once it has lost its gas phase.

Taking the present minimum rate of degassing magma (800 kg s^{-1}) for the last 2000 years of steady activity, at least 20 km^3 of unobserved magma has been degassed. This magma rises from a deep source into the edifice where it loses its volatiles and a small amount of heat to keep the conduit system open (Giberti *et al.* 1992). There is no evidence that this magma is extruded under sea water or added to the edifice (Allard *et al.* 1994). Another possibility is that the ascending magma, as it loses the gas phase, cools and becomes denser, may undergo some kind of convection in the feeding system which connects the narrow upper conduits to large magmatic reservoirs at depth (Giberti *et al.* 1992; Stevenson & Blake 1994). The existence of storage zones is consistent with the steady activity (Giberti *et al.* 1992), the uniform chemistry of the lavas (for the last 5000 years) containing large amounts of phenocrysts (25–50% by volume) (Capaldi *et al.* 1978; Gillot, 1984; Francalanci *et al.* 1989), and a residual gravity high corresponding to the island (Capaldi *et al.* 1978).

Indirect evidence indicates the existence of a shallow magma reservoir. Giberti *et al.* (1992)

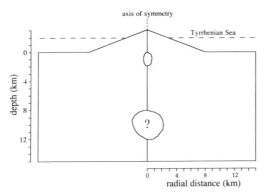

Fig. 1. Schematic model of the Stromboli volcanic system. The edifice is 3000 m high, mostly submarine. The plumbing system is assumed to include two magma reservoirs fed from depth and connected to the surface by a conduit filled with magma. The shallow reservoir is located at the base of the edifice (about 1 km³ in volume). We vary the depth and volume of the deeper reservoir (see text).

analysed the thermal and gas budget of Stromboli and they reached the conclusion that the upper conduits are a few metres in radius (which is consistent with the results obtained by Neuberg *et al.* (1994) Vergniolle & Brandeis (1994)) and they are not deeper than a few hundred metres (in accord with Chouet *et al.* (1974) and Settle & McGetchin (1980)). This implies the existence of a shallow magma reservoir within the subaerial edifice. Giberti *et al.* (1992) did not take into account the possibility of thermal convection in magma conduits. However, degassing-induced convection allows conduits of several kilometres in length connected with a deeper chamber (Stevenson & Blake, 1994). Petrological data (Capaldi *et al.* 1978; Francalanci *et al.* 1989) and seismic velocity anomalies (Morelli *et al.* 1975) suggest the presence of a storage zone located at 10–14 km depth (Fig. 1). The steady activity of Stromboli cannot be fed directly by such a deep magma chamber. Large volumes (800–1600 kg s⁻¹) convecting in long and narrow conduits (with velocity of the order of 1 cm s⁻¹) for the last 2000 years would make the plumbing system unstable. Additional evidence points to the existence of a magma reservoir at a few kilometres depth: seismicity is weak and shallow (Capaldi *et al.* 1978; De Fino *et al.* 1988; Ntepe & Dorel 1990; Neuberg *et al.* 1994; Martini 1994, pers. comm.); pit craters are formed after prolonged effusive activity (Arnaud, 1988); and the dynamics and thermodynamics of Strombolian explosive activity requires accumulation of gas

at shallow depth before the eruption (Jaupart & Vergniolle 1988, 1989; Giberti *et al.* 1992; Allard *et al.* 1994) (Fig. 1).

Description of the model

We investigate the mechanical stability of Stromboli by using the schematic model shown in Fig. 1. The model is axisymmetric around the vertical *z* axis. The volcanic edifice is approximated by a cone, 8 km in radius at its base, 3 km high, and with its summit at about 1 km above sea level. The plumbing system includes a shallow magma chamber having the shape of a prolate spheroid about 1 km³ in volume (horizontal semiaxis 0.5 km; vertical major semiaxis 1 km), located at the base of the edifice and connected to the summit by an open conduit (10 m in radius). This magma chamber is also connected by a wider conduit to a deep spherical reservoir, which is fed from deeper levels. Since in this work we shall be interested in the upper part of the volcanic system, we anticipate that the details of this lower part of the feeding system do not influence the stability of the edifice. We shall discuss this point in the next section.

The country rocks are assumed to be homogeneous, isotropic and linearly elastic. We choose the standard value $\nu = 0.25$ for Poisson's ratio and $\rho = 2700 \, \text{kg m}^{-3}$ for the density of the magma and host medium. In this context, the stress field is independent of the rigidity modulus. The stress field is calculated by using a finite-element numerical method within a vertical cylinder, 30 km in diameter and 18 km in height including the edifice (Fig. 1). These dimensions have been chosen so as to make the calculated far-field stresses practically unaffected by the presence of the feeding system and the edifice. The structure of Fig. 1 was split into about 1650 quadrangular elements. We varied the number and the dimensions of the elements to establish the sensitivity of the calculated stress fields to element size. In the edifice and in the neighbourhood of the feeding system the mesh is fine (Fig. 2). The elements near the upper conduit have horizontal dimensions of a few metres. In the far field a coarser mesh turns out to be adequate (Sartoris *et al.* 1990). We use cylindrical coordinates (*z*-axis pointing downward) with the origin at the base of the edifice. Negative stress corresponds to compression.

The upper conduits are open and filled with magma. Thus, stress boundary conditions corresponding to the hydrostatic pressure due to the weight of magma are imposed on the walls

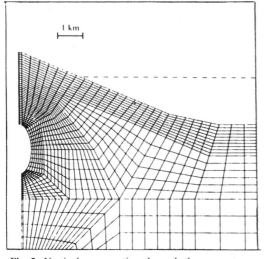

Fig. 2. Vertical cross-section through the symmetry axis of the finite-element mesh (detail). The structure of Fig. 1 was split into about 1650 quadrangular elements.

of the feeding system. On the top of the model, we include the effect of the hydrostatic pressure due to the sea (P_{sea}), while leaving unconstrained the displacements on the subaerial part of the edifice. Only horizontal displacements are allowed on the bottom of the model. On the vertical side of the cylinder ($r = 15\,\text{km}$) we impose three types of boundary conditions:

(a) No horizontal displacements (hereafter NHD). This implies that the regional stresses are

$$\sigma_r = \sigma_\theta = \nu\sigma_z/(1 - \nu)$$
$$= -\nu(P_{sea} + \rho gz/(1 - \nu)) \quad (1)$$

The hydrostatic pressure due to the sea P_{sea} (at $r = 15\,\text{km}$) corresponds to 20 MPa. In our case ($\nu = 0.25$), the horizontal component of the regional stress is one-third of the vertical component. This condition is widely used in the literature.

(b) Lithostatic regional stresses (LITH), i.e.

$$\sigma_r = \sigma_\theta = \sigma_z = -(P_{sea} + \rho gz) \quad (2)$$

The standard state of stress of the crust is close to the lithostatic limit in the absence of tectonic forces (McGarr, 1988).

(c) Non-axisymmetric regional stresses (NAS). For this case, we use a 3-D model. We take $\sigma_z = -(P_{sea} + \rho gz)$ and we have to choose the appropriate horizontal stresses for the Stromboli zone.

An important feature of this central volcano is that dykes, fractures, faults, eruptive fissures, and parasitic vents developed preferentially along a direction SW–NE (Pasquarè *et al.* 1993). This confirms that the stress is non-axisymmetric and suggests that the most compressive horizontal stress $|\sigma_h|_{max}$ is directed along the main structural trend SW–NE (Zoback 1992). These data collected on the subaerial edifice do not allow a stress regime to be chosen.

Neri *et al.* (1995) investigated the focal mechanisms of earthquakes in the southern Tyrrhenian sea, less than 40 km deep. In the Aeolian Islands, the earthquakes with magnitude less than 4 are located between 8 and 15 km and they have heterogeneous focal mechanisms, indicating a high degree of rock fracturing. Three events of magnitude larger than 4 occurred at about 20 km depth (at the Moho depth level) and they are characterized by strike-slip focal mechanisms (Neri *et al.* 1995). These focal mechanisms resulted from a strike-slip regime or were possibly determined by pre-existing faults. Geological studies (Frazzetta *et al.* 1982; Ghisetti & Vezzani 1982) and DSS surveys (Finetti & Del Ben 1986) show two transcurrent faults (the Sisifo and Vulcano faults) crossing the Aeolian Islands and they are still active (Neri *et al.* 1995).

Taking into consideration the data mentioned above, we consider only the case in which the horizontal stress (σ_h) is related to vertical stress (σ_v) by the condition:

$$|\sigma_h|_{min} < |\sigma_v| < |\sigma_h|_{max} \quad (3)$$

corresponding to a strike-slip stress regime. We assume that σ_h varies according to the equation:

$$\sigma_h = \sigma_v - \Delta(z)\cos(2\theta) \quad (4)$$

where $\sigma_v = -P_{sea} - \rho gz$ and $\Delta(z)$ is a positive function depending on depth. The angles $\theta = 0$ and $90°$ correspond to the directions of maximum and minimum compression, respectively. The dependence on depth of $\Delta(z)$ was chosen in accordance with the following arguments.

The shallow rocks are faulted and fractured and do not allow a large stress difference (frictional shear-stress release). The friction is proportional to the normal stress to the plane of the fracture (Coulomb criterion) and approximately proportional to depth. The maximum shear stress

$$(\sigma_1 - \sigma_3)/2 = (|\sigma_{hz}|_{max} - |\sigma_h|_{min})/2 = \Delta(z)$$

increases approximately linearly with depth for the first few kilometres and it reaches a constant value at some depth in the crust (Lliboutry 1982). Therefore, the quantity $\Delta(z)$ is defined by:

$$\Delta(z) = \begin{cases} \Delta_0 z/z_0 & z \leq z_0 \\ \Delta_0 & z \geq z_0 \end{cases} \qquad (5)$$

The maximum shear stress Δ_0 in intraplate regions is of the order of 10 MPa and in major shear zones it may exceed 50–100 MPa (Lliboutry 1982; England & Molnar 1991). We take $z_0 = 3$ km and we vary the value for Δ_0 within the range 0–20 MPa . If $\Delta_0 = 0$, the NAS condition is equivalent to the LITH condition (Fig. 3).

To analyse the mechanical stability of the model, we chose two simple failure criteria:

(1) The development of tensile (positive) tangential stress in the elements adjacent to the wall of the conduit and reservoir is assumed to be a sufficient condition for instability. The stress gradient near the surface of the feeding system is large and the numerical method used in this work yields values of stress averaged over one element. Thus, we slightly underestimate the tangential stresses on the wall. This criterion includes, implicitly, a finite tensile strength of the host rocks.

(2) In compression we adopted the Coulomb criterion for shear failure:

$$|\tau| = S_0 + \mu|\sigma_n| \qquad (6)$$

where τ and σ_n are the shear and normal stresses. The parameters S_0 and μ are the cohesion term and the coefficient of internal friction, respectively. As mentioned before, we are concerned with the stability of the upper part of the volcanic system. The rocks in the edifice, above the shallow chamber, are presumably fractured. In this case, frictional shear failure may occur. We take two values for S_0, 0 and 10 MPa (Lliboutry 1982). The value $S_0 = 0$ is appropriate to the slopes of the subaerial edifice that mainly consist of highly fractured rocks and loose materials. The value $S_0 = 10$ MPa corresponds to the zone near the wall of the feeding system. We take $\mu = 0.85$ (Byerlee, 1978). Near the surface of the edifice, rainwater and seawater may penetrate into the fractures. The Coulomb criterion applied to a material containing pore-water has to be replaced by

$$|\tau| = S_0 + \mu(|\sigma_n| - p) = S_0 + \mu_{eff}|\sigma_n| \qquad (7)$$

where p is the pore water pressure and μ_{eff} is an effective value of the coefficient of internal friction. At depth h below the surface of the edifice the water pressure is $p = \rho_w g h$ and it is more than one-third of the overburden pressure. We estimate the value of μ_{eff} for the slopes of the edifice:

$$\mu_{eff} = \mu(|\sigma_n| - p)/|\sigma_n| \approx 2\mu/3 \approx 0.6 \qquad (8)$$

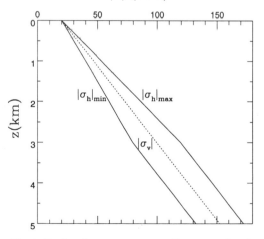

Fig. 3. Regional stresses corresponding to a strike-slip regime versus depth. The absolute value of the vertical component is $|\sigma_v| = |\sigma_{LITH}| = P_{sea} + \rho g z$. The hydrostatic pressure due to the sea P_{sea} (at $r = 15$ km) corresponds to 20 MPa. The maximum shear stress $\Delta(z) = (|\sigma_h|_{max} - |\sigma_h|_{min})/2$ increases linearly and it reaches a constant value at 3 km depth (see text).

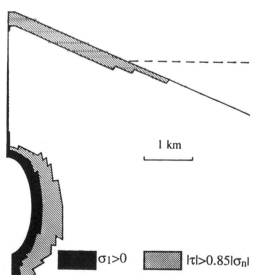

Fig. 4. Zones corresponding to elements in which σ_1 is tensile and those in which frictional shear failure $(S_0 = 0, \mu = 0.85)$ may occur, with regional stresses $\sigma_h = \sigma_v/3$.

Results and discussion

Influence on stability of the deeper part of the feeding system

The deep part of the magmatic system is poorly known. First, we evaluate the influence of the deeper part of the feeding system on the stress field in the edifice. We considered two extreme limits:

(1) the plumbing system is limited to the shallow reservoir connected to the surface (no conduits and reservoir at depth);

(2) the deep plumbing system consists of a spherical magma chamber, with centre at 8.5 km below sea-level and variable radius (1–2 km for top at 8.5–7.5 km below summit), which is fed by a conduit (radius 100 m) and connected by a conduit (radius 100 m) to the shallow reservoir.

We calculated the stress difference at the base of the edifice (3 km below the summit) for these two extreme cases. For the NHD boundary conditions, we found that the maximum difference is about 15% (concerning the σ_r component). For the LITH regional stress, the maximum difference

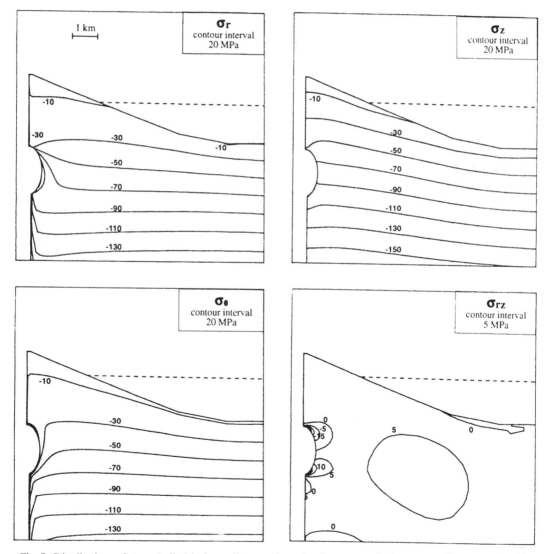

Fig. 5. Distributions of stress (cylindrical coordinates; minus sign for compression) corresponding to Eqn 2 with lithostatic regional stresses.

is about 4%. We conclude that the presence of the deeper chamber has practically no influence on the stability of the edifice.

Axisymmetric regional stress

In axially symmetric problems,

$$\sigma_{r\theta} = \sigma_{z\theta} = 0 \qquad (9)$$

i.e. the hoop stress σ_θ is a principal stress. We assume that no shear stresses are generated by magma flow on the wall of conduits and reservoirs. Therefore the other principal stresses on these surfaces are the normal stress

$$\sigma_n = -\rho g h \qquad (10)$$

and the tangential stress

$$\sigma_t = (\sigma_r \cos^2 \alpha - \sigma_z \sin^2 \alpha)/\cos 2\alpha \qquad (11)$$

where ρ is the density of the magma, h is the distance from the summit, and α is the angle between the z axis and the normal to the surface. While the normal stress σ_n is a boundary condition (which is known), the tangential stresses σ_t and σ_θ must be calculated on the wall of the feeding system. We now evaluate where tensile failure and shear failure might occur in the upper part of the volcanic system under axisymmetric conditions and two different boundary conditions.

NHD boundary conditions. The NHD boundary conditions imply that the regional stresses are given by equation (1). In this case, the hoop stress σ_θ takes positive values (i.e. tensile) on the wall of the upper conduit at a depth greater than 1300 m. The tangential stress σ_θ increases rapidly with depth along the conduit (10 MPa at 1800 m; 20 MPa at 2100 m) and reaches the value of about 100 MPa near the top of the shallow chamber. On the entire wall of the chamber σ_θ is greater than 30 MPa. In these conditions, the wall ruptures and emplacement of vertical dykes occurs.

The zones corresponding to elements in which the principal stresses are positive and to elements in which frictional shear failure may occur are shown in Fig. 4. The principal stress σ_1 (when positive) corresponds to σ_θ; σ_2 is tensile near the top of the chamber.

The magmatic feeding system is mechanically unstable. This result is consistent with the conclusion reached by Sartoris *et al.* (1990).

LITH boundary conditions. The distributions of stress corresponding to regional stresses given by equation (2) are shown in Fig. 5.

In the elements adjacent to the wall of the upper conduit and reservoir, the principal tangential stress σ_t, given by equation (9), is negative and does not contribute to instability. The zones in which the principal stress σ_θ is tensile reduce to a few elements at the top of the shallow reservoir. These positive values are determined by the sharp angle at the intersection of the upper conduit and reservoir. In reality, this angle is smoothed by detachment of pieces of rock and magma convection. In the elements adjacent to the wall of the feeding system the fractures are welded and frictional shear failure cannot occur ($S_0 = 10$ MPa, $\mu = 0.85$).

In Fig. 6 the Coulomb criterion was applied with $S_0 = 0$, which is appropriate for the slopes of the edifice, and two values of μ, $\mu = 0.85$ (dry rocks) and $\mu_{eff} = 0.6$ (rocks containing porewater). The two values of μ do not yield very different results. On the surface of the subaerial edifice frictional shear failure occurs and may induce sector collapses of the edifice. The load of the sea increases the stability of the edifice.

The magmatic feeding system is mechanically stable and the subaerial edifice is at the limit of instability.

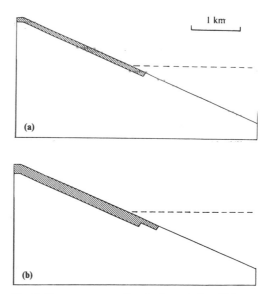

(a)

(b)

Fig. 6. Zones corresponding to elements in which frictional shear failure may occur, with lithostatic regional stresses. The Coulomb criterion was applied to the slopes: (**a**) $S_0 = 0$, $\mu = 0.85$ (dry rocks); (**b**) $S_0 = 0$, $\mu_{eff} = 0.6$ (rocks containing porewater). Notation as in Fig. 4.

A non-axisymmetric model

NAS boundary conditions. The results corresponding to regional stresses given by equations (3–5) are shown in Figs 7–9.

The stress distribution of σ_θ is shown in Fig. 7 in planes at angles $\theta = 0$ (maximum horizontal compression) and $\theta = 90°$ (minimum horizontal compression), with $\Delta_0 = 10$ and 20 MPa.

For $\Delta_0 = 10$ MPa and $\theta = 0$, σ_θ is slightly positive (a few MPa) in the elements adjacent to the wall of the upper conduit and it reaches higher values near the top of the reservoir. For $\theta = 90°$, σ_θ is positive in a couple of elements near the top of the chamber. Frictional shear failure may occur near the wall of the chamber corresponding to the direction of maximum compression ($S_0 = 10$ MPa, $\mu = 0.85$). The magmatic feeding system is at the limit of mechanical instability. Frictional shear failure ($S_0 = 0$ MPa, $\mu = 0.85$) occurs on the slopes of the subaerial edifice (Fig. 8; cf. the discussion of the LITH case). If we use $\mu_{eff} = 0.6$, the shear zone greatly increases on the slopes in the direction of maximum compression and it is slightly affected in the direction of minimum compression.

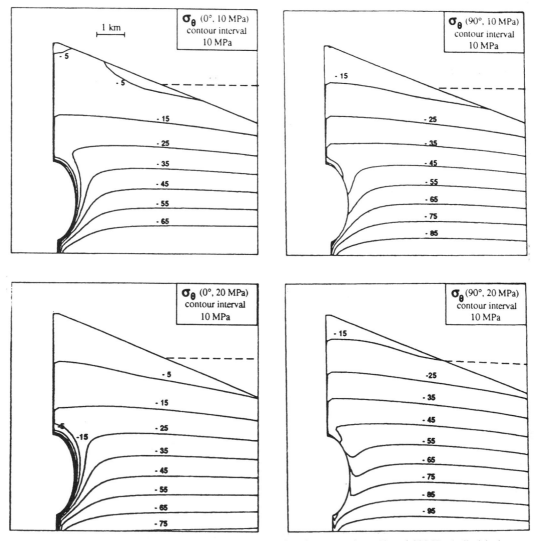

Fig. 7. Stress distribution of σ_θ with non-axisymmetric regional stresses: $\Delta_0 = 10$ and 20 MPa (cylindrical coordinates; minus sign for compression). The angles $\theta = 0$ and 90° correspond to the maximum and minimum horizontal compression, respectively.

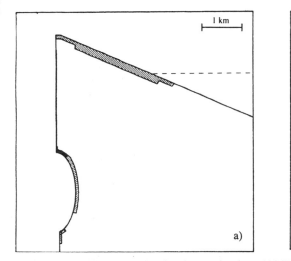
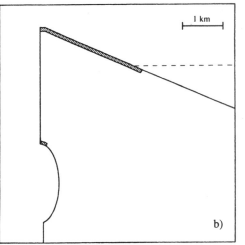

Fig. 8. Non-axisymmetrical regional stress for $\Delta_0 = 10\,\text{MPa}$: (**a**) $\theta = 0$; (**b**) $\theta = 90°$. Zones corresponding to elements in which σ_1 is tensile and those in which frictional shear failure ($S_0 = 0$, $\mu = 0.85$) may occur. The value of the parameter $S_0 = 0$ is appropriate for the slopes. With $S_0 = 10\,\text{MPa}$, the shear zone near the wall of the chamber shrinks upward (about 50%) for $\theta = 0$ and it disappears for $\theta = 90°$. Notation as in Fig. 4.

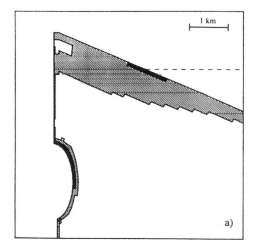
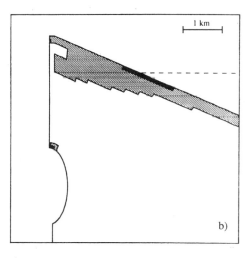

Fig. 9. Same as Fig. 8 with $\Delta_0 = 20\,\text{MPa}$.

For $\Delta_0 = 20\,\text{MPa}$ and $\theta = 0$, σ_θ is positive in the elements adjacent to the wall of the conduit and the upper hemisphere of the reservoir (20–25 MPa). In the edifice there is a tensile zone and an extended zone of frictional shear failure (Fig. 8). The volcanic system is mechanically unstable.

Conclusions

The shallow reservoir buffers the effects of the deep plumbing system in the edifice. With realistic boundary conditions (LITH, NAS), whether we include or neglect the deeper chamber in the model, the change of the actual stress in the edifice amounts to a few percent. The lower part of the magmatic feeding system has no influence on the stability of the edifice.

The boundary condition of zero horizontal displacement (NHD) implies that the horizontal regional stress is one-third of the vertical component. With this horizontal component of regional stress, the Stromboli volcanic system is largely unstable. We can conclude that the NHD boundary condition is unrealistic for the Stromboli region. Furthermore, any volcanic system with an open and magma-filled plumbing system and NHD boundary conditions, is mechanically unstable. This result is consistent with the conclusion reached by Sartoris *et al.* (1990).

The lithostatic boundary condition (LITH) implies that the horizontal regional stress is equal to the vertical stress. The magmatic feeding system is mechanically stable under the LITH condition. Even in this case, the situation would be different if the upper conduits were obstructed, because the pressure on the wall of the feeding system might increase above the present value. The previous case (LITH) implies that the regional horizontal stress is isotropic. This state of stress may exist in some places, but it is not common in the Earth's crust (Zoback 1992) and especially in the Southern Tyrrhenian Sea (Gasparini *et al.* 1982; Iannaccone *et al.* 1985; Pasquarè *et al.* 1993; Neri *et al.* 1995). We considered a non-axisymmetric regional stress corresponding to a strike-slip regime (NAS). Tensile stresses tangential to the wall of the feeding system, as in hydraulic fracturing, first develop on those parts of the wall facing the direction of maximum regional compression. The stability of the plumbing system of Stromboli volcano allows us to place an upper limit on the maximum shear stress $\Delta_0 = (|\sigma_h|_{max} - |\sigma_h|_{min})/2$. For $\Delta_0 = 10\,\text{MPa}$, the magmatic feeding system is at the limit of mechanical instability.

We note that in spite of the feeding system stability, the slopes of the subaerial edifice are unstable and subject to landslides. The steep edifice is at the limit of gravitative instability independent of the boundary conditions. Stromboli has had many collapses in its past history (Pasquarè *et al.* 1993; Tibaldi 1994). Such collapses might induce an instability of the magmatic feeding system.

This work was financially supported by the Gruppo Nazionale di Vulcanologia, Italy. We thank Stephen Blake and Simon Day for their constructive reviews.

References

ALLARD, P., CARBONELLE, J., METRICH, N., LOYER, H. & ZETTWOOG, P. 1994. Sulphur output and magma degassing budget of Stromboli volcano. *Nature*, **368**, 326–330.

ANDERSON, E. M. 1936. The dynamics of the formation of cone-sheets, ring-dykes and cauldron subsidence. *Proceedings of the Royal Society of Edinburgh*, **56**, 128–157.

——1938. The dynamics of sheet intrusion. *Proceedings of the Royal Society of Edinburgh*, **58**, 242–251.

ARNAUD, O. N. 1988. *Stromboli: a Morphological Study*. Kagoshima International Conference, Japan.

BLACKBURN, E. A., WILSON, L. & SPARKS, R. S. J. 1976. Mechanics and dynamics of Strombolian activity. *Journal of the Geological Society, London*, **132**, 429–440.

BLAKE, S. 1981. Volcanism and the dynamics of open magma chambers. *Nature*, **289**, 783–785.

——1984. Volatile oversaturation during the evolution of silicic magma chambers as an eruption trigger. *Journal of Geophysical Research*, **89**, 8237–8244.

BYERLEE, J. 1978. Friction of rocks. *Pure and Applied Geophysics*, **116**, 615–626.

CAPALDI, G., GUERRA, I., LO BASCIO, A. *ET AL.* 1978. Stromboli and its 1975 eruption. *Bulletin Volcanologique*, **41**, 259–285.

CHEVALLIER, L. & VERWOERD, W. J. 1988. A numerical model for the mechanical behavior of intraplate volcanoes. *Journal of Geophysical Research*, **93**, 4182–4198.

CHOUET, B., HAMISEVICZ, N. & McGETCHIN, T. R. 1974. Photoballistics of volcanic jet activity at Stromboli, Italy. *Journal of Geophysical Research*, **79**, 4961–4976.

DE FINO, M., LA VOLPE, L., FALSAPERLA, S. *ET AL.* 1988. The Stromboli eruption of December 6, 1985 to April 25, 1986: volcanological, petrological and seismological data. *Rendiconti della Società Italiana di Mineralogia e Petrologia*, **43**, 1021–1038.

ENGLAND, P. & MOLNAR, P. 1991. Deviatoric stress in actively deforming belts from simple physical models. *In*: WHITMARSH, R. B., BOTT, M. H. P., FAIRHEAD, J. D. & KUSZNIR, N. J. (eds) *Tectonic Stress in the Lithosphere*. The Royal Society, London, 151–164.

FINETTI, I. & DEL BEN, A. 1986. Geophysical study of the Tyrrhenian opening. *Bollettino di Geofisica Teorica ed Applicata*, **28**(110), 75–155.

FRANCALANCI, L., MANETTI, P. & PECCERILLO, A. 1989. Volcanological and magmatological evolution of Stromboli volcano (Aeolian Islands): the roles of fractional crystallization, magma mixing, crustal contamination and source heterogeneity. *Bulletin of Volcanology*, **51**, 355–378.

FRAZZETTA, G., LANZAFAME, G. & VILLARI, L. 1982. Deformazioni e tettonica attiva a Lipari e Vulcano (Eolie). *Memorie della Società Geologica Italiana*, **24**, 293–297.

GASPARINI, C., IANNACCONE, G., SCANDONE, P. & SCARPA, R. 1982. Seismotectonics of the Calabrian arc. *Tectonophysics*, **84**, 267–286.

GHISETTI, F. & VEZZANI, L. 1982. Different styles of deformation in the Calabrian Arc (Southern Italy): implications for a seismotectonic zoning. *Tectonophysics*, **85**, 149–165.

GIBERTI, G., JAUPART, C. & SARTORIS, G. 1992. Steady-state operation of Stromboli volcano, Italy: constraints on the feeding system. *Bulletin of Volcanology*, **54**, 535–541.

GILLOT, P. Y. 1984. *Datation par la méthode du potassium argon des roches volcaniques récentes (pléistocènes et holocénes). Contribution à l'étude chronostratigraphique et magmatique des provinces volcaniques de Campanie, des Iles Eoliennes, de Pantelleria (Italie du Sud) et de la Réunion (Océan Indien)*. PhD thesis, Paris.

GUDMUSSON, A. 1986. Possible effect of aspect ratios of magma chambers on eruption frequency. *Geology*, **14**, 991–994.

IANNACCONE, G., SCARCELLA, G. & SCARPA, R. 1985. Subduction zone geometry and stress patterns in the Tyrrhenian Sea. *Pure and Applied Geophysics*, **123**, 819–836.

JAUPART, C. & VERGNIOLLE, S. 1988. Laboratory models of Hawaiian and Strombolian activity. *Nature*, **300**, 427–429.

—— & ——1989. The generation and collapse of a foam layer at the roof of a basaltic magma chamber. *Journal of Fluid Mechanics*, **203**, 347–380.

KOIDE, H. & BHATTACHARJI, S. 1975. Formation of fractures around magmatic intrusions and their role in ore localization. *Economic Geology*, **70**, 781–799.

LLIBOUTRY, L. 1982. *Tectonophysique et Géodynamique*. Masson, Paris.

MCGARR, A. 1988. On the state of lithospheric stress in the absence of applied tectonic forces. *Journal of Geophysical Research*, **93**, 13 069–13 617.

MORELLI, C., GIESE, P., CASSINIS, R. *ET AL.* 1975. Crustal structure of Southern Italy: a seismic refraction profile Puglia-Calabria-Sicily. *Bulletin de Géophysique Théorique et Appliquée*, **18**, 183–210.

NERI, G., CACCAMO, D., COCINA, O. & MONTALTO, A. 1995. Geodynamic implications of earthquake data in the Southern Tyrrhenian sea. Preprint.

NEUBERG, J., LUCKETT, R., RIPEPE M. BRAUN, T. 1994. Highlights from a seismic broadband array on Stromboli volcano. *Geophysical Research Letters*, **21**, 749–752.

NTEPE, N. & DOREL, J. 1990. Observations of seismic volcanic signals at Stromboli volcano (Italy). *Journal of Volcanology and Geothermal Research*, **43**, 235–251.

ODÉ, H. 1957. Mechanical analysis of the dyke pattern of the Spanish Peaks area, Colorado. *Geological Society of America Bulletin*, **68**, 567–576.

PARFITT, E. A., WILSON L. & HEAD III, J. W. 1993. Basaltic magma reservoirs: factors controlling their rupture characteristics and evolution. *Journal of Volcanology and Geothermal Research*, **55**, 1–14.

PASQUARÈ, G., FRANCALANCI, L., GARDUÑO, V. H. & TIBALDI, A. 1993. Structure and geologic evolution of the Stromboli volcano, Aeolian Islands, Italy. *Acta Vulcanologica*, **3**, 79–89.

PHILLIPS, W. J. 1974. The dynamic emplacement of cone sheet. *Tectonophysics*, **24**, 69–84.

POLLARD, D. D. 1973*a*. Equations for stress and displacement fields around pressurized elliptical holes in elastic solids. *Mathematical Geology*, **5**, 11–25.

——1973*b*. Derivation and evaluation of a mechanical model for sheet intrusions. *Tectonophysics*, **24**, 233–269.

RIPEPE, M., ROSSI, M. & SACCOROTTI, G. 1993. Image processing of explosive activity at Stromboli. *Journal of Volcanology and Geothermal Research*, **55**, 335–351.

ROBERTS, J. L. 1970. The intrusion of magma into brittle rocks. *Journal of Geology, Special Issue*, **2**, 287–338.

ROBSON, G. R. & BARR, K. G. 1964. The effect of stress on faulting and minor intrusions in the vicinity of a magma body. *Bulletin of Volcanology*, **27**, 315–330.

RYAN, M. P. 1988. The mechanics and three-dimensional internal structure of active magmatic systems: Kilauea volcano, Hawaii. *Journal of Geophysical Research*, **93**, 4213–4248.

SAMMIS, C. G. & JULIAN, B. R. 1987. Fracture instabilities accompanying dike intrusion. *Journal of Geophysical Research*, **92**, 2597–2605.

SARTORIS, G., POZZI, J. P., PHILIPPE, C. & LE MOÜEL, L. L. 1990. Mechanical stability of shallow magma chambers. *Journal of Geophysical Research*, **95**, 5141–5151.

SETTLE, M. & MCGETCHIN, T. R. 1980. Statistical analysis of persistent explosive activity at Stromboli 1971: implications for eruption prediction. *Journal of Geophysical Research*, **8**, 45–58.

STEVENSON, D. S. & BLAKE, S. 1994. *Dynamics of degassing volcanic conduits*, preprint.

SWANSON, D. A. 1972. Magma supply rate at Kilauea volcano 1952–1971. *Science*, **175**, 169–170.

TAIT, S. R., JAUPART, C. & VERGNIOLLE, S. 1989. Pressure, gas content and eruptive periodicity of a shallow crystallising magma chamber. *Earth and Planetary Science Letters*, **92**, 107–123.

TIBALDI, A., 1994. Diking, collapses and sea level changes at the Stromboli volcano, Aeolian arc, Italy. Conference on *Volcano Instability on the Earth and Other Planets*, The Geological Society of London, London.

VERGNIOLLE, S. & BRANDEIS, G. 1994. Origin of the sound generated by Strombolian explosions. *Geophysical Research Letters*, **21**, 1959–1962.

WADGE, G. 1982. Steady state volcanism: evidence from eruption histories of polygenetic volcanoes. *Journal of Geophysical Research*, **87**, 4035–4049.

ZOBACK, M. L. 1992. First- and second-order patterns of stress in the lithosphere: the world stress map project. *Journal of Geophysical Research*, **97**, 11 703–11 728.

Hydrothermal pore fluid pressure and the stability of porous, permeable volcanoes

S. J. DAY

Department of Geography and Geology, Cheltenham & Gloucester College of Higher Education, Francis Close Hall, Swindon Road, Cheltenham GL50 4AZ, UK, and Department of Geological Sciences, University College London, Gower Street, London WC1E 6BT, UK

Abstract: Lateral collapses of large volcanoes are commonly associated with phreatic explosions and other evidence for the presence of pressurized hydrothermal pore fluids within the volcanoes prior to collapse. Furthermore, hydrothermal alteration of volcanic edifices is a major factor in increasing susceptibility to collapse. This is generally held to be because of a reduction in effective friction coefficient μ through alteration. However, this is inconsistent with an analysis of the factors affecting the strength of fluid-saturated rocks and volcanic debris in terms of the Rubey & Hubbert equations for shear failure of such materials. Instead, this analysis indicates that reductions in the strength of volcanic materials are mainly due to the effect of high pore pressure relative to confining pressure, expressed as the ratio λ of the two. Consideration of field and seismic evidence, together with simple calculations, indicates that high values of, and large increases in, λ are produced by a variety of mechanisms: heating of confined pore water by intrusions; degassing of intrusions; discharges of highly pressurized fluids from depth through clastic dykes; and by deformation associated with faulting. The sensitivity of pore fluid pressures to perturbation by these mechanisms is however highly dependent upon the permeability of their host rocks, which may itself be subject to rapid changes by fracturing, faulting and other processes. The rapidity of temperature changes and other mechanisms for pressurization in volcanic edifices means that the resultant pore pressure changes are large even in quite highly permeable rocks, but the effects are unpredictable. Detection of the development and spreading of high pore pressures within active volcanoes may however be possible by careful monitoring of patterns of seismicity.

In a review of historical and Holocene lateral collapses of volcanoes, Siebert *et al.* (1987) emphasize the existence of a broad range of lateral collapses, which they divide into Bezymianny type, Bandai type and Unzen type. The defining characteristics of these are summarized in Table 1.

Bezymianny-type collapses, such as the 1980 collapse of Mount St Helens (Lipman & Mullineaux 1981) and the prehistoric collapse of Socompa (Francis *et al.* 1985), are readily explained in terms of an increase in the load on the volcano in the shape of a new intrusion of magma into it, typically as a cryptodome. If this load increase cannot be supported by the edifice, catastrophic failure results. Bandai- and Unzen-type collapses, in contrast, are not preceded by intrusions of juvenile material into the volcanoes affected. In some cases these collapses may be induced, at least in part, by external changes in the loading of the edifice such as regional or tectonically induced tilting of the volcano (Johnson 1987; Stewart *et al.* 1993); changes in sea level around coastal and near-coastal volcanoes (Wallmann *et al.* 1988; Nakada & Yokose 1992); or erosion of the flanks of volcanoes leading to collapse through debuttressing. An alternative possibility is that collapse

Table 1. *Hydrothermal and magmatic activity associated with the three types of lateral collapse defined by Siebert* et al. *(1987)*

Type	Explosive activity	Hydrothermal discharges	Pre-collapse doming and intrusion
Bezymianny	Magmatic and phreatic	?	Yes
Bandai	Phreatic	Yes	No
Unzen	None	Yes	No

From McGuire, W. J., Jones, A. P. & Neuberg, J. (eds) 1996, *Volcano Instability on the Earth and Other Planets*, Geological Society Special Publication No. 110, pp. 77–93.

may be caused by weakening of the rocks making up the volcano, leading to failure under the same loads which had previously been supported. This paper considers how changes in the material properties of porous, permeable rocks and unconsolidated debris may be a primary cause of Bandai- and Unzen-type collapses. It also considers the extent to which such changes, which in many cases are a consequence of intrusion emplacement, may contribute to Bezymianny-type collapses.

A further feature of Bandai- and Unzen-type collapses pertinent to the subject of this paper is their association with phreatic explosions and non-explosive but copious hydrothermal discharges, respectively (Siebert *et al.* 1987). These discharges occur syn- and post-collapse and result from decompression of hydrothermal systems within the volcano beneath and to the side of the collapse itself. For present purposes their significance is that they indicate the presence of abundant hydrothermal fluids in pores and fractures within the volcanoes prior to collapse. Any syn- and post-collapse hydrothermal discharges in Bezymianny-type collapses are, as a rule, obscured by the powerful magmatic eruptions characteristic of this collapse type, but the common, although not ubiquitous, occurrence of phreatic explosions prior to this type of collapse (Siebert *et al.* 1987) again points to the presence of abundant and highly pressurized hydrothermal fluids within the volcanoes concerned.

In addition to the evidence of phreatic and hydrothermal activity associated with historic lateral collapses, the frequent occurrence of hydrothermally altered material and of mud-rich debris flow deposits within sequences associated with older collapses has been noted by numerous authors, and the development of hydrothermal systems and the associated alteration cited as a contributory factor in the collapses (Crandall 1971; Siebert 1984; Siebert *et al.* 1987). However, some notable exceptions to this rule do occur, such as Socompa (Francis *et al.* 1985). No comprehensive survey of alteration associated with volcanic lateral collapse structures on Earth presently exists, although Siebert *et al.* (1987) consider the association to be very common. In the absence of such a data set, and the occurrence of 'dry' collapses such as Socompa, the overall importance of alteration and hydrothermal fluids as a causal or contributory mechanism to lateral collapse of volcanoes cannot be assessed. However, the common association between hydrothermal alteration and lateral collapses indicates that pore fluids and/or hydrothermal alteration

may have an important effect in promoting collapses: the purpose of this paper is to consider, in a largely qualitative manner, the mechanisms by which this effect may occur.

Material properties relevant to the development of catastrophic volcanic edifice failures

Large-scale lateral collapses of volcanoes begin by slip on discrete brittle shear or fault zones, although once movement has begun the fault blocks disaggregate in part or in total to produce various types of debris avalanche. The observed collapse of Mount St Helens provides the clearest example of this process (Voight 1981; Voight *et al.* 1981). The properties of the rocks and unconsolidated clastic deposits making up a volcano which determine its susceptibility to catastrophic failure are, therefore:

(1) Strength, with respect to shear fracturing and to slip on pre-existing faults (generally expressed in terms of the critical shear stress required to produce deformation). This determines whether the volcanic edifice will deform at all under a given load.
(2) Slip-strength variation, or variation in strength with fault displacement. If a fractured material exhibits slip-hardening (increasing strength with amount of slip on fault surfaces) movement will be by small, self-limiting increments and the overall deformation will be creep-like, whereas if slip-weakening occurs catastrophic failure is possible.

The material properties which determine whether a given material is slip-weakening or slip-hardening, and over what ranges of deformation rate, are poorly understood (see discussion in Scholz 1990, 73–91). It is therefore difficult to predict under what circumstances deformation will change from progressive or gradual to catastrophic. The remainder of this paper will therefore concentrate on the effects of pore fluids upon rock strength: in a sense this is a more fundamental issue as rock strength with respect to brittle failure must be exceeded before any type of brittle deformation, whether progressive or catastrophic, can occur.

The fundamental equation for the brittle strength of materials containing a pressurized pore fluid (here taken to mean fluid in intergranular pore space or in small distributed fractures) was first defined by Rubey & Hubbert (1959a):

$$\tau_c = \tau_0 + (1 - \lambda)\mu S \tag{1}$$

where τ_c = critical shear stress required to produce a fracture or cause slip on a pre-existing fracture; τ_0 = cohesive strength of rock or other material, or cohesive strength of fracture in the case of a pre-existing fracture (generally very small or zero); λ = pore pressure as a fraction of lithostatic load; μ = effective coefficient of friction; S = stress normal to plane of fracture.

A useful derivative of equation (1) is an expression for the critical angle of inclination θ_c of a slope on which a block of material will first begin to slide: actual sustainable slopes on the flanks of volcanoes are greatly dependent upon the geometries of the edifice and of the failure surface(s) but the following equation, which assumes zero cohesive strength on the slide surface, gives an indication of the dependence of θ_c upon λ and μ:

$$\tan \theta_c = (1 - \lambda)\mu \qquad (2)$$

These equations, an extension of the Coulomb brittle failure criterion, apply both to development of fractures and to slip on pre-existing fractures without change in form but with different values of the constants τ_0 and μ. Similar relationships can be written for the modified Griffith (McClintock & Walsh 1962) and other failure criteria, involving the same material properties, but that above will be used for simplicity.

I now consider known variations in the terms τ_0, μ and λ in order to evaluate their relative contributions to variations in material strength: the most important material properties for present purposes will be those whose range of natural values produces the larger proportional variations in equations (1) and (2).

Values of τ_0

Determinations of τ_0 are commonly made experimentally by deformation of small samples (Paterson 1978; Hoek & Bray 1981). These yield values for intact rock of up to 10 to 40 MPa in the case of crystalline rocks (Brace 1964; Jaeger & Cook 1971), would be appropriate to massive holocrystalline lavas and intrusive rocks; Hoshino et al. (1972) similarly determined values of τ_0 for shales and sandstones in the range 5 to 20 MPa, which would be appropriate to lithified volcaniclastic rocks. Values of τ_0 at the upper end of this range, if present in natural materials, would dominate the strength of the rock (equation (1)) at values of S corresponding to depths of up to several kilometres, and certainly within all but the largest volcanic

edifices. However, values measured on small samples are unlikely to be representative of the much larger volumes of rock and fragmental material making up volcanic edifices because of the presence in these of abundant fractures and networks of interlinked fractures (see discussion in Scholz 1990, 28–29). Values of tensile strength for large fractured rock masses (determined, for example, from slope stability relationships (Hoek & Bray 1981)) are generally non-zero but much reduced compared to values determined experimentally. The reduction is in general a function of the abundance and size of open fractures and of the degree of cementation of granular materials. Since the effects of hydrothermal alteration include sealing of such fractures by mineral precipitation, cementation of granular materials, and plastic creep deformation of altered rocks to seal fractures mechanically, it is to be anticipated that if anything, hydrothermal alteration will most often increase the tensile strength of most volcanic materials. In any case, however, the values of τ_0 are in general so small on the large scale that they will have comparatively minor effects on the overall stability of volcanoes.

Values of μ

Weakening of volcanic edifices by hydrothermal alteration is commonly thought of in terms of a reduction in the effective coefficient of friction μ, caused by an increase in the proportion of clay minerals. Examples of this view are contained in the review by Siebert et al. (1987). Paterson (1978) and Byerlee (1978) review experimental studies which show that the presence of montmorillonitic clay mineral gouge linings on pre-existing fracture surfaces reduces μ from values of about 0.6, characteristic of immature, unlined fault surfaces, to values in the range 0.3 to 0.5. However, clay gouges differ from statically altered clay-rich rocks in that any remaining non-clay minerals in gouges are comminuted by abrasive wear. Hoek & Bray (1981, 112–115) review studies of hydrothermally altered rocks including kaolinized granites which found that values of μ remained high in these rocks, and comparable to those in unaltered rocks of the same type: it was suggested by them that the high friction coefficients of the altered rocks was due to the presence of large angular grains of non-clay minerals. The values of μ in hydrothermally altered volcanic rocks are therefore likely to be highly dependent upon mineralogy and the presence or absence of large relict crystals: for example, an altered quartz porphyry is likely to have a higher effective coefficient of friction than altered aphyric basic rocks with a similar overall clay content. In any case the range of values of μ produced by alteration is relatively small compared to the effects of variations in λ discussed below, and comparable to the difference in values of μ for pre-existing fractures and for unfractured rocks (in the range 0.8 to 1.0 (Paterson 1978).

Values of λ

Values of λ in non-volcanic settings have been extensively studied, particularly in thrust belts (Rubey & Hubbert 1959a, b; Davis et al. 1983), sedimentary basins (Rubey & Hubbert 1959a, b; McGarr & Gay 1978), and within active upper crustal fault zones (Sibson 1981, 1987, 1990; Byerlee 1990; Rice 1992; Axen 1992; Chester et al. 1993). Except at shallow depths (less than 5 to 10 km) in undeformed rocks and in dehydrated basement rocks, where measured values of λ are, respectively, around 0.4 (corresponding to hydrostatic pressure gradients) and less than 0.4 (owing to metamorphic dehydration reactions (McGarr & Gay 1978)), measured values of λ commonly approach unity, in compacted sediments and within fault zones in particular (note, however, the possibility of wide variations in λ proposed by Nur & Walder (1992)). In view of the various usages of the terms overpressure and lithopressure in the works noted above, I define, for the purposes of this paper, overpressure conditions as corresponding to values of λ in excess of the hydrostatic value but less than 1; lithopressure conditions as corresponding to values of λ equal to 1; and superpressure as values of λ significantly in excess of 1.

Pore fluid pressures in volcanic edifices are less well known. However, the very high permeabilities associated with vigorous convection in open hydrothermal fields mean that fluid pressure gradients within them are unlikely to rise much above hydrostatic values with $\lambda \approx 0.01$–0.4, depending on the temperatures and hence the densities of the fluids (Helgeson & Kirkham 1974a, b, 1976; Helgeson et al. 1981; Norton 1984, 1988). At the other extreme, the occurrence of phreatic explosions implies the local development of superpressured conditions, in which fluid pressures are sufficient to cause tensile failure of the rocks in which the initial rupture occurs; from equation (1) this implies maximum values of λ given by:

$$\lambda_{max} = 1 + \left(\frac{\tau_0}{P}\right) \qquad (3)$$

Table 2. *Variations in sustainable slope angle θ_c, in degrees, for a simple sliding block (Rubey & Hubbert 1959a) for $\tau_0 = 0$ and various values of μ and λ (see text for discussion)*

λ	μ			
	1	0.8	0.6	0.3
0	45	39	31	17
0.2	39	33	26	13
0.4	31	26	20	10
0.6	22	18	13	7
0.8	11	9	7	3
1.0	0	0	0	0

where P is the lithostatic load at the depth of rupture. The development of high pore fluid pressures in volcanic terranes is also indicated by a variety of field observations in exhumed or incised rocks which are discussed below in the context of field evidence for different mechanisms for producing high pore fluid pressures.

Comparison of the natural ranges of the material properties τ_0, μ and λ in this section indicates that variations in λ are likely to have the greatest effect upon the strength and thus the stability of volcanoes, although the effects of the others may be significant under certain circumstances. Table 2 illustrates this for λ and μ by showing values of θ_0 (equation (2)) for the natural ranges of λ and μ.

It will be noted that whilst at the lower limit of natural values of μ, θ_c remains significant, as λ approaches unity the value of θ_c approaches zero (although in practice any tensile strength present in the material will allow a small residual slope angle to be maintained). It follows that a primary explanation for the common association of hydrothermal alteration with volcano collapses should be sought in the mechanisms by which high pore fluid pressures can be produced and the circumstances under which they can be maintained. Whilst any reduction in μ which does occur as a result of alteration will also weaken the volcanoes affected, this will be relatively minor compared to the effects of increases in pore pressure to near-lithostatic values.

Mechanisms for producing high values of λ in volcanic edifices

Having shown in the previous section that variations in λ over the range of natural values can greatly reduce the strength of volcanoes, I now consider evidence for the operation of a variety of mechanisms which may increase λ, and in particular produce values of λ which approach or exceed unity. The approach used here complements the mathematical approach of Elsworth & Voight (1996) by considering possible effects in more general terms and in the context of various lines of geological and geophysical evidence from field studies of active volcanoes and, in particular, from incised volcanic edifices in which the basal sections and infrastructures of volcanic collapses are exposed by erosion. Structural studies of incised volcanic edifices (as opposed to the numerous studies of intrusive complexes at and below the initial base level of the volcano) are unfortunately extremely rare at present; the examples of exhumed structures used in this paper are taken lateral collapse structures in the Pliocene Roque Nublo Group of Gran Canaria, Canary Islands which are the subject of ongoing structural studies by the author.

Heating of pore fluids: aquathermal effects in volcanic terranes

The extreme temperature gradients common in geothermal and volcanic fields, coupled with the frequent emplacement of minor intrusions, imply a potential for rapid changes in temperature through emplacement of intrusions within volcanic edifices; heating by larger intrusions at greater depths; changes in the efficiency of heat transfer in hydrothermal systems through collapse or occlusion by mineral precipitation of pore space, changed fluid fluxes, or episodes of fracturing. The effects of such temperature changes upon fluid pressure distributions are likely to be extremely complex: I first consider the limiting case of temperature changes in zero-permeability rocks where the most likely cause of rapid temperature increase is emplacement of minor intrusions.

Emplacement of hot magma bodies into water-rich sediments and consequent heating and expansion of the pore fluids has been associated with fluidization of the sediment to produce peperitic intrusions (Kokelaar 1982; Busby-Spera & White 1987; Branney & Suthren 1988). The bulk expansion of the sediment associated with its fluidization is significant (Wilson 1980) and requires the development of pore fluid pressures equal to or in excess of the confining pressure on the rocks ($\lambda \geq 1$). A similar phenomenon, degassing of volatile-rich sediments such as coals on heating by intrusions, has been invoked to explain the particularly strong development of peperitic structures in and around intrusions emplaced into coal seams

(Walker & Francis 1987). In these cases the abundance of fluid leads to high local fluid–magma ratios, efficient convective heat transfer away from the magma–host sediment boundary and efficient fluid–coolant interaction (Wohletz 1983), hence the development of the distinctive brecciation of the intrusive magma into cauliform inclusions in the mobilized host sediment.

Rubey & Hubbert (1959a) show, however, that the mechanical effects of a pore fluid pressure increase upon static rock strength are independent of the actual pore fraction in the rock. Thus, emplacement of intrusions into more consolidated but fluid-saturated materials with a lower pore fraction may have nearly as drastic an effect upon their strength as fluidization has upon water-rich materials. As discussed by Elsworth & Voight (1996) the effect of thermal expansion upon pore pressures in the vicinity of an intrusion is dependent upon the permeability of the host rock and hence the extent to which the pressure increase is dissipated (but also spread over a greater volume) by fluid flow away from the intrusion. Here I consider the limiting case of porous but impermeable rock in order to evaluate the sensitivity of thermally induced pore pressure increases upon the properties of the pore fluid. Since most pore fluids are H_2O-rich, and the thermodynamic properties of water are well-known, the following discussion considers pore fluids approximating to pure water in their properties.

Norton (1984) notes that the net fluid pressure increase in a constant-volume pore network caused by heating is dependent on the ratio of fluid thermal expansivity α_f to fluid compressibility β_f (equation 12, Norton 1984):

$$\left(\frac{\partial P_f}{\partial T_f}\right) = \alpha_f / \beta_f \qquad (4)$$

This ratio varies considerably over the pressure range of hydrothermal systems, as shown by the dotted lines in Fig. 1. Steam and low-density supercritical hydrous fluids, because of their high compressibility, have values of α/β as low as $0.01\,\mathrm{MPa\,°C^{-1}}$, whereas liquid water and high-density supercritical fluid water have values of α/β as high as 1–$2\,\mathrm{MPa\,°C^{-1}}$, in the temperature range 50–$300°C$. In this temperature range values of α/β vary only slightly with pressure, making it possible to define an approximate expression for the temperature increase ΔT_c required to raise the reduced pore pressure λ at constant volume from an initial value λ_0 to 1 at a given initial temper-ature T and rock confining pressure P:

$$\left(\frac{(1-\lambda_0)P\beta_f}{\alpha_f}\right) \approx \Delta T_c \qquad (5)$$

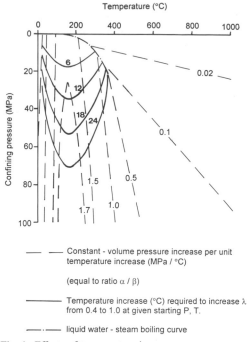

Temperature (°C)

Confining pressure (MPa)

—— — Constant - volume pressure increase per unit temperature increase (MPa / °C)

(equal to ratio α / β)

———— Temperature increase (°C) required to increase λ from 0.4 to 1.0 at given starting P, T.

—— · —— liquid water - steam boiling curve

Fig. 1. Effects of temperature increases upon pore pressure at constant volume (zero permeability) for water-filled pore space.

Setting $\lambda_0 = 0.4$ (a typical hydrostatic value for liquid water) and solving equation (5) at various values of T and P in the range noted above yields the solid contours in Fig. 1: the numbers attached to each contour show the value of ΔT_c for the combinations of T and P along the contour line. It should be noted that these remarkably small values of ΔT_c are confined to the region of high α/β: values of ΔT_c for steam-filled porous rocks in particular will be much higher, implying that the constant-volume pore pressure increases resulting from intrusion emplacement will be most significant when the pore fluid is initally relatively cool, dense and incompressible. Elevation of pore pressures by heating of high-density, relatively incompressible aqueous fluids was recognized in the context of sediments in sedimentary basins by Barker (1972): the process, termed aquathermal pressuring by Barker, will of course be more effective in volcanic settings where thermal gradients are much greater. It should also be noted that the pressure increase will tend to drive heated high-density pore fluid away from the boiling curve, to which it can only be returned by massive decompression: hence, perhaps, the contrast between the relatively mild hydrothermal or

fumarolic activity prior to collapses, and the violent phreatomagnatic lateral blasts and phreatic explosions which accompany collapse and decompression in Bezymianny- and Bandai-type collapses respectively.

A further interesting implication of equation (5) is that, provided efficient mechanisms of heat transfer exist, a relatively small intrusion can produce large increases in λ (at constant pore volume) in a much greater volume of host rock. At relatively low porosity, the latter will have a similar specific heat capacity to the intrusion: typically, $1-1.5 \, \text{kJ} \, \text{kg}^{-1} \, {}^{\circ}\text{C}^{-1}$ (Carmichael et al. 1977). Hence, assuming the latter cools through a temperature range of 700°C and releases latent heat of the order of $160-400 \, \text{kJ} \, \text{kg}^{-1}$ (Nicholls & Stout 1982), it will be capable of producing fluid lithopressuring ($\lambda = 1$) in a volume of rock up to $1000/\Delta T_c$, or 40 to 200, times greater than its own volume provided that the heat from it can be uniformly distributed through that volume. Whilst this is an extreme case which would only be approached in very special circumstances such as emplacement of an intrusion into a highly permeable aquifer or convecting hydrothermal system efficiently sealed by impermeable cap rocks, it nevertheless suggests that the intrusions which cause Bezymianny-type collapses might do so as much through heating and thermal pore pressurisation of the volcanoes into which they are emplaced, that is to say by aquathermal effects, as by oversteepening of the flanks of the volcanoes.

All of the above discussion assumes that dissipation of the increase in pore fluid pressure by fluid flow away from the heat source is negligible. This is unlikely to be the case if only because of the existence of a finite pre-existing permeability (even if only very small) in the volcanoes concerned: these effects are modelled by Elsworth & Voight (1996). In practice, however, a more important effect is likely to be the development of fracture permeability as the pressurised volume grows, leading to partial decompression of that volume coupled to injection of fluid, still at relatively high pressure, into surrounding rocks. This is a much more complex process than that modelled by Elsworth & Voight, who assume a constant permeability: I consider its general characteristics below.

Mechanical effects of intrusion emplacement upon pore pressures: the role of degassing

Elsworth & Voight (1996) consider the effects of intrusion emplacement upon the pore pressures within, and the stability of, a porous host edifice in terms of an excess magma pressure applied to one side of a wedge, plus the additional load from the weight of the (assumed) planar or disc-like intrusion itself. In addition to these two terms, degassing of volatiles from crystallizing intrusions is a potential source of increases in pore pressure through (i) an increase in the mass of fluid that has to be accommodated in the pore space; (ii) heating of existing pore fluids by an influx of hot magmatic fluids; (iii) ascent of highly pressurized pore fluids released at greater depths. The latter is considered in a subsequent section as it is a special case of linkage of high- and low-pressure fluid reservoirs.

The contents of dissolved water-rich volatiles in magmas at or near their liquidus temperatures at pressures of 100 to 300 MPa (typical for shallow magma chambers) typically vary from much less than 1 wt% in the case of tholeiitic basic magmas (Byers et al. 1986) to perhaps as much as 10 wt% in hydrous silicic magmas. On exsolution these volatiles do however have a very low density owing to their high temperature, $100–500 \, \mathrm{kg \, m^{-3}}$ at 600–1000°C and 100–300 MPa (Helgeson et al. 1981). Degassing of a hydrous silicic magma body at these pressures would therefore create a volume of fluid in the range 50–250% of the magma body volume. Cooling to more typical hydrothermal system temperatures of around 300°C will increase the density of these fluids to values around $800 \, \mathrm{kg \, m^{-3}}$ (corresponding to a total fluid volume of about 30% of the magma body volume) but will also, as noted above, greatly decrease their compressibility. Furthermore, such cooling will be matched by heating of the host rocks and pore fluids. In either case it is evident that degassing of silicic magma bodies on crystallization under these conditions, would substantially increase pore pressures through a large volume of the host rock unless permeabilities were high enough to permit fluid escape, for example through macroscopic fractures. The common concentration of fumarolic precipitates from exsolved magmatic fluids in fracture zones indicates that the latter alternative is a common one. The corollary, as with the effects of heating upon pore pressures and thus upon edifice stability, is that the effects of magmatic fluid exsolution in actual volcanoes will be critically dependent upon their permeability.

Pressurization by transfer of fluid from deeper to shallower levels within volcanic edifices: the importance of clastic dykes

Clastic dykes: evidence from surface phenomena and seismic swarms. Eruptions of water-rich mud, breccia and hydrothermal water have been recorded from a number of active volcanoes and volcanic hydrothermal fields (Salton Sea volcanic field, California (Ellsworth 1992); Suoh volcanic field, Sumatra (Stehn 1934; GVN 1994); Tokachi-dake, Yake-dake and Usu volcanoes, Japan (Murai 1963; Morimoto & Ossaka 1964; Oinouye 1917, respectively)) as well as being associated with Unzen-type collapses (Siebert et al. 1987). At both the Salton Sea and Suoh fields, the eruptions were associated with large earthquakes on adjacent faults: possible causes of this association are considered further below. A corollary of these occurrences is that mud or mud–breccia intrusions, generally referred to as clastic dykes, must be a feature of the subsurface geology of these and similar volcanoes. Hydrous mud volcanoes are also a ubiquitous feature of subaerial and submarine accretionary prisms; breccia and mud dykes which may have fed such volcanoes have been found in a number of exhumed accretionary prisms (see, for example, Pickering et al. 1990).

These phenomena are surface expressions of the movement of pressurized water-rich fluids through discrete fractures. Nur (1974) proposed that an earthquake swarm at Matsushiro, Japan was caused by migration of hydrothermal fluids. Similarly, Bonafede (1991) attributes uplift and seismicity in the Campi Flegrei caldera around a very shallow focus to pressurization of a shallow aquifer by fluids ascending from a deep high-pressure fluid source along fractures. The observed eruptive activity and inferred subsurface activity such as that proposed by Nur and Bonafede implies the frequent occurrence of corresponding intrusions of mud-rich breccia and mudrock. Such intrusions should be exposed in incised volcanoes but have only very rarely been identified in volcanic terranes. A possible reason for this is that preferential erosion of the mud matrix leads to very poor exposure of these rocks under normal circumstances. Mehl & Schmincke (1993) note the presence of numerous clastic dykes in the collapse structures of the Roque Nublo Group on Gran Canaria: these are exposed in an area of great topographic relief and relatively dry climate but are nonetheless preferentially eroded relative to rocks around them.

Fracturing, clastic intrusion and fluid flow: effects on pore pressure distribution. One of the most important effects of clastic, fluid-filled intrusion formation in volcanic edifices will be to allow large-scale fluid movement and consequent redistribution of pore pressures. Porous-medium or Darcian flow of pressurized pore water is considered by Elsworth & Voight (1996) as a potential means of spreading local over-pressurization of pore fluids from the vicinity of intrusions into a much larger volume of rock. However, fluid flow through porous solids is driven by a pressure gradient which, depending on the permeability of the host medium, is commonly steep. Pressure gradients in fractures filled with flowing fluids have been dealt with extensively in the context of magma-filled sheet intrusions (most recently, by Spence *et al.* 1987; Lister 1990; Lister & Kerr 1991; Rubin 1993); critically, these gradients are small compared to those needed to drive porous-medium flow over comparable distances (Sleep 1988).

The potential therefore exists for short-circuiting of porous-medium flow, even in permeable rocks, by macroscopic fracturing of the rock and flow of mobilized mud or more water-rich fluids in those fractures. In this case an increased pore pressure in the sink region at the top of the fracture, a distance Δz above the source region, will be generated given by:

$$\lambda_s P_s - \rho_f g \Delta z - \Delta P_{vf} = \lambda_1 P_1 \qquad (6)$$

where λ_s and λ_1 are the reduced pore pressures in the source and sink regions respectively; P_s, P_1 are the confining pressures in the source and sink regions; ρ_f is the fluid density; g is the acceleration due to gravity; and ΔP_{vf} the pressure drop associated with viscous fluid flow within the fracture. The magnitude of the term ΔP_{vf} depends on the sizes and geometries of the fractures or fracture networks under considera-tion, flow rates in them, and the viscosity of the fluids. It has been discussed extensively in the context of silicate magma-filled fractures (see references above) and will not be considered here. Neglect of this term in the present context can be justified for two reasons: firstly, in the case of water-rich fluids the viscosity will commonly be very low and, secondly, flow rates are not required to be high in order to avoid thermal freezing, as is the case with silicate magmas (Lister & Kerr 1991; Rubin 1993). Under these circumstances the ΔP_{vf} term is likely to rapidly approach zero as the source and sink regions approach mechanical equilibrium.

Equation (6) can be simplified considerably by neglecting the ΔP_{vf} term and assuming that the confining pressures are equal to the lithostatic loads in the source and sink regions:

$$\lambda_s \rho_r g z_s - \lambda_h \rho_r g \Delta z = \lambda_1 \rho_r g (z_s - \Delta z) \qquad (7)$$

(note that by the definition of reduced pore pressure, the reduced hydrostatic pore pressure is equal to the ratio ρ_f/ρ_r). Then:

$$\lambda_s z_s - \lambda_h \Delta z = \lambda_1 (z_s - \Delta z) \qquad (8)$$

It will be noted from equation (8) that the value of λ_1 at mechanical equilibrium between source and sink regions increases with the height of the fracture as a fraction of the depth of the source and also with the excess of source region pore pressure over its hydrostatic value. If the latter is large, with λ_s close to unity, superpressurization of the sink region (values of $\lambda_1 > 1$) is likely to occur.

Overall, the effectiveness of this process in producing pore pressure increases in a low-pressure, near-surface aquifer depends on a number of factors: whether the intrusions vent at the surface; the fluid pressure in the source region; the sensitivity of pressures in the low-pressure aquifer to addition of fluids from below; and the fluid flow-induced reduction in overpressure. As noted above, this last term is likely to be small if the fluids are of low viscosity and not subject to solidification on cooling.

Surface venting of clastic intrusions? Whether clastic or mud dykes propagate to and vent at the surface will depend on the same factors which control propagation of magma-filled fractures (see references above), with the addi-tion of a leakage term to allow for loss of fluid from the intrusion into porous wall rocks: it is to be anticipated that modelling of this process, the reverse of the drainage process considered by Sleep (1988), will be highly intractable. Other points to note, however, are that the fragmental, poorly lithified and/or partly plastic behaviour of the materials making up pyroclastic-rich and hydrothermally altered volcanoes (particularly in the near-surface parts of the edifices where lithification is less intense) will cause them to be inefficient stress transmitters and thus resistant to dyke propagation (Rubin 1993): relatively large fluid overpressures at the clastic dyke tips will be required for them to propagate all the way to the surface.

Fluid overpressures in source regions. The amount of overpressuring (in the sense of λ_s exceeding unity) in the source region feeding a clastic intrusion or intrusions is limited by the amount of overpressure required for fracture propagation and thus drainage of fluid to begin. As noted by Anderson (1938), Phillips (1972) and Sibson (1987) in the contexts of both igneous intrusions and hydrothermal vein systems, the requirement for the development of tensile fractures is that fluid pressure exceed the minimum stress σ_3, not the lithostatic load.

If σ_3 is less than the lithostatic load, as it is by varying amounts in all except compressive stress regimes, the value of $(\lambda_s - \lambda_h)$ in the fluid source region may be quite small when failure occurs: the pressurization effect in the regions into which the fluid ascends will be correspondingly reduced (see equation (8), above).

The reduction in $(\lambda_s - \lambda_h)$ due to this effect will however be greatly dependent upon the shear strength of the source region. This is itself a function of the pore pressure, as discussed in the section on material properties, above, because this determines the maximum possible reduction in σ_3 relative to the lithostatic load. The presence of a highly pressurized, weak region deep in a volcanic edifice, particularly if it shows long-term creep or quasiplastic behaviour and therefore maintains a high pore fluid pressure over time, may therefore lead to a reduction in the strength of the rest of the edifice through propagation of highly pressurized water- or mud-filled fractures into those other parts of the edifice. Such behaviour is analogous to that proposed by Byerlee (1990), Scholz (1990), Rice (1992) and Axen (1992) to explain the relative weakness of large to crustal-scale fault zones which root into the quasiplastic region of the crust. Release of pressurized fluids from the latter during prograde metamorphism during faulting and high-strain-rate deformation in the root zones leads to the development of high pore pressures in the fault zones during interseismic periods (the direct applicability of this mechanism to fault zones within volcanic edifices is considered further below). Quantifying this effect is extremely difficult owing to the problems of modelling fluid flow into, and out of, propagating fluid-filled fractures that were discussed by Sleep (1988). The rapid and, most significantly, pervasive deformation of certain volcanoes built upon weak clay-rich substrates (van Wyke de Vries & Borgia this volume) may in part reflect pressurization of the edifice released by fluids from their substrates.

Determination of values of λ in source regions from field observations. Although treatment of many of the factors determining redistribution of pore pressures by fluid flow through clastic intrusions is presently rather intractable, the more basic issue of values of λ in clastic dyke source regions (λ_s, defined above) can be addressed by field observations. As noted by Phillips (1972), fluid-filled fractures formed at moderate values of λ have a restricted range of orientations around the local σ_3 direction at the time of their formation. This range of orientations increases with λ. In the extreme case of

$\lambda \approx 1$, the initial fractures will have random orientations (unless the host rock is anisotropic, with a strong variation in τ_0 with direction). Sheet intrusions, once they begin to form, propagate either in their initial plane or else rotate towards the σ_3 orientation if this changes (Anderson 1938). Consequently, wide variations in the azimuth of clastic dykes will be indicative of their propagation from regions of high λ_s. Caution should be exercised in the interpretation of the reverse case, however, since propagation of clastic dykes, as with other types of sheet intrusion, into a region of high deviatoric stress will lead either to their rotation in the plane of σ_3 (a process whose operation may be recognized by strong and systematic segmentation of the intrusions) or to suppression of unfavourably orientated intrusions: the presence of a swarm of clastic dykes with uniform orientation would not necessarily imply low λ_s in their source.

High pore pressures associated with deformation

Quasiplastic creep and cataclasis are both mechanisms by which the framework around pores may be collapsed, leading to the development of pore pressures equal to the local lithostatic load ($\lambda = 1$). It also leads to substantial reductions in permeability, except during fault movements when transient fractures develop within fault zones (Sibson 1981, 1990). Measured permeabilities are particularly low in fault gouge and fine-grained cataclasite. Creep deformation leading to collapse of pores will be an important mechanism for increasing pore pressures in unconsolidated or partially consolidated volcaniclastic rocks, as it is in non-volcanic sediments, and will also be important in clay-rich hydrothermally altered rocks as discussed in the previous section. The effects of elevated fluid pressures upon faulting are emphasized here, since as noted above the development of discrete faults is essential to the catastrophic collapse process in volcanoes.

The process of fault pressurization is self-perpetuating as the development of high pore fluid pressures weakens the rocks in the fault zone, promoting further deformation in that zone. Owing to the local reduction in permeability, and low intrinsic permeability in the host rocks, the pressurization may be quite localized (Byerlee 1990; Rice 1992; Chester *et al.* 1993) but as will be seen this may not necessarily be the case. Deformation of fluid-saturated porous rocks and consequent lithopressurization has been recognized as a mechanism for rock weakening in thrust belts (Rubey & Hubbert 1959a, b; Davis et al. 1983), in mature strike-slip fault zones (Scholz 1990; Byerlee 1990; Rice 1992) and in extensional detachment faults (Axen 1992). Its characteristic geometrical consequence in near-surface dip-slip faulting is the development of low-angle faults and, in extreme cases, gravity sliding in regions of relatively subdued topography (Rubey & Hubbert 1959a).

In non-volcanic geological settings this fault self-pressurization process is generally associated with large, long-lived fault zones with large total slips (of the order of tens of kilometres or more) and relatively high displacement rates (Scholz 1990; Wesnousky 1988). In contrast, faults within volcanic edifices are typically short-lived and small, and have relatively small displacements unless they actually act as lateral collapse slip surfaces, but slip rates on them may be extremely high, several orders of magnitude greater than those associated with tectonic faults. For example, total slip on the faults active at Mount St. Helens prior to the May 1980 lateral collapse totalled some 200 metres in a little under 3 months (Voight et al. 1981), giving a slip rate of the order of 1 km/year, as compared to the slip rate of the San Andreas fault zone, of the order of 0.00004 km/year (Thatcher 1992).

A number of observations suggest that fault-pressurization processes may operate in and around faults in unstable volcanic edifices. Deformation (commonly but not always lateral spreading) on low-angle faults has been identified in a number of volcanoes (Borgia et al. 1990; van Wyke de Vries & Borgia this volume). van Wyke de Vries & Borgia (this volume) describes mud diapirs developed in and adjacent to an annular thrust belt around the flanks of Concepcion volcano, Nicaragua. The spatial and temporal association of mud diapirism and faulting at Concepcion suggests that the pressurization and mobilization of the poorly consolidated sediments to produce these diapirs resulted from escape of pressurized fluids from the faults, and/or in situ fluid pres-surization due to creep around the faults. Fluid discharges from faults during or immediately after earthquakes, due to creation of high transient permeabilities by coseismic fracturing, are a common feature of non-volcanic faults (Sibson 1981, 1990, 1992; Nur & Walder 1992). Similar transient flow events involving hot hydrothermal fluids in volcanic areas may account for the association of phreatic eruptions with earthquakes in the Salton Sea and Suoh volcanic fields, noted above.

Detailed descriptions of major low-angle faults in incised volcanoes are unfortunately rare, in part because of the tendency of cataclasite and gouge-rich faults to be eroded out relative to the adjacent intact rocks and therefore poorly exposed. However, close examination of volcanic faults, as with tectonic faults (for example, Chester et al. 1993) may reveal much about their behaviour. Figures 2 and 3 shows a relatively late fault in the Ayacata formation of the Roque Nublo Group, Gran Canaria, exposed in a road-cut north of the village of Ayacata (Ejercito Grid Reference 396 933). This fault has a shallow dip (orientation 080/18 N) and an oblique slip vector from asymmetric gouge marks in the roof contact of 036/14 N, antithetic to the overall southwestward movement direction for lateral collapse deposits and related structures in the Roque Nublo Group (Brey & Schmincke 1980; Torrado 1992; Mehl & Schmincke 1993). The latter congruency and the lack of evidence for rotation of contemporaneous structures (Torrado 1992) suggest that the fault is close to its original orientation and that its shallow dip is a primary feature. This is in itself indicative of high λ during fault movement. The fault consists of up to two metres of lithified fine-grained banded gouge below an undulating upper contact, with abundant veins and intrusions of mobilized gouge mud cutting the banding but in various states of deformation: note that the banding may itself represent intensely deformed and transposed earlier veins. The smaller veins root into paler gouge bands within the exposure (Fig. 3), indicating that they were produced by local mobilization of gouge mud. This and the varied orientations of the veins and larger intrusions suggest the development of values of λ close to or in excess of unity within the fault zone.

Available radiometric dating (Torrado 1992 and refs therein) brackets the age of formation of the Ayacata formation and its subsequent deformation to between 3.1 and 2.7 Ma. The duration of movement on the fault is therefore constrained to be less than 400 000 years, and is probably much less than that. The extremely rapid maturation of the fault may reflect a number of factors: high deformation rates; highly reactive host rocks undergoing alteration to clay-rich materials; abundant and reactive pore fluids; high thermal gradients in the host rocks.

The development of high pore fluid pressures within fault zones is likely to lead to development of high pore pressures in surrounding rocks in the up-dip direction in particular, due to

Fig. 2. Road-cut exposure of the gouge-rich Ayacata fault, cutting Ayacata formation breccias and a small brecciated gabbro intrusion (in hanging wall), near Ayacata, Gran Canaria. View looking northwest; overhanging upper fault surface is about 3 m above road level in centre of field of view.

Fig. 3. Detail of large and small mobilized gouge mud intrusions cutting banded gouge, from centre of field of view in Fig. 2. Note clasts of banded gouge in larger intrusion. Compass length 10 cm.

creep deformation (Chester *et al.* 1993) and especially discharges of fluids during seismicity (Sibson 1990; Nur & Walder 1992). The high permeability of many volcanic edifices and the relatively small slips on the faults (and hence the restricted development of low-permeability damage zones around the faults) means that these processes are likely to be even more pronounced in volcanic edifices than in the vicinity of tectonic faults. Whilst in the case of tectonic faults large amounts of such leakage would lead to depressurization of the fault zones, at least in the short term (over longer interseismic periods fluid pressures appear to be restored, see Sibson 1992), the much higher slip rates of volcanic faults in pre-collapse periods, as in the case of Mount St. Helens, would allow correspondingly higher rates of fluid leakage although the precise form of slip rate–pressurization rate relationships are poorly known (Scholz 1990; Byerlee 1990; Rice 1992; Axen 1992).

A further factor which may need to be considered in volcanic edifice related deformation, which is in general not relevant to tectonic faults, arises in cases where the faults are mechanically linked to intrusive complexes or dyke swarms. In such situations fault movement will be associated with intrusion injection either in the fault zones themselves or in adjacent areas. As a result, heated, pressurized fluids generated in or around the intrusions by the aquathermal and gas-mixing processes discussed above are likely to be injected into the fault zones. Mixing of magma or other hot material with fluid-rich fault gouge or breccia in fault zones may lead to particularly rapid heating and pressurization.

It is therefore to be anticipated that the development of, and movement on, pressurized fault zones could contribute to progressive overall weakening of the volcanoes in which they occur rather than to localized weakening around developing fault zones themselves. It may be possible to resolve this issue either by considering patterns of seismicity, especially aftershocks associated with large earthquakes, in volcanic edifices – Sibson (1981), Li *et al.* (1987) and Scholz (1990, 205–210) discuss criteria for recognizing fluid migration related aftershock swarms – or by detailed mapping of fault zones and associated clastic dykes in exhumed collapse structures. Such work would be best carried out in incipient or 'aborted' collapse structures, as it is comparatively easy to determine the distribution of faults and clastic dykes developed in the period leading up to the collapse when the structure has deformed in a coherent fashion throughout.

Sustaining elevated pore pressures in permeable volcanic edifices: an alternative explanation for the association of previous hydrothermal alteration with lateral collapses

The discussion thus far indicates that a variety of mechanisms exist whereby pore fluid pressures in volcanoes may be increased, leading to weakening and deformation. However, whether such pore pressure increases can be sustained over long periods or through large volumes of rock depends critically on the extent to which high pore pressures are dissipated by fluid flow to low-pressure regions and in particular to surface discharges. Consideration of this aspect of the problem of deformation in permeable volcanic edifices leads to some possible explanations of the association of volcano instability with hydrothermal alteration noted in the introduction to this paper.

The extent to which this occurs depends on the permeabilities of the rocks making up the volcano concerned, and to a lesser extent upon their porosities, but also upon the rates at which pore pressure changes are generated. In non-volcanic settings, the development of high pore pressures is in general critically dependent upon the presence of very low-porosity mudrocks, either as a large part of the sequence as a whole or as caprocks, whilst the development of fractures almost invariably leads to a reduction to near-hydrostatic values (Sibson 1990; Nur & Walder 1992). This is a reflection of low rates of pore pressure increase, whether by compaction or by the aquathermal effect (Barker 1972).

In volcanic settings, however, the much more rapid rates of heating, deformation or other mechanisms of pore pressure increase may lead to elevated pore pressures over a wider permeability range. At low permeabilities, λ will be sensitive to perturbations resulting from heating of the host rocks or from compaction of the matrix and a consequent reduction in pore volume. However, since low permeability restricts fluid migration, the dispersal or spreading of high pore pressures through fluid migration from high-λ to initially low-λ regions will be slow. At high permeabilities, values of λ will be effectively buffered by rapid fluid migration in response to any pressure increase, provided that a large-capacity sink for the fluid exists, such as surface runoff from the volcano in the case of systems connected to the free surface. Such buffering will be particularly effective in the case of gradual changes, such as those induced by heating following intrusion emplacement, but may be less so when large volumes of fluid are introduced suddenly, as after a fracturing event at depth (Nur & Walder 1992). It follows that the permeability of rocks will affect not only their overall sensitivity to perturbations in pore pressure but also their sensitivity to particular mechanisms for changing pore pressures. Furthermore, the details of the permeability structure and distribution within a volcanic edifice may be important: the structure most vulnerable to weakening by pore pressure increase would be one in which a high-permeability interior is enclosed by low-permeability rocks towards the exterior of the edifice. In this case pore pressures could rise rapidly throughout the interior of the volcano, and be contained by the low-permeability carapace until catastrophic failure of the latter occurred. Such a structure could either result from the eruptive history of the volcano (for example, early scorias and coarse pyroclastic rocks being mantled by later lahars or welded ignimbrites) or from subsequent hydrothermal or fumarolic alteration. Anderson & Burnham (1965) and Frantz et al. (1981) show that silicate solubilities in supercritical aqueous fluids increase with pressure and temperature, so such alteration will tend to dissolve the interiors of volcanic edifices, creating high-permeability zones, whilst precipitating minerals in the cooler exterior parts of the edifice and reducing permeabilities there. A similar effect might result from weathering of the exterior of a volcano to produce a clay-rich, low-permeability exterior carapace, or for thermal fracturing of the initially hot core of the volcano by an inward-propagating hydrothermal system (Lister 1974).

The mechanisms of volcano deformation may also have a strong effect on its permeability and the way in which this evolves as pore pressure increases. If the volcano is composed of relatively strong, brittle materials, deformation in response to a change in strength or in external load will cause fracturing and an overall increase in permeability, although whether this leads to escape of fluid and reductions in λ, or merely to spreading of the region of high λ will of course depend upon the structure of the fractures and in particular whether they extend to the surface or to another large-volume fluid sink. For example, in a layered structure composed of strong, brittle and weak quasiplastic materials such as an alternating sequence of lavas and altered clay-rich pyroclastic rocks (Gudmundsson 1986), fracturing of the strong materials would merely result in a more widespread distribution of the highly pressurized fluids since these would still be trapped within the

volcano by the impermeable quasiplastic layers. Such impermeable barriers might also be produced by clay-rich fault zones or by granulation seams in particulate rocks (Woodcock & Underhill 1987).

The effects of porosity upon the sensitivity of volcanoes to perturbations in λ are likely to be less pronounced because porosity varies over a much smaller range than permeability (Norton 1988). High-porosity rocks and unconsolidated materials (such as fresh scoria) will however tend to be less sensitive to thermal or deformational perturbation than low-porosity rocks (such as compacted clay-rich materials as well as fresh massive lavas or intrusive rocks) because, respectively, of higher thermal capacities resulting from the presence of more water (which, in the high density field, has a much higher thermal capacity than most rocks (Norton 1984)), and greater overall compressibility.

It will be noted from this discussion that because of their low initial permeabilities, tendency to deform by creep rather than by the development of through-going fracture systems, and generally low porosities, hydrothermally altered rocks will tend to experience larger and more sustained increases in λ in response to a given thermal or mechanical perturbation than most fresh rocks. Furthermore, hydrothermal alteration of volcanic edifices as a whole may lead to the development of low-permeability carapaces. These trends, in addition to the weakness of clay-rich altered rocks with respect to creep deformation and consequent pore pressure increases as discussed above, are likely to account for the marked association of lateral collapses with previous hydrothermal alteration of the volcanoes affected by them (Siebert et al. 1987), rather than any intrinsic difference in the physical strength of hydrothermally altered rocks, as compared to the corresponding unaltered rocks.

Implications of the importance of pore pressure variations for modelling and prediction of volcano stability

It has been shown in general, qualitative terms in this paper that rapid variations in λ may result from a variety of effects: temperature changes; degassing of magma bodies; influx or drainage of pressurized pore fluids; and deformation. These changes in λ may have a dramatic effect upon the strength of a volcano; in particular, increases in λ to near or even greater than unity will eliminate all but any residual tensile or cohesive strength and may therefore be powerful agents for triggering lateral collapses. Whether such increases occur, however, will greatly depend upon the permeability structure and other aspects of the mechanical behaviour of the volcano concerned. This has implications for monitoring and prediction of the behaviour of water-saturated volcanoes in which the development of high pore pressures may precipitate potentially catastrophic instability.

Whilst it is a relatively simple matter to incorporate a known pore pressure distribution, or simply a constant value of λ, into a model for volcano stability by including it in an effective friction coefficient μ (see, for example, Paul *et al.* 1987), incorporating actual variations in λ into predictive models of volcanic edifices is likely to prove a more intractable problem. Elsworth & Voight (1996) address the problem in part but their methods are restricted to cases of fixed (although perhaps spatially variable) permeability. As they note, their models are liable to break down when lithopressured or superpressured pore fluids develop because rapid permeability increases will result from hydro-fracturing (clastic dyke formation) or explosive brecciation of the rocks. Even if a satisfactory model for the mechanics of a porous, water-saturated volcano could be developed its application to an actual volcano would be problematic because, as shown in this paper, the pore pressure distribution and evolution within it would be dependent upon a large number of factors: temperature distributions; porosity and permeability distributions; rock rheology and fault geometries, amongst others. Most of these are not well known and are likely to undergo rapid changes during a volcanic or volcanotectonic crisis.

Given the difficulties of attempting to model and thus predict the evolution of pore pressures in volcanoes approaching instability, a more profitable approach to specific prediction of volcanic collapses caused by edifice weakening might be to attempt to monitor changes in λ, and in particular to attempt to detect the occurrence of regions of near-lithopressured pore fluids, directly. This might best be done by observations of patterns of seismicity. Firstly, as was noted by Rubey & Hubbert (1959a, b), the development of high λ results in slip on near-horizontal fault planes: detection of movement on such planes directly, via determination of focal plane solutions, or indirectly, by identification of shallowly dipping to subhorizontal zones of microseismicity, would be one means of recognizing that high pore pressures were

present in the region affected. Secondly, the gradual spreading of high pore pressures through development of pressurized fracture zones would result in a gradually expanding seismic front, enclosing a region of relative seismic quiescence. The development of such zones before and after major earthquakes on pressurized large faults has been considered by Sibson (1981), Li *et al.* (1987) and Scholz (1990, 205–210) and may also be explicable in terms of pore fluid migration. Furthermore, the occurrence of earthquake swarms (ones in which there is no dominant single event) has been closely linked to volcanism (Sykes 1970) and to migration of highly pressurized pore fluids in particular (Nur 1974).

In more general terms, the conclusion that weakening of volcanic edifices is most likely to result from the development of high pore fluid pressures explains and reinforces the empirical association of a tendency to lateral collapses with hydrothermal alteration of the volcanoes affected. Furthermore, the conclusion that this relationship primarily results from permeability reduction during alteration rather than a reduction in the effective friction coefficient suggests that it may be possible to further refine hazard estimates on the basis of an understanding of the relationships between alteration and mechanisms of permeability reduction. Detailed study of the patterns of alteration and fluid flow in incised volcanoes has long been carried out in relation to studies of epithermal mineralization: similar studies may prove to be of value in understanding volcano instability.

Fieldwork in Gran Canaria was made possible by Commission of the European Communities Environment Programme Contract EV5V-CT92–0170; the generosity of Bill McGuire; and the efforts of individuals and organizations too numerous to mention in removing the UK from the European Exchange Rate Mechanism. Dave Prior provided invaluable guidance in the field of deformation-related fluid flow, and an anonymous reviewer made many improvements to the manuscript and a variety of stimulating criticisms.

References

ANDERSON, E. M. 1938. The dynamics of sheet intrusion. *Proceedings of the Royal Society of Edinburgh*, **58**, 242–251.
ANDERSON, G. M. & BURNHAM, C. W. 1965. The solubility of quartz in supercritical water. *American Journal of Science*, **263**, 494–511.
AXEN, G. J. 1992. Pore pressure, stress increase and fault weakening in low-angle normal faulting. *Journal of Geophysical Research*, **97**, 8979–8991.

BARKER, C. 1972. Aquathermal pressuring – role of temperature in development of abnormal pressure zones. *Bulletin of the American Association of Petroleum Geologists*, **56**, 2068–2071.

BONAFEDE, M. 1991. Hot fluid migration: an efficient source of ground deformation. Application to the 1982–1985 crisis at Campi Flegrei, Italy. *Journal of Volcanology and Geothermal Research*, **48**, 187–198.

BORGIA, A., BURR, J., MONTERO. L. D. & ALVARADO, G. E. 1990. Fault propagation folds induced by gravitational failure and slumping of the Central Costa Rica Volcanic Range: implications for large terrestrial and martian volcanic edifices. *Journal of Geophysical Research*, **95**, 14 357–14 382.

BRACE, W. F. 1964. Brittle fracture in rocks. *In*: JUDD, W. R. (ed.) *State of Stress in the Earth's Crust*. Elsevier, Amsterdam, 111–174.

BRANNEY, M. J. & SUTHREN, R. J. 1988. High-level peperitic sills in the English Lake District: distinction from block lavas, and implications for Borrowdale Volcanic Group stratigraphy. *Geological Journal*, **23**, 171–187.

BREY, G. & SCHMINCKE, H.-U. 1980. Origin and diagenesis of the Roque Nublo breccia, Gran Canaria (Canary Islands) – Petrology of Roque Nublo volcanics II. *Bulletin Volcanologique*, **43**, 15–33.

BUSBY-SPERA, C. J. & WHITE, J. D. L. 1987. Variation in peperite textures associated with differing host–sediment properties. *Bulletin of Volcanology*, **49**, 765–775.

BYERLEE, J. D. 1978. Friction of rocks. *Pure and Applied Geophysics*, **116**, 615–626.

——1990. Friction, overpressure and fault normal compression. *Geophysical Research Letters*, **17**, 2109–2112.

BYERS, C. D., GARCIA, M. O. & MUENOW, D. W. 1986. Volatiles in basaltic glasses from the East Pacific Rise at 21°N: implications for MORB sources & submarine lava flow morphology. *Earth and Planetary Science Letters*, **79**, 9–20.

CARMICHAEL, I. S. E., NICHOLLS, J., SPERA, F. J., WOOD, B. J. & NELSON, S. A. 1977. High-temperature properties of silicate liquids: applications to the equilibration and ascent of basic magmas. *Philosophical Transactions of the Royal Society of London, Series A*, **286**, 373–431.

CHESTER, F. M., EVANS, J. P. & BIEGEL, R. L. 1993. Internal structure and weakening mechanisms of the San Andreas Fault. *Journal of Geophysical Research*, **98**, 771–786.

CRANDELL, D. R. 1971. *Post-glacial lahars from Mt. Rainier Volcano*. Washington. United States Geological Survey Professional Paper **677**.

DAVIS, D., SUPPE, J. & DAHLEN, F. A. 1983. Mechanics of fold-and-thrust belts and accretionary wedges. *Journal of Geophysical Research*, **88**, 1153–1172.

ELLSWORTH, W. L. 1992. Earthquake history 1769–1989. *In*: WALLACE, R. E. (ed.) *The San Andreas Fault System*. United States Geological Survey Professional Paper, **1515**, 153–187.

—— & VOIGHT, B. 1996. Evaluation of volcano flank instability triggered by dyke intrusion. *This volume*.

FRANCIS, P. W., GARDEWEG, M., O'CALLAGHAN, L. J., RAMIREZ, C. F. & ROTHERY, D. A. 1985. Catastrophic debris avalanche deposit of Socompa volcano, North Chile. *Geology*, **13**, 600–603.

FRANTZ, J. D., POPP, R. K. & BOCTOR, N. Z. 1981. Mineral–solution equilibria – V. Solubilities of rock forming minerals in supercritical water. *Geochimica Cosmochimica Acta*, **45**, 69–77.

GVN 1994. Suoh. *Bulletin of the Global Volcanism Network*, **19**(2), 9–10.

GUDMUNDSSON, A. 1986. Formation of crustal magma chambers in Iceland. *Geology*, **14**, 164–167.

HELGESON, H. C. & KIRKHAM, D. H. 1974a. Theoretical prediction of the thermodynamic behavior of aqueous electrolytes at high pressures and temperatures. I. Summary of the thermodynamic/electrostatic properties of the solvent. *American Journal of Science*, **274**, 1089–1198.

—— & ——1974b. Theoretical prediction of the thermodynamic behavior of aqueous electrolytes at high pressures and temperatures. II. Debye–Huckel parameters for activity coefficients and relative partial molal properties. *American Journal of Science*, **274**, 1199–1261.

—— & ——1976. Theoretical prediction of the thermodynamic behavior of aqueous electrolytes at high pressures and temperatures. III: Equation of state for aqueous species at infinite dilution. *American Journal of Science*, **276**, 97–240.

——, —— & FLOWERS, G. C. 1981. Theoretical prediction of the thermodynamic behavior of aqueous electrolytes at high pressures and temperatures. IV: Calculations of activity coefficients, osmotic coefficients, and apparent molal and standard and relative partial molal properties to 600°C and 5 kb. *American Journal of Science*, **281**, 1249–1536.

HOEK, E. & BRAY, J. W. 1981. *Rock Slope Engineering* (3rd edn). E. & F. N. Spon, London.

HOSHINO, K., KOIDE, H., INAMI, K., IWAMURA, S. & MITSUI, S. 1972. *Mechanical Properties of Japanese Tertiary Sedimentary Rocks under High Confining Pressures*. Geological Survey of Japan Report **244**.

JAEGER, J. C. & COOK, N. G. W. 1971. *Fundamentals of Rock Mechanics*. Chapman & Hall, London.

JOHNSON, R. W. 1987. Large-scale volcanic cone collapse: the 1888 slope failure of Ritter volcano, and other examples from Papua New Guinea. *Bulletin of Volcanology*, **49**, 669–679.

KOKELAAR, B. P. 1982. Fluidisation of wet sediments during the emplacement and cooling of various igneous bodies. *Journal of the Geological Society of London*, **139**, 21–33.

LI, V. C., SEALE, S. H. & CAO, T. 1987. Postseismic stress & pore readjustment & aftershock distributions. *Tectonophysics*, **144**, 37–54.

LIPMAN, P. W. & MULLINEAUX, D. R. 1981. *The 1980 Eruptions of Mount St. Helens, Washington*. United States Geological Survey Professional Paper **1250**.

LISTER, C. R. B. 1974. On the penetration of water into hot rock. *Geophysical Journal of the Royal Astronomical Society*, **39**, 465–509.

LISTER, J. R. 1990. Buoyancy-driven fluid fracture: the effects of material toughness and of low-viscosity precursors. *Journal of Fluid Mechanics*, **210**, 263–280.

—— & KERR, R. C. 1991. Fluid-mechanical models of crack propagation and their application to magma transport in dykes. *Journal of Geophysical Research*, **96**, 10 049–10 077.

MCCLINTOCK, F. A. & WALSH, J. B. 1962. Friction of Griffith cracks in rock under pressure. *In*: *Proceedings of the 4th National Congress of Applied Mechanics*, Vol. 2. American Society of Mechanical Engineering, New York, 1015–1021.

MCGARR, A. & GAY, N. C. 1978. State of stress in the earth's crust. *Annual Review of Earth and Planetary Sciences*, **6**, 405–436.

MEHL, K. W. & SCHMINKE, H.-U. 1993. Multiple sector collapse of the Pliocene Roque Nublo stratocone on Gran Canaria (Canary Islands)? *III Congreso Geologica de Espana y VIII Congreso Latinoamericano de Geologica, Salamanca 1992*. Actas Tomo I, 448–452.

MORIMOTO, T. & OSSAKA, H. 1964. Low-temperature mud-explosion of Mt. Yake, Prefs. Nagano-Gifu, central Japan, on 17th June 1962 as an example of endogenous katamorphism of volcanic rock at the destructive stage of the volcano. *Bulletin Volcanologique*, **27**, 49–50.

MURAI, S. 1963. A brief note on the eruption of the Tokachi-dake volcano of June 29 and 30, 1962. *Tokyo University Earthquake Research Institute Bulletin*, **41**, 185–208.

NAKADA, M. & YOKOSE, H. 1992. Ice age as a trigger of active Quaternary volcanism and tectonism. *Tectonophysics*, **212**, 321–329.

NICHOLLS, J. & STOUT, M. Z. 1982. Heat effects of assimilation, crystallization and vesiculation in magmas. *Contributions to Mineralogy and Petrology*, **81**, 328–339.

NORTON, D. L. 1984. Theory of hydrothermal systems. *Annual Review of Earth and Planetary Sciences*, **12**, 155–177.

——1988. Metasomatism and permeability. *American Journal of Science*, **288**, 604–618.

NUR, A. 1974. Matsushiro, Japan earthquake swarm: confirmation of the dilatancy–fluid diffusion model. *Geology*, **2**, 217–221.

—— & WALDER, J. 1992. Hydraulic pulses in the Earth's crust. *In*: EVANS, B. F. & WONG, T.-F. (eds) *Fault Mechanics and Transport Properties of Rocks*. Academic Press, London, 463–474.

OINOUYE, T. 1917. A few interesting phenomena on the eruption of Usu. *Journal of Geology*, **25**, 258–288.

PATERSON, M. S. 1978. *Experimental rock deformation – the brittle field*. Springer-Verlag, Berlin.

PAUL, A., GRATIER, J. P. & BOUDON, J. 1987. A numerical model for simulating deformation of Mount St. Helens volcano. *Journal of Geophysical Research*, **92**, 10 299–10 312.

PHILLIPS, W. J. 1972. Hydraulic fracturing and mineralisation. *Journal of the Geological Society of London*, **128**, 337–359.

PICKERING, K. T., AGAR, S. M. & PRIOR, D. J. 1990. Vein structure and the role of pore fluids in early wet-sediment deformation, Late Miocene volcaniclastic rocks, Miura Group, S.E. Japan. *In*: KNIPE, R. J. & RUTTER, E. H. (eds) *Deformation Mechanisms, Rheology and Tectonics*. Geological Society, London, Special Publication, **54**, 417–430.

RICE, J. R. 1992. Fault stress states, pore pressure distributions, and the weakness of the San Andreas Fault. *In*: EVANS, B. F. & WONG, T.-F. (eds) *Fault Mechanics and Transport Properties of Rocks*. Academic Press, London, 475–504.

RUBEY, W. M. & HUBBERT, M. K. 1959a. Role of fluid pressure in mechanics of overthrust faulting. I: Mechanics of fluid-filled porous solids and its application to overthrust faulting. *Bulletin of the Geological Society of America*, **70**, 115–166.

—— & ——1959b. Role of fluid pressure in mechanics of overthrust faulting. II: overthrust belt in geosynclinal area of Western Wyoming in light of fluid-pressure hypothesis. *Bulletin of the Geological Society of America*, **70**, 167–206.

RUBIN, A. M. 1993. Tensile failure of rock at high confining pressure: implications for dyke propagation. *Journal of Geophysical Research*, **98**, 15 919–15 935.

SCHOLZ, C. H. 1990. *The Mechanics of Earthquakes and Faulting*. Cambridge University Press, Cambridge.

SIBSON, R. H. 1981. Fluid flow accompanying faulting: field evidence and models. *In*: SIMPSON, D. W. & RICHARDS, P. G. (eds) *Earthquake Prediction: an International Review*. American Geophysical Union Maurice Ewing Series **4**, 593–603.

——1987. Earthquake rupturing as a mineralising agent in hydrothermal systems. *Geology*, **15**, 701–704.

——1990. Conditions for fault-valve behaviour. *In*: KNIPE, R. J. & RUTTER, E. H. (eds) *Deformation Mechanisms, Rheology and Tectonics*. Geological Society, London, Special Publication, **54**, 15–28.

——1992. Implications of fault-valve behaviour for rupture nucleation and recurrence. *Tectonophysics*, **211**, 283–293.

SIEBERT, L. 1984. Large volcanic debris avalanches: characteristics of source areas, deposits and associated eruptions. *Journal of Volcanology and Geothermal Research*, **22**, 163–197.

——, GLICKEN, H. & UI, T. 1987. Volcanic hazards from Bezymianny- and Bandai-type eruptions. *Bulletin of Volcanology*, **49**, 435–459.

SLEEP, N. H. 1988. Tapping of melt by veins and dikes. *Journal of Geophysical Research*, **93**, 10 255–10 272.

SPENCE, D. A., SHARP, P. W. & TURCOTTE, D. L. 1987. Buoyancy-driven crack propagation: a mechanism for magma migration. *Journal of Fluid Mechanics*, **174**, 135–153.

STEHN, C. C. 1934. Die semivulkanischen explosienen des Pematang Bata in de Soeoh-Senke (Sud-Sumatra) im Jahre 1933. *Natururk Tijdschrift voor Nederlands–Indies*, **94**(1).

STEWART, I., McGUIRE, W., VITA-FINZI, C., FIRTH, C., HOLMES, R. & SAUNDERS, S. 1993. Active faulting and neotectonic deformation on the eastern flank of Mount Etna, Sicily. *Zeitschrift für Geomorphologie NF*, **94**, 73–94.

SYKES, L. R. 1970. Earthquake swarms and sea-floor spreading. *Journal of Geophysical Research*, **75**, 6598–6611.

TORRADO, F. 1992. *The Petrology of the Roque Nublo Volcanic Group, Gran Canaria*. PhD thesis, University of Las Palmas.

THATCHER, W. 1992. Present-day crustal movements and the mechanics of cyclic deformation. *In*: WALLACE, R. E. (ed.) *The San Andreas Fault System, California*. United States Geological Survey Professional Paper, **1515**, 189–205.

VAN WYK DE VRIES, B. & BORGIA, A. 1996. The role of basement in volcano deformation. *This volume*.

VOIGHT, B. 1981. Time scale for the first moments of the May 18th eruption. *In*: LIPMAN, P. W. & MULLINEAUX, D. R. (eds) *The 1980 Eruptions of Mount St. Helens, Washington*. United States Geo-logical Survey Professional Paper, **1250**, 69–92.

——, GLICKEN, H., JANDA, R. J. & DOUGLASS, P. M. 1981. Catastrophic rockslide avalanche of May 18. *In*: LIPMAN, P. W. & MULLINEAUX, D. R. (eds) *The 1980 Eruptions of Mount St. Helens, Washington*. United States Geological Survey Professional Paper, **1250**, 347–377.

WALKER, B. H. & FRANCIS, E. H. 1987. High-level emplacement of an olivine–dolerite sill into Namurian sediments near Cardenden, Fife. *Transactions of the Royal Society of Edinburgh, Earth Sciences*, **77**, 295–307.

WALLMANN, P. C., MAHOOD, G. A. & POLLARD, D. D. 1988. Mechanical models for correlation of ring-fracture eruptions at Pantelleria, Strait of Sicily, with glacial sea-level drawdown. *Bulletin Volcanologique*, **50**, 327–339.

WESNOUSKY, S. G. 1988. Seismological and structural evolution of strike-slip faults. *Nature*, **335**, 340–343.

WILSON, C. J. N. 1980. The role of fluidisation in the emplacement of pyroclastic flows: an experimental approach. *Journal of Volcanology and Geothermal Research*, **8**, 231–249.

WOHLETZ, K. H. 1983. Mechanisms of hydrovolcanic pyroclast formation: grain size, scanning electron microscopy, and experimental studies. *Journal of Volcanology and Geothermal Research*, **17**, 31–63.

WOODCOCK, N. H. & UNDERHILL, J. R. 1987. Emplacement-related fault patterns around the Northern Granite, Arran, Scotland. *Bulletin of the Geological Society of America*, **98**, 515–527.

The role of basement in volcano deformation

BENJAMIN VAN WYK DE VRIES[1] & ANDREA BORGIA[2]

[1] *Department of Earth Sciences, The Open University, Walton Hall, Milton Keynes, MK7 6AA, UK*
[2] *Instituto Nazionale di Geofisica, Roma, Italy*

Abstract: Growing volcanoes load their basements, causing isostatic flexure, compaction and brittle and ductile deformation. Deformation of basement in turn exerts stress onto the edifice, which also responds by deforming. This deformation will be gradual or catastrophic, depending on the nature of the cone, and the properties of the underlying rocks. The physical properties of substratum, most especially the viscosity, can vary greatly. Thus a substratum of lava will support a volcano to a greater extent than fine clastic rocks. Compaction, crustal flexure, and sagging (a result of viscous flow of substratum) create a depression below the volcano. In the cone this induces compression, which increases with increasing sagging. However over long time spans, or in low viscosity substratum, sagging generates volcano spreading, where elastic compression is relaxed. The role of basement in volcano stability at four Nicaraguan stratocones 1.5–2 km high, constructed of similar materials on three types of basement has been studied. San Cristobal volcano has a volcanic basement of lava and ignimbrite, which has sagged by small amounts. Mombacho volcano has a basement of volcanic and marine strata. Sagging occurs, but spreading is slow. Compressive stresses have been released in the cone by thrust faulting. These structures have probably been exploited by three sector collapses. Concepción and Maderas volcanoes rest on sedimentary strata of weak mudstones, and large amounts of sagging and spreading have occurred. The study shows that spreading promotes gradual deformation in the volcano, because slopes are reduced and stresses relaxed. Catastrophic failure is favoured when compression is dominant, because stresses are large enough to fracture rock and produce decollements. Fracturing also promotes hydrothermal circulation, which further weakens the construct.

Volcanic constructs are unstable when the material they are made of, or on which they stand, is unable to maintain the stresses placed upon it. Milne (1878) first suggested that the shape of a volcano is a function of the deformation of the construct under its load. The effect of weak substrata was investigated by Van Bemmelen (1949) who showed that the substrata of many Javan volcanoes were unable to support the volcano load. Large extensional structures were formed on and around the cones and compressional structures developed from near the base to many tens of kilometres away. Another mode of deformation, that of subsidence caused by volcano loading, was addressed by Suzuki (1968). He showed that similar cones in Japan and Indonesia caused different styles of deformation in different age substratum. In thick young (Quaternary–Pliocene) sediments a broad 'fold' developed at the base of the volcano. On older rocks, or with a thin young cover, normal faults developed, downthrowing toward the volcano. He interpreted this style of deformation as being due to the elastic response of the substratum and crust, rather than to brittle and ductile deformation. He estimated the rate of sinking of the Iizuna volcano to be about 2 mm/a. If the basement and crust are thick and

strong, then neither of the above processes are important. In this case Shteynberg and Solov'yev (1974) showed that volcanic cones with 30° slopes of more than 2 km height produce enough load on their lower parts to exceed the tensile strength of volcanic rocks at their base, and start to deform. Dieterich (1988) suggests that a volcanic edifice is in a state of critical equilibrium, governed by the load of the volcano, the angle of internal friction of the rocks and the friction of the base. Borgia *et al.* (1990) and Borgia & Treves (1991) studied a number of volcanoes on Earth and Mars that stand on different substrata which show different evidence of deformation. Finally Merle & Borgia (1996) present analogue experiments that attempt to determine the physical parameters which control spreading. Despite these no systematic study of the role of the substratum on deformation of real volcanoes has yet been done.

The rocks underneath volcanoes range from very strong and coherent, like igneous and metamorphic basement, to weak and incoherent, such as clay-rich sedimentary sequences, or evaporites. Different rock types react to loading in different ways and will feed stresses back into edifices that vary accordingly. Loading has the initial effect of producing a depression of the

From McGuire, W. J., Jones, A. P. & Neuberg, J. (eds) 1996, *Volcano Instability on the Earth and Other Planets,* Geological Society Special Publication No. 110, pp. 95–110.

basement beneath the volcano, by crustal subsidence and substratum compaction. Outward movement of rocks from under the cone by plastic or viscous flow may also occur. We call this latter effect sagging; it is similar to crustal subsidence, but is more localized. (In crustal subsidence the crust subsides into the mantle as the mantle flows aside; in sagging a ductile crustal layer flows aside and the brittle overlayer subsides.) With large amounts of outward flow, radial thrusting and diapirism occur, and the sagging causes the volcano to spread. All but the latter extreme effect of sagging have the same effect on stress in the cone and on the style of volcano deformation.

We investigate the role of the substratum on the deformation of volcanic constructs by considering similar volcanoes built on different substrata. In order to simplify the approach we chose situations with similar tectonic setting, negligible external tectonic stresses and where substratum geology is simple. We examine four conical stratocones erupted onto nearly flat surfaces. These are San Cristobal, Mombacho, Concepción and Maderas in Nicaragua (Fig. 1). Each is constructed in a similar way, but has a different style of deformation. San Cristobal has no observable deformation. Mombacho has compressive features at its foot and on the flanks, and has also collapsed on three sides.

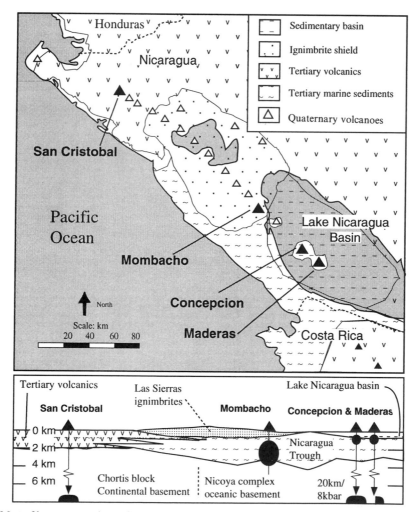

Fig. 1. (a) Map of basement geology of western Nicaragua modified from van Wyk de Vries (1993). The locations of the four volcanoes considered here, San Cristobal, Mombacho, Concepción and Maderas are shown. **(b)** Section through crust along the volcanic arc, showing location of intrusive complexes at each volcano; from van Wyk de Vries (1994).

Concepción and Maderas have a central rifting zone and a compressional belt around the cone. The major variable in the geological environment is the lithology of the basement, which is volcanic at San Cristobal, sedimentary at Concepción, and a combination of the two at Mombacho.

Basement control on volcano deformation: field evidence from Nicaragua

Basement geology

The volcanoes we consider here stand in the Nicaraguan Depression on the Central American volcanic arc (Fig. 1). Weyl (1980) suggests that the crustal basement at San Cristobal in the northwest of Nicaragua is probably Palaeozoic continental crust of the Chortis block, while to the south, under the other volcanoes, it is more probably oceanic, related to the Nicoya complex of Costa Rica.

The substratum at San Cristobal is probably made of a thin veneer of sediment (the Totogalpa formation; Weyl 1980) and certainly overlain by the Tertiary volcanic El Coyol group

(Pliocene), which are mostly stratovolcanoes interleaved with ignimbrite sheets (Fig. 1). The thickness of the volcanic pile is approximately 2 km.

In the central area at Mombacho the El Coyol group gives way to a $c.\,5\,\mathrm{km}$ thick marine sequence of the Nicaraguan Trough (Schmidt 1989). The marine rocks in the Nicaragua Trough are of Cretaceous to Pliocene age. They are mainly fine to medium-grained clastic rocks with occasional conglomerate beds and few limestones (Weyl 1980). These are covered by $c.\,500\,\mathrm{m}$ of Quaternary ignimbrites from the Las Sierras and Malpaisillo centres (van Wyk de Vries 1993). To the south the sedimentary sequence is increasingly deformed creating a coastal range, behind which a $c.\,500\,\mathrm{m}$ thick lacustrine sequence of Lake Nicaragua has developed. Concepción and Maderas have been erupted onto this lacustrine sequence (Fig. 1).

Volcano construction

All the volcanoes considered here are built of accumulations of pyroclastics and lava mostly

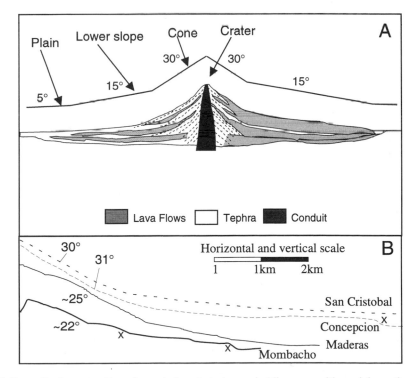

Fig. 2. (A) Generalized construction of a central vent stratocone in Nicaragua with no deformation, showing slope angles and main units. **(B)** Slope profiles for the four Nicaraguan volcanoes considered here. X marks the position of scarps at Concepcin and Mombacho.

ejected from a central vent (Fig. 2). The deposits observed at each are similar.

1. Scoria layers which thin rapidly away from the vent. On the cone they may be between 1 and 50 m thick, but at the base rarely exceed 1 m. Near the vent they are occasionally found as agglutinate, with small clastogenic lava flows less than 1 km long and 1–3 m thick.

Table 1. *Physical features, deformation styles, and deformation process at the volcanoes under study*

	San Cristobal	Mombacho	Concepción	Maderas
1. Physical features				
Volcano size (qualitative)	Large	Medium	Small	Small
Type of crustal basement	Coninental	Oceanic	Oceanic	Oceanic
Type of substratum	Tertiary volcanic rocks on metamorphic base, with possibly thin sediments below Tertiary	Coherent ignimbrites on Tertiary–Cretaceous marine flysch	Weak Quaternary lake sediments	Weak Quaternary lake sediments
Constraints on spreading:				
A. Buffering	Casita buffers the south east flank of San Cristobal	Non significant buffering effect to north west from Apoyo Volcano	None, flat lake bed	flat lake bed
B. Basal loading	Loma la Teta, Certo Moyotepe and El Chonco load the lower slopes	None	None	None
C. Slope of base	0°	2° slope to SE	0°	0°
State of volcanic activity	Vigorous fumarolic activity	Mild fumarolic activity	Mild fumarolic activity	Inactive
Time since last major growth phase	500 years	500–1000 years	40 years	>3000 years
Depth of magmatic system	Major system in lower crust (*c.* 8 kbar). No significant shallow system	Minor lower crustal system (8 kbar), major shallow system (*c.* 1 kbar)	Major system in lower crust (*c.* 8 kbar), feeding minor shallow system (*c.* 1 kbar)	Major system in lower crust (*c.* 8 kbar), feeding minor shallow system (*c.* 1 kbar)
Hydrothermal manifestations	Fumaroles restricted to summit	Fumarolic field and hot springs over wide area	Fumaroles restricted to summit	No hydrothermal manifestations
2. Deformation features	No structures	Thrusting along base and within volcano. Scarps 100 m high. Slumps and sector collapses	Summit extension (*c.* 5 cm per year). Basal thrusting and diapirism. Minor slumping of north flank	Leaf grabens with 150 m scarps. Steep lower flanks and gentle summit slopes. Slow slumping of West flank
3. Stress strain state	Elastic deformation compression, no relaxation	Elastic deformation Compressional faulting, hydrothermal weakening, partial relaxation	Spreading, elastic stresses, relaxing	Spreading elastic stresses relaxed

2. Lava flows, which are 1–3 m thick and 50–100 m wide on the steep cone, and which become 10–80 m thick and 1–2 km wide once they reach the base of the cone.
3. The distribution of lava and scoria is asymmetrical due the prevailing winds: the deposits on the western side are 75% pyroclastic and 25% lava flows, while on the eastern side the proportions are reversed. Summits are to the west (down wind) of craters, and hence more lava flows run down the eastern flanks.

A generalized cross-section of one of these volcanoes is shown in Fig. 2. It comprises an upper slope dominated by tephra, a lower slope dominated by lava flows and lahar deposits, and a basal plain dominated by tephra, lahar deposits, and alluvium that fans out from the main gullies.

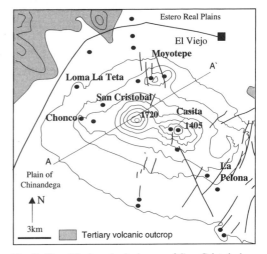

Fig. 3. Simplified geological map of San Cristobal, showing main structural features and location of vents. Line A–A′ is the line of section shown in Fig. 10A.

Description of volcanoes

The topography now seen at Concepción and San Cristobal corresponds closely to the idealized form in Fig. 2 while Maderas and Mombacho depart strongly from it. At Maderas the summit area is less steep, while the flanks are steeper. At Mombacho the profile is, in general, less steep, except at the scarps near the base and on the flanks.

The Concepción and San Cristobal volcanoes have grown rapidly in historic times, adding up to 100 m to their summit heights. Mombacho has had recent eruptions adding 200–300 m to its western flank, but no deposits added to the east side, since the two major sector collapses. Maderas has no historic record of activity and may have been inactive for a few thousand years.

San Cristobal volcano

The basement at San Cristobal is made of Pre-Mesozoic continental crust, overlain by about 2 km of El Coyol Tertiary volcanic rock (Fig. 1 and Table 1). About 30 km to the northeast the continental Totogalpa sandstone formation is found between the two. This formation may continue under San Cristobal, perhaps as a shallow marine temporal equivalent. The El Coyol volcanic sequence stands out to the south, north and east about 5 km from the base of the cone with up to 300 m of relief. Their relief decreases towards the volcano suggesting some subsidence under its load.

San Cristobal is the most recently active part of a complex comprising two other major older centres, Casita and La Pelona (Fig. 3). Casita is a 1400 m high volcanic ridge formed of interleaved deposits erupted from two vents; La Pelona is a stratocone truncated by a 4 km wide caldera (Hazlet 1987). San Cristobal has grown on the northwest base of Casita and has subsidiary centres situated at its own base: El Chonco to the northwest, Loma La Teta to the north and Cerro Moyotepe to the northeast. Casita volcano buffers the volcano to the southeast inhibiting any possible spreading towards this side. The subsidiary centres, loading the base, are stabilizing factors and act against spreading. Apart from some strong north-oriented extensional faulting on Moyotepe, there is no relevant faulting at San Cristobal, either on the cone or at the base. The slope profile conforms to the idealized construction (Fig. 2).

Mombacho volcano

The crust at Mombacho is probably oceanic crust of the Cretaceous Nicoya complex (Fig. 1 and Table 1). Marine strata of the Pre-Rivas, Rivas and Brito formations cover this to a thickness of about 5 km. These are overlain by about 200 m of Las Sierras ignimbrite (van Wyk de Vries 1993).

Mombacho volcano has repeatedly grown and collapsed (van Wyk de Vries 1993). The volcano now consists of two main peaks

separated by two sector collapses, one to the
north-northeast and one to the south. The most
recent addition is centred 300 m to the northwest of these, building a half cone about 300 m
thick (Fig. 4). The base of the edifice, which
has a radius of about 5–6 km is a gentle plain
covered by pumice from the Apoyo ignimbrite,
tephra from Mombacho, and by hummocky
deposits of the debris avalanches. South of
Mombacho regional strike-slip faulting is north-
east-oriented. North-oriented splays of this
system extend toward Mombacho, favouring
the emplacement of cinder cones at its western
base.

The two scars of the sector collapses are
well preserved. The southern scar is horse-
shoe shaped similar to that at Mt. St. Helens,
although there are no post-collapse dome or
pyroclastic deposits in the associated avalanche.
The northern collapse scar is shallower and
longer, extending to the base of the cone. The
existence of two other sector collapses is inferred
from their deposits. The southeast collapse
deposit is similar to the southern one, while the
east collapse deposit is instead made of toreva-
like blocks (Reiche 1937).

In the basement rocks there are no signs of
structures associated with the volcano. In
contrast, within the cone, steeply inclined

strata are associated (Figs 2 and 8) with
marked increases in slope angle of the flanks.
These zones are interpreted as being the result of
thrust faulting (van Wyk de Vries 1994; see Fig.
10). The highest of these occurs on the east
flank, at 350 m elevation and has about 100 m of
uplift.

Concepción volcano

The crust at Concepción is oceanic, as at
Mombacho (Weyl 1980), and is overlain by
about 5 km of marine sediments. In addition
these are covered by about 500 m of lacustrine
sediments. The lake sediments are mainly unconsolidated mudstones, with subordinate volcanic
sandstones in the upper part of the sequence.
These sandstones are only a few metres thick to
the east, but thicken to over 100 m on the western
side of the volcano. This area is also the site of the
thickest tephra deposits, due to the prevailing
wind. To the east total tephra thickness amounts
to less than a few metres, while to the west it
exceeds 50 m.

Concepción volcano is 1700 m high, with a
radius of about 5 km (Fig. 5). The upper 1200 m
of the cone mostly rises at 32°, though a sector
to the north and west, which is not covered by

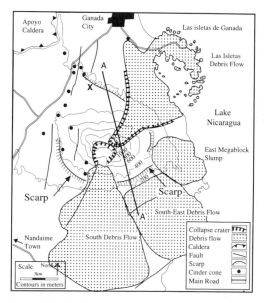

Fig. 4. Mombacho volcano showing collapse scars,
avalanches and major structural features. Line A–A′ is
the line of section in Fig. 10B. Near-vertical pyroclastic
and alluvial strata are found at location X.

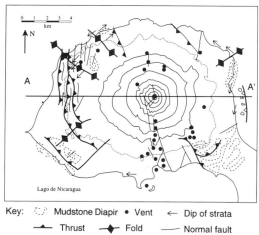

Fig. 5. Simplified geological map of Concepción
volcano, showing main structural and morphological
features, including areas of mudstone diapirism, radial
folding, and tangential thrusting with associated fault
propagation folds. Normal faults and fractures with
associated vents bisecting the cone are also shown. The
line A–A′ is the line of section in Fig. 10C.

recent deposits has a more gentle slope of 28°. Below this at about 400 m elevation, slopes angles decrease rapidly and are made of lava and talus fans (van Wyk de Vries 1993)

North–south trending fractures and faults bisect the central crater and are associated with subsidiary eruption centres (spatter and cinder cones, fissures, and maars). The ground surrounding the cone is formed of recently folded, faulted, and uplifted lake sediments with a veneer of volcanic and volcaniclastic deposits. The structures can be classified into three types (Borgia & van Wyk de Vries 1994; see also Fig. 5).

(1) Radial folding: folds in lake sediments caused by the initial crustal subsidence of the volcanic edifice. These cause radial hills and valleys.

(2) Tangential thrusting and associated fault-related folds, with radial shortening: caused by spreading of the edifice and intrusive system. These create tangential ridges and a trough around the volcano.

(3) Mudstone diapirs and chaotic soft-sediment deformation: caused by squeezing of the mudstones under the load of edifice, of individual lava flows and sediment fans. This deformation style causes moundy, chaotic topography, with hollows.

Maderas volcano

The basement and substratum at Maderas are identical to those of Concepción (van Wyk de Vries 1986). Maderas is 1400 m high, with a radius of 5 km (Fig. 6). Its lower slopes rise straight from Lake Nicaragua thus there is little knowledge of the geology off-shore. Bathymetric maps, however, show a trench-like feature 20–40 m deep around its southwestern shore.

The edifice is cut by many faults with a dominant central leaf graben (Merle & Borgia 1996) oriented north–south, with at least 140 m of vertical displacement. Other faults define less clearly other leaf grabens, or crescentic half grabens. The west side is also cut by a slump fault with about 100 m displacement. The geology of the base of the volcano is exposed in the northwest at El Istián, where at the foot, mudstones crop out. The steep faults pass into the mudstones. By analogy with Concepción, brittle deformation seems confined to the edifice, whereas ductile flow characterizes the substratum.

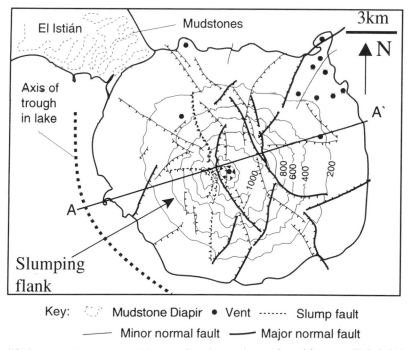

Fig. 6. Simplified structural and topographic map of Maderas volcano adapted from van Wyk de Vries (1986). Of particular note are the major faults, which create leaf graben and crescentic half graben. Also note slump feature on west side and trough in lake. The line A–A' is the line of section in Fig. 10D.

Dimensional analysis of volcano and basement

To compare the dynamics of deformation of these different volcanoes one may use dimensionless numbers, usually the ratios between characteristic geometric parameters, or between the forces at play. Merle & Borgia (1996) use a set of dimensionless numbers to scale their analogue experiments of volcanic spreading to real volcanoes. We attempt the same here (Table 2).

Π_1, the ratio between height and radius of a volcano, is a measure of its stability. As spreading of the volcano occurs H decreases proportionally faster than R thus Π_1 decreases over time; major constructive events will increase it again.

Π_2, the thickness of brittle substratum versus the height of the volcano, is a measure of how high a volcano may grow before the brittle substratum will fail, leading to spreading. For Π_2 larger than 0.4 no spreading occurs, only elastic deformation is possible. Since D does not change much during spreading, this number acts opposite to Π_1.

Π_3, the brittle ductile ratio of the substratum, is a measure of the mode of deformation of the substratum. For a value much larger than 1 no spreading occurs; for values around 1 a fold and thrust belt develops around the base of the volcano; for values much smaller than 1 instead, a belt of concentric diapirs grows.

Π_4, the ratio between the density of the volcano versus the density of the substratum, is a measure of the buoyancy response of the substratum. It is one of the parameters involved in determining the fault density within a volcano and the rate of spreading.

Π_5, the ratio between gravity and viscous forces, is a measure of the rate of deformation and also of the amount of deformation for any given substratum viscosity and time span of deformation.

In addition to these numbers we use Π_6, the ratio between the time since the last major eruptive phase and the time of viscoelastic relaxation (the Maxwell time) as a measure of the time needed to relax the elastic stresses placed onto the edifice by eruption and basement deformation. Of the aforementioned Π-numbers the most important to define the state of

Table 2. *Physical parameters and Π-numbers of the volcanoes studied, and of the numerical models*

Variable	Symbol	San Cristobal	Mombacho		Concepcion		Maderas	Models	
			Before	After	East	West		A	B
Volcano height	H (m)	1745	1800	1344	1610		1394	2000	2000
Volcano radius	R (m)	8000	5250		5000	4500	5000	6000	6000
Brittle layer	D (m)	2000	200		1	100	1	10 000	0
Ductile layer	T (m)	100	5000		500		500	0	10 000
Density volc	ρ_v (kg m^{-2})	2700	2700		2700		2700	2700	2700
Density seds	ρ_s (kg m^{-2})	2700	2400		2000		2000	2200	2200
Elasticity	λ (Pa)	1×10^{11}	1×10^{10}		1×10^{9}		1×10^{9}	2×10^{10}	2×10^{10}
Poisson's ratio	None	na	na		na		na	0.25	0.25
Yield Stress	Pa	na	na		na		na	na	5×10^{6}
Viscosity	μ (Pa s)	1×10^{21}	1×10^{19}		1×10^{17}		1×10^{17}	na	na
Gravity	g (m s^{-2})	9.81	9.81		9.81		9.81	9.81	9.81
Life time of volcano	t_o (s)	3×10^{11}	3×10^{11}		3×10^{11}		3×10^{11}	na	na
Time since last major growth	t_a (s)	1.6×10^{10}	3.2×10^{10}		1.6×10^{9}		1.6×10^{11}	na	na

Π numbers	Equation	San Cristobal	Mombacho		Concepción		Maderas	A	B
Π_1	H/R	0.22	0.34	0.26	0.32	0.36	0.24	0.3	0.3
Π_2	D/H	1.15	0.11	0.15	0.0006	0.03	0.0006	na	na
Π_3	D/T	20.00	0.04		0.002	0.2	0.002		na
Π_4	ρ_v/ρ_s	1.00	1.13		1.35		1.35	na	na
Π_5	$(\rho g H t_o)/\mu$	0.01	1.50	1.06	134.48		116.44	na	na
Π_6	$(\lambda t_a)/\mu$	1.6	32		16		1577	na	na

na indicates that no value is known or none is applicable.

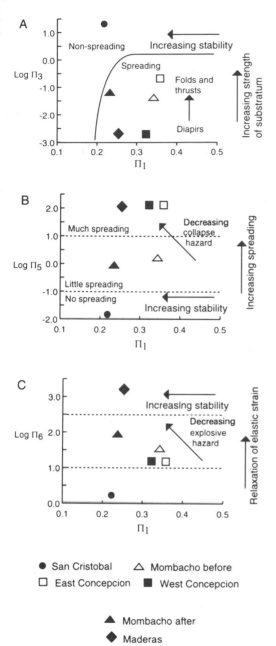

Fig. 7. Plots of Π-numbers for the four volcanoes considered. (A) (Π_3/Π_1) shows the fields of spreading and non-spreading volcanoes. The spreading boundary is taken from Merle and Borgia (1995). (B) (Π_5/Π_1) indicates spreading rate and the relative hazard of collapse. (C) (Π_6/Π_1) gives an indication of the rate of elastic strain relaxation by viscous flow in the substratum and the relative hazard of explosive eruption. Numbers are included for east and west Concepcin, and for Mombacho, before and after sector collapse.

stress and deformation of a volcano are Π_1, Π_3, Π_5, Π_6. Figure 7 plots the last three numbers as a function of the first. Figure 7A (Π_3/Π_1) shows the geometric relation between the dimensionless numbers of volcano and of basement that lead to spreading; this diagram does not give an indication of the rate of spreading, but only of the geometric capacity of the system to spread. In addition, this figure indicates the style of deformation: the small value of Π_3 at Concepción East indicates that concentric diapirs will grow around the base, while the intermediate values of Π_3 at Concepción West and Mombacho indicate that a fold and thrust belt will form. The different styles of deformation on the east and west of Concepción result because of the prevailing winds, with tephra and volcaniclastic sands (D) being thicker on the west side (larger Π_3) relative to the east (smaller Π_3).

A plot of Π_5 versus Π_1 (Fig. 7B) indicates the total amount of spreading that should have taken place during the life of a volcano or, for a given volcanic age and height to radius ratio, the rate of spreading. San Cristobal has a very minimal rate of spreading, Mombacho has a relatively slow rate of spreading, while Concepción and Maderas are fast spreading. The difference between the last two represents the time passed since the last major constructive process; thus, given enough time with no eruptions, Concepción may evolve towards a structural setting similar to that of Maderas. On the other hand, spreading on Mombacho is so small that other processes may have a major control on the structural evolution (for instance, volcanic activity, erosion, or sector collapse). A large amount of spreading leads to a more stable volcano, one with a smaller Π_1; equally sector collapse will reduce Π_1 and favour stability. Mombacho was in a critical state before its cone was sectioned, but since then lies near to the stable field (Fig. 7A). Concepción as well is in a critical state; its rate of spreading, however, may be fast enough to make the volcano evolve to a more stable condition before any collapse structure may develop.

Figure 7C (Π_6/Π_1) illustrates the state of the elastic stresses within the volcanic edifice built by the last major eruptive phase. At San Cristobal almost all elastic stress still needs to relax; both at Mombacho and at Concepción they have already started to relax, while at Maderas they should be almost completely relaxed. Since the presence of a large unrelaxed elastic stress tends to inhibit the formation of extensional fractures and effusive eruptions, San Cristobal seems to be the volcano most in danger of having powerful explosive eruptions.

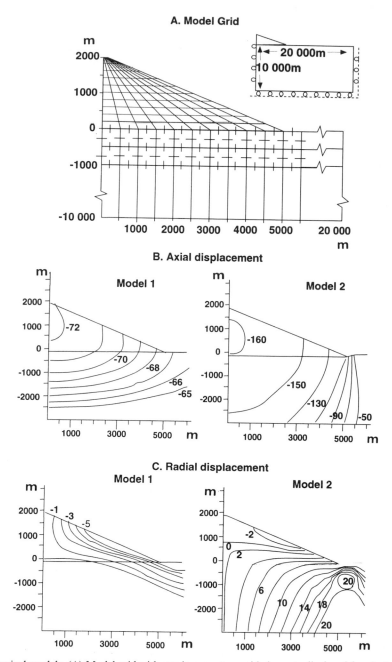

Fig. 8. Numerical models. (**A**) Model grid with one in every two grid elements displayed for clarity. Inset shows whole model with boundary conditions. (**B & C**) Displacement fields calculated from the numerical models: 1 (elastic), and 2 (elastoplastic). (**B**) Axial displacement; (**C**) radial displacement. Contours are in metres, with the convention: positive = upward or outward, negative = downward or inward.

Numerical models of volcano stress

We use Nike2d, an implicit finite-element code for analysing elastic and elastoplastic deformation (Engelmann & Hallquist 1991), to make simple axisymmetric finite-element models of the stresses in a volcano. The two models presented simulate the behaviour of an elastic cone on (1) elastic and (2) elastoplastic basements. The models are a gross simplification of reality, but they serve to show possible differences in the stress and strain rate fields that could arise in a volcano overlying basements with different rheological properties. They differ from the model for Hawaii presented by Borgia (1994), where the only effect of basement deformation considered is that of a decollement.

In each model the volcano is simulated by a truncated cone, 2×10^3 m high, 5×10^3 m in basal radius and 100 m in plateau radius at the summit; the latter simulates the crater area and avoids triangular elements in the grid (Fig. 9). Basements are 10×10^3 m deep and 20×10^3 m in radius, and tested to be large enough to avoid significant boundary effects. The model's grid has 3600 quadrilateral elements with sides of about 250 m at the base of the cone, that reduce to about 10 m at the summit (Fig. 8). The bottom of the model is fixed in the axial direction, while the right side is fixed in the radial direction; thus, the bottom right corner node is fixed in space. The left side of the grid is the axis of the model, movement is free in the axial direction, but no movement can occur in the radial direction. Since the base of the model is fixed in the axial direction there is no simulation of the isostatic crustal flexure, which would increase the stresses in the volcano and the basement. This contribution, however, may not be significant for small volcanoes on weak basement, since most of the deformation will be limited to the immediate substratum. The material properties used are shown in Table 2. The value of the yield strength of the elastoplastic basement is chosen to reproduce the 100–200 m of sagging observed at Japanese stratocones of similar dimensions by Suzuki (1968), and are consistent with the values given for real rocks (Clark 1966).

The distributions of axial and radial displacements are shown in Fig. 8. The axial, radial and tangential stresses resulting from the modelling are presented in Fig. 9. The discontinuity in stresses, shown between the cone and the basement, is only apparent. It is related to the fact that the stresses shown are the components of the stress tensor parallel to the model's axes and not to the axes of the principal stress ellipsoid. Indeed, the principal stresses and the strains are continuous across the boundary.

In the first model (Figs 8 and 9) the basement responds elastically to the load of the cone (no plastic deformation is allowed); the inflection of the basement due to elastic compaction places the cone under compression. This is analogous to the elastic models for Olympus Mons of Thomas et al. (1990), and for Hawaii of Borgia (1994). As expected, the axial stress is compressional, increasing downward and mimicking, as a first approximation, the topography. Radial compression is greater than tangential. In the upper part of the cone radial and tangential stresses are larger than the vertical component, but with depth (as the load increases) the vertical component begins to dominate (compare Fig. 9A with 9B and 9C). The displacement fields show that, due to the elastic compaction, particles move downward and towards the axis of symmetry (Fig. 8). The largest axial displacement is along the axis, while the largest radial displacement is at the base of the cone.

In the second model, the basement has a relatively low yield strength so that it gives way by plastic deformation under the load of the volcano, while this is sagging into it. The axial stress is extensional in the nucleus of the volcano and increases, becoming compressional, both upward and downward. The radial and tangential stresses are both compressional in the upper part of the cone and extensional in the lower part. As for the first model, the axial displacement is downward below the volcano, while on the contrary, the radial displacement is away from the axis of symmetry. In fact, the lower part of the cone is brought into extension in the radial and tangential directions, as the basement material flows outward from underneath the cone.

Near the cone surface stresses in an elastic basement model are up to ten times smaller than those in the yielding basement model, and at the base about twice as large. This indicates that the feed-back stresses in the construct increase with increasing amounts of sagging. In both models, however, maximum compressional and extensional stresses tend to be higher than the strength of fractured volcanic rocks (Clark 1966). Thus, faulting should be considered as the norm at medium sized volcanoes.

Discussion and conclusions

The stress imposed on a volcano and its substratum will deform them with a typology that is a function of rheology of the materials involved, of the geometry, and of the boundary conditions of the system. Of these, the rheology of the materials is of primary importance in determining the rate of deformation and whether the behaviour is elastic, brittle, plastic, viscous, etc., or more commonly a combination of these. In addition, there is a strong feedback between stress and deformation in the volcano and in the substratum: the deformation of the substratum under the stress imposed by the load of the volcano feeds back stress into the volcano, in turn influencing its deformation. Therefore, in studying the tectonics of a volcano one cannot avoid considering the role played by the type and rheology of substratum.

The four volcanoes studied show this influence in controlling volcano deformation. Their

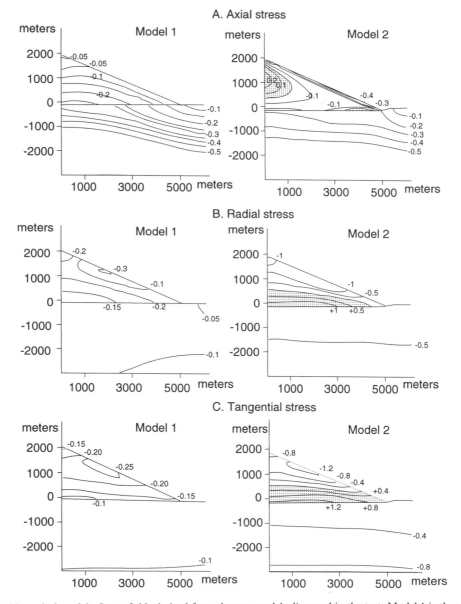

Fig. 9. Numerical models. Stress fields derived from the two models discussed in the text. Model 1 is the purely elastic substratum model, and model 2 is the elastoplastic substratum model. The stress fields along the three axes of the model are shown: (**A**) axial; (**B**) radial and (**C**) tangential. Values are to 10^8 Pa. Shaded portion indicates area of tensile stress. Conventions in the package are: compressive stress = negative, and tensile stress = positive.

location with respect to other stress sources is similar: they lie away from crustal fault zones on stable blocks and tend to be surrounded by lowlands.

San Cristobal (Figs 3 and 10) is set on a strong volcanic substratum that allows only a small amount of elastic deformation and compaction to occur. Thus, feedback stresses are small and not sufficient to induce faulting within the edifice.

Mombacho (Figs 4 and 10), on the other hand, stands on a thick sequence of flysch of lower strength (Table 1). Elastic deformation, compaction, and perhaps also sagging of the substratum are greater. Therefore, the stress fed back into the volcano is larger and a substantial amount of deformation is expected. As the numerical model shows (Fig. 9A) stress up to 5×10^7 Pa may occur within the flanks, which can produce not only elastic deformation but also the substantial faulting observed within the flanks of the volcano.

Concepción (Fig. 5) overlies a very weak mudstone substratum where most of the deformation is accomplished by sagging (i.e. radial viscous flow) of the mudstone. Feedback stresses into the volcano are large enough (Fig. 9B) to produce substantial brittle and viscous deformation with radial and concentric folding, diapirism, and distal uplift, a pattern that is significantly different from that observed at Mombacho. Despite the large amount of deformation observed around the base, the cone itself displays only minor extensional fracturing. This contradiction may be due to the fact that most of the upper part of the volcano was recently constructed (Table 1); thus, there has not been enough time for the deformation to become a dominant factor in modelling the morphology of the cone.

Finally, at Maderas (Fig. 6) the basement is similar to that of Concepción. Unlike that, however, the edifice is deeply faulted and has a well developed complex structure with leaf graben and triangular horsts (Merle & Borgia 1996). The most obvious explanation for this difference is that, contrary to the situation at Concepción, Maderas stopped erupting more than 1000 years ago (Table 2). Thus, the morphology results from the cumulative deformation acquired during this period.

One other major difference can be observed between San Cristobal, Mombacho, Concepción, and Maderas. The second has been dissected by at least four major sector collapses, while the others have been stable through time. By reducing the height-to-radius ratio (Π_1) spreading will tend to flatten the cones making

them more stable (Dieterich 1988; Merle & Borgia 1996), as is clearly the case of Maderas. Thus, one might expect that San Cristobal, being the least spreading, should also be the most prone to collapse. This not being the case, other factors must come into play.

We postulate two such factors, which may operate concurrently. The first involves the reverse faults created by elastic compression of the edifice that may have been reactivated as detachment surfaces for collapse. At San Cristobal, which has no structures, this factor is minimized. In contrast, at Mombacho, where there has been considerable compressive deformation, the reactivation of these structures as detachment surfaces for collapse may become a prominent factor. At Concepción and Maderas, the time over which elastic stresses are relaxed is much shorter than at Mombacho (Fig. 7), thus there is not sufficient time for the development of faulting created by the elastic compression.

Our second proposal is that hydrothermal alteration may weaken the rocks that make up the volcano, favouring the inception of collapse (Lopez & Williams 1993). In fact, of the four volcanoes studied only Mombacho has a well developed hydrothermal system with associated hot springs, fumaroles, and highly weathered rocks (Table 1). The acceptance of this idea shifts the question to why only Mombacho has a well developed hydrothermal system and how does spreading come into play? Borgia (1994) and work in progress allow us to propose the following speculative scenario:

(a) spreading forces into extension the lower part of a volcanic cone inducing fracturing and faulting (see Fig. 9, numerical model 2);

(b) extension allows the magma to rise, accumulate and de-gas close to the base of the volcano, feeding a geothermal system within the volcanic edifice;

(c) fracturing and faulting of the volcano by sagging and spreading create an optimal pathway for the development of a geothermal system with large-scale rock–water interaction and consequent alteration of rocks.

Therefore, since at San Cristobal there is no spreading, magma cannot accumulate close to the surface (Table 1) because of the existence of a compressive stress field (see Fig. 9, numerical model 1). A geothermal system cannot develop within the volcano, the rock skeleton is not weakened by alteration, and no collapses may occur.

At Mombacho sagging and spreading have faulted the cone, allowing an active magmatic

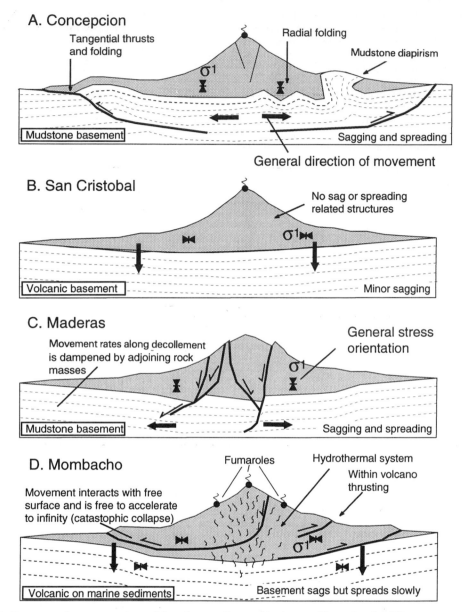

Fig. 10. Representative cross-sections of the volcanoes discussed in the text, illustrating the different responses of cones to different substrata. (**A**) San Cristobal: on Tertiary volcanic rock. Minor sagging occurs with no plastic or viscous flow in the substratum. The volcano is subjected to compression, but with the small degrees of sagging, stresses are not large enough to initiate failure in the unaltered rocks. (**B**) Mombacho volcano: on marine rocks under ignimbrite layers. Substratum response is by sagging with slow viscous spreading. Compressional structures form in the cone. Preferential deformation occurs along hydrothermally altered, or active hydrothermal zones. Movement rates are not dampened by adjoining masses, but can interact with the free surface. Movement on decollements can thus accelerate to catastrophic failure. (**C**) Concepción: on mudstone substratum with low viscosity. Sagging occurs, but the dominant process is the outward flow of substratum, either as diapirs or along decollement planes. This causes spreading and rapid relaxation of compressive stresses. (**D**) Maderas volcano: on mudstone basement similar to Concepción. Leaf graben have formed as the volcano has spread and relaxed. A slump feature has formed in the cone but has not led to sector collapse. This is due to reduced slopes, and sharing of deformation between substratum and volcano. Movement rates are dampened by the resistance of the adjoining substratum.

system to form close to the surface. Thus, rocks have become geothermally altered and structurally weak. However, spreading has not been sufficiently fast to decrease Π_1 to the point where no collapse could reasonably occur.

At Concepción and Maderas there is a higher degree and rate of spreading than at Mombacho and, in fact, very active superficial magmatic systems exist (Table 1). The geology, however, shows no significant hydrothermal system within the cones. We think that the sequence of ductile impermeable lake mudstones seals the fractures induced by spreading inhibiting the rise of the hydrothermal systems into the volcanic cones. Thus, even if Concepción has a Π_1 large enough to be unstable and permit collapse, its rocks are unaltered and sufficiently strong to hold the load of the cone.

Finally, the process of spreading may also relate to the style of eruption (Borgia 1994). If the compressive stress field, that characterizes a new growing volcano, is not relaxed by spreading, this stress may inhibit magma ascent allowing the build-up of larger magmatic pressures and consequent explosive eruptions. In fact, most of the early activity at Concepción is characterized by major Plinian explosions, which took place probably before spreading had relaxed much of the compressive stress field produced by elastic deformation (van Wyk de Vries & Borgia 1993).

If this reasoning is correct, stratocones built on stronger substratums are more stable, but they may produce the most destructive eruptions. The calderas of Casita and La Pelona just to the southeast of San Cristobal, may be the final product of this type of evolution and suggest that San Cristobal, as well, could produce large caldera-forming explosions.

We are grateful to Peter Francis, who considerably improved the original text and to Andy Pullen for introducing us to Nike2D. The Nicaraguan work has been made possible by INETER, especially by the efforts of Helman Taleno, Wilfreid Strauch and Orlando Membreñez. The work has been supported by NERC grant (GR9/837) and for B. van Wyk de Vries continues to be supported by a Leverhulme Trust Grant.

References

BORGIA, A., 1994. The dynamic basis of volcanic spreading. *Journal of Geophysical Research*, **99**, 17 791–17 804.

—— & TREVES, B. 1991. Volcanic plates overriding the ocean crust: structure and dynamics of Hawaiian volcanoes. *In*: PARSON, L. M. (ed.) *Ophiolites and their Modern Analogues.* Geological Society, London, Special Publication, **60**, 277–299.

—— & VAN WYK DE VRIES, B. 1994. Spreading at Concepción volcano, Nicaragua. *In*: *Abstracts of Volcano Instability on the Earth and Other Planets*, Geological Society, London.

——, BURR, J., MONTERO, L. D., MORALES, W. & ALVARADO, G. E. 1990. Fault propagation folds induced by gravitational failure and slumping of the Central Costa Rica Volcanic Range: implications for large terrestrial and Martian volcanic edifices. *Journal of Geophysical Research*, **95**, 14 357–14 382.

CLARK, S. P. 1966. *Handbook of Physical Constants.* Geological Society of America Memoir **97**, 587.

DIETERICH, J. H. 1988. Growth and persistence of Hawaiian volcanic rift zones. *Journal of Geophysical Research*, **93**, 4258–4270.

ENGELMANN, D. & HALLQUIST, R. 1991. *A Nonlinear, Implicit, Two-dimensional Finite Element code for Solid Mechanics. User Manual.* Lawrence Livermore National Laboratory, National Technical Information Service, US Department of Commerce, Springfield, VA.

FRANCIS, P. W. 1994. Large volcanic debris avalanches in the Central Andes. *In*: *Abstracts of Volcano Instability on the Earth and Other Planets.* Geological Society, London.

HAZLET, R. H. 1987. Geology of San Cristobal volcanic complex, Nicaragua. *Journal of Volcanology and Geothermal Research*, **33**, 233–240.

LOPEZ, D. L. & WILLIAMS, S. N. 1993. Catastrophic volcanic collapse; relation to hydrothermal alteration. *Science*, **260**, 1794–1796.

MERLE, O. & BORGIA, A. 1996. Scaled experiments of volcanic spreading. *Journal of Geophysical Research*, in press.

MILNE, J. F. G. S. 1878. On the form of volcanoes. *Geological Magazine*, **5**, 337–345.

REICHE, P. 1937. The Toreva block, a distinctive landslide type. *Journal of Geology*, **45**(5), 538–548.

SCHMIDT, H. 1989. *Sequenszstratigraphie des Neogenen Inselborge Schelfes im 'Forearc' – Bereich Costa Ricas und Nicaraguas.* PhD thesis, Technische Universität, Berlin.

SHTEYNBERG, G. S. & SOLOV'YEV, TS. V. 1974. The shape of volcanoes and the position of subordinate vents. *Izvestiya Earth Physics*, **5**, 83–84.

SUZUKI, T. 1968. Settlement of volcanic cones. *Bulletin of the Volcanological Society of Japan*, **13**, 95–108.

THOMAS, P. J., SQUYRES, S. W. & CARR, M. H. 1990. Flank tectonics of Martian volcanoes. *Journal of Geophysical Research – B Solid Earth and Planets*, **95**, 14 345–14 355.

VAN BEMMELEN, R. W. 1949. *The Geology of Indonesia. General Geology of Indonesia and Adjacent Archipelagos*, **1A**, Government Printing Office, The Hague.

VAN WYK DE VRIES, B. 1986, *Volcanic and Seismic Hazard on Isla de Ometepe, Lago de Nicaragua, Nicaragua.* INETER archives, Managua, Nicaragua.

——1993. *Tectonics and Magma Evolution of Nicaraguan Volcanic Systems.* PhD thesis, Open University, Milton Keynes, UK.

——1994. Spreading at medium-sized stratocones. *In: Abstracts of Volcano Instability on the Earth and Other Planets.* Geological Society, London.

—— & BORGIA, A. 1993. Spreading at Concepción volcano, Nicaragua. *In: EOS Abstracts of the American Geophysical Union,* December 1993.

WEYL, R. 1980. *Geology of Central America.* Borntraeger, Berlin.

Slope stability and eruption prediction on the eastern flank of Mount Etna

J. B. MURRAY[1] & B. VOIGHT[2]

[1] Department of Earth Sciences, The Open University,
Milton Keynes, MK7 6AA, Bucks., UK
[2] Earth System Science Centre, Pennsylvania State University,
University Park, PA 16802, USA

Abstract: Recent work applying knowledge of the failure of materials to volcanic eruptions in Kamchatka, Alaska and mainland USA, has shown that inverse rate analysis of seismic data can accurately predict eruption times up to 2 or 3 weeks in advance. We find evidence that application of the same principles to ground deformation data on Mt Etna's eastern flank prior to the eruptions of 1985 and 1989 provides good eruption time predictions more than 3 months in advance. The same data also point to an eruption triggering mechanism involving an interplay between slope creep and magma pressure that has not been described before.

This work is based on 1982–90 vertical ground deformation measurements (Murray 1990), derived from repeated measurements of levelling benchmarks along the upper eastern flank of Mt Etna, shown in Fig. 1. Accelerating subsidence of a 1 km wide section of this flank between 1982 and 1986 initially caused concern. The downward movement, which increased from an annual rate of 2 cm in 1982–83 to 137 cm in 1985–86 (Fig. 2), resembled slope creep prior to landslides (Radbruch-Hall 1978; Muller 1964), and inverse rate plots predicted failure late in 1985. The fear was that a major slope failure

might occur, possibly accompanied by depressurization of a magma reservoir and subsequent eruption. This large event did not occur, but an eruption down this flank in 1985 (McClelland et al. 1989) was accompanied by a small slope failure in the form of a rockslide, with extensive cracking of the eastern flank and associated shallow earthquakes. Post-1986 data from Etna suggest that the slope stability crisis of 1982–86 was repeated at a smaller scale prior to the 1989 eruption, and before the present eruption which began in December 1991, though the inverse rate method cannot be used for the latter because of insufficient data points in 1990.

The inverse rate method

Work on volcanic eruptions in Kamchatka, Alaska and mainland USA (Voight 1988; Voight & Cornelius 1991) has prompted a reinterpretation of the ground deformation data in terms of a valuable eruption prediction method. The remarkably simple phenomenological law $\Omega'^{-\alpha}\Omega'' - A = 0$ (where Ω is an arbitrary quantity such as strain or displacement, and A and α are constants) adequately describes the terminal stages of failure under constant stress of many different materials. This law has been adapted for the prediction of volcanic eruptions as well as landslides (Voight 1988, 1989; Voight & Cornelius 1991); the east flank situation may have characteristics of both types of event.

The method may be applied by plotting inverse rates of ground movement against time. Failure occurs shortly before the inverse rate curve intersects the time abscissa (Fig. 3), i.e.

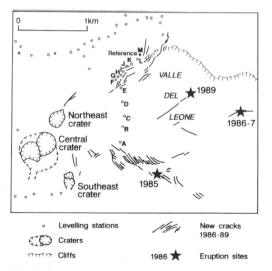

Fig. 1. September 1989 eruptions. The 25 km of levelling lines provide height data on over 200 benchmarks to an accuracy of about 1 cm in 10 km.

From McGuire, W. J., Jones, A. P. & Neuberg, J. (eds) 1996, *Volcano Instability on the Earth and Other Planets*, Geological Society Special Publication No. 110, pp. 111–114.

shortly before the movement becomes infinite.
The inverse rate curve may be linear or curved
depending upon the value of the power constant
a which empirically is usually 2 ± 1, and the
conditions of loading, which may be variable.
The situation on Etna during 1982–86 is shown
in Fig. 3a. Although the time scale is different
and the number of points is small (four series

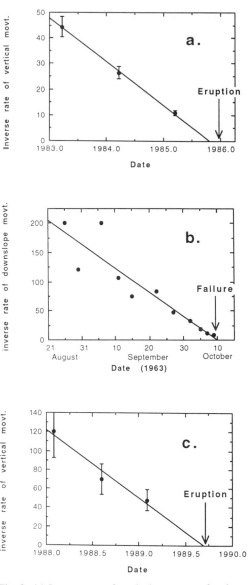

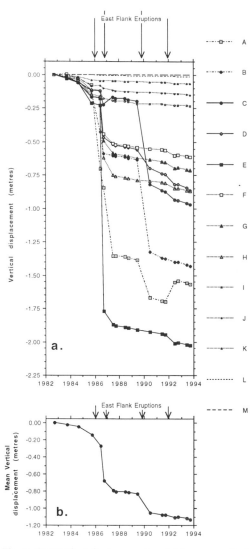

Fig. 2. (a) Vertical displacement and (b) mean vertical
displacement of benchmarks. Positions of the
benchmarks are shown in Fig. 1. Times of the onset of
east flank eruptions are arrowed. Note the accelerating
subsidence of benchmarks 1982–85, and to a smaller
extent 1987–89. During eruptions, some benchmarks
dropped much more than others as complex local
fracturing broke up the slope.

Fig. 3. (a) Inverse rate of vertical movement for the
eruption that began on 25 December 1985. Only rates
derived from measurements made before the eruption
have been used, the dates plotted being the mean of the
two dates on which the height determinations were
made. The least squares straight line cuts the x axis
near the end of 1985. Error bars refer to precisions of
height determinations relative to the reference point M
shown in Fig. 1. (b) As (a), but showing the inverse
mean downslope movement of markers prior to the
Vaiont landslide of 9 October 1963; note the difference
in time scale. Data from Muller (1964). (c) As (a), but
for the period 1988–89, prior to the east flank eruption
which began on 27 September 1989. Note the larger
relative errors due to the smaller preliminary
movement.

of measurements producing three mean rates of movement in three years), the straight line relationship of the inverse rate is similar to that observed prior to a landslide (Fig. 3b), with failure predicted at the end of 1985.

Instead of slope failure, an eruption occurred down the eastern flank on 25 December 1985, accompanied by a small slope failure (Fig. 1). Further large downhill movements (Fig. 2) preceded a second eruption in November 1986. Extensive ground cracking (Fig. 1) occurred between December 1985 and November 1986, defining a sector of the eastern flank measuring 1 to 2 km north–south and of unknown east–west extent. It is presumably this sector that was creeping downslope 1982–85.

A further eruption occurred on the upper eastern flank in September 1989 (Fig. 1), and examination of the movement of benchmarks in 1987 to 1989 (Fig. 2) shows an accelerating downward movement similar to that in 1982–85, but at a much smaller scale. The inverse rate also shows an approximate straight line relationship (Fig. 3c), but because the movements are smaller, the errors on the inverse rate are larger, and the best fit straight line indicates failure at the end of August 1989. The actual eruption began on 27 September. Large downward movements also preceded the October 1986 eruption, but only two measurements of the network were possible between the 1985 and 1986 eruptions, precluding any inverse rate analysis.

Before considering the implications of this analysis, it is worth commenting on the errors in the geodetic measurements, and how these propagate through. All the data presented here were derived by levelling with a Zeiss Ni2 self-levelling level and micrometer (replaced with a Wild Na2000 digital level since 1991) and an invar staff. In the first two years, these data were part of a closed levelling loop 12 km in circumference, which gave a mean closing error averaging 10 mm. In the 1984 eruption, 1.5 km of this loop was lost under loose Aa lava that it was not possible to level across, but since 1987 the loop was again closed with trigonometric levelling. Levelling accuracy a can be expressed as $\pm a\sqrt{K}$ mm, where K is the length of the loop levelled in km (Murray et al. 1995), so errors at station A are not expected to exceed 3 mm, and will be lower than this at other stations.

Since the method relies on the inverse of the measured rate, it is clear that the smaller the movement, the larger the percentage error for each inverse data point. Hence it could be possible to represent the inverse rate curves of Fig. 3 by a higher order curve than a straight line, particularly in the case of Fig. 3c (1989 eruption). However, it is equally clear from the paucity of data that one would not be justified in departing from the simple case.

Eruption triggering mechanism

As well as their predictive potential, these observations suggest an eruption triggering mechanism which has not previously been described. The area affected encompasses some of the steepest slopes on the summit cone, locally in excess of 35°, and since 1955 repeated eruptions from the Northeast Crater have built up an enormous field of lavas near the summit, reaching a maximum of over 240 m thick, with a volume in excess of 420 million m^3 and a mass of the order of 10^{12} kg. (Murray 1988). Continuing eruption of flows of limited length could be leading to overloading, oversteepening and consequent slope failure. Geological evidence indicates that a number of similar events have occurred on Etna's eastern flank in the past few thousand years (Kieffer 1970; McGuire 1982).

The following mechanism is proposed to account for these recent observations on the upper eastern flank. Firstly, overloading and oversteepening provoke slope instability and consequent accelerating downslope creep, but only when the magma pressure within the volcano exceeds a certain critical level. As this pressure increases, so does the tensile stress near the surface, until a critical value is exceeded and creep begins, creating a decrease in effective tensile strength of the rock, due to stable crack growth and other damage mechanisms. As soon as the tensile strength drops below the point where the magma pressure can exceed the overload, fractures open between magma and the surface, and eruption begins. This relieves the pressure within the edifice, and slope movement ceases. Cessation of movement after the two eruptions of magma in 1985 and 1986 is seen in Fig. 2.

Future prediction

The possibility of using the inverse rate method with geodetic data to forecast future volcanic events at Etna has been encouraged by the correlation (within a few weeks) between the intersection of the inverse subsidence rate curves with the time abscissa, and east flank eruptions that occurred in 1985 and 1989. Predicted dates will depend upon the choice of benchmarks used for the analysis; those used in Figs 3a and 3c were those that moved most before the eruption. Using different combinations of the benchmarks which moved most over the entire period gives closer dates (1985 Nov. 23 ± 33 days and 1989 Sep. 11 ± 56 days) but poorer straight line fits (correlation coefficients of 0.85 instead of 0.99). Further application of this method should focus on data collected at a high frequency, such as continuously recorded electronic distance measurement or tilt, in order to facilitate short-term forecasts. This may allow the fitting of higher order curves to the data, which might in turn lead to investigation of the constant load assumption and the detailed validity of the inverse-rate law.

This project was financed by a NATO collaborative research grant, EU Epoch contract No. EPOC CT 900032, EU Science project No. ERB40002PL900491-(90400491), PIRPSEV (CNRS-INSU, France), Earthwatch (USA) and NERC (England). Kern Ltd, Sokkisha Ltd, and Dr Ramsay Wilson of the South Bank University loaned equipment, and constructive criticism of the original manuscript by S. J. Day and A. D. Pullen has substantially improved the quality of this paper. Most importantly the willing assistance in the field of Dominique Decobecq, Jane Moss, Helen Cunnigham, Liz Bisbee, Gerry Byrne, Nina Hass, Connie Hastert, Fiona McGibbon, Connor O'Rourke, Ervin Schowengerbt, Margie Singer, David Stevenson, Ben van Wyk de Vries, Martin Wilding and many others is most gratefully appreciated.

References

KIEFFER, G. 1970. Les depôts détritiques et pyroclastiques du versant oriental de l'Etna. *Atti dell' Accademia Gioenia di Scienze Naturale di Catania*, sér. 7 **2**, 3–32.

MCCLELLAND, L., SIMPKIN, T., SUMMERS, M., NIELSEN, E. & STEIN, T. C. (eds) 1989. *Global Volcanism 1975–1985*, Prentice-Hall, New Jersey, 75.

MCGUIRE, W. J. 1982. Evolution of the Etna volcano: information from the southern wall of the Valle del Bove caldera. *Journal of Volcanology and Geothermal Research*, **13**, 241–271.

MULLER, L. 1964. The rock slide in the Vaiont Valley. *Rock Mechanics and Engineering Geology*, **2**(3/4), 148–212.

MURRAY, J. B. 1988. The influence of loading by lavas on the siting of volcanic eruption vents on Mt Etna. *Journal of Volcanology and Geothermal Research*, **35**, 121–139.

—— 1990. High-level magma transport at Mount Etna volcano, as deduced from ground deformation measurements. *In*: RYAN, M. P. (ed.) *Magma Transport and Storage*. Wiley, Chichester, 357–383.

——, PULLEN, A. D. & SAUNDERS, S. 1995. Ground deformation surveying of active volcanoes. *In*: MCGUIRE, W. J., KILBURN, C. R. J. & MURRAY, J. B. (eds) *Monitoring Active Volcanoes: Strategies, Procedure and Techniques*. UCL Press, London, 113–150.

RADBRUCH-HALL, D. H. 1978. Gravitational creep of rock masses on slopes. *In*: VOIGHT, B. (ed.) *Rockslides and Avalanches 1*. Elsevier, Oxford, Ch. 17.

VOIGHT, B. 1988. A method for the prediction of volcanic eruptions. *Nature* **332**, 125–130.

—— 1989. A relation to describe rate-dependent material failure. *Science*, **243**, 200–203.

—— & CORNELIUS, R. R. 1991. Prospects for eruption prediction in near real-time. *Nature*, **332**, 125–130.

Tsunami waves generated by volcanic landslides: an assessment of the hazard associated with Kick 'em Jenny

M. S. SMITH & J. B. SHEPHERD

Environmental Science Division, IEBS, Lancaster University, Lancaster, LA1 4YQ, UK

Abstract: Landslides and rock falls generating tsunamis constitute a serious element of risk at steep-sided volcanoes located in close proximity to water, especially when the volcano's structure is cut by faults or altered by fumaroles and where there has been a history of subsidence or signs of incipient caldera formation. Approximately 5% of known tsunami events have been generated by volcanoes, producing some of the most destructive tsunamis on record. A preliminary study suggests that Kick 'em Jenny is a prime candidate for tsunamigenic events on a potentially hazardous scale, possibly affecting the whole of the eastern Caribbean region. An estimate of the potential height of tsunami waves generated following slope failure on the flanks of Kick 'em Jenny has been found using the basic solitary wave theory combined with equations of energy conservation. Generally, landslide-generated tsunamis possess little energy and, unless they are confined in a bay or channel, are only hazardous close to the source. However, the results show that with the low-lying Grenadine Islands situated a few kilometres to the east, even a relatively small landslide event at Kick 'em Jenny has the potential to produce waves that would prove hazardous to both coastal populations and ships.

Tsunamis are formed following any large-scale, short-duration disturbance of the free surface of the ocean, and the majority are related to tectonic displacements associated with earthquakes at plate boundaries. However, tsunamis can also be generated by erupting volcanoes, landslides or underwater explosions. A preliminary study (Smith & Shepherd 1993) suggests that Kick 'em Jenny is a prime candidate for tsunamigenic events on a potentially hazardous scale, possibly affecting the whole of the eastern Caribbean region (Fig. 1). The travel times for a tsunami wave system propagating from a Kick 'em Jenny source are illustrated in Fig. 2. The average velocity of a tsunami wave propagating across the Caribbean is $400-500 \, km \, h^{-1}$, rising to a maximum of around $600 \, km \, h^{-1}$ in deep water. within 25 minutes of initiation at a Kick 'em Jenny source, the leading wave of a tsunami system would reach the whole of the coastline of Grenada, all of the Grenadine Islands and the west coast of St. Vincent. Within one hour the Leeward Islands to the north and the northern coast of Trinidad to the south would be inundated, and within two hours the tsunami would reach all of the islands of the eastern Caribbean and most of the Venezuelan coastline. These results emphasize the need for a rapid response to possible tsunami-generating events.

The causes of tsunamis of volcanic origin have been studied by Latter (1982) who described ten different potential tsunamigenic sources in volcanism (Table 1). Mass movements account for at least 20% of the total volcanic tsunami recorded. Furthermore, volcanic landslides and subsequent eruptions have been the cause of in excess of 20 000 deaths in the past 400 years, with six major events in the last century (Siebert *et al.* 1987).

Background

Kick 'em Jenny is an asymmetrical submarine volcano located *c.* 9 km to the north of Grenada on the western flank of the Lesser Antilles arc platform (Fig. 3). The volcano was first identified by visual observation of a series of explosive eruptions in 1939 (Devas & McAdam-Sherwin 1939) and was precisely located by seismological techniques in 1965 (Shepherd & Robson 1967). The first accurate bathymetric survey of the volcano was carried out in 1972 from a surface ship (Sigurdsson & Shepherd 1974), at which time the summit of the volcano was approximately 200 m below sea level. Since then a series of underwater eruptions has increased the height of the volcano by about 60 m (an average growth rate of *c.* $4 \, m \, a^{-1}$) according to the most recent survey carried out by a submersible in 1989 (Sigurdsson 1989). During the intervening period between these two surveys the volcano was modified considerably by underwater explosions, lava flows and pyroclastic flows and the summit crater appears to have been breached by a landslide. The vent is now extensively carpeted with extremely fresh volcanic rubble.

The volcano has erupted at least ten times in the last 55 years making it by far the most active volcano in the Lesser Antilles island arc. The

From McGuire, W. J., Jones, A. P. & Neuberg, J. (eds) 1996, *Volcano Instability on the Earth and Other Planets*, Geological Society Special Publication No. 110, pp. 115–123.

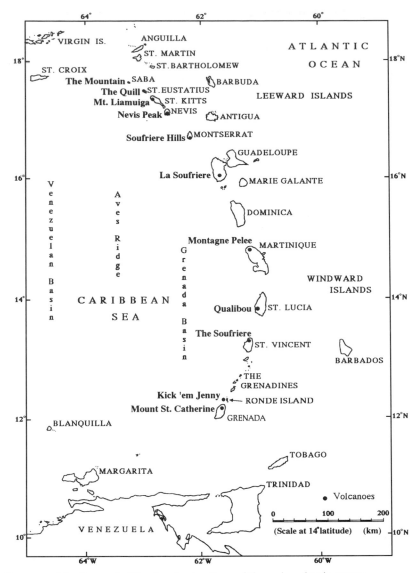

Fig. 1. Outline map of the Lesser Antilles showing locations of the main volcanic centres.

eruptions have generally been identified by the recording of extremely strong underwater acoustic signals, similar to the T-phase generated by large submarine earthquakes. Kick 'em Jenny is currently one of the most powerful T-phase generators anywhere in the world. Signals associated with the eruptions are regularly felt not only in the nearby Grenadine Islands, but also at distances of up to 400 km from the volcano. This indicates extremely energetic eruptions, a highly efficient T-phase generating mechanism, or most probably both. The likely explanation of these acoustic signals is that they are generated by the collapse of a steam cupola formed above the vent by an explosive interaction between molten magma and cold sea-water. Previous eruptions of Kick 'em Jenny have been largely suppressed by the overlying water pressure, but future eruptions are likely to become increasingly more violent as the confining pressure is reduced owing to continued shoaling of the summit (Smith & Shepherd 1993).

Numerous large arcuate depressions have been found along the length of the backarc providing evidence of previous gravity slides (Sigurdsson *et al.* 1980; Roobol *et al.* 1983).

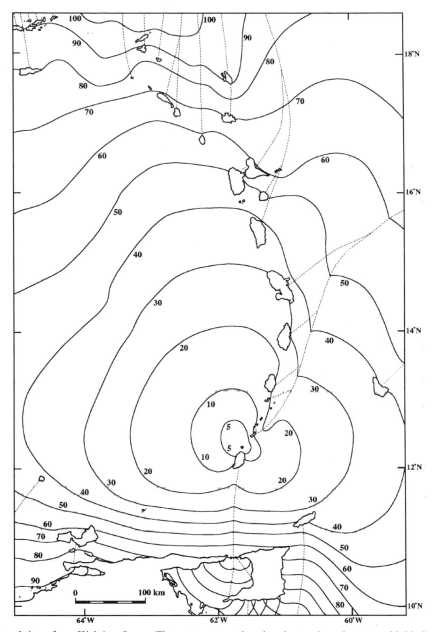

Fig. 2. Travel times from Kick 'em Jenny. The contours are given in minutes since the tsunami initiation at the Kick 'em Jenny source. The dashed lines indicate the regions most likely to experience a chaotic sea surface due to the crossing of adjacent wave-paths.

These structures correspond to the steepest slopes where the 1000 m contour most closely approaches the islands. The backarc slopes of the Lesser Antilles average angles of 10° into the Grenada basin in contrast to the 1° slopes of the Atlantic side. The flanks of Kick 'em Jenny locally reach angles of up to 30° as can be seen from the cross-sections drawn through the centre of the volcano (Fig. 4).

Landslide generation of tsunamis

Landslide and rock falls generating tsunamis constitute a serious element of risk at steep-sided

Table 1. *Mechanisms of volcanogenic tsunamis (after Latter 1982)*

Probable cause of volcanic tsunamis	% of total
(1) Earthquakes accompanying eruptions	22
(2) Pyroclastic flows impacting on water	20
(3) Submarine explosions	19
(4) Caldera collapse or subsidence	9
(5) Avalanches of cold rock	7
(6) Base surges with accompanying shock waves	7
(7) Avalanches of hot material	6
(8) Air-waves from explosions	4.5
(9) Lahars (mudflows) impacting on water	4.5
(10) Lava avalanching into the sea	1

volcanoes located in close proximity to water, especially when the volcano's structure is cut by faults or altered by fumaroles, and where there has been a history of subsidence or signs of incipient caldera formation. However, landslide-generated tsunamis generally possess little energy and, unless they are confined in a bay or channel, are only hazardous close to the source.

The mechanism by which tsunamis are generated following submarine landslides is outlined in Fig. 5. Evidence exists for submarine gravity slides occurring on very shallow angled slopes down to approximately 0.5°, although these movements require very fine-grained, unconsolidated material and large initiating

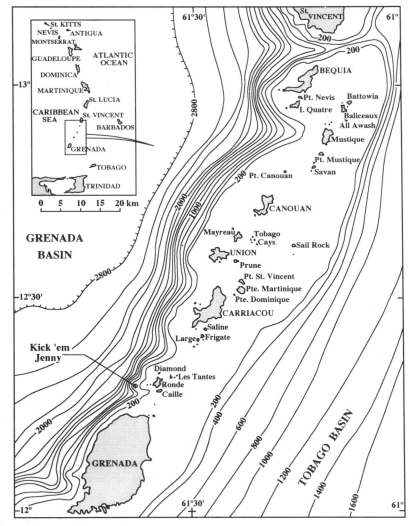

Fig. 3. Bathymetric map of the Grenadines (after Westercamp *et al.* 1985). The bathymetric contours are given in metres below sea level.

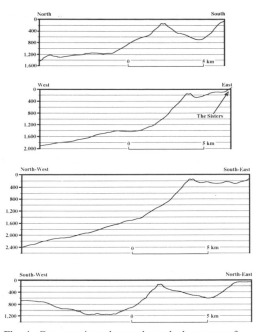

Fig. 4. Cross-sections drawn through the centre of Kick 'em Jenny. The exaggeration between the vertical and horizontal scales is 2 : 1 and the vertical scale is given in metres below sea level.

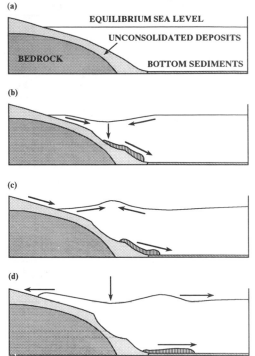

Fig. 5. Schematic sequential cross-sections showing waves generated by a subaqueous slide (after McCulloch 1985). (**a**) Pre-slide conditions. (**b**) Start of the sliding; local drawdown at the head of the slide. (**c**) Water rushes in from all directions to restore the water level and the sea recedes far from the coast. The inward flow of water towards the area of the slide is so strong that a mound of water is generated above the source. (**d**) The unstable mound collapses under gravity and tsunami waves are generated (probably a series) that radiate away from the oscillatory mound.

forces (Terzaghi 1956). Submarine landslides are invariably initiated by an increase in pore-water pressure, often associated with external forces such as extreme tidal movements, storm waves and seismic loading. In the Kick 'em Jenny example, the most likely initiating force is seismic loading from both local earthquakes and the T-phase generated during eruptions of the volcano itself.

Geotechnical studies (Seed 1968) suggest that ground motion whose horizontal acceleration is in excess of 0.13g (130 gal) at the sea floor should be sufficient to produce slope failure. Kick 'em Jenny is in an area of low seismicity – low, that is, in the context of the Lesser Antilles. Based on the data included in an eastern Caribbean earthquake catalogue for the period AD 1530 to 1993 (Shepherd *et al.* 1994), an iso-acceleration map for the southern Lesser Antilles has been constructed (Fig. 6) using a method developed by Woodward-Clyde Consultants (1982). The iso-acceleration map indicates that the ground acceleration at Kick 'em Jenny, with a 10% probability of exceedance in any 50 year period, is *c.* 0.14g (140 gal). Table 2 lists 12 historic earthquakes of magnitude greater than 6.4 that have occurred within

200 km of Kick 'em Jenny; as with the iso-acceleration map, the ground accelerations at Kick 'em Jenny were calculated using the method developed by Woodward-Clyde Consultants (1982). Of the 12 events summarized in Table 2, three have exceeded the 0.13g ground acceleration that may be sufficient to initiate slope failure on the flanks of Kick 'em Jenny, the most recent of which occurred in 1957.

The T-phase acoustic waves from several recent eruptions of Kick 'em Jenny have been felt at intensity 4 (Modified Mercalli scale) in Sauteurs, Grenada, and at intensity 2 as far north as Martinique (250 km from the volcano). the T-phase waves generated by the 1965 eruption were felt at intensity 5 on the north coast of Grenada (Shepherd & Robson 1967); this intensity roughly corresponds to a ground acceleration of 0.01 to 0.02g. Assuming inverse

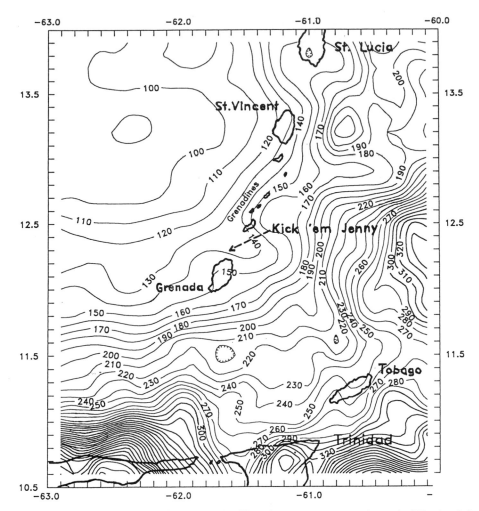

Fig. 6. Iso-acceleration map for the southern Lesser Antilles. The contours are at an interval of 10 gal and signify a 10% probability of exceedance in any 50-year period.

first-power geometrical spreading for the T-phase, the ground acceleration on the flanks of Kick 'em Jenny during the 1965 eruption (i.e. at a distance of one kilometre from the vent) was of the order 0.1 to 0.2g. According to Shepherd & Robson (1967), this vibration was practically continuous for one hour. The ground acceleration was probably even greater than this during the 1939 eruption. Furthermore, the T-phase waves generated by future eruptions of Kick 'em Jenny may become even more powerful as the vent ascends towards the sea surface.

In order to provide an accurate hazard assessment, detailed, up-to-date information is needed on both the grain size and the gross morphology of Kick 'em Jenny, so that slope

stability analysis can be carried out on the volcano's flanks. A proposed side-scan sonar survey, due to take place in 1995, will provide the necessary data. Until this time, the analysis is largely based upon data collected during the 1972 and 1985 bathymetric surveys.

Quantitative evaluation of tsunami generation

Based on the solitary wave theory and by assuming conservation of wave energy, Streim & Miloh (1975) developed a simple approach to estimate the height of tsunamis generated on the

Table 2. *Summary of the data from historic earthquakes of magnitude greater than 6.4 that have occurred within 200 km of Kick 'em Jenny*

Date	Position	Depth (km)	Magnitude	Intensity (MM)	Hypocentral distance to KeJ (km)	Ground acceleration at KeJ (gal)
1766	(11.00°N, 62.50°W)	100	7.75	9	205.14	166.92
1825	(11.00°N, 62.00°W)	75	6.5	7	165.84	81.16
1834	(13.00°N, 61.00°W)	100	6.5	7	141.97	91.09
1844	(12.00°N, 61.75°W)	100	6.5	6	108.62	70.81
1846	(11.50°N, 62.00°W)	100	6.5	6	141.91	57.72
1888	(11.30°N, 62.20°W)	–	7.0	8	132.03	147.84
1910	(12.00°N, 60.50°W)	100	7.19	5	145.16	35.38
1923	(11.00°N, 62.76°W)	100	6.5	5	223.22	25.60
1926	(10.88°N, 62.40°W)	5	6.5	5	182.50	29.41
1935	(10.64°N, 62.77°W)	102	6.5	6	250.69	36.80
1957	(10.86°N, 62.77°W)	6	6.69	9	211.17	163.71
1968	(10.79°N, 62.68°W)	105	6.4	8	234.66	98.41

coast of Israel by mass movements on the ocean floor. Murty (1979) reapplied their results to the slide-generated waves observed in the Kitimat Inlet, British columbia in 1975. It was found that the agreement between the observed and theoretical results was good considering the assumptions and uncertainties involved. The theoretical results of Striem & Miloh (1975) are therefore used to estimate the potential heights of the tsunamis generated by various hypothetical landslide events on the flanks of Kick 'em Jenny.

Striem & Miloh (1975) assumed that, given a landslide scar of breadth b, depth h and length l (Fig. 7), the net (submerged) potential energy E_p released by a failure is given by

$$E_p = gbh(\rho_s - \rho_w)(D_0 - D_s) \qquad (1)$$

where ρ_s and ρ_w are the specific densities of the sea-bottom material and sea water, respectively, D_s is the depth at the centre of gravity of the scar and D_0 is the depth at the end of the slope. Assuming that the displacement of the sea floor generates a solitary surface wave (as suggested by laboratory experiments – Prins 1958; Wiegel 1964) then the total energy E_w per unit width of crest of such a single wave is given by

$$E_w = \frac{g}{8} \frac{\rho_w}{\sqrt{3}} (HD)^{3/2} \qquad (2)$$

where D is the local water depth and H denotes the wave height (Ippen 1966). To adapt this to a three-dimensional problem it is assumed that the wave energy is uniformly distributed over a finite width b, equated with the width of the scar.

It is further assumed that only a fraction μ of the potential energy E_p released by the landslide is actually transformed into wave energy. This energy fraction was estimated by experimental analysis to be of the order of 1–2% (Wiegel 1955). Provided $D_s \leq D \leq D_0$, the height H of

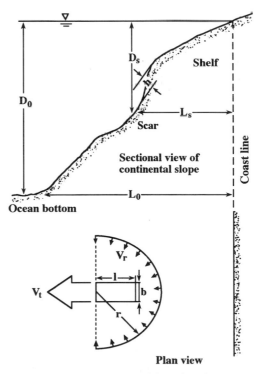

Fig. 7. Schematic illustration of the submarine landslide (after Striem & Miloh 1975).

the generated wave is derived from equations (1) and (2) as

$$H = \frac{1}{D} \{8\sqrt{3}\mu l h(\delta - 1)(D_0 - D_s)\}^{2/3}$$

(3)

$$\text{where } \delta = \frac{\rho_s}{\rho_w}$$

If the energy, instead of being contained in a single solitary wave, is distributed evenly among m identical solitary waves, the height H_m of the m wave is given by

$$H_m = H m^{-2/3}, \quad m = 2, 3, 4, \ldots$$

(4)

using equation (3), initial tsunami heights above Kick 'em Jenny can be calculated for a variety of landslide volumes. Assuming $D = D_0 = 2500$ m, $D_s = 500$ m, $\mu = 0.01$ and $\delta = 2$ for slope failures on the western flanks of the volcano, initial wave heights are plotted in Fig. 8 as function of landslide length and thickness.

Upon dispersion across the Caribbean to the Leeward Islands in the north, the hypothetical wave systems illustrated in Fig. 8 would become insignificant since the amplitude decay is proportional to the inverse power of the distance from the source (Kajiura 1963). However, over short distances (<100 km) and considering the amplification effect due to shoaling at the coastlines which can increase open water wave amplitudes by a factor of 3 or 4 in the Caribbean (Smith & Shepherd 1993), a realistically sized tsunamigenic landslide occurring on Kick 'em Jenny's flanks would be very destructive. For example, a landslide 30 m thick and 2 km long would generate a tsunami with an initial wave height

of $c.\,26$ m. Upon dispersion, the tsunami would decay to 2–3 m on the northern coast of Grenada and 1.5–3 m on the coasts of the southern Grenadine Islands. Depending on the local coastline configuration and hydrography, the corresponding potential run-up heights on these islands would be in the range 4–12 m and 3–12 m, respectively. Since many of the islands are low-lying with a large proportion of the communities concentrated along the coastlines, even tsunamis towards the bottom end of these ranges would prove to be a considerable hazard.

It should be noted that the final tsunami height estimated at each coastline is subject to two sets of large uncertainties: the first set concerns the proportion of the energy of a submarine landslide which is converted into tsunami wave energy. This determines the initial height of the wave at the source. The amount of amplification due to shoaling of the waves at each coastline constitutes the second set of uncertainties.

Discussion

It has previously been shown that Kick 'em Jenny is a prime candidate for tsunamigenic events in the near future, following explosive shallow-submarine eruptions (Smith & Shepherd 1993). However, the majority of tsunamigenic events associated with volcanoes are caused by catastrophic slope failures. Evidence exists for previous submarine gravity slides along the length of the Lesser Antilles backarc and on Kick 'em Jenny itself. The steep angles reached by the submarine flanks of Kick 'em Jenny indicate that only relatively small forces would be require to initiate instability; it has been shown that instability could be initiated by seismic loading from both regional earthquakes and the powerful T-phase generated during eruptions of the volcano.

Although the morphological data required for an accurate slope stability analysis are not yet available, we have estimated the height of potential tsunami waves generated by various hypothetical landslide events on the western flank of Kick 'em Jenny. Despite the assumptions involved, the results using the basic solitary wave theory developed by Striem and Miloh (1975) show that although the initial waves generated at the source would be very hazardous to ships, they are unlikely to propagate with large amplitudes to the Leeward Islands located in the north of the arc. However, for the southern Grenadine Islands and Grenada, even a relatively small landslide event at Kick 'em Jenny would present a considerable hazard with

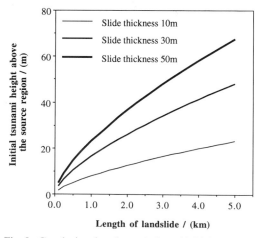

Fig. 8. Graph showing the variation of initial tsunami wave height at the Kick 'em Jenny source with changing landslide dimensions (length and thickness).

potential run-up heights of up to 12 m predicted. Within 25 minutes of initiation the wave systems generated by Kick 'em Jenny would inundate all of the coastlines of Grenada and the Grenadines, making precautionary evacuation of the areas most likely to be affected impossible. It is important, therefore, that slope stability analysis is carried out on the flanks of Kick 'em Jenny in order to assess the likelihood of such an event occurring.

M.S.S. thanks the Science and Engineering Research Council for a research studentship.

References

DEVAS, R. P. & MACADAM-SHERWIN, T. 1939. Manifestations of volcanic activity observed July 24, 1939 from Gunton Estate House, Grenada. Typescript dated 25 July 1939.

IPPEN, A. T. (ed.) 1966. *Estuary and Coastline Hydrodynamics*. McGraw Hill, New York.

KAJIURA, K. 1963. the leading wave of a tsunami. *Bulletin of the Earthquake Research Institute*, **41**(3), 535–571.

LATTER, J. N. 1982. Tsunamis of volcanic origin: summary of causes, with particular reference to Krakatoa, 1893. *Bulletin of Volcanology*, **44**, 467–490.

MCCULLOCH, D. S. 1985. *Evaluating Tsunami Potential (evaluating earthquake hazards in the Los Angeles region)*. United States Geological Survey Professional Paper **1360**, 325–382.

MURTY, T. S. 1979. Submarine slide-generated water waves in Kitimat Inlet, British Columbia. *Journal of Geophysical Research*, **84**(C12), 7777–7779.

PRINS, J. E. 1958. Characteristics of waves generated by a local disturbance. *Transactions of the America Geophysical Union*, **39**(5) 865–874.

ROOBOL, M. J., WRIGHT, J. V. & SMITH, A. L. 1983. Calderas or gravity-slide structures in the Lesser Antilles Island Arc. *Journal of Volcanology and Geothermal Research*, **19**, 121–134.

SEED, H. B. 1968. Landslides during earthquakes due to soil liquefaction. *Journal of the Soil Mechanics and Foundations Division of the American Society of Civil Engineers*, **94**(SM5), 1053–1122.

SHEPHERD, J. B. & ROBSON, G. R. 1967. The source of the T-phase recorded in the Eastern Caribbean on October 24, 1965. *Bulletin of the Seismological Society of America*, **57**, 227–234.

——, LYNCH, L. L. & TANNER, J. G. A revised earthquake catalogue for the Eastern Caribbean region 1530–1993. *Proceedings of the Caribbean Conference on Natural Hazards: Volcanoes, Earthquakes, Windstorms, Floods*. 11–15 October 1993, St. Anns, Trinidad (in press).

SIEBERT, L., GLICKEN, H. & UI, T. 1987. Volcanic hazards from Bezymianny- and Bandai-type eruptions. *Bulletin of Vocanology*, **49**, 435–459.

SIGURDSSON, H. 1989. Submarine investigations in the crater of Kick 'em Jenny volcano. *Bulletin of the Scientific Event Alert Network*, **4**, 45–49.

—— & SHEPHERD, J. B. 1974. Amphibole-bearing basalts from the submarine volcano Kick 'em Jenny in the Lesser Antilles island arc. *Bulletin of Volcanology*, **37**, 891–910.

——, SPARKS, R. S. J., CAREY, S. N. & HUANG, T. C. 1980. Volcanogenic sedimentation in the Lesser Antilles arc. *Journal of Geology*, **88**, 523–540.

SMITH, M. S. & SHEPHERD, J. B. 1993. Preliminary investigations of the tsunami hazard of Kick 'em Jenny submarine volcano. *Natural Hazards*, **7**, 257–277.

STRIEM, H. L. & MILOH, T. 1975. *Tsunamis Induced by Submarine Slumpings off the Coast of Israel*. Israel Atomic Energy Commission, Tel Aviv.

TERZAGHI, K. 1956. *Varieties of Submarine Slope Failures*. Proceedings of the eighth Texas conference on soil mechanics and foundation engineering, Special Publication **29**, Houston, Texas.

WESTERCAMP, P. D., ANDREIFF, P., BOUYSSE, P., MASCLE, A. & BAUBRON, J. C. 1985. *Géologie de l'archipel des Grenadines (Petites Antilles méridionales) étude monographique*. Document, de Bureau des Recherches Geologiques et Minieres 92. Orléans Cedex, France [in French].

WIEGEL, R. L. (ed.) 1955. Laboratory studies of gravity waves generated by the movement of a submerged body. *Transactions of the American Geophysical Union*, **36**(5), 759–774.

——1964. *Oceanographical Engineering*. Prentice-Hall, Englewood Cliffs, NJ.

WOODWARD-CLYDE CONSULTANTS 1982. *Development and Initial Application of Software for Seismic Exposure Evaluation*. Report for NOAA, Vol. II.

A simple model for the genesis of large gravitational landslide hazards in the Canary Islands

J. C. CARRACEDO

Volcanological Station of the Canary Islands, Consejo Superior de Investigaciones Científicas, PO Box 195, 38206 La Laguna, Tenerife, Canary Islands, Spain

Abstract: Natural hazards in the Canarian Archipelago are mainly in relation to volcanism (at least five islands with Holocene eruptive activity, 17 eruptions in the last 500 years) and massive gravitational landslides related to edifice overgrowth and dyke intrusion. In the volcanically active islands, the emission vents tend to group in clearly aligned clusters, evolving to form steep ridges that behave as true polygenetic active volcanoes with clear rift affinities, and constitute by far the most probable location of any future volcanic eruption in the archipelago. Tunnels excavated for water mining show a narrow band of tightly packed parallel dykes running through the centre of the rifts. The rift zones play a key role in the growth and shape of the island edifices and in the generation of massive landslides. Cumulative gravitational stresses related to the growth of the volcanic edifices and more ephemeral mechanisms associated with intense eruptive phases, such as dyke wedging, increase of slope angles and strong local seismicity associated with magma movement can finally exceed the trigger-threshold of gravitational slides. This mechanism may be the explanation for the numerous horseshoe-type valleys and calderas developed in the Canary Islands. The geometry of these rift zones is frequently three-branched at 120°C (Mercedes-Benz star configuration), suggesting a least-effort fracturing by magma-induced upwelling. The rift zones play a major role in the distribution of geological hazards: eruptive vents and the failure planes of gravitational landslides are located preferentially along these volcanic lineaments.

The Canarian Archipelago is a volcanically active, 400 km long alignment of seven islands off the African continental margin opposite Cape Juby. The islands were formed through multiple volcanic episodes (Carracedo 1979; Schmincke 1982) with different evolutionary histories on each island. The present volume and shape of each island is the result of the accretion of several volcanoes, whose activity is frequently independent, and usually of relatively short duration. Palaeomagnetic stratigraphy carried out in several islands shows as a common pattern the presence of a few polarity units, generally under 0.5 Ma (Carracedo 1979; Carracedo & Soler 1995). Repetitive processes of relatively fast development of volcanoes, instability and often instantaneous mass-wasting destruction have been a common feature in the volcanic history of the Canary Islands.

The islands can be separated into three groups (Fig. 1): (1) Tenerife, La Palma, Lanzarote and probably Hierro, which have had eruptions in historic time (<500 years); (2) Fuerteventura and Gran Canaria, with subhistoric volcanism (> 500 years); (3) Gomera, without Quaternary eruptions and probably extinct. However, it should be noted that longer periods without eruptions in Lanzarote, Gran Canaria and Fuerteventura were followed by renewed activity.

Growth of the Canary Island volcanoes

Time and space distribution of recent volcanism in the Canary Islands

The analysis of the historic volcanism in the Canary Islands (last 500 years) does not reveal any significant pattern in the distribution in time of eruptive activity. Inter-eruptive periods vary from 1 to 237 years with a mean value of about 30 years for the entire archipelago (Fig. 2)

There is, however, a definite pattern in the spatial distribution of recent volcanism (Fig. 3). Recent (late Pleistocene–Holocene) as well as historic emission centres are clearly associated with active rifts, whose main characteristics are described below. Very few of the Holocene vents and none of the historic ones are located outside these volcano-tectonic features.

Canary Islands rifts

In the islands with Quaternary volcanic activity, the construction of the island-volcanoes has been closely controlled by rift-type volcano-tectonic features, characterized by a tight cluster of recent emission centres piled up along narrow dorsal ridges known locally in Spanish as *dorsales*. The Canarian rifts show some of the main features of

From McGuire, W. J., Jones, A. P. & Neuberg, J. (eds) 1996, *Volcano Instability on the Earth and Other Planets*, Geological Society Special Publication No. 110, pp. 125–135.

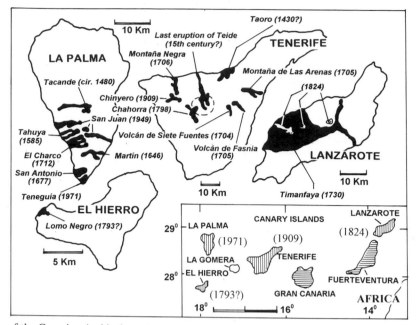

Fig. 1. Map of the Canarian Archipelago showing the location and age of historic volcanic eruptions. The inset map shows the islands with historic (last 500 years) volcanism (vertical stripes); those with Quaternary volcanism (horizontal stripes); and those without Quaternary volcanism (no stripes). The dates of the historic eruptions are indicated in parentheses.

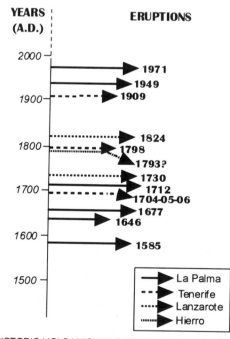

HISTORIC VOLCANISM IN THE CANARY ISLANDS

Fig. 2. Time distribution of volcanic activity in the historic record (last 500 years) of the Canarian Archipelago.

Hawaiian rifts (such as forceful injection of dykes associated with extension), but lack some important ones such as direct connection with central shallow underlying magma chambers and summit calderas (Carracedo *et al.* 1992). At erosional windows, a coherent (Walker 1992) swarm of feeding dykes can be observed, with increasingly dense packing with depth and towards the axis of the rifts.

The presence of hundreds of kilometres of infiltration galleries (2×2 m near-horizontal tunnels up to 8 km long, excavated for the purpose of intercepting groundwater) allows the direct observation of the deep structure of the dyke swarms that appear as the inner structure of the rifts (Carracedo 1994). As observed in the galleries, the inner structure of the rifts is characterized by a relatively narrow (3–5 km margin to margin in the upper part), wedge shaped band of predominantly pyroclastic formations densely intruded by hundreds of dykes parallel or subparallel to the axis of the rift.

The density and parallelism of the dykes increases with depth. Another common feature of the rifts are open, secondary fractures parallel to the general trend, probably associated with relaxation after intense intrusion phases.

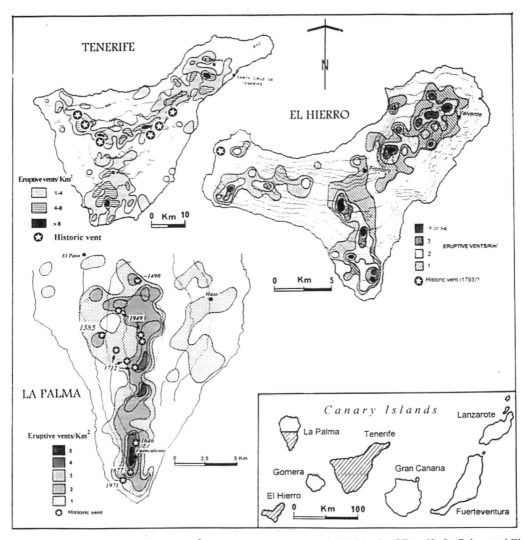

Fig. 3. Concentration (eruptive vents/km²) of recent emission centres in the islands of Tenerife, La Palma and El Hierro. A complex, 120° stellate rift arrangement has formed in Tenerife and El Hierro, whereas a single, extremely fast growing, high aspect ratio rift has developed in the southern part of La Palma. Note that very active rifts are only present in the western islands of the Archipelago, the most probable present location of the Canarian hotspot according to Holik *et al.* (1991).

The presence of the rifts was first inferred by MacFarlane & Ridley (1968) by means of gravity measurements in Tenerife. These authors explained the local Bouguer anomaly showing a three-pointed star shape coinciding with topographic ridges as reflecting unusually high concentrations of dykes along fissure zones. The regular geometry of these major fissure zones, at 120° to one another, could have been generated by inflation of the volcano due to magma intrusion.

Two main types of rifts can be defined in terms of geometry: single, as in La Palma, or triple, as in Tenerife and Hierro (Fig. 3). In the latter complex scheme, a stratovolcano-type central volcano of differentiated (trachytic-phonolitic) magmas (Teide–Pico Viejo volcanic complex) has developed at the triple junction in the more evolved island of Tenerife, whereas in Hierro, an island at an earlier stage of building, this central activity is not present.

Mass-wasting destruction of the island volcanoes

Since the eruption of Mount St. Helens in 1980, massive landslides have gained acceptance as a possible common and key factor in the mass-wasting destruction of mature, unstable volcanoes. Huge landslides associated with unstable, rift-zone-bounded, unbuttressed flanks appear to be responsible to a great extent for the destruction and loss of volume of most volcanic oceanic islands. This has been extensively documented in the islands of Hawaii, Reunion, Tristan da Cunha, etc.

In the Canaries, there are two main types of large depressions that open toward the sea: straight-walled and arcuate head basins such as the Orotava and Güimar valleys in Tenerife and crescent-shaped coastal embayments like the El Golfo in El Hierro (Fig. 4). Their genesis has been the subject of a long debate. Faulting and collapse in giant gravitational landslides is now preferred to a mainly erosional origin (Carracedo 1994; Masson 1994).

The model proposed for the genesis of the rifts provides a new scheme that may explain the sources of accumulative tensional stresses that can finally trigger mass movements capable of creating these depressions.

Extensional stresses, probably related to phases of intense eruptive activity, tend to build up in the rifts until the rupture threshold is reached, triggering massive landslides. These tensional stresses are of three different types: (1) *non-volcanic, long-lasting stresses* resulting from the growth and progressive gravitational instability of the volcanoes; (2) *volcanic long-lasting cumulative stresses*, such as (a) the wedging effect of the dykes forcefully intruded between the parallel sheets of the intrusive complex, (b) the progressive increase in elevation and consequent instability of volcanoes in intense magmatic phases, (c) progressive loading of the volcanoes by new volcanic materials; and (3) *volcanic ephemeral stresses* in the eruptive processes, such as (a) the strong local seismicity originated by magma-fracting and forceful dyke intrusions, (b) the dynamically sustained increase in slope angles due to magma swelling, (c) the thermal plasticity at the rift axis as the feeding dykes progress to the surface. The sum of these coherent tensional stresses may reach a critical point, at which an eruptive event may trigger release.

The results of these tensional mechanisms vary with the type of rift. In single structures, landslides may occur perpendicularly to the rift

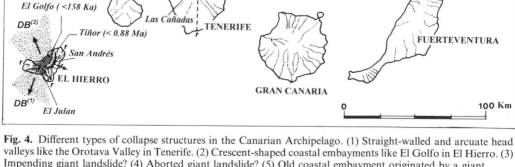

Fig. 4. Different types of collapse structures in the Canarian Archipelago. (1) Straight-walled and arcuate head valleys like the Orotava Valley in Tenerife. (2) Crescent-shaped coastal embayments like El Golfo in El Hierro. (3) Impending giant landslide? (4) Aborted giant landslide? (5) Old coastal embayment originated by a giant landslide? (6) Rift. DB, debris flow originated by giant landslides ([1]Holcomb & Searle 1991; [2]Masson 1994; [3]A. B. Watts pers. comm. Ages of El Hierro collapses after Guillou *et al.* (1995) and Carracedo *et al.* (1995)).

axis, either on one side of the axis (as in the southern rift of La Palma, Figs 4 and 6) or on both sides (as in the NE rift of Tenerife, Fig. 4). In complex, three-branched rifts, generally two of the branches concentrate the tensional stresses and the least active one functions as a buttress. This is clearly observed in Tenerife and Hierro, where the NE and NW branches have been more active than the S branch, and the main mass slides were directed seaward in the opposite (northern) direction (as in Las Cañadas or El Golfo depressions, see Fig. 4). Recently, Holcomb and Searle (1991) found evidence in the GLORIA sonographs of a giant gravitational slide in the Julan embayment, south-west Hierro (Fig. 6), suggesting a period of intense activity of NW and S rift zones at a different stage of the volcanic evolution of the island.

On the other hand, Masson et al. (1992) found evidence based on GLORIA side-scan sonar images and sediment cores collected northwest of the Canary Islands of a debris-flow deposit probably related to a Holocene single slope failure in one of the islands of the Archipelago; later TOBI surveys and coring seem to confirm that this deposit is volcanic debris apparently related to the partial collapse of El Hierro that originated the El Golfo embayment (Masson 1994). Recently, volcanic and magnetic stratigraphy and radiometric dating in El Hierro have shown the presence of three volcanic cycles separated by two giant landslides at about 0.88 Ma and between 158 and 38 ka respectively (Guillou et al. 1995; Carracedo et al. 1995).

A simple model for the genesis of eruptive and giant gravitational landslide hazards in the Canary Islands

Three-armed patterns seem to be a common scheme in the arrangement of volcanic vents in oceanic volcanoes. The presence of three rift zones radiating from the summit of the Hawaiian shields with angles of about 120° between them was mentioned by Wentworth & Macdonald in 1953. The observation pointed out by Macdonald (1972) that the shape of the Hawaiian shields is greatly influenced by the geometry and strength of the rifts is also applicable to the Canarian islands and, probably, to many other oceanic volcanoes. When the rifts are poorly developed the eruptions tend to take place from vents radiating in all directions from the summit, forming an island or volcano that is more or less circular (Gomera, Gran Canaria, Taburiente volcano in La Palma, etc.). Conversely, if the rifts

are very active, the geometry of the ground plan of the island or volcano is elongate if a single rift is involved (Cumbre Vieja in La Palma) or lobate, in the form of a three-pointed star, in the case of a triple-rift complex (Tenerife, El Hierro).

Coherent dyke swarms have been proposed as a common feature and a key factor in the development of oceanic island volcanoes by Walker (1992). Updoming magma pressure, swell and eventual rupture and consequent injection of blade-type dykes is a synthesis of the repetitive process that, by progressively increasing anisotropy, forces the new dykes to wedge their path parallel to the main structure (Carracedo et al. 1992). The result is a narrow, dense swarm of parallel or subparallel dykes.

The geometry of the complex Canarian rifts is characterized by three branches symmetrically separated by angles of 120° (Fig. 5). In the asymmetric model proposed by Walker (1992) for the Hawaiian Islands the injection of dyke wedges along two collinear rifts would induce asymmetric growth causing the rifts to become non-collinear and set up extensional stresses which would be relieved by the formation of an orthogonal rift. As stated previously, the two-branched rift stage has not been found in the Canaries, and the three-branched stage consistently shows a symmetric pattern with angles of 120°. The geometry of the Canarian rifts points rather to a least-effort fracture as a result of magma-induced vertical upward loading. This Mercedes-Benz triple fracturing is the one that minimizes the value of external load among all the possible fracturing mechanisms that may develop in a homogeneous and isotropic plate undergoing upward vertical thrust. The shape of function for this least-effort failure has been described by Luongo et al. (1991) as:

$$f(\alpha_1, \alpha_2)$$
$$= \frac{\tan\left(\frac{a_1}{2}\right) + \tan\left(\frac{a_2}{2}\right) + \tan\left(p - \frac{a_1}{2} - \frac{a_2}{2}\right)}{\sin(\alpha_1) + \sin(\alpha_2) + \sin(2\pi - \alpha_1 - \alpha_2)}$$

in which α_1 and α_2 are the angles between fractures and $\alpha_3 = 2\pi - \alpha_1 - \alpha_2$. The minimum value of the function is 2 determined by $\alpha_1 = \alpha_2 = 2.09\,\text{rad} = 120°$, and therefore:

$$\alpha_1 = \alpha_2 = \alpha_3 = 120°$$

The distribution of eruptive vents and related dyke swarms along perfectly arranged 120°-separated triple rifts in Tenerife and El Hierro islands strongly supports this model. On the other hand, the single rift that has developed in the southern part of La Palma may be related to

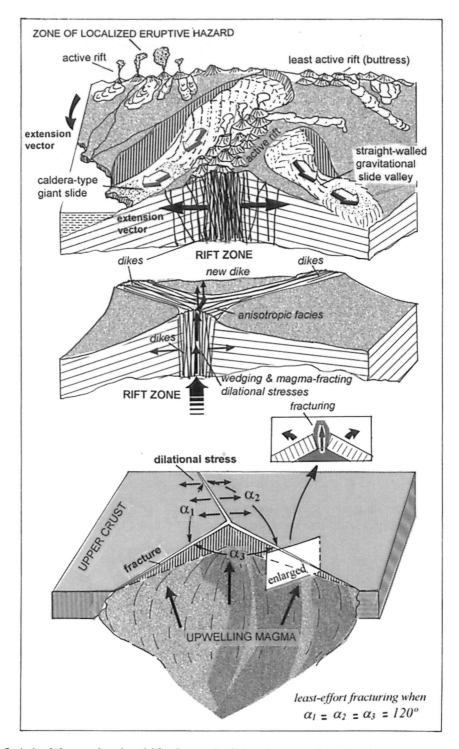

Fig. 5. A simple hotspot-based model for the genesis of Mercedes-type stellate rifts. This model is appropriate for the assessment of both eruptive and massive gravitational landslide hazards in the Canary Islands.

the crustal structure at the place where the upwelling magma was located, mainly the anisotropy of the crust due to the presence or absence of previous tectonic fabric signatures. There is no evidence of the two-branched stage in the Canary Islands. Although this could be explained by this stage being a very short-lived, transitional phase in the evolution of these structures, we favour the model of alternative single or triple rift arrangements as the result of fracturing by magma updoming in anisotropic or isotropic crust frameworks.

The present depth of the magmatic bodies that have generated the rifts is difficult to estimate. The brittle–ductile discontinuity at which the rifting starts may have varied with the evolution of the rifts. Long-term location of the focal depth of seismic events underneath the rifts, now in progress by means of a newly deployed seismic network (Carracedo et al. 1993), may help to define the upper boundary of the bodies of magma that sustain the rifts.

Implications of the existence of rift zones in volcanic hazards assessment

Volcanic hazards assessment and surveillance in the Canarian Archipelago (seven main islands, 1.7 million inhabitants, seven to eight million tourists per year) have not yet been sufficiently attempted. This is probably due, among other factors, to the formerly widespread assumption that there are not distinct zones or volcanic edifices – other than the Teide stratovolcano – where future eruptions may be preferentially localized. However, this is far from true, since there are well defined zones – the rifts previously described – where most of the recent eruptive activity has concentrated.

The main risk factors associated with volcanism in the Canary Islands, eruptive and massive gravitational slides, can now be analysed taking into consideration the presence of these rifts. Since most of the recent volcanism and all the historic eruptions are located in the rifts, they function, from the point of view of volcanic surveillance and risk mitigation, as polygenetic active volcanic edifices and constitute by far the most probable location of any future volcanic eruption in the archipelago. There is, therefore, a compelling reason to focus volcanic surveillance on these active edifices.

Volcanic hazards associated with the basaltic fissure-type eruptions at the rifts are generally small in magnitude. Damage is usually caused by tephra fall within a radius of a few hundred metres

around the vent and by small volume and low velocity lava flows, whose courses are closely controlled by the topography. An exception is the 1730 eruption of Lanzarote, in which 3–5 km^3 of volcanic products were emitted over 6 years, covering 23% of the island with pyroclastic ejecta and lava flows (Carracedo et al. 1992).

In complex and evolved rifts, as in Tenerife, long-lasting central-type composite volcanoes (Teide–Pico Viejo) with more differentiated magmas have developed at the junction of the rifts. Explosive eruptive mechanisms and even high-energy plinian episodes have frequently occurred in this stratovolcano, active as recently as the 15th century. The Teide complex is nested in the caldera of Las Caadas, in the unbuttressed northern flank of the island, bounded by rifts which have been highly active in recent times. The growth of this stratovolcano (3718 m high and 1700 m on the caldera floor), the instability towards the north coast and the dilation stresses expected in the forceful emplacement of dyke-type conduits in any new fissure eruption emplaced in these rifts, pose a significant hazard to the island and emphasize the need for the study and surveillance of this central edifice and its associated rifts.

Massive landslides developed on the flanks of rifts are relatively common in the Canaries and represent a significant hazard. Forceful emplacement of dykes could be responsible for incipient displacement of unstable, unbuttressed flanks of rifts. This is illustrated by the opening in the 1949 eruption in La Palma of broadly curving circular faults (Bonelli Rubio 1950), probably as a result of the stresses trying to collapse the west flank of the southern rift which has slope angles exceeding 30% (Fig. 6). An earlier but similar process may have generated the slide calderas of Taburiente and Cumbre Nueva to the north, a mass-wasting response to the overgrowth of the rift, nearly 5 km high from the sea floor.

Associated tsunamis (Moore & Moore 1984) also pose an important hazard to the islands nearby, considering the densely populated areas on the coast of La Palma, Tenerife and Gran Canaria.

Another massive gravitational slide feature that may not yet be fully developed and may constitute a potential risk is the SE flank of El Hierro. This island has exceptionally well-represented triple 120° star geometry rifts with three correlative golfo-type giant gravitational slides (Fig. 6). The N and NW slides are concluded processes, the NW being probably the older (Holcomb & Searle 1991). However, in the SE part of El Hierro, long, arcuate en-echelon

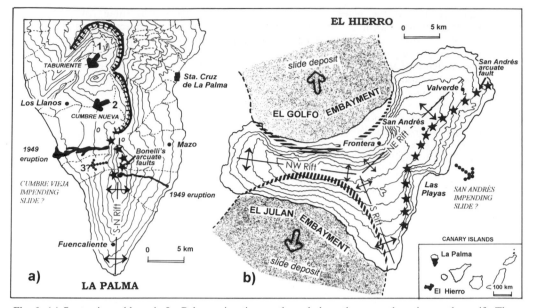

Fig. 6. (a) Successive calderas in La Palma, migrating southward along the presently active southern rift. These horseshoe-type calderas are consistently directed towards the west flank of the rift, probably an inherited feature related to the shape and structure of the submarine part of the island edifice. The stars show arcuate en-echelon faults opened during the 1949 eruptive event (Bonelli Rubio 1950) that may indicate the earliest stage of formation of a new caldera. (b) Horseshoe-type embayments associated with the Mercedes-type triple rift of El Hierro. The Julan and El Golfo embayments seem to be large landslides related to the partial collapse of the island edifice in independent events (Holcomb & Searle, 1991; Masson et al. 1992; Masson 1994), probably triggered by the cumulative stresses associated with the rifts already mentioned. The SE sector of the island is bordered by a 15 km long, arcuate fault, with en-echelon drops up to 80–100 m. Field observations suggest that this is an old, aborted feature, but more detailed studies should be carried out before completely discarding this feature as a main potential hazard for El Hierro and, by triggering tsunamis, to the neighbouring islands.

faults developed (see Fig. 6). This gravitational failure caused the collapse of the triangular SE part of the island, with subvertical drops in excess of 80–100 m in some places, and the formation of a smaller embayment (Las Playas) at the southern end of the faults. This partial collapse could be a relatively old feature, predating the N and probably the NW slides. Lava flows filling the Las Playas embayment give ages of 38 and 146 ka (Guillou et al. 1995; Carracedo et al. 1995) while the fault planes that outcrop at the bottom of gulches have been smoothed by erosion. An interesting problem not completely resolved

from the natural hazards point of view, is to clarify whether this feature is in fact a relatively old, aborted event or, like the Bonelli faults in La Palma, an impending process that could be triggered by future eruptions in the island.

The concentration of recent eruptive vents in El Hierro shows that the NE and S rifts that bound this semi-collapsed part of the island seem to be in fact the most active in recent times. Taking into consideration the risk posed by potential flank collapses and associated tsunamis to the population of the island and to the facing Canarian islands (the densely populated

Fig. 7. (A) Contrasting evolutionary patterns and volcanic hazard sources in the western and eastern islands of the Archipelago. The main factors controlling these differences are the activity of a hotspot and the lateral variation of the structure, thickness and rigidity of the crust in the oceanic (western end) and the transitional (eastern end, near the African coast) sectors of the volcanic chain. (B) Iso-Q_0 map of the Canarian Archipelago (Canas et al. in press). The shaded areas indicate zones of high seismic attenuation or high anelasticity that may point to the presence of a strong asthenosphere, probably hotspot-rejuvenated crust. The high anelastic zone between Tenerife and Gran Canaria has been the source of recent, relatively strong seismicity (several events >4.5), as well as the vicinity of El Hierro. In both scenarios seismicity could be related to the activity of the asthenospheric plume.

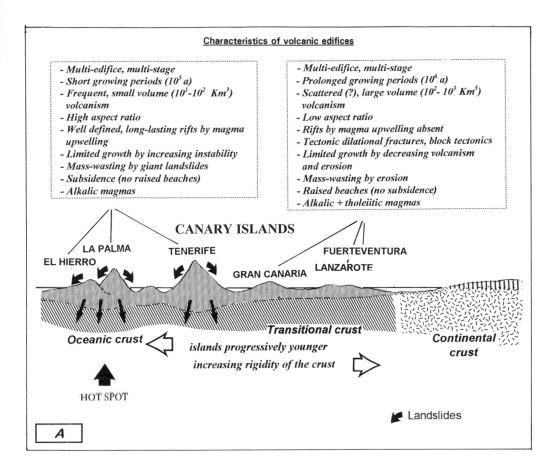

Characteristics of volcanic edifices

- *Multi-edifice, multi-stage*
- *Short growing periods (10^5 a)*
- *Frequent, small volume (10^1-10^2 Km^3) volcanism*
- *High aspect ratio*
- *Well defined, long-lasting rifts by magma upwelling*
- *Limited growth by increasing instability*
- *Mass-wasting by giant landslides*
- *Subsidence (no raised beaches)*
- *Alkalic magmas*

- *Multi-edifice, multi-stage*
- *Prolonged growing periods (10^6 a)*
- *Scattered (?), large volume (10^2-10^3 Km^3) volcanism*
- *Low aspect ratio*
- *Rifts by magma upwelling absent*
- *Tectonic dilational fractures, block tectonics*
- *Limited growth by decreasing volcanism and erosion*
- *Mass-wasting by erosion*
- *Raised beaches (no subsidence)*
- *Alkalic + tholeiitic magmas*

CANARY ISLANDS

LA PALMA TENERIFE FUERTEVENTURA
EL HIERRO LANZAROTE
GRAN CANARIA

Oceanic crust Transitional crust Continental crust

islands progressively younger
increasing rigidity of the crust

HOT SPOT

Landslides

A

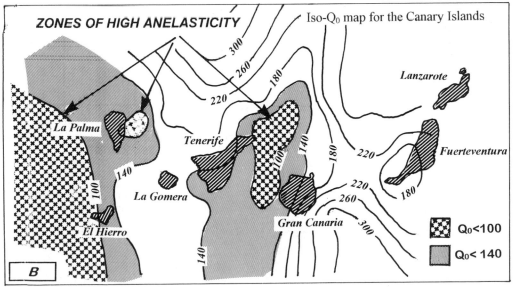

ZONES OF HIGH ANELASTICITY   Iso-Q_0 map for the Canary Islands

300
260
180
220
Lanzarote
La Palma
Tenerife
140
100
180
220
Fuerteventura
140
100
La Gomera
180
220
El Hierro
Gran Canaria
260
300
140
180

$Q_0 < 100$
$Q_0 < 140$

B

southern tourist resorts of Gomera, Tenerife and Gran Canaria), this geological feature should be extensively investigated from the geological, geophysical and marine points of view.

Implications of the contrasting origin and evolution of the eastern and western Canarian islands in volcanic hazards assessment

The rifts represent long-lived, volcano-tectonic features that constitute the key factor controlling the development of some insular edifices, possibly changing their location, rate of activity and configuration as the different islands evolved. Active rifts are well displayed only in those islands with important recent eruptive activity. In fact, historic activity has occurred only in the islands having rifts, which seems to suggest that these features developed in places where magmatism is presently more active and crustal conditions favour the development of steady magma plumbing systems that facilitate sustained eruptive activity.

The fact that only the western islands show well-defined, long-lasting rifts originated by magma upwelling requires some further analysis. Since the rifts are predominant in the young island, they could represent features related to the early, non-evolved stages of the building of the island's edifices.

In contrast with purely oceanic islands like Hawaii, Tahiti and La Reunion, the Canarian island chain is located in a passive margin, in close proximity to the Moroccan continental margin (see inset in Fig. 2). A more convincing model would relate the presence or absence of the rifts to two main factors.

(1) The activity of a hotspot located at present under the western end of the archipelago. The motion of the African plate for the last 60 Ma (Morgan 1983) would be compatible with a quasi-stationary plume that roughly fits the age scheme and trend of the Canarian chain for the last 20–30 Ma, and which would presently be located under the island of Hierro (see Fig. 10 in Holik et al. 1991).

(2) The lateral variation of the structure, thickness and rigidity of the crust.

Analysis of the geoid anomalies in the area of the Canarian Archipelago led Filmer & McNutt (1988) to infer the local lithosphere to be very rigid, without any indication of shallow reheating related to mantle plume activity. However, Holik et al. (1991) detected the presence at the north end of the archipelago of a chaotic seismic facies that they interpret as being volcanic in origin. They also detected a low velocity anomaly at the base of the crust, which they propose reflects the signature of thermal rejuvenation and underplating of the oceanic crust as a result of the earlier activity of the Canarian hotspot around 60 Ma before present. Recently, Watts (1994) found the elastic thickness of the lithosphere to be considerably lower than would be expected for the age of the crust underlying the Canary Islands. A likely explanation is thermal weakening or re-heating by a hotspot.

The combined influence of a hotspot and the lateral variation of the thickness and rigidity of the crust may explain the contrasting characteristics of the volcanic edifices in the western and eastern parts of the Canarian Archipelago, indicated schematically in Fig. 7.

The iso-Q_0 map obtained with the analysis of coda waves (Canas et al. 1995) shows important lateral variations of Q_0, pointing out zones of high anelasticity of the crust under La Palma and El Hierro (the probable present location of the Canarian hotspot according to Holik et al. (1991)), and between Tenerife and Gran Canaria (see Fig. 7B). The highly anelastic zone between Tenerife and Gran Canaria has been the source of recent, relatively strong seismicity (several events >4.5), as well as the neighbourhood of El Hierro. We speculate that in both cases the origin of the regional seismicity may be related to magmatism associated with the hotspot activity rather than to purely tectonic processes associated with differential displacements of the African plate.

Financial support for this work by the Spanish DGICYT Project PB92-0119 and helpful comments by Angus Duncan, Phil Weaver, Robin Holcomb, Bill McGuire, and Douglas Masson are very gratefully acknowledged.

References

BONELLI RUBIO, J. M. 1950. *Contribución al Estudio de la Erupción del Nambroque o San Juan (Isla de La Palma)*. Instituto Geografico y Catastral, Madrid.

CANAS, J. A., PUJADES, L. G., BLANCO, M. J., SOLER, V. & CARRACEDO, J. C. 1995. Coda-Q distribution in the Canary Islands. *Tectonophysics*, **246**, 245–261.

CARRACEDO, J. C. 1979. *Paleomagnetismo e Historia Volcánica de Tenerife*. Aula de Cultura de Tenerife, 1–82.

——, 1994. The Canary Islands: an example of structural control on the growth of large oceanic-island volcanoes. *Journal of Volcanology and Geothermal Research*, **60**.

—— & SOLER, V. 1995. Shallow paleomagnetic inclinations in the island of Lanzarote and the question of the age of the Canarian Archipelago. *Geophysical Journal International*, **122**, 393–406.

——, GARCÍA-FERNÁNDEZ, M., JIMÉNEZ, M. J. & SOLER, V. 1993. A newly-deployed permanent seismic network to monitor active volcanism of the Canary Islands. *WOVO Workshop on Volcano Observatories, Surveillance of Volcanoes and Prediction of Eruptions.* Guadaloupe Island.

——, GUILLOU, H., LAJ, J., KISSEL, K. PÉREZ TORRADO, J. F. & RODRÍGUEZ BADIOLA, E. 1995. Volcanic history of the island of El Hierro, Canarian Archipelago. *Abstact, EGU 8 Meeting*, Strasbourg.

——, RODRÍGUEZ BADIOLA, E. & SOLER, V. 1992. The 1730–1736 eruption of Lanzarote: an unusually long, high magnitude fissural basaltic eruption in the recent volcanism of the Canary Islands. *Journal of Volcanology and Geothermal Research*, **53**, 239–250.

DUFFIELD, W. A., STIELTJES, L. & VARET, J. 1981. Huge landslide blocks in the growth of Piton de la Fournaise, La Réunion, and Kilauea Volcano, Hawaii. *Journal of Volcanology and Geothermal Research*, **12**, 147–160.

FILMER, P. E. & McNUTT, M. K. 1988. Geoid anomalies over the Canary Islands group. *Marine and Geophysical Research*, **11**, 77–87.

GUILLOU, H., CARRACEDO, J. C., LAJ, J., KISSEL, K. PÉREZ TORRADO, J.F & RODRÍGUEZ BADIOLA, E. 1995. K-Ar ages and geomagnetic reversals from lavas of El Hierro, Canary Islands. *Abstact, EGU 8 Meeting*, Strasbourg.

HOLCOMB, R. T. & SEARLE, R. C. 1991. Large landslides from oceanic volcanoes. *Marine Geotechnology*, **10**, 19–32.

HOLIK, J. S., RABINOWITZ, P. D. & AUSTIN, J. A. 1991. Effects of Canary hotspot volcanism on structure of oceanic crust off Morocco. *Journal of Geophysical Research*, **96-B7**, 12039–12067.

LUONGO, G., CUBELLIS, E., OBRIZZO, F. & PETRAZZUOLI, S. M. 1991. A physical model for the origin of volcanism of the Tyrrhenian margin: the case of the Neapolitan area. *Journal of Volcanology and Geothermal Research*, **48**, 173–185.

MACDONALD, G. A. 1972. *Volcanoes*. Prentice-Hall, Englewood Cliffs, New Jersey.

MACFARLANE, D. J. & RIDLEY, W. I. 1968. An interpretation of gravity data for Tenerife, Canary Islands. *Earth and Planetary Science Letters*, **4**, 481–486.

MASSON, D. G. 1994. *TOBI Surveys and Coring of Debris Flows West of the Canaries*. Institute of Oceanographic Science, Deacon Laboratory, Report no. **239**.

——, KIDD, R. B., GARDNER, J. V., HUGGET, Q. J. & WEAVER, P. P. E., 1992. Saharan Continental Rise: facies distribution and sediment slides. *In*: POAG, C. W. & DE GRACIANSKY, P. C. (eds) *Geologic Evolution of Atlantic Continental Rises*. Van Nostrand Reinhold, New York, 327–343

MOORE, G. W. & MOORE, J. G., 1984. Deposit from a giant wave on the island of Lanai, Hawaii. *Science*, **226**, 1312–1315.

MORGAN, W. J. 1983. Hotspots tracks and the early rifting of the Atlantic. *Tectonophysics*, **94**, 123–139.

SCHMINCKE, H. U. 1982. Volcanic and chemical evolution of the Canary Islands. *In*: VON RAD, V., HINZ, K., SHARTEIN, M. & SEIBOLD, E. (eds) *Geology of the Northwest African Continental Margin*. Springer-Verlag, New York, 273–306.

WALKER, G. P. L. 1992. Coherent intrusion complexes in large basaltic volcanoes – a new structural model. *Journal of Volcanology and Geothermal Research*, **50**, 41–54.

WATTS, A. B. 1994. Crustal structure, gravity anomalies and flexure of the lithosphere in the vicinity of the Canary Islands. *Geophysical Journal International*, **119**, 648–666.

WENTWORTH, C. K. & MACDONALD, G. A. 1953. *Structures and Forms of Basaltic Rocks in Hawaii*. US Geological Survey Bulletin, **994**.

Topographic characterization and monitoring of volcanoes via airborne laser altimetry

JAMES B. GARVIN

NASA Goddard Space Flight Center, Geodynamics Branch, Code 921, Greenbelt, MD 20771 USA

Abstract: High spatial and vertical resolution airborne laser altimetry surveys of selected volcanic landforms have been used to investigate the metre-scale topographic characteristics of such features. Geodetic-quality airborne laser altimeter cross-sections of the Mount St. Helens dacite lava dome were acquired during the interval from 1987 to 1993; such data indicate that mass wasting of the flanks of the dome has outpaced episodic construction over the past seven years. Massive slumping of the south inner crater walls of the Mount St. Helens amphitheatre has been documented. Laser altimeter cross-sections of Mount Rainier have been compared with Mount St. Helens, Mount Adams, and with the Icelandic lava shield Skjaldbreidur in terms of local slope distributions, revealing basic similarities between the flanks of Rainier and St. Helens at length scales less than 5 m. When simple edifice shape parameters such as aspect ratio (H/D) are compared against total inferred edifice volume (V), Cascades stratovolcanoes such as Rainier and St. Helens fall along the extrapolation of the trend displayed for simple Icelandic lava shields. Cylindrical harmonic expansions involving laser altimeter cross-sections of volcanoes can be used mathematically to model the three-dimensional shapes of such features on the basis of only a few tens of coefficients and hence can be utilized to reduce the apparent extreme topographic complexity of major stratocones to terms that permit quantitative comparison with simpler volcanoes. In the future, geodetic airborne laser altimetry may be suitable as one of the many useful remote sensing methods for monitoring active volcanoes. A summary of the basic techniques associated with airborne laser altimetry in the context of volcanoes is provided.

Topography has been used historically to describe volcanic landforms (Becker 1885; Williams 1932; Lacey *et al.* 1981; Pike & Clow 1981), and it has long been recognized that the three-dimensional shape properties of volcanoes can be related to several of the critical variables involved in their construction and evolution, including eruption style, vent geometry, mass or volume eruption rate, and magma composition. While morphologic characterization of evolving volcanoes has developed as an important source of information over the past decades (e.g. BVSP 1981; McGuire *et al.* 1995), rapid and high-precision methods for determining the often complex topography of volcanoes have only recently emerged as a contributor of valuable quantitative data. Traditional methods for measuring the topography of landforms are often inadequate for volcanoes, in part due to the sometimes rapidly changing relief associated with activity, and also because of difficulties of field access. Indeed, airborne and spaceborne remote sensing techniques which permit measurement of dynamic landscape topography are a critical element of so-called 'global change research programs' in many countries. Furthermore, topographic changes often take place at spatial scales that have not been previously accessible with traditional topographic mapping

systems (i.e. stereogrammetry with metric aerial photographs), and hence new methods are required for observation of local-scale topographic properties of active landforms such as volcanoes.

In the investigation described in this report, a new technique for topographic remote sensing is described in the context of volcanology. Since the middle 1980s, a small group of scientists and engineers at the National Aeronautics and Space Administration (NASA) have been developing airborne and spaceborne laser altimeter methods for measurement of metre and sub-metre scale relief of terrestrial surfaces (e.g. Bufton *et al.* 1991; Garvin 1993), and in particular of volcanic landforms (Garvin & Williams 1990, 1992). Other methods for topographic remote sensing have also emerged in the past decade, including synthetic aperture radar (SAR) interferometry (Evans *et al.* 1992; Mouginis-Mark & Garbeil, 1993), which can efficiently address 10 m scale topographic properties of landscapes.

Here we report on NASA's evolving efforts with respect to airborne laser altimetry as a topographic remote sensing tool in the context of volcanology. Particular attention is given to preliminary efforts to use airborne laser altimetry for topographic monitoring of active or recently active volcanoes, including the Mount

From McGuire, W. J., Jones, A. P. & Neuberg, J. (eds) 1996, *Volcano Instability on the Earth and Other Planets*, Geological Society Special Publication No. 110, pp. 137–152.

St. Helens dacite lava dome. The prime objective in NASA's airborne laser altimetry efforts has focused upon metre and sub-metre precision topographic measurements in both vertical and horizontal dimensions (Bufton *et al*, 1991; Garvin & Williams 1992), in contrast with the wide-swath (*c.* 10 km or greater) and lower-precision emphasis of the interferometric SAR efforts (Evans *et al.* 1992). Basic characterization of the metre-scale topographic cross-sections of a broad variety of volcanic landforms has always been and remains a major goal associated with laser altimetry observations of volcanoes.

A brief summary of the laser altimeter remote sensing technique is provided, after which examples of data are discussed, with emphasis on the results achieved to date for Mount St. Helens and other Cascades stratovolcanoes. The intent is to demonstrate how metre-resolution topographic data can be used to characterize and potentially to monitor geomorphic changes at volcanoes. In essence, this is a 'techniques' paper in which examples of a new class of observations are described (i.e. metre-scale topography) and a limited set of preliminary results using such data are presented. Because of the extremely high-spatial and vertical resolution inherent with airborne laser altimeter topographic data, we have explored ways of mathematically modelling the cross-sectional shapes of complex volcanoes to reduce their topographic complexity to a manageable and systematic set of parameters. The approach we have taken involves cylindrical harmonic expansions using laser altimeter topographic cross-sections. Finally, we have investigated how volcano shapes and volumes derived from laser altimeter data permit one to classify volcanic edifices in terms of their constructional histories. It is our contention that geodetic-quality airborne laser altimeter surveys of active or potentially active volcanoes should be included as part of basic volcano monitoring programmes (e.g. Tazieff & Sabroux 1983; Tilling 1989; McGuire *et al.* 1995) now under development.

Background and approach

Laser altimetry as a method for remote sensing of terrestrial and planetary surface topography has existed since the 1960s. Indeed, the Apollo orbital spacecraft used a primitive laser altimeter to measure the global shape of the Moon as early as 1971, and airborne laser altimeters have been in limited use around the Earth for various remote sensing purposes since the late 1970s (Bufton 1989; Garvin 1993). Excellent descriptions of the basic method are available in the literature (e.g. Bufton 1989; Bufton *et al.* 1991; Garvin & Bufton 1992). The laser altimeter instruments used in our investigation of volcanoes are pulsed, time-of-flight sensors which involve an all-solid-state laser transmitter (typically a Q-switched, diode-pumped Nd : YAG variety), a receiving telescope (which acts as the altimeter 'antennae'), and various supporting altimeter electronics to detect the backscattered pulses of laser radiation and measure their time-of-flight from transmission to reception at very high temporal resolution (i.e. <1 ns). The simple elegance of these laser altimeter sensors is related to their extremely narrow transmitter and receiver fields of view. It is typical of the diverging laser beam transmitted from a moving platform (i.e. aircraft or spacecraft) to subtend an angle of only 1–2 milliradians, which translates into an illuminated footprint on the Earth's surface approximately 1–10 m in diameter from typical aircraft remote sensing altitudes.

It has been empirically observed that the internal vertical structure of most metre-diameter patches of unvegetated terrain is never much greater than 0.5 m (Garvin *et al.* 1995); hence, the laser altimeter receiver electronics (Fig. 1) can relatively easily detect the backscattered laser radiation with high reliability and in a robust manner. As will be described later, it is typical for the NASA airborne laser altimeter systems to achieve a 99% measurement success rate (i.e. successful acquisition of a valid and reproducible ranging observation) over unvegetated terrain, independent of the local slope. This is made possible as a consequence of the narrow field of view (i.e. less than a few milliradians) and relative absence of coherent fading (i.e. speckle modulation) that plagues microwave altimeters. Indeed, with most laser altimeters, each laser pulse results in a successful ranging measurement, and no averaging is required. Figure 1 schematically illustrates the components of the NASA profiling airborne laser altimeter (known by the acronym 'ALAS') as used for most of the remote sensing of the volcanoes discussed in this paper. This instrument is a highly evolving one due to improvements in technology, and as of spring 1994 two independent and embellished laser altimeter systems have been spawned from the 1993 state-of-the art ALAS sensor, both facilitating cross-track coverage.

Critical to the success of laser altimetry as a remote sensing tool for characterizing and monitoring volcanoes is horizontal and vertical

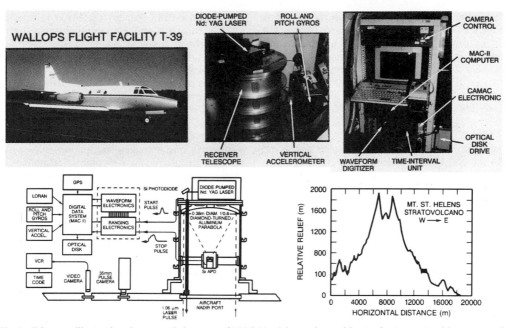

Fig. 1. Diagram illustrating the general elements of NASA's airborne laser altimeter instrument, with an example of a dataset for Mt. St. Helens. See text and Bufton *et al.* (1991) for details.

resolution. By pulsing the nadir-oriented laser transmitter 50 or more times a second from a moving aircraft platform, horizontal sampling on the order of 1 to 2 m is achieved, which allows for contiguous footprint profiling of terrain. In addition, each laser pulse is 'timed' to within a few hundreds of picoseconds by the altimeter receiver ranging electronics, yielding on the order of 5 cm vertical resolution. However, the motion of the platform on which the altimeter is configured dictates the final precision of the acquired data, as pointing knowledge is critical to assign each measurement to its proper position on the Earth's surface, ideally in a centre-of-mass coordinate system (i.e. relative to the geoid). This is accomplished using kinematic Global Positioning System (GPS) methods in which GPS receivers aboard the aircraft and on the ground at a fixed reference point are used simultaneously to determine the trajectory of the aircraft, usually to within tens of centimetres in a vertical sense. Horizontal positional recovery involves both GPS and a ring laser gyro package which measures the aircraft roll and pitch orientation at high sample rate and precision. It is not our intention to present a rigorous error analysis of the NASA airborne laser altimeter system here; suffice it to say that careful analysis of the error budget associated

with this system suggests that final vertical accuracies in the 15 to 50 cm range are routinely achieved, with hori-zontal positional accuracy to within 1 to 2 m (Bufton *et al.* 1991; Garvin 1993). From the six years of airborne laser altimeter experiments involving volcanic targets, it is our estimation that vertical accuracies are typically better than 1 m RMS (and better than 0.5 m after 1992), and horizontal accuracies are usually better than 10 m RMS (and good to 1–2 m after 1992). Future airborne laser altimeter sensors operated by NASA will make use of multibeam and raster scanning methods to achieve greater coverage and better statistical positioning accuracies (Blair *et al.* 1994).

Airborne laser altimeter surveys of volcanoes within North America, Iceland, and the Azores archipelago have been accomplished since 1986 as part of NASA-supported investigations in volcanology. Topographic cross-sections of Mount St. Helens summit region (and the dacite lava dome) have been acquired with NASA laser altimeter systems since 1987, with continuously improving reliability and accuracy. Results from the 1993 geodetic-quality laser altimeter surveys will be presented here, in comparison with lower-accuracy measurements from 1987, 1989, and 1990. Future plans call for routine raster-scanning airborne laser altimeter surveys of Mount St. Helens and Mount Rainier using swath-mapping and multi-beam laser altimeter systems now under development at NASA under the aegis of the 'Topography and Surface Change Initiative' within NASA's Mission to Planet Earth programme.

Examples of laser altimeter data

Mount St. Helens

Topographic characterization of the post-1980 Mount St. Helens volcanic system is an important component of Cascades Volcano Observatory efforts to study the evolution of an active stratovolcano in the continental US (Swanson & Holcomb 1990; Holcomb & Colony 1987; Chadwick & Swanson 1989; Tilling 1989). Indeed, Swanson & Holcomb (1990) conducted a comprehensive investigation of the temporal topographic and volumetric evolution of the Mount St. Helens summit dacite dome (hereafter MSH dome) for the period from its birth in 1980 to 1986, when major construction apparently

ceased. Since 1987, our interest has been focused upon measuring and characterizing the topography, shape, and volume of the MSH dome at metre-length scales using airborne laser altimetry. Between 1987 and 1989, these efforts have centred upon statistical characterization using sets of orthogonal topographic cross-sections acquired with non-GPS assisted airborne laser altimetry. In 1990, successful kinematic GPS tracking of the laser altimeter aircraft platform resulted in our first geodetic-quality, sub-metre vertical accuracy measurements. Finally, in September of 1993, extremely high precision laser altimeter cross-sections were acquired in north–south and west–east orthogonal directions over the MSH dome centre with no more than a few tens of centimetres vertical error and with positional accuracy in the 1–2 m RMS range. These data can ideally serve as the basis for continued geodetic topographic monitoring of the MSH dome and of the entire edifice.

Figure 2 illustrates four laser altimeter cross-sections of the MSH dome, all of which

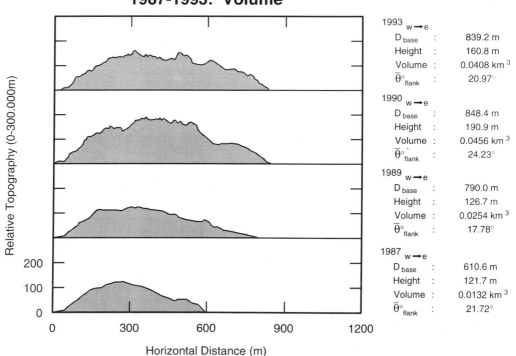

Mount St. Helens Dome
1987-1993: Volume

1993	w → e		
	D base	:	839.2 m
	Height	:	160.8 m
	Volume	:	0.0408 km^3
	$\bar{\theta}°$ flank	:	20.97

1990	w → e		
	D base	:	848.4 m
	Height	:	190.9 m
	Volume	:	0.0456 km^3
	$\bar{\theta}°$ flank	:	24.23°

1989	w → e		
	D base	:	790.0 m
	Height	:	126.7 m
	Volume	:	0.0254 km^3
	$\bar{\theta}°$ flank	:	17.78°

1987	w → e		
	D base	:	610.6 m
	Height	:	121.7 m
	Volume	:	0.0132 km^3
	$\bar{\theta}°$ flank	:	21.72°

Relative Topography (0-300.000m)

Horizontal Distance (m)

Fig. 2. Airborne laser altimeter cross-sections of Mt. St. Helens summit lava dome acquired between 1987 and 1993. All profiles illustrate west to east cross-sections, with 2–4 m spatial resolution. Simple dimensional statistics are listed to the right of each profile; all values are derived solely from the laser altimeter profiles themselves. Vertical axes have 100 m tick marks.

approximately represent a west to east topographic profile. The 1990 and 1993 cross-sections were reduced using kinematic GPS solutions for the aircraft platform position, and are co-registered to within approximately 20 m on the MSH dome surface. The dimensional parameters listed in association with each laser altimeter cross-section were derived exclusively from the profile data. Thus, the volumes listed in Fig. 2 were derived by means of simple numerical integration of the laser altimeter profiles under the assumption of circular symmetry, and as such are for comparison purposes only. The major differences in volume between 1987 and 1989 are partly a consequence of the limited horizontal positional accuracy of the pre-GPS tracked data. However, it is more interesting to observe the apparent decrease of volume from 1990 and 1993, as these data have been geolocated via GPS techniques to within c. 20 m in horizontal position. Basal diameters of the

lava dome are objectively measured using the largest breaks in slope between the apparent base of the MSH dome and the walls of the MSH amphitheatre crater. It is not clear why the dome appears to have enlarged in a west to east direction between 1987 and 1990, but the positional accuracy of the 1987 and 1989 laser altimeter surveys is dependent upon simultaneous bore-sighted VHS video and photographic data, and does not utilize kinematic GPS positioning, which was not readily available to us until 1990. Hence, part of the reason for the tremendous volumetric discrepancy is most probably related to horizontal positional accuracy of the 1987 data, which may have been off-centre by as much as 100 m.

Figure 3 illustrates a 10 m spatial resolution perspective view of the relief of Mount St. Helens acquired in June of 1992 via the NASA Airborne interferometric SAR sensor known as TOPSAR (Evans et al. 1992). The TOPSAR

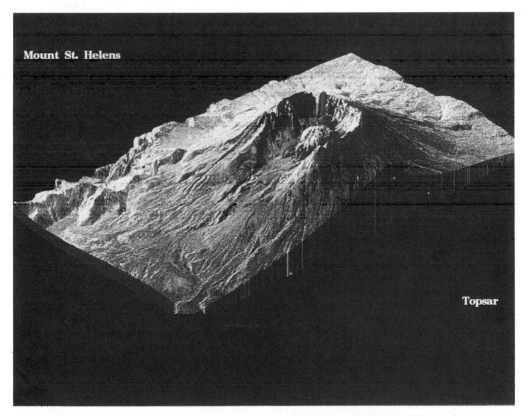

Fig. 3. Perspective view of synthetic aperture radar backscatter draped over airborne SAR interferometric topography at 10 m spatial resolution and c. 3 m vertical resolution. Data from the NASA TOPSAR system, provided to us courtesy of H. Zebker of Jet Propulsion Laboratory. TOPSAR data collected in June of 1992. These data are not geolocated; see text for details.

system permits wide-swath (up to 10 km) surveys of several meter precision topography (Zebker et al. 1992), and the image presented in Fig. 3 uses the SAR backscatter as an overlay to the TOPSAR topography. We have attempted to use the 1992 TOPSAR dataset for the MSH dome in comparison with our 1993 geodetic laser altimeter measurements in order to refine the past several years of geomorphic evolution of the feature. Unfortunately, the TOPSAR data are presently uncontrolled, and must be registered to a controlled reference, such as a topographic map, none of which are available for the entire MSH edifice since the late 1980s. Our efforts to compare digitally the 1992 TOPSAR data for MSH with our 1993 laser altimeter data are ongoing on the basis of common geolocation of both datasets to a recent Landsat Thematic Mapper image (30 m resolution), and future georeferenced TOPSAR acquisitions for MSH dome are anticipated in 1995. Many of the topographic changes at the MSH dome occur at horizontal spatial scales less than 10–20 m, and may necessitate repeat geodetic laser altimeter surveys for adequate measurement. Figure 4 suggests that 50 m horizontal scale changes can also be anticipated over a multi-year time frame.

Figure 4 is a digital intercomparison of a 1987 NASA laser altimeter survey of the north to south cross-section of the MSH dome with that acquired in September of 1993. We have geolocated these two profiles on the basis of photographic and video records from the 1987 surveys, and using the geodetic positioning control we were able to achieve in 1993. The two cross-sections are spatially positioned to an accuracy of c. 15 m RMS with respect to one another, and should be adequate for comparing the statistical nature of the topographic evolution of the MSH dome in a N–S direction. Relative to the 1987 dome, the 1993 cross-section suggests major slumping of the flanks, and mass-wasting of material from the central 400 m of the upper carapace. The apparent loss of 0.0131 km³ of volume between 1987 and 1993 can be partially explained by continued deposition of mass-wasted materials from the dome flanks and from the inner amphitheatre walls within the summit crater. We have detrended the two profiles illustrated in Fig. 4 by identifying basal ground control points in each dataset and then removing the tilt associated with the matched segments of each in order to facilitate a more meaningful and objective multi-temporal intercomparison. The result of this analysis

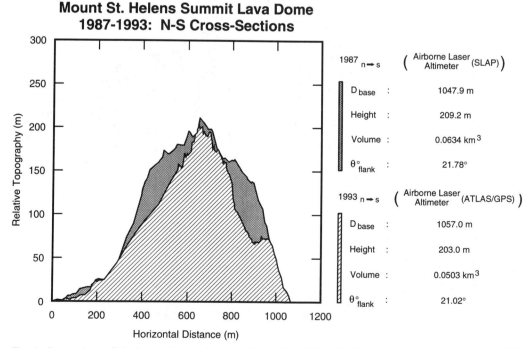

Fig. 4. Comparison of the laser altimeter topographic profiles of Mt. St. Helens summit lava dome from 1987 and 1993, in a north to south orientation. Statistics at right are derived from each laser profile. The geodetic-quality 1993 data are shown shaded in black, while the 1987 data are shaded in grey. See text for details.

(Fig. 4) suggests an integrated erosion rate less than or equal to $2.2 \times 10^6 \, m^3 \, a^{-1}$, albeit as an upper bound, and the total annual erosion rate is probably in the vicinity of $1.0 \times 10^6 \, m^3 \, a^{-1}$, on the basis of uncertainties associated with inner wall slumping and positional accuracy of the two profiles. This is on the order of the episodic volume growth of the dome in the 1980–86 constructional period (Swanson & Holcomb 1990). In essence, the comparison depicted in Fig. 4 is a harbinger of what is now routinely possible with the geodetic precision of the post-1993 laser altimeter systems, mostly as a result of kinematic GPS aircraft tracking and GPS-assisted aircraft flight operations. The pattern of degradation suggested by the comparison of the 1987 and 1993 dome cross-sections is reliable; however, the magnitudes of dome materials lost by means of flank collapse and mass-wasting are only approximations because of the assumptions associated with the numerical integrations used to estimate volumes (i.e. circular symmetry of the dome). In addition, the uncertainties

associated with the absolute positional accuracy of the 1987 pre-GPS data are large enough to contribute 10–20% errors in the volume computations, which assume that both the 1987 and 1993 profiles intersect at the lava dome centre. Reflights of the orthogonal cross-sections acquired in 1993 using a swath-mapping laser altimeter now under final development at NASA (Blair *et al.* 1994) should permit precise tracking of dome erosion volumes and pathways in future years, commencing in 1995.

Major slumping episodes involving the inner crater walls of the MSH amphitheatre have been documented since the early 1980s (Swanson & Holcomb 1990). Between 1987 and 1993 one major slump was measured via laser altimetry. A slump of the southern, inner crater wall of the amphitheatre occurred between 1990 and September of 1993, as documented by the vertical aerial photographs that were acquired as part of the laser altimeter surveys in these years. Figure 5 illustrates the cross-sectional nature of the tongue-shaped slump deposit that

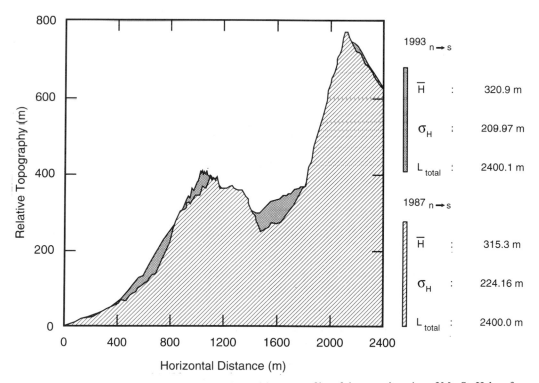

Fig. 5. As in Fig. 4 a comparison of airborne laser altimeter profiles of the summit region of Mt. St. Helens from 1987 and 1993, illustrating (see dark grey zone between 1500 and 1900 m on the horizontal axis) the topography of a recent slump deposit. See text for details.

apparently resulted from failure of the southern amphitheatre wall, probably in late 1992 or early 1993 (i.e. it is not documented in the June 1992 TOPSAR data, but appears in our 1993 laser altimeter and photographic data). The slump deposit is shown in cross-section, relative to the 1987 north to south topography of the summit region of Mount St. Helens. The slump is probably several tens of metres thick, and displays wave-like deformation features with wavelengths in excess of 40 m (i.e. visible only in highly enlarged profile segments), suggesting features akin to those predicted by Baloga (1987) for lava flows. While we fortuitously profiled the centre-line of this feature in 1993, we were not able to acquire orthogonal cross-sections of its frontal rampart or lobe. A first-order volume balance between the observed 1993 cross-sectional topography of the slump and previously acquired topographic data suggests that is has a maximal volume of $0.005 \, km^3$. Further analysis of this newly formed erosional feature is in progress.

When the E–W and N–S profiles for the 1993 MSH summit lava dome are contrasted (i.e. compare Fig. 2 and Fig. 4), it is apparent that the topology of this landform is not that of a simple quasi-circular viscous dome. Indeed, a 20% difference in the volume computed by means of numerical integration of each profile can be observed (i.e. $0.0408 \, km^3$ for W–E versus $0.0596 \, km^3$ for N–S). Even when the profiles are detrended and their basal contours matched, there are disparities in the volumes computed.

Mathematical modelling of the two orthogonal MSH dome profiles from 1993, although only minimally constrained (Table 1), suggests a model volume of $0.053 \, km^3$. The suggestion is that the MSH lava dome, at least at the time of the geodetic laser altimeter overflights in September of 1993, is an irregular landform, undergoing mass-wasting toward the north, and episodic exogenic construction in its central regions. The orthogonal laser altimeter cross-sections illustrate and document the irregular topographic character of the evolving summit lava dome; indeed, its surface ruggedness, as determined from analysis of laser altimeter echoes (Garvin et al. 1995) is remarkable, with several metres of vertical structure within 2 m diameter laser footprints. The dissimilarity between orthogonal cross-sections of a feature such as the MSH lava dome demonstrates the pitfalls associated with interpretation of one-dimensional cross-sections of complex volcanic landforms, and argues for more comprehensive and areally extensive laser altimeter datasets before definitive conclusions can be realized. Mathematic modelling methods, such as those presented later in this paper (Table 1), permit objective, albeit limited, interpretations of sparse datasets such as laser altimeter transects. NASA plans call for extensive laser altimeter topographic remote sensing of Mt. St. Helens in 1995, with acquisition of at least six different azimuths of multi-beam data in order to assess directional effects associated with high precision topographic cross-sections.

Table 1. *Details of cylindrical harmonic analysis method as it applies to volcanoes described in terms of their topography (cross-sections or DEM). The* $J_n()$ *and* $J_m()$ *denote the Bessel functions which are fitted to the topography*

Quantifying Shapes of Volcanoes

Cylindrical harmonic model approach

- Ideal for landforms with 'regular' topologies and circular symmetry (i.e. volcanoes).
- Cylindrical harmonics have circular symmetry, are orthogonal, and mathematically complete (with fast convergence).
- Surface cylindrical harmonics $f(r, \theta)$ are given by:

$$f(r, \theta) = \sum_{n \geq 0} \sum_{s \geq 0,1} [A_{n,s} \cos n\theta + (B_{n,s} \sin n\theta)] J_n(\lambda_s r)$$

where the λ_s represent the roots of the Bessel functions of order n.
- Once we have computed the coefficients (i.e. the $A_{n,s}$ and $B_{n,s}$ terms) for the cylindrical harmonics to model the surface relief of a volcano, we can use them to compute volumes, surface areas, etc.:

$$V = \int_{Z_{min}}^{Z_{max}} \int_0^1 \int_0^{2\pi} [A_{m,n} \cos(m\theta) + B_{m,n} \sin(m\theta)] J_m(\lambda r) r \, d\theta \, dr \, dz$$

where $r \, d\theta \, dr \, dz$ is an element of volume in cylindrical coordinates.

Cascades edifices

As part of the geodetic laser altimeter surveys of 1993, we acquired multiple edifice-scale topographic cross-sections of Mount Rainier (three), Mount Adams (two), and orthogonal profiles of Mount St. Helens (two). Examples of the resulting cross-sections are illustrated in Fig. 6. Representative examples are shown for Mt. Adams and Mt. Rainier, relative to the orthogonal pair for Mt. St. Helens. In addition, we have included a cross-sectional profile of the Icelandic Skjaldbreidur lava shield, acquired in 1991 (Garvin & Williams 1992). Skjaldbreidur is the type-locality of a basaltic lava shield volcano (Whitford-Stark 1975; Thorarinsson 1967; Walker 1965; Pike & Clow 1981; Garvin & Williams 1990) and is useful for comparison purposes because of its symmetric and simple topographic cross-section. Figure 6 illustrates the vast differences in shape and volume as one progresses from simple shields such as Skjald-breidur to dormant andesitic stratocones such as Mt. Adams and Mt. Rainier. Average flank slopes, computed for horizontal baselines of 2 to 4 m, range from 6.5° at lava shields to over 18° for less active stratocones such as Mt. Adams. The recently glacially sculpted summit of Mt. Rainier has probably lowered its effective average flank slope from over 20° to the observed 17.5°. We have de-termined the basal diameters of each of the volcanoes depicted in Fig. 6 on the basis ofthe largest inflection point in the gradient of the profile so that the estimate is purely objective. These estimates may vary from those determined on the basis of morpho-logic parameters and field measurements (Pike & Clow 1981; Hammond 1989). However, they provide a systematic basis for comparison, as do the numerically integrated (using the laser profiles) volumes. Evidence of major flank slumps and possible debris avalanche deposits can be observed in the SE to NW cross-section of Mt. Rainier, attesting to its potential for future hazards (Crandell & Mullineaux 1967; Tazieff & Sabroux 1983; Tilling 1989).

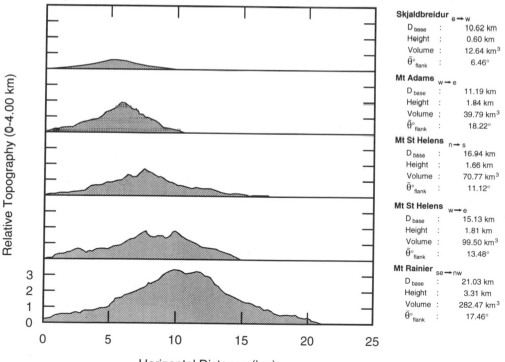

Fig. 6. Comparison of five laser altimeter topographic cross-sections of major volcanic edifices in the Cascades (lower four), and in Iceland (Skjaldbreidur, at top). Vertical scale is in 1000 m intervals between tick marks; horizontal axis is in 5 km intervals. Values listed at right are derived exclusively from the laser profiles and are for comparison purposes only.

One simple means of comparing high-resolution cross-sections of disparate edifices is illustrated in Fig. 7. In this case, the local slope distribution computed from each of the topographic cross-sections shown in Fig. 6 is presented in the form of a cumulative probability distribution. It is important to note that these slope values are computed using a very short baseline of less than 4 m. Thus, in the case of small escarpments the effective local slope as sampled with the laser altimeter's 2 m footprint could approximate 90°. The cumulative percentage of slopes greater than or equal to a given local slope listed on the horizontal axis for each of the four volcanoes depicted in Fig. 6 is plotted in Fig. 7 and the best-fitting power law relating each cumulative percentage to local slope is tabulated. The quality of the fit of the power law is indicated using an R^2 correlation coefficient; the closer the R^2 value is to 1.0, the better the correlation. The cumulative slope frequency distribution for the lava shield falls off rapidly with increasing local slope, as indicated by the power-law exponent of −1.2. In contrast, the three Cascades stratocones follow very different slope distributions, with Mount Rainier displaying the most rapid fall-off in local gradients (80% of its local slopes are less than 30°). Mount Adams, the most inactive of the three Cascades stratocones shows the least rapid fall-off in local slopes, with 80% of slopes less than 60°. These slope curves suggest that Rainier is transitional between the long-period dormancy of Mt. Adams, and the recent eruptive activity of Mt. St. Helens. Evidence suggests that Skjaldbreidur was formed in the past few thousands of years (Thorarinsson 1967; Walker 1965), and has retained a minimally eroded topographic expression. Figure 7 illustrates the kind of statistical analysis of local (and longer wavelength) slopes that may be of use in assessing the probability of future volcanic activity at major edifices for which detailed field surveys have not yet been undertaken.

Morphometric analysis

It is sometimes instructive to compare various volcanic landforms using simple 'shape' and size

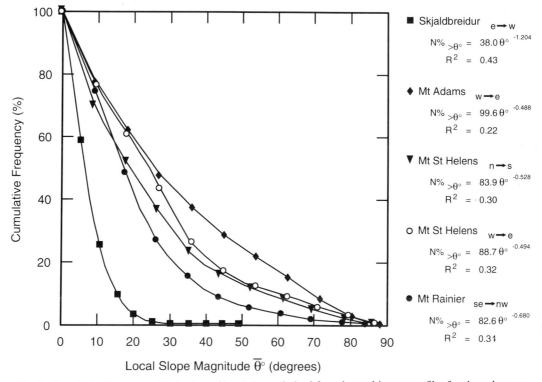

Fig. 7. Cumulative frequency distribution of local slopes derived from laser altimeter profiles for the volcanoes illustrated in Fig. 6. Each curve depicts the cumulative percentage of local slopes greater or equal to a given value of slope along the horizontal axis. Power-law fits are listed at right for each curve, as computed by least-squares regression methods. Correlation coefficients (R^2) closest to 1.0 indicate the best fits. See text for details.

parameters (Blake 1990; Pike & Clow 1981; Anderson & Fink 1990; Lacey *et al.* 1981). While we seek to develop more robust and physically motivated descriptors of volcano shape, we can use a simple parameter such as aspect ratio (height H divided by basal diameter D: H/D) to quantify 'shape'. Furthermore, it is relatively straightforward to estimate the volume of a discrete volcano, either from a topographic map or model or using simple numerical integration techniques (Garvin & Williams 1990, 1992). Blake (1990) and others have compared lava dome aspect H/D against inferred volume V in order to analyse behavioural differences between end-member morphologic varieties of such simple volcanoes. In Fig. 8 we have plotted H/D versus V for the Cascades volcanoes surveyed by means of laser altimetry (Figs 6 and 7), as well as with the general trends we have established for Icelandic table mountains and lava shields (Garvin & Williams 1995). The Icelandic trends (ITM and ILS in Fig. 8) are derived empirically from analysis of digital elevation model data for all of Iceland, and involve many tens of volcanoes; laser altimeter data have also been used to ensure validity (see Garvin & Williams 1992). The Cascades stratocones define a narrow, polygonal field in H/D versus V space, which appears to fall on the extrapolation of the trend displayed for classical Icelandic lava shields such as Skjaldbreidur. Such shields do not typically exceed about 100 km^3 in volume (or 20 km in basal diameter). The Icelandic table mountain empirical trend (ITM in Fig. 8) clearly illustrates how the effect of an eruption constraint such as ice can change the shape and volume productivity of simple basaltic volcanoes. Even the presence of summit glaciers on the Cascades stratocones has not influenced their volumetric growth to the extent that the ice sheet overburden has affected the table mountains. The plotted position of the Cascades stratocones in Fig. 8 suggests that these non-basaltic edifices none-theless display, to first order, shapes that resemble volumetrically scaled lava shields, many of which erupt monogenetically in a totally effusive manner. This observation sug-gests that in spite of the great precision of the laser altimeter topographic cross-sections for these volcanoes, simple shape parameters such as aspect (H/D) are inadequate to describe their physical properties.

On the basis of the results depicted in Fig. 8 we have developed a more rigorous mathema-tical approach for characterizing the two and three-dimensional shapes of volcanoes, as described in terms of topographic profiles or

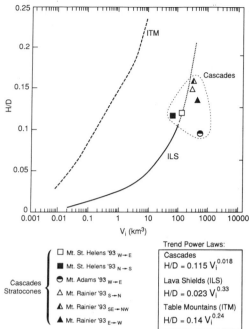

Volcanic Edifices: Morphometric Analysis

	Trend Power Laws:
	Cascades
Cascades Stratocones	$H/D = 0.115 \ V_i^{0.018}$
□ Mt. St. Helens '93 W→E	Lava Shields (ILS)
■ Mt. St. Helens '93 N→S	$H/D = 0.023 \ V_i^{0.33}$
◑ Mt. Adams '93 W→E	Table Mountains (ITM)
△ Mt. Rainier '93 S→N	$H/D = 0.14 \ V_i^{0.24}$
▲ Mt. Rainier '93 SE→NW	
▲ Mt. Rainier '93 E→W	

Fig. 8. Correlation of aspect ratio (H/D) against edifice volume V_i (in km^3) for Cascades stratocones measured with airborne laser altimetry (see Fig. 6). ITM trend is that derived empirically for table mountain volcanoes in Iceland from a DEM, and ILS is that for Icelandic lava shields derived in a similar manner. Cascades volcanoes field shown with dashed line. Power law trends relating H/D to volume V_i are listed in the box to the lower right. All three trends are statistically different, although the Cascades trend appears to follow the natural extrapolation of the lava shield trend to larger diameters. See text for details.

digital elevation models (Garvin *et al.* 1995). For the purposes of this investigation, we will only summarize the essence of the method and present two examples. Table 1 outlines the mathematical fundamentals of the approach we have adopted. We use surface cylindrical harmonics to model the topography of any volcano described in terms of a single profile, a set of profiles, or a three-dimensional digital elevation model or DEM. The method is particularly useful for parsimoniously reducing the tremendous data volume associated with a typical DEM for a volcano from millions of data values (Mouginis-Mark & Garbeil 1993) into a manageable set of a few tens of coefficents which fully describe the mathematical essence of the landform, in a process analogous to spherical harmonics as they are used to quantify the

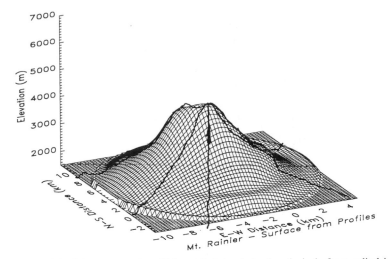

Fig. 9. 'Wire-frame' model of the topography of Mount Rainier derived exclusively from cylindrical harmonic analysis (degree 16 model) of three airborne laser altimeter profiles described in the text (note the three profiles superimposed). Vertical axis is relief in metres, and the two horizontal axes represent relative (to centre of the edifice) dimensions in E–W and N–S directions (in km). Surface area and volume data derived from the cylindrical harmonic model are as follows: SA = 194.3 km^2, and V = 169.76 km^3. See text and Table 1 for details.

overall shapes of entire planets. Essentially this technique makes use of Bessel functions to depict the shapes of cone-like objects in a cylindrical coordinate framework. The real advantage of this method for quantifying shapes of volcanoes is its objectivity; the cylindrical harmonics can be extended to a high enough degree and order to fit virtually any topographic surface, and from the derived coefficients volumes, surface areas, and other dimensional parameters can be directly computed (Table 1). Furthermore, if only a few topographic profiles are available, we can use cylindrical harmonics to model the entire three-dimensional shape of an edifice even without a uniform grid of elevation values (i.e. DEM). Figure 9 illustrates the three-dimensional topography of the upper 80% of the relief of Mt. Rainier as synthesized from cylindrical harmonics derived from only three independent geodetic airborne laser altimeter profiles. The model surface area and volume of the edifice can then be computed using straightforward mathematical methods (see Table 1). Figure 10 further illustrates the potential of this technique for MSH; in this case, a set of four independent 1990 laser altimeter transects have been used to model the upper kilometre of the edifice on the basis of a degree 9 cylindrical harmonic representation (i.e. over 30 coefficients). It is important to observe that the cylindrical harmonic approach is best suited for use with a complete DEM in order to minimize Bessel function fit errors; when it is used with

sparse data such as provided by laser altimeter cross-sections for MSH or Mt. Rainier (Figs 9, 10), it performs most reliably where the data density is highest, such as in the upper reaches of these edifices.

Using this technique with more than three cross-sections would of course reduce the spatial errors and permit development of a simple mathematical model for any complex volcanic edifice. The elegance of this approach lies in its absolute objectivity; one can display the amplitude spectrum from the cylindrical harmonics computed from the topography of any volcano and fully describe subtle shape variations in terms of only a few tens of coefficients. For example, in Fig. 11 cylindrical harmonic models of shield volcanoes on Earth (Skjaldbreidur), Mars (Olympus Mons), and Venus (Sif Mons) are illustrated, along with their relatively similar amplitude spectra. The major escarpment that surrounds the Olympus Mons vol-cano on Mars shows up in the higher order terms in the amplitude spectrum. Each of these models was computed on the basis of a DEM input dataset. We believe that using this approach in combination with laser altimetry and SAR interferometry could provide the basis for characterizing hazardous volcanoes relative to non-hazardous varieties in terms of their existing topographic characteristics. This approach has been adopted for a NASA-supported multi-year study of the topography of the summit region of Mt. Rainier, scheduled to commence in 1995.

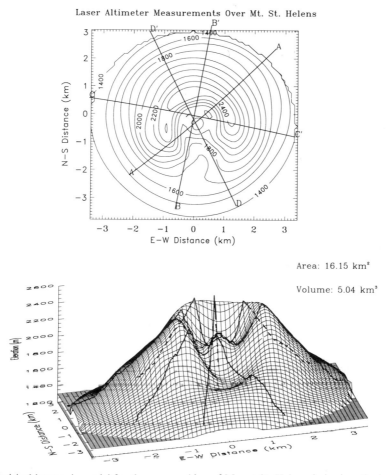

Fig. 10. Cylindrical harmonic model for the upper *c.* 1 km of Mount St. Helens derived on the basis of four independent 1990 geodetic laser altimeter cross-sections. A perspective view of the model result with the laser altimeter profiles used as input superimposed is illustrated at the bottom. A plan view of the horizontal location of the four laser altimeter profiles relative to the topography of the summit region of MSH is shown at top. Surface area and volume are also listed for that part of the edifice which has been modelled.

Summary

Airborne laser altimetry has been developed into a remote sensing tool of value in volcanological studies requiring detailed knowledge of local-scale topographic slopes. NASA airborne laser altimeter surveys of volcanoes in the Cascades mountains of the northwestern US have been used to document erosion at the MSH summit lava dome, as well as edifice slope distributions that could be related to the eruptive histories of now dormant volcanoes such as Mt. Rainier. Geodetic-quality airborne laser altimetry now offers the possibility of monitoring the sub-metre (horizontal and vertical) topographic characteristics of active and recently active volcanoes at sufficient resolution to potentially document zones at which slope failure could occur (McGuire 1994). Annual topographic surveys of active or dangerous volcanoes could be arranged using airborne laser altimetry, perhaps in combination with airborne and spaceborne interferometric SAR, to monitor changes associated with potential eruptive activity or associated with ongoing eruptions. Modelling the detailed shapes of volcanoes using simple parameters such as aspect ratio (H/D) may be misleading, and more rigorous mathematical

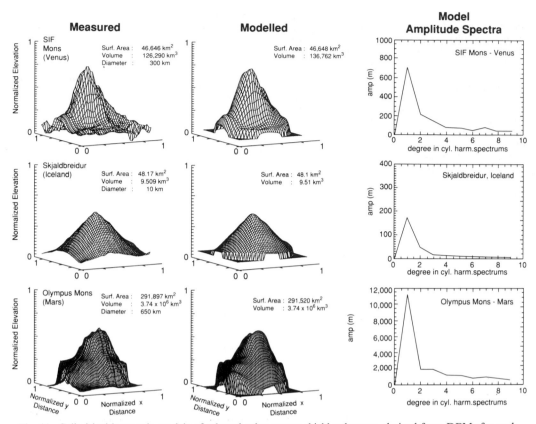

Fig. 11. Cylindrical harmonic models of selected solar system shield volcanoes, derived from DEMs for each volcano. In each case, the raw DEM data are illustrated in wire-frame form at left, while the model result is shown in the middle, also in wire-frame style. Amplitude spectra are plotted at right. The topographic data are plotted in normalized format (relative to the maximum relief and basal dimensions of each edifice). Sif Mons (top) is on Venus, and the DEM is from the Magellan global altimetry data. Skjaldbreidur (Earth: Iceland) is in the middle, and a DEM derived from a digitized 1 : 250 000 topographic map has been used for this lava shield. Olympus Mons (Mars) is illustrated below; a DEM produced by the US Geological Survey at 1 km horizontal resolution has been used in this case. Note the basic similarity of the amplitude spectra for each volcano. Degree and order 9×5 models were used in all three cases. Surface area and volume statistics are listed adjacent to the input DEMs and the models.

methods are suggested. Cylindrical harmonics fitted to the topographic cross-sections or to DEM of volcanoes offer an improved method for quantifying volcano shapes and should be applied in studies of potentially dangerous volcanoes such as Mt. Rainier and others. Geodetic airborne laser altimetry should evolve to include swath-mapping (however limited) capabilities to ensure that repeat overflights can revisit previously measured regions.

Aircraft laser altimetry of volcanoes would never have been possible without the engineering contributions of Jack L. Bufton, James B. Abshire, and most recently J. Bryan Blair, all of NASA's Goddard Space Flight Center. Scientific contributions to aircraft laser altimetry in volcanology have largely involved Richard S. Williams Jr of the US Geological Survey, with additional assistance from David J. Harding of NASA/GSFC and James Frawley of Herring Bay Geophysics. The NASA airborne laser altimetry effort with respect to volcanoes has been supported by P. J. Mouginis-Mark, M. Baltuck, and most recently by Earnie Paylor, of NASA's Solid Earth Processes Branch. We are grateful for their support of these efforts since 1986, under RTOP 465-44-03, and 465-67-02. Flight operations have been expertly handled by David Pierce of NASA's Wallops Flight Facility, and pilots Virgil Rabine, John Riley, and Robert Gidge have been instrumental in acquiring the data we sought using sensors with 1–2 m wide swaths. Bill

Krabill and colleagues of NASA/WFF have developed the kinematic GPS techniques needed to provide geodetic quality data. David Rabine has expertly reduced much of the GPS and laser altimeter data in recent years. James J. Frawley (Herring Bay Geophysics) has developed unique visualization and shape modelling codes for use in volcano studies over the years. M. Taylor (SSAI) has developed laser altimeter profile analysis tools that have provided many of the results illustrated in this paper. W. Lazenby (NASA/WFF) has provided outstanding photographic support of all of our volcano flight missions over the years. David E. Smith (NASA/GSFC) has encouraged these efforts from the outset, and we are grateful for his support. Finally, Cindy, newly born Zachary Kellen, and Georgie (Bouvier des Flandres) Garvin have supported the author on many occasions throughout this research.

References

ANDERSON, S. W. & FINK, J. H. 1990. The development and distribution of surface textures at the Mount St. Helens Dome. *In*: FINK, J. H. (ed.) *Lava Flows and Domes*. Springer-Verlag, New York, 25–46.

BALOGA, S. 1987. Lava flows as kinematic waves. *Journal of Geophysical Research*, **92**, 9271–9279.

BECKER, G. F. 1885. The geometric forms of volcanic cones and the elastic limits of lava. *American Journal of Science*, **30**, 293–382.

BLAIR, J. B., COYLE, D. B., BUFTON, J. L., & HARDING, D. J. 1994. Optimization of an airborne laser altimeter for remote sensing of vegetation and tree canopies. *International Geology And Remote Sensing Symposium (IGARSS) 1994 Digest*, Volume **II**, 939–941.

BLAKE, S. 1990. Viscoplastic models of lava domes. *In*: FINK, J. H. (ed.) *Lava Flows and Domes*. Springer-Verlag, New York, 88–126..

BUFTON, J. L. 1989. Laser altimetry measurements from aircraft and spacecraft. *Proceedings of the IEEE*, **77**, 463–477.

——, GARVIN, J. B., CAVANAUGH, J. F., RAMOS-IZQUIERDO, L., CLEM, T. D., & KRABILL, W. B. 1991. Airborne lidar for profiling of surface topography. *Optical Engineering*, **30**, 72–78.

BVSP 1981. *Basaltic Volcanism on the Terrestrial Planets*. Pergamon, New York.

CHADWICK, W. W. & SWANSON, D. A. 1989. Thrust faults and related structures in the crater floor of Mount St. Helens volcano, Washington. *Geological Society of America Bulletin*, **101**, 1507–1519.

CRANDELL, D. R. & MULLINEAUX, D. R. 1967. *Volcanic Hazards at Mt. Rainier*. US Geological Survey Bulletin, **1238.**

EVANS, D. L., FARR, T., ZEBKER, H., VAN ZYL, J. & MOUGINIS-MARK, P. J. 1992. Radar interferometry studies of the Earth's topography. *EOS, Transactions of the American Geophysical Union*, **73**(52), 553–558.

GARVIN, J. B. 1993. Mapping New and Old Worlds with Laser Altimetry. *Photonics Spectra*, **37**, 67–75.

—— & BUFTON, J. L. 1992. Lunar orbital laser altimeter observations for lunar base site selection, in *NASA CR-3166*, Vol. **I**, 209–218.

—— & WILLIAMS, R. S. JR. 1990. Small domes on Venus: Probable analogs of Icelandic lava shields. *Geophysical Research Letters*, **17**, 1381–1384.

—— & ——1992. Remote sensing studies of the geomorphology of Surtsey, 1987–1991. *Journal of the Surtsey Research Society*, **X**, 57–81.

——, HARDING, D. J., BLAIR, J. B. & BUFTON, J. L. 1995. Determination of planetary surface vertical structure at meter scales using laser altimeter echo recovery, *EOS, Transactions of American Geophysical Union, Spring 1995 Meeting*, **76**(17), 192.

HAMMOND, P. E. 1989. Guide to the geology of the Cascade Range (IGC Field Trip T306), *In: Sedimentation and Tectonics of Western N. America*, Vol. **1**, 28th International Geological Congress, Washington, DC.

HOLCOMB, R. T. & COLONY, W. E. 1987. Large scale maps of a growing lava dome, Mount St. Helens, Washington (abstract). *International Union of Geology and Geophysics (IUGG) Assembly XIX Abstracts*, Vol. **2**, 417.

LACEY, A., OCKENDON, J. R. & TURCOTTE, D. L. 1981. On the geometrical form of volcanoes. *Earth and Planetary Science Letters*, **54**, 139–143.

McGUIRE, W. J. (ed.) 1994. *Volcano Instability*. Abstract volume for Symposium held at Geological Society of London, 16–17 May 1994, (University College London).

——, KILBURN, C. & J. MURRAY, (eds) 1995. *Monitoring Active Volcanoes: Strategies, Procedures, and Techniques*, UCL Press, London.

MOUGINIS-MARK, P. J. & GARBEIL, H. 1993. Digital topography of volcanoes from radar interferometry; An example from Mt. Vesuvius, Italy. *Bulletin of Volcanology*, **55**. 566.

PIKE, R. J. & CLOW, G. 1981. *Revised classification of terrestrial volcanoes and catalog of topographic dimensions, with new results on edifice volume*, US Geological Survey Open File Report **81–1039**.

SWANSON, D. A. & HOLCOMB, R. T. 1990. Regularities in growth of the Mount St. Helens dacite dome, 1980–1986. *In*: Fink J. H. (ed.) *Lava Flows and Domes*. Springer-Verlag, New York, 3–24.

TAZIEFF, H. & SABROUX, J.-C. 1983. *Forecasting Volcanic Events*. Elsevier, Amsterdam.

THORARINSSON, S. 1967. Some problems of volcanism in Iceland. *Geologische Rundschau*, **57**, 1–20.

TILLING, R. I. (ed.) 1989. *Volcanic Hazards*. American Geophysical Union, Washington, DC.

WALKER, G. P. L. 1965. Some aspects of Quaternary volcanism in Iceland. *Leicester Literary and Philosophical Society Transactions*, **59**, 25–40.

WHITFORD-STARK, J. L. 1975. Shield volcanoes. *In*: FIELDER, G. & WILSON, L. (eds) *Volcanoes of the Earth, Moon, and Mars*. St. Martins Press, New York, 66–74.

WILLIAMS, H. 1932. The history and character of volcanic domes. *Bulletin of the Department of Geological Sciences, Univ. of California Publication*, **21**, 51–146.

ZEBKER, H. MADSEN, S., MARTIN, J., WHEELER, K., MILLER, T., YOUNG, Y., ALBERTI, G., VETRELLA, S. & CUCCI, A. 1992. The TOPSAR interferometric radar topographic mapping instrument. *IEEE Transactions: Geoscience and Remote Sensing*, **30**, 933–940.

Coastal elevation changes in eastern Sicily: implications for volcano instability at Mount Etna

C. FIRTH[1], I. STEWART[1], W. J. MCGUIRE[2,3], S. KERSHAW[1]
& C. VITA-FINZI[2]

[1] Neotectonics Research Centre, Division of Geography & Geology, Brunel University,
Borough Road, Isleworth, London TW7 5DU, UK
[2] Department of Geological Sciences, University College London, Gower Street,
London WC1E 6BT, UK
[3] Centre for Volcanic Research, Cheltenham & Gloucester College HE, Francis Close Hall,
Swindon Road, Cheltenham GL50 4AZ, UK

Abstract: The eastern flank of Mount Etna, Sicily has been recognized as being unstable, and three contrasting models have been proposed to account for this phenomenon, these being deep-seated spreading, shallow sliding and tectonic block movements. These models are examined by making reference to the rates and patterns of crustal movement along the eastern coastline of Sicily as determined from palaeoshoreline data. The south-eastern coastline of Sicily (Portopalo to Catania) provides no evidence of Holocene emergence. In contrast the volcanic coastline (Catania to Capo Schiso) and the northeastern shoreline (Taormina to Milazzo) display widespread evidence of coastal emergence. Radiocarbon dated remains indicate that both the volcano and northeastern Sicily have been uplifted at a rate exceeding $1.5\,\mathrm{mm\,a^{-1}}$ during Holocene times, although more recent rates of uplift may have been greater. The pattern of uplift suggests that the northeastern coastline of Sicily, including the volcanic edifice, is apparently uplifting as a coherent unit, with superficial flank movements being superimposed on a regionally uplifting sub-volcanic basement.

Evidence from structural, morphological and geophysical studies indicate that a 30 km wide sector of the eastern flank of Mount Etna, Sicily, is unstable and slumping seaward. Guest *et al.* (1984) first drew attention to the possibility that the eastern slopes of the volcano might be sliding slowly seaward, and Hughes *et al.* (1990) illustrated how this behaviour was resulting in longer duration eruptions in this sector of the volcano. Sliding has clearly been operating throughout historic and late prehistoric times, and while the precise timing of the initiation of instability within the lifecycle of the volcano remains to be established, it is likely to have persisted over at least tens of thousands of years. Although the extent and kinematics of this mobile sector are now reasonably well resolved, being delineated to the north and south by active strike-slip fault zones (sinistral and dextral, respectively) and to the west by eastward-directed extension along persistent volcanic rift zones (Fig. 1), the mechanisms driving flank collapse remain contentious. In particular, three contrasting models have been proposed: (1) deep-seated spreading, (2) shallow sliding, and (3) tectonic block movements.

In this paper we use evidence for late Quaternary coastal elevation changes on the eastern coast of Sicily to compare the magnitudes, rates and patterns of crustal movements on the volcanic edifice with those affecting the adjacent basement blocks. The use of palaeoshorelines represents a new approach to the study of volcano instability at Mount Etna and yields data which set current instability models in the context of a regionally deforming tectonic framework.

Volcano instability models for Mount Etna: an overview

Although gravitational instability is recognized as an inherent feature of many terrestrial and planetary volcanoes, the extent to which this mechanism is involved in edifice collapse at Mount Etna is disputed. For example, according to a 'deep-seated' spreading model (Borgia *et al.* 1992; Borgia 1994), both the volcanic edifice and its uppermost basement are spreading eastwards under gravity along a thrust fault at depth (*c.* 5 km) (Fig. 2a). Within the framework of this model, spreading produces extensional structures in the summit region and compressional deformation at the base of the volcano, but within the sliding block internal deformation accommodates movement along the deeper décollement. An alternative gravitational mechanism is proposed by Lo Giudice & Rasà (1986, 1992), who

From McGuire, W. J., Jones, A. P. & Neuberg, J. (eds) 1996, *Volcano Instability on the Earth and Other Planets*, Geological Society Special Publication No. 110, pp. 153–167.

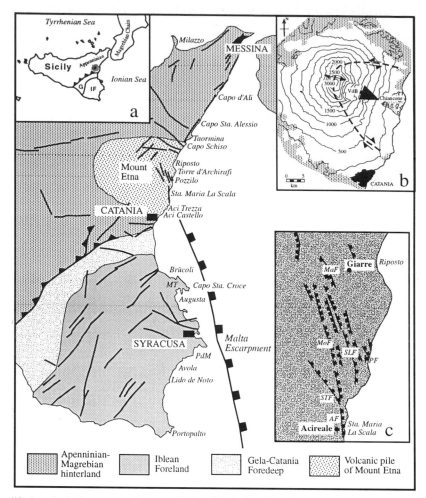

Fig. 1. Simplified geological structure of eastern Sicily with the location of the main coastal sites listed in italics (*MT*, Monte Tauro Peninsula, *PdM*, Penisola della Maddalena). Active faults denoted as solid lines; the line with triangular barbs delimits a major thrust fault. Inset map (**a**) shows the regional geological setting (G, Gela-Catania Foredeep; IF, Iblean Foreland). Modified from CNR-PFG (1985). Inset map (**b**) shows the detailed morphology of the volcano. The thick dashed lines delimit the mobile sector, with the general direction of flank movement indicated by the solid arrow. The main expressions of instability within the mobile zone are the amphitheatre-like Valle del Bove (VdB) and the extensive fanglomerate deposit (the Chiancone). Heavy stippled ornament shows the outcropping sub-Etnean sedimentary basement. Inset map (**c**) shows the Timpe fault zone, a network of normal fault strands (solid square barbs denote downthrown side) comprising the Acireale Fault (AF), the Santa Tecla Fault (STF), the Moscarello Fault (MoF), the Santa Leonardello Fault (SLF), the Macchia Fault (MaF) and the Pozzillo Fault (PF).

consider the uppermost portion of Etna's eastern flank to be a thin unstable slice which is structurally detached from the main volcanic body at a shallow level (<3 km) and, as a result, is sliding seaward under its own weight (Fig. 2b). Such 'shallow sliding' is accommodated by brittle deformation along seismotectonic lines which, although related to regional tectonic axes, are not dynamically coupled to deeper fault movements. Instead, such 'thin-skinned' sliding (i.e. not

involving the sub-volcanic basement) results in distributed near-surface seismicity, pervasive ground fracturing and aseismic creep on faults (Rasa *et al.* 1996).

Despite this recent emphasis on gravity as a principal driving force for edifice collapse, the location of Mount Etna at the intersection of a number of major active fault zones has long focused attention on the role of tectonic movements in the volcano's long-term behaviour

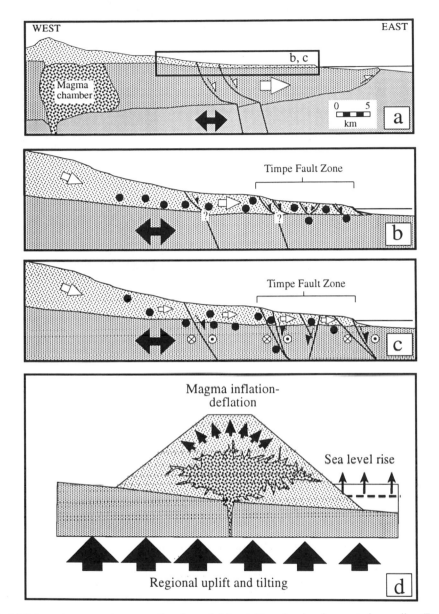

Fig. 2. (a) Schematic west-east cross-section through Mount Etna showing deep-seated spreading (Borgia *et al.* 1992, fig. 3c) in which the volcanic pile and uppermost sub-Etnean basement are spreading eastwards (white arrow) along a low-angle thrust which emerges seaward as a shallow fault-propagation fold. Local extensional structures (the Timpe) are attributed to differential compaction as it is thrust over a regionally extending basement (divergent black arrows). See Fig. 1 for key to ornamentation. (b) Schematic west–east cross-section of the area shown in (a) and illustrating the 'shallow sliding' scenario. In this second scenario, shallow earthquakes (solid circles) and superficial fault movements (small arrows) combine to accommodate thin-skinned gravitational collapse of a volcanic pile which is dynamically decoupled from a regionally extending basement. (c) Schematic west–east cross-section of the area shown in (a) and illustrating the tectonic block movements scenario. In this third scenario, earthquakes are more deep-seated and aligned along basement faults, and fault movements involve both normal and dextral strike-slip. Instability occurs by differential sliding within independent crustal blocks, rather than on a single décollement surface as in (b). (d) Schematic section highlighting other potential instability mechanisms at Mount Etna. See text for explanation.

(Cristofolini *et al.* 1977; Ghisetti & Vezzani 1982; Lo Giudice *et al.* 1982). The Timpe fault zone (Fig. 2c), widely regarded as the landward prolongation of a major extensional structure (the Malta Escarpment), is viewed by some workers as responsible for the significant uplift of the Etnean area (Kieffer 1972; Adorni & Carveni 1993). Although significant dextral strike-slip movement is apparent along the Timpe fault zone (Kieffer 1972; Stewart *et al.* 1993), prominent topographic escarpments ('Timpe'), ranging from 20–30 m in height where the fault zone is distributed, to 180 m where the fault zone is more localized, testify to differential vertical movements of Mount Etna's eastern flank. The alignment of both shallow and more deep-seated (<5 km) earthquake activity along the Timpe, and related structures (Pantane *et al.* 1994; Montalto *et al.* 1996) suggests that these fault zones take up regional deformation, rather than being local accommodation structures (e.g. Borgia *et al.* 1992) or shallow detached phenomena (Rasa *et al.* 1996). Furthermore, according to Kieffer (1972), the dislocation of lahar units related to prehistoric (post-Trifoglietto) volcanic collapse indicates that violent eruptive activity is intimately associated with tectonic movements, suggesting a link (direct or indirect) with internal volcanic processes. As a result, a third possible instability model involves tectonic uplift and dislocation along active transtensional fault zones (Kieffer 1977, 1985), accompanied perhaps by superficial sliding on independent shallow slip surfaces (Montalto *et al.* 1996) rather than on the single shallow décollement proposed by Lo Giudice & Rasa (1992).

In addition to these relatively simple though conflicting scenarios, three other potential instability mechanisms may operate at Mount Etna. Firstly, although the nature of high-level magma storage remains a matter of conjecture (e.g. Chester *et al.* 1985; Hirn *et al.* 1991), some workers note that edifice swelling related to magma emplacement would also contribute to flank instability (Lo Giudice & Rasa 1992; Montalto *et al.* 1996) (Fig. 2d). While this contribution is speculative, a second mechanism, that of regional uplift of the volcanic edifice and its basement, is apparent from the present-day exposure of pre-Etnean Quaternary marine clays at elevations of up to 750 m on the flanks of Mount Etna (Labaume *et al.* 1990). Evidence of recent coastal emergence suggests that uplift of the Etnean area continues at the present day (Platania 1904; Blanc & Molinier 1955; Kieffer 1972). As well as increasing the general potential for gravitational instability, regional uplift has resulted in the seaward tilting of the volcanic

pile, thereby further promoting its eastward-directed collapse (Fig. 2d). A third but as yet equally poorly constrained factor is the role of sea-level change.

Resolving the pattern of late Quaternary relative sea-level movements along Mount Etna's adjacent coastline is important for several reasons. Firstly, sea-level changes themselves may contribute to flank instability, either directly by edifice erosion or debuttressing, or indirectly by crustal loading and unloading in response to changing ocean volumes (McGuire 1992). Secondly, sea level serves as a useful reference datum with which to compare contemporary rates and magnitudes of movements of both the volcanic edifice and its underlying basement. As a result, the incidence of coastal emergence or submergence along Sicily's eastern

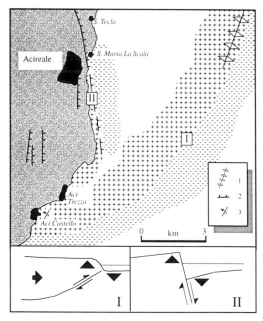

Fig. 3. Map view illustration of expected patterns of coastal uplift (crosses) and subsidence (dashes) associated with contrasting modes of flank movement within the southeastern sector of Mount Etna's mobile zone. In the first scenario (**I**), active growth of a fault-propagation fold at the leading edge of the deep sliding wedge produces inferred domal uplift along an arcuate belt from Aci Castello to a NE–SW trending offshore ridge (Borgia *et al.* 1992). Uplift dissipates northwards away from the active fold trace, while subsidence predominates to the south. In the second scenario (**II**), uplift occurs in the footwall of the coastal-bounding Acireale fault, resulting in the formation of a steep 40 m high coastal escarpment and associated subsidence in its immediate hangingwall (Kieffer 1985).

shoreline provides a potential means of discriminating whether uplift of the Etnean area reflects regional geodynamics, localized fault movements, gravity-induced sliding or spreading, or internal magma-related volcanic deformation. Finally, the coastal record constitutes a framework within which the conflicting models discussed above may be evaluated. For example, coastal uplift documented at Aci Trezza may be explained in terms of coseismic elevation of the footwall of the Timpe fault zone (Kieffer 1972). Alternatively, Borgia *et al.* (1992) attribute uplift of this area to axial doming above an alleged emerging fault-propagation fold invoked to mark the leading edge of 'deep-seated spreading' and to explain possibly overturned pillow lavas at Aci Castello. Although both schemes predict crustal uplift at Aci Trezza, the wider pattern of relative sea-level change predicted by these contrasting mechanisms is very different (Fig. 3).

In the following section we demonstrate how data on the altitude and form of low-level marine notches and platforms, combined with analysis and dating of elevated palaeoshoreline fauna, can elucidate the spatial and temporal pattern of shoreline changes along the eastern coast of Sicily over recent millenia.

Coastal elevation changes in eastern Sicily

It has long been recognized that relict (raised or submerged) marine features provide an ideal opportunity to determine crustal movements in coastal areas (e.g. Fairbridge 1961). The standard procedure (e.g. Shennan 1987) is to reconstruct the relative sea-level history of the area (relative altitude of the sea at known times) and then compare this with a eustatic (global) sea-level curve in order to determine the extent and rates of crustal movement during the period in question. The procedure is hampered by the fact that to date it has proved impossible to determine a precise global sea-level curve (Kidson 1982) or even regional curves (Pirazzoli 1991). However, if a general global eustatic curve, such as the one derived by Fairbanks (1989), is adopted, regional variations in crustal uplift can be determined.

Morphological and biological sea-level indicators

Although a wide range of coastal features (morphological and biological) has been used in such studies (e.g. Laborel & Laborel-Deugen 1994), it has been recognized that care needs to be adopted in the interpretation and utilization of such data (van de Plassche 1986). It is generally accepted that accurate shoreline changes can only be determined if the relict features can be related to former sea levels and dated. For example, features such as notches in sheltered locations or certain species of coralline algae and vermetids maintain a consistent relationship to mean sea level and so prove to be good indicators of former sea levels.

Mediterranean coastlines are particularly suited to palaeoshoreline studies since a wide variety of marine features develop in a narrow altitude band due to the restricted tidal range (0.2–0.5 m). This altitude band is even more restricted in locations sheltered from storm wave activity. A variety of palaeoshoreline features were identified from the coast of eastern Sicily, including marine notches, the boreholes of the mollusc *Lithophaga,* coralline algal ridges (trottoir) and vermetid gastropod constructions. The relationship of these key morphological and biological features to mean sea level is illustrated in Fig. 4; the apices of notches and the upper surfaces of coralline algal ridges and vermetid constructions generally coincide with mean sea level while the highest *Lithophaga* borings delimit the low tide level. Those interested in the detailed use of these phenomena to reconstruct shoreline movements are directed to Van de Plassche (1986) and Laborel & Laborel-Deugen (1994).

The present study is based on a field survey of the entire eastern coast of Sicily (from Portopalo in the south to Milazzo in the north). Large sections of the coast were examined, revealing a number of coastal sites where relict notches, combined with the upper limit of biotic sea-level indicators, permit relative sea-level movements to be determined. Where marine notches were identified, detailed profiles of the cliffs were produced, using either an Electronic Distance Measuring (EDM) total station or a tape measure and Abney level. In the latter case, profile segments as short as 0.05 m were measured. In each case the profile was related to present sea level or present mean sea level as determined from morphological (active notches) or biological (active algal and vermetid reefs) evidence. The location of *Lithophaga* borings, vermetid gastropod constructions and coralline algal ridges along these profiles was also noted as was their general lithological and structural setting. At other sites, a sketch profile of the cliff-line was produced and then the altitude of selected features (*Lithophaga* borings, coral and shell samples) above mean sea level was determined by using an EDM total station, an Abney level survey or a hand-held

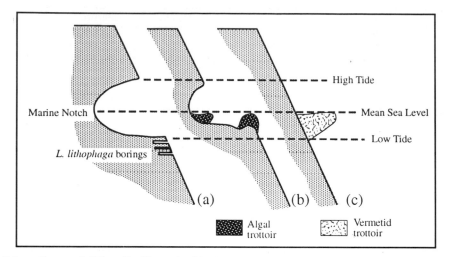

Fig. 4. Schematic coastal cliff profiles illustrating idealized relationship of (**a**) notches and *Lithophaga* borings, (**b**) coralline algal ridges (trottoir), and (**c**) vermetid constructions to various marine levels.

digital barometer. At some of these sites, a detailed analysis of the Quaternary sedimentary deposits was undertaken, making reference to clast size, shape and sorting.

The shoreline elevation data determined from each site were then compared with the eustatic sea-level curve of Fairbanks (1989). Such a comparison allows estimates to be made of the rates of crustal movements and, in particular, highlight any relative differences in coastal elevation changes across the region.

Here we consider Sicily's eastern coastline in terms of three contrasting geological sections. The first section, from Portopalo to Catania, corresponds to the eastern edge of the Iblean foreland, a thick post-Triassic carbonate platform bounded offshore by the Malta Escarpment, and, further north, to the marine limit of a Pliocene–Quaternary filled tectonic depression (the 'Gela-Catania Foredeep'). The second section, from Catania to Capo Schiso, comprises the volcanic coastline of Mount Etna's eastern flank, including the large mobile sector of the volcano. The third section, from Taormina to Milazzo, is set within the sub-Etnean hinterland of the Apenninian–Maghrebian mountain chain. All the localities discussed here are shown on Fig. 1.

The southern coastline: Portopalo to Catania

A range of palaeoshoreline features, including raised beaches, abrasion platforms, marine caves and erosional strandlines, have been documented to the south of Catania, particularly in the coastal strip between Syracusa (Di Grande & Raimondo 1982) and the Monte Tauro peninsula north of Augusta (Bordonaro *et al.* 1984). Here at least six elevated marine levels are recognized, with the higher levels attributed to Pliocene to Lower Pleistocene stillstands, while the lower two palaeoshorelines are interpreted as Tyrrhenian (late Pleistocene) in age (Bordonaro *et al.* 1984). These multiple shorelines result in a stepped coastal morphology which is particularly well developed along the Mount Tauro peninsula, where the modern cliffs are capped by a broad (up to 500 m wide) raised platform which is backed by an extensively degraded marine cliffline. At Capo St. Croce, at the southern end of Monte Tauro peninsula, a staircase sequence of notches, benches and shoreline deposits is elevated in the footwall of an emergent normal fault (340/70°E), and extends to a height of 15 m above present-day sea level (Fig. 5). The fault plane, however, is misleadingly fresh, being undercut by a well-defined notch and unconformably overlain by cemented sands and colluvium, demonstrating that it has not been active recently. Nearby, marine deposits bearing the diagnostic Tyrrhenian fauna *Strombus bubonius* are found within only a few metres of present day sea-level while Holocene marine phenomena are absent (Di Grande & Neri 1988), indicating that the emergent shoreline levels at this site are late Pleistocene in age.

According to Di Grande (pers. comm.) a decade of intensive field surveys along the

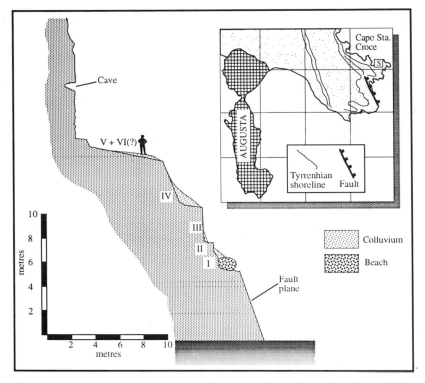

Fig. 5. Detailed profile of series of coastal notches (I–VI) developed in the immediate footwall of a normal fault at Capo Santa Croce, near Augusta. Inset map shows the location and orientation of the fault, the positions of inferred Tyrrhenian shorelines and the site of *Strombus bubonius* shells (S) indicative of Tyrrhenian deposits (after Di Grande & Neri 1988, Fig. 1).

southern coastline has failed to reveal emergent Holocene shorelines. Although the long-term pattern recorded by relict Pleistocene shorelines is one of net tectonic emergence, the pattern revealed by archaeological and historical evidence is one of marine inundation. The remains of the Roman port of Syracusa (Schmiedt 1972 cited in Mulargia *et al.* 1991), for example, together with Greek–Roman stone quarries at Maddalena Peninsula (Di Grande & Raimondo 1982) and just north of Portopalo are presently found below sea level. The extent to which net submergence during recent millenia reflects rises in eustatic sea level or crustal subsidence can not be ascertained, but it is clear that little or no tectonic uplift has been experienced during Holocene times.

The volcanic coastline: Catania to Capo Schiso

The volcanic coastline of Mount Etna is not ideal for the preservation of relict marine features, with modern lavas burying much of the coastal stratigraphy and the resulting rocks being unsuitable hosts for marine fauna. Furthermore, it is often difficult to discriminate between erosional marine forms (e.g. notches, erosional surfaces) and primary volcanic forms, such as the tops of lava flows and hollows related to former lava tubes. Despite these difficulties, coastal elevation changes have been documented at various points along the volcanic coastline. Kieffer (1972), for example, noted raised beaches at Pozzillo, where a 15 m high terrace was cut into mid-Holocene deposits, and at Aci Castello, where a pebbly beach is surmounted by a lava flow dating from AD 1169. Within that lava flow itself, Platania (1904) described coralline-encrusted marine shells at a height of 5.4 m inferring an average historical emergence of 7.5 mm a^{-1}. Recent coastal emergence is also inferred by pottery found in marine deposits at a height of 2 m at Acireale and 3 m at Capo Schiso, the latter sherds dating from 700–400 BC (Kieffer 1972). In contrast, according to Platania (1904), submerged roads and ancient buildings on the coastal strip between Torre d'Archirafi and Riposto testify to historical

(a)

(b)

(c)

(d)

(e)

(f)

subsidence, as does the presence of once emergent rocks which, at the turn of the century, were again found below sea level.

In addition to these previous accounts, we report raised notches and associated marine deposits at a number of sites, principally Aci Castello, Aci Trezza, Sta. Maria La Scala, and Capo Schiso (Fig. 1). At Aci Castello, for example, shallow (<0.5 m deep) raised notches occur at 1.75 and 2.9 m above mean sea level, these being fronted by a sloping beach. Both notches are partially infilled with encrustations of coralline algae. Similarly at Capo Schiso, shallow raised notches infilled with algae and vermetids occur at 0.9 and 2.0 m above mean sea level, respectively. The age of organic remains collected from these two sites is still to be determined, but the shape of the notches (with well developed roofs but poorly defined floors) suggests that relative sea level has been falling at these sites (Pirazzoli 1986), interrupted by periods of sea-level stability during which the notches developed.

A site where elevated marine deposits have long been recognized (e.g. Lyell 1858; Platania 1904) is at Aci Trezza, where a group of basalt pinnacles (the Faraglioni or Isole dei Ciclopi) is partly covered by a reef deposit containing *Spondylus* and other molluscs as well as vermetid material, and rises to 6.5 m above sea level (Fig. 6b). The reef deposit has been bored by *Lithophaga* to a maximum height of 6 m and exhibits multiple erosional under-cuts that reflect the combined effect of wave action and weathering in the splash zone. Prominent and consistent erosional levels, however, are displayed at elevations of 0.5, 1.0, 2.0, 2.5 and 3.8 m (Fig. 7).

Kieffer (1972) had previously reported from the coast around Aci Trezza algal concretions at heights up to 8 m containing molluscs whose modern counterparts live at depths of as much as 100 m below sea level. On balance, Kieffer concluded that there had been as much as 15 m emergence. Specimens of *Spondylus gaederopus* 3–6 m above sea level yielded a ^{14}C age of 5900 + 120 a BP. According to Kieffer (1972) X-ray analysis showed that these specimens contained as much as 25% calcite, consistent with the mixed mineralogy of the genus, and therefore indicating no recrystallization. Despite this, the possibility exists that the high calcite content indicates that some aragonite replacement is apparent and the age is thus probably a minimum. The result, however, is comparable with ages of in situ *Lithophaga* shells dated by Accelerator Mass Spectrometry (Table 1) and reported in Stewart et al. (1993). The results suggested that Aci Trezza had experienced 6–11 m of emergence during the last 7000 years (the ambiguity stemmed, as is often the case, from uncertainty over the eustatic correction to be applied).

Here we report an additional age determination from Aci Trezza, from in situ *Lithophaga* shells at a height of 1.55 m (Table 1). In addition, the previous age data have been corrected for isotopic fractionation to a value of $\delta^{13}C = 0$‰ and calibrated to calendar years using the data of Stuiver & Reimer (1993) and corrected for sea-level changes using the global data of Fairbanks (1989). The data now indicate uplift rates of 1.8–3.0 mm a^{-1}.

Fig. 6. (a) View looking northwest along an exhumed fault plane at Capo Sta. Croce, near Augusta. In the emergent footwall of the fault are a series of erosional benches draped largely in colluvial debris but with a marine beach deposit (B) occupying a prominent notch immediately above the 7 m high fault plane. A well-defined notch is currently developing at the base of the fault plane in relation to present-day sea level. See profile in Fig. 5. (b) Basaltic stack at Aci Trezza encrusted by a carbonate reef carapace up to a height of 7 m above sea level. The reef comprises mollusc and vermetid material and is extensively bored by *Lithophaga*, numerous shells of which remain in growth position. Radiocarbon dating of these shells indicates a time-averaged uplift rate of 2.6 mm a^{-1} over the last 8000 years. Figure gives indicative scale. (c) General view of the bay at Mazzaro, immediately east of Taormina, where a series of shallow notches have developed on the steep and sheltered limestone cliffs. The upper notch can be traced around the coastline at an altitude of 4.3–4.8 m above present mean sea level and, on the dated coral sample nearby (see (d)), is thought to be around 4300 years old. Below this a series of shallow notches are present at 3.8 m 1.6 m and 0.9 m above mean sea level. (d) Part of a branching coral colony of *Cladocora caespitosa* within a matrix of quartz clasts and carbonate-clay matrix, collected at 3.4 m above sea level from Isola Bella bay, east of Taormina (see Profile A in Fig. 8). The coral displays a well-preserved internal structure, with X-ray analysis revealing no recrystallisation, and was dated by first-order radiocarbon assay as 4295 ± 205 a BP. (e) A limestone block immediately south of Capo Sta. Alessio exhibiting evidence of three former shorelines. The lower two are defined by prominent coastal notches at 0.8 m and 1.8 m above present-day sea level, while the upper shoreline corresponds to the planated top of the block which occurs at a height of around 3.5 m. The form of the block is shown in Profile E in Fig. 8. Figure gives indicative scale. (f) A well-defined coastal notch at the northern end of the Milazzo peninsula, elevated relative to modern vermetid constructions developing at present-day sea level. The notch is developed at a height of 2 m above sea level (see Profile H in Fig. 8). Figure gives indicative scale.

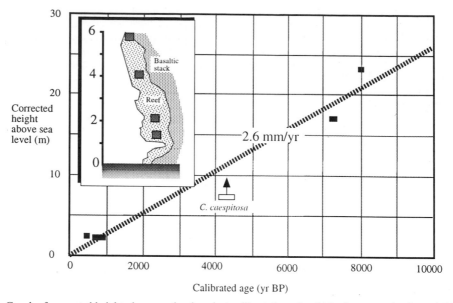

Fig. 7. Graph of corrected height above sea level against calibrated age for *Lithophaga* samples from Aci Trezza (solid boxes) and a *Cladocora caespitosa* (coral) sample from Taormina (white boxes) (see Table 1 for data). The upward-pointing arrow indicates that the age estimate for the coral is likely to be a minimum due to poor resolution of its original depth. Sea-level correction after Fairbanks (1989). All the results are minima and the sizes of boxes are proportional to inferred error (1σ). An idealized best-fit line gives an indication of the time-averaged uplift rate, though it is recognized that uplift is likely to have been episodic rather than continuous. Inset diagram shows a vertical profile of the sample site, with boxes indicating the actual heights of *Lithophaga* samples depicted in the main graph.

In summary, the shell dates combined with the marine notches indicate that the volcanic coastline has undergone net emergence over the last 7700 years. Such a trend, however, contrasts with the short tidal gauge record which indicates that, from 1895 to 1921, mean sea level at Catania rose at a rate of $0.6\,\mathrm{mm\,a^{-1}}$. Although little confidence can be placed on the results based on such a short record, it appears to indicate recent coastal subsidence or a eustatic rise in water level. According to Kieffer (1971), over the period between 1920 and 1970, however, there

Table 1. *Accelerator Mass Spectrometry dates for* Lithophaga *samples collected from Aci Trezza and a first-order age determination for a coral* (Cladocora caespitosa) *collected from Taormina. The age data are presented along with appropriate corrections*

Elevation (m)	^{14}C age (a^{-1} BP)	Species	Lab no.	δ^{13}C (‰)*	Cal. age (a^{-1} BP)†	Corr. sea level (m)‡	Uplift rate ($mm\,a^{-1}$)
Aci Trezza							
1.55	1270 ± 160	*Lithophaga*	Beta-70673	3.2	790 ± 160	2.35	1.85
2	1160 ± 170	*Lithophaga*	OxA-2484	0.8	485 ± 55	2.5	2.1
4	7060 ± 90	*Lithophaga*	OxA-2485	1.6	7250 ± 85	17	2.4
6	7600 ± 100	*Lithophaga*	OxA-2486	0.5	8010 ± 80	23	3.0
Taormina							
3.4	4200 ± 120	*Cladocora caespitosa*	UCL-362	n.d	4295 ± 205	>6.65	>1.6

* Normalized to δ^{13}C = 0‰ except for UCL-362 for which no ^{13}C value has been obtained.
† Age calibration after Stuiver & Reimer (1993). No apparent age correction as no local determinations are available but subtraction of $400\,a^{-1}$ from all ages is reasonable (Stiros *et al.*1992).
‡ Sea-level calibration after Fairbanks (1989) plus 0.5 for depth below high water for *Lithophaga*.

has been about 0.3 m of uplift of the coastline from Aci Trezza to Santa Maria La Scala, which he attributed to tectonic movements. The development of notches along the coastline confirms that coastal emergence has involved both periods of rapid uplift (possibly coseismic) and periods of relative sea-level stability during which the crust and sea level were rising in unison. Thus, although we report generalized uplift rates, uplift is likely to be pulsed, with higher average uplift rates ($c.\,4$–$5\,\mathrm{mm\,a^{-1}}$) indicated for the last millenium (Table 1 and Fig. 6).

The northern coastline: Taormina to Milazzo

The northern coastline of eastern Sicily is heavily urbanized and thus many of its relict marine features have been destroyed. Despite this, raised notches associated with marine fauna have been identified at a number of localities (Fig. 8). Of particular importance is at Taormina, where algal constructions and shallow notches have developed on the steep and sheltered limestone cliffs (Fig. 6c) (Ottman & Picard 1954; Blanc & Molinier 1955). The upper notch is 0.5 m deep and can be traced around the coastline at an altitude of 4.3–4.8 m above present mean sea level. The floor of this notch is relatively poorly

developed which suggests that once it formed, relative sea level fell gradually (Pirazzoli 1986). Below this a series of shallow notches are present at 0.9, 1.6 and 3.8 m above mean sea level. These features thus indicate a relative fall in sea level which has been interrupted by short periods of relative stability.

Although Ottman & Picard (1954) described vestiges of a vermetid construction associated with the uppermost notch, its age has remained undetermined. The freshness of elevated marine borings, however, together with the occurrence of Roman pottery cemented by calcareous algae, was cited as evidence for historical emergence (Ottman & Picard 1954). Here we report a first-order age determination on a coral (*Cladocora caespitosa*) (Fig. 6d), collected from a narrow platform at an elevation of 3.4 m (Profile A in Fig. 8), of $4295 \pm 205\,\mathrm{a}$ BP (Table 1). Careful preparation of the sample (the corals were split lengthwise and cleaned mechanically before being screened by X-ray diffraction to ensure a pure aragonitic composition) makes us reasonably confident about this age. The depth range of this coral, however, is poorly constrained and may be up to several metres to a few tens of metres (H. Zibrowius pers. comm.). Thus the uplift rate of $1.5\,\mathrm{mm\,a^{-1}}$ shown in Table 1 assumes no palaeodepth correction and so constitutes a minimum uplift rate, with the true uplift rate increasing with coral depth

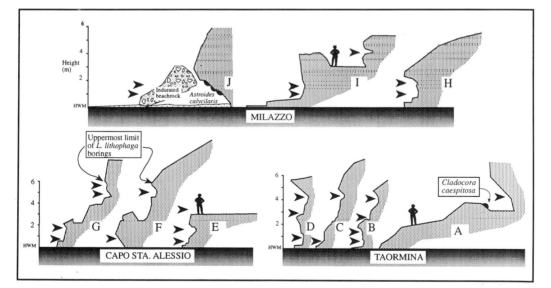

Fig. 8 Vertical coastal profiles from Milazzo, Capo Santa Alessio and Taormina, with black arrowheads indicating the inferred positions of prominent notches. Heavy stipple represents bedrock (mainly limestone), light stipple represents unconsolidated beach deposits and gravel texture represents indurated beachrock. HWM: high water mark.

(Table 1). If it is assumed that the coral is contemporaneous with the prominent uppermost notch, located 1.0 m above, this would infer an uplift rate of 1.8 mm a^{-1}.

At Capo Sta. Alessio and Capo D'Ali the cliff profiles are both notched and bored by *Lithophaga* up to an altitude of 5.7 m (Fig. 8). At Capo St. Alessio the highest notch is a shallow feature (0.2 m deep) with a poorly defined floor. The centre of the notch lies 5.5 m above mean sea level and it immediately overlies a corniche of serpulids, algae, bivalves and coral. Below this, three further shallow notches occur at 0.8 m, 1.8 m and 3.8 m (Fig. 6e). The field evidence thus indicates that relative sea level stood at least 5.7 m above present level and the subsequent fall was interrupted by four periods of stability. These features are considered to be Holocene in age and radiocarbon dates of *Lithophaga* shells are awaited so that rates of crustal uplift can be determined.

A longer term emergence record is provided from the Milazzo peninsula (Fig. 1) where both Pleistocene and Holocene marine phenomena are found elevated. Here, an attempt was made to extend the uplift chronology into pre-Holocene times by dating the well known deposits (e.g. Ottman & Picard 1954) which attain heights of 55–60 m and include bored boulders within richly fossiliferous marine sands. Because deposits at this elevation were likely to be too old for reliable radiocarbon dating, a search was made for corals which would be amenable to U-series dating. Corals (*Cladocora caespitosa*) were successfully located, but X-ray diffraction showed that their aragonite had been completely replaced by calcite. One cannot exclude, however, the possibility that careful searching will, in due course, yield sufficient coral for a reliable age determination.

At a lower level, Roman pottery, cemented by calcareous algae and infilling fissures in a former marine platform, occur at a height of 0.6 m above modern sea level, indicating that late Quaternary coastal uplift had continued into historical times (Ottman & Picard 1954). Field surveys reveal that there are three well defined notches at 0.8, 1.8 and 5.1 m above mean sea level (Fig. 6f). A few kilometres immediately north of the port of Milazzo, on the eastern side

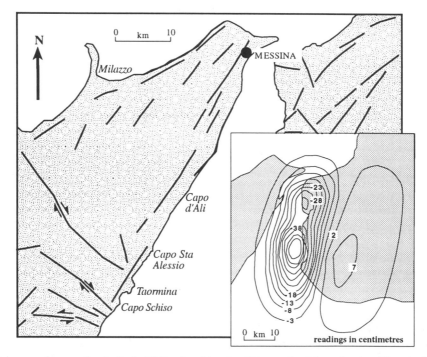

Fig. 9 Main map shows active faults (solid lines) and key localities north of the volcanic edifice at which geomorphological evidence of coastal uplift is found. Inset map shows an isoline map of coseismic deformation accompanying the 1908 Messina Straits earthquake (redrawn from Valensise & Pantosti 1992), illustrating coastal subsidence of the eastern side of the Straits. Rapid subsidence documented by tide gauge records at Messina between 1909 and 1923 may be related to continued post-seismic deformation in the same sense as that experienced during the 1908 event, thereby accounting for its conflict with the general late Holocene trend.

of the peninsula, in situ corals (*Astroides calycilaris*) occur at an elevation of 2.0 m on the overhanging roof of a prominent notch, protected seaward by an indurated boulder and pebble deposit (Profile J in Fig. 8).

In summary, all the geomorphic evidence from the northeastern coastline of Sicily is indicative of crustal uplift. The radiocarbon dated material from Taormina suggests an uplift rate of at least 1.5 mm a^{-1} during the last 4500 years. Despite this, and the inferences of historical emergence, tide-gauge data suggest that the Messina area experienced rapid submergence by 1.6 m between 1909 and 1923 (Emery & Aubery 1991). Although apparently conflicting with the longer term record, we suggest that this is a short-term anomaly which reflects extended crustal subsidence following the large (M = 7.5) Straits of Messina earthquake which induced 0.5 m of coseismic inundation of the Messina coastline (Fig. 9) (Pirazzoli 1987). The prevailing sense of coastal elevation changes in northeastern Sicily, however, is one of net emergence.

Implications for instability models

The main observation arising from the present study is that both the coastal flank of Mount Etna and the volcano's underlying allochthonous basement are uplifting in a broadly consistent manner. Thus uplift rates determined for the volcanic edifice appear to be comparable to, if slightly higher than, those determined for the hinterland. Indeed, the extent of this uplift may persist further along the northern coastline than documented in this study, since Ottman & Picard (1954) noted elevated marine phenomena as far west as Palermo. In contrast, the southeastern coast of Sicily can be considered as a separate structural block which is essentially stable relative to its rising northern counterpart.

It is important to incorporate such regional geodynamics into current models of flank collapse at Mount Etna (Kieffer 1985). Although we document late Quaternary uplift of the region, the occurrence of marine clays of Quaternary age at altitudes in excess of 750 m on the eastern flanks of the volcano testifies to significant uplift over at least the last 200 000 years. Reconstruction of the form of the contemporary sub-Etnean basement reveals that uplift has resulted in a surface which dips steeply seaward, a condition that further favours seaward collapse. Perhaps more significantly, Labaume *et al.* (1990) interpret shearing within these sub-Etnean clays to indicate eastward-directed gravity sliding of material off the nascent Gela

'nappe', even before the formation of the Etna edifice. Such behaviour reveals the ability of these marine clays to deform and slide under gravity without the need for any additional loading due to the subsequent accumulation of volcanic materials. Later southward-directed thrusting of the sub-Etnean basement into these marine deposits, however, has accentu-ated this potential by forming two clay horizons along which potential décollement may occur: one at the base of the volcanic pile and a second beneath the allochthonous mass at depths of up to 5 km below current sea level (Fig. 2) (Labaume *et al.* 1990). While Lo Giudice & Rasa (1986) infer edifice sliding on the former, Borgia *et al.* (1992) infer spreading along the latter.

These observations suggest that Mount Etna developed on an unstable substratum and that subsequent regional tectonic movements have served to maintain, if not promote, continued instability (Kieffer 1985). Superimposed upon this framework is a regional tectonic stress regime characterized by NNE–SSW compression but which, in the Etnean area, has recently become overprinted by an east–west tensile stress regime (Bousquet *et al.* 1988). It is this regime which appears to dominate both coseismic and aseismic movements along active faults within the mobile sectors, as well as the persistent reactivation of volcanic rift zones which effectively constitute the western boundary of the mobile sector (Kieffer 1985).

The continuity of coastal emergence between the volcanic edifice and its northern basement has some implications for instability models which emphasize the independent nature of Mount Etna's mobile flank. The coastal elevation changes documented here, for example, provide no support for the differential coastal uplift predicted by Borgia *et al.*'s (1992) large-scale spreading of a deep-seated portion of Mount Etna's substratum (Fig. 3). Indeed, such behaviour has been described elsewhere within a framework of basement subsidence rather than the basement uplift documented here. Instead, a picture emerges of a volcanic edifice growing and developing upon the eastern margin of a clay-draped allochthonous thrust mass undergoing persistent, distributed uplift. Clearly, within such a setting, gravity ought to be a significant driving force for superficial as well as more deep-seated instability, and the clay formation immediately underlying the edifice appears to be a prime candidate for a decoupling horizon. Nevertheless, the recognition that despite seaward sliding of the coastal flank, the volcanic coastline is emerging rather than subsiding, suggests that any subsidence related to flank collapse must be overprinted by tectonic uplift. The precise mechanism by which such uplift is accomplished awaits a much improved uplift chronology for the Etnean region, but again the continuity of uplift within the study area suggests that it is not dominated by localized fault-delimited block movements (Montalto *et al.* 1996) but instead reflects the actions of regional tectonics (Kieffer 1985).

Conclusions

While the southeastern coastline of Sicily displays no geomorphological evidence of recent coastal emergence, elevated Holocene marine phenomena on the volcanic coastline of Mount Etna and further north within the Apenninian–Magrebian hinterland testify to regional crustal uplift. Radiocarbon dating of elevated marine deposits both on the volcano, at Aci Trezza, and off the volcano, at Taormina, indicate comparable rates of coastal emergence of $1.8–3.0 \, \text{mm} \, \text{a}^{-1}$ and $>1.5 \, \text{mm} \, \text{a}^{-1}$, respectively, although uplift rates may have been more rapid ($4.0–5.0 \, \text{mm} \, \text{a}^{-1}$) during the most recent millenium. Short-term fluctuations in the rate and sense of crustal movements are likely to reflect localized tectonic movements. Although such movements are responsible for the independent motion of discrete parts of the coasts, the long-term pattern of coastal elevation changes is one of persistent emergence.

The continuity of emergent coastal features argues for broadly coherent uplift of the region from Catania to Milazzo rather than any independent mobility of the volcanic flanks, with little difference between the uplift rate for the Etnean area and that recorded at Taormina to the north. Persistent uplift in the Etna region during Quaternary times has resulted in the growth and development of the volcanic pile on a clay-draped substrate which dips sharply seaward. Within such a framework, edifice instability in general, and the mobility of the eastern flank in particular, is unlikely to be attributable to deep-seated processes driven by loading of the growing volcanic pile. Instead, the available data from the coastal record support the contention of superficial flank movements being superimposed on a regionally uplifting sub-volcanic basement.

This research was supported by the Commission of the European Communities, DG XII, Environment Programme, Climatology and Natural Hazards Unit, in the framework of contract EV5V-CT92–0170. We thank Steve Hirons (UCL) for help with X-ray diffraction, Helmut Zibrowius (Marseilles) and Brian Rosen (Natural History Museum) for coral identification, and Andy Cundy and Stephen Pearson (Brunel) for field assistance. Discussions with Marco Neri and Angelo Di Grande greatly improved our understanding of the late Quaternary coastal evolution of Sicily, while the paper benefited from helpful reviews by David Chester, John Guest and Guy Kieffer. This is contribution 156 of the Joint Research School of Geology and Geophysics, University and Birkbeck Colleges, London.

References

ADORNI, G. & CARVENI, P. 1993. Geomorphology and seismotectonic elements in the Giarre area, Sicily. *Earth Surface Processes and Landforms*, **18**, 275–283.

BLANC, J. J. & MOLINIER, R. 1955. Les formations organogenes consdruites superficiellement en Méditerranée occidentale. *Bulletin Institute Océanographie*, **1067**.

BORDONARO, S., DI GRANDE, A. & RAIMONDO, W. 1984. Lineamenti geomorfostratigrafici pleistocenici tra Melilli, Augusta e Lentini (Siracusa). *Bolletino dell'Academia Gioenia di Scienze Naturali, Catania*, **17**, 65–88.

BORGIA, A. 1994. Dynamic basis of volcanic spreading. *Journal of Geophysical Research*, **99**(B9), 17 791–17 804.

——, FERRARI, L. & PASQUARE, G. 1992. Importance of gravitational spreading in the tectonic and volcanic evolution of Mount Etna. *Nature*, **357**, 231–235.

BOUSQUET, J-C., LANZAFAME, G. & PAQUIN, C. 1988. Tectonic stresses and volcanism: in situ stress measurement and neotectonic investigations in the Etna area (Italy). *Tectonophysics*, **149**, 219–231.

CHESTER, D. K., DUNCAN, A. M., GUEST. J. E. & KILBURN, C. R. J. 1985. *Mount Etna, The Anatomy of a Volcano*. Chapman & Hall, London.

CNR – PFG 1985. Neotectonic Map of Italy. *Quaderni de la Ricerca Scientifica*, **114**.

CRISTOFOLINI, R., GHISETTI, F., RIUSCETTI, M. & VEZZANI, L. 1977. Neotectonics, seismicity and volcanic activity in North-eastern Sicily. *Proceedings of VI Colloquium on the Geology of the Aegean Region*, **2**, 757–766.

DI GRANDE, A. & NERI, M. 1988. Tirreniano a *Strombus b.* a M. Tauro (Augusta-Syracusa). *Rendiconti della Scoietà Geologica Italiana, Roma*, **11**, 57–58.

—— & RAIMONDO, W. 1982. Linee di costa Plio-Pleistoceniche e schema litostratigrfico del Quaternario Siracusano. *Geologica Romano*, **21**, 279–309.

EMERY, K.O & AUBERY, D. G. 1991. *Sea Levels, Land Levels and Tide Gauges*. Springer-Verlag, New York.

FAIRBANKS, R. G. 1989. A 17,000-year glacio-eustatic sea level record – Influence of glacial melting rates on the Younger Dryas event and deep-ocean circulation. *Nature*, **342**, 637–642.

FAIRBRIDGE, R. W. 1961. Eustatic changes in sea level. *In*: AHRENS, L. H., PRESS, F., Kalervo, R. & RUNCORN, S. K. (eds) *Physics and Chemistry of the Earth*. Pergamon Press, New York, **4**, 99–185.

GHISSETTI, F. & VEZZANI, L. 1982. Different styles of deformation in the Calabrian Arc (southern Italy); implications for a seismotectonic zoning. *Tectonophysics*, **85**, 149–165.

GUEST, J. E., CHESTER, D. K. & DUNCAN, A. M. 1984. The Valle del Bove, Mount Etna: its origin and relation to the stratigraphy and structure of the volcano. *Journal of Volcanology and Geothermal Research*, **21**, 1–23.

HIRN, A., NERCESSIAN, A., SPAIN, M., FERRUCCI, F. & WITTLINGER, G. 1991. Seismic heterogeneity of Mt. Etna: Structure and activity. *International Journal of Geophysics*, **105**, 139–153.

HUGHES, J. W., GUEST, J. E. & DUNCAN, A. M. 1990. Changing styles of effusive eruption on Mount Etna since AD 1600. *In*: RYAN, M. (ed.) *Magma Transport and Storage*. Wiley, Chichester, 385–406.

KIDSON, C. 1982. Sea level changes in the Holocene. *Quaternary Science Reviews*, **1**, 121–151.

KIEFFER, G. 1971. Dépot et niveaux marins et fluviatiles de la région de Catane (Sicile). *Mediterranée*, 5/6, 591–626.

——1972. Succession, ampleur et modalités des mouvements tectoniques récents à la base orientale de l'Etna (Sicile). *Comptes Rendus de l'Academie des Sciences, Paris*, **275**, 1339–1342.

——1977. Donnees nouvelles sur lorigine de la Valle del Bove et sa place dans l'histoire volcanologique de l'Etna. *Comptes Rendus de l'Academie des Sciences, Paris*, **285**, 1391–1393.

——1985. *Evolution Structurale et Dynamique d'un Grand Volcan Polygenique: Stades d'Edification et Activite actuelle de L'Etna (Sicile)*. Thèse etat, University Clermont-Ferrand II.

LABAUME, P., BOUSQUET, J-C. & LANZAFAME, G. 1990. Early deformations at a submarine compressive front: the Quaternary Catania foredeep south of Mt. Etna, Sicily, Italy. *Tectonophysics*, **177**, 349–366.

—— & LABOREL-DEGUEN, F. 1994. Biological indicators of relative sea-level variations and co-seismic displacements in the Mediterranean Region. *Journal of Coastal Research*, **10**, 395–415.

LO GIUDICE, E. & RASA, R. 1986. The role of the NNW structural trend in the recent geodynamic evolution of northeastern Sicily and its volcanic implications in the Etnean area. *Journal of Geodynamics*, **25**, 309–330.

—— & ——1992. Very shallow earthquakes and brittle deformation in active volcanic areas: The Etnean region as an example. *Tectonophysics*, **202**, 257–268.

——, PATANE, G., RASA, R. & ROMANO, R. 1982. The structural framework of Mount Etna. *In*: Romano, R. (ed.) *Mount Etna Volcano*. Memorie della Società Geologica Italiana, **23**, 125–158.

LYELL, C. 1858. On lavas consolidated on steep slopes. *Philisophical Transactions*, 703.

McGUIRE, W. J. 1992. Changing sea levels and erupting volcanoes: cause and effect. *Geology Today*, **8**, 141–144.

—— & SAUNDERS, S. J. 1993. Recent earth movements at active volcanoes – a review. *Quaternary Proceedings*, **3**, 33–46.

MONTALTO, A., VINCIGUERRA, S., MENZA, S. & PATANE, G. 1996. Recent seismicity of Mount Etna: implications for flank instability. *This volume*.

MULARGIA, F., ACHILLI, V., BROCCIO, F. & BALDI, P. 1991. Is a destructive earthquake imminent in southeastern Sicily? *Tectonophysics*, **188**, 399–402.

OTTMANN, F. & PICARD, J. 1954. Sur quelques mouvements tectoniques récentes sur le côtes nord et est de la Sicile. *Comptes Rendus de l'Academie des Sciences, Paris*, **239**, 1230–1231.

PATANE, G., MONTALTO, A., IMPOSA, S. & MENZA, S. 1994. The role of refional tectonics, magma pressure and gravitational spreading in earthquakes of the eastern sector of Mt. Etna volcano (Italy). *Journal of Volcanology and Geothermal Research*, **61**, x–xx.

PIRAZZOLI, P. A. 1986. Marine notches. *In*: VAN DE PLASSCHE, O. (ed.) *Sea-level Research: A Manual for the Collection and Evaluation of Data*. Geo Books, Norwich. 361–400.

——1987. Sea-level changes in the Mediterranean. *In*: TOOLEY, M. J. & SHENNAN, I. (eds) *Sea-level Changes*. Basil Blackwell, Oxford, 152–181.

——1991. *World Atlas of Holocene Sea-level Changes*. Elsevier Oceanographic Series, **58**, Elsevier, Netherlands.

PLATANIA, G. 1904. Sur les anomalies de la gravité et les bradysismes dans la région de l'Etna. *Comptes Rendus de l'Academie des Sciences, Paris*, **2**, 4–16.

RASA, R., AZZARO, R. & LEONARDI, O. 1996. Aseismic creep on faults and flank instability at Mount Etna volcano, Sicily. *This volume*.

SHENNAN, I. 1987. Holocene sea-level changes in the North Sea region. *In*: TOOLEY, M. J. & SHENNAN, I. (eds) *Sea-level Changes*. Basil Blackwell, Oxford, 109–151.

STEWART, I. S., McGUIRE, W. J., VITA-FINZI, C., FIRTH, C., HOLMES, R. & SAUNDERS, S. 1993. Active faulting and neotectonic deformation on the eastern flank of Mount Etna, Sicily. *Zeitschrift für Geomorphologie N.F. Supplement*, **94**, 73–94.

STIROS, S. C., ARNOLD, M. A., PIRAZZOLI, P. A., LABOREL, J. & PAPAGEORGIOU, S. 1992. Historical co-seismic uplift in Euboea Island (Greece). *Earth and Planetary Science Letters*, **108**, 109–117.

STUIVER, M. & REIMER, P. J. 1993. Extended ^{14}C database and revised CALIB radiocarbon calibration program. *Radiocarbon*, **35**, 215–230.

VALENSISE, G. & PANTOSTI, D. 1992. A 125 Kyr-long geological record of seismic source repeatability: the Messina Straits (southern Italy) and the 1908 earthquake (Ms 7.5). *Terra Nova*, **4**, 472–483.

VAN DE PLASSCHE, O. 1986. *Sea-level research: A Manual for the Collection and Evaluation of Data*. Geo Books, Norwich.

Recent seismicity of Mount Etna: implications for flank instability

A. MONTALTO[1], S. VINCIGUERRA[2], S. MENZA[3] & G. PATANÈ[2]

[1] *Dipartimento di Scienze della Terra, University of Pisa, Pisa, Italy*
[2] *Istituto di Geologia e Geofisica, University of Catania, Catania, Italy*
[3] *Osservatorio Sismologico di Protezione Civile, Acireale, Italy*

Abstract: This study considers seismic activity recorded beneath the low eastern flank of Etna during the period between April 1989 and December 1991 with the aim of placing some seismological constraints on the investigation of slope instability related to the gravitational sliding of this unsupported side of the volcano. The seismicity essentially consists of rather superficial ($z < 10$ km for more than 90% of cases), low-magnitude (usually $M < 3$) earthquakes. Foci of earthquakes are clustered on the main fault systems crossing the region, such as the Santa Tecla fault and the San Leonardello fault system, that have in recent times produced earthquakes of unusually high intensity covering the whole of the Etnean area. The broad picture of seismicity may be partially attributed to the accumulation of stress related to the seaward displacement of moving blocks in the vicinity of the Valle del Bove and adjacent regions in response to the storage and release of elastic energy associated with frequent episodes of magma intrusion. We propose that eastward sliding probably involves a complicated ensemble of moving blocks, resting on shallow independent décollements rather than on a single, widespread decoupling surface.

Etna, the largest volcano in Europe (altitude 3300 m, basal diameter about 40 km) is located on the eastern coast of Sicily (Italy). Both summit and flank eruptions take place, with almost annual frequency (Gasperini *et al.* 1990). Frequent changes in the eruptive style have been suggested based on the study of the stratigraphic and compositional features of the older volcanic piles, that are mainly exposed within the Valle del Bove (see Fig. 1), a horse-shoe-shaped depression (probably a caldera) in the eastern flank of the cone (McGuire 1982, 1983; Guest *et al.* 1984). Within this depression, important tectonic trends are attested by the orientation of the dykes exposed in its cliff walls, which reflect the principal surface traces of magma intrusion. Moreover, the persistence of a dilatation area located about 1 km SE of the summit craters has been detected by Murray & Guest (1980), and has been associated with the presence of a shallow plexus of interconnecting fissures which should work as a short-term store (or 'clearing house') for the primary magma rising from a deeper reservoir.

The general stress field acting on the eastern sector of Etna appears to result from an interplay between tectonic stresses, magmatic intrusion and gravity-induced sliding or spreading, although the precise relationship remains to be established (Hughes *et al.* 1990; Patanè *et al.* 1994).

In recent years, gravitational sliding and spreading have been observed in a number of volcanoes in the world, determining the mechanical instability of volcanic flanks (Borgia *et al.*

1990; Thomas *et al.* 1990; McGuire 1993; McGuire & Saunders 1993). Such behaviour has been proposed by a number of authors to explain the recent history of the eastern flank of Mt. Etna using evidence derived from ground deformation studies (Murray & Guest 1980, 1982; McGuire *et al.* 1990, 1993; Bonaccorso & Davis 1993), structural investigations (Neri *et al.* 1991; Borgia

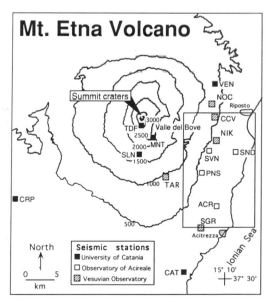

Fig. 1. Location map showing positions of the seismic stations and the sector of the eastern flank subjected to hypocentral computation and energy estimation of earthquakes.

From McGuire, W. J., Jones, A. P. & Neuberg, J. (eds) 1996, *Volcano Instability on the Earth and Other Planets*, Geological Society Special Publication No. 110, pp. 169–177.

et al. 1992; Lo Giudice & Rasà 1992) and seismic analyses (Cosentino *et al.* 1982; Patanè *et al.* 1984; Gresta *et al.* 1990; Patanè *et al.* 1994). All models stress the seaward displacement of the eastern flank of the volcanic pile, unbuttressed on a clay-rich layer, in contrast to the remainder of the edifice, which is topographically buttressed and which rests on a more competent substratum. Sliding of the eastern sector of the volcano is favoured by a strong seaward dip characterizing the surface of the sedimentary basement (Ogniben 1966; Lentini 1982; Stewart *et al.* 1993).

In this paper we analyse the seismicity that occurred between April 1989 and December 1991 within a sector located on the low eastern flank of the volcano (Fig. 1), with the aim of placing some seismological constraints on the nature of slope instability related to gravitational sliding of this unsupported side of Etna.

Seismotectonic and structural framework of the lower eastern flank

Etna is located in a seismically active region astride the complex tectonic zone marking the boundary between the African and European plates (McKenzie 1970; Barberi *et al.* 1973; Lentini 1982). Major fault scarps located on the seaward side of the volcano have been interpreted by various authors (see, for example, Borgia *et al.* 1990; McGuire *et al.* 1990) as clear evidence of the gravitational instability of the unbuttressed eastern flank. At lower altitudes, and particularly between Acireale, Santa Venerina and Giarre (see Fig. 2 for location), this is one of the most seismotectonically active parts of the volcano. This is demonstrated by the high frequency of earthquake occurrence closely associated with fault systems for which there is clear evidence at the surface in the form of morphological features and ground fractures (Patanè 1975, 1982; Lo Giudice *et al.* 1982; Cristofolini *et al.* 1982; Azzaro *et al.* 1989a; Patanè *et al.* 1994). Another feature which testifies to the active nature of this region is the bradyseismic behaviour which has been reported along the coast between Acitrezza and Riposto (see Fig. 1 for location) since the beginning of this century (Platania 1904). This bradyseismic behaviour is currently marked by uplift to the south of Acireale and subsidence between Pozzillo (see Fig. 2 for location) and

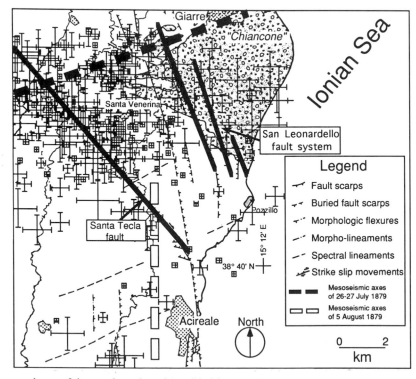

Fig. 2. Structural map of the area investigated (modified from Lo Giudice *et al.* 1982) and epicentral distribution of events during April 1989 - December 1991. Error bars are shown.

Riposto to the north. Stratigraphic observations by De Fiore (1919) have suggested, however, that episodes of uplift and subsidence may have occurred in the recent past. Some such morpho-lineaments have been explained by Cristofolini *et al.* (1979) and Romano (1982) in terms of regional tectonic trends crossing the eastern sector of the volcano. The orientations of these features define a sharp structural alignment along a bearing of 150–170°. Other important alignments are also defined by the morpho-structural lineaments trending NE–SW, N–S, and WNW–ESE, and by the orientation of the main mesoseismic axes associated with seismic events in the region on 26–27 July 1879 and 5 August 1879 (Imbò 1935), 19 March 1952 and 19 October 1984 (Patanè *et al.* 1994). Further-more, the area investigated shows, to the north of Acireale, a distributed zone of horsts and grabens forming a system of fault and buried fault scarps trending NNW–SSE, that represents the extension of the Malta–Iblean Escarpment. In contrast to the south and west of Acireale, faults and partially buried faults trend predomi-nantly north–south. Finally, field observations of a relict fault surface associated with the Santa Tecla fault (see Fig. 2), have identified slicken-sides defining a clear sense of dextral strike-slip, with a pitch of about 45 (Lo Giudice *et al.* 1982; Stewart *et al.* 1993).

Presentation and analysis of seismic data (April 1989–December 1991)

Methodology and data set

Seismic activity recorded in the low eastern flank of Etna between April 1989 and December 1991 has been considered for the present investiga-tion. Time–space–magnitude patterns of earth-quakes are evaluated together with estimations of the focal mechanisms associated with a limited number of selected events. Data have been acquired by means of three local networks operated in this sector of the volcano (Fig. 1) by the University of Catania (UCT), the Seismolo-gical Observatory of Acireale (SOACR), and the Vesuvian Observatory (VO). The recording sites are equipped with analogue 1s-vertical seism-ometers (UCT and SOACR) and 3D digital stations (UCT and VO). The magnitude of events has been calculated by means of the following relation, that uses the coda duration estimated on the paper drum recordings of the ACR station:

$$M_L = 2.36 \log D - 1.57 \qquad (1)$$

where D is the coda duration in seconds.

Energy has been obtained by using the Richter (1956) relation:

$$\log E = 9.9 + 1.9 M_L - 0.024 M_L^2 \qquad (2)$$

where E is energy in erg.

The activity recorded over the period investi-gated essentially consisted of rather surficial ($z < 10$ km for more than 90% of cases) low-magnitude (usually $M < 3$) earthquakes. These occur against a background of very weak microevents with negative magnitude ($M < -1$) that are generally recorded at only one or, at most, two stations.

Analysis and interpretations

Figure 3 shows the temporal distribution (a) and the cumulative energy release (b) associated with those earthquakes of $M \geq 2$ occurring within the sector illustrated in Fig. 1. The graph shows that the most significant episode of energy release took place near the end of June 1989, when a cluster of 14 events was recorded with a maximum magnitude of 3.1 (28 June, 21:36 GMT). This activity affected an area located about 5 km NW of Acireale in a depth range between 2 and 7 km. Post-June 1989 seismicity was characterized by a near regular trend, both in terms of the number and energy of events, the only exceptions being minor events during June–August 1990 and October–November 1991.

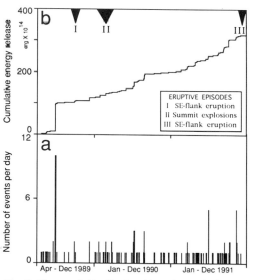

Fig. 3. Temporal distribution (a) and cumulative energy release (b) of shocks with $M \geq 2$ occurring within the rectangular sector shown in Fig.1 during April 1989 - December 1991. The main episodes of volcanic activity are reported.

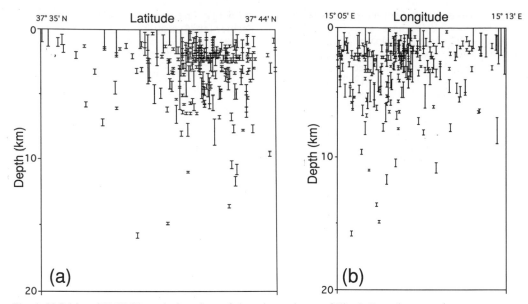

Fig. 4. N-S (**a**) and E–W (**b**) vertical sections of the epicentral map of Fig. 2. Error bars are shown.

Figure 2 also shows the locations of all events. Hypocentral computation was undertaken using a modified version of the program HYPO71 (Lee & Lahr 1975), and the velocity model proposed for the region by Hirn *et al.* (1991). Hypocentre uncertainties are within 2 km for both the horizontal and the vertical axes, while the root-mean-square is less than 0.3 s.

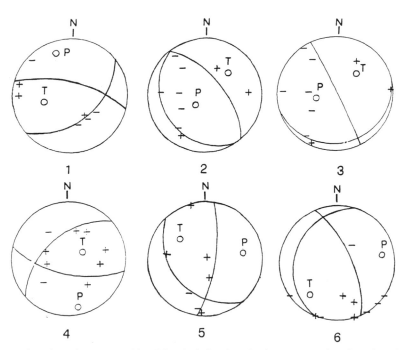

Fig. 5. First-motion plots of events considered for single focal mechanism computation. See Fig. 6 for hypocentre locations and Table 1 for focal parameters. Error bars are shown.

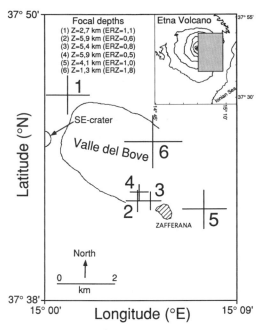

37° 50'

Focal depths
(1) Z=2,7 km (ERZ=1,1)
(2) Z=5,9 km (ERZ=0,6)
(3) Z=5,4 km (ERZ=0,8)
(4) Z=5,9 km (ERZ=0,5)
(5) Z=4,1 km (ERZ=1,0)
(6) Z=1,3 km (ERZ=1,8)

Etna Volcano

SE-crater

Valle del Bove

ZAFFERANA

North

0   2
km

Latitude (°N)

37° 38'
15° 00'   Longitude (°E)   15° 09'

Fig. 6. Epicentral distribution, focal depths, and sector location of events considered in Fig. 5.

The observed seismicity is mainly related to the Santa Tecla fault (trending NW–SE, see Fig. 2) which, in the recent past, generated earthquakes of unusually high intensity for the Etna region (Azzaro *et al.* 1989*b*; Lo Giudice & Rasà 1992; Patanè *et al.* 1994). Only a few earthquakes affect the San Leonardello fault system (which trends NNW–SSE). Epicentres are also scattered where the mesoseismic axes of the 26–27 July 1879 earthquakes (Fig. 2 and Imbò 1935) approach the Santa Tecla fault. The two vertical cross-sections shown in Fig. 4a, b,

reveal that foci are largely concentrated in the upper 5 km, with a gradual deepening of hypocentres along a NW direction. This is in agreement with previous observations (Azzaro *et al.* 1989*b*; Patanè *et al.* 1994) which stress that hypocentres are usually very shallow on the 'San Leonardello' fault system, while also deeper earthquakes affect the Santa Tecla fault. This feature suggests that the activity of the San Leonardello fault system is strictly related to the sliding processes, while deeper seismicity occurring on the Santa Tecla fault is likely the effect of tectonic stress.

Single fault-plane solutions have been determined for those events marked by obvious polarity of the P-wave arrivals at a minimum of seven stations, and first-motion plots for these events are shown in Fig. 5, while Fig. 6 shows their locations on an epicentral map together with focal depths and associated hypocentral uncertainties. Other focal parameters are shown in Table 1 while Table 2 contains the same data for seven pairs of earthquakes used in the computation of composite fault-plane solutions. Fault planes and auxiliar planes have been differentiated on the basis of structural inferences on the ground surface, which were carried out by the authors. First-motion plots and epicentre locations for these are shown in Figs 7 and 8 respectively.

Focal mechanisms for both sets of events (Figs 5 and 7) are mainly related to the movement on structures broadly trending NNW–SSE, NW–SE and WNW–ESE (hereafter referred to as the 'main' pattern). A few events, however, are characterized by focal mechanisms related to fault planes oriented roughly along NE–SW and NNE–SSW trends (hereafter named the 'secondary' pattern). Both normal and reverse faults are evidenced, along

Table 1. *Focal parameters of events considered in Figs 5 and 6*

No.	Date	h : min (GMT)	Origin	Magnitude	Fault plane	Auxiliar plane	P axis	T axis
1	31.5.89	8 : 10	34, 26	2, 4	Strike N105°E Dip 63°	Strike N51°E Dip 40°	Strike N144°E Dip 14°	Strike N70°E Dip 53°
2	28.6.89	21 : 36	30, 01	3, 1	Strike N140°E Dip 64°	Strike N146°E Dip 26°	Strike N45°E Dip 60°	Strike N56°E Dip 30°
3	28.6.89	22 : 03	39, 17	2, 9	Strike N155°E Dip 87°	Strike N76°E Dip 13°	Strike N86°E Dip 40°	Strike N60°E Dip 42°
4	28.6.89	22 : 05	48, 32	2, 8	Strike N103°E Dip 60°	Strike N49°E Dip 45°	Strike N170°E Dip 3°	Strike N67°E Dip 62°
5	28.6.89	22 : 26	13, 30	2, 4	Strike N8°E Dip 71°	Strike N137°E Dip 29°	Strike N88°E Dip 22°	Strike N139°E Dip 40°
6	28.12.89	0 : 06	10, 39	2, 2	Strike N156°E Dip 70°	Strike N19°E Dip 26°	Strike N80°E Dip 12°	Strike N40°E Dip 30°

Table 2. *Focal parameters of events considered in Figs 7 and 8*

No.	Date	h:min (GMT)	Origin	Magnitude	Fault plane	Auxiliar plane	P axis	T axis
A	24.2.90	0:23	11,68	2,6	Strike N133°E; Dip 70°	Strike N88°E; Dip 26°	Strike N28°E; Dip 40°	Strike N80°E; Dip 58°
B	23.3.90	23:40	13,01	2,1				
C	18.6.89	15:44	02,67	2,1	Strike N94°E; Dip 73°E	Strike N94°E; Dip 16°E	Strike N18°E; Dip 52°E	Strike N13°E; Dip 38°E
D	18.6.89	15:44	37,70	2,1				
E	27.6.89	20:38	05,19	2,0	Strike N140°E; Dip 40°E	Strike N37°E; Dip 32°	Strike N3°E; Dip 40°	Strike N102°E; Dip 18°
F	03.8.91	20:02	12,44	1,9				
G	24.3.91	2:35	33,60	2,1	Strike N144°E; Dip 61°E	Strike N154°E; Dip 29°	Strike N51°E; Dip 74°	Strike N60°E; Dip 16°
H	16.11.91	1:04	50,26	2,1				
L	07.5.91	20:26	53,03	1,7	Strike N161°E; Dip 49°E	Strike N166°E; Dip 41°	Strike N70°E; Dip 4°	Strike N2°E; Dip 90°
M	07.5.91	21:06	45,35	2,1				
N	07.8.91	13:32	22,88	2,0	Strike N129°E; Dip 61°E	Strike N119°E; Dip 30°	Strike N56°E; Dip 75°	Strike N39°E; Dip 20°
P	13.10.91	·10:50	46,16	2,3				
Q	19.3.91	1:38	51,00	1,5	Strike N98°E; Dip 69°E	Strike N145°E; Dip 29°	Strike N22°E; Dip 30°	Strike N151°E; Dip 35°
R	19.3.91	1:40	45,88	1,5				

both the main and secondary pattern, while strike-slip movements are greater along the secondary pattern. Furthermore, earthquakes ascribed to movements along fault planes belonging to the main pattern are generally deeper ($Z_{max} = 7 \pm 1.7\,\text{km}$) than events associated with active structures of the secondary pattern.

Implications for the kinematics of the eastern flank

The unbuttressed eastern sector of Etna is decoupled from the rest of the volcanic pile by three major boundary structures: the Pernicana fault to the north, the Mascalucia–Trecastagni fault system to the south, and an extensive

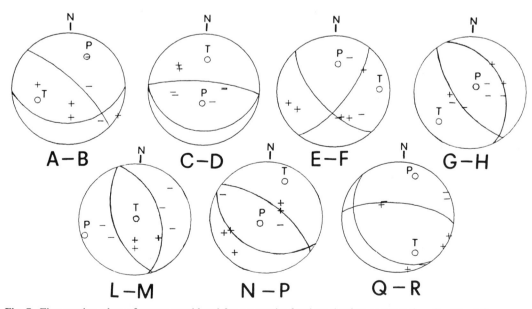

Fig. 7. First-motion plots of events considered for composite focal mechanism computation. See Fig. 8 for hypocentre location and Table 2 for focal parameters.

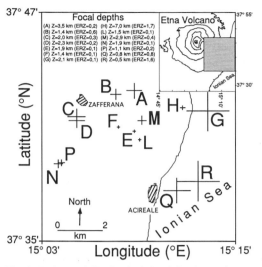

Fig. 8. Epicentral distribution, focal depths, and sector location of events cosidered in Fig. 7.

region running approximatively N–S through the summit craters and along the western rim of Valle del Bove to the west (Fig. 9). The Pernicana fault is considered by a number of authors (Luongo *et al.* 1989; Lo Giudice & Rasà

Fig. 9. Sketch model of gravitational sliding on the eastern sector of Etna (modified from Borgia *et al.* 1992 and Stewart *et al.* 1993). The inset shows a hypothetical section through the Pernicana falt which , according to Patanè *et al.* (1994) is a reverse fault. This contradicts the distensive pattern of the associated surficial structures evidenced by ground observations of Luongo *et al.* (1989) and Lo Giudice & Rasà (1992). (a = Volcanic outcrop; b = sedimentary layer).

1992; Azzaro *et al.* 1989*a*) as a normal fault with a significant component of left strike-slip. These features appear to contradict the compressive focal mechanisms determined for seismic events in the area which suggest the occurrence of thrust faulting (see Patanè *et al.* 1994 and Fig. 9 inset). The Mascalucia–Trecastagni fault system is characterized by oblique-slip movements comprising both normal and dextral components of dip-slip and strike-slip displacement (Lo Giudice & Rasà 1992; Stewart *et al.* 1993; Patanè *et al.* 1994). The broad pattern of displacement observed at the surface may be at least partially attributed to stress accumulation in the lower eastern flank in response to the seaward displacement of moving blocks in the Valle del Bove and adjacent regions. This, in turn, may result from the release either seismically or aseismically of elastic energy associated with the episodes of magma intrusion which are frequent in this sector of the volcano. McGuire *et al.* (1990) have shown that dyke emplacement in the vicinity of the headwall of the Valle del Bove produces appreciable decoupling, displacement and successive downhill collapsing of megablocks in this area. Such behaviour, resulting from a combination of tectonic, gravitational and magmatic forces explains the occurrence of extensional structures in the region of major decoupling which separates the eastern flank from the remainder of the edifice.

We interpret the pattern of shallow lowenergy seismicity discussed earlier in terms of a broad stress field which might be expected to result from the above described mechanism. Both thrusting and extension occur in close spatial association defining block movements which result in complex surface stress patterns. Such behaviour is evidenced by the range of computed focal mechanisms shown in Figs 5 and 7. Moreover, both the focal mechanisms and the hypocentral distributions of the shallowest earthquakes support a mechanism of shallow sliding of a complicated ensemble of adjacent blocks on a number of independent horizons, rather than on a single, widespread surface. Relative displacements between these blocks neatly explain the close proximity of compressive and distensive faulting.

Sliding seems to occur only at shallow depths, largely within the volcanic pile. At greater depths, the stress field is primarily dominated by the regional tectonic forces. The deeper tectonic seismicity associated with the Santa Tecla fault supports the hypothesis of Stewart *et al.* (1993) that such a structure marks the southern border of a large depression filled by a thick sequence of volcanically derived fan conglomerates known as the Chiancone (Lentini 1982 and Fig. 2).

Finally, faulting with a marked strike-slip component typifies both those structures trending ENE–WSW (the orientation of the 26–27 July 1879 mesoseismic axes) and those aligned WNW–ESE (belonging to the 'main' pattern). Also such behaviour, at least at shallow depths, can reflect the seaward sliding of this sector of the volcano, and may explain the relatively modest morphological expression of these structures with respect to those trending NNW–SSE and NW–SE (both belonging to the main pattern), where dip-slip movements are dominant.

Conclusion

In the low eastern flank of Etna episodes of brittle failure of both the volcanic pile and upper part of the sedimentary basement are evidenced by recent seismicity, the broad pattern of which supports models of seaward sliding of the eastern flank. We suggest that gravitational sliding takes place where the frictional decoupling of crustal blocks operated by tectonic and magmatic forces encourages the movement of shallow structures. This occurs under the pushing of instable components downhill from the highest boundary of the buttressed sector of the volcano, which is located near the western rim of Valle del Bove (see Fig. 9). The seismicity recorded between April 1989 and December 1991 prevaled near the Santa Tecla fault, which is the main structure crossing the region investigated. Earthquakes also occurred on other adjacent structures with very clear morphologic evidence, such as the S. Leonardello fault system. The seismic activity of these secondary structures displays very superficial foci, which suggests that they are probably associated with the eastward migration of unsupported rigid blocks upon shallow independent décollements. On the contrary, the Santa Tecla fault is likely involved in merely tectonic processes, as testified by the recording of deeper earthquakes. The close spatial association of distensive and compressive faulting mechanisms along adjacent structures suggests that the temporal evolution of the local stress field is dynamically controlled by the continuous seaward migration of de-coupled megablocks.

We wish to thank the Vesuvian Observatory of Naples for providing integration to our data by means of their recordings operated on the eastern flank of Etna. This work was carried out with the scientific coordination and the financial support of the National Group for Volcanology, Italy. Grants MPI 40% have been used. One of us (A.M.) is financially supported by the Doctorate School of the University of Pisa (Italy). N. Peacock is acknowledged for revision of the English text.

References

AZZARO, R., LO GIUDICE, E. & RASÀ, R. 1989a. Note macrosismiche e considerazioni sismotettoniche. *In*: *Attività Etna 1988*. Monographs, CNR **IV**: 40–56.

——, CARVENI, P., LO GIUDICE, E. & RASÀ, R. 1989b. Il terremoto di Codavolpe (basso versante orientale Etneo) del 29 Gennaio: Campo macrosismico e fratturazione cosismica. *Bollettino GNV-CNR*, **1**, 1–12.

BARBERI, F., GASPARINI, P., INNOCENTI, F. & VILLARI, L., 1973. Volcanism in Southern Tyrrhenian Sea and its geodynamic implications. *Journal of Geophysical Research*, **78**, 5221–5232.

BONACCORSO, A. & DAVIS, P. M. 1993. Dislocation modelling of the 1989 dike intrusion into the flank of Mount Etna, Sicily. *Journal of Geophysical Research*, **98**, 4261–4268.

BORGIA, A., BURR, J., MONTERO, W., MORALES, L. D. & ALVADARO, G. 1990. Fault propagation folds induced by gravitational failure and slumping of the Central Costa Rica Volcanic Range: Implications for large Terrestrial and Martian Volcanic edifices. *Journal of Geophysical Research*, **95**, 14 357–14 382.

——, FERRARI, L. & PASQUARÈ, G. 1992. Importance of gravitational spreading in the tectonic and volcanic evolution of Mount Etna. *Nature*, **357**, 231–235.

CRISTOFOLINI, R., LENTINI, F., PATANÈ, G. & RASÀ, R. 1979. Integrazione di dati geologici, geofisici e petrologici per la stesura di un profilo crostale in corrispondenza dell'Etna. *Bollettino Societá Geologica Italiana*, **98**, 239–247.

——, PATANÈ, G. & RECUPERO, S. 1982. Morphologic evidence for ancient volcanic centres and indications of magma reservoirs underneath Mt. Etna, Sicily. *Geografia Fisica e Dinamica Del Quaternario*, **5**, 3–9.

COSENTINO, M., LOMBARDO, G., PATANÈ, G., SCHICK, R. & SHARP, A. D. L. 1982. Seismological researches in Mount Etna: state of art and recent trends. *In*: ROMANO, R. (ed.) *Mount Etna Volcano*. Memorie della Società Geologia Italia **23**, 159–202.

DE FIORE, O. 1919. *L'Etna – I fenomeni eruttivi e sismici loro topografia e meccanismo*. Officina Tipografica La Stampa Catania.

GASPERINI, P., GRESTA, S. & MULARGIA, F. 1990. Statistical analysis of seismic and eruptive activities at Mt. Etna during 1978–1987. *Journal of Volcanology and Geothermal Research*, **40**, 317–325.

GRESTA, S., LONGO, V. & VIAVATTENE, A. 1990. Geodynamic behaviour of eastern and western sides of Mount Etna. *Tectonophysics*, **179**, 81–92.

GUEST, J. E., CHESTER, D. K. & DUNCAN, A. M.
1984. The Valle del Bove, Mount Etna: its origin
and relation to the stratigraphy and structure of
the volcano. *Journal of Volcanology and Geothermal Research*, **21**, 1–23.

HIRN, A., NERCESSIAN, A., SAPIN, M., FERRUCCI, F.
& WITTLINGER, G., 1991. Seismic heterogeneity
of Mt. Etna: structure and activity. *Geophysics
Journal International*, **105**, 139–153.

HUGHES, J. W., GUEST, J. E. & DUNCAN, A. M. 1990.
Changing styles of effusive eruption on Mount
Etna since AD 1600. In *Magma Transport and
Storage*, John Wiley, London, 385–405.

IMBÒ, G. 1935. *I Terremoti Etnei*. Accademia
Nazionale dei Lincei, Casa Editrice F. Le
Monnier, Firenze.

LEE, W. H. K. & LAHR, J. C. 1975. *HYPO71: A
computer programme for determining hypocenter,
magnitude, and first motion pattern of local
earthquakes*. US Geological Survey Open-file
Report, 75–311.

LENTINI, F. 1982. The geology of the Mt. Etna
basement. *In*: ROMANO, R. (ed.) *Mount Etna
Volcano*. Memorie della Società Geologica Italiana, **23**, 7–25.

LO GIUDICE, E., PATANÈ, G., RASÀ, R. & ROMANO, R.
1982. The structural framework of Mount Etna. *In*:
ROMANO, R. (ed.) *Mount Etna Volcano*. Memorie
della Società Geologia Italia, **23**, 125–158.

— & RASÀ, R. 1992. Very shallow earthquakes and
brittle deformation in active volcanic areas: the
Etnean region as an example. *Tectonophysics*,
202, 1–12.

LUONGO, G., DEL GAUDIO, C., OBRIZZO, F. &
RICCO, C., 1989. Movimenti lenti del suolo
all'Etna mediante livellazioni di precisione. *Bollettino Gruppo Nazionale per la Vulcanologia,
CNR*, **1989–1**, 345–361.

MCGUIRE, W. J. 1982. Evolution of the Etna volcano:
information from the southern wall of the Valle
del Bove caldera. *Journal of Volcanology and
Geothermal Research*, **13**, 241–271.

—1983. Prehistoric dyke trends on Mount Etna;
implications for magma transport and storage.
Bulletin in Volcanology, **46**, 9–22.

—1993. Volcano instability and hazard. *Geoscientist*, **4**(3), 9–11.

— & SAUNDERS, S. 1993. Recent earth movements
at active volcanoes: a review. In *Quaternary
Proceedings* 3, Quaternary Research Association,
Cambridge: 33–46.

—, PULLEN, A. D. & SAUNDERS, S. J. 1990. Recent
dyke-induced large-scale block movement at
Mount Etna and potential slope failure. *Nature*,
343, 357–359.

—, SAUNDERS, S. & PULLEN, A. 1993. Rifting at
Mount Etna. *WOVO News, Osservatorio Vesuviano edn*, **4**, 16–18.

MCKENZIE, D. P. 1970. The plate tectonics of the
Mediterranean region. *Nature*, **226**, 239–243.

MURRAY, J. B. & GUEST, J. E. 1980. Vertical ground
deformation by precise levelling techniques. *UK
Research on Mount Etna, 1977–79*. The Royal
Society, London, 18–20.

— & — 1982. Vertical ground deformation on
Mount Etna; 1975–1980. *Geological Society of
America Bulletin*, **93**, 1160–1175.

NERI, M., GARDUNO, V. H., PASQUARÉ, G. &
RASÀ, R. 1991. Studio strutturale e modello
cinematico della Valle del Bove e del versante
orientale etneo. *Acta Vulcanogica*, **1**, 17–24.

OGNIBEN, L., 1966. Lineamenti idrogeologici
dell'Etna. *Rivista di Mineralogia Siciliana*, **100–102**, 1–24.

PATANÈ, G. 1975. I terremoti di Santa Maria
Ammalati e di Guardia dell'Agosto 1973. *Rivista
di Mineralogia Siciliana*, **154–156**, 199–206.

—1982. Seismological observation at Mt. Etna from
the instrumental data. *In*: ROMANO, R. (ed.)
Mount Etna Volcano. Memorie della Società
Geologica Italiana, **23**, 82–190.

—, GRESTA, S. & IMPOSA, S. 1984. Seismic activity
preceding the 1983 eruption of Mt. Etna. *Bulletin
of Volcanologique*, **74**, 941–952.

—, MONTALTO, A., IMPOSA, S. & MENZA, S. 1994.
The role of regional tectonics, magma pressure
and gravitational spreading in earthquakes of
the eastern sector of Mt. Etna volcano. *Journal
of Volcanology and Geothermal Research*, **61**,
253–266.

PLATANIA, G. 1904. Sur les anomalies de la gravit_ et
les bradisismes dans la region orientale de l'Etna.
Comptes Rendus de l'Academie des Sciences Paris,
137, 859–860.

RICHTER, C. F. 1956. *Elementary Seismology*. Freeman, San Francisco, CA.

ROMANO, R., (ed.) 1982. *Mount Etna Volcano*.
Memorie della Società Geologica Italiana, Vol.
23.

STEWART, I. S., MCGUIRE, W. J., VITA FINZI, C.,
FIRTH, C., HOLMES, R. & SAUNDERS, S. 1993.
Active faulting and neotectonic deformation on
the eastern flank of Mount Etna, Sicily. *Zeitschrift fur Geomorphologie N.F. Supplement*, **94**,
73–94.

THOMAS, P. J., SQUYRES, S. W. & CARR, M. H. 1990.
Flank tectonics of Martian volcanoes. *Journal of
Geophysical Research*, **95**, 14345–14356.

Aseismic creep on faults and flank instability at Mount Etna volcano, Sicily

R. RASÀ[1], R. AZZARO[2] & O. LEONARDI[3]

[1] Dipartimento di Fisica della Materia, Geofisica e Fisica dell'Ambiente,
Università di Messina, Salita Sperone 31, 98166 Messina, Italy
[2] GNDT C/O Istituto Internazionale di Vulcanologia – CNR,
Piazza Roma 2 95123 Catania, Italy
[3] Ufficio Tecnico Comunale, via Piano Consolazione 18, 95022 Acicatena, Italy

Abstract: This paper presents new data on the nature and significance of shallow fault creep in the Etna region. Sixteen sites where creep behaviour is obvious, have been identified, both from analysis of historical records, and from field surveys. Creep rates at each site vary considerably, from 0.5 to 2.3 cm a^{-1}, and two extreme types of aseismic slip are recognized; (a) near-continuous, long-period movement along the aseismic segments of faults, and (b) spasmodic, short-lived, pre- and post-seismic movement related to seismically active fault segments. At most creep sites active displacements range from purely extensional to dip-slip. In some cases oblique-slip movements prevail, whereas purely strike-slip movements have been detected at only a single site. The overall creep kinematics indicate that surface creep on faults is a mode of discontinuous strain restricted to the faults displacing a sector of the eastern flank of the volcanic edifice bordered by the Pernicana fault, the NE Rift, the SE Rift and the Trecastagni-Mascalucia fault zone. We suggest that this mobile sector of the sea-facing flank of the volcano, including its uppermost clay-rich basement, is slowly sliding southeast under the control of a main deep-seated detachment surface.

Very slow aseismic slip along a fault, at an average rate typically ranging from 3.5–6.5 mm a^{-1} (Lienkaemper et al. 1991) to 1–2 cm a^{-1} (Dickinson & Grantz 1968), is known as fault creep. Following recognition of the tectonic origin of this phenomenon in California (Steinbrugge & Zacher 1960; Tocher 1960), this mode of frictional sliding without appreciable seismic energy release and stress drop has been investigated by both laboratory fracture studies (Brace & Byerlee 1966; Byerlee & Brace 1968) and field observations, such as those which recorded the well known episodes of rapid creep along the San Andreas fault following the 1966, Parkfield earthquake (Scholz et al. 1969).

Faults are now widely believed to move in a strongly heterogeneous manner, and different sections of the same fault can reveal displacement histories governed either by stick-slip behaviour, when a sudden very high slip rate generates seismic waves and stress drop, or by stable-sliding behaviour, when continuous creep occurs without accompanying earthquakes (Brune 1968; Engelder 1973).

Most fault creep occurs as long-period, low slip-rate displacement punctuated by prominent displacement episodes, called 'creep events' by Wesson (1988). These occur both as afterslip following a coseismic surface displacement (Lienkaemper et al. 1991) and as pre-seismic slip, immediately prior to earthquakes (Kanamori & Cipar 1974; Dieterich 1978).

Since the last century some examples of surface faulting without significant seismic energy release on Mount Etna volcano have been occasionally reported by several authors (O. Silvestri 1883; A. Silvestri 1893; De Fiore 1908–11; Imbò 1935) who recognized the phenomenon because of the considerable damage aseismic creep caused in the more densely urbanized areas. Apart from a few recent studies on episodic creep behaviour (Lo Giudice & Longo 1986; Lo Giudice 1988; Azzaro et al. 1989b, 1991), few specific contemporary investigations have been undertaken on fault movements showing this mode of slip.

A number of recent papers (Kieffer 1985; Borgia et al. 1992; Lo Giudice & Rasà 1992; Ferrucci et al. 1993; Kieffer & Tanguy 1993) have stressed the significance of the location of Etna on a mobile substratum beneath the eastern flank of the volcano. Therefore, the active faults concentrated in this unbuttressed, seaward-facing, eastern flank (Fig. 1) are important in accommodating, in a brittle manner, the large strains affecting this segment of the volcanic pile together with the shallow levels of its underlying sedimentary basement. A number of models, incorporating the seismic and structural evidence for instability of the eastern flank at different scales,

From McGuire, W. J., Jones, A. P. & Neuberg, J. (eds) 1996, *Volcano Instability on the Earth and Other Planets*,
Geological Society Special Publication No. 110, pp. 179–192.

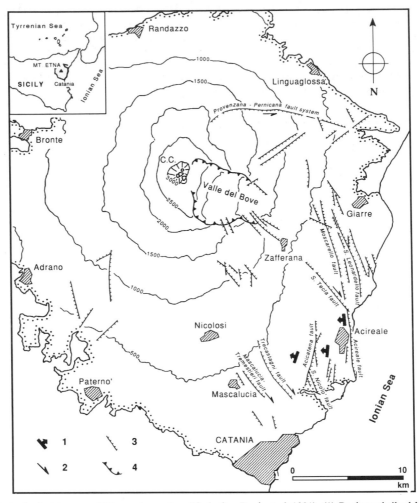

Fig. 1. Tectonic sketch map of Etna volcano (modified after Rasà *et al.* 1981). (1) Backward-tilted blocks; (2) oblique-slip displacements; (3) main faults; (4) rim of the Valle del Bove depression.

have been proposed (McGuire *et al.* 1990, 1991; Borgia *et al.* 1992; Lo Giudice & Rasà 1992), all of which focused in various ways on the important role played by gravity. Major problems include the question of whether this slowly eastward-gliding megastructure is strongly controlled by the pre-existing large scale structural setting of the Etna region (Lo Giudice *et al.* 1982; Lo Giudice & Rasà 1986*a*; McGuire & Pullen 1989; Ferrucci *et al.* 1992) and the related questions of both the depth and nature – ductile or brittle – of the detachment surface.

Since stable sliding constitutes a significant slip mechanism operating on the faults displacing the Mount Etna edifice, creep-data analysis may be viewed as being crucial for understanding the nature of flank deformation. This paper presents

a preliminary account of historical creep records from the literature together with the description of sites at which creep has been detected by systematic surveys. In all, 16 'creep sites' have been identified and two localities, in particular at Acicatena and East Pernicana, have been fully investigated because of impressive evidence of long-term aseismic slip.

Creep sites

All the 16 creep sites identified are confined to the eastern flank of the volcano. For each site, the principal features of the creep process are presented, including average fracture trends, the nature of the surface displacements, and related topographic features. For a comprehensive view, most data are also summarized in a graphical form in Fig. 2.

In some cases the average creep rates determined from cumulative displacements observed across reference lines are supplied. These non-instrumental measurements should be regarded

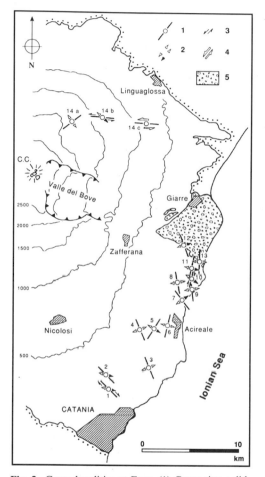

Fig. 2. Creep localities at Etna. (1) Creep site: solid line indicates the prevailing trend of ground cracks and fractures on man-made features; (2) average direction of extension: black arrow indicates the downthrown side when dip-slip is appreciable; (3) oblique-slip displacements; (4) strike-slip displacement with negligible dip separation; (5) Chiancone Formation (sandy fanglomerates). Index of creep sites: 1, Santa Agata li Battiati; 2, Tremestieri; 3, Crocefisso–Nizzeti; 4, Aci San Antonio; 5, Acicatena; 6, Aciplatani; 7, Santa Tecla; 8, San Giovanni Bosco–Guardia; 9, Stazzo; 10, Scillichenti; 11, Pozzillo Soprano; 12, San Leonardello; 13, Torrente Fago; 14, Provenzana–Pernicana fault system: a, Guardia Romana, b, Piano Pernicana, c, Rocca Campana.

as a crude approximation, because creep rate typically jumps to a high value following the occurrence of significant earthquakes along the same fault, thereafter progressively decaying (Wesson 1988). We believe that only detailed instrumental data recorded using creep meters (wires or road extensiometers), and geodetic monitoring, along with trenching, will provide a real measure of the temporal evolution of the surface fault creep acting at each locality.

Santa Agata li Battiati

Creep episodes at a locality south of Santa Agata li Battiati village (Villaggio Primavera) have been reported as far back as 1973 (Lo Giudice 1988). More recently, three days prior to the 25 October, Fleri, macroseismic ($M = 3.9$) earthquake of the October–November 1984 seismic crisis which affected the eastern flank of the volcano (Gresta *et al.* 1987), a set of open soil cracks trending NW–SE developed in a narrow sheaf in the same area (Azzaro *et al.* 1989*b*). Fractures up to 300 m in length propagated rapidly (5–6 h) causing right-lateral, oblique offset of the road SP 3/II° and some buildings. Cumulative lateral displacement reached a maximum value of 5–6 cm, and a few centimetres both in heave and throw (downthrown side to the east), were observed. The creep features observed were probably due to surface aseismic slip occurring along a concealed fault with the same trend and kinematics as the Mascalucia–Tremestieri fault (Fig. 1). At present, there is no evidence of active creep.

Tremestieri

Aseismic slip occurred along the Mascalucia–Tremestieri fault in 1960 and related offsets of some buildings on the fault line south of Tremestieri village are still visible (Lo Giudice 1988). Subsequently, a composite event (Wesson 1988) characterized by two distinct phases of pre- and post-seismic creep pulses occurred along the southern segment of the same fault during the August 1980 very shallow seismic sequence, which affected the northern segment of the fault itself (Lo Giudice & Longo 1986).

Surface pre-seismic slip started on 21 August, two days prior to the main shock of the seismic sequence, and open surface cracks slowly propagated northwards for about 1 km along the fault trace over a period of about 12 h (Lo Giudice & Rasà 1992). The fractures were aligned along a bearing of 140°, and characterized by a right-lateral oblique displacement which offset the road SP 3/II°, together with boundary walls and buildings. Creep was renewed abruptly in the form of post-seismic slip immediately after the seismic sequence ended and gradually decayed to zero after some hours of rapid slip.

Further aseismic ruptures, with similar kinematics along the fault trace, repeatedly opened during the course of the 1984 and 1986 seismic sequences, and it is likely that the ground breaks associated with surface slip reported by Silvestri (1883) as occurring just west of Tremestieri village during the 1883 seismic and eruptive crisis, can also be interpreted as another stable-sliding episode affecting the Mascalucia–Tremestieri fault. Currently, stable-sliding processes on this fault seem to be inactive.

Crocefisso–Nizzeti

A prominent creep event occurred near the southern tip of the Timpa di San Nicoló fault scarp (Fig.1) in December 1988 (Azzaro *et al.* 1989*b*). Creep features, such as open ground cracks and fractures through some buildings and boundary walls, developed along a strip (70–80 m wide, 500 m long) trending NW–SE, revealing predominantly extensional displacement on a centimetric scale (3 cm in heave, 1 cm in throw) with no observed lateral component. Aseismic displacement still prevails at a very low creep rate, as evidenced by the minor disruption of man-made features built after 1989.

In this area, a discontinuous thin lava cover some metres thick overlies the Sicilian bluish clays (Francaviglia 1959) which here represent the sedimentary basement of the volcano. Nearby, this sedimentary formation crops out widely along the coast, where it is pervasively affected by surficial mass-movements (Platania 1899–1900; Scalia 1900; Sbaratta 1927–31; Sturiale 1967; Di Grande & Lo Giudice 1987). This leads to some ambiguity in the interpretations of the true nature of the previously described breakage features as creep movements along a fault, and the latter may be simply related to the movements of a disrupted volcanic slab slipping over the unstable, underlying clays.

Aci San Antonio

A creep episode took place during the summer of 1980 in the southeast outskirts of Aci San Antonio village and an impressive trench 4 m in width and 50 m in length opened along a contemporaneous ground-crack zone striking NW–SE (Lo Giudice 1988). The same author

indicated extensional slip without lateral components, but the subsequent evolution of the phenomenon is unknown. At present there is no evidence of active creep.

Acicatena

Long-lived aseimic creep along faults continuously causes severe damage to structures in Acicatena village (Lo Giudice 1988). Both here, and in the neighbouring area, the local stratigraphic succession revealed by detailed geological mapping and well-log interpretation from

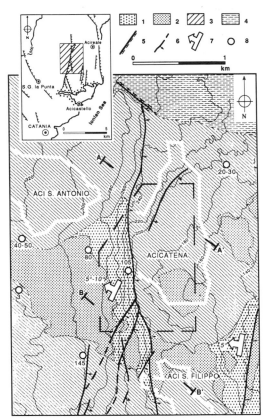

Fig. 3. Geology of Acicatena area. (1) Lava flows with subordinate horizons of tephra and tuffaceous sediments (Pre-Trifoglietto Unit; Upper Pleistocene); (2) brown tuffs with graded pumice layers (Trifoglietto Unit; Upper Pleistocene); (3) undated lava flows with poorly preserved surface features (Recent Mongibello Unit; Holocene); (4) lava flow with well- preserved surface features (394 BC; Mt. Gorna eruption?); (5) buried fault scarp; (6) fault; (7) backward-tilted blocks; (8) water well: number indicates top altitude (m a.s.l.) of the sedimentary basement. A–A', B–B' are the locations of the cross-sections in Fig. 4. Inset area defined by dashed lines is enlarged in Fig. 5. The edges of the villages are shown by a thick white line.

hydrogeological studies, is essentially made up of a volcanic rock sequence, including both lava and pyroclastic formations, overlying the bluish marly clays of the sub-volcanic basement (Fig. 3). The volcanic cover, ranging in thickness from 100 to 300 m, is displaced by local small-scale block faulting (Fig. 4). On a larger scale, this area can be seen to be part of a sector of the southeastern flank of the volcano which is broken into three, gently westward tilted sub-blocks separated by the Trecastagni, Acicatena and Acireale faults which are held responsible for the backward rotation of individual blocks (Fig. 1).

Acicatena itself lies on the western border of the intermediate block, and is bounded by the steep Acicatena fault scarp (Timpa di Acicatena). Strong creep effects, such as the formation of close sets of open cracks offsetting buildings and roads, have been recognized along a highly urbanized, recent fault scarp branching from the main fault and crossing Acicatena village, while similar features have also been observed along the main fault itself (Fig. 5).

Cumulative measurements carried out on different sampled areas along the fracture zone indicate horizontal aseismic slip rates ranging from 0.9 to 1.7 cm a^{-1} (A and C respectively in Fig. 5) with movements being predominantly extensional with only minor vertical displacement.

Inhabitants report episodic sinking effects and breakage of irrigation pipelines in this fracture zone prior to urban expansion, which took place in the early 1960s, while Platania (1922) cites evidence suggesting that aseismic fault slip occurred as far back as the beginning of this century. Because historical (Imbò 1935) and

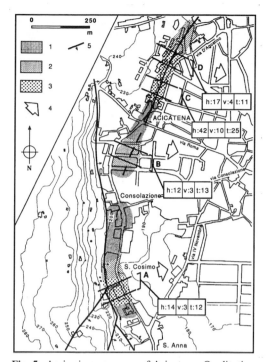

Fig. 5. Aseismic creep map of Acicatena. Qualitative levels of damage: (1) minor; (2) moderate; (3) major; (4) extensional direction; (5) fault. Numbers relating to A–D sampled areas indicate cumulative horizontal (h), vertical (v) displacement (cm), and lapsed time (t) since the first evidence of damage (years). The downthrown side of the fault is towards the east.

recent (Azzaro *et al.* 1989*b*) macroseismic studies reveal an absence of shallow seismic activity on both the Acicatena fault and the related structure, we believe that this fault system moves by stable sliding. The creep rate increased abruptly during the August 1980, October 1984, April 1985 seismic crises affecting the eastern flank of the volcano.

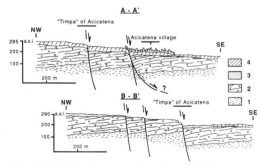

Fig. 4. Geological cross-sections through Acicatena area. (1) Bluish marly clays (Lower and Middle Pleistocene); (2) lava flows with subordinate horizons of tephra and tuffaceous sediments (Pre-Trifoglietto Unit; Upper Pleistocene); (3) brown tuffs with graded pumice layers (Trifoglietto Unit; Upper Pleistocene); (4) undated lava flows with poorly preserved surface features (Recent Mongibello Unit; Holocene).

Aciplatani

Silvestri (1879) reported the occurrence of a long fracture which opened during the 1879 eruption extending from the Acireale cemetery to a few kilometres south of Aciplatani village, where it vanished. The fracture developed aseismically without associated earthquakes (Imbò 1935) and crossed Aciplatani village causing great damage. The close alignment of the fracture line to a fault scarp which occurs about 1.5 km east of the Acicatena fault scarp (Timpa di Acicatena) with the same NNE–SSW strike, suggests that the former continues northwards, crossing the Aciplatani village without morphological expression of faulting.

Subsequently Silvestri (1893) reported a new, long crack following the same fault, which developed aseismically (Arcidiacono 1893) five days prior to the end of the 1886 eruption (7 June 1886). This fracture, with a maximum opening not exceeding 5 cm, crossed the village causing a similar offset.

Seven years later (9 April 1889), the onset of aseimic slip was once again observed in the same area (De Fiore 1908–11; Imbò 1935), occurring in a narrow zone, 1 km long and up to 8 m wide, in which densely spaced NNE–SSW trending cracks developed. Subsidence observed along the crushed strip suggested that mainly extensional kinematics characterized this event.

All the creep effects reported for the Aciplatani area come from observations made by authors during the last century, with no evidence for this behaviour being visible today.

Santa Tecla

Active surface creep occurs near the southeastern tip of the Santa Tecla fault scarp, along a strip where N30°W striking cracks and other creep features, such as sinks and depressions, continually develop in agricultural land. This fracture zone is more than 600 m long and 50 m wide, and crosses the southern part of Santa Tecla village, offsetting the SP 2/I° road, buildings and boundary walls, and vanishing near the coast. Cumulative displacements (15–20 cm) reveal a prevailing extensional movement, with a slight right-lateral component.

The first evidence for aseismic slip became apparent in the late 1970s when a creep rate of about $1 \, cm \, a^{-1}$ was recognized. A sharp, post-seismic increase in this rate was observed immediately after seimic activity (February and December 1986) on the Santa Tecla fault and nearby tectonic structures (Azzaro *et al.* 1989*b*).

San Giovanni Bosco–Guardia

Local inhabitants reported episodic creep pulses, causing damage to man-made structures, and the formation of soil cracks between the villages of San Giovanni Bosco and Guardia, occurring along a linear zone trending about N10°W. Field data appear to indicate purely extensional movements on the concealed section of a fault to the north which is morphologically expressed in the form of the Timpa di Moscarello.

Stazzo

A discontinuous, 400 m long fracture, broadly trending N10°W, characterized by purely extensional displacement of up to 2 cm, crosses the road linking Santa Tecla and Stazzo and other minor roads in the area. The crack has developed along the southern continuation of a fault scarp that is locally called the Timpa di San Leonardello. There are no reliable data concerning the onset of slip, and it is likely that given the absence of surficial seismicity since 1980 (Azzaro *et al.* 1989*b*, 1992), the breakage developed aseismically.

Scillichenti

Discontinuous N10°E striking cracks up to 200 m long have developed along the San Leonardello fault trace, causing fissuring of the two roads connecting Scillichenti to Stazzo village, just to the west of Cimaloro.

Available field evidence reveals the ambiguous nature of displacement across the fracture. Right-lateral, oblique slip (5–7 cm vertical and lateral) can be observed on the northern road, whereas purely dip-slip displacement (up to 15 cm) is visible on the southern one, with only a negligible horizontal component of the dip separation.

Because of the absence of seismicity along this section of the San Leonardello fault, the currently active fracturing must be ascribed to stable sliding with a mean creep rate not exceeding $0.5 \, cm \, a^{-1}$ revealed by analysis of the offsets of man-made structures.

Pozzillo Soprano

A set of currently active fractures trending N10°E has developed for about 600 m along a 100 m wide strip at the foot of the San Leonardello fault scarp, causing the offset of buildings, roads, and walls in the eastern part of Pozzillo Soprano village. Both extensional and vertical components of movement have been observed, but field evidence for the timing of the onset of creep, and markers which clearly explain the kinematics of the slip, are absent.

San Leonardello

Soil cracks have been detected in a narrow zone at the southern side of San Leonardello village where the road SS 114 crosses the Dagala torrent. At this site fractures breach a church and some buildings, and aseismic displacement is still active. Fractures reveal a prevailing dip slip, with a sluggish creep rate which increased suddenly after local seismic activity, such as the Codavolpe earthquake ($M = 3.5$, 29 January 1989) which affected the same fault about 1.5 km to the north (Azzaro *et al.* 1989*a*).

Torrente Fago

Some uncertain creep effects, such as the breakage of the Fago torrent bridge (road SP 2/I-II°) and slight deformation of walls in the nearby area, are reported as possible creep effects. This site lies at the northern tip of a fault scarp developed near the coast to the north of Pozzillo village.

Provenzana–Pernicana fault system

On the upper northeast flank of the volcano high surficial seismicity and marked, coseismic and aseimic brittle deformation are closely related to the activity of the Provenzana–Pernicana fault system (Gresta *et al.* 1986; Lo Giudice & Rasà 1986*b*; Azzaro *et al.* 1988). The overall kinematics have been clarified by Azzaro *et al.* (1991) and Lo Giudice & Rasà (1992). In the western part (Provenzana fault) the system displays purely dip-slip movements

and can be considered part of the NE Rift, which is a NE-trending zone of active magma injection connected to the summit craters. In contrast, the eastern part (Pernicana fault) decouples the eastern flank of the edifice from the rest of the volcanic pile by left-lateral, oblique-slip, normal movements.

The whole system shows discontinuous evidence of different modes of active creep and three main creep sites are currently recognized.

(i) Soil cracks up to 1 m wide, sometimes arranged 'en echelon' and trending about NE–SW, occur where the Provenzana fault joins the Pernicana fault (Guardia Romana locality; Fig. 2 site 14a). There is no obvious evidence of a visible fault and displacements can be explained by purely extensional strain. The timing of the onset of the fracture field is unknown, but the well-preserved appearance of the cracks in an area subject to considerable physical weathering suggests that it may be very recent.

(ii) Coseismic surface faulting followed by minor afterslip pulses, both showing oblique-slip movements, with normal and sinistral components respectively, have often been observed along the central, strongly seismo-genic (Lo Giudice & Rasà 1986*a*; Azzaro *et al.* 1988) sector of Pernicana fault (Piano Pernicana locality; Fig. 2 site 14b). The transient

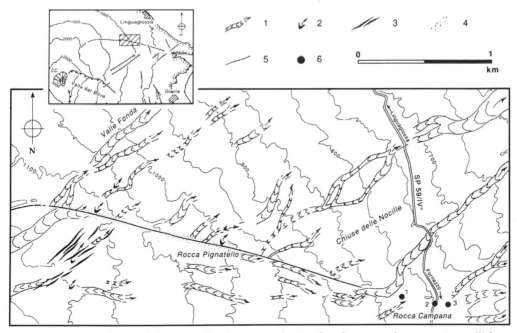

Fig. 6. Morphological map of the eastern Pernicana area showing flow features and mesostructures: (1) lava channels with flow directions; (2) rootless vents; (3) main ground cracks; (4) crush zones; (5) foot of the fault scarp; (6) sample sites (see text).

Fig. 7. Road SP 59/IV° 'Fornazzo–Linguaglossa' (sample site 2 of Fig. 6). Creep on the Pernicana fault offsets the central white line and boundary walls (view from south).

post-seismic creep commonly exhibited along this 'locked' section of the fault may be explained by seismic failure-induced relaxation of stress perturbations.

(iii) About 4 km eastwards, the Pernicana fault scarp tends to disappear, although the fault trace can be easily recognized by the damming effect on the Recent Mongibello lava units and by the distortion suffered by the lava-flow paths (Fig. 6). The dislocation line has developed as a discontinuous crush zone and distinctive aseismic slip is evident in the Rocca Campana locality (Fig. 2; site 14c). The nature of the surface displacement here is purely left-lateral. Secular aseismic slip is evident, as shown by the different magnitude of the offset measured in man-made features of varying ages. At the point where the fault crosses the road SP 59/IV°, strike separation measures 3 cm on the centre-line painted in 1992, and 80 cm on the boundary walls which are between 54 and 58 years old (Fig. 6 sample site 2; Fig. 7). Just to the east of the road a severely damaged house built in 1972 (Fig. 6 sample site 3) is offset by 40 cm, and about 200 m further west a neglected cart track dated between 1830 and 1850 has slipped 3.5 m (Fig. 6 sample site 1; Fig. 8).

It should be stressed that neither examination of historical data nor recent macroseismic investigations have revealed the existence of seismic activity along this sector of the Pernicana fault.

Discussion

Given the widespread distribution of creep phenomena determined from historical and

contemporary observations (Table 1), shallow stable sliding may be considered to be a significant mode of slip on the faults displacing Etna's eastern flank. It could certainly be argued

Fig. 8. Neglected cart track (sample site 1 on Fig. 6) showing left-lateral displacement due to secular creep on the Pernicana fault (view from north).

Table 1. *Creep data in the Etna area (site numbers as in Fig. 2).*

Site no.	Localities	Indicators of slip*	Average strikes of ruptures	Kinematics	Modes of slip	Associated faults	Source of data
1	Santa Agata li Battiati	b, c	135°	Dextral, oblique slip	Episodic	Concealed fault	Lo Giudice (1988) Azzaro et al. (1989b)
2	Tremestieri	a, b, c	135°	Dextral, oblique slip	Pre, post-seismic	Mascalucia–Tremestieri fault	Lo Giudice & Longo (1986) Lo Giudice (1988) Lo Giudice & Rasà (1992)
3	Crocefisso-Nizzeti	a, b, c	155°	Extensional, with minor vertical components	Episodic	San Nicolò fault	This study Azzaro et al. (1989b)
4	Aci San Antonio	a	155°	Purely extensional	Episodic	Concealed fault	Lo Giudice (1988)
5	Acicatena	b, c	025°	Extensional, with minor vertical components	Long-period	Acicatena fault	This study Platania (1922)
6	Aciplatani	a, b, c	170° 015°	Purely extensional	Episodic	Concealed fault	Silvestri (1879, 1893) De Fiore (1908–11)
7	Santa Tecla	a, b, c	140°	Extensional, with minor dextral components	Episodic	Santa Tecla fault	This study
8	San G. Bosco-Guardia	a, b, c	170°	Purely extensional	Episodic	Moscarello fault	This study
9	Stazzo	c	170°	Purely extensional	Episodic	San Leonardello fault	This study
10	Scillichenti	c	010°	Dextral, oblique slip	Episodic	San Leonardello fault	This study
11	Pozzillo Soprano	b, c	010°	Extensional, with vertical components	Episodic	San Leonardello fault	This study
12	San Leonardello	a, b, c	160°	Vertical, with minor extensional components	Episodic	San Leonardello fault	This study
13	Torrente Fago	c	005°	Purely extensional?	Episodic?	Torrente Fago fault	This study
14a	Guardia Romana	a	055°	Purely extensional	Post-seismic?	Provenzana–Pernicana system	This study
14b	Piano Pernicana	a, c	095°	Sinistral, oblique slip	Post-seismic	Provenzana–Pernicana system	This study
14c	Rocca Campana	a, b, c	095°	Purely left-lateral	Long-period	Provenzana–Pernicana system	This study

* Indicators of slip: cracks/dislocations in: a, soil; b, buildings; c, other cultural features (curbs, guard-rails, walls, fences, etc.).
† Episodic slip: creep events without close association with local earthquakes. Long-period slip: long-term, near continuous, aseismic slip punctuated by prominent creep pulses.

that permanent deformation due to aseismic slippage has often been overlooked, with respect to the permanent strain caused by very shallow seismic failures, especially in evaluating the magnitude of overall permanent deformation affecting this side of the edifice and its shallow basement. If it is assumed that the surficial seismicity exhibited in this sector is related to faults moving in a stable manner, it is also not unreasonable to suggest that creep movements within discrete individual fault zones may load locked fault segments leading to failure during subsequent earthquakes.

Creep rates, even if approximated, range from 0.5 to 2.3 cm a^{-1}, and the local creep histories are complex. Long-term (e.g. Acicatena) up to secular creep (e.g. Provenzana–Pernicana system), and both pre-seismic and post-seismic (e.g. Tremestieri), and multiple as well as episodic creep pulses have been recognized. This requires different creep laws at different sites. Even along the same fault, the form of individual creep events may be similar at a single site, but differ from one site to the next (e.g. Stazzo, Scillichenti, Pozzillo Soprano and San Leonardello, creep sites which are all related to the activity of the San Leonardello fault).

Eruptive crises rarely appear to have triggered fault creep, and no obvious relationship has been established between eruptions and creep activity. This may depend on the different eruptive mechanisms and it may be inferred that additional, transient stresses induced by magma moving inside the volcano are high enough to perturb the state of stress acting in the intermediate and lower eastern slopes of the volcano only in a few cases. Conversely, this suggests that many historical eruptive events related to steeply dipping intrusions issuing from the central feeding zone, have been ruled by a gravity-controlled stress regime as proposed by McGuire & Pullen (1989).

Even if at present there is little observational data to study the relative timing of eruptive activity and creep episodes, considerable attention should be focused on the Provenzana–Pernicana system. Since the Provenzana fault can be regarded as a structure belonging to the NE Rift, then the Pernicana fault accommodates by left-lateral movements the E–W extensional strains which severely stretch the Rift itself. If so, the creep movements along the Pernicana fault may be partially due to repeated pressurized magma injections along the rift structure. In a preliminary way this hypothesis appears to be unrealistic, since the steady-state mode of creep shown by the eastern tip of the Pernicana structure (Fig. 9) seems to indicate a 'passive'

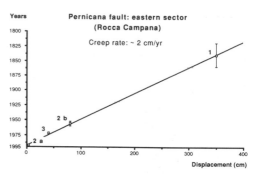

Fig. 9. Average creep rate along the eastern tip of Pernicana fault estimated by left-lateral offsets on: (1) neglected cart truck; (2) road SP 59/IV° 'Fornazzo–Linguaglossa': (**a**) central white line, (**b**) road boundary walls; (3) severely damaged house.

mode of rifting rather than an 'active' one. Nevertheless, in-depth investigations of the creep movements along the Pernicana fault by continuous instrumental monitoring and close cross-correlation of the creep data to the eruptive activity of the NE Rift are clearly required to address the problem adequately.

Finally, creep movements in the Etna area present a significant problem for planning and civil protection authorities. In the densely urbanized areas characteristic of the eastern flank, aseismic slip causes local destructive effects comparable to those caused by earthquakes. Any all-encompassing hazard assessment analysis of Etna should include data relating to problems associated with creep phenomena.

Conclusions

All the recognized creep sites are confined to the eastern sector of the volcano between the Pernicana fault, where secular creep at an average rate of about 2 cm a^{-1} accommodates by left-lateral slip the large extensional strains which occur along the NE Rift, and the Trecastagni–Mascalucia fault zone, where both coseismic and aseismic right-lateral slip take place. Lateral movements at other creep sites are trivially small compared to dip-slip movements with predominantly extensional component. Furthermore, the large extensional strains revealed by the creep displacements act approximately in an E–W direction, whereas no creep features indicating active N–S extension have been found (Fig. 2).

This kinematic picture is consistent with a dynamic picture emerging from the stress field map of the area (Fig. 10) proposed by Ferrucci

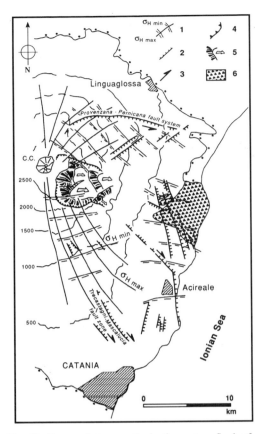

Fig. 10. Proposed stress paths in the eastern flank of Mt. Etna volcano (slightly modified from Ferrucci *et al.* 1993). (1) Maximum (σH_{max}) and minimum (σH_{min}) stress trajectories in the horizontal plane. Inferred stress paths are determined from tectonic and volcano-tectonic data including parasitic cone distribution, crater rim shapes, occurrence and orientation of dry and eruptive fissures, dyke swarms and faults; (2) main active faults; (3) lateral-slip sites; (4) rim of the Valle del Bove depression; (5) major slide features related to the evolution of the Valle del Bove (after Guest *et al.* 1984); (6) Chiancone Formation.

et al. (1993). It suggests that instability does not affect the whole eastern flank of the volcano as claimed by Borgia *et al.* (1992), but is restricted to a sector of the eastern flank structurally bordered by the Pernicana fault, the NE Rift, the SE Rift and the Trecastagni–Mascalucia fault zone (Lo Giudice & Rasà 1992). This mobile sector is locally dismembered into minor sub-blocks of volcanics, some of which are back-tilted, as in the Acicatena–Acireale area, which are decoupled from the remaining edifice, and slowly moving southeast together with the upper levels of the sedimentary basement (Fig. 4). The

presence of such back-rotated sub-blocks, in addition to the high surface stretching suffered in this sector of the volcano as revealed by a predominance of east–west extensional movements at nearly all the creep sites along the coast, confirm an overall eastward gliding tendency purely ruled by gravity (Kieffer 1985; Gresta *et al.* 1990; McGuire *et al.* 1991; Neri *et al.* 1991).

The Pernicana fault, NE Rift, SE Rift and Trecastagni–Mascalucia fault zone are discrete structural elements which coalesce into the arcuate structure embracing the seaward sliding sector. Both structural evidence and creep pattern suggest that this entire horse-shoe-shaped structure may be regarded as a complex, detached normal-fault system (Harding & Lowell 1979) which flattens to near-horizontal at depth allowing a large portion of the fault motion to be translated directly into extension (Fig. 11). Similar slowly gliding megablocks, characterized by cycloidal rupture surfaces and marked by planar motion, are common in many tectonic environments (Bally 1983). Typically they are relatively undeformed, but the movement is usually complex in details, involving translation and backward rotation of minor sub-blocks.

A primary problem is the interference between the horse-shoe fault system bounding the mobile sector and the main, deep-seated normal-fault zones displacing the crust beneath the volcano (Ghisetti & Vezzani 1982; Lo Giudice *et al.* 1982). In spite of specific investigations on this matter, the regional tectonic setting leads us to suppose that the NNW–SSE fault zone and the NE–SW fault zone (Lo Giudice & Rasà 1986*a*; McGuire & Pullen 1989; Ferrucci *et al.* 1992) play a major role in laterally driving the southern and the western border of the sliding megablock, respectively, whereas no evidence supports a deep structural control exerted by a regional structure on the northern border (i.e. Pernicana fault). Since Etna is located (Ferrucci *et al.* 1992) in a transitional zone separating crustal domains with contrasting tendencies toward active uplift (Sicilian continental crust) and subsidence (Ionian oceanic crust), we also propose that the gravity-induced movements characterizing this sector of the eastern flank may be genetically linked to large-scale tectonic behaviour.

It should be stressed that in the gravitational model proposed here the block moves under the influence of its own body forces, and the mechanism results in a megaslide implying a progressive flattening at depth of the main detachment surface. This flattening may be related to an increase in sub-surface fluid

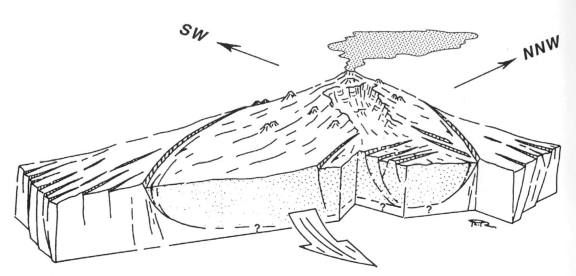

Fig. 11. Speculative block diagram showing the southeast sliding sector of Mt. Etna's sea-facing flank, not to scale. According to this interpretation the main detachment zone involves the upper levels of the clay-rich substrate, but its depth and nature are not determined. Arrows indicate the trends of the two main, deep-seated regional fault zones displacing the crust beneath the volcano. We suggest that the southern boundary (SE Rift, Trecastagni–Mascalucia fault zone) of the decoupled sector is closely controlled, in terms of its depth, by the NNW–SSE fault zone, whereas the northern one (Pernicana fault) offsets structures of the NE–SW zone at least at the surface. The offset drawn on the southern boundary is emphasized for graphical reasons, no obvious downfaulting along the SE-Rift and the Trecastagni–Mascalucia fault zone being observed in the field because of the high rate of resurfacing which affects this area (historical lava flows and pyroclastic cones).

pressure with depth which reduces the load-bearing strength of the sub-volcanic sedimentary sequence involved (Fyfe *et al.* 1978) or, alternatively, to the presence at depth of a pre-existing sub-horizontal weakness plane or zone. However, depth and type of failure along the basal detachment (laminar plastic flow, shear surface, chaotic slide-flow zone) are open questions which cannot be constrained by the surface-creep data presented in this study, and detailed geological, geophysical and geodetic investigations are required to improve this sliding model.

This work was supported by grants no. 93.02414 and no. 94.01619 by CNR – Gruppo Nazionale per la Vulcanologia, which is gratefully acknowledged. Thanks go to M. Macpherson for improving the English manuscript. We also thank W. McGuire and I. Stewart for very useful comments and amendments to an earlier version of this paper.

References

ARCIDIACONO, S. 1893. Fenomeni geodinamici che precedettero, accompagnarono e seguirono l'eruzione etnea del Maggio–Giugno 1886. *Atti della Accademia Gioenia di Scienze Naturali in Catania*, serie 4°,**VI**, memoria XXI.

AZZARO, R., BIRRITTA, G., LO GIUDICE, E. & RASÀ, R. 1992. Eventi macrosismici nell'area etnea nel periodo 1989–1991 ed implicazioni sismotettoniche. *Bollettino della Accademia Gioenia di Scienze Naturali in Catania*, **25** (339), 375–394.

——, BUDETTA, G., DEL NEGRO, C. & RASÀ, R. 1991. Dinamica del sistema Provenzana-Pernicana (M. Etna) e primi risultati di misure magnetiche. *Atti 10° Convegno del Gruppo Nazionale di Geofisica della Terra Solida, Roma*, **2**, 909–921.

——, CARVENI, P., LO GIUDICE, E. & RASÀ, R. 1989a. Il terremoto di Codavolpe (basso versante orientale etneo) del 29 Gennaio 1989: campo macrosismico e fratturazione cosismica. *Bollettino del Gruppo Nazionale per la Vulcanologia*, **1**, 1–12.

——, LO GIUDICE, E. & RASÀ, R. 1988. Il terremoto di Piano Pernicana (Etna Nord) del 28/10/1988. Campo macrosismico e quadro deformativo fragile associato all'evento. *Bollettino del Gruppo Nazionale per la Vulcanologia*, 22–40.

——, —— & —— 1989b. Catalogo degli eventi macrosismici e delle fenomenologie da creep nell'area etnea dall'agosto 1980 al dicembre 1989. *Bollettino del Gruppo Nazionale per la Vulcanologia*, **1**, 13–46.

BALLY, A. W. 1983. *Seismic Expression of Structural Styles*. American Association of Petroleum Geologists Studies in Geology, Series **15**.

BORGIA, A., FERRARI, L. & PASQUARÈ, G. 1992. Importance of gravitational spreading in the tectonic and volcanic evolution of Mount Etna. *Nature*, **357**, 231–234.

BRACE, W. F. & BYERLEE, J. D. 1966. Stick slip as a mechanism for earthquakes. *Science*, **153**, (3739), 990–992.

BRUNE, J. N. 1968. Seismic moment, seismicity and rate of slip along major fault zones. *Journal of Geophysical Research*, **73**(2), 777–784.

BYERLEE, J. D. & BRACE, W. F. 1968. Stick slip, stable sliding, and earthquakes – effect of rock type, pressure, strain rate, and stiffness. *Journal of Geophysical Research*, **73**(18), 6031–6037.

DE FIORE, O. 1908–11. Il periodo di riposo dell'Etna: 1893–1907. *Rendiconti e Memorie della Regia Accademia di Scienze, Lettere e Arti degli Zelanti di Acireale*, Memorie della Classe di Scienze, serie 3°, **VI**, 57–128.

DICKINSON, W. R. & GRANTZ, A. (eds) 1968. *Proceedings of a Conference on Geologic Problems of the San Andreas Fault System*. Stanford University Publication, Geological Sciences, **11**, 376 pp.

DIETERICH, J. H. 1978. Preseismic fault slip and earthquake prediction. *Journal of Geophysical Research*, **83**(B8), 3940–3948.

DI GRANDE, A. & LO GIUDICE, A. 1987. Osservazioni geologiche nei dintorni di Acicastello (Catania). *Bollettino della Accademia Gioenia di Scienze Naturali in Catania*, **20**(330), 317–327.

ENGELDER, J. T. 1973. The influence of quarz fault-gouge on sliding mode and stick-slip stress drops. *Transactions of the American Geophysical Union*, **54**(4), 465 pp.

FERRUCCI, F., GRESTA, S., PATANÈ, D. & RASÀ, R. 1992. Inferences on the magma feeding system at Mt. Etna volcano from seismological, structural and volcanological data. *Atti 11° Convegno del Gruppo Nazionale di Geofisica della Terra Solida*, Roma, **1**, 455–460.

——, RASÀ, R., GAUDIOSI, G., AZZARO, R. & IMPOSA, S. 1993. Mt. Etna: a model for the 1989 eruption. *Journal of Volcanology and Geothermal Research*, **56**, 35–56.

FYFE, W. S., PRICE, N. J. & THOMPSON, A. B. 1978. *Fluids in the Earth's Crust*. Elsevier Scientific Publishing Company, Amsterdam.

FRANCAVIGLIA, A. 1959. L'imbasamento sedimentario dell'Etna e il golfo pre-etneo. *Bollettino del Servizio Geologico Italiano*, **81**(4–5), 593–684.

GHISETTI, F. & VEZZANI, L. 1982. Different styles of deformation in the Calabrian Arc (southern Italy); implications for a seimotectonic zoning. *Tectonophysics*, **85**, 149–165.

GRESTA, S., LONGO, V. & VIAVATTENE, A. 1990. Geodynamic behaviour of eastern and western sides of Mount Etna. *Tectonophysics*, **179**, 81–92

——, CALTABIANO, T., CRISTOFOLINI, R., ET AL. 1986. L'eruzione dell'Etna del dicembre 1985. Integrazione di dati sismologici, tiltmetrici e vulcanologici. *Atti 11° Convegno del Gruppo Nazionale di Geofisica della Terra Solida*, Roma, **1**, 647–659.

——, GLOT, J. P., PATANÈ, G., POUPINET, G. & MENZA, S. 1987. The October 1984 seismic crisis at Mount Etna. Part I: Space-time evolution of the events. *Annales Geophysicae*, **5B**, 6 671–680.

GUEST, J. E., CHESTER, D. K., & DUNCAN, A. M. 1984. The Valle del Bove, Mount Etna: its origin and relation to the stratigraphy and structure of the volcano. *Journal of Volcanology and Geothermal Research*, **21**, 1–23.

HARDING, T. P. & LOWELL, J. D. 1979. Structural styles, their plate tectonic habitats and hydrocarbon traps in petroleum provinces. *American Association of Petroleum Geologists Bulletin*, **63**(7), 1016–1058.

IMBÒ, G. 1935. *I Terremoti Etnei*. Pubblicazioni della Commissione Italiana per lo Studio delle Grandi Calamitá, Regia Accademia Nazionale dei Lincei, Roma, **5**, parte 1.

KANAMORI, H. & CIPAR, J. J. 1974. Focal processes of the great Chilean earthquake May 22, 1960. *Physics of the Earth and Planetary Interiors*, **9**, 128–136.

KIEFFÈR, G. 1985. *Evolution Structurale et Dynamique d'un Grand Volcan Polygénique: Stades d'Édification et Activitè Actuelle de l'Etna*. Thèse Doctorat Ès Sciences, Université de Clermont-Ferrand

—— & TANGUY, J. C. 1993. L'Etna: évolution structurale, magmatique et dynamique d'un volcan 'polygénique'. *Mémoire de la Société Géologique de France*, **163**, 253–271.

LIENKAEMPER, J. J., BORCHARDT, G. & LISOWSKI, M. 1991. Historic creep rate and potential for seismic slip along the Ayward fault, California. *Journal of Geophysical Research*, **96**(B11), 18 261–18 283.

LO GIUDICE, E. 1988. Particolari aspetti del rischio sismico nell'area etnea. *In*: FAMOSO, N. (ed.) *Atti Convegno Internazionale 'L'organizzazione territoriale delle aree sismiche e vulcaniche'*, Zafferana E.-Randazzo 1985, 59–85.

—— & LONGO, V. 1986. *La Crisi Sismica Etnea dell' Agosto–Settembre 1980*. Istituto Internazionale di Vulcanologia–CNR Catania, Open File Report **4/86**.

—— & RASÀ, R. 1986a. The role of the NNW structural trend in the recent geodynamic evolution of North-Eastern Sicily and its volcanic implications in the Etnean area. *Journal of Geodynamics*, **5**, 309–330.

—— & —— 1986b. *Relazione Preliminare sulla Crisi Sismica Etnea del Dicembre 1985–Febbraio 1986*. Istituto Internazionale di Vulcanologia – CNR Catania, Open File Report **3/86**.

—— & —— 1992. Very shallow earthquakes and brittle deformation in active volcanic areas: the Etnean region as example. *Tectonophysics*, **202**, 257–268.

——, PATANÈ, G., RASÀ, R. & ROMANO, R. 1982. The structural framework of Mount Etna. *In*: ROMANO, R. (ed.) *Mt. Etna Volcano*, Memorie della Societá Geologica Italiana, **23**, 125–158.

McGUIRE, W. J. & PULLEN, A. D. 1989. Location and orientation of eruptive fissures and feeder-dykes at Mt. Etna: influence of gravitational and regional stress regimes. *Journal of Volcanology and Geothermal Research*, **38**, 325–344.

——, MURRAY, J. B., PULLEN, A. D. & SAUNDERS, S. J. 1991. Ground deformation monitoring at Mt. Etna: evidence for dyke emplacement and slope instability. *Journal of the Geological Society, London*, **148**, 577–583.

——, PULLEN, A. D. & SAUNDERS, S. J. 1990. Recent dyke-induced large-scale block movement at Mt. Etna and potential slope failure. *Nature*, **343**, 357–359.

PLATANIA, G. 1899–1900. Aci Castello. Ricerche geologiche e vulcanologiche. *Atti e Rendiconti della Regia Accademia di Scienze, Lettere e Arti degli Zelanti di Acireale*, Classe di Scienze, **10**, 1–56.

——1922. *Origine dei Terrazzi dell'Etna*. Pubblicazione dell'Istituto di Geografia Fisica, Università di Catania.

NERI, M., GARDUNO, V. H., PASQUARÈ G. & RASÀ, R. 1991. Studio strutturale e modello cinematico della Valle del Bove e del versante nord-orientale etneo. *Acta Vulcanologica*, **1**, 17–24.

RASÀ, R., ROMANO, R. & LO GIUDICE, E. 1981. Morphotectonic Map of Mt. Etna. Scale 1 : 100 000. *In*: ROMANO, R. (ed.) *Mt. Etna Volcano*, Memorie della Società Geologica Italiana, **23** [for 1982].

SBARATTA, R. 1927–31. Sulle sabbie vulcaniche intercalate nelle argille di Capo Molini (Catania). *Rendiconti e Memorie della Regia Accademia di Scienze, Lettere e Arti degli Zelanti di Acireale*, memorie della Classe di Scienze, serie 4°, **II**.

SCALIA, S. 1900. Revisione della fauna post-pliocenica dell argilla di Nizzeti presso Acicastello (Catania). *Atti della Accademia Gioenia di Scienze Naturali in Catania*, serie IV°, **13**,, memoria **19**.

SCHOLZ, C. H., WYSS, M. & SMITH, S. W. 1969. Seismic and aseismic slip on the San Andreas Fault. *Journal of Geophysical Research*, **74**(8), 2049–2069.

SILVESTRI, A. 1893. L'eruzione dell'Etna del 1886. *Atti della Accademia Gioenia di Scienze Naturali in Catania*, serie IV°, **6**, memoria **11**.

SILVESTRI, O. 1879. Fenomeni dell'Etna successivi all'ultima eruzione. *Bullettino del Vulcanismo Italiano*, anno **VI**, (8–11, agosto–novembre), 119–124.

——1883. Sulla esplosione etnea del 22 marzo 1883 in relazione ai fenomeni vulcanici (geodinamici ed eruttivi) presentati dall'Etna durante il quadriennio compreso dal gennaio 1880 al dicembre 1883. Osservazioni e studi. *Atti della Accademia Gioenia di Scienze Naturali in Catania*, serie III°, **17**.

STEINBRUGGE, K. V. & ZACHER, E. G. 1960. Creep on the San Andreas fault – Fault creep and property damage. *Bulletin of the Seismological Society of America*, **50**, 389–396.

STURIALE, C. 1967. Su alcune piroclastiti del basso versante meridionale dell'Etna. *Rendiconti della Societá Mineralogica Italiana*, anno **23**, 427–452.

TOCHER, D. 1960. Creep on the San Andreas fault – Fault creep rate and related measurements at Vineyard, California. *Bulletin of the Seismological Society of America*, **50**, 396–404.

WESSON, L. W. 1988. Dynamics of fault creep. *Journal of Geophysical Research*, **93**(B8), 8929–8951.

The boundaries of large-scale collapse on the flanks of Mount Etna, Sicily

DEREK RUST[1] & MARCO NERI[2]

[1] Neotectonics Research Centre, Brunel University, Isleworth, TW7 5DU, UK
[2] Istituto Internazionale di Vulcanologia, Catania, Piazza Roma, 2-95123, Italy

Abstract: Proposals for flank collapse on Etna find agreement from recent authors but models differ considerably in the scale and nature of the instability. Our work, including a new compilation of subsurface data, identifies the Ragalna system of linked faults and cinder cones as defining the southern margin of a very wide sector of flank instability comprising over 50% of the volcanic edifice. The Mascalucia and Trecastagni faults, previously identified as the southern boundary, occur within this sector and are now regarded as two examples of a number of relatively superficial faults accommodating differential movement. By comparison, faulting on the Ragalna system has produced very fresh-appearing scarps up to 20 m in height associated with dominantly dip-slip displacement. This pattern is expected on a boundary fault, the unstable side of which is moving downslope. The problem of the enigmatic triangular horst which abruptly terminates the surface expression of the Ragalna system at its upslope end may now be viewed in the light of new scale-model experiments which predict that such features are the likely result of spreading within a volcanic edifice. This helps explain the lack of a clear surface connection between the obviously active Ragalna faulting and the summit rifting. If this explanation is correct the Ragalna system assumes similar continuity and dimensions as the Pernicana – a system of linked structures generally accepted as defining the northern boundary of instability. The scale of the collapse is well within that predicted by the model experiments. Topographic buttressing on the northwestern arc of the volcano is mirrored by the absence of such support on the unstable southeastern arc where the flanks are bordered either by the sea or by a sedimentary trough (Gela–Catania Foredeep) occupied by recent plastic clays close to sea level. In addition, the rapidly growing volcanic edifice, approaching 3.5 km in some 300 ka, straddles the thrusted nappes of the Appennine–Maghrebian Chain to the northwest and the weak sediments of the Gela–Catania Foredeep to the southeast, with their contact beneath the volcano probably contributing to the location of the unstable sector. Minimum long-term slip rates determined from outcrop information on the Ragalna, and determined independently from subsurface data on the basal detachment underlying the collapsing sector are similar, arguing for a mechanical connection as would be expected if the Ragalna system formed the boundary to the basal detachment. A deep detachment model is consistent with focal depths on the Ragalna and with recent data on the timing of regional deformation in the Chain compared to the later timing of local (collapse-induced) deformation within the Etnean realm. The amplitude and wavelength of the local deformation, particularly on the southern margin of the volcano, is inconsistent in magnitude with that expected mechanically if the detachment was relatively superficial. A deep detachment is also indicated by the space requirements of a plutonic sequence postulated on geological and geophysical grounds below the summit region of the volcano.

Large-scale flank instability has been documented on a number of active volcanoes, notably in Hawaii and La Reunion (Duffield *et al.* 1982; Denlinger & Okubo 1995). On Mount Etna two recent papers have focused on the potential for large-scale gravity-induced collapse of the eastern flank of the volcano (Borgia *et al.* 1992; Lo Giudice & Rasà 1992). However, as a result of differences in the position of the boundaries of the proposed collapsing sector, particularly the position of its southern margin and of its lower limit within the volcanic edifice, the two papers differ considerably in their models of the scale and nature of collapse. These proposed structures have important hazard implications for the densely populated flanks of the volcano, increasing the need to resolve uncertainties in the extent and nature of the instability; any model must be based on firm evidence concerning these variables. The present paper reports new field and subsurface data and, in combination with existing information, aims to better define the activity level and boundaries of the instability, both in map view and cross-section.

From McGuire, W. J., Jones, A. P. & Neuberg, J. (eds) 1996, *Volcano Instability on the Earth and Other Planets*, Geological Society Special Publication No. 110, pp. 193–208.

Pernicana fault system

Both proposed models focus on the eastern and southeastern flanks of the volcano, identifying unstable segments radiating from the summit area and bounded on the north by the Pernicana fault. Field study of this fault has established a link with the main NE rift zone of the volcano via a right-stepping en echelon series of fractures (Neri *et al.* 1991) and together these structures represent a well defined line of active left-lateral displacement (Figs 1 and 2). The

importance of this system can be clearly established on the basis of historical seismicity, associated ground rupture and geodetic determinations (Lo Giudice 1986; Azzaro *et al.* 1989*b*, *c*; Borgia *et al.* 1994; Neri *et al.* 1994). Moreover, a compilation of published and previously unpublished hydrogeological data, prepared during the course of this study, has enabled a new contour map of the Etnean subsurface to be produced and the expression of the Pernicana fault on this compilation indicates a long history of displacement (Fig. 3).

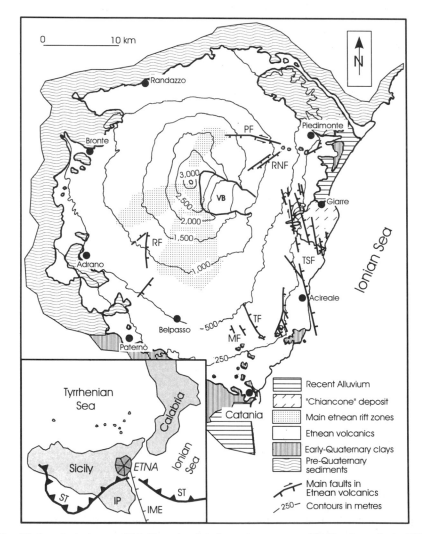

Fig. 1. Simplified geological map of Mt Etna showing the main structures. PF, Pernicana fault; RNF, Ripa della Naca faults; TF, Trecastagni fault; MF, Mascalucia fault; RF, Ragalna fault system; TSF, Timpe fault system; VB, Valle del Bove. Inset map: IP, Iblean Plateau; ST, Sole thrust of Appenine–Maghrebian Chain (rocks within the Chain are shown as Pre-Quaternary sediments on the main map); IME, Iblean–Malta Escarpment. See Fig. 8 for cross-section. Map based primarily on Romano (1979) and Rasè *et al.* (1982).

Fig. 2. Aerial view looking westwards along the strike of the active left-lateral Pernicana fault in the northern part of Mt Etna. See Fig. 1 for location of fault.

Mascalucia and Trecastagni faults

These two faults are important to both collapse models. The Lo Giudice & Rasà (1992) model identifies these faults as defining the southern margin of the collapsing sector. The Borgia *et al.* (1992) model on the other hand, while using the faults to define the southern margin of principal collapse, also suggest that more limited instability is occurring farther to the south and west, within a sector whose southwestern boundary is defined by the Ragalna fault (Fig. 1). Evidence for the importance of the Mascalucia–Trecastagni faults comes primarily from macroseismic determinations using the felt areas of very shallow seismicity, together with ground cracks recorded along the line of the faults (Lo Giudice & Rasà 1992). In the subsurface these authors suggest that a prominent ridge trending SSE from the summit area is made up of sedimentary basement which delimits their collapsing sector (Lo Giudice & Rasà 1992, fig. 8). This ridge is also apparent on the new subsurface map shown in Fig. 3 but the present authors interpret it to

be the result of intrusions within a broad zone extending generally southwards from the summit of the volcano. This zone is probably not a deep-seated structure, and intrusion of dykes is likely to be limited at lower altitudes within this ridge (McGuire & Pullen 1989). To the southeast of the rift zone the mapped position of the Trecastagni fault is poorly reflected in the subsurface contours (Fig. 3).

At the surface the two faults are far less convincing as a boundary to the collapsing sector than the Pernicana and Ragalna faults. They occur as two isolated structures, exhibiting relatively subdued geomorphic expression (Rust 1993*a*), about 2 km long and about 2.5 km apart at about the same altitude on the volcano, and do not appear to constitute two en echelon segments of a more continuous line of faulting.

Ragalna system

Large-scale aerial photographs and field examination of the relatively unstudied Ragalna fault system and associated structures some 12 km farther to the west on the volcano suggest that the boundary to the collapsing sector occurs there (Figs 1 and 4). The Ragalna fault can be traced as a series of linked structures extending for as much as 10 km in an overall NNE direction towards the summit area of the volcano, and may link with the rifting in the upper part of the volcano (Figs 1 and 4; Rust 1993*b*). The system includes a series of small and recently active cinder cones which appear to form a transfer zone between the ends of two fault segments (Fig. 4), and linear fresh-appearing fault scarps up to 5 km long and 20 m high (Fig. 5). These structures clearly indicate that the Ragalna system accommodates a significant level of activity. The scarps themselves are developed in volcanic sequences mapped as very late Pleistocene and Holocene in age by Romano (1979) and De Rita *et al.* (1991), as shown in Fig. 4b. Scarp heights and ages of the associated volcanics suggest a long-term dip-slip component of movement up to approximately 1.4 mm a^{-1}. In addition, a series of open fissures were also discovered along one segment of the fault, possibly indicating tectonic activity (Fig. 6).

Examination of the fault system in the field indicates dominantly dip-slip extensional displacement, and deflections in drainage crossing the fault are consistent with a component of right-lateral slip (Fig. 4b). In addition, the left-stepping arrangement of the axes of an en echelon series of late Pleistocene–early

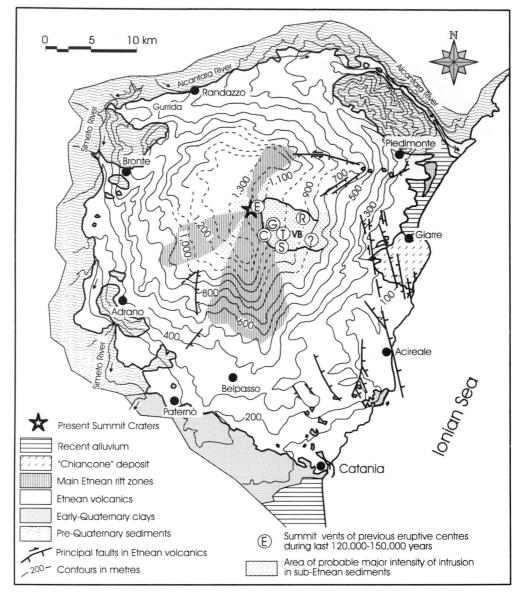

Fig. 3. Simplified contours on the reconstructed sub-Etnean surface, together with adjacent outcrops and Etnean structures. VB, Valle del Bove. Previous eruptive centres (from youngest to oldest): E, Ellittico; C, Cuvigghiuni; G, Serra Giannicola Grande; S, Salifizio; T, Trifoglietto; R, Rocca Capra; ?, Calanna? Note the present summit close to the Ellittico vent. The positions of the previous eruptive centres are taken from Coltelli *et al.* (1994), Calvari *et al.* (1994) and Romano (1982).

Holocene lava domes mapped by Romano (1979) and Rasà *et al.* (1982), and their close spatial association with the faulting, is consistent with a component of right-lateral movement (Fig. 4a). The age and arrangement of the lava domes further suggest that the linked structures have played a relatively long-standing role in accommodating right-lateral displacement in this part of the volcano. This suggestion is consistent with the subsurface expression of the fault as indicated in Fig. 3.

The well-defined triangular pattern created by active faults in the Ragalna system, with the triangle apex pointing towards the volcano summit and dip-slip faulting on either side leaving the triangle as a horst (Figs 1 and 4b), demands explanation. Attempts in the field and on aerial photographs to find a continuation of this structure in the direction of the volcano summit are hampered by dense vegetation and very recent lava flows. The linear margins of lava flows, trending downslope on the volcano, are in this area close to the strike of possible continuations of the active Ragalna structures.

Confident distinction between the two features relies heavily on field observation of tilted and disrupted blocks of tabular lava coinciding with the linear crest of a fault scarp. Such features can be observed along the mapped part of the Ragalna system shown in Fig. 4 but in the younger lavas nearer the summit a throughgoing linear series of these characteristic forms cannot be recognized. However, the clear evidence for a relatively long history of active movement on

(a)

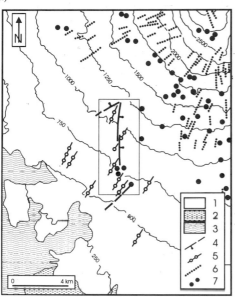

(b)

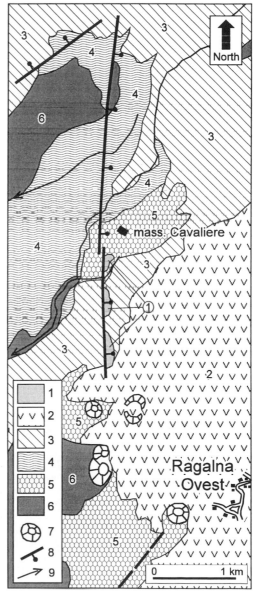

Fig. 4. (a) Map of Ragalna system of faults and cinder cones within the volcanic sequence on the southern flank of Mount Etna. The left-stepping en echelon arrangement of lava domes associated with the system suggests a component of right-lateral displacement. 1, Etnean volcanics; 2, Sub-Etnean clays; 3, Appennine–Maghrebian Chain; 4, faults with bar on downthrown side; 5, axes of lava domes; 6, eruptive fissures; 7, cinder cones. See text for further explanation and Fig. 1 for location. Box indicates area of Fig. 4b. Map uses data from Romano (1979) and Rasà *et al.* (1982). (b) Geological map of the northern part of the Ragalna system. See (a) for location. 1, Recent alluvium; 2, historical lavas; 3, lavas related to the Recent Mongibello phase (<8000 years); 4, ignimbrites related to the final stage of the Ellittico centre *c.* 14 000 years); 5, autoclastic lava domes related to the Ellittico centre (40 000–14 000 years); 6, lavas related to the Ellittico centre (40 000–14 000 years); 7, cinder cones; 8, fault with bar and ball on downthrown side; 9, drainage crossing the faults. Map also includes data from Romano (1979) and De Rita *et al.* (1991).

Fig. 5. Panorama of a linear scarp developed on part of the Ragalna fault system in the southern part of Mt Etna. View is westwards from Masseria Cavaliere (see Fig. 4b).

the mapped fault traces implies transfer of displacement to other linked structures. This is particularly true for the triangular-shaped horst structure at the summit end of the system because of the relatively abrupt termination of such a pronounced feature of active faulting. The downslope end of the system, by comparison, indicates gradually diminishing offset and apparently ends at a small and relatively degraded cinder cone.

Fig. 6. A series of open fissures developed on the N–S striking fault scarp within the Ragalna system SSW of Masseria Caveliere (see Fig. 4b). The fissures may be influenced by local gravity-induced movements affecting the scarp face.

These observed features coincide well with the structures produced in recent scale-model experiments of the spreading and collapse of volcanic edifices (Merle & Borgia 1995). These experiments produced triangular horsts separated by wide downslope-narrowing graben structures, with dip-slip displacement on the bounding faults supplemented by a minor strike-slip component offsetting the wedge-shaped graben relatively downslope. Additionally, the amount of fault offset diminishes downslope towards the base of the edifice, again coinciding with observations on the Ragalna system. Consequently, based on these model experiments, the abrupt termination of fault activity at the upslope end of the system may simply represent the high-standing apex of a relatively stable horst. Upslope from this apex the model indicates a wide depressed zone of rifting. On Etna the apex on the Ragalna system does closely approach the summit rift zones (Fig. 3), and the surface expression of any throughgoing structure within the rifts can be expected to be obscured by very recent lavas within this structural low.

Seismicity

A review of available seismological data for Etna confirms the active status of the structures identified above. For example, the earthquake sequence of 15–16 December 1991 began with a mainshock ($M = 4.5$) located about 2 km SW of the summit, followed by a pattern of aftershocks ($M_{max} = 2.6$) which spread towards the SW for 6–7 km. The distribution of aftershocks allowed the fault plane to be unambiguously constrained and fault-plane solutions revealed right-lateral displacement (Ferrucci & Patane 1993). Similar results are indicated by fault-plane solutions obtained by Cristofolini et al. (1981) from earthquakes recorded during November 1977–January 1978, and by a fault-plane solution and the macroseismic field from a shallow (<5 km) event on the mapped part of the Ragalna fault (Gresta & Patane 1987). These findings are consistent with a possible link between the Ragalna system and the summit area rift zones, and with the suggested component of right-lateral displacement on the system.

Such instrumental data as above are at present unfortunately limited. Seismic energy is almost continuously released at Mt. Etna in the form of temporal and/or spatial clusters, the largest magnitudes seldom reaching $M = 4.0$, and more than 80% of these events have focal depths of <5 km (Gresta et al. 1990). Because of this the events are localized in terms of felt area and macroseismic investigations are regarded as the best means of epicentre and hypocentre determination (Rasà pers. comm. 1994). This is, however, inevitably likely to introduce a bias in earthquake distribution maps towards the more densely populated eastern flank of the volcano. The effect of such a bias in comparing the importance of the Ragalna system with the Mascalucia and Trecastagni faults may be significant because the events used by Lo Giudice & Rasà (1992) to characterize the behaviour of the latter faults, and covering the period from 1980 to 1989, have very shallow foci (1–2 km) and very restricted felt areas. Such events may be poorly constrained in the more sparsely populated and higher altitude terrain of the Ragalna system. Nevertheless, maps of macroseismic activity for the southern and eastern flanks during the 1980–89 period clearly show a significant number of events (up to intensity VII) centred on the Ragalna system (Azzaro et al. 1989c: Benina et al. 1984). It should be noted that events on the eastern flank are generally shallow (1–2 km) whereas those recorded on the Ragalna system are generally deeper (4–7 km).

Hydrogeological, outcrop and seismic profile data on Etnean basement

The topography and nature of the Etnean basement is regarded in both models as an important influence on the stability of the volcanic edifice. The Lo Giudice & Rasà (1992) model postulates a relatively shallow detachment beneath the volcanic sequence of Etna itself, consistent with the very shallow seismicity determined macroseismically on the eastern flank. The Borgia et al. (1992) model suggests a detachment as deep as about 5 km occurring chiefly within weak sediments of the Gela–Catania Foredeep which occupy the junction between the Iblean Foreland to the south and the southward verging thrusted nappes of the Appennine–Maghrebian Chain to the north (Lentini 1982; Fig. 1).

Our analysis of the instability models employs published work and previously unpublished hydrogeological reports (Fig. 7) to produce a new subsurface contour map beneath Etna (Fig. 3); new cross-sections through the volcano have also been compiled (Fig. 8). It should be noted that the borehole information is generally limited to the lower slopes of the volcano (Fig. 7), and wells often penetrate only a few metres below the water table, usually still within

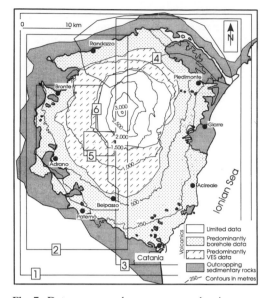

Fig. 7. Data source and coverage map showing areas of sub-Etnean basement studied by previous authors and used in the reconstruction shown in Fig. 3.
1. Ogniben (1966); Compagnia Mediterranea Prospezioni (unpublished, 1979); Loddo *et al.* (1989).
2. Aureli (1973); 3. Ferrara (1975, 1977). 4. Aureli & Musarra (1975). 5. Lo Giudice *et al.* (1981).
6. Patella & Quarto (1987).

the volcanics overlying the clay-rich sedimentary basement (Ogniben 1966). Much of the more recent hydrogeological data comes from indirect geoelectric and gravity surveys using in particular Vertical Electrical Sounding (VES) methods, but uncertainty about the depth of sedimentary basement remains because experience shows that the low resistivity of sedimentary rocks (Patella & Quarto 1987; Loddo *et al.* 1989) is sometimes very similar to the low-resistivity of groundwater in volcanics (M. Patane, pers. comm. 1994). Overall, these limitations tend to produce an underestimate of the thickness of the volcanic pile and, due to very limited borehole and VES data (Fig. 7), this uncertainty is particularly true in the summit area.

Despite these notes of caution the reconstructions clearly indicate features within the subsurface which are consistent with surface mapping (Fig. 3). The principal Etnean structures, such as the Timpe fault system for example (Figs 1 and 3), are clearly expressed on this reconstructed surface. In the northeast sector of the volcano the Pernicana and Ripa della Naca faults are clearly associated with a subsurface ridge which continues on strike to coincide with outcrops of sedimentary basement (Figs 1 and 3). Similar subsurface ridges are

associated with the Ragalna fault system, and the more detailed work of Patella & Quarto (1987) in this area of the volcano shows correspondence between the subsurface and surface expressions of the system. Such consistent relationships provide confidence in the accuracy of the map overall, although the inferred contours of a buried mountain of some 1300 m located to the northwest of the present summit craters should be regarded with caution because they occur in the summit region where data quality is relatively poor (Fig. 7).

Outcrops of early Quaternary sub-Etnean clays occur on the south and to a limited extent on the southeast of the volcano (Fig. 3), and are characterized by well-developed shears and slickensides (Fig. 9). Borgia *et al.* (1992) suggest that the E–W trends of anticline–syncline structures mapped within these sediments are the result of southward-directed spreading movement of the sector of the volcano between the Mascalucia and Trecastagni faults and the Ragalna fault. The smaller-scale deformation structures, which include conjugate shears, also indicate a generally N–S sense of compression (Labaume *et al.* 1990). Overall, the orientation of these structures is consistent with the view that right-oblique displacement is occurring on the Ragalna system to accommodate southward-directed movement within the volcanic edifice.

Commercial (AGIP) seismic profile and borehole records which transect the anticline–syncline axes are presented by Ferrari (1991) and Borgia *et al.* (1992) and indicate a 400 m compressional offset of a 50 m thick lava flow which is petrographically identical to the Etnean basal tholeiites dated by Gillot & Romano (1987) at *c.* 300 ka (Ferrari, pers. comm. 1994). Borgia *et al.* (1992) interpret this offset as the result of an active southward-verging fold associated with their postulated deep detachment as it climbs towards the surface as a thrust near the southern margin of the volcano (Fig. 8a). Interestingly, the minimum rate of thrust displacement calculated by these authors on this structure by means of section balancing is 2 mm a^{-1}, similar to the rate of about 1.4 mm a^{-1} suggested above for the dip-slip component of displacement on parts of the Ragalna system. Augmenting this with the probable right-lateral slip component is likely to increase the similarity between the two rates and appears to reinforce the proposal that this system forms the boundary to active collapse deformation on this flank of Etna.

Outcrops of the sub-Etnean clays in the coastal zone of the southeastern sector of the volcano

(Fig. 3) contain small-scale structures related to generally WNW–ESE directed compression. However, these structures, as well as the small-scale structures described above to the south of the volcano, are thought by Labaume *et al.* (1990) and Bousquet *et al.* (1988) to be largely synsedimentary, resulting from instability associated with nappe emplacment during formation of the Appennine–Maghrebian Chain, rather than by gravity-induced sliding of the volcanic edifice as suggested by the Borgia *et al.* (1992) model. This problem may be resolved through

(a)

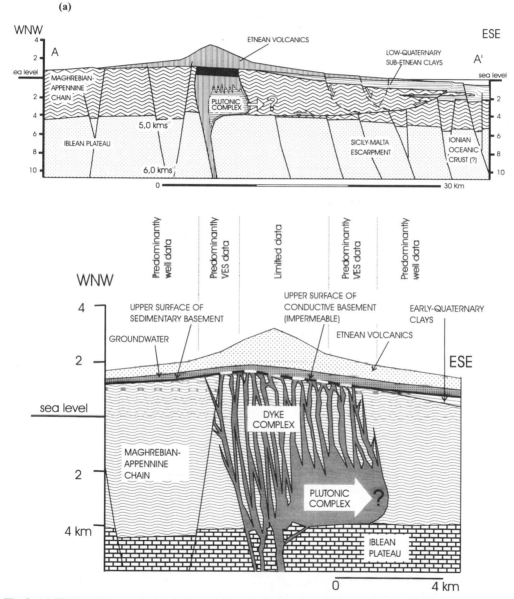

Fig. 8. **(a)** WNW–ESE cross-section below Mt Etna (redrawn after Borgia *et al.* 1992, and including data from Morellia *et al.* 1975 and Finetti 1982) showing the plutonic complex interpreted from seismic, gravity and structural data. Also shown is the possible detachment associated with the plutonic complex and rising from a depth of about 5 km. See also inset map in Fig. 1 and cross-section trace on Fig. 11. **(b)** Schematic cross-section showing possible relationships beneath the central part of Mt Etna. Note the pervasive dyking interpreted to occur above the plutonic complex. See **(a)** for context and Fig. 7 for data sources.

recent work by Lentini *et al* (1991) and Pedley & Grasso (1991) on the timing of deformation in the Chain in the Catania–Gela Foredeep, and in the Iblean Plateau. These areas lie to the south of Etna and beyond any local deformation associated with the edifice itself (Fig. 1). This work indicates that major plate-margin under-thrusting took place in Mio-Pliocene times and ceased after the early Pleistocene. Moreover, the folding associated with the later phases of this regional deformation characteristically produces low-amplitude long-wavelength folds, unlike the

Fig. 9. (a) Outcrop and (b) hand specimen photographs of the sub-Etnean clays which crop out particularly to the south of Mt Etna (Fig. 1). Both photographs show the highly sheared and slickensided nature of the clays.

style of deformation associated with the sub-Etnean clays within the Etnean domain. The timing of this regional deformation, together with the AGIP data outlined above on the deformed *c.* 300 ka old basal Etnean tholeiites, suggests that the outcrop-scale compressional deformation structures found in coastal exposures of the sub-Etnean clays may be related to movement within the volcanic edifice. Basal Etnean tholeiites crop out in the form of pillow lavas at the well known Acicastello exposure on the coast between Catania and Acireale (Fig. 1). Here the sequence has been uplifted and deformed, and now dips near vertically within coastal cliffs (Di Re 1963; Fig 10).

It is noteworthy that Labaume *et al.* (1990) draw attention to the difficulty in discriminating between synsedimentary gravity-induced deformation in the sub-Etnean clays and thrust-related structures. Additionally, they emphasize the low shear strength of the clays and the likelihood of high pore-pressures from interstitial water, both factors serving to facilitate and concentrate deformation within this unit (Fig. 9). These authors also note that the sub-Etnean clays now crop out at an altitude of 750 m near the community of Vena on the eastern flank of the volcano, in fact occurring as windows along the crest of the ridge at the

eastern end of the Pernicana fault (Fig. 3). This information, together with recent work (Firth *et al.* 1996) on late Holocene uplifted coastal carbonate reefs at Acireale which indicates uplift at $0.8–1.4\,\mathrm{mm\,a^{-1}}$, has been used to suggest a persistent pattern of uplift and eastward tilting beneath Etna, further suggesting that such a pattern is likely to produce a long history of superficial instability in the growing edifice. However, the coincidence of the highest clay outcrops with a ridge which appears to be genetically related to the Pernicana fault raises a question about the extent to which these outcrops in such easily deformed clays are more than a localized phenomenon associated with active faulting. Figure 3 shows that many of the remaining outcrops of the sub-Etnean clays, particularly to the north of Catania, occur as small windows closely associated with active structures such as the Trecastagni fault. It may be that the uplift and tilting of these clays in the Etnean realm is actually more modest than suggested by these isolated outcrops and, particularly in view of the recent work on the timing of regional deformation outlined above, it may be that the present distribution and structural character of the clays, together with the data on late Holocene coastal uplift, can be largely attributed to deformation of a plastic substrate as a result of loading by the volcanic edifice.

Fig. 10. Aerial view of the steeply dipping Etnean basal tholeiitic pillow lavas exposed at Acicastello, on the coast between Catania and Acireale (Fig. 1). View is NNE on strike with the near-vertical contact between the pillow lavas to the left of the photograph beneath the tower and hyaloclastites to the right making up the seaward end of the castle promentary. Flat-lying recent lavas underlie the promenade at the extreme lower left of the photograph.

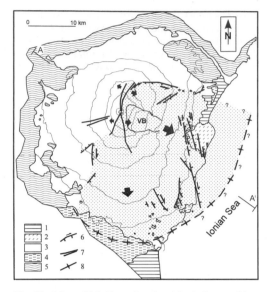

Fig. 11. Map of Mt Etna showing (shaded) unstable segment with arrows indicating radially directed spreading. The segment as a whole may be underlain by a deep-seated detachment as suggested by the interpretation of section A–A[1] shown in Fig. 8a. The arcuate anticlinal structure fringing the southern margin of the volcano, together with its possible extension offshore, is probably related to the detachment. Faults shown within the segment are active and accommodate differential movement. Differential movement is also likely in section, particularly in the part of the segment centred on the more northerly arrow. Here very shallow seismicity suggests dislocation within a relatively superficial layer made up predominantly of the volcanic sequence itself. 1, Recent alluvium; 2, 'Chiancone' deposit; 3, Etnean volcanics; 4, Early Quaternary clays; 5, Pre-Quaternary sediments; 6, principal faults within Etnean volcanics; 7, limits of principal Etnean rift zones; 8, fold axis, with question marks indicating uncertainty in its offshore projection.

Overall, the available evidence is consistent with a belt of active compressional deformation bordering the volcano at the foot of its southern and southeastern flanks, and appears to strengthen the suggestion of Borgia *et al.* (1992) that a ridge-like bathymetric feature offshore of the eastern flank is similar in origin (Fig. 11). Similar marginal bulge structures were produced in the scale-model experiments of Merle & Borgia (1995) although these experiments did not attempt to model the possible influence on spreading of regional uplift.

Intrusive bodies and space considerations

Geological mapping within the Valle del Bove has revealed evidence for a spatial and temporal

sequence of volcanic centres, beginning with the oldest centre farthest downslope and continuing through progressively younger centres upslope towards the presently active summit area (McGuire 1982; Romano 1982; Neri 1992; Coltelli *et al.* 1994; Calvari *et al.* 1994; Fig. 3). This mapping, and the idea that the sequence is related to a long-term history of downslope movement towards the southeast, is consistent with the interpretation of seismic data by Sharp *et al.* (1980) and Hirn *et al.* (1991) which concludes that a high-velocity plutonic complex associated with past eruptive centres extends southeastwards from the present summit. Seismic tomography work by Cardaci *et al.* (1993) also reinforces this interpretation, as does the gravimetric survey of Loddo *et al.* (1989). The Borgia *et al.* (1992) model proposes that movement on a deep-seated detachment accommodates the space requirements of such a plutonic complex and this is shown in our cross-section reconstruction (Fig. 8a). Similar space considerations and directions of dilation have been documented for high-level dykes around the Valle del Bove by McGuire *et al.* (1991) and Ferrari *et al.* (1991). It is also noteworthy that the broad zone of flank eruptions and associated intrusives which extends southwards from the summit of Etna occurs within the large unstable sector defined by the Pernicana and Ragalna fault systems (Fig. 3). This suggests the possible role of intrusives in accounting for the greater width of the feature during movement across a linear magma source beneath the basal detachment underlying the sector. These data together indicate a long and continuing history of deep-seated flank instability on Etna, possibly with movement aided by intrusions in a similar way to the flank movements on Kilauea in Hawaii (Duffield *et al.* 1982; Denlinger & Okubo 1995).

Discussion and conclusions

The foregoing analysis of recently available and previously unpublished data suggests that the boundaries and nature of instability on the flanks of Mount Etna can be refined, with the consequent sharpening of focus for further studies and hazard monitoring of this important phenomenon. In particular the previously little-studied Ragalna system of faults and related structures is identified as the southern boundary to a wide sector of flank instability whose northern boundary is defined by the Pernicana fault system (Fig. 1). Although, of the two, the Ragalna has received relatively little attention, it exhibits striking evidence of recent faulting activity, and is clearly a seismogenic structure with recent instrumented seismicity suggesting links to the active rifting in the summit region.

The problem of the enigmatic triangular horst which abruptly terminates the surface expression of the Ragalna system at its upslope end may now be viewed in the light of new scale-model experiments which predict that such features are the likely result of spreading within a volcanic edifice. This experimental evidence may help to explain the lack of a clear surface connection between the obviously active Ragalna faulting and the summit rifting. If this explanation is correct the Ragalna system assumes similar continuity and dimensions to the Pernicana, a system of linked structures generally accepted as defining the northern boundary of instability.

Accepting the Pernicana and Ragalna systems as forming the boundaries between unstable and relatively stable parts of Mount Etna defines a collapsing sector with an arc of some 35 km involving more than 50% of the edifice (Fig. 11). Firstly, this scale of collapse is well within that predicted by the recent model experiments discussed above; an experiment buttressed in a similar way to Mount Etna produced a wide pattern of collapse very similar to that observed on the volcano itself. Second, the topographic buttressing in the northwestern arc of the volcano is mirrored by the absence of such support on the southeastern arc. Here the flanks are bordered either by the sea or by a sedimentary trough (Gela–Catania Foredeep) occupied by recent plastic clays close to sea level. A third factor is the rapid rate at which the volcano is being constructed: the basal lavas are only some 300 ka in age yet the edifice is now close to 3.5 km in height. In addition, this rapid accumulation has taken place at the boundary between the thrusted nappes of the Appennine–Maghrebian Chain to the northwest and the weak sediments of the Gela–Catania Foredeep to the southeast. The fact that the contact between these two units to the southwest of the volcano lies approximately on strike with the Ragalna system suggests that the sub-Etnean continuation of this contact may govern the scale and location of the instability (Kieffer 1985; Fig. 1).

The subsurface data provide further evidence of the role of the Ragalna system and the instability of the flank segment it bounds. The similarity between minimum long-term slip rates determined from outcrop information on the Ragalna, and that determined from subsurface data on the basal detachment underlying the collapsing sector argue for a direct mechanical connection, as would be expected if the Ragalna system formed the boundary to the basal detachment. Moreover, at a minimum slip rate of some 1.4 mm a^{-1} the Ragalna system must be regarded as exhibiting a significant level of activity. The series of aligned fissures (Fig. 6) warrants further investigation but they are a localized occurrence and their position near the crest of a fault scarp suggests the possible role of local slope instability. Such fissures have not been observed elsewhere on the fault and it may be that creep behaviour, which is documented on the Pernicana, Mascalucia and Trecastagni faults for example, is uncharacteristic. A possible explanation may involve the typically deeper seismicity on the Ragalna, and the consequent possibility that displacement is largely restricted to that accompanying significant seismic events. The inaccessibility of the fault and the lack of older cultural features to record creep displacement may also be significant.

Turning to the disagreement between the two collapse models on the depth of the detachment, here the recent data concerning the timing of regional deformation in the Chain, in comparison to the later timing of local deformation within the Etnean realm, argues for a deep detachment as proposed by Borgia et al. (1992). Recent uplift on the coastal margin of the volcano may be a response to movement on this detachment. The amplitude and wavelength of the folds mapped in the sub-Etnean clays, particularly on the southern margin of the volcano (Ferrari 1991; Borgia et al. 1992), appears to be larger than would be expected mechanically if the detachment was relatively superficial. A deep detachment also appears to be indicated by the space requirements of a plutonic sequence postulated on geological and geophysical grounds below the summit region of the volcano (Fig. 8a). An alternative view is that the complex represents one single large intrusion, now solidified, associated with the Trifoglietto centre. Support for this view comes from cumulate material collected from pyroclastic sequences and thought to be derived from compositional layering within a single large chamber (McGuire pers. comm. 1995). The present authors, however, hold the view that the complex is more likely to represent a series of intrusions around the main volcanic conduit, associated with the present as well as the older volcanic centres (Figs 2 and 8b).

The active status of the Mascalucia and Trecastagni faults is not in question, although they appear to have received unwarranted attention in attempts to use them in defining the southern boundary of instability. In comparison to the faults of the Ragalna system they occur in relatively densely populated neighbourhoods, a factor which may influence the reports from the small felt areas associated with the very shallow events documented by macroseismic methods. Their overall surface expression appears less active than the Ragalna faulting. This is unexpected if the faults mark the true boundary between stable and unstable sectors of the volcano; such a role would be expected to produce a significant component of dip-slip displacement, and consequently a pronounced fault scarp, as a result of the downslope movement on one side of the fault. This pattern is displayed by the Ragalna fault scarps but the Mascalucia and Trecastagni faults appear to be dominantly strike-slip structures (Lo Giudice & Rasà 1992). This, together with their characteristically very shallow seismicity, appears more consistent with the function of accommodating differential movement within a larger collapsing sector, rather than marking its boundary. This function is likely to be shared by other similar structures within the sector. An example may be provided by the very shallow event on 29 January 1989, with a restricted felt area centred near Codavolpe on the lower eastern flank of the volcano, and attributed to displacement on the NNW–SSE striking S. Leonardello fault (Azzaro et al. 1989a). The Ragalna system, with its characteristically deeper seismicity, is indicated as the best candidate for the role of southern bounding fault to the sector as a whole. A better under-standing of the behaviour of this fault, by such means as geodetic determinations and palaeoseismological investigations for example, and in combination with similar studies on the Pernicana fault, is suggested as a means of characterizing the movement pattern of the unstable sector as a whole.

This work was in part supported by the Commission of the European Communities, DG XII, Environment Programme, Climatology and Natural Hazards Unit, Contract EV5V-CT92–0170. D.R. would also like to acknowledge assistance provided by Brunel University towards the cost of fieldwork. The work has benefited considerably from reviews, comments and discussions involving Raffaele Azzaro, Andrea Borgia, Luca Ferrari, Stefano Gresta, Emanuele Lo Giudice, Bill Mcguire, Riccardo Rasà and Iain Stewart.

References

AURELI, A. 1973. Idrogeologia del fianco occidentale etneo. *Atti 2o Convegno Internazionale. Acque Sotterranee*, 28 Aprile – 2 Maggio, Palermo.

—— & MUSARRA, F. 1975. Idrogeologia del bacino del Fiume Alcantara (Sicilia). *Atti 3o Convegno Internazionale. Acque Sotterranee*, 1–5 Novembre, Palermo.

AZZARO, R., CARVENI, P., LO GIUDICE, E. & RASÀ, R. 1989a. Il terremoto di Codavolpe (basso versante orientale etneo) del 29 Gennaio 1989: campo macrosismico e fratturazione cosismica. *Bollettino del Grappo Nazionale per la Vulcanologia, CNR*, **1**, 1–12.

——, LO GIUDICE, E. & RASÀ, R. 1989b. Note Macrosismiche e Considerazioni Sismotettoniche. Attività Etna 1988, Monographics CNR Istituto Internazionale de Vulcanologia, 40–56, Catania.

——, —— & ——1989c. Catalogo degli eventi macrosismici e delle fenomenologie da creep nell'area Etnea dall' Agosto 1980 al Dicembre 1989. *Bollettino del Grappo Nazionale per la Vulcanologia, CNR*, **1**, 13–46.

BENINA, A., IMPOSA, S., GRESTA, S. & PATANÈ, G. 1984. Studio macrosismico e strumentale di due terremoti tettonici avvenuti sul versante meridionale dell'Etna. *Atti del 3o Convegno Annali. Gruppo Nazionale Geofisica Terra Solida*, Roma, 931–940.

BORGIA, A., FERRARI, L. & PASQUARÈ, G. 1992. Importance of gravitational spreading in the tectonic and volcanic evolution of Mount Etna. *Nature*, **357**, 231–235.

BORGIA, A., GARDUNO, V. H., NERI, M., PASQUARÈ, G., & TIBALDI, A. 1994. Dislocation rate, kinematics, and evolution of the system rift of northeast-Pernican fault, Mt. Etna, Italy. *Project Seavolc, Interim Report*, April 1994, 10pp.

BOUSQUET, J-C., LANZAFAME, G. & PAQUIN, C. 1988. Tectonic stresses and volcanism: in-situ stress measurement and neotectonic investigations in the Etna area (Italy). *Tectonophysics*, **149**, 219–231.

CALVARI, S., GROPPELLI, G. & PASQUARÈ, G. (in press) Preliminary geological data on the south-western walls of Valle del Bove, Mt Etna (Sicily). *Acta Vulcanologica*, **5**.

CARDACI, C., COVIELLO, M., LOMBARDO, G., PATANÈ, G. & SCARPA, R. 1993. Seismic tomography of Etna volcano. *Journal of Volcanology and Geothermal Research*, **56**, 357–368.

COLTELLI, M., GARDUNO, V. H., NERI, M., PASQUARÈ, G. & POMPILIO, M. 1994. Geology of the northern wall of Valle del Bove. *Acta Vulcanologica*, **5**, 15–30.

CRISTOFOLINI, R., FICHERA, R., & PATANÈ, G. 1981. Osservazioni morfotettoniche sul settore occidentale dell'Etna. *Geografia Fisica e Dinamica Quaternaria*, **4**, 55–63.

DENLINGER, R. P. & OKUBO, P. 1995. Structure of the mobile south flank of Kilauea volcano, Hawaii. *Journal of Geophysical Research*, **100**, B12, 24 499–24 507.

DE RITA, D., FRAZZETTA, G. & ROMANO, R. 1991. The Biancavilla-Montalto ignimbrite (Etna, Sicily). *Bulletin Volcanologique*, **53**, 121–131.

DI RE, M. 1963. Hyaloclastite and pillow lavas of Acicastello (M. Etna). *Bulletin Volcanologique*, **25**, 281–297.

DUFFIELD, W. A., STIELTJES, L. & VARET, J. 1982. Huge landslide blocks in the growth of Piton De La Fournaise, La Reunion, and Kilauea volcano, Hawaii. *Journal of Volcanology and Geothermal Research*, **12**, 147–160.

FERRARA, V. 1975. Idrogeologia del fianco orientale dell'Etna. *Atti 3o Convegno Internazionale. Acque Sotterranee*, 1–5 Novembre, Palermo.

——1977. Moderne conoscenze sull'Idrogeologia dell'Etna. *Idrotecnica*, **3** (maggio–giugno), 87–91.

FERRARI, L. 1991. *Evoluzione Vulcanologica e Strutturale del Monte Etna e suoi Rapporti con il Vulcanismo Ibleo*. Tesi di Dottorato, IV Ciclo, Univ. Milano.

——, GARDUNO, V. H. & NERI, M. 1991. I Dicchi della Valle del Bove, Etna: Un metodo per stimare le dilatazioni di un apparato vulcanico. *Memorie della Società Geologica Italiana*, **47**, 495–508.

FERRUCCI, F. & PATANÈ, D. 1993. Seismic activity accompanying the outbreak of the 1991–1993 eruption of Mt. Etna (Italy). *Journal of Volcanology and Geothermal Research*, **57**, 125–135.

FIRTH, C., STEWART, I., McGUIRE, W. J., KERSHAW, S. & VITA-FINZI, C. 1996. Coastal elevation changes in eastern Sicily: implications for volcano instability at Mount Etna. *This volume*.

GILLOT, P. & ROMANO, R. 1987. Potassium-Argon dating of Mount Etna volcano. *Symposium on Volcanology*, Hilo, Hawaii, (poster).

GRESTA, S. & PATANÈ, G. 1987. Review of seismological studies at Mount Etna. *Pure and Applied Geophysics*, **125**, 951–970.

——, LONGO, V. & VIAVATTENE, A. 1990. Geodynamic behaviour of eastern and western sides of Mount Etna. *Tectonophysics*, **179**, 81–92.

HIRN, A., NERCESSIAN, A., SAPIN, M., FERRUCCI, F. & WITTLINGER, G. 1991. Seismic heterogeneity of Mount Etna: structure and activity. *Geophysical Journal International*, **105**, 139–153.

KIEFFER, G. 1985. *Evolution Structurale et Dynamique d'un Grand Volcan Polygenique: Stades d'Edification et Activite' Actuelle de L'Etna (Sicily)*. Annals Scientifique del' Université de Clermont-Ferrand.

LABAUME, P., BOUSQUET, J. C. & LANZAFAME, G. 1990. Early deformations at a submarine compressive front: the Quaternary Catania foredeep south of Mt Etna, Sicily, Italy. *Tectonophysics*, **177**, 349–366.

LENTINI, F. 1982. The geology of the Mt. Etna basement. *In*: ROMANO, R. (ed.) *Mount Etna Volcano*. Memorie della Società Geologica Italiana, **23**, 7–25.

——, CARBONE, S., CATALANO, S., GRASSO, M. & MONACO, C. 1991. Presentazione della Carte Geologica della Sicilia Centro-Orientale. Memorie della Società Geologica Italiana, **47**, 145–156.

LO GIUDICE, E. & RASÀ, R. 1986. *Relazione Preliminare sulla Crisi Sismica Etnea del Dicembre 1985 – Febbraio 1986*. CNR-Istituto Internazionale de Vulcanologia, Open File Report **3/86**.

—— & ——1992. Very shallow earthquakes and brittle deformation in active volcanic areas. The Etnean region as an example. *Tectonophysics*, **202**, 257–268.

——, PANDOLFO, C. & PATANÈ, G. 1981. Dynamic evidence and hydrogeological implications of structures in recent volcanic areas. A multidisciplinary approach in the Etnean area. *Acqua & Aria*, **7** (Sept.).

LODDO, M., PATELLA, D., QUARTO, R., RUINA, G., TRAMACENERE, A. & ZITO, G. 1989. Application of gravity and deep dipole geoelectrics in the volcanic area of Mt. Etna (Sicily). *Journal of Volcanology and Geothermal Research*, **39**, 17–39.

McGUIRE, W. J. 1982. Evolution of the Etna volcano: information from the southern wall of the Valle del Bove caldera. *Journal of Volcanology and Geothermal Research*, **13**, 241–271.

—— & PULLEN, A. D. 1989. Location and orientation of eruptive fissures and feeder dykes at Mount Etna: influence of gravitational and regional tectonic stress regimes. *Journal of Volcanology and Geothermal Research*, **38**, 325–344.

——, MURRAY, J. B., PULLEN, A. D. & SAUNDERS, S. J. 1991. Ground deformation monitoring at Mt Etna; evidence for dyke emplacement and slope instability. *Journal of the Geological Society, London*, **148**, 577–583.

MERLE, O. & BORGIA, A. (in press). Scaled experiments of volcanic spreading. *Journal of Geophysical Research*.

NERI, M. 1992. Esempio di applicazione della normativa. *Carta Geologica D'Italia, 1 : 50000, Guida al Rilevamento*. Servizio. Geologico Nazionale, Quaderni, Serie III, **1**, 100–107.

——, GARDUNO, V. H., PASQUARÈ, G. & RASÀ, R. 1991. Studio strutturale e modello cinematico della Valle del Bove e del settore nord-orientale etneo. *Acta Vulcanologica*, **1**, 17–24.

——, GROPPELLI, G. & TIBALDI, A. 1994. *Installazione di Tre Fessurimetri e Prime Misure Lungo un Muro Deformato dalla Faglia della Pernicana (Mt. Etna)*. CNR, Istituto Internazionale de Vulcanologia, Open-File Report **1/94**, Catania.

OGNIBEN, L. 1966. Lineamenti idrogeologici dell'Etna. *Rivista Mineralogica Siciliana*, **XVII**, 100–102.

PATELLA, D. & QUARTO, R. 1987. Interpretation of shallow Schlumberger soundings in the western sector of Mt. Etna, Sicily. *Bollettino Geofisica Teoretica e Applicata*, **XXIX**, **116**, 309–320.

PEDLEY, M. & GRASSO, M. 1991. Sea-level change around the margins of the Catania–Gela Trough and Hyblean Plateau, southeast Sicily (African–European plate convergence zone): a problem of Plio-Quaternary plate buoyancy? *In*: MACDONALD, D. I. M. (ed.) *Sedimentology, Tectonics and Eustacy; sea-level changes at active margins*. Special Publications of the International Association of Sedimentologists, **12**, 451–464.

RASÀ, R., ROMANO, R. & LO GIUDICE, L. 1982. Morphotectonic map of Mt. Etna. *In*: ROMANO, R. (ed.) *Mount Etna Volcano*. Memorie della Società Geologica Italiana, **23**.

ROMANO, R. (ed.) 1979. *Geological Map of Mt. Etna*. CNR, Progetto Finalizzato Geodinamica, Istituto Internazionale di Vulcanologia, Catania, 1 : 50 000 scale.

——1982. Succession of the volcanic activity in the Etnean area. *In*: ROMANO, R. (ed.) *Mount Etna Volcano*. Memorie della Società Geologica Italiana, **23**, 27–48.

RUST, D. J. 1993*a*. Recognition and assessment of faults within active strike-slip fault zones: a case study from the San Andreas fault in southern California. *Zeitschrift fur Geomorphologie*, **94**, 207–222.

——1993*b*. Structures accommodating active deformation on the southern flank of Mount Etna, Sicily. *Proceedings, Geological Society Tectonic Studies Group, Annual Meeting*, Dublin, 62.

SHARP, A. D. L., DAVIS, P. M. & GRAY, F. 1980. A low velocity zone beneath Etna and magma storage, *Nature*, **287**, 587–591.

Volcanological and structural evolution of Roccamonfina volcano (Italy): origin of the summit caldera

D. DE RITA[1] & G. GIORDANO[2]

[1] Dipartimento di Scienze Geologiche, III Università di Roma,
Via Ostiense 169, 00154 Roma, Italia
[2] Dipartimento di Scienze della Terra, Università di Roma 'La Sapienza',
P. le Aldo Moro 5, 00185 Roma, Italia

Abstract: Roccamonfina volcano (Roman Magmatic Province) sits at the margin of the NE-trending Garigliano graben. The most important episodes in the volcano's history (630–50 ka BP) have been controlled by tectonic activity associated with the graben's master-faults. Roccamonfina volcano comprises two main parts: a stratovolcano developed inside the graben, and a complex of centres developed on the south-eastern horst. The summit of the stratovolcano is truncated by a horse-shoe shaped caldera (dimensions 6.5 km by 5.5 km) with the longest axis trending NW. The caldera opens towards the SE along NE-trending faults, which belong to the same system as the graben faults. Stratigraphical evidence indicates that caldera collapse was not caused by explosive eruptive events emplacing ignimbrites, or by sector collapse preceding ignimbrite eruptions. Geomorphological and structural observations, together with geophysical evidence, suggest that collapse of the volcano summit occurred as a mechanical re-adjustment to the high rate of the Garigliano graben extension during a climax of the regional tectonism at around 400 ka BP. The present elliptical shape of the collapsed area is due to the superposition of a linear NE-trending graben structure in the east, and a sector collapse in the west.

Roccamonfina volcano is located south of Rome and belongs to the alkali-potassic volcanic province of central Italy, which developed during late-Pleistocene times (650–630 ka BP. Radicati di Brozolo *et al.* 1988) coincident with extension at the margin of the Tyrrhenian sea. The volcano's position is marked by an elliptical caldera rim, 6.5 km by 5.5 km in diameter, interpretations of the origin of this are presented in a number of papers (e.g Giannetti 1979; Chiesa *et al.* 1985; Watts 1987; Radicati di Brozolo *et al.* 1988; Ballini *et al.* 1989a; Cole *et al.* 1992; Capuano *et al.* 1992).

Here we aim to investigate the relationship between the activity of the volcano and the origin of the summit caldera. We have analysed the stratigraphical relationships between pyro-clastic deposits and the caldera and have undertaken geomorphological and structural studies. We have also re-interpreted existing geophysical and drilling data from the Rocca-monfina area (Ippolito *et al.* 1973; Nicotera & Civita 1969; Barbier *et al.* 1970; Cassa per il Mezzogiorno 1979; Watts 1987; Frezzotti *et al.* 1988; Ballini *et al.* 1989a; Capuano *et al.* 1992; Giordano *et al.* 1995a).

We document here the role of regional tectonics in the development of the collapse and in the evolution of Roccamonfina volcano, starting by summarizing data from previous works, and then presenting our data together with a proposed new interpretation of the collapse origin.

Previous studies

The first study of Roccamonfina caldera related the collapse event to the first intermediate-volume ignimbrite unit recognized in the Roccamonfina stratigraphy (Giannetti 1979). This deposit, dated at 385 ka BP, was named the Brown Leucitic Tuff (BLT) by Luhr & Giannetti (1987) who recog-nized that the BLT draped the caldera rim and suggested, therefore, that the collapse occurred during a poorly defined earlier event. More recently Cole *et al.* (1992) subdivided the BLT deposit into several eruptive units separated by palaeosoils. The last unit draping the caldera rim was called the Campagnola Tuff and these authors linked the initial collapse event to some of the underlying units.

Chiesa *et al.* (1985) also related the collapse to the eruption of the BLT, but they suggested, from the shape of the caldera, a mechanism of lateral sector collapse toward the east. This kind of interpretation also appears to be supported by data from a deep borehole (Watts 1987; Ballini *et al.* 1989a) drilled at the geometrical centre of the caldera, which encountered the base of the volcanic products at almost the same depth as

From McGuire, W. J., Jones, A. P. & Neuberg, J. (eds) 1996, *Volcano Instability on the Earth and Other Planets,* Geological Society Special Publication No. 110, pp. 209–224.

in the surroundings (about 200 m b.s.l.), indicating no subsidence. This deep borehole, named Gallo 85-1, encountered a layer of juvenile-free breccia about 170 m thick, which has been interpreted as a conduit breccia (Ballini *et al.* 1989*a*) or as the co-ignimbrite breccia of the BLT (Watts 1987).

Gravimetric data do not show a relative minimum corresponding to the position of the caldera (Watts 1987; Frezzotti *et al.* 1988; Capuano *et al.* 1992) and Capuano *et al.* (1992) express doubts about the existence of a remnant magma chamber in the upper crust. Finally it is worth noting the work of Radicati di Brozolo *et al.* (1988), who dated intracalderic lavas at 397 ka.

The structural setting of Roccamonfina volcano

Roccamonfina volcano is located in a topographical depression, surrounded by the Mesozoic–Cenozoic calcareous basement blocks of the Aurunci Mountains to the NW, Mount Massico to the SW, Mount Maggiore to the SE, and Mounts Cesima and Camino to the N (Figs 1 and 4). The blocks expose mostly Triassic to Cretaceous shelf carbonates overlain by Miocene flysch shortened by the Apennine orogenesis (Barbier *et al.* 1970; Bartole 1984; Patacca *et al.* 1990). Some authors have suggested that Roccamonfina is located at the eastern margin of an eastward-thrusted allochthonous Mesozoic–Cenozoic sedimentary sequence (Barbier *et al.* 1970; Watts 1987), but hydrogeological evidence (Celico 1983) and structural evidence seem to exclude the presence of shallow thrusts beneath the volcano.

Starting in the Late Miocene, crustal extension associated with rifting of the Tyrrhenian basin caused the development of the horst and graben structural character of the area. Roccamonfina lies at the intersection of a main NW-trending tectonic depression and the transverse, NE-oriented Garigliano graben. The main evolution of these minor graben during the Early Pleistocene was controlled by the extensional Mount Massico fault at the northwestern border of the Mount Massico structure (Fig.1) (Nicotera & Civita 1969; Ippolito *et al.*1973).

Volcanic evolution of Roccamonfina

A revised stratigraphy of Roccamonfina volcano, according to the recommendations of the International Subcommission of Stratigraphic Classification (Salvador 1987), is summarized below

(see Table 1 for a comparison with previous schemes). The stratigraphy had been subdivided into three main supersynthems which correspond to different epochs of volcanic activity (Figs 2 and 3).

Supersynthem of Roccamonfina (Epoch I: 630–400 Ka BP)

This epoch lasted from the onset of volcanism until the main caldera collapse event. During this epoch 100–120 km^3 of erupted products were emplaced (Giannetti 1979).

Magma reached the surface via dykes preferentially aligned along regional NE-trending faults (Bosi 1994). Several small centres developed over a wide area (about 1000 km^2, see Fig. 4) at about 600 ka BP (Bergomi *et al.* 1969; Sgrosso & Aiello 1963; Di Girolamo *et al.* 1991). Following this early activity, the stratovolcano of Roccamonfina, mainly comprising leucite-tephrite lava flows and strombolian to subplinian pyroclastics, developed inside the Garigliano graben along a NE-trending fault system.

SE of the NE-trending Mount Massico fault, upon the Mount Massico horst, only several small centres developed. This bimodality in the volcanic structure is strongly supported by geoelectrical, gravimetric data, and borehole data (Fig. 4) (Barbier *et al.* 1970; Cassa per il Mezzogiorno 1979; Giordano *et al.* 1995*a*). The absence of the stratovolcano lavas just SE of the Mount Massico fault indicates that the Mount Massico horst had the form of a topographic ridge, and was surmounted by lavas of the growing stratovolcano only at a later stage.

The products described above are overlain by the BLT. We have carefully investigated the relationship between this deposit and the caldera rim, as its emplacement has been held responsible for the collapse. The BLT is distributed all around the stratovolcano with the exception of the NW sector (Fig. 2). It is a complex eruptive unit comprising several pyroclastic flow, pyroclastic surge, and plinian fall deposits (Fig. 5) forming a continuous sequence of depositional events which are not separated by palaeosoils. Cole *et al.* (1993) have identified this unit as the last one of a sequence of leucitophyric ignimbrites. Our stratigraphy indicates, however, that pyroclastic flow deposits are rarely present below and when present they are mainly mudflows or ignimbrites of small volume related to Epoch I activity (Fig. 5). So we agree with the interpretation of Luhr & Giannetti (1987), who considered the BLT as a single eruption unit.

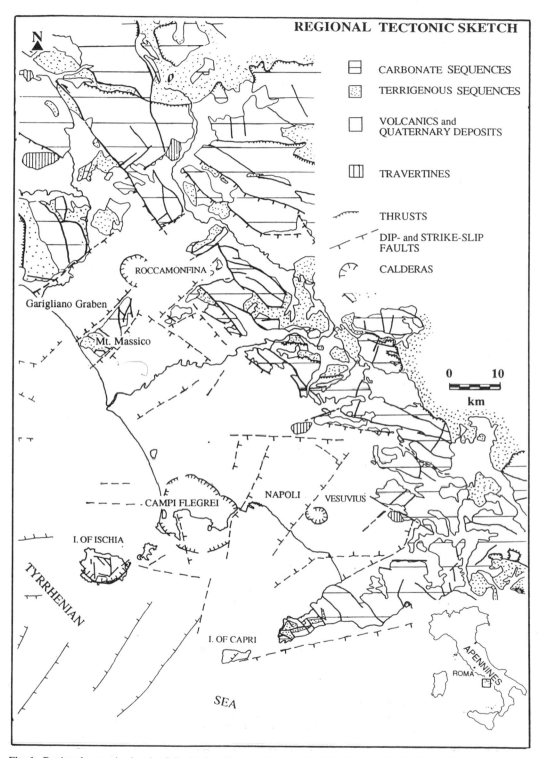

Fig. 1. Regional tectonic sketch of the Latian–Campanian margin of the Tyrrhenian Sea basin. Modified after Consiglio Nazionale delle Ricerche (1987).

The BLT drapes the caldera wall at Mount Torecastiello and rests on the deposits of three small edifices that lie along the collapsed rim of the volcano: Mount Atano, Mount Tuororame, and Mount Capitolo (Fig. 6). Their stratigraphical relationships with the products of Epoch I (Fig. 7), and the internal flowage lineations of the Mount Capitolo lavas (Fig. 8) indicate that these centres developed after the caldera collapse, implying a long time gap between the collapse and the BLT eruption.

The BLT has a high content of lithic clasts which increases upward in several breccia layers (Fig. 5) (as also noted for the Campagnola Tuff by Cole *et al.* 1993). Almost all the lithic clasts come from the stratocone, but some are from the sedimentary basement and from the subvolcanic system. No areas of particular breccia concentration have been observed around the volcano. The presence of breccias and lithic-concentration zones at the top of the unit and the absence of any debris avalanche deposit at the base contradict the interpretation of Chiesa *et al.* (1985) and Watts (1987), who proposed that the eruption of the BLT was caused by sector collapse as in the case of the 1980 Mount St. Helens eruption.

Bore-hole data from the eastern sector of the volcano (see Fig. 4 for locations) provide no

Table 1. *Epochs of Roccamonfina volcano activity and comparisons with previous stratigraphies*

This work

Age (ka)	Stage	Major Events	Comments
53 (1)	Epoch III	Yellow Trachytic Tuff (YTT) Intracalderic lava domes Intracalderic phreatomagmatic eruptions	About 1 km³ of magma DRE erupted Volcanic centres aligned along N-trending lineaments
230 (2)	Epoch II	WTT Galluccio WTT S. Clemente WTT Aulpi WTT Cupa	About 10 km³ of magma DRE erupted. Highly explosive activity Pericalderic centres aligned along NE-trending lineaments
385 (3)		Brown Leucitic Tuff (BLT)	
630 (4)	Epoch I	Gravitational collapse of the volcano summit Development of a NE-trending graben structure along the eastern flank of the growing stratovolcano Stratovolcano building Strong eccentric activity	About 100 km³ of mainly lavas erupted The stratovolcano develops into the NE-trending Garigliano graben, by the emplacement of mainly lavas and minor strombolian to subplinian fall deposits, small volume ignimbrites, and reworked materials SE of the Mt. Massico fault a complex of small volcanic centres develops

Previous stratigraphies

Stage	Luhr & Giannetti (1987)	Cole *et al.* (1992)	Ballini *et al.* (1989)
Stage II	YTT Intracalderic lava domes Intracalderic phreatomagmatic eruptions WTT	Conca Ignimbrite Intracalderic lava domes Intracalderic phreatomagmatic eruptions Upper Galluccio Tuff (caldera collapse) Middle Galluccio Tuff (caldera collapse) Lower Galluccio Tuff (caldera collapse)	WTT sup. WTT medio WTT inf.
Stage I	BLT Caldera collapse related to magma withdrawal Central stratocone building	Campagnola Tuff (caldera collapse) Several leucitophyric ignimbrites (caldera collapses) Central stratocone building	Lateral sector collapse(?) BLT Central stratocone building

The ages are from (1) Radicati di Brozolo *et al.* (1988), (2) Giannetti (1990), (3) Luhr & Giannetti (1987), and (4) Ballini *et al.* (1989*a*).

evidence of lithologies related to sector collapse events. Above and below the identified BLT deposits only fluvial and lacustrine reworked pyroclastics interbedded with fall layers and mudflow deposits are present (Barbier *et al.* 1970; Cassa per il mezzoggiorno 1979; Giordano *et al.* 1995*a*).

The collapse of the Roccamonfina summit had already occurred at the time of the BLT eruption, and the latter was not preceded by a sector collapse. According to the ISSC suggestions (Salvador 1987), the BLT has then to be considered the first unit erupted during the subsequent epoch.

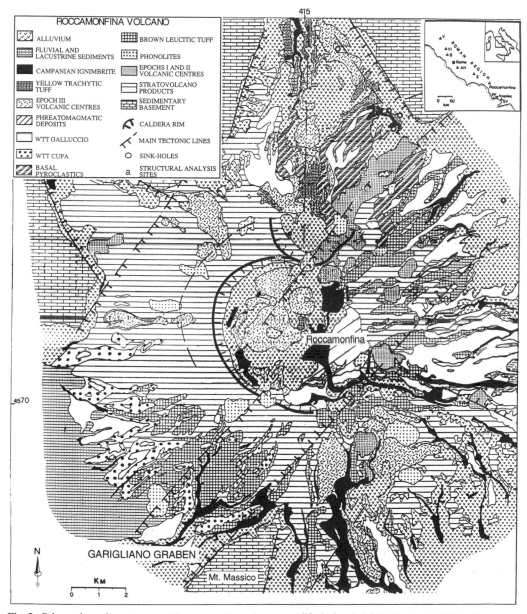

Fig. 2. Schematic geological map of Roccamonfina volcano, modified after Luhr & Giannetti (1987). Kilometric coordinates in this figure and others are from UTM system, 33TVF zone.

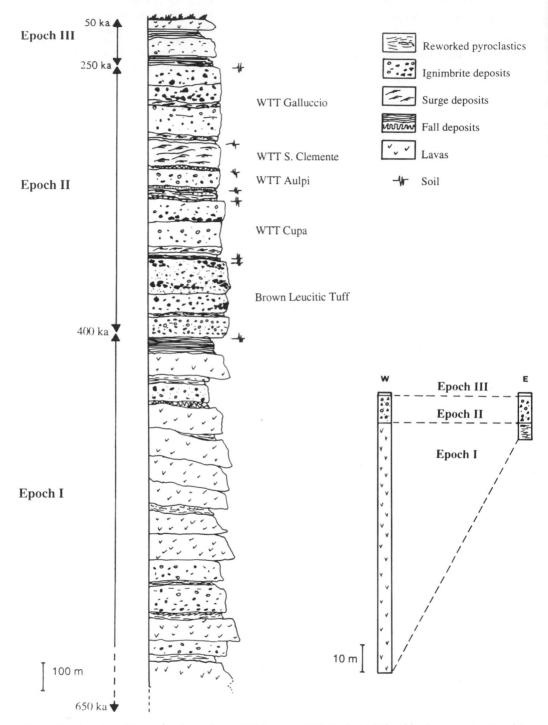

Fig. 3. Stratigraphy of Roccamonfina volcano. Thickness and lithological relationships between the W and E sectors are also indicated.

Supersynthem of the Riardo Basin (Epoch II: 385–250 ka BP)

This epoch comprises highly explosive eruptions from vents located inside the caldera, probably along NE-trending faults. The related major ignimbrite units, of small to intermediate volume, are the Brown Leucitic Tuff (BLT of Luhr & Giannetti (1987) or Campagnola Tuff of

Cole *et al.* (1992)) and several subsequent complex trachytic eruption units, ranging in age between 327 and 230 ka BP (White Trachitic Tuff (WTT) of Giannetti & Luhr (1983), Ballini *et al.* (1989*b*), Giannetti (1990); Galluccio Tuff eruption of Cole *et al.* (1993); WTT Cupa, WTT Aulpi, WTT S. Clemente and WTT Galluccio synthems of De Rita *et al.* (1994) and of Giordano (1995)). The total DRE (dry rock

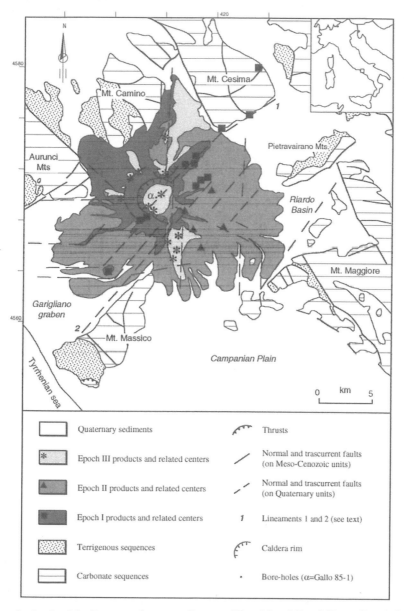

Fig. 4. Tectonic sketch of the Roccamonfina area. Centres of Epoch I and Epoch II are aligned along NE-trending fault systems, and centres belonging to Epoch III along N-trending lineaments.

equivalent) volume erupted during the Epoch II explosive eruptions ranges between 8.5 and 11 km^3, according to the estimations of previous authors (Luhr & Giannetti 1987; Cole *et al.* 1993). This range of values has been obtained by adding the total lithic clast volume, ranging between 2.4 and 3.4 km^3, and the calculated DRE magma volume, ranging between 6.1 and 7.6 km^3, taking into account an estimated vitric loss of about 50% of the present deposits.

Supersynthem of Vezzara (Epoch III; 250–50 ka BP)

This is the last eruptive epoch of the Roccamonfina district, involving the emplacement of two lava domes (Mount S. Croce and Mount Lattani) inside the collapsed area along a NE-trending fracture system. Effusive and explosive activity occurred from many parasitic centres aligned along N-trending lineaments (Fig. 4) which completely cut the pre-existing volcanic structure. The total volume erupted during this epoch was about 1 km^3.

Geomorphological observations

The Roccamonfina caldera is elliptical in shape (dimensions 6.5 by 5.5 km) with its maximum diameter trending NW (Figs 4 and 6). The western rim forms a perfect semi-circle, with elevations ranging between 933 and 650 m whereas the eastern rim is not well defined and has a mean elevation of 550 m. A Landsat image (Fig. 9) shows that the geometry of the rim is

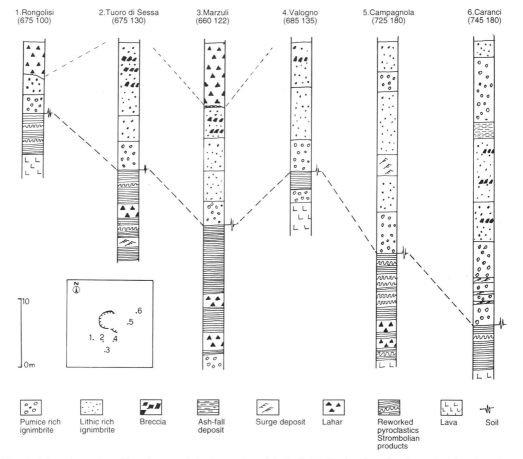

Fig. 5. Selected stratigraphic columns of the Brown Leucitic Tuff (BLT), showing also the underlying deposits. Field evidence shows that the BLT has to be considered the first intermediate-volume eruption in the history of the Roccamonfina volcanic. Location coordinates are given in parentheses.

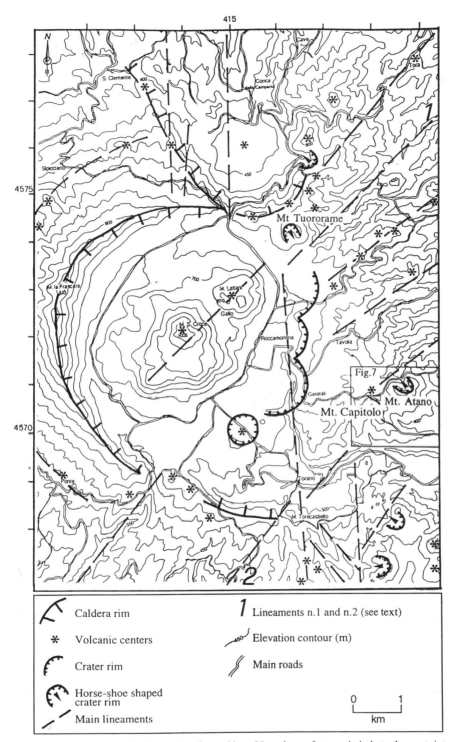

Fig. 6. Geomorphological map of the Roccamonfina caldera. Note the perfect semi-circle to the west, interrupted by the NE-trending lineaments no. 1 and no. 2, which define a graben structure, as indicated by the horse-shoe shapes of Mounts Tuororame and Atano and by topographic elevations. The box indicates the area represented by the geological map in Fig. 7.

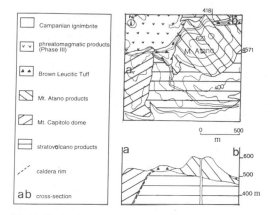

Legend:

☐ Campanian ignimbrite

∨ ∨ phreatomagmatic products (Phase III)

▲ ▲ Brown Leucitic Tuff

◿ Mt. Atano products

◿ Mt. Capitolo dome

☐ stratovolcano products

⌁ caldera rim

a b cross-section

Fig. 7. Geological map of the Mount Atano and Mount Capitolo area. Stratigraphic relationships indicate that the BLT eruption occurred after the emplacement of the intracalderic dome of Mount Capitolo.

strictly controlled by NE-trending lineaments, two of which play a major role in defining the geometry of the caldera. Lineament no. 1 of Fig. 6 cuts the western semi-circular caldera rim

lowering the volcano to the southeast, and represents the extension toward the southwest of the structural lineament bordering Mount Cesima (Fig. 4). Lineament no. 2 (Fig. 6) limits the southeastern caldera rim, and represents the extension toward the northeast of the Mount Massico fault (Fig. 4).

It is interesting to note that the pericalderic centres are not developed along radial or tangential fracture systems, but where NE-trending lineaments intersect the caldera rim. Field relationships indicate that centres belonging to Epochs I and II are aligned along NE-trending lineaments (Fig. 4). Both Mount Tuororame, along lineament no. 2, and Mount Atano, along lineament no. 1, exhibit horse-shoe forms truncated by NE-trending lineaments (Fig. 6); Mount Atano is open toward the NW whereas Mount Tuororame is open toward the SE, suggesting that the two NE-trending lineaments define a graben structure.

Landsat images and air-photo analyses also reveal NW-trending lineaments. Centres of Epoch III are aligned along N-trending lineaments (Fig. 4) which are the most recent and cut all others (see also Frezzotti *et al.* 1988).

Fig. 8. Lavas of the Mount Capitolo dome with flowage lineations toward left, which is the internal caldera direction. Faults and fractures are NE-trending. Hammer for scale.

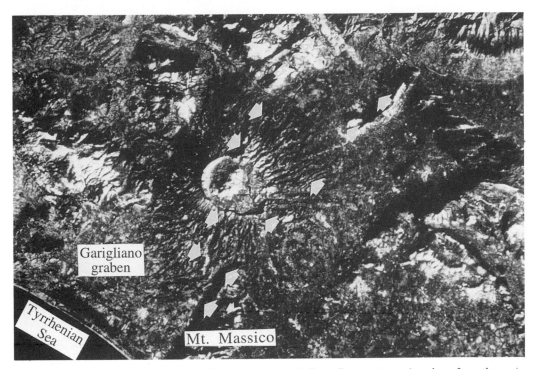

Fig. 9. Landsat image of the Roccamonfina area. Arrows indicate lineaments no. 1 and no. 2 as shown in Figs 4 and 6.

Finally it is noteworthy that on the western side of the volcano, most of the parasitic centres lie at altitudes between 650 and 550 m suggesting the existence of a tangential discontinuity (Figs 4 and 6)

Structural analysis

In the Roccamonfina area NE- and NW-trending fracture patterns predominated throughout the history of the volcano (Fig. 4), while N- and E-trending patterns have also been active during more recent times. These structural patterns are in agreement with the regional structure of the sedimentary basement. By analysing the relationships between these lineaments we seek to establish the temporal sequence of their movements.

The NE-trending system

This is the most important system and occurs everywhere in the region; the most significant outcrops have been analysed at the northwestern margin of Mount Massico, where NE-trending faults cut the entire volcanic sequence (Figs 2 and 10g). These faults are coincident with lineament no. 2 described in the previous section. Joints are filled with halloysite and/or carbonate. The faults are extensional and caused a net dip-slip of about 40–50 m in the last 300 ka (this age is determined on the basis of the structures cutting the WTT deposits). Movement has continued in more recent times resulting in the cutting of the Campanian Ignimbrite deposit (erupted at about 33 ka BP from Campi Flegrei, about 60 km to the south (Barberi *et al.* 1978). Downthrows are toward the NW. This same fault system cuts the eastern rim of the caldera where we have observed brittle fractures in the lava dome of Mount Capitolo (Figs 6, 7 and 10d). Toward the NE (Fig. 10a and b) this fault system intersects the deposits of Epoch I and the four WTT eruption deposits. Here, NE-trending dykes have also been observed. Structural data taken along lineament no. 1, described in the previous section, show that the lineament corresponds to a fault system with downthrow toward the SE (Fig. 10i and l; Bosi 1994).

The NE-trending system is widely present in the eastern sector of the volcano, where it controlled development of an extensional basin

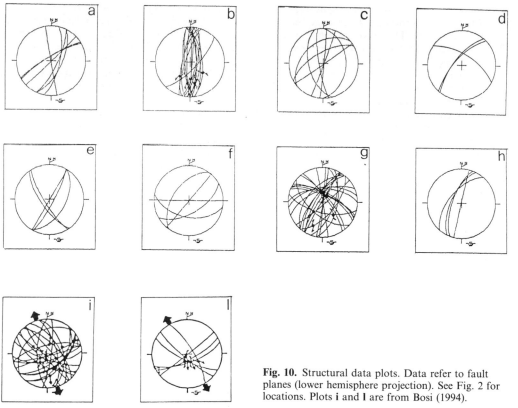

Fig. 10. Structural data plots. Data refer to fault planes (lower hemisphere projection). See Fig. 2 for locations. Plots **i** and **l** are from Bosi (1994).

along NE- and NW-trending lineaments during the early Pleistocene (Riardo Basin of Fig. 4; Giordano *et al.* 1995*a, b*). The development and distribution of this structural pattern and the alignment of dykes and centres from the early stage of the volcanism suggest that it has controlled volcanism throughout the growth of Roccamonfina.

The NW-trending system

This system is of regional significance because the Tyrrhenian basin opened along this trend (Patacca *et al.* 1990). Two important elements have been observed. The first intersects the eastern sector of the volcano, from Mount Maggiore to the caldera rim (Fig. 4). Normal faults lowering the NE sector (also evidenced by gravity anomalies; Watts 1987; Capuano *et al.* 1992) have also been observed. The second element is an important fault that borders Mount Cesima (Fig. 4) and which has been active from the Pliocene until recent times (Bosi 1994). This element cuts the entire pyroclastic sequence of Roccamonfina with a normal component of motion.

The E–W system

This system appears to be limited to the Garigliano area (Fig. 4) and is revealed primarily by morphological anomalies in the fluvial network. Field evidence suggests that this system has been operating as a transfer system (Fig. 10f and g; see also Giordano *et al.* 1995*b*).

The N–S system

This is the youngest system, cutting all the deposits cropping out around the volcano (Fig. 10b and c). It seems to be particularly active along a narrow belt intersecting the central sector of the volcano. Most of the centres of Epoch III are aligned along this system (Fig. 4).

Discussion and conclusions

The data presented above can be briefly summarized as follows:

(1)   The main collapse(s) of Roccamonfina caldera occurred before the eruption of

the BLT, which is the first eruption (385 ka; Luhr & Giannetti, 1987) large enough (about 3.5 km³ DRE) to cause a collapse.

(2) The elliptical caldera morphology is strictly controlled by NE-trending faults; in particular the eastern rim which coincides with the Mount Massico Fault (lineament no. 2).

(3) The Mount Massico Fault controlled the complex development of Roccamonfina; a stratovolcano developed in the Garigliano graben, and parasitic activity occurred within the graben as well as on the southeastern horst.

(4) There are no deposits related to a lateral sector collapse in the eastern sector of the volcano.

We stress the roles of regional tectonics and of the structure of the sedimentary basement in the origin of the Roccamonfina caldera. We interpret the summit depression of Roccamonfina volcano as a collapse structure that originated through regional extension. In support of this thesis it is important to note that:

(1) Estimates of the volume of failed material range from 17 km³ to 20 km³. These values have been calculated considering the probable maximum height (1700–1800 m) of the stratovolcano (Bergomi *et al.* 1969), the depth of the caldera floor (reached by the Gallo 85-1 deep-well; Watts 1987; Ballini *et al.* 1989*a*) (Fig. 11), and the steepness of

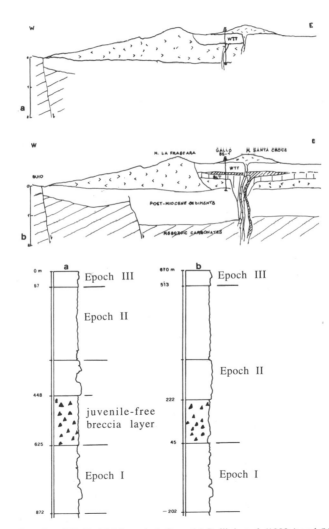

Fig. 11. Simplified stratigraphy of Gallo 85-1 bore-hole from (**a**) Ballini *et al.* (1989*a*) and (**b**) from Watts (1987).

the caldera walls. The total estimated DRE volume erupted during the Epoch II explosive eruptions ranges from 6.1 to 7.6 km³. A maximum of about 3 km³ of lithics, currently embedded in the deposits, could be added to these values.

(2) Gravimetric data (Watts 1987; Capuano *et al.* 1992) show that the gravimetric minima related to the Garigliano graben form a narrow belt close to the maxima related to Mount Massico, and that there are no relative minima corresponding to the caldera.

(3) There is a surprising correspondence between the position of the gravity slopes, which define the Garigliano graben and lineaments no. 1 and no. 2 (see previous sections), implying that the geometric centre of the caldera, where the deep-hole Gallo 85-1 was drilled (Fig. 4), does not correspond to the depo-centre of the basin, which is displaced toward the SE.

(4) Radiometric data (Radicati di Brozolo *et al.* 1988) indicate an age older than 400 ka BP for the collapse.

The model for the origin of the collapse of Roccamonfina summit is schematically presented in Fig. 12. The early stages of the volcanic activity (about 600 ka BP) were characterized by the development of two distinct domains (Fig. 12). To the west, inside the Garigliano graben the stratovolcano grew, while along the eastern flank of the volcano, contemporaneous activity of the Mount Massico Fault and associated antithetic faults produced a linear NE-trending graben structure (about 500 ka BP; Fig. 12). A climax of the regional extensional tectonism, which, by comparison with regional data, probably occurred around 400 ka BP (Ciaranfi *et al.* 1983; Cavinato *et al.* 1993; Bosi 1994; Giordano *et al.* 1995*a, b*), resulted in an increase in the rate of downthrow along the graben faults. The collapse of the summit of the volcano was due to

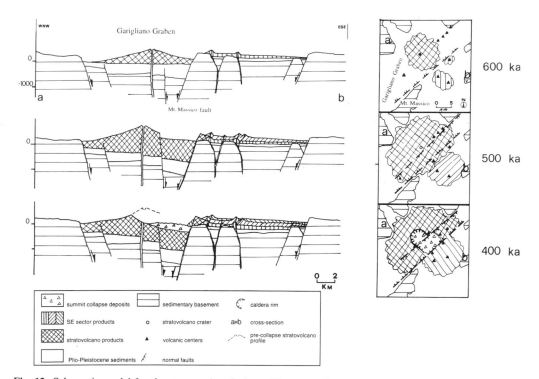

Fig. 12. Schematic model for the structural evolution of Roccamonfina caldera. At about 600 ka BP the stratovolcano was growing within the Garigliano graben, while a complex of eccentric centres was developing on the Mount Massico horst. The eastern flank of the stratovolcano is continuously downthrown by activity of the Mount Massico fault and associated antithetic faults (500 ka BP). A climax in the rate of extension causes gravitational collapse of the summit at about 400 ka BP. The vertical scale of the cross-sections is given in metres with respect to sea level.

gravitational instability induced by the high rate of extension (about 400 ka BP; Fig. 12). Thus, the summit slid along pre-existing volcano-tectonic tangential discontinuities.

The final elliptical shape of the collapsed area is due to the superposition of a linear NE-trending graben structure to the east and a sector collapse from the west (Fig. 12). We interpret the juvenile-free breccia of the Gallo 85-1 slim-hole (Fig. 11) as the megabreccia related to this eastward-directed summit gravitational collapse. The absence of related collapse deposits from the eastern sector is in agreement with the existence of the Mount Massico horst as a ridge throughout the life of Roccamonfina.

This model provides an explanation for all available data, in particular the shape of the caldera; the radiometric ages of intracaldera lavas; observed stratigraphic relationships; the volume of the caldera versus the volume of the ignimbrite units; geolectrical and gravimetric data, and especially the absence of a gravity low associated with the caldera structure; the absence of Epoch I lavas and collapse deposits in the eastern sector; and the stratigraphy of the Gallo 85-1 borehole and in particular the absence of any evidence for caldera subsidence in this area (Fig. 11).

In conclusion we note that the collapse occurred during Epoch I when around $100 \, km^3$ of mainly lavas had been erupted. This has implications for the rate of extension required and its influence on the volcanic activity. The significantly lower volume of magma erupted during Epoch II (about $10 \, km^3$ DRE), and the occurrence of time-spaced violent explosions (BLT and subsequent WTT eruptions), mainly characterized by evolved magmas, seem to indicate a much lower rate of extension after 400 ka BP, which allowed the closure of the subvolcanic system and the establishment of a magma chamber in the upper crust. These explosive eruptions, however, may have caused further limited collapses contributing to the present complex morphology of the Roccamonfina summit area.

We are grateful to Prof. Ray A. F. Cas, and to Drs Michael J. Branney, Jim Luhr and Paul Cole for critical reviews of the manuscript and for improving the English.

References

BALLINI, A., BARBERI, F., LAURENZI, M. A., MEZZETTI, F. & VILLA, I. M. 1989a. Nuovi dati sulla stratigrafia del vulcano di Roccamonfina. *Bollettino Gruppo Nazionale di Vulcanologia*, **2**, 533–555.

——, FRULLANI, A. & MEZZETTI, F. 1989b. La formazione piroclastica del Tufo Trachitico Bianco del vulcano di Roccamonfina. *Bollettino Gruppo Nazionale di Vulcanologia*, **2**, 557–574.

BARBERI, F., INNOCENTI, F., LIRER, L., MUNNO, R., PESCATORE, T. & SANTACROCE, R. 1978. The Campanian Ignimbrite: a major prehistoric eruption in the neapolitan area (Italy). *Bulletin Volcanologique*, **41**, 1–22.

BARBIER, E., BURGASSI, P. D., CALAMAI, A., CATALDI, R. & CERON, P. 1970. Relationships of geothermal conditions to structural and hydrogeological features in the Roccamonfina region (northern Campania). *Journal of Volcanology and Geothermal Research*, **38**, 603–610.

BARTOLE, R. 1984. Tectonic structure of the Latian-Campanian shelf (Tyrrhenian sea). *Bollettino di Oceanografia Teorica e Applicata*, **2**(3), 197–230.

BERGOMI, C., CATENACCI, C., CESTARI, G., MANFREDINI, M. & MANGANELLI, V. 1969. *Note illustrative alla Carta Geologica d'Italia alla scala 1:100000, foglio 171: Gaeta e vulcano di Roccamonfina*. Servizio Geologico Italiano.

BOSI, V. 1994. *Evoluzione neotettonica del Lazio meridionale Campania settentrionale, in corrispondenza della terminazione meridionale della linea tettonica 'Ortona-Roccamonfina'*. PhD thesis, Università 'La Sapienza', Roma, Italia.

CAPUANO, P., CONTINISIO, R. & GASPARINI, P. 1992. Structural setting of a typical alkali-potassic volcano: Roccamonfina, southern Italy. *Journal of Volcanology and Geothermal Research*, **53**, 355–369.

CASSA PER IL MEZZOGIORNO 1979. *Censimento dei Dati Idrogeologici dell'Area di Intervento del Progetto Speciale 29*, Roma.

CAVINATO, G., DE RITA, D., MILLI, S. & ZARLENGA, F. 1993. Correlazione tra i principali eventi tettonici, sedimentari, vulcanici ed eustatici che hanno inteessato l'entroterra (conche intrappenniniche) e il margine costiero tirrenico laziale durante il Pliocene superiore ed il Pleistocene. *Studi Geologici Camerti*, Special volume, 109–114.

CELICO, P. 1983. Idrogeologia dei massicci carbonatici, delle piane quaternarie e delle aree vulcaniche dell'Italia centro-meridionale. *Quaderni CASMEZ*, 4/2.

CHIESA, S., CORNETTE, Y., GILLOT, P. Y. & VEZZOLI, L. 1985. New interpretation of Roccamonfina volcanic history. *IAVCEI, Sicily* (abstract).

CIARANFI, N., GHISETTI, F., GUIDA, M. ET AL. 1983. *Carta Neotettonica dell'Italia Meridionale*. CNR PFG, publication no. **515**, Bari.

COLE, P. D., GUEST, J. E. & DUNCAN, A. M. 1993. The emplacement of intermediate volume ignimbrite: a case study from Roccamonfina volcano, Southern Italy. *Bulletin of Volcanology*, **55**, 467–480.

——, ——, ——, CHESTER, D. K. & BIANCHI, R. 1992. Post-collapse volcanic history of calderas on a composite volcano: an example from Roccamonfina, Southern Italy. *Bulletin of Volcanology*, **54**, 504–520.

CONSIGLIO NAZIONALE DELLE RICERCHE, 1987. Progetto Finalizzato Geodinamica. Neotectonic map of Italy. *Quaderni della Ricerca Scientifica*, **114**, 4.

DE RITA, D., GIORDANO, G. & MILLI, S. 1994. A stratigraphic–sedimentological approach to the volcanic risk evaluation: an example from Roccamonfina volcano (Southern Italy). *EGS 19th General Assembly*, Grenoble, 25–29 April 1994 (abstract).

DI GIROLAMO, P., MELLUSO, L. & MORRA, V. 1991. Magmatic activity northeast of Roccamonfina volcano (Southern Italy): Petrology, geochemistry and relationship with campanian volcanics. *Neues Jahrbuch für Mineralogie Abhunellurgen*, **163**, 271–289.

FREZZOTTI, M., MOLIN, D. & NARCISI, B. 1988. Correlazione tra caratteri strutturali e sismicità storica dell'area di Roccamonfina. *Memorie della Società Geologica Italiana*, **41**, 1307–1316.

GIANNETTI, B. 1979. The geology of the Roccamonfina caldera (Campanian province, Italy). *Giornale di Geologia*, **2**(43), 187–206.

——1990. Strutture neotettoniche presenti nel Tufo trachitico bianco del vulcano di Roccamonfina. *Bollettino del Servizio Geologico d'Italia*, **109**, 195–206.

—— & LUHR, J. F. 1983. The White Trachitic Tuff of Roccamonfina volcano (Roman Region, Italy). *Contribution to Mineralogy Petrology*, **84**, 235–252.

GIORDANO, G. 1995. *Evoluzione vulcanologico-strutturale del vulcano di Roccamonfina, con implicazioni circa l'evoluzione strutturale della depressione sommitale*. PhD thesis, Università di Roma 'La Sapienza'.

——, NASO, G., SCROCCA, D., FUNICIELLO, R. & CATALANI, F. 1995a. Processi di estensione e circolazione di fluidi a bassa termalità nella piana di Riardo (Caserta, Appennino centro-meridionale). *Bollettino della Società Geologica Italiana*, in press.

——, —— & TRIGARI, A. 1995b. Evoluzione tettonica di un settore peculiare del margine tirrenico: l'area compresa tra Lazio e Campania. Prime considerazioni. Atti del Convegno 'Geodinamica e tettonica attiva del sistema Tirreno-Appennino', *Studi Geologici Camerti*, Special volume, in press

IPPOLITO, F., ORTOLANI, F. & RUSSO, M. 1973. Struttura marginale tirrenica dell'Appennino campano: reinterpretazioni dei dati di antiche ricerche di idrocarburi. *Memorie della Società Geologica Italiana*, **12**, 227–250.

LUHR, J. F. & GIANNETTI, B. 1987. The Brown Leucitic Tuff of Roccamonfina volcano (Roman Region, Italy). *Contribution to Mineralogy Petrology*, **95**, 420–436.

NICOTERA, P. & CIVITA, M. 1969. Idrogeologia della bassa piana del Garigliano (Italia Meridionale). *Memorie Instituto Geologia Applicata*, Napoli, **11**, 1–48.

PATACCA, E., SARTORI, R & SCANDONE, P. 1990. Tyrrhenian basin and Apenninic arcs: kinematic relations since late Tortonian times. *Memorie della Società Geologica Italiana*, **45**, 425–452.

RADICATI DI BROZOLO, F., DI GIROLAMO, P., TURI, B. & ODDONE, M. 1988. 40Ar/39Ar and K/Ar dating of K-rich rocks from Roccamonfina volcano, Roman comagmatic region, Italy. *Geochimica et Cosmochimica Acta*, **52**, 1435–1441.

SALVADOR, A. 1987. Unconformity-bounded stratigraphic units. *Geological Society of America Bulletin*, **98**, 232–237.

SGROSSO, I. & AIELLO, R. 1963. Bocca eruttiva presso Presenzano (Caserta). *Bollettino della Società Naturalisti in Napoli*, **72**.

WATTS, M. D. 1987. Geothermal exploration of Roccamonfina volcano, Italy. Geothermics, **16**, 517–528.

Structural evolution of the Bracciano volcano-tectonic depression, Sabatini Volcanic District, Italy

D. DE RITA[1], M. DI FILIPPO[2] & C. ROSA[3]

[1] *Dipartimento di Scienze Geologiche, Terza Università di Roma,*
Via Ostiense 169, 00154 Rome, Italy
[2] *Dipartimento di Scienze della Terra, Università degli Studi di Roma 'La Sapienza',*
Piazzale Aldo Moro 5, 00185 Rome, Italy
[3] *Dottorato di Ricerca – Dipartimento di Scienze della Terra, Università degli Studi di Roma*
'La Sapienza', Piazzale Aldo Moro 5, 00185 Rome, Italy

Abstract: The Latian volcanoes of Central Italy form several K-rich volcanic districts, some of which are characterized by large volcano-tectonic depressions filled with lakes. The development of these large depressions (>8 km in diameter) occurred from 0.4–0.3 Ma BP, during a climax of regional extension. Analysis of geophysical and deep drilling data and detailed field analysis, allows reconstruction of the evolution of the Bracciano volcano-tectonic depression in the Sabatini Volcanic District, northwest of Rome. This depression developed during the Upper Pleistocene inside a NE-trending half-graben structure. The evolution of the half-graben has been driven by NE-trending regional faults which were reactivated during volcanism. Magma rose along these faults and came to rest at 4–7 km depth, probably as a laccolithic body, and was then erupted with emplacement of large volume ignimbrites. A lava plateau recognized by drilling data in the southern and western sectors of the depression is interpreted as being associated with NE-striking swarms of feeder dykes. The final downsagging was caused by NE and NW-trending regional faults after 0.17 Ma. The eastern depression morphology was modified by late Pleistocene N-trending strike-slip faults which were accompanied by intense hydromagmatic activity. Hydromagmatic craters are distinguished in the eastern margin of the area and in the southeastern part of Lake Bracciano in high-frequency seismic sections.

Within the Pliocene extensional structures that occupied the western margin of the Italian Peninsula (Fig. 1), volcanism developed from late Pliocene to late Pleistocene, because of rifting in the Tyrrhenian basin and post-orogenic extension in the Apennines (Serri *et al.* 1992; Locardi 1985; Lavecchia & Stoppa 1990; Peccerillo & Manetti 1985; Conticelli *et al.* 1986). This volcanism, forming the Latian Volcanic Province, is subdivided into districts each characterized by either central or areal volcanism. The central volcanism is characterized by the early formation of a stratovolcano and the subsequent collapse of this volcano into a caldera; finally, in some cases, a new cone grows inside the previous depression and is cut by a new caldera (for instance, the Colli Albani Volcanic District; De Rita *et al.* 1988). The areal volcanism is characterized by distributed activity and a main depression >8 km in diameter (for instance, the Sabatini Volcanic Districts; De Rita *et al.* 1993). This depression is commonly referred to as either a large caldera (Cioni *et al.* 1993; Nappi *et al.* 1991) or a volcano-tectonic depression (Amodio *et al.* 1987; De Rita *et al.* 1983). The depressions associated with the areal volcanism

began to form around 0.4 Ma, coincident with a peak in post-orogenic extension, and 0.2 Ma after the beginning of volcanic activity (Cavinato *et al.* 1993). Several thermal springs and gas emissions (H_2S, CO_2) occur along the structures associated with the depressions (De Rita *et al.* 1993).

In this paper we reconstruct the volcano-tectonic history of the Bracciano Depression (BD) of the Sabatini Volcanic District (SVD), on the basis of the correlation and interpretation of detailed geologic and structural surveys, numerous stratigraphic sections, well logs, high-frequency seismic sections, and gravity and magnetic surveys (Table 1).

Pre-volcanic setting

In the Bracciano area the Pliocene extensional tectonism, cutting the thrust sheets of the Apennine orogeny, formed a NW-trending graben that is bordered to the east by the normal faults of the Monte Soratte horst and extends westward to the Baccano–Cesano horst (Baldi *et al.* 1974; Locardi *et al.* 1976; Fig. 2). This

From McGuire, W. J., Jones, A. P. & Neuberg, J. (eds) 1996, *Volcano Instability on the Earth and Other Planets,*
Geological Society Special Publication No. 110, pp. 225–236.

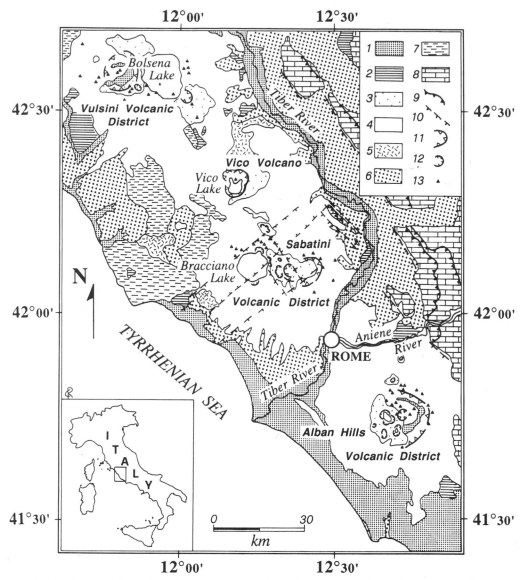

Fig. 1. Sketch map of the Latian volcanic area, central Italy. Legend: (1) continental and marine sediments (upper Pleistocene to Holocene); (2) travertine; (3) hydromagmatic units; (4) Tolfa Cerite Manziate acidic volcanic district; (5) K-alkaline volcanic products; (6) Plio-Pleistocene marine sediments; (7) Cretaceous–Oligocene marls and marly limestones; (8) Meso-Cenozoic limestones and marls; (9) thrusts; (10) normal faults; (11) calderas; (12) craters; (13) scoria cones. (Modified after De Rita *et al.* 1983.)

latter is interrupted by NE-trending faults and is interpreted to be the culmination of a Miocene thrust sheet structure (Funiciello *et al.* 1979; De Rita *et al.* 1983).

The graben and the horst cut an allochthonous Cretaceous–Oligocene flysch sequence, comprising marls and marly limestones on average 1000 m thick (Fazzini *et al.* 1972), which covers a Meso-Cenozoic sequence of pelagic limestones 1500 m thick (Funiciello *et al.* 1976*a*,*b*, 1979). Below the volcanic products, Plio-Pleistocene marine sediments (clays, sandy clays and conglomerates) infill the graben for more than 500 m (Barberi *et al.* 1994), while on the Baccano–Cesano horst they are either absent or very thin.

Table 1. *Summary of data presented in this paper.*

Field analysis	1 : 25 000 scale mapping (1 : 10 000 around Bracciano Lake); more than 50 stratigraphical sections
Deep well logs analysis	23 exploratory deep wells and 49 boreholes for heat flow survey
High frequency seismic sections	see Fig. 5
Gravimetric survey	see Fig. 6
Magnetic survey	see Fig. 7

Volcanic sequences

The siting of volcanic activity in the SVD, the styles of eruptions, and the relationships and distribution of volcanic units are strongly controlled by the pre-volcanic lithology and structure (De Rita & Sposato 1986; this work Fig. 2). In fact, the first K-rich volcanic activity begins at the eastern margin of the graben close to Monte Soratte at about 0.6 Ma (Cioni *et al.*

1993; Figs 2 and 3). Succeeding activity, at 0.5–0.4 Ma (Cioni *et al.* 1993), moved westward to the area of Sacrofano, at the boundary between the graben and the Baccano–Cesano (BC) horst (De Rita *et al.* 1983).

At about 0.43 Ma (Cioni *et al.* 1993; Fig. 3), coincident with the peak of regional extension (Cavinato *et al.* 1993), volcanism spread westward (Fig. 4a) to the NE-trending faults that cut the northern part of BC horst. This episode (the first to be located in the Lake Bracciano area) erupted a large volume (about $10 \, km^3$) of trachy-phonolitic ignimbrite, the Sabatinian Red Tuff with Black Scoria (SRTBS), that was emplaced all the way to the periphery of the SVD and was influenced by the pre-existing topography, being absent on the BC horst (Cavarretta *et al.* 1990).

Our data (Table 1) show that after the eruption of the SRTBS, from 0.40 Ma to 0.28 Ma (Fornaseri 1985), the continuing regional extension was accompanied by strombolian and effusive activity, and by the subsidence of the BC horst (Fig. 4a). Interbedding of scoria cones with lava flows, geometry of these flows, and pre-effusive morphology indicate that the

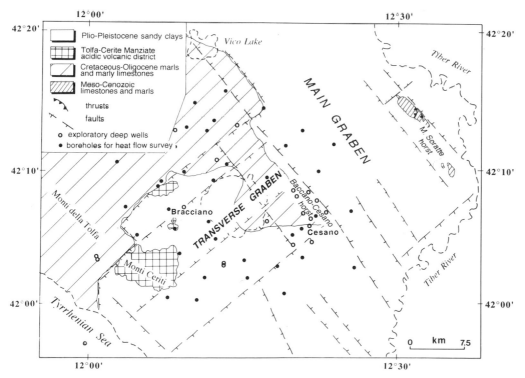

Fig. 2. Pre-volcanic geological and structural sketch map. The Baccano–Cesano horst had its maximum elevation at the southeast margin of Lake Bracciano.

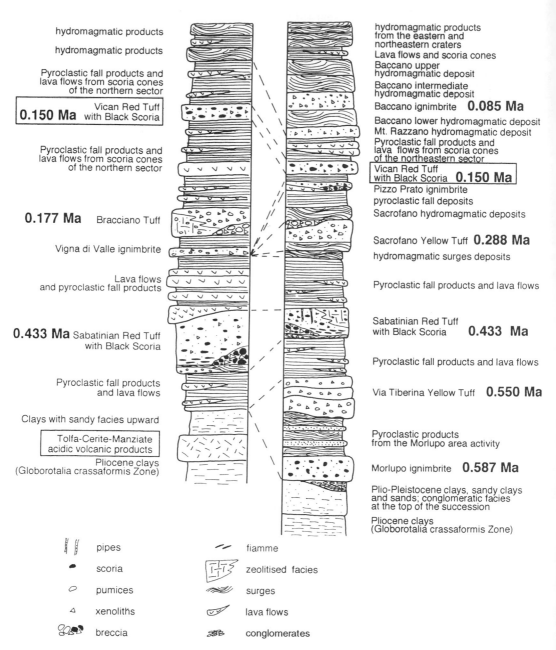

WESTERN SECTOR   EASTERN SECTOR

hydromagmatic products

hydromagmatic products

Pyroclastic fall products and lava flows from scoria cones of the northern sector

0.150 Ma Vican Red Tuff with Black Scoria

Pyroclastic fall products and lava flows from scoria cones of the northern sector

0.177 Ma Bracciano Tuff

Vigna di Valle ignimbrite

Lava flows and pyroclastic fall products

0.433 Ma Sabatinian Red Tuff with Black Scoria

Pyroclastic fall products and lava flows

Clays with sandy facies upward

Tolfa-Cerite-Manziate acidic volcanic products

Pliocene clays (Globorotalia crassaformis Zone)

hydromagmatic products from the eastern and northeastern craters
Lava flows and scoria cones
Baccano upper hydromagmatic deposit
Baccano intermediate hydromagmatic deposit
Baccano ignimbrite **0.085 Ma**
Baccano lower hydromagmatic deposit
Mt. Razzano hydromagmatic deposit
Pyroclastic fall products and lava flows from scoria cones of the northeastern sector
Vican Red Tuff with Black Scoria **0.150 Ma**
Pizzo Prato ignimbrite
pyroclastic fall deposits
Sacrofano hydromagmatic deposits

Sacrofano Yellow Tuff **0.288 Ma**

hydromagmatic surges deposits

Pyroclastic fall products and lava flows

Sabatinian Red Tuff with Black Scoria **0.433 Ma**

Pyroclastic fall products and lava flows

Via Tiberina Yellow Tuff **0.550 Ma**

Pyroclastic products from the Morlupo area activity

Morlupo ignimbrite **0.587 Ma**

Plio-Pleistocene clays, sandy clays and sands; conglomeratic facies at the top of the succession

Pliocene clays (Globorotalia crassaformis Zone)

pipes
scoria
pumices
xenoliths
breccia

fiamme
zeolitised facies
surges
lava flows
conglomerates

Fig. 3. Schematic stratigraphic sections of the Sabatini Volcanic District. The field data are complemented by deep-drilling data (ENEL 1992) carried out in the area during a geothermal power evaluation programme. At the base of the K-alkaline sequence, the *c.* 2 Ma acid volcanism of the Tolfa Cerite Manziate District is indicated. Geochronological data from Fornaseri (1985), Cioni *et al* (1993) and Bonadonna & Bigazzi (1970).

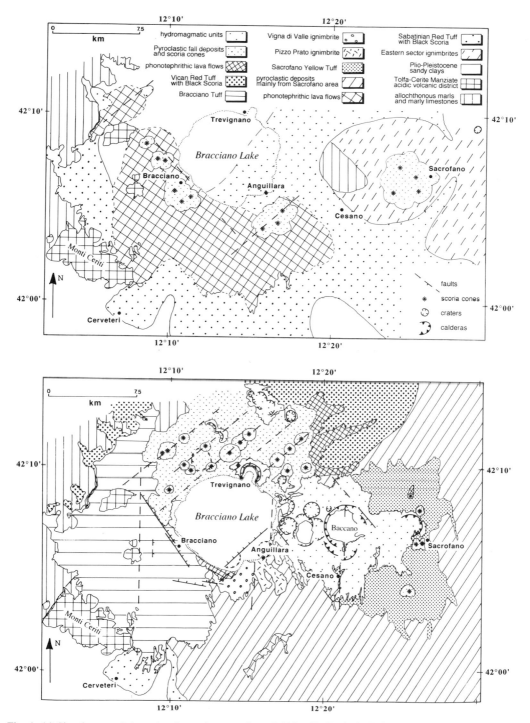

Fig. 4. (**a**) Sketch map of the volcanic products at about 0.4 Ma. (**b**) Geological sketch map of the volcanic products in the SVD.

vents were located south and west of the Lake Bracciano area, perhaps at the intersection of NE-trending faults with the faults bounding the BC horst.

After the lavas, three ignimbrite sheets were erupted between 0.28 Ma and 0.17 Ma (Bonadonna & Bigazzi 1970; Fig. 3) from fault systems just north of those that erupted the lavas (Fig. 4b). Co-ignimbrite breccias indicate that the first vent was located close to the village of Anguillara, on the southeastern margin of the lake, the second at its southern margin, and the third at its northwestern margin (Cioni & Sbrana 1991), north of Bracciano town (Fig. 4b). Minor effusions of lava from the same fracture system succeeded the ignimbrites. Lavas were also emplaced north of the lake, where they are interbedded with scoria cones aligned mostly NE and NW (Fig. 4b). At this time the Bracciano Depression had partially formed, as shown by a lava that flowed towards its centre. The last volcanic activity, from 0.17 Ma to less than 0.08 Ma (Fornaseri 1985; Fig. 3), erupted hydromagmatic products from craters aligned N–S and E–W around the eastern margin of the lake.

Structure of the Bracciano Depression

High-frequency Uniboom seismic lines were recorded along paths radial to Lake Bracciano. Two tangential profiles were also recorded in the southern part of the lake, where preliminary data suggested a more complicated morphology (Fig. 5). By contouring the first seismic reflector a new bathymetric map of Lake Bracciano (Fig. 5) was obtained. Interpretation of the seismic sections was carried out on the assumption that the lake was an enclosed sedimentary environment without important tributaries and with a low sedimentation rate.

The new bathymetric map of Lake Bracciano (Fig. 5) indicates that the present morphology is due to the superposition of different tectonic

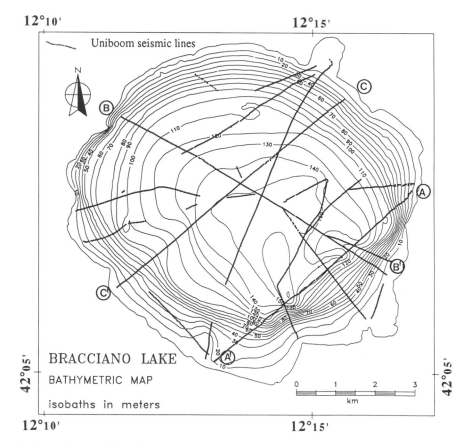

Fig. 5. Bathymetric map of Lake Bracciano.

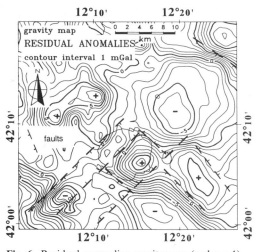

Fig. 6. Residual anomalies gravity map (order n-1).

lineaments. The southwestern and the north-eastern margins of the lake are defined by NW-trending ridges whereas the southeastern margin is clearly limited by a steep, NE-striking slope. On these, N-trending lineaments are superposed at the eastern margin of the present lake, where hydromagmatic craters are evident in the field. The lake is deepest in the south.

The residual anomalies gravity map (Fig. 6) shows that the Bracciano Depression is located at the intersection of NW and NE-trending gravity lows representing the main graben (Toro 1976) and a minor, NE-trending, transverse graben (Fig. 2). The faults controlling the development of this secondary graben are the same ones bordering the BC horst and controlling the sinking of the Bracciano Depression. The transverse graben may be subdivided into two parts: a southern part of Messinian age, where the

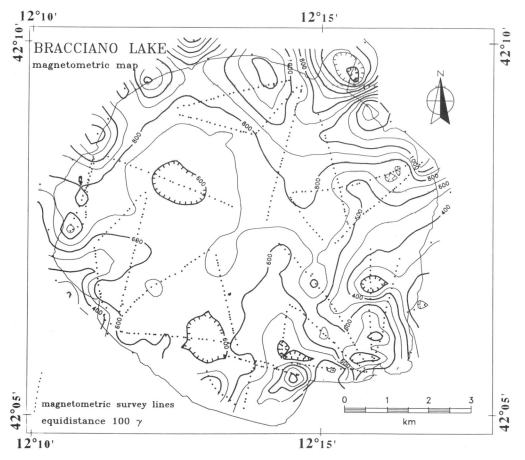

Fig. 7. Magnetometric map of Lake Bracciano.

Monti Ceriti volcanoes developed (De Rita *et al.* 1994), and a northern part of Upper Pliocene age (Buonasorte *et al.* 1991), presently occupied by the Bracciano Depression. The fault system controlling the development of the Monti Ceriti graben has been studied in detail (De Rita *et al.* 1994; Faccenna 1993). Because the fault system controlling the formation of the Bracciano Depression is part of the same system, the graben inside which it developed may have evolved in the same manner as the Monti Ceriti graben. The northern, NE-striking fault

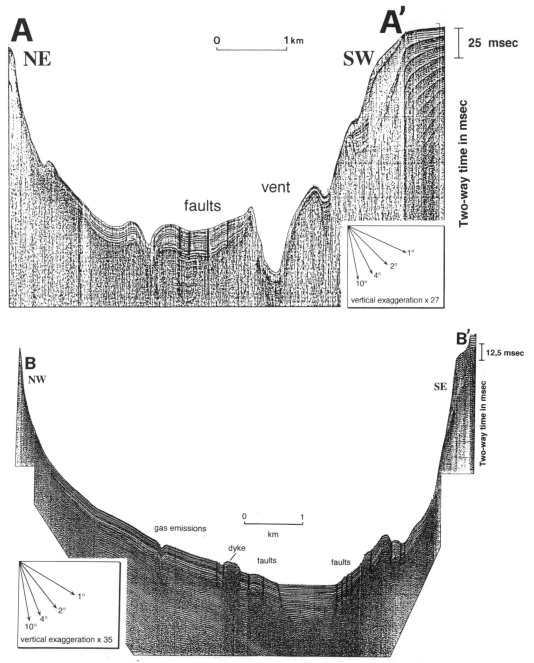

Fig. 8. (**a, b, c**) Uniboom high-frequency seismic sections (see Fig. 5 for locations of sections).

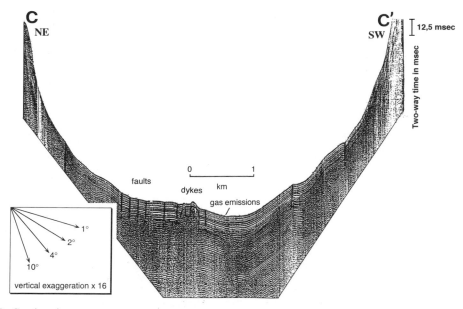

Fig. 8. Continued.

is the main fault of a half-graben structure. The asymmetric shape of the transverse graben, whose deepest part is located toward the northern margin, is clearly delimited by an important regional fault (see the residual anomalies gravity map in Fig. 6). Deep-drilling data indicate that the deepest part of the transverse graben is filled by younger sediments.

The magnetometric map (Fig. 7) shows the presence of magnetic dipoles in the southeastern part of the lake which coincides with the BC horst. Dipoles are also present in the northern part of the Bracciano area (Di Filippo *et al.* 1982). The extension and the high values of the residual anomalies (between 500 and 1000 g) may be attributed to the presence of solidified subsurface magma bodies such as lava flows or dykes. The geometry of the dipoles suggests an alignment of dykes or eruptive vents emplaced along NE-trending regional fractures re-activated during the development of the Bracciano Depression. This interpretation is consistent with the data of Molina & Sonaglia (1969) who recognized, from analysis of anomalies of the vertical component of the earth's magnetic field, the presence of an ellipsoidal, magmatic body located at shallow depths below the Bracciano area (around 7–10 km), whose associated apophyses reach to within 1 km of the surface.

The Uniboom high-frequency seismic sections (Fig. 8a, b, c) show the irregular bathymetry of the lake, whose recent sedimentary sequence appears almost undisturbed but is strongly controlled by the pre-existing topography. The most recent sedimentary layers are onlapping onto the older strata indicating that the basin has been actively sinking until recent times. Most of the ridges and cavities interrupting the continuity of the strata can be interpreted as dykes, ridges formed due to faults, and gas pipes. These characteristics are more evident in the southeastern part of the Lake. In the Anguillara area (Fig. 8a) it is also possible to recognize a circular depression, interpreted to be a crater related to the late hydromagmatic activity developed along N-trending fracture systems during the last phase of extensional tectonism (from 0.17 to less than 0.08 Ma).

Conclusions

The Bracciano volcano-tectonic depression developed inside a NE-trending half-graben formed during the Pliocene as a result of regional extensional tectonism affecting the Tyrrhenian margin of the Italian Peninsula. Explosive volcanic sequences issued from the reactivated faults which had controlled the half-graben collapse. Hence, the pre- and synvolcanic evolution of the Bracciano volcano-tectonic depression is controlled by regional extensional tectonism. Evidence for the half-graben structure includes: (a) the geometry of the NE-trending main fault, which crops out at the extreme northwestern

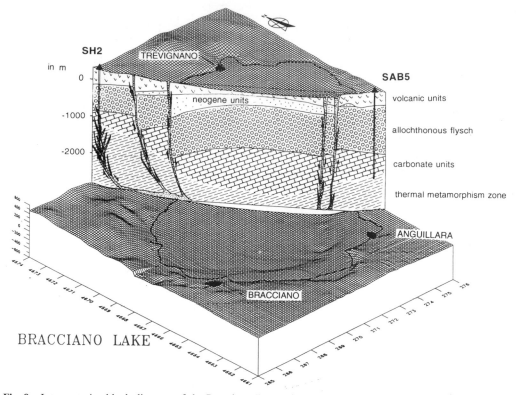

Fig. 9. Interpretative block diagram of the Bracciano Depression area.

margin of the depressed area; (b) the asymmetry of the structurally depressed area, which according to gravimetric information is deepest near the northwestern margin of the lake; (c) deep well data which indicate that the depression is infilled with Pliocene clay-rich sediments which thin to the SE; and (d) the analogy with other similar regional situations (De Rita *et al.* 1994; Faccenna *et al.* 1994).

During a phase of intense extensional tectonic activity magma rose to shallow depths (about 4–7 km) along the main NE-trending fault, forming a magmatic body whose geometry could be interpreted as being similar to a laccolith (Molina & Sonaglia 1969). Magma may have risen as far as a sharp thrust discontinuity (basal decollement horizon) between the sedimentary sequence and the underlying Palaeozoic crystalline basement (Bally *et al.* 1986), which gravimetric and deep-drilling data indicate lies 4–7 km below the Bracciano area (Di Filippo & Toro 1993). Extensional faults intersected the magmatic body approximately 0.4–0.3 Ma, during a climax of the regional extension, triggering the explosive eruption of the SRTBS.

Further magma then erupted to form a thick sequence of lava flows which issued from NE-striking swarms of feeder dykes in the southern area of the depression. The southern area of the present lake is cross-cut by dykes intruding the calcareous substratum along NE-trending faults which controlled central block subsidence (Fig. 9). The magma from these dykes forms a lava plateau which crops out to the south and west of the lake.

After 0.17 Ma the Bracciano Depression suffered its maximum subsidence during which lava effusions and scoria cone eruptions occurred in the northern area. The lake morphology has since been modified by the superposition of N–S strike-slip tectonism which affected pre-existing structures in the Central Latium area almost from around 0.17 Ma to Late Pleistocene times (Faccenna 1993). This tectonic phase controlled the focus of the hydromagmatic activity, on the eastern margin of the lake. We ascribe to this activity the further collapse of the southeastern part of the Bracciano Depression which is at the present time the deepest part.

We are grateful to C. Leah Moore for helpful suggestions for improving the English of the first version of the manuscript. We also thank Andrea Borgia, Mike Branney, and an anonymous reviewer for critical and fruitful comments which have greatly improved the manuscript.

References

AMODIO, M., DE RITA, D., DI FILIPPO, M., GALADINI, F. & SPOSATO, A. 1987. Evoluzione geologico-strutturale del bacino vulcano-tettonico di Bolsena (Complesso Vulcanico Vulsino). *CNR – Bollettino del Gruppo Nazionale per la Vulcanologia*, **1987**, 21–36.

BALDI, P., DECANDIA, F. A., LAZZAROTTO, A. & CALAMAI, A. 1974. Studio geologico del substrato della copertura vulcanica laziale nella zona dei Laghi di Bolsena Vico e Bracciano. *Memorie della Società Geologica Italiana*, **13**, 575–606.

BALLY, A. W., BURBI, L., COOPER, C. & GHELARDONI, R. 1986. Balanced sections and seismic reflection profiles across the central Apennines. *Memorie della Società Geologica Italiana*, **35**, 257–310.

BARBERI, F., BUONASORTE, G., CIONI, R. *ET AL.* 1994. Plio-Pleistocene geological evolution of the geothermal area of Tuscany and Latium. *Memorie descrittive della Carta Geologica d'Italia*, **49**, 77–135.

BONADONNA, F. P. & BIGAZZI, G. 1970. Studi sul Pleistocene del Lazio. VIII – Datazione di tufi intertirreniani della zona di Cerveteri (Roma) mediante il metodo delle tracce di fissione. *Bollettino della Società Geologica Italiana*, **89**, 463–473.

BUONASORTE, G., CARBONI, M. G. & CONTI, M. A. 1991. Il substrato plio-pleistocenico delle vulcaniti sabatine: considerazioni stratigrafiche e paleoambientali. *Bollettino della Società Geologica Italiana*, **110**, 35–40.

CAVARRETTA, G., DE RITA, D., ROSA, C. & SPOSATO, A. 1990. Caratteri geologico-petrografici del 'tufo rosso a scorie nere' sabatino. *Convegno Scientifico Annuale del Gruppo Nazionale per la Vulcanologia, Ravenna*, 18–20 Dicembre 1990 (poster).

CAVINATO, G. P., DE RITA, D., MILLI, S. & ZARLENGA, F. 1993. Correlazione tra i principali eventi tettonici, sedimentari, vulcanici ed eustatici che hanno interessato l'entroterra (conche intrappenniniche) ed il margine costiero laziale durante il Pliocene superiore ed il Pleistocene. *Studi Geologici Camerti, volume speciale* (1992/1), 109–114.

CIONI, R. & SBRANA, A. 1991. L'evoluzione del Complesso Vulcanico Sabatino. *Workshop: Evoluzione dei Bacini Neogenici e loro rapporti con il magmatismo Plio-Quaternario nell'area Tosco-Laziale*, Pisa, 10–12 Settembre 1991.

——, LAURENZI, M. A., SBRANA, A. & VILLA, I. M. 1993. 40Ar/39Ar chronostratigraphy of the initial activity in the Sabatini Volcanic Complex (Italy). *Bollettino della Società Geologica Italiana*, **112**, 251–263.

CONTICELLI, S., MANETTI, P., PECCERILLO, A. & SANTO, A. 1986. Caratteri petrologici delle vulcaniti potassiche italiane: considerazioni genetiche e geodinamiche. *Memorie della Società Geologica Italiana*, **35**, 775–783.

DE RITA, D. & SPOSATO, A. 1986. Correlazione tra eventi esplosivi ed assetto strutturale del substrato sedimentario nel Complesso Vulcanico Sabatino. *Memorie della Società Geologica Italiana*, **35**, 727–733.

——, BERTAGNINI, A., CARBONI, M. G. *ET AL.* 1994. Geological–petrographical evolution of the Ceriti Mountains area (Latium, Central Italy). *Memorie Descrittive della Carta Geologica d'Italia*, **49**, 231–323.

——, FUNICIELLO, R., CORDA, L., SPOSATO, A. & ROSSI, U. 1993. Volcanic Units. *In*: DI FILIPPO, M. (ed.) *Sabatini Volcanic Complex. Quaderni de 'La ricerca scientifica'. Progetto Finalizzato 'Geodinamica' – Monografie Finali*, **11**, 33–79.

——, —— & PAROTTO, M. 1988. *Carta Geologica del Complesso Vulcanico dei Colli Albani.* CNR, Roma.

——, ——, ROSSI, U. & SPOSATO, A. 1983. Structure and Evolution of the Sacrofano-Baccano Caldera, Sabatini Volcanic Complex, Rome. *Journal of Volcanology and Geothermal Research*, **17**, 219–236.

DI FILIPPO, M. & TORO, B. 1993. Gravimetric Study of Sabatini Area. *In*: DI FILIPPO, M. (ed.) *Sabatini Volcanic Complex. Quaderni de 'La ricerca scientifica'. Progetto Finalizzato 'Geodinamica' – Monografie Finali*, **11**, 95–99.

——, MAINO, A. & TORO, B. 1982. La prospezione gravimetrica del Lago di Bracciano (Italia Centrale) effettuata con l'ausilio del sottomarino 'F.A. Forel'. *Bollettino della Società Geologica Italiana*, **103**, 277–283.

ENEL – Università degli Studi di Roma 'La Sapienza', Dipartimento di Scienze della Terra 1992. *Aggiornamento delle caratteristiche geologiche di superficie e profonde del Lazio Settentrionale*, ENEL, internal report.

FACCENNA, C. 1993. *Tettonica quaternaria e stili deformativi lungo il margine tirrenico laziale.* Tesi di dottorato V Ciclo – Dipartimento di Scienze della Terra, Università degli Studi di Roma 'La Sapienza'.

——, FUNICIELLO, R., BRUNI, A., MATTEI, M. & SAGNOTTI, L. 1994. Evolution of a transfer-related basin: the Ardea basin (Latium, central Italy). *Basin Research*, **6**, 35–46.

FAZZINI, P., GELMINI, R., MANTOVANI, M. P. & PELLEGRINI, M. 1972. Geologia dei Monti della Tolfa (Lazio Settentrionale, Provincie di Viterbo e Roma). *Geologica Romana*, **11**, 65–144.

FORNASERI, M. 1985. Geochronology of volcanic rocks from Latium (Italy). *Rendiconti della società Italiana di Mineralogia e Petrologia*, **40**, 73–106.

FUNICIELLO, R., LOCARDI, E., LOMBARDI, G. & PAROTTO, M. 1976*a*. The sedimentary ejecta from phreatomagmatic activity and their use for location of potential geothermal areas. *Proceedings of the International Congress on Thermal Waters, Geothermal Energy and Volcanism of the Mediterranean Area*, Atene, 22–25.

——, —— & PAROTTO, M. 1976*b*. Lineamenti geologici dell'area sabatina orientale. *Bollettino della Società Geologica Italiana*, **95**, 831–849.

——, MARIOTTI, G., PAROTTO, M., PREITE-MARTINEZ, M., TECCE, F., TONEATTI, R. & TURI, B. 1979. Geology mineralogy and stable isotope geochemistry of the Cesano Geothermal Field (Sabatini Mts. Volcanic System, Northern Latium, Italy). *Geothermics*, **8**, 55–73.

LAVECCHIA, G. & STOPPA, F. 1990. The Tyrrhenian zone: a case of lithospheric extension control of intra-continental magmatism. *Earth and Planetary Science Letters*, **99**, 336–350.

LOCARDI, E. 1985. Neogene and Quaternary mediterranean volcanism: the Tyrrhenian example. *In*: STANLEY, D. J. & WEZEL, F. C. (eds) *Geological Evolution of the Mediterranean Basin*. Springer Verlag, New York, 273–291.

——, LOMBARDI, G., FUNICIELLO, R. & PAROTTO, M. 1976. The main volcanic groups of Latium (Italy): relations between structural evolution and petrogenesis. *Geologica Romana*, **15**, 279–300.

MOLINA, S. & SONAGLIA, A. 1969. Rilevamento geomagnetico degli apparati vulcanici Vicano e Sabazio. *Annali di Geofisica*, **22**, 147–162.

NAPPI, G., RENZULLI, A. & SANTI, P. 1991. Evidence of incremental growth in the Vulsinian calderas (central Italy). *In*: VERMA, S. P. (ed.) *Calderas: Genesis, Structure and Unrest. Journal of Volcanology and Geothermal Research*, **47**, 13–31.

PECCERILLO, A. & MANETTI, P. 1985. The Potassium alkaline volcanism of central-southern Italy: a review of the data relevant to petrogenesis and geodynamic significance. *Transactions of the Geological Society of South Africa*, **88**, 379–394.

SERRI, G., INNOCENTI, F., MANETTI, P., TONARINI, S. & FERRARA, G. 1992. Il magmatismo neogenico-quaternario dell'area tosco-laziale-umbra: implicazioni sui modelli di evoluzione geodinamica dell'Appennino settentrionale. *Studi Geologici Camerti, volume speciale* (1991/1), 429–463.

TORO, B. 1976. Gravimetry and deep structure of the Sabatinian and Alban Volcanic area (Latium). *Geologica Romana*, **15**, 301–310.

Transport and emplacement mechanisms of mass-flow deposits on Monte Vulture volcano, Basilicata, southern Italy

A. M. DUNCAN[1], P. D. COLE[2,1], J. E. GUEST[2] & D. K. CHESTER[3]

[1]*Department of Geology, University of Luton, Luton, LU1 3JU, UK*
[2]*Planetary Image Centre, University College London, 33/35 Daws Lane, Mill Hill, London, NW7 4SD, UK*
[3]*Department of Geography, University of Liverpool, Liverpool, L69 3BX, UK*

Abstract: The Lahar Facies of Mt Vulture, which forms a broad apron around the base of the cone, is composed predominantly of mass-flow deposits. There is a spectrum of lithological types ranging from monolithologic units which may be of a primary pyroclastic flow origin and are composed entirely of juvenile material, to polylithologic deposits, containing a range of clast types, interpreted to be cold debris-flow deposits. Some debris-flow deposits show evidence of being hot on emplacement. Debris-flow deposits are interbedded with lapilli-fall layers and lava flows suggesting formation contemporaneous with eruptive activity. Some debris-flow deposits travelled no more than 3 km from their source. Many flows were apparently non-erosive, although there is one example where a debris-flow eroded clasts from the top of a lava flow. The presence of fractured 'jigsaw' blocks and large fragile blocks of pyroclastic material rules out turbulent flow and high shear for much of the transport prior to emplacement. Multiple grading and abundant development of reverse grading with large lava blocks rafted on, or protruding through, the upper surface of flow units implies that the lahars were high-concentration, high-strength flows in which differential shearing produced discontinuous multiple grading. Locally, individual debris-flow deposits have convex upper surface profiles with internal grading paralleling the surface, strongly supporting a conclusion that these debris-flow deposits were emplaced en masse.

The purpose of this paper is to describe and interpret the field relationships of mass-flow deposits on the slopes of Monte Vulture volcano, Basilicata, southern Italy. Study of these deposits provides important insights into their mechanisms of transport and emplacement. We suggest that these mass-flow deposits were formed by a number of flow mechanisms which range from cold debris flows, through hot debris flows, to pyroclastic flows. We do not envisage this range as being continuous, but rather of different types of flow, which may in part be gradational.

Mass-flow deposits are abundant within the Lahar Facies of Guest *et al.* (1988), which forms a broad apron around much of the lower flanks of the cone of Monte Vulture (Fig. 1). The Lahar Facies is composed of mass-flow deposits, principally debris-flow deposits and some primary pyroclastic-flow deposits. These mass-flow deposits are typically interbedded with lapilli-fall layers and locally lavas (Fig. 2). Some of the debris-flow materials occur within an envelope of lapilli-fall layers demonstrating a syn-eruptive relationship.

We use the term 'mass-flow deposit' as a general term to describe units in this sequence,

because detailed field investigation demonstrates that they have been generated by a variety of different types of flow mechanism. The sequence includes both debris-flow deposits and pyroclastic-flow deposits. The broad similarity of these different kinds of deposit implies a commonality of styles of emplacement from these different flow types.

Monte Vulture is the only volcano of the Italian Roman Province which lies on the eastern side of the Apennines (Fig. 1). The geology of Monte Vulture has been described by Hieke Merlin (1967), La Volpe *et al.* (1984), Guest *et al.* (1988) and La Volpe & Principe (1991). The volcano is composed of strongly undersaturated alkalic products of the Italian high-K series. The earliest activity (*c.* 1 Ma) involved eruption of phonolitic/trachytic pyroclastic flows (Crisci *et al.* 1983). This was followed by a cone-building phase with eruption of more strongly undersaturated magmas, tephrites and foidites (De Fino *et al.* 1986). Explosive activity deposited thick tephra beds to the east and southeast of the volcano and reworking of this material on the higher slopes of the volcano formed an apron of mass-flow deposits on the lower slopes of the cone, the

From McGuire, W. J., Jones, A. P. & Neuberg, J. (eds) 1996, *Volcano Instability on the Earth and Other Planets*, Geological Society Special Publication No. 110, pp. 237–247.

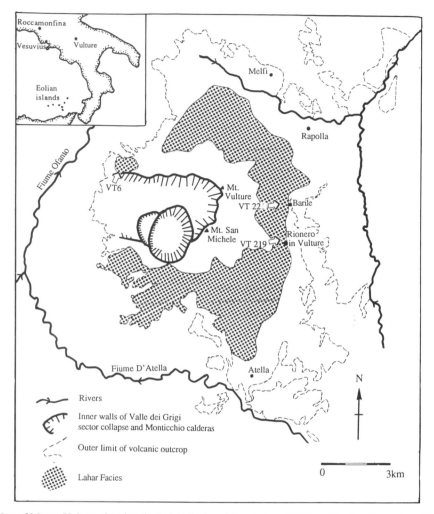

Fig. 1. Map of Monte Vulture showing the Lahar Facies of Guest *et al.* (1988) and the location of localities. Inset shows location of Monte Vulture in southern Italy.

Lahar Facies of Guest *et al.* (1988). La Volpe & Principe (1991), however, interpreted these to be predominantly block-and-ash-flow deposits; see also Guest *et al.* (1991). We found little evidence to support a block-and-ash-flow origin although the Lahar Facies does contain probable primary pyroclastic-flow deposits. These deposits comprise predominantly vesicular scoriaceous material, including bombs, and it is most unlikely that they were generated by the collapse of a lava dome, as is the case for block-and-ash-flow deposits (Cas & Wright 1987). The cone-building phase was terminated by caldera collapse followed by gravitational collapse of the western flank sector to form the Valle dei Grigi. The last activity of Vulture was the

phreatomagmatic eruptions about 40 000 a BP forming two maar-like lakes, the Laghi di Monticchio.

Field relationships

Quarries immediately northwest of Rionero in Vulture and west of Barile (Fig. 1) provide excellent 2D and some 3D exposures of the mass-flow deposits. Geometrically the deposits occur either in-filling channels or have a sheet-like form (Fig. 2). Within channels lapilli-fall layers underlie the mass-flow deposits (see Figs 2 and 3), implying that the channels were excavated by earlier fluvial activity rather than

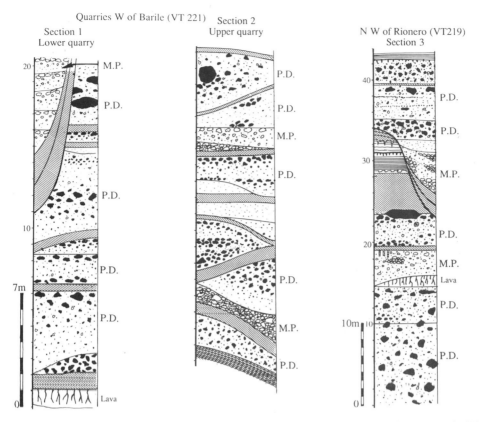

Fig. 2. Sections through the Lahar Facies on the east side of Monte Vulture. Diagonal hatch represents lapilli-fall layers. P.D., polylithologic debris-flow deposit. M.P., monolithologic pyroclastic-flow deposit. Open symbols are vesicular clasts, closed symbols are dense lithic blocks.

being eroded by the flows that fill them. Flow deposits occurring in sheets are the more abundant type and range from single massive homogeneous units several metres thick to deposits composed of several discontinuous sub-units.

Lithologically there appears to be a spectrum of mass-flow deposits ranging from monolithologic deposits, which are almost totally composed of juvenile material, to those containing a variety of clast types. The monolithologic deposits are composed of clasts with a range of vesicularity from dense blocks to scoria. Many clasts have cauliform shapes, breadcrusted outer surfaces and some clasts have spindle bomb shapes suggestive of being derived as juvenile ballistic projectiles resulting from mild explosive activity (Fig. 4). The monomict composition of mainly vesicular juvenile clasts and the presence of rare gas escape pipes suggest that these may be primary pyroclastic-flow deposits. It could be, however,

that these deposits formed by rapid reworking of fresh primary material while still hot. This is similar to the situation on Mount Pinatubo, described by Rosi *et al.* (1994), with reworked deposits being generated by avalanching from fresh pyroclastic-flow deposits. Such a process will form products with the characteristics of primary flow deposits. On the other hand some of the mass-flow deposits are polylithologic, contain many lithic (i.e. derived) clasts which are angular, non-vesicular and are of varying lithology. These deposits we consider to be emplaced by debris flows. Some hydrothermally altered lithic clasts are also present. There are also, however, polylithologic deposits with a significant content of juvenile clasts together with massive lava blocks. The lava blocks, up to 2 m across, often show well developed radial jointing (Fig. 5), probably formed during cooling, indicating that some of the clasts were hot on emplacement. These deposits we also consider to be of a debris-flow origin. The mass-

Fig. 3. Monolithologic mass-flow deposits filling a channel at a quarry just outside Rionero in Vulture. The channel-filling deposits are underlain by lapilli-fall beds.

flow deposits, therefore, range between two lithological end members implying that there may be a spectrum of flow types involved ranging from primary pyroclastic flows, through debris flows rich in juvenile material and hot blocks to cold debris flows.

We use the term 'mass-flow deposit' as a general term to describe the units within the Lahar Facies. We restrict the terms debris-flow deposit and pyroclastic-flow deposit to those units which we can identify according to the criteria described above.

Fig. 4. The upper, clast-rich part of a monolithologic deposit considered to be of a primary pyroclastic-flow origin. Note the abundance of vesicular juvenile material and the spindle bomb

Fig. 5. Block with well developed radial jointing in a polylithologic deposit. The radial cooling joints indicate that the flow was hot on emplacement (see Smith & Lowe 1991).

Evidence for transport and emplacement mechanisms

This section describes the field relations that give important information regarding the transport and emplacement mechanisms that operated to form these mass-flow deposits.

Flow Fronts

The quarry immediately to the west of Barile (VT 221 – Fig. 1), 3 km from the summit of the volcano, shows excellent exposures, running east–west, parallel to the flow direction displaying massive debris-flow deposits

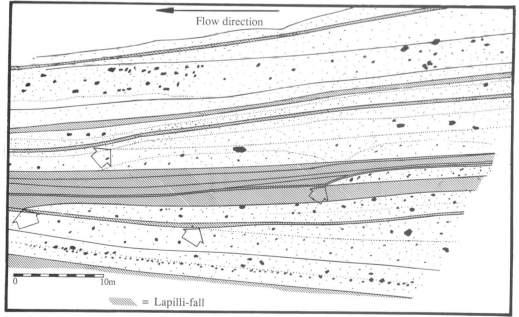

Fig. 6. Sketch of quarry wall at site VT 221 (lower quarry) showing flow deposits interbedded with lapilli-fall layers (diagonal cross-hatch). Steep flow fronts are highlighted with open arrows. Flow direction was from right to left.

interbedded between lapilli-fall layers (Fig. 6). Many of the debris-flow deposits can be seen to terminate with distinctive flow fronts. The flow fronts are geometrically well defined with no evidence of truncations suggestive of erosion. These features, therefore, are primary implying that some of the debris flows terminated at this point. This indicates that some of the flows came to a halt before reaching the foot of the volcano.

Grading styles

Reverse grading of dense clasts is common within many of the mass-flow deposits. Individual reverse graded units do not normally exceed *c*. 2 m in thickness. An abundance of reverse grading coupled with the presence of protruding blocks indicate that the flows had high particle concentrations at least during the final stages of transport and emplacement (Lowe 1982). High particle concentrations may have caused dispersive pressures that forced clasts upwards, so producing reverse grading (Bagnold 1954). Multiple grading is a feature typical of many debris-flow deposits on Vulture (Figs 7, 8 and 9). A debris-flow deposit several metres in thickness is often composed of a number of distinct sub-units. As many as five sub-units have been observed in one debris-flow

deposit. Sub-units are defined by concentrations of coarse clasts occurring in distinct horizons. Reverse grading is predominant but some sub-units are ungraded. Normal grading is rare. Individual, coarse horizons range from 0.3 to 2 m in thickness but are more commonly 0.5–1 m thick. In exposures cut parallel to flow direction, individual sub-units are broadly continuous and in some places may be traced over at least 50–100 m before grading into a massive unit. These sub-units are separated by discontinuous fine-grained layers (Figs 8a and b). In exposures cut perpendicular to flow direction, the sub-units are less continuous. Between sub-units gradational contacts suggest contemporaneous emplacement of several sub-units within one debris-flow unit. The presence of normal and reverse grading within a single unit as shown in Fig. 7 may suggest changing flow conditions in the transport stage over time. Differential shear within a single flow could produce several graded layers in a similar fashion to that described by Cas & Landis (1987). Dispersive forces would move coarser clasts away from the zones of high shear leading to reverse grading. The several reverse graded sub-units within a single debris-flow deposit may indicate that there were a number of zones of high shear within the lahar. This could have been caused by pulsing of different parts of the flow generating anastomosing lobes within the same flow.

Fig. 7. A polylithologic debris-flow deposit exposed in the quarry at site VT 219 illustrating multiple grading. Both normal and reverse grading are well developed in this unit. It is underlain by a thin (<10 cm) lapilli-fall layer and overlain by a thin discontinuous pyroclastic-surge deposit.

Convex upper surfaces

Excellent exposures reveal that the debris-flow deposits have convex upper surfaces (Figs 8a and b). Grading within the deposit parallels the upper surface (Figs 8a and b) indicating that the concave upper surface was an integral feature of the flow and was not a late stage process. This morphology suggests that the debris-flow came to rest en masse and possessed a yield strength. The debris-flow deposit illustrated in Fig. 8 is under- and overlain by lapilli-fall, where the flow unit pinches out and the lapilli-fall merges into a single unit. This implies that in this particular case the debris-flow deposit was emplaced during the existence of a continuous convecting eruption column.

Fragile blocks

Also of interest in the debate on emplacement mechanisms is the fragile nature of some of the components of the debris-flow deposits. Debris-flow deposits on the east flank of the volcano contain lava blocks that have a network of fine

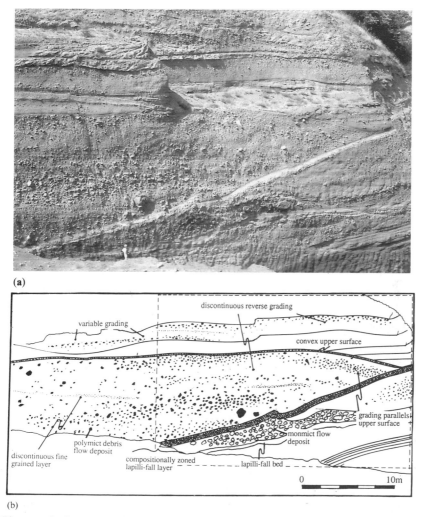

(a)

(b)

Fig. 8. (a) Photograph of exposure of debris-flow deposits at the upper quarry to the west of Barile VT 221. The face is cut perpendicular to flow. Shows different grading styles. Note the convex upper surface of the main debris-flow deposit. **(b)** Explanatory diagram of the quarry face. Area enclosed by the dashed line is illustrated in the photograph.

fractures and disintegrate on removal from the exposure. The nature of these fractures is quite distinct from the radial fractures attributed to cooling of hot clasts. These fragile blocks resemble in part the jigsaw cracks or brecciated blocks that have been described from debris avalanche deposits (Glicken 1991) and have been interpreted as resulting from clast collisions during flow (Smith & Lowe 1991). Fragile blocks of bedded pyroclastic material up to 4 m long and 2 m high are present within debris-flow deposits on the western side of the volcano (Figs 9a and b). In the same debris-flow deposit blocks of similar pyroclastic material *c*. 3 m long protrude from the upper surface of the unit. Delicate blocks of undisturbed pyroclastic material within debris-flow deposits on Mt St Helens have been described

(a)

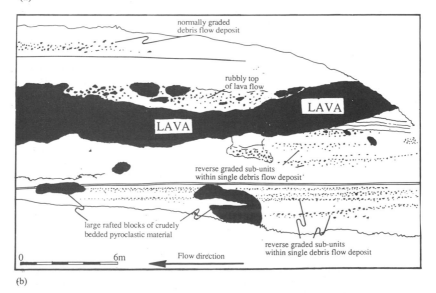

(b)

Fig. 9. (a) Photograph showing large outsized blocks of pyroclastic material both within and protruding through the upper surface of a polylithologic debris-flow deposit (base). Note reverse graded sub-units within both the debris-flow deposits below the lava. Flow direction was from right to left. (b) Explanatory diagram of the photograph.

from both prehistoric (Scott 1988) and 1980 lahars (Brantley & Waitt 1988). This suggests that for much of the transport stage these fragile clasts must have been transported in a non-turbulent manner with 'gentle handling' (see Fisher & Schmincke 1984, p. 307) in order to be preserved within the final deposit.

Transport of outsized clasts

Debris-flow deposits, on the southeastern slopes of the volcano have massive lava blocks, up to 3 m across, protruding from the upper surface of flow units. Recent research on high density turbidity currents (Postma *et al.* 1988) has explained the emplacement of similar large clasts by a process involving the development of a rheological interface which divides a more viscous, non-turbulent inertia flow below from a less viscous, more dilute turbulent flow above. The larger clasts are transported downflow and upwards 'gliding' on this interface as it rises through the decelerating and depositing flow. Best (1992) has suggested that a similar process may have operated to enable clasts to 'float' on the surface of the mass flows generated by the 1971 eruption of Volcan Hudson, Chile. Some caution needs to be exercised, however, in relating features seen in subaerial debris-flow deposits too closely to processes observed in subaqueous sediment flows. The concentrations of coarse clasts in the Vulture debris-flow deposits, however, do not show the imbrication textures which might be expected if the clasts were being driven along an interface between a lower dense flow and an overlying, faster moving turbulent layer (see Postma *et al.* 1988). This, taken together with the evidence for convex margins and the transport of fragile clasts discussed above, makes it likely that the lahars that formed these debris-flow deposits had sufficient strength to allow such large blocks to be transported and indeed to have some rafted on top of the flow.

Erosion by flows and clast scavenging

Within the Lahar Facies southeast of the volcano many thin lapilli-fall layers, 0.1–2 m in thickness, are interbedded between the mass-flow deposits (Figs 2 and 3). The generally constant thickness and uninterrupted nature of these lapilli layers suggests that the mass flows were not erosive in this area. Only one exposure of mass-flow deposits shows evidence for erosion of underlying material. On the western flank of the volcano a debris-flow deposit rests on top of

a lava flow. The lava flow has an extensive rubbly upper surface composed of loose scoriaceous material. At the top of a sloping surface, a zone at the base of the debris-flow deposit is strongly enriched in lava clasts (Figs 10a and b). This zone of lava clasts extends upwards and laterally downslope into the debris-flow deposit where the clast concentration becomes more diffuse. This is evidence that the lahar entrained scoria clasts as it moved over the scoriaceous/rubbly top of the lava flow. Furthermore this indicates that a velocity gradient was present within the lahar and strongly implies laminar motion at this stage in the flow.

Discussion and conclusions

The Lahar Facies of Monte Vulture is composed of a spectrum of mass-flow deposits that range from monomict units of a primary pyroclastic flow character through debris-flow deposits, which show evidence for clasts being hot on emplacement to polymict debris-flow deposits. In addition there are some materials which were probably deposited by hyperconcentrated stream flow (Guest *et al.* 1988). These mass-flow deposits were generated during eruptive episodes as they are intimately associated with lapilli-fall layers. The debris-flow deposits show good evidence for laminar flow and internal shear during transport with individual portions coming to a halt en masse while other parts continued to move forming a series of anastomosing lobes.

Non-volcanic debris flows contain appreciable clay and it is this clay-rich matrix that is considered to make them cohesive (Lowe 1979; Naylor 1979). Young volcaniclastic debris flows on the other hand, tend to contain very little clay, apart from that derived from hydrothermally altered material. In fact Smith & Lowe (1991) state that most volcanic debris flows are non-cohesive and regard them as water-saturated granular flows. Furthermore they also suggest that debris-flow deposition is not always en masse. They cite examples of large volume, far travelled flows that leave deposits significantly thinner than the flows themselves and veneers of debris-flow matrix (Smith & Lowe 1991, p. 63). This argument is similar in many ways to the recent debate on ignimbrite emplacement where evidence for progressive aggradation is present in some deposits (Branney & Kokelaar 1992, 1994) but en masse emplacement seems more likely in others (Sparks 1976; Freundt & Schmincke 1986; Cole *et al.* 1993).

As described above several features of these debris-flow deposits suggest that these flows had a yield strength and came to rest en masse. It seems likely that many of the flows that produced these debris-flow deposits on Monte Vulture had a negligible clay content. It is possible that there are several other mechanisms of generating cohesion in volcanic debris flows. Their strength results from (a) grain collisions and (b) cohesion between silt and ash sized particles (Smith & Lowe 1991). The clasts in volcanic debris flows are much more irregular than the sand grains in sedimentary debris flows and therefore cohesion between clasts is likely to be more effective.

These debris-flow deposits are at the small volume end of the spectrum having short run-out distances. It is possible that there is a continuum of debris-flow types from small volume short run-out lahars, that were probably responsible for these deposits which were emplaced en masse, through to the larger volume long run-out types which left veneers of deposits rather than coming to rest as a whole.

(a)

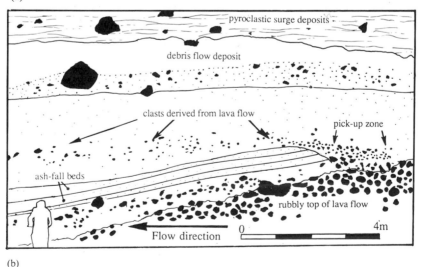

(b)

Fig. 10. (a) Photograph illustrating a polylithologic debris-flow deposit showing scoriaceous clasts derived from the rubbly top of the lava flow below. Note the debris-flow eroded through the ash-fall beds on top of the lava flow. Flow direction was from right to left. **(b)** Explanatory diagram of the photograph.

We thank Annamaria Perrotta and Claudio Scarpati for constructive discussion in the field and Grant Heiken and Gary Smith for helpful comments on an earlier version of this manuscript.

References

BAGNOLD, R. A. 1954. Experiments on gravity-free dispersion of large solid spheres in a Newtonian fluid under shear. *Proceedings of Royal Society of London*, **A225**, 49–63.

BEST, J. L. 1992. Sedimentology and event timing of a catastrophic volcaniclastic mass flow, Volcan Hudson, Southern Chile. *Bulletin of Volcanology*, **54**, 299–318.

BRANNEY, M. J. & KOKELAAR, B. P. 1992. A reappraisal of ignimbrite emplacement: changes from particulate to non-particulate flow during progressive aggradation of high-grade ignimbrite. *Bulletin of Volcanology*, **54**, 504–520.

—— & ——1994. Reply to comment by Wolff & Turbeville. *Bulletin of Volcanology*, **54**, 504–520.

BRANTLEY, S. R. & WAITT, R. B. 1988. Interrelations among pyroclastic surge, pyroclastic flow, and lahars in Smith Creek valley during first minutes of 18 May 1980 eruption of Mt St Helens, USA. *Bulletin of Volcanology*, **56**, 134–137.

CAS, R. A. F. & LANDIS, C. A. 1987. A debris-flow deposit with multiple plug-flow channels and side accretion deposits. *Sedimentology*, **34**, 901–910.

—— & WRIGHT, J. V. 1987. *Volcanic Successions, Modern and Ancient*. Allen & Unwin, Hemel Hempstead.

COLE, P. D., GUEST, J. E. & DUNCAN, A. M. 1993. The emplacement of intermediate volume ignimbrites: a case study from Roccamonfina Volcano southern Italy. *Bulletin of Volcanology*, **55**, 467–480.

CRISCI, G., DE FINO, M., LA VOLPE, L. & RAPISARDI, L. 1983. Pleistocene ignimbrites of Monte Vulture (Basilicata, Southern Italy) *Neues Jahrbuch für Geologie Palaontologie Monatshefte*, **12**, 731–746

DE FINO, M., LA VOLPE, L., PECCERILLO, G. PICCARRETA, G. & POLI, G. 1986. Petrogenesis of Monte Vulture volcano (Italy): inferences from mineral chemistry, major and trace element data. *Contributions to Mineralogy and Petrology*, **92**, 135–145

FISHER, R. V. & Schmincke, H-U. 1984. *Pyroclastic Rocks*. Springer-Verlag, Berlin.

FREUNDT, A. & SCHMINCKE, H-U. 1986. Emplacement of small volume pyroclastic flow deposits at Laacher See (East Eiffel, Germany). *Bulletin of Volcanology*, **48**, 39–59.

GLICKEN, H. X. 1991. Sedimentary architecture of large volcanic-debris avalanches. *In*: FISHER, R. V. & SMITH, G. A. (eds) *Sedimentation in Volcanic Settings*. SEPM special publication **45**, 99–106.

GUEST, J. E., DUNCAN, A. M. & CHESTER, D. K. 1988. Monte Vulture Volcano (Basilicata, Italy): an analysis of morphology and volcaniclastic facies. *Bulletin of Volcanology*, **50**, 244–257.

——, —— & ——1991. Reply to comment by La Volpe & Principe. *Bulletin of Volcanology*, **53**, 228–229.

HIEKE MERLIN, O. 1967. I prodotti vulcanici del Monte Vulture (Lucania). *Memorie degli Istituto di Geologia e di Mineralogia Univ Padova*, **26**, 3–67.

LA VOLPE, L. & PRINCIPE, C. 1991. Comment on Guest et al 1988. *Bulletin of Volcanology*, **53**, 222–227.

——, PATELLA, D., RAPISARDI, L. & TRAMACERE, A. 1984. The evolution of the Monte Vulture volcano (Southern Italy): inferences from volcanological, geological and deep dipole electrical soundings data. *Journal of Volcanology and Geothermal Research*, **22**, 147–162.

LOWE, D. R. 1979. Sediment gravity flows: Their classification and application to natural flows and deposits. *In*: DOYLE, L. J. & PILKEY, O. H. (eds) *Geology of Continental Slopes*. SEPM special publication **27**, 75–82.

——1982. Sediment gravity flows II. Depositional models with special reference to the deposits of high-density turbidity currents. *Journal of Sedimentary Petrology*, **52**, 279–297.

NAYLOR, M. A. 1979. The origin of inverse grading in muddy debris-flow deposits – a review. *Journal of Sedimentary Petrology*, **50**, 1111–1116

POSTMA, G., NEMEC, W. & KLEINSPEHN, K. L. 1988. Large floating clasts in turbidites a mechanism for their emplacement. *Sedimentary Geology*, **58**, 47–61.

ROSI, M., SELF, S. & TORRES, R. 1994. Potential role and importance of secondary pyroclastic flow processes in ignimbrite sequences. *IAVCEI Commission on Explosive Volcanism, Newsletter*, No. **25**.

SCOTT, K. M. 1988. *Origins, Behavior and Sedimentology of Lahars and Lahar Runout Flows in the Toutle Cowlitz River System*. US Geological Survey Professional Paper **1447-A**.

SMITH, G. A. & LOWE, D. R. 1991. Lahars: volcano-hydrologic events and deposition in the debris flow -hyperconcentrated continuum. *In*: FISHER, R. V. & SMITH, G. A. (eds) *Sedimentation in Volcanic Settings*. SEPM special publication **45**, 59–70.

SPARKS, R. S. J. 1976. Grain size variations in ignimbrites and implications for the transport of pyroclastic flows. *Sedimentology*, **23**, 147–188.

Recent uplift of Ischia, southern Italy

GIORGIO BUCHNER[1], ANTONINO ITALIANO[2] & CLAUDIO VITA-FINZI[3]

[1] *Via S. Alessandro 23, I-80077 Porto d'Ischia, Italy*
[2] *ENEL SOIC, Via P.E. Imbriani 42, I-80132 Napoli, Italy*
[3] *Research School of Geological and Geophysical Sciences, University College, Gower St, London WC1E 6BT, UK*

Abstract: Radiocarbon dating of fossil bivalves and corals from Ischia, in southern Italy, shows that parts of the island have undergone some 70 m of uplift in the last 8500 years. Historical evidence reportedly suggests that during the last two millennia parts of the north coast were submerged by up to 4 m whereas the southern coast underwent as much as 25 m of emergence. The ^{14}C results, which represent an average uplift rate of about 9 mm a^{-1}, supplement studies based on potassium–argon dating of volcanic deposits which indicate that the Monte Epomeo horst at the centre of the island has risen by at least 800 m during the last 33 000 years, and micropalaeontological evidence, which points to some 700 m of emergence in the same time period. Eyewitness accounts suggest that some of the movement was coseismic. Prolonged uplift has created a steep topography prone to slope failure.

The volcanic island of Ischia, off Naples, has long been recognized as tectonically active. As early as 1814 Giovan Battista Brocchi reported marine molluscs on the island, and in a letter to Roderick Murchison dated 6 November 1828 Charles Lyell (1881) announced his discovery on Ischia of up to 30 species 'at a greater height than any of Brocchi's sub-Apennines, and belonging to a formation decidedly more recent'.

Other nineteenth century students of Ischia's marine fossil record include R. A. Philippi, S. A. Spada-Lavini and E. Van den Broek. These scholars, and their twentieth century successors, were of course unable to specify the age of the faunas until radiometric dating of some of the volcanic deposits in question. Nevertheless the apparent modern aspect of the faunas alerted them to the possibility that uplift had been rapid.

Three major structural units are generally recognized on Ischia: the Monte Epomeo horst, the Ischia Graben, and the highs of Castello d'Ischia, Punta Chiarito, Punta Imperatore and Monte Vico (Fig. 1). The fault pattern reflects the interplay between the regional stress field and the influence of a magma chamber (Fusi *et al.* 1990). The volcanic evolution of Ischia has been divided into five main phases (Vezzoli 1988): pyroclastic activity >150 000 a BP; emplacement of lava domes 150 000–75 000 a BP; pyroclastic activity 55 000–33 000 a BP; explosive and effusive activity 28 500–18 000 a BP; and scattered eruptions 10 000 a BP–AD 1302. In the 1970s the Green Tuff of Monte Epomeo, at the core of the island, was thought to have a K/Ar age of about 700 000 a but Gillot *et al.* (1982) later obtained a K/Ar age of 55 000 ± 3500 a BP for the ash and demonstrated that it had accumulated between 75 000 ± 2000 and 33 000 ± 2000 a BP. In their view uplift of the Monte Epomeo horst from sea level by at least 800 m occurred subsequently.

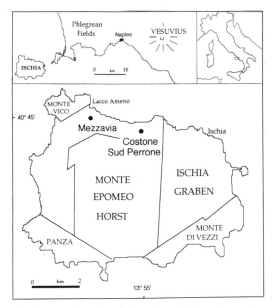

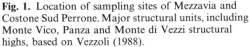

Fig. 1. Location of sampling sites of Mezzavia and Costone Sud Perrone. Major structural units, including Monte Vico, Panza and Monte di Vezzi structural highs, based on Vezzoli (1988).

Radiocarbon dating

The present study is an attempt to establish the extent of late Quaternary deformation on Ischia

From McGuire, W. J., Jones, A. P. & Neuberg, J. (eds) 1996, *Volcano Instability on the Earth and Other Planets*, Geological Society Special Publication No. 110, pp. 249–252.

by applying the radiocarbon method to coastal features. The ^{14}C method is of course applicable only to the last 40 000 years or so; the variant used here for three of the samples encompasses only the last 16 000 years by virtue of the procedures used in sample preparation (Vita-Finzi, 1991).

The search for dependable fossil shorelines was thwarted by the destruction caused by building and road construction. But a set of well documented marine fossils collected and stored over the years by Paul and Giorgio Buchner has made it possible to date the key locations of Mezzavia and Costone Sud Perrone (Figs 1 and 2). The samples were screened with the help of acetate peels, X-ray diffraction and scanning electron microscopy. Mechanical abrasion was followed by selective acid leaching. The corals were sectioned to ensure the complete removal of matrix from the chambers (Fig. 3). The three first-order samples were prepared using silver nitrate and desiccant traps and a 1:1 mixture of Carbosorb and Permafluor V; counting was carried out on a Packard Tricarb 2260 XL liquid scintillation counter for 1000 minutes (Vita-Finzi, 1991).

At Mezzavia, Scacchi (1841) reported shells at a height of 40 m which had retained their original coloration and thus appeared to reflect a recent shoreline. Two species were collected from this deposit by P. and G. Buchner. Their radiocarbon ages are in excellent agreement (Table 1), suggesting that redeposition of the molluscs took place soon after their death and that their ages provide a good guide to that of the waterline. The data indicate some 57 m of uplift in less than 6000 years. A specimen of the coral *Cladocora caespitosa* from Costone Sud Perrone, 10 m higher, was dated by first-order

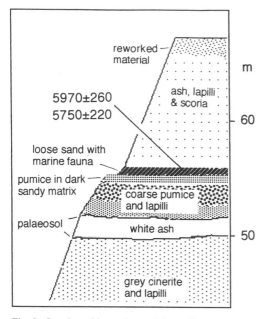

Fig. 2. Stratigraphic section at Mezzavia. Archaeological material dating from *c.*4000 a BP has been recovered from the surface of the sequence. Elevation is shown on the right. The dated material discussed in the paper came from the loose sand horizon at about 55 m above sea level.

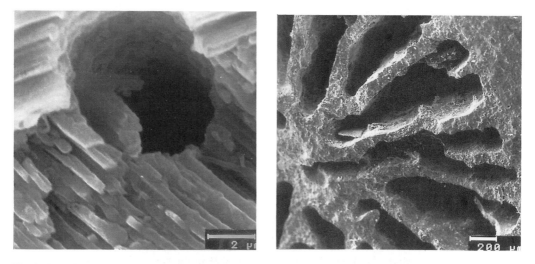

Fig. 3. Scanning electron micrographs of (**a**) *Glycymeris* sp. from Mezzavia and (**b**) *Cladocora caespitosa* from Costone Sud Perrone showing absence of contamination by secondary carbonate on the surface or within natural cavities.

Table 1. *First-order ^{14}C ages on marine deposits from Ischia*

Site no.	Locality	Elevation (m)	Corrected height*	Species	^{14}C age (a BP)	XRD†	Calibrated age‡ (a BP)	Lab. no.
1	Mezzavia	55	57	*Glycymeris* sp.	5600 ± 200	A	5970 ± 260§	UCL-357
1	Mezzavia	55	57	*Venus verrucosa*	5400 ± 200	A	5750 ± 220§	UCL-358
2	Costone Sud Perrone	65	71	*Cladocora caespitosa*	7900 ± 300	A	8350 ± 340§	UCL-363
2	Costone Sud Perrone	65	71	*Cladocora caespitosa*	8450 ± 80	A	8770 ± 340‖	Beta-74919

* After Flemming & Webb (1986)
† Powder X-ray diffraction. A = aragonite with no detectable (>0.5%) calcite
‡ After Stuiver & Braziunas (1993)
§ Not normalized as $\partial^{13}C$ not determined
‖ Normalized to 0‰ ($\partial^{13}C = -3.5$‰)

and conventional methods. The two ages overlap at one s.d. (Table 1) but as the depth at which the coral grew cannot be specified the result serves only as a minimum value for emergence, namely 71 m in the last 8500 years.

Discussion

The average implied by the data reported in this paper, assuming continuous movement until the present day, is about $9 \, \text{mm a}^{-1}$ (Fig. 4). In addition to the K/Ar ages already mentioned there is palaeontological evidence to suggest that uplift has decelerated. The faunal record of the Monte Epomeo area (Barra *et al.* 1993) indicates that the Green Tuff accumulated in water depths of 70–120 m. The deposits now stand as high as 620 m above sea level; on the basis of their proposed age and without regard to changes in

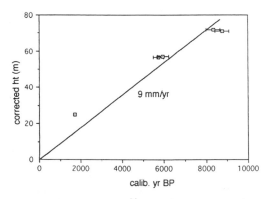

Fig. 4. Plot of calibrated ^{14}C ages in years BP against corrected elevation in metres. The data point at lower left represents the post-Roman uplift reported by Buchner (1986). A graph of uplift at $9 \, \text{mm a}^{-1}$ is shown for reference.

Quaternary sea level the corresponding average rate of uplift is 21–$22 \, \text{mm a}^{-1}$.

The difference may stem partly from the prevalence of spasmodic rather than uniform uplift. Buchner (1986) cites a petition from the islanders to Charles I of Anjou which mentions submergence of an unspecified part of Ischia during an earthquake in 1275. Moreover, differential deformation is to be expected from the island's structural pattern. Various authors have detected Quaternary tilting of the Monte Epomeo horst towards the SSE. According to Buchner (1986) the northeast experienced 5–7 m of subsidence during the Roman period in contrast with as much as 25 m of uplift in the south immediately afterwards. Tidal records kept between 1890 and 1910 at Porto d'Ischia, on the northeastern coast, indicate net submergence by 60 mm (Grablovitz 1911).

The historical record also illuminates the effect of seismicity on slope stability. Late Quaternary uplift has produced a topography with gradients of 1:4, and it is hardly surprising that earthquakes such as that of 1228 should trigger mass movement (Buchner 1986). It remains to be seen whether there is a corresponding isostatic effect which promotes further uplift, and what the relationship is between volcanicity and the movements recorded here. There is an obvious need to link the record on Ischia with events at Pozzuoli and elsewhere in the Gulf of Naples.

This is Contribution No. 59 of the Research School of Geological and Geophysical Sciences, University and Birkbeck Colleges. The research was supported by the Commission of the European Communities, DG XII, Environment Programme, Climatology and Natural Hazards unit, in the framework of contract EV5V-CT 92-0170 directed by W. J. McGuire. We thank G. Rolandi for advice, and J. Davy for the SEMicrographs.

References

BARRA, D., CINQUE, A., ITALIANO, A. & SCOR-ZIELLO, R. 1993. Il Pleistocene superiore marino di Ischia: paleoecologia e rapporti con l'evoluzione tettonica recente. *Studi Geologici Camerti*, Special volume for 1991–92, 231–243.

BROCCHI, G. B. 1814. *Conchiologia Fossile Subapennina con Osservazioni Geologiche sugli Apennini e sul Suolo Adiacente*. Stamperia Reale, Milano.

BUCHNER, G. 1986. Eruzioni vulcaniche e fenomeni vulcano-tettonici di età preistorica e storica nell'isola d'Ischia. *In: Tremblements de Terre, Éruptions Volcaniques et Vie des Hommes dans la Campanie Antique*. Bibliotèque de l'Institut Français, Naples, **VII**, 145–188.

FLEMMING, N. C. & WEBB, C. O. 1986. Tectonic and eustatic coastal changes derived from archaeological data. *Zeitschrift für Geomorphologie Supplementband*, **62**, 1–29.

FUSI, N., TIBALDI, A. & VEZZOLI, L. 1990. Vulcanismo, risorgenza calderica e relazioni colla tettonica regionale nell'isola d'Ischia. *Memorie della Società Geologica Italiana*, **45**, 971–980.

GILLOT, P.-Y., CHIESA, S. , PASQUARÈ, G. & VEZZOLI, L. 1982. >33 000-yr K–Ar dating of the volcano-tectonic horst of the Isle of Ischia, Gulf of Naples. *Nature*, **299**, 242–244.

GRABLOVITZ, G. 1911. Il mareografo d'Ischia in relazione ai bradisismi. *Bollettino della Società Sismologica Italiana*, **15**, 144–153.

LYELL, C. 1881. *Life Letters and Journals of Sir Charles Lyell, Bart.* Murray, London, 2 vols.

SCACCHI, A. 1841. Notizie geologiche sulle conchiglie che si trovan fossili nell'isola d'Ischia e lungo la spiaggia tra Pozzuoli e Monte Nuovo. *Antologia Scienze Naturali*, **I**, 33–48.

STUIVER, M. & BRAZIUNAS, T. 1993. Modeling atmospheric ^{14}C influences and ^{14}C ages of marine samples to 10 000 BC. *Radiocarbon*, **35**, 137–189.

VEZZOLI, L. (ed.) 1988. *Island of Ischia*. CNR, Rome.

VITA-FINZI, C. 1991. First-order ^{14}C dating, Mark II. *Quaternary Proceedings*, **1**, 11–17.

Deception Island (Bransfield Strait, Antarctica): an example of a volcanic caldera developed by extensional tectonics

J. MARTÍ[1], J. VILA[2] & J. REY[3]

[1] *Instituto de Ciencias de la Tierra, CSIC, c/Luis Solé Sabaris s/n, 08028 Barcelona, Spain*
(Present address: Department of Geology, University of Bristol, Wills Memorial Building,
Queen's Road, Bristol BS8 1RJ, UK)
[2] *Department of Astronomy and Meteorology, Facultat de Físiques, and Eduard Fontseré*
Geophysical Studies Lab., Institut d'Estudis Catalans, Martí i Franqués s/n,
08028 Barcelona, Spain
[3] *Spanish Institute of Oceanography, Centro Oceanográfico de Fuengirola,*
Puerto Pesquero, s/n, 29640 Fuengirola, Málaga, Spain

Abstract: Deception Island has traditionally been considered as a collapse caldera formed by subsidence into a magma chamber of a group of overlapping volcanoes along arcuate and radial faults. In fact, the morphological features of Deception Island (horseshoe shape, location of post-caldera vents apparently along concentric faults, existence of a depression in the centre of the island, concentration of post-caldera activity along the 'ring fault', etc.) support this idea. However, a detailed revision of the structure of Deception Island combining field geology, high resolution seismic profiles and analysis of local and regional seismicity, indicates that most of the structural features identified as evidence for supporting the model of caldera formed by collapse of a magma chamber have been misunderstood. Post-caldera volcanic activity is not restricted to the border of the depression, but appears both inside (submarine volcanism) and outside (subaerial volcanism) the hypothetical ring fault. Nearly all the post-caldera vents are located on linear faults, and seismic profiles indicate that most of these linear faults, which are parallel or normal to the spreading axis of Bransfield Strait, can be traced outside of the island. The postulated ring fault results from these intersecting linear faults in the interior of the island where they define a depression. No arcuate faults were identified on the border of the depression. The structure of the depressed sector of the island is also defined by several blocks limited by a nearly orthogonal network of normal faults. This geometry is also indicated by the epicentral location of more than 100 seismic events, which define a linear distribution of earthquakes following the main regional normal faults across the entire island. This contrasts with the circular pattern found in collapse calderas with well defined ring fault systems (i.e. Long Valley, Rabaul, Campi Flegrei). Moreover, the presence of radial faults, postulated by previous authors, has not been proved. The existence of a well developed system of radial faults reflects the pushing action of a shallow magma chamber and should normally imply the intrusion of dykes through these fractures. Very few dykes, always of basaltic composition, have been identified in Deception Island and were intruded along linear regional faults. Because the central depression exists we cannot deny the existence of the caldera depression at least in a morphological sense. However, we propose a mechanism of caldera formation contrasting to the one proposed by previous authors. The tectonic features of Deception Island indicate the existence of a tensional stress field in all directions at the surface, compatible with the regional stress field which has characterized the Bransfield Strait at least during the last 4 Ma. This favoured the normal faulting of the island and the subsidence of the central blocks without the formation of any ring fault system. After the formation of the depression at the centre of the island submarine and subaerial volcanic activity has continued along the nearly orthogonal network of normal faults

Deception Island, located on the spreading centre of the Bransfield Strait marginal basin, is a young (<0.75 Ma, Valencio *et al.* 1979; Smellie 1988) horseshoe-shaped stratovolcano 25 km in submerged basal diameter (Smellie 1988) and about 15 km in diameter of the emerged zone. A sea-flooded depression known as Port Foster occupies the central part of the island. Deception Island has been very active during its entire history, although periods of contrasting style of activity can be distinguished. It is presently the most active volcano of the South Shetland Islands–Antarctic Peninsula group, with eruptions

From McGuire, W. J., Jones, A. P. & Neuberg, J. (eds) 1996, *Volcano Instability on the Earth and Other Planets,*
Geological Society Special Publication No. 110, pp. 253–265.

known to have taken place in 1842, 1967, 1969 and 1970.

Deception Island has traditionally been considered as a collapse caldera formed by subsidence of a group of overlapping volcanoes along arcuate and radial faults (Hawkes 1961; Gonzalez Ferran & Katsui 1970; Baker *et al.* 1975; Smellie 1988, 1989), to the extent that it has been used as a reference model of a ring fault system bounding a collapse caldera depression (Walker 1984; Newhall & Dzurisin 1988). The morphological features of Deception Island (horseshoe shape, existence of a depression in the centre of the island, location of post-caldera vents apparently along concentric faults, etc.) support this idea. However, no detailed study of the tectonic structure of Deception Island exists.

Since the 1986–87 austral summer, a Spanish working group with the financial support of the Spanish National Programme of Antarctic Research has carried out studies with the aim of characterizing the volcanic activity and the tectonic structure of Deception Island. In order to identify the main tectonic features of Deception Island and surrounding areas, field geology, high resolution seismic profiles, and analysis of local and regional seismicity have been carried out. The results obtained from these studies do not support the generally assumed structural model of Deception Island, despite the fact that the central depression exists. This paper documents the tectonic structure of Deception Island on the basis of field geology, interpretation of seismic profiles and location of seismic events and proposes a new model for the formation of the central depression of Deception Island.

Tectonic setting and characteristics of the Bransfield Strait

Bransfield Strait is a narrow (<60 km) marginal basin separating the South Shetland Islands from the northern end of the Antarctic Peninsula (Fig. 1). The Pacific margin of the Antarctic Peninsula has been characterized by a complex tectonic history which includes a sequence of successive ridge–trench collisions that probably started in the south of the Peninsula some 50 Ma ago (Barker 1982; Henriet *et al.* 1992). The transition from compression to extension in that region was probably related to the cessation of subduction of the South Shetland Islands at about 4 Ma when the offshore spreading centre (the Drake Rise) ceased (Barker 1982; Barker & Dalziel 1983; Garrett & Storey 1987).

The opening of the Bransfield rift started some 2 Ma ago (Weaver *et al.* 1982; Gonzalez-Ferran 1991; Henriet *et al.* 1992) and generated a new microplate, the South Shetland Plate (Fig. 1), bounded by the Shackleton and Hero Fracture Zones to the east and west, respectively, by the South Shetland Trench to the north, and by the Bransfield rift on the south. Shallow earthquakes occur along these bounding fracture zones and in the Bransfield Strait, but a few earthquakes are associated with the South Shetland Trench (Pelayo & Wiens 1989). These authors suggest continued but largely aseismic subduction along the South Shetland Trench, and that diffuse extension rather than typical organized mid-ocean spreading characterizes Bransfield Strait where large normal faulting occurs. Thus, the tectonic model proposed by Pelayo & Wiens (1989) for the South Shetland Plate (Fig. 1) includes active back-arc spreading in the Bransfield Strait, slow subduction along an active South Shetland Trench, and diffuse convergence between the South Shetland and Scotia plates at the Shackleton Fracture Zone.

The Bransfield basin shows a characteristic graben structure, with tilted blocks and rotational faults developed in a regime of continental extension (Jeffers & Anderson 1991; Henriet *et al.* 1992). The Bransfield basin is segmented longitudinally into three sub-basins which differ in width, depth and structural style (Jeffers & Anderson 1991). Geophysical evidence, including magnetics, seismic refraction, and seismicity, suggests that the segmentation is tectonically controlled and does not merely reflect differences in the surface morphology of the basin (Ashcroft 1972; Parra *et al.* 1984; Jeffers & Anderson 1991). The edge of the Bransfield basin is defined by a spreading centre with which Deception, Penguin and Bridgeman islands and some submerged volcanic vents are associated. Deception Island is located near the intersection between the tensional axis of the Bransfield basin and the extension of the Hero Fracture Zone.

Geology of Deception Island

Stratigraphy

Volcanic rocks of Deception Island have been traditionally divided into pre- and post-caldera products (Hawkes 1961; González-Ferrán & Katsui 1970; Baker *et al.* 1975; Smellie 1988). A syn-caldera group has also been considered by some authors (Baker *et al.* 1975). Marti & Baraldo (1990) proposed a new stratigraphy for the subaerial volcanic rocks of Deception Island. These authors divide the island into two main groups of rocks, pre- and post-caldera respectively, identifying two formations in the pre-caldera group: the Basaltic Shield Formation (BSF) and the Yellow Tuff Formation (YTF).

The BSF is composed of basaltic lava flows and palagonitized tuffs and forms the shield structure which makes up the largely unexposed basement of the island. The YTF constitutes the main part of the island and comprises thick sequences of palagonitized pyroclastic flow deposits of andesitic composition and dry surge deposits with minor air-fall deposits and lava flows. The YTF can be divided into a lower member of massive pyroclastic flow deposits

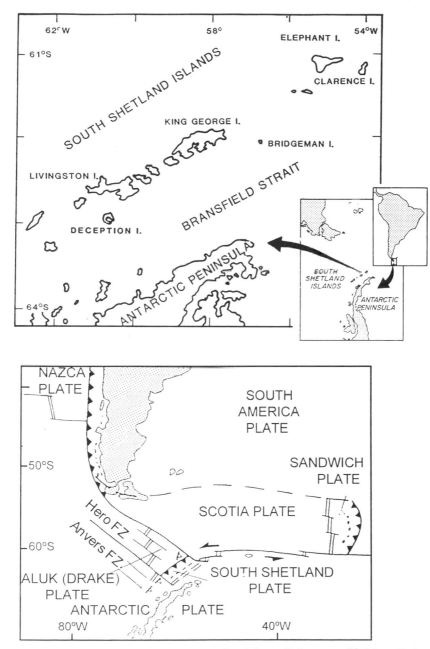

Fig. 1. Location map of Deception Island and plate tectonics of the studied area, modified from Barker (1982).

which form a nearly continuous outcrop that extends from Macaroni Point to the south of Entrance Point (Fig. 2), and an upper member formed of pyroclastic surges and some associated air-fall and thin pyroclastic flow deposits, which only appears in small exposures.

Phreatomagmatic episodes were common during the formation of the YTF (Marti & Baraldo 1990), which seems to be derived, at least for the lower member, from the explosive activity of a central vent producing radially distributed products. This central vent would have been destroyed during the formation of the central depression. Post-caldera volcanism, which occurs inside and outside of the depression, is mainly represented by several small vents which have acted independently, generating both strombolian and phreatomagmatic deposits.

All exposed rocks have normal magnetic polarity, indicating that they are younger than 0.7 Ma (Valencio *et al.* 1979). On the basis of K–Ar data, Keller *et al.* (1991) suggest that most of the subaerial part of the island was built after 0.2 Ma.

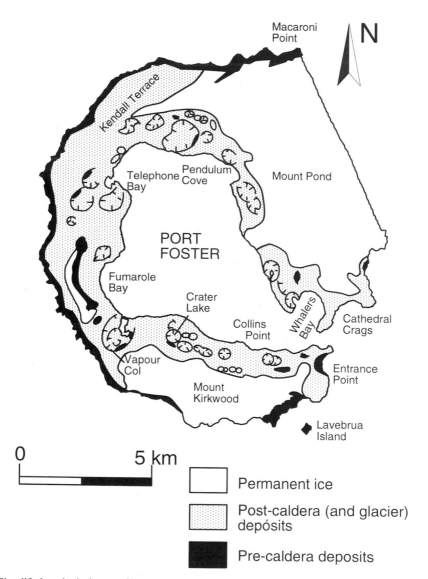

Fig. 2. Simplified geological map of Deception Island, showing the distribution of the pre- and post-caldera volcanic deposits (after Martí & Baraldo 1990).

Tectonic structure

The tectonic structure of the subaerial part of Deception Island has been established on the basis of field geology, remote sensing and aerial photograph analyses. The existence of a dense network of tectonic lineations, many crossing the entire island, has been identified (Fig. 3). A NE–SW oriented tectonic trend, parallel to the expansion axis of the Bransfield Strait, is clearly predominant on the island (also indicated by Smellie 1988, 1989). However, NW–SW and N–S oriented faults are also present. In those cases where the sense of movement of faults could be established, they nearly always showed a normal sense of movement and the dip of the fault plane was nearly vertical. This suggests that most of these faults are extensional normal faults. Most of the faults affect both pre- and post-caldera rocks.

Post-caldera volcanic activity is not restricted to the border of the depression, but appears outside the hypothetical ring fault. Nearly all the post-caldera vents are located on linear faults. According to this, the postulated ring fault (e.g. Hawkes 1961; González-Ferrán & Katsui 1970; Baker et al. 1975; Smellie 1988) seems to be the result of the intersection of these linear faults in the interior of the island where they define a depression. No arcuate faults have been identified in the border of the caldera. This observation is also supported by geomorphological data (Criado et al. 1992). Moreover, the presence of radial faults, postulated by some previous authors, has never been proved. Very few dykes have been identified in Deception Island. These dykes are always of basaltic composition and intruded along linear regional faults affecting both the pre- and post-caldera sequences. Occasionally the dykes display multiple intrusions textures.

Seismic reflection profiles

Methodology

Several seismic reflection profiles were obtained by the Spanish Institute of Oceanography during the 1987–88 and 1988–89 austral summers inside Port Foster, around Deception Island and throughout Bransfield Strait. During the first season a narrow network of high resolution seismic profiles was carried out in the interior of Port Foster using a Geopulse (300 joules) and a Trisponder positioning system (see Rey et al. 1989). During the second season, several continuous seismic reflection profiles were obtained with a Sparker (4500 joules) on the external platform of Deception Island (Fig. 4) and in the interior of the bay (Port Foster) using a satellite positioning system. A mud penetrator (3.5 kHz) was also used in both seasons. The density of distribution of the seismic profiles (see Rey et al. 1989) allowed the detailed identification of the reflectors from the seismic units intersected. This also made it possible to interpret the structure and morphology of these units and to relate them to the geological and volcanological evolution of the area in recent times. The morphology and tectonic structure of the upper units have been analysed in more detail than the lower ones because of the better definition in the high resolution seismic profiles recorded with Geopulse and the mud penetrator.

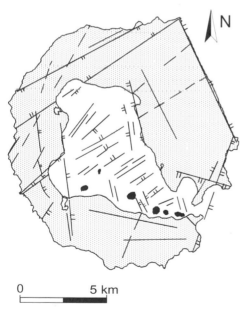

N

0   5 km

Fig. 3. Simplified tectonic map of Deception Island, based on field geology, remote sensing and continuous seismic reflection profiles, showing the distribution of the main normal faults (tick on downthrow side) and structural lineations (straight lines) as well as submerged volcanic vents (in black).

Interpretation of seismic profiles

The interior bay of Deception Island has a regular morphology, as indicated by the continuity of bathymetric lines (Rey et al. 1989, 1992). It is characterized by the presence of a littoral platform with an average width of 700 m. A break of slope on the platform occurs at a

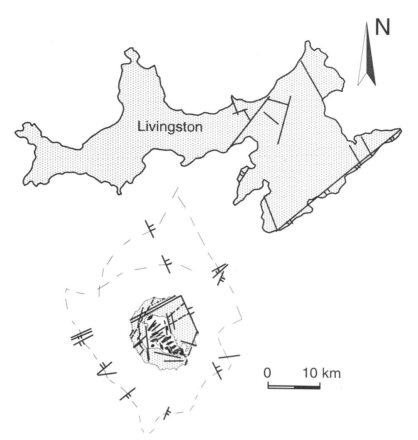

Fig. 4. Tectonic scheme of Deception Island (this work), eastern part of Livingston Island (Santanach *et al.* 1992), and surrounding submarine areas (Rey *et al.* 1989; this work). Discontinuous lines represent seismic reflection surveys.

depth of 50–60 m and is followed by a steep incline down to a depth of 120 m. Beyond this point the floor of the bay is uniform and gently dipping towards the centre of the bay, where it reaches a maximum depth of 195 m. Only three submerged volcanic edifices and a few sedimentary structures locally disturb the uniformity of the depression floor.

The interpretation of the Sparker seismic profile, that was carried out inside Port Foster (see Figs 5 and 6) in terms of seismic sequences, shows the existence of three different formations (Rey *et al.* 1989, 1995). Formation C is the sequence of recent volcanic deposits produced during the last eruptions. These units have a maximum thickness of 72 m (80 milliseconds for a seismic velocity of 1800 m/s). Formation B comprises the volcanic sequences of the main part of the post-caldera group. It can be interpreted as a thick body which includes several seismically stratified reflectors

with a high reflection value, and has been locally deformed or fractured. The upper limit of this formation corresponds to a reflector with high acoustic intensity, occasionally discontinuous, highly fractured, and intruded by serveral dykes. This reflector is unconformably overlain by Formation C. Formation A would represent the pre-caldera sequences of the Yellow Tuff Formation. Similar sequences of rocks can be identified in the seismic profiles carried out around the island (Fig. 7) indicating than the subaerial geology of Deception Island continues significantly far out in the Bransfield Strait.

Interpretation of seismic profiles clearly indicates the effects of Quaternary neotectonics on the volcanic rocks, and the structural and morphological variations which affect the uppermost to the deepest deposits (see Rey *et al.* 1989, 1995). The existence of a well developed linear fracture system is apparent both inside and

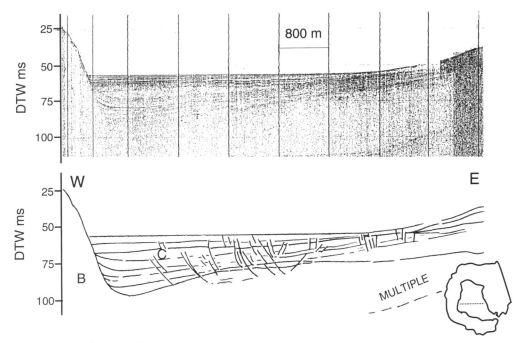

Fig. 5. Interpretation of a seismic reflection profile (Geopulse 300 joules) showing the distribution of the most recent units of Formation C and their stratigraphical relationships with Formation B. Note the unconformity defined by the reflectors of each formation at the left side of the cross-section.

outside the island, juxtaposing the direction of the regional lineations and those identified on land (Figs 3 and 4). This system of normal fractures reflects the regional extensional tectonics which affects the area, as indicated by the correspondence of the structural lineations in Deception Island and surrounding areas and in the Bransfield basin. It is important to emphasize the presence of a major normal fault oriented NE–SW in the interior of Port Foster. This major fault also affects the pre-caldera rocks with a displacement between the two sides of the fault plane corresponding to more than 300 milliseconds of travel time. This normal fault has also been recognized on land, outside the island, and was also identified by Grad *et al.* (1992) in their study of the upper crustal structure of Deception Island. Associated with this major fault there are younger extensional faults which affect recent shallower units, developing half-graben structures which consequently cause the collapse of Formation B. These tectonic structures are in concordance with regional tectonics. Seismic profiles suggest that they are still active, as indicated by the fact that the deepest fractures also affect the most recent sediments.

Seismicity

General aspects

Since the austral summer of 1986–87, continuous monitoring of seismic activity has been carried out at Deception Island. General characteristics of the seismicity at Deception Island and surrounding areas are discussed in the present section. Information on seismic stations, processing procedure and detailed description of seismic phenomena (volcanic seismicity, volcanic tremors and geophysical features) have been given earlier (Ortiz *et al.* 1992; Vila 1992; Vila *et al.* 1992*a, b*). Here, we will note the relation between the seismicity in the area and the regional tectonic settings of the Bransfield basin, trying to correlate the seismic results with those obtained from field geology and seismic reflection.

The seismicity that we will try to connect with tectonics is different from seismicity directly related to volcanism at Deception Island. This is because the sources of the events located outside the island probably do not involve volcanic processes such as dynamic motion of gas, fluid and solid. The extremely heterogeneous

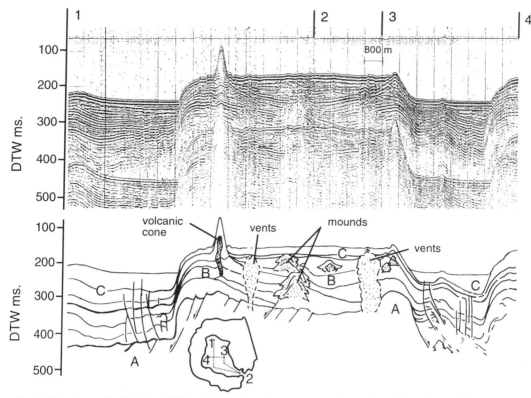

Fig. 6. Seismic profile (Sparker 4500 joules) showing the structure at the interior of Port Foster. The stratigraphical relationships between pre- (Formations A and B), and post-caldera (Formation C) rocks are clearly defined.

propagation paths, the anisotropy and the absorption present in volcanic areas could be reflected in data collected. Taking into account these fact-ors, measurements should be analysed statistically and the results understood globally, not by focusing on the analysis of individual events.

As described by Vila (1992), analogue and digital seismic networks, specially designed for Antarctic operation, were set up in the island. These networks consisted of six vertical 1 Hz component FM telemetry stations set with the VHF 170 MHz band and, in the case of the digital network, the sampling rate was 64 sps. The seismic stations were located considering the previous studies of petrology and volcanology of Deception Island, results of which have suggested a collapse caldera structure in the central part of the island and a continuation of the seismic activity associated with the concentric faults around the edge of the caldera. Then, a circular distribution of the seismic stations was chosen.

Even though seismic studies at Deception Island began during the Antarctic Summer Expedition of 1986–87 and have been continuing in order to improve understanding of the area, results shown in this section correspond only to the Antarctic Summer Expeditions of 1986–87, 1987–88 and 1988–89. This is because those expeditions were specially directed towards the study of general aspects of the seismicity.

Selection of events and data analysis

Despite the fact that it is often difficult to differentiate between events of volcanic (particularly volcano-tectonic) and tectonic origins, earthquake activity in volcanic areas is usually called 'volcanic seismicity'. An earthquake is 'considered' volcanic if it is directly related to magmatic processes such as magma injection or gas expansion, but this relationship is usually hard to demonstrate. The study has been made

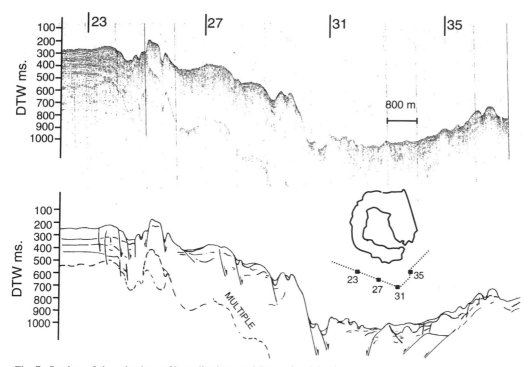

Fig. 7. Section of the seismic profile realized around Deception Island.

using the whole data collected except for 'volcanic tremors' (easy to define in Deception Island) which were the object of a separate work (Vila *et al.* 1992*a*).

The statistical study of the seismicity, made using data from the Antarctic Summer Expeditions of 1986–87 and 1987–88, showed that seismic activity was distributed around the island. During the periods of observation (January and February of each year), the number of events was stationary at a rate of about 1000 events per month with a released seismic energy of about 3×10^{13} erg/day (Vila *et al.* 1992*b*).

The Antarctic Summer Expedition of 1988–89 aimed to locate the earthquakes, and to determine whether the microseismic activity followed certain patterns. Throughout this study, we have used the velocity model deduced by Vila *et al.* (1992*b*), consisting of a first layer with a velocity of 1.5 km/s (water saturated) and a thickness of 0.6 km, followed by another layer with velocity of 1.7 km/s and thickness of 0.3 km, followed by a 4.5 km/s velocity layer with mean thickness of 5.2 km over a half-space with a velocity of 6 km/s. For S-wave velocity, $V_p = 3^{1/2} V_s$ has been assumed.

From 28 December 1988 to 25 February 1989, more than 2000 events were recorded by the seismic network, over 1000 of them digitally. Only events recorded by a minimum of three stations were located, resulting in 118 located events, mainly on the island. Locations were determined in two steps. First, a location in real time was done as part of the volcano surveillance with special emphasis given to the statistical distribution. The allowed maximum RMS error was 0.3 s and the focal depth was restricted to 2.5, 5 and 7.5 km. Second, to im-prove the accuracy of the location, the allowed RMS error was 0.1 s at each station, and the focal depth was allowed to vary freely with 100 m steps. These restrictive conditions reduced the number of located events to 66.

Epicentre maps determined after the first (Fig. 8) and after the second step (Fig. 9) present similar distribution patterns. It should be noted from Figs 8 and 9 that the epicentral distribution obtained considering a fixed depth and RMS error of 0.3 s (Fig. 8) or a variable depth and RMS error of 0.1 s (Fig. 9) are nearly the same. Both figures show an E–W general trend that we interpret as due to the activity of a system of fractures crossing the island along the main regional trends defined by the Bransfield Strait rift. This could be interpreted as evidence of the structural continuity of Deception Island and the Bransfield rift, and confirms the impossibility of separating, from a seismic point of view, Deception Island from the rest of Bransfield Strait rift.

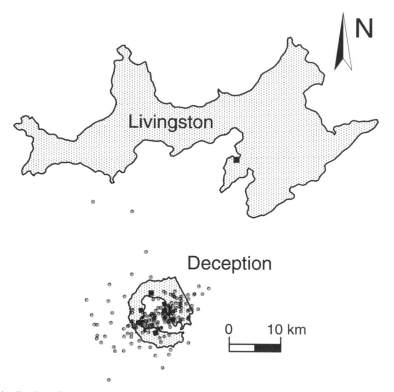

Fig. 8. Distribution of located seismic events during the Antarctic Summer Expedition 1988–89 (RMS <0.3 s). Modified from Vila *et al.* (1992a).

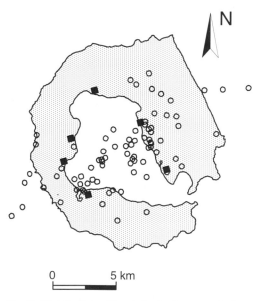

Fig. 9. Distribution of located seismic events during the Antarctic Summer Expedition 1988–89 (RMS < 0.3 s). Note the continuity of lineations outside the island.

Discussion and conclusions

Detailed revision of the structure of Deception Island has been carried out. Field geology, high resolution seismic profiles and analysis of local and regional seismicity, indicate that most of the structural features identified as evidence for explaining the internal depression as a ring fault structure bounding a collapse caldera, have been misunderstood.

Field geology and remote sensing analysis have indicated the existence of a nearly orthogonal system of linear fractures and normal faults which affect both pre- and post-caldera rocks and which has repeatedly been used as a pathway for magma rising to the surface over the entire history of the island. Post-caldera and recent volcanic activity have been associated with these fractures, rather than with any ring fault system. Interpretation of high resolution seismic profiles has revealed that many fractures and faults observed on land can also be traced in the submarine areas of Port Foster and offshore.

Location of seismic events in volcanic areas where ring faults have been clearly evidenced follows a typical circular pattern. Such ring faults have been invoked for various calderas including Campi Flegrei (Aster & Meyer 1988; Aster *et al.* 1992), Long Valley (Savage & Clark 1982; Vasco *et al.* 1988) or Rabaul (Mori & McKee 1987). At Deception Island, the distribution of earthquake epicentres does not define a circular pattern which could represent ring faults associated with the formation of the central depression by caldera collapse. The distribution of earthquakes mainly follows the SW–NE trend of the Bransfield Strait defined by the network of linear fractures affecting the island and surrounding areas. The distribution of magnetic and gravimetric anomalies also disagrees with the existence of circular tectonic patterns at Deception Island (Ortiz *et al.* 1992).

The evidence presented here clearly shows that the fracturing system which affects Deception Island reflects the regional tectonics that controlled the whole history of extension in the Bransfield Strait. This is also supported by the fact that the main tectonic lineations observed in the eastern sector of Livingston Island, which have been active in the last 4–2 Ma (Santanach *et al.* 1992), follow the same pattern as the fracturing system of Deception Island, some of the main fractures being continuous between the two islands. On the contrary, none of the tectonic features that appear when a local stress field is developed by inflation and decompression of a shallow magma chamber, such as radial and concentric fractures and dykes (Anderson 1936; Roberts 1970; Gudmundsson 1988; Martí *et al*, 1994), have been identified in Deception Island.

The tectonic features of Deception Island indicate the existence of a continuous extension, in all directions at the surface, originated by a lateral simple shear stress around Deception Island (see Rey *et al.* 1995) resulting from a complex regional stress field that has characterized the Bransfield Strait at least over the last 4 Ma. It is inconsistent with the tensional stress field that is produced by the inflation of a shallow magma chamber (Roberts 1970; Gudmundsson 1988). In that case the formation of radial and concentric, inward and outward dipping faults, should be expected to appear superimposed on regional tectonic features. Only a few dykes of basaltic composition intruding along linear faults, occasionally showing multiple intrusions, have been observed in Deception Island.

Existence of a shallow magma chamber seems plausible according to the nature and composition of the Yellow Tuff Formation pre-caldera rocks (i.e. Weaver *et al.* 1979). However, in this highly fractured medium the stresses produced by the growing magma chamber could have been rapidly accommodated by readjustment of blocks causing rapid intrusion and subsequent eruption of resident magma. The presence of a highly fractured medium surrounding the magma chamber would also permit sea water to access the chamber producing hydrovolcanic eruptions which would weaken the country rocks. This would account for a very short residence time of deep magmas at shallow levels and prevent significant overpressure. This is consistent with the relatively poor degree of differentiation of the pre-caldera pyroclastics and their hydrovolcanic character (Martí & Baraldo 1990). There is no evidence for the presence of pure magmatic explosive eruptions associated with the Yellow Tuff Formation. After a prolonged period of hydrovolcanic explosions the blocks of country rock, previously separated by the effect of regional tectonics, could sink into the remaining chamber throughout the movement of the pre-existing normal faults, rather than creating a ring fault system as occurs in typical collapse calderas (Williams 1941; Smith & Bailey 1968; Williams & McBirney 1979; Druitt & Sparks 1984; Gudmundsson 1988; Martí *et al.* 1994).

The volume of magma ($>55\,\text{km}^3$) extruded during the eruption of the lower member of the Yellow Tuff Formation could account for the formation of the central depression by caldera collapse. However the formation of the caldera is clearly unrelated to the eruption of that sequence of pyroclastic flow deposits. This is indicated by the fact that the caldera also affected the Yellow Tuff Formation upper member which is discontinuously distributed along the island.

In conclusion, if any collapse caldera event took place in Deception Island this cannot only be explained as a direct consequence of volcanic activity. We suggest that Port Foster is a volcano-tectonic depression created by the passive normal faulting of blocks previously separated by extensional tectonics without the formation of any ring fault system.

This research was (in part) supported by the Plan Nacional de la Antártida (CICYT, Spain). We would like to thank Dr C. A. Rinaldi (Instituto Antártico Argentino) for helping us in the logistic and subsistence arrangements for the field seasons. Prof. J. G. Viramonte is thanked for offering us the opportunity to collaborate with the Volcantar Project (Argentine) and for his helpful discussions on the geology of Deception Island. The seismic reflection surveys were carried out through the Exantarte 87–88 and 88–89 projects on the Buque Oceanográfico Las Palmas. Seismic data were obtained during the Antarctic Summer Expedition 1988–89 with the support of the research project ANT88-0303-C09-05 co-ordinated by Prof. Ramón Ortiz. We owe a heavy debt of gratitude to Dr Manuel Catalan, leader of the oceanographic expeditions and J. Martí is grateful for a Fleming Award and EC contract (ERBCHBICT93052) of the Human Capital and Mobility Programme. J. Vila is supported (in part) by the DGICYT under Grant PB90-0599-C03–03. J. L. Smellie is thanked for his helpful review of the manuscript. This forms Contribution no. 82 of the Department of Astronomy and Meterology of the University of Barcelona.

References

ANDERSON, E. M. 1936. The dynamics of the formation of cone-sheets, ringdykes, and couldron subsidences. *Proceedings of the Royal Society of Edinburgh*, **56**, 128–163.

ASHCROFT, W. A. 1972. *Crustal Structure of the South Shetland Islands and Bransfield Strait*. British Antarctic Survey Scientific Reports, **66**, 43.

ASTER, R. C. & MEYER, R. P. 1988. Three-dimensional velocity structure and hypocenter distribution in the Campi Flegrei caldera, Italy. *Tectonophysics*, **149**, 195–218.

——, ——, DE NATALLE, G. *ET AL.* 1992. Seismic investigation of the Campi Flegrei: a summary and synthesis of results. *In*: GASPARINI, P., SCARPA, R. & AKI, K. (eds) *Volcanic Seismology*. Springer-Verlag, 462–483.

BAKER, P. E., MCREATH, I., HARVEY, M. R., ROOBOL, M. & DAVIES, T. G., 1975. *The Geology of the South Shetland Islands: Volcanic Evolution of Deception Island*. British Antarctic Survey Scientific Reports, **78**.

BARKER, P. F. 1982. The Cenozoic subduction history of the Pacific margin of the Antarctic Peninsula: ridge crest-trench interactions. *Journal of the Geological Society of London*, **139**, 787–801.

— & DALZIEL, I. W. D. 1983. Progress in geodynamics in the Scotia Arc Region *In*: CABRE, R. (ed.) *Geodynamics of the Eastern Pacific Region, Caribbean and Scotia Arcs*. American Geophysical Union, Washington, DC, Geodynamic Series, **9**, 137–170.

CRIADO, C., ARCHE, A. & VILAS, F. 1992. Mapa geomorfological preliminar de la isla Decepción, Islas Shetland del Sur. *In*: MARTINEZ-LOEPEZ, J. (ed.) *Geología de la Antártida Occidental*. Simposios T 3, III Congreso Geológico de España y VIII Congreso Latinoamericano de Geología. Salamanca, España, 293–304.

DRUITT, T. & SPARKS, R. S. J. 1984. On the formation of collapse calderas. *Nature*, **310**, 679–681.

GARRETT, S. W. & STOREY, B. C. 1987. Lithospheric extension on the Antarctic Peninsula during Cenozoic subduction. *In*: COWARD, M. P., DEWEY, J. F. & HANCOCK, P. L. (eds) *Continental Extension Tectonics*. Geological Society Special Publication, **28**, 419–431.

GONZALEZ-FERRAN, O. 1991. The Bransfield Strait rift and its active volcanism. *In: Geological evolution of Antarctica*. Cambridge University Press, Cambridge, 505–509.

—— & KATSUI, Y. 1970. Estudio integral del volcanismo cenozoico superior de las Islas Shetland del Sur, Antártica. *Instituto Antártico Chileno Serie Científica*, **1**, 123–174.

GRAD, M., GUTERCH, A. & SPRODA, P. 1992. Upper crustal structure of Deception Island area, Bransfield Strait, West Antarctica. *Antarctic Science*, **4**, 469–476.

GUDMUNDSSON, A. 1988. The formation of collapse calderas. *Geology*, **16**, 808–810.

HAWKES, D. D. 1961. *The Geology of the South Shetland Islands, II. The Geology and Petrology of Deception Island*. Falkland Islands Dependencies Survey Scientific Reports, **27**.

HENRIET, J. P., MEISSNER, R., MILLER, H. & THE GRAPE TEAM. 1992. Active margin processes along the Antarctic Peninsula. *Tectonophysics*, **201**, 229–253.

JEFFERS, J. D. & ANDERSON, J. B. 1991. Sequence stratigraphy of the Bransfield Basin, Antarctica: Implications for tectonic history and hydrocarbon potential. *In*: ST. JOHN, B. (ed.) *Antarctica as an Exploration Frontier – Hydrocarbon Potential, Geology, and Hazards*. Americal Association of Petroleum Geologists, Tulsa, Oklahoma, Studies in Geology, **31**, 13–29.

KELLER, R. A., FISK, M. R., WHITE, W. M. & BIRKENMAJER, K. 1991. Isotopic and trace element constraints on mixing and melting models of marginal basin volcanism, Bransfield Strait, Antarctica. *Earth and Planetary Science Letters*, **111**, 287–303.

MARTÍ, J. & BARALDO, A. 1990. Pre-caldera pyroclastic deposits of Deception Island (South Shetland Islands). *Antarctic Science*, **2**, 345–352.

——, ABLAY, G. J., REDSHOW, L. & SPARKS, R. S. J. 1994. Experimental studies on collapse calderas. *Journal of the Geolocial Society*, **151**, 919–929.

MORI, J. & MCKEE, C. O. 1987. Outward dipping ring fault structure at Rabaul Caldera as shown by earthquake locations. *Science*, **235**, 193–195.

NEWHALL, C. G. & DZURISIN, D. 1988. Historical unrest at large calderas of the World. *US Geological Survey Bulletin*, **1855**.

ORTIZ, R., VILA, J., GARCÍA, A. *ET AL.* 1992. Geophysical features of Deception Island. *In*: NATIONAL INSTITUTE OF POLAR RESEARCH (ed.) *Recent Progress in Antarctic Earth Science*. Terra Scientific Publishing Company, Tokyo, 143–152.

PARRA, J. C., GONZALEZ-FERRAN, O. & BANNISTER, J., 1984. Aeromagnetic survey over the South Shetland Islands, Bransfield Strait and part of the Antarctic Peninsula. Revista Geológica de Chile, **23**, 3–20.

PELAYO, A. & WIENS, D. 1989. Seismotectonics and relative plate motions in the Scotia Sea region. *Journal of Geophysical Research*, **94**, 7293–7320.

REY, J., DE ANDRES, J. R. & FERNANDEZ-LOPEZ, J. M. 1989. Tectónica reciente en los depósitos submarinos de la bahía de Decepción. *In*: CASTELLVÍ, J. (ed.) *Actas del III Symposium Español de Estudios Antarticos*. 258–270.

——, SOMOZA, L. & HERNANDEZ-MOLINA, F. J. 1992. Formas de los sedimentos submarinos superficiales en el Puerto Foster, Isla Decepción, Islas Shetland del Sur. *In*: MARTINEZ-LÓPEZ, J. (ed.) *Geología de la Antártida Occidental*. Simposios T 3, III Congreso Geológico de España y VIII Congreso Latinoamericano de Geología. Salamanca, España, 163–172.

——, —— & MARTINEZ-FRIAS, J. 1995. Tectonic, volcanic and hydrothermal event sequence on Deception Island (Antarctica). *Geo-Marine Letters*, **15**, 1–8.

ROBERTS, J. L. 1970. The intrusion of magma into brittle rock. *In*: NEWALL, G. & RAST, N. (eds) *Mechanisms of Igneous Intrusion*. Geological Journal Special Issue, **2**, 287–338.

SANTANACH, P., PALLÀS, R., SÀBAT, F. & MUÑOZ, J. A. 1992. La fracturación en la Isla Livingston, Islas Shetland del Sur. *In*: MARTINEZ-LÓPEZ, J. (ed.) *Geología de la Antártida Occidental*. Simposios T 3, III Congreso Geológico de España y VIII Congreso Latinoamericano de Geología. Salamanca, España, 141–151.

SAVAGE, J. C. & CLARK, M. M. 1982. Magmatic resurgence in Long Valley caldera, California: Possible cause of the 1980 Mammoth Lakes earthquakes. *Science*, 531–533.

SMELLIE, J. L. 1988. Recent observations on the volcanic history of Deception Island, South Shetland Islands, *British Antarctic Survey Bulletin*, **81**, 83–85.

——, 1989. Deception Island. *In*: DALZIEL, I. W. D. (ed.) *Tectonics of the Scotia Arc, Antarctica*. Field Trip Guidebook T 180, 28th International Geological Congress, American Geophysical Union, Washington, DC, 146–152.

SMITH, R. L. & BAILEY, R. A. 1968. Resurgent couldrons. *The Geological Society of America Memoir*, **116**, 613–662.

VALENCIO, D. A., MENDIA, J. E. & VILAS, J. F. 1979. Paleomagnetism and K-Ar age of Mesozoic and Cenozoic igneous rocks from Antactica, *Earth and Planetary Science Letters*, **45**, 61–68.

VASCO, D. W., JOHNSON, L. R. & GOLDSTEIN, N. E. 1988. Using surface displacement and strain observation to determine deformation at depth, with an application to Long Valley caldera, California. *Journal of Geophysical Research*, **93**(B4), 3232–3242.

VILA, J. 1992. *Estudis geofísics a l'Illa Decepción. Shetland del Sud, Antàrtida*. PhD Thesis, Departament de Geologia Dinàmica, Geofísica i Paleontologia, University of Barcelona.

——, MARTÍ, J., ORTIZ, R., GARCÍA, A. & CORREIG, A. 1992a. Volcanic tremors at Deception Island, South Shetland Island, Antarctica. *Journal of Volcanology and Geothermal Research*, **53**(1–4), 89–102.

——, ORTIZ, R., CORREIG, A. & GARCÍA, A. 1992b. Seismic activity on Deception Island. *In*: National Institute of Polar Research (ed.) *Recent Progress in Antarctic Earth Science*. Terra Scientific Publishing Company, Tokyo, 153–161.

WALKER, G. P. L. 1984. Downsag calderas, ring faults, caldera sizes and incremental caldera growth. *Journal of Geophysical Research*, **89**, 8407–8416.

WEAVER, S. D., SAUNDERS, A. D., PANKHURST, R. J. & TARNEY, J. 1979. A geochemical study of magmatism associated with the initial stages of back-arc spreading. The Quaternary volcanics of Bransfield, from South Shetland Islands. *Contribution to Mineralogy and Petrology*, **68**, 151–169.

——, ——, & TARNEY, J. 1982. Mesozoic–Cenozoic volcanism in the South Shetland Islands and the Antarctic peninsula. a geochemical nature and plate tectonic significance. *In*: CRADDOCK, C. (ed.) *Antarctic Geoscience*. University of Wisconsin Press, Madison, Wisc., 263–273.

WILLIAMS, H. 1941. Calderas and their origin. *Bulletin of the Department of Geological Sciences, University of California*, **25**, 239–346.

—— & MCBIRNEY, A. R. 1979. *Volcanology*. Freeman, Cooper & Co., San Francisco.

Destructive mass movements associated with Quaternary volcanoes in Hokkaido, Japan

HIROMITSU YAMAGISHI

Geological Survey of Hokkaido, Kitaku, Kita 19, Nishi 12, Sapporo 060, Japan

Abstract: Hokkaido, the northern island of Japan, is situated on the North American Plate between the Pacific Plate and the Eurasian Plate; it is set on an island arc subducted by the two latter plates. Hence, Hokkaido has many Quaternary volcanoes. Most of these volcanoes have the andesitic to dacitic composition diagnostic of island arcs. They are remarkably unstable due to steepness of the upper slopes, structural fragility, and post-hydrothermal alteration. Consequently, in Hokkaido, many destructive mass movements occur from the Quaternary volcanoes. They are represented by debris avalanches from stratovolcano or lava dome collapses, hydrologic mass flows due to rainfalls, and slides associated with caldera formation.

The term 'mass movement' is defined as a process involving downslope movement of material due to gravity. Factors influencing mass movement are slope, water, vegetation, bedrock structure, rock type, and weathering (Cazeau *et al.* 1976). In particular, young volcanoes and volcanic rocks are prone to mass movement (Eisbacher & Clague 1984) because of their steep slopes, soft materials, and typically scarce vegetation. Therefore, mass movements are very common on andesitic and dacitic Quaternary volcanoes, which are explosive and have relatively steep slopes.

Hokkaido has 14 active volcanoes which are mostly andesitic to dacitic in composition. Mass movements from these volcanoes are triggered by not only eruptions and earthquakes, but also heavy rainfalls. Such mass movements are very destructive and are represented by debris avalanche, pyroclastic flow and hydrologic mass flow.

The purpose of this paper is to review the destructive mass movements associated with Quaternary volcanoes by showing several examples.

Giant collapses from Quaternary volcanoes

In Hokkaido, giant collapses of stratovolcano or lava domes, occur on Oshima Ohshima (1 in Fig. 1), Esan Skyzawa-yama (2 in Fig. 1), Komagatake Volcano (3 in Fig. 1), Usu Volcano (5 in Fig. 1), Shiribetsudake (6 in Fig. 1), Niseko Volcano (7 in Fig. 1), Shikaribetsu Volcano (8 in Fig. 1), Tokachidake Volcano (9 in Fig. 1), Irumukeppu-yama (10 in Fig. 1), Onnebetsu-dake (11 in Fig. 1), and Minami-dake (12 in Fig. 1).

Oshima Ohshima (1 in Fig. 1) is a basaltic volcanic islet 50 km offshore of the Oshima Peninsula. It is 10×12 km and has an amphitheatre-shaped crater opening toward the east. A central cone 300 m high and 300 m across has formed built in the crater. This crater was opened by catastrophic collapse due to explosions on 29 August 1741, generating large debris avalanches and causing a catastrophic tsunami that hit the west shore of the Oshima Peninsula, killing 1467 people (Katsui *et al.* 1977; Katsui & Yamamoto 1981).

Esan Skyzawa-yama (2 in Fig. 1), situated at the southern margin of the Oshima Peninsula, consists of several lava domes of pyroxene andesite (Katsui *et al.* 1983), and has an amphitheatre-shaped wall, which was thought to be a volcanic crater from where a debris avalanche occurred, forming a large mound in front.

Komagatake Volcano (3 in Fig. 1), located on the southern part of the Oshima Peninsula, has a history of two debris avlalanches. The deposits are called the Komagatake debris avalanche deposits (AD 1640) and the Kurumisaka debris avalanche deposits (*c.* 22 500 years BP) (Katsui *et al.* 1975, 1985). This volcano also has a history of erupting pyroclastic flows in 1640, 1856, 1929, associated with pumice falls during a Plinian eruption (Katsui *et al.* 1975). In particular, the 1929 pyroclastic flow was associated with pyroclastic surge, and followed by hydrologic mass flows several days leter.

Usu Volcano (5 in Fig. 1), situated at the southwestern margin of the Toya Caldera Lake, was formed by a large ash flow *c.* 0.1 Ma BP. The volcano was formed by repeated eruptions of lava flows and scoriae of basalt and mafic andesite in the early Holocene. After the construction of the stratovolcano 7000–8000 years BP, the summit was broken by a violent explosion resulting in the Zenkoji debris avalanche toward the southern foot of the volcano.

From McGuire, W. J., Jones, A. P. & Neuberg, J. (eds) 1996, *Volcano Instability on the Earth and Other Planets*, Geological Society Special Publication No. 110, pp. 267–279.

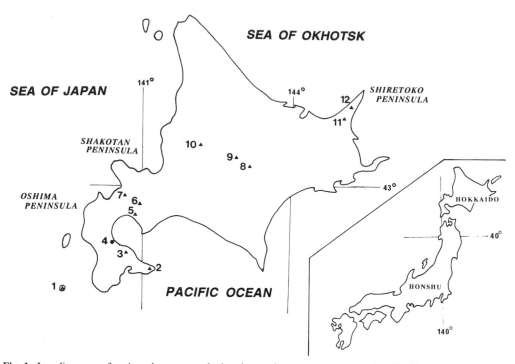

Fig. 1. Locality map of main volcanoes producing destructive mass movements described in this paper. Solid triangles with numbers indicate locations of Quaternary volcanoes producing debris avalanches, pyroclastic flows, and hydrologic mass flows. 1 Oshima Ohshima, 2 Esan Skyzawa-yama, 3 Komagatake Volcano, 5 Usu Volcano, 6. Shiribetsu-dake, 7 Niseko Volcano, 8 Shikaribetsu Volcano, 9 Tokachidake Volcano, 10 Irumukeppu-yama, 11 Onnebetsu-dake, 12 Minami-dake. Solid circle with number 4 indicates locality of the Nigorikawa Caldera.

Later, magma from this volcano became dacitic. In addition, it erupted pumice air falls in 1663 and pyroclastic flows in 1769, 1822, and 1853, followed by the formation of lava domes at the summit (Yokoyama *et al.* 1973; Soya *et al.* 1981).

Shiribetsu-dake (6 in Fig. 1), situated in the north of the Oshima Peninsula and southeast of the Yotei Volcano, has an amphitheatre-shaped collapse wall on the western face (Fig. 2) from which a debris avalanche has flowed toward the west. The debris avalanche is composed many flow mounds, one of which is a mountain 773 m high, called Gunjin-yama (Yamagishi 1993).

Niseko Volcano (7 in Fig. 1) forms a mountain range which is arranged in an E–W direction to the north of the Oshima Peninsula. Yamagishi (1993) found debris avalanche deposits beneath a basaltic lava flow at the southern foot of the volcano. The debris avalanche deposit has many flow mounds cored by lava block more than 5 m across. The deposit is composed of angular lava fragments, some of which show impact joints, and the others have cooling-contraction prismatic joints.

Shikaribetsu Volcano (8 in Fig. 1), situated in central Hokkaido, has a history of erupting debris avalanche deposits, pumice flow deposits and several block-and-ash flow deposits (Wright *et al.* 1980; Fig. 3; Yamagishi 1977). The debris avalanche deposits (Eishin debris avalanche deposit) are arranged in three zones up to 200 to 500 m wide and 1.5 to 2 km long. These zones are represented by earth mounds 1 to 5 m high and 5 to 10 m across. The earth mounds are composed of subrounded pebbles of altered andesite in the matrix of clayey pumiceous sands. The pumice flow deposit is 5 to 10 m thick, and is composed of hornblende hypersthene andesite pumice fragments up to 5 cm across. The block-and-ash flow deposits are Ogigahara block-and-ash flow, Pankechin block and ash flow, Shinkai block-and-ash flow, and Nitta block-and-ash flow. All of them consist of monolithologic lava fragments containing hornblende and hypersthene as phenocrysts. The Ogigahara block-and-ash flow deposit has a flat surface, while the other deposits have hummocky surfaces. The Shinkai block-and-ash flow

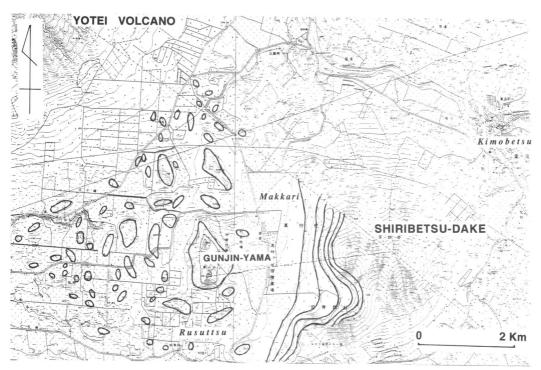

Fig. 2. Topographic map of Shiribetsu-dake and debris avalanche deposits consisting of flow mounds.

deposit contains many blocks showing prismatic joints on the surface (jointed block; Francis *et al.* 1974; Fig. 4a), indicating quenching. The Pankechin block-and-ash flow deposit has fragments showing jigsaw cracking (Fig. 4b; Ui 1985) that indicates collision impact during transportation. This debris avalanche deposit includes large mounds, 414 m and 424 m high (Fig. 3), which are composed of huge lava blocks with regular jointed cores a few tens of metres across, at a distance of several kilometres from the volcano of the lava dome group. These mounds have slid toward the south, maintaining the original internal structure of the lava dome. Palaeomagnetic data indicate that the Ogigahara block-and-ash flow and Pankechin block-and-ash flow deposits were emplaced at temperatures above 500°C (Ando & Yamagishi 1975; Yamagishi 1977).

These debris avalanche deposits were probably produced by repeated collapse of lava domes with minor explosions, because the lava dome group is composed of more than ten domes, some of which have collapsed, and the explosion products, including bread-crust bombs, are found at the southern foot of the dome group.

Tokachidake Volcano (9 in Fig. 1) is a stratovolcano situated in the Tokachidake Range, central Hokkaido. This volcano has a history of collapse of its central cone by explosions, generating debris avalanches, that have been transformed into hydrologic mass flow (lahar in 1926; Fig. 10) by melting snow on the summit of the mountain (Ishikawa *et al.* 1971). The mass flow flooded the towns of Kamifurano and Biei, killing 144 people. The total volume of this mass flow was estimated at $1.9 \times 10^6 \, \text{m}^3$ (Yamagishi 1993). This volcano produced several pyroclastic flows (scoria flows) 2000 to 3000 years ago, indicated by the radiocarbon dating of included carbonized trunks.

Irumukeppu-yama (10 in Fig. 1) is a stratovolcano that was formed 2.5 million years ago. The eastern foot of the volcano is occupied by debris avalanche deposits up to 50 m thick, whose surfaces are characterized by hummocky flow mounds. The deposits include blocks with jigsaw cracks (Ui 1985) and cooling contraction prismatic joints (Yamagishi 1993).

The northwest face of Onnebetsu-dake (11 in Fig. 1) on the Shiretoko Peninsula is characterized by a smooth slope on which two hills as much as 50 m high, slid down toward the north (Fig. 5). The smooth slope probably implies rapid sliding of the hill (Yamagishi 1993). These hills are fringed with many small mounds on the surfaces. The hills collapsed by further sliding,

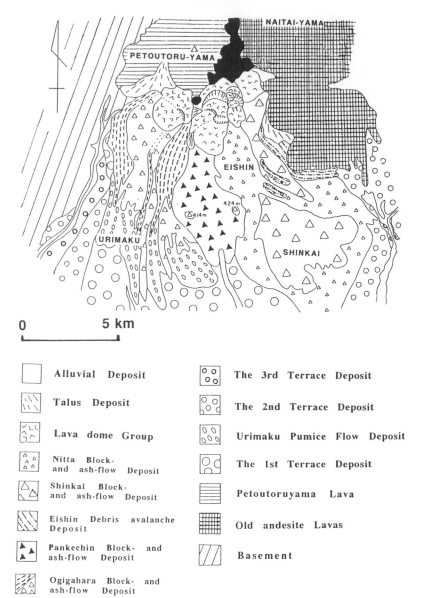

Fig. 3. Geologic map of Shikaribetsu Volcano and related mass-movement deposits (modified from Yamagishi 1977).

forming secondary scarps and large mounds in front. Several hollows were formed between the hills and mounds.

Minami-dake (12 in Fig. 1), on the Shiretoko Peninsula, east Hokkaido, is one of several large craters opened toward the west, at the south end of the Shiretoko Iwo-zan (Katsui *et al.* 1982). This crater was formed by a huge collapse producing debris avalanche deposits which are scattered with five lakes between the mounds

of the deposits along the coast facing Sea of Okhotsk.

Hydrologic mass flows following volcanic eruptions

Usu Volcano

Before its 1977–1978 eruptions, Usu Volcano (5 in Fig. 1) was covered by a deep forest.

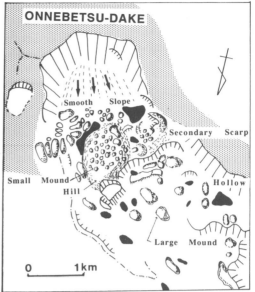

Fig. 5. Giant collapse deposits from the Onnebetsu-dake. Notice the large hill with many small mounds on the surface.

Fig. 4. (a) Jointed block in the Shinkai block- and ash-flow deposit at Shikaribetsu Volcano (8 in Fig. 1). Note prismatic joints on the surface, indicating quenching. (b) Jigsaw-cracked block in the Pankechin block-and-ash flow deposit at Shikaribetsu Volcano (8 in Fig. 1).

However, the 1977–1978 eruptions devastated the summit and slopes of the volcano, and numerous hydrologic mass flows were generated (Yamagishi *et al.* 1982).

The Plinian eruptions began in the morning of 7 August 1977. These Plinian eruptions took place four times by August 14 (the first stage eruptions; Katsui *et al.* 1978). Immediately after these eruptions, blocky mass flows were generated along the valleys on the southwest slope in August and September 1977 (Fig. 6 upper, and Fig. 7a). They were triggered by precipitation of 20 to 40 mm/day. The total amount of these mass flows was estimated at 50 000 m³. The surfaces of the slopes were covered by a crust of mortar-like ash ejected during the rainy weather. The mass flows were mainly caused by flash floods resulting from surface runoff of rain water on the devastated upper slopes and gully erosion in the valleys. Along the valley walls, previous landslides were reactivated by erosion of the lower slopes. Airfall pumices were reworked as pumice flows by precipitation on

the northern slopes, but they were highly viscous; therefore, they did not reach the foot of the slopes but formed viscous tongue-shaped lobes (Fig. 7b). These mass flows display no stratification and are clast-supported; however, distinct reverse grading indicates debris flow mechanism defined by Smith (1986) and Smith & Lowe (1991).

The first stage eruptions ended with the eruption on 14 August and then the second stage eruptions began with phreatic explosions in November 1977, and continued intermittently with phreatomagmatic eruptions in September 1978 (Niida *et al.* 1980). In particular, on 12 September 1978, the largest phreatomagmatic eruptions produced fine-grained, white, hot ash materials as much as 50 cm thick on the upper slope; these materials flowed down slopes and valleys as a powder avalanche (Fig. 7c). Rainfall wetted the falling ash and avalanche deposits, and then the surfaces of the deposits were dried up, forming desiccation cracks. The interior of the deposits were still mobile, however, and continued to move like pahoehoe lava. Immediately after the Second Stage Eruptions, hydrologic mass flows such as mudflows, occurred frequently on not only the southern slopes, but also the northern ones (Fig. 6 lower). On 24 October 1978, they were generated in most valleys on the northeast slope and spread to the Toya and Sobetsu-Onsen Spas, triggered by

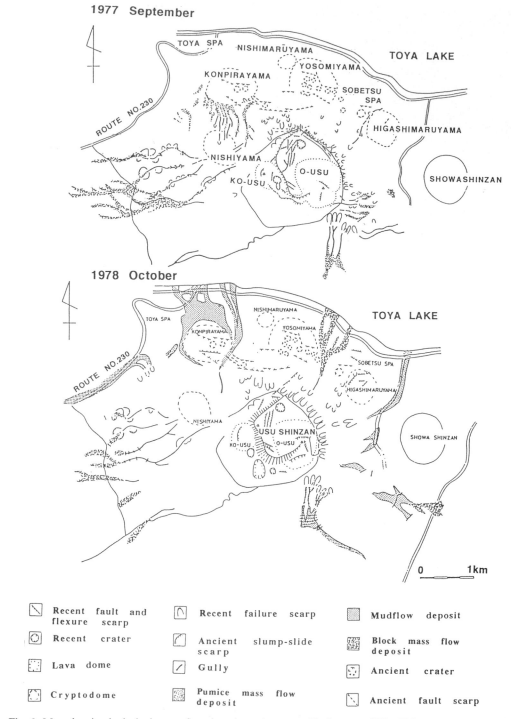

Fig. 6. Map showing hydrologic mass flow deposits and geomorphic features of Usu Volcano (5 in Fig. 1) after the first stage eruptions in 1977 (upper) and during the second stage eruptions in 1978 (lower).

Fig. 7. (a) Block mass flow deposits spread toward the southern foot of Usu Volcano (September 1978). Note size grading toward the right-hand side. **(b)** Highly viscous pumice mass flow spread onto the northern valley slope of Usu Volcano (September 1977). **(c)** White, dry ash flow 10 cm thick moving downvalley, derived from phreatomagmatic eruptions of 12 September 1978, Usu Volcano. **(d)** Highly fluid mass flow deposits, burying the first floor of the water plant at Usu Volcano (October 1978).

maximum-intensity rainfall of 24–29 mm/day, in which hourly rainfall reached 5–14.5 mm. The mudflows striking the Toya Spa travelled at a velocity of as much as 10 m s^{-1} (Fig.7d), killing three people. Maximum thickness of the mudflows exceeded 2 m in the alluvial fan on the valley plain. The main body of the mudflow transport continued for 15 to 20 minutes. The total volume was estimated to be 120 000 m^3 (Kadomura *et al.* 1980). The formation of the mudflows was due in large part to the fine-grained nature of the ejecta on the summit and upper slope, generated by the phreatic to phreatomagmatic eruptions, together with accumulation of debris from rock fall and sliding triggered by earthquake swarms. These thick fine-grained materials on the summit and upper slope formed an impermeable crust, resulting in a drastic decrease in water infiltration capacity and contributing to repetition of the mudflows. Simultaneously, the fine-grained materials penetrated into the interstices between the underlying pumices of the first stage eruptions, causing a decrease in viscosity of the mass flow of the reworked pumice. They would be hyperconcentrated flood flows because of the clast-supported

fabric and the large percentage of water versus low percentage of materials (Smith 1986).

During volcanic activities from 1977 to 1980, the northern caldera rim was subjected to tensional stress due to northeastward movement of Usu Shinzan, showing a U-shape in plan view (Fig. 6 lower), caused by oblique upheaval of a cryptodome associated with earthquake shaking (Yamagishi *et al.* 1982). These movements expanded the caldera rim and the earthquake shattered the surface. In particular, the northeast caldera rim moved horizontally *c.* 170 m toward the northeast, and rose about 20 m due to oblique upheaval of Usu Shinzan cryptodome. Consequently, the outer rim slope increased by 20° while the inner rim slope decreased in inclination by the same degree. Finally, the steepened northeast rim slope became prone to sliding (Figs 8a and 8b) because of dip-slipping of unconsolidated ash and pumice deposits on the surfaces. On the northeast alluvial fan where Sobetsu Spa is located, small hydrologic mass flows due to rainfall were generated, mostly from the somma lava slope (Fig. 6 lower). Such mass flows were originated from blocks of the lavas, together

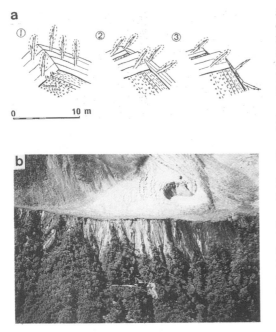

Fig. 8. (a) Schematic model of sliding due to steepening of outer caldera rim wall of Usu Volcano. (1) The caldera rim is composed of somma lava overlain by air-fall pumice (Us-b) and ash (Us-b₁). (2) Since the eruptions of 1977, the rim was crossed and the outer wall steepened due to uplifting of the Usu Shinzan. (3) Finally, the top of the rim began to slip. (b) Oblique aerial photograph of sliding slope of the northeast caldera rim of Usu Volcano.

a hot volcanic avalanche which induced a disastrous lahar through snow melt. The lahar flowed 25 km from the crater with a velocity of as much as 60 km/hour and killed 144 people (Katsui *et al.* 1990). The total volume of the lahar has been estimated to be $2 \times 10^7 \text{m}^3$ (Yamagishi 1993).

Tokachidake Volcano burst into moderate phreatic activity from a new vent on the southwest wall of the 62-II Crater on 16 December 1988, after a 26 year period of dormancy since a large-scale scoria eruption in 1962 (Katsui *et al.* 1990). Since the eruption on 16 December 1988, 23 phreatic and vulcanian eruptions took place from the vent until 5 March 1989 (Katsui *et al.* 1990). These eruptions were associated with small-scale block-and-ash flows (as defined by Wright *et al.* 1980), ejection of ballistic blocks and bombs (Yamagishi & Feebrey 1994), and fallout ash (Miyaji *et al.* 1990). Five block-and-ash flows were generated, and these were always associated with pyroclastic surges (Fig. 9a). The

with a matrix of ash and pumice; they were matrix-supported en masse deposits (Smith 1986). The total volume of the deposits was estimated to be 26 000 m³ (Kadomura *et al.* 1980). In addition, a small debris avalanche occurred from the northeast steepened rim slope on 24 April 1981. The avalanche was generated from the top of the slope 310 m in elevation, and debris moved in a winding flow; its length was 825 m. The marginal toe of the avalanche is 30 m wide, and 1.5 m thick. The total volume was estimated to be 8000 m³, and the maximum flow velocity was determined to be 41 m s⁻¹ based on the duration the elastic wave pattern for the debris avalanche as recorded in a seismogram (Kadomura *et al.* 1983).

Tokachidake Volcano

Tokachidake Volcano (9 in Fig. 1) has recorded historical eruptions since 1857. In particular, the eruption of 1926 broke a central cone to produce

Fig. 9. (a) Block-and-ash flow moving downward on the northwest slope of the 62-II Crater of the Tokachidake Volcano (9 in Fig. 1); photo was taken by airplane on 25 December 1988. (b) Gully erosion along the block-and-ash flow at Tokachidake Volcano caused by the heavy rainfall on 23 August 1989. Photo was taken on 6 July 1990.

block-and-ash flows travelled on snow less than 1.2 km along a NW valley with levees developed on both sides of the flows. Sixty hours after the eruption of 25 December the deposits, consisting of non-vesiculated polygonal blocks, had a maximum temperature of 92°C at 50 cm depth in the distal parts of the flow (Katsui *et al.* 1990). The marginal toes of the block-and-ash flows diverged into two parts (Figs. 10 and 11a).

After the 1988–1989 eruptions of Tokachidake Volcano, considerable rainfall (30 mm in 3 hours) on 23 August 1989, generated hydrologic mass flows forming gullies as much as 7 m wide and 5 m deep (Fig. 9b) of 1000 m^3 in volume, running more than 2 km along valleys and depositing debris including boulders as much as 50 cm across. It was possible to measure the velocity of the flows because they cut the seismometer cable. A velocity of 2–4 m/s was calculated by Yamagishi *et al.* (1991). This value

is comparable to the velocity of 3.8 m/s calculated by Rodolfo (1989), for the Typhoon Saling debris flow on 18 October 1985, on Mayon Volcano, Philippines. The mass flows were probably debris flow or hyperconcentrated flood flow (Smith & Lowe 1991), evidenced by the clast-supporting fabric of the flows which have reverse grading or no stratification.

Furthermore, on 12 August 1994, heavy rainfalls of more than 100 mm in 5 hours triggered three events of hydrologic mass flows, which were recognized by vibration on the seismograph located on the slopes of the Tokachidake Volcano (Okada pers. comm. 1994). The largest mass flow occurred at 21:13–21:30 (Okada pers. comm. 1994). The flow was generated from gullies (Fig. 11a, quadrangle A in Fig. 10) that ran from the rim of Taisho Crater to the cottage of Fig, 10, and emplaced a debris fan including boulders up to

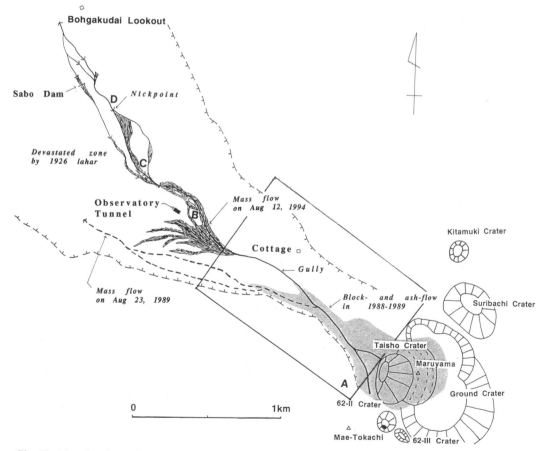

Fig. 10. Map showing gully erosion and hydrologic mass flows on 23 August 1989 and 12 August 1994 at Tokachidake Volcano.

50 cm across on the underlying lava toe, close to the observatory tunnel (Fig. 10). This flow was followed by flowing of water-rich fine-grained materials toward the Bohgakudai Lookout of Fig. 10. Such water-rich mass flow left lag deposits of boulders up to 50 cm across on one side margin (Fig. 11b , B in Fig. 10) and double-level terrace sediments up to 50 cm high, which are coarse-grained and clast-supported, were left in the lower channel (Fig. 11c, C in Fig 10; Rodolfo 1989). Both of the terrace sediments were sharply and vertically truncated, indicating that central portions of each flow passed downstream, leaving shallow channels.

The streamline from the observatory tunnel to Bohgakudai Lookout of Fig. 10 has distinct knickpoints (Fig. 11d, D in Fig. 10), which indicates that water-rich flows eroded previous stream beds rather than highly concentrated mass flows. The total volume of the mass flows on 12 August 1994 was estiamted to be as much as 8000 m³.

Water flooding by heavy rainfall on the upper slope of Tokachidake Volcano was transformed into hydrologic mass flows, such as debris flow and hyperconcentrated flood flow (Smith & Lowe 1991), by bulking (incorporation of over-ridden sediments into the flow; Scott 1988) by erosion of the 1988–1989 block-and-ash flow sediments and the 1926 lahar sediments, so increasing the proportion of material content to water content while passing through the gullies on the upper stream. After the first deposition (B in Fig. 10), the mass flow evolved to hypercon-centrated flood flow with further dilution downstream.

Slides related to caldera formation

Nigorikawa Caldera (4 in Fig. 1) is a crater-lake-type caldera 3 km in diameter, situated north of Komagatake Volcano (see Fig. 1) on the Oshima Peninsula. This caldera was formed by eruption of an ash fall, followed by an ash flow 11 670–12 900 years BP (Ando 1983). Geo-thermal drilling cores have revealed that caldera-filling deposits 1500 m thick, a hornblende lava dome, slide deposits 150 m thick, lacustrine deposits 350 m thick and alluvial deposits 100 thick, are filed up in ascending order (Ando 1983). In particular, the slide deposits are

Fig. 11. (**a**) Aerial photo of the northwest slope (A quadrangle of Fig. 10) of Tokachidake Volcano. Note the gullies along the remnants of the block-and-ash flow by the 1988–1989 eruptions. (**b**) Lag blocks on the margins of the stream (B in Fig. 10) by the mass flows on 12 August 1994. (**c**) Two terrace deposits (C in Fig. 10) by the mass flows on 12 August 1994. (**d**) Knickpoint (D in Fig. 10) by dilute streams on 12 August 1994.

regarded as caldera-collapse breccias (cf. Lipman 1976). Lipman presumed that the internal caldera cross-section of the middle Tertiary San Juan volcanic field in Colorado, USA, is funnel-shaped, 60° to 70° with walls, and the bottom exists at a depth of 1800 m.

Southwest of the caldera, along the 490–630 m elevation range, a V-shaped trench 2 km long and 200 m wide has been recognized (Fig. 12). A small trench is aligned along the eastern wall of the trench. From the V-shaped trench, two large-scale slides 3–5 km wide and long developed toward the Nigorikawa Caldera and the Kamabetsugawa River. Both of the slides show cracks and secondary scarps, parallel and/or oblique to the V-shaped trench and are associated with small slides in and around them. Airphoto interpretation has revealed that the processes of sliding and formation of the V-shaped trench were related to the collapse of the Nigorikawa Caldera (Hokkaido Branch Landslide Society of Japan 1985). The slide facing the caldera moved first toward the caldera (First Slide in Fig. 12), associated with small slides, just after the eruption of ash fall and occurrence of the ash flow, which were accompanied with caldera collapse. Consequently, the western wall of the V-trench was formed. The interpretation that the sliding was related to collapse of the caldera, is supported by the fact that the upper caldera-filling deposits include slide deposits regarded as caldera-collapse breccias at the margin of the caldera (Ando 1983).

However, after the caldera was filled with lacustrine materials, slide deposits and alluvial deposits, the first slide became stable. On the other hand, the slide facing the Kamabetsugawa River moved toward the river (Second Slide in Fig. 12), as a result of erosion of the river wall. This led to the eastern wall of the V-shaped trench being formed, followed by the small trench on the wall. The V-shaped trench, therefore, was developed as a result of the two large-scale slides.

Conclusion and summary

There are many Quaternary volcanoes and calderas in Hokkaido, Japan. They have been

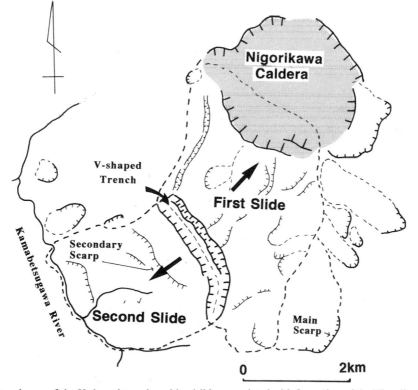

Fig. 12. Local map of the V-shaped trench and landslides associated with formation of the Nigorikawa Caldera (4 in Fig. 1). Modified from Hokkaido Branch of Landslide Society of Japan (1985).

prone to destructive mass movements, such as pyroclastic flows, hydrologic mass flows and slides during or just after eruptions.

Some of the volcanoes are still active, as shown by eruptions of Usu Volcano in 1977–1978 and Tokachidake Volcano in 1988–1989. Both of the volcanoes have a history of not only erupting pyroclastic flows, but also producing hydrologic mass flows due to rainfall during or just after the eruptions. Active stratovolcanoes such as Oshima-Ohshima, Komagatake Volcano, Usu Volcano and Tokachidake Volcano have produced debris avalanches, some of which have transformed into hydrologic mass flows as shown by the 1926 lahar of Tokachidake Volcano. Collapse of ancient lava domes or stratovolcanoes also produced debris avalanches at Esan Skyzawa-yama, Niseko, Shiribetsu-dake, Irumukeppu-yama, Shikaribetsu Volcano, Onnebetsudake and Minami-dake. Formation of calderas, such as Nigorikawa Calderas, is in places, associated with large-scale slides. Caldera formation also is associated with large-scale slides.

I am indebted to Robert Schuster and Peter Francis and an anonymous referee for critical comments on my draft.

References

ANDO, S. 1983. Structure of Nigorikawa Caldera viewing from drilling data. *Monthly Chikyu,* **5**, 116–121 (in Japanese).

—— & YAMAGISHI, H. 1975. Hill topography on the Nuee Ardente deposits of Shikaribetsu Volcano, Hokkaido. *Bulletin of the Volcanological Society of Japan,* **20**, 31–36 (in Japanese with English abstract).

CAZEAU, C. J., HATCHER, JR., R. D. & SIEMANKOWSKY, F. T. 1976. *Physical Geology – Principles, Processes, and Problems.* Harper & Row.

EISBACHER, G. H. & CLAGUE, J. J.1984. *Destructive Mass Movements in High Mountains: Hazard and Management.* Geological Survey Canada, Paper **84-16**, 28–43.

FRANCIS, P. W., ROOBOL, M. J., WALKER, G. P. L., COBOLD, P. B. & COWARD, M. P., 1974. The San Pedro and San Pablo Volcanoes of North Chile and their hot avalanche deposits. *Geologische Rundschau,* **63**, 357–388.

HOKKAIDO BRANCH OF LANDSLIDE SOCIETY OF JAPAN, 1985. *Landslides in Hokkaido.* Civil Engineering Association of Hokkaido.

ISHIKAWA, T., YOKOYAMA, I., KATSUI, Y. & KASAHARA, M. 1971. *Tokachi-dake, its Volcanic Geology, History of Eruption, Present State of Activity and Prevention of Disasters.* Committee for Prevention of the Natural Disasters of Hokkaido, Sapporo (in Japanese).

KADOMURA, H., OKADA, H., IMAGAWA, T., MORIYA, I. & YAMAMOTO, H., 1983. Erosion and mass movements on Mt. Usu accelerated by crustal deformation that accompanied its 1977–1982 volcanism. *Journal of Natural Disaster Science,* **5**, 33–62.

——, YAMAMOTO, H., IMAGAWA, T. *ET AL.* 1980. Erosion and mudflows at Usu Volcano after the 1977–1978 eruption: August 1977–December 1979, *Environmental Science, Hokkaido,* **3**, 155–184.

KATSUI, Y., OBA, Y. *ET AL.*, 1978 Preliminary report on the 1977 eruption of Usu Volcano. *Journal of Faculty of Science, Hokkaido University, Ser. 4,* **18**, 385–408.

—— & YAMAMOTO, M. 1981. The 1741–1742 activity of Oshima-Oshima Volcano, north Japan. *Journal of the Faculty of Science, Hokkaido University, Ser. 4,* **4**, 527–536.

——, KAWACHI, S., KONDO, Y. *ET AL.* 1990. The 1988–1989 explosive eruptions of Tokachidake, central Hokkaido, its sequence and mode. *Bulletin of Volcanological Society of Japan, Ser. 2,* **35**, 111–129.

——, SUZUKI, T., SOYA, T. & YOSHIDA, Y.1985. *Geological map of Hokkaido-Komagatake Volcano, scale 1:50,000.* Geological Survey of Japan.

——, YOKOYAMA, I., EHARA, Y., YAMASHITA, H. & NIIDA, K. 1977. *Oshima-Ohshima, its Volcanic Geology, History of Eruption, Present State of Activity and Prevention of Disasters.* Committe for Prevention of the Natural Disasters of Hokkaido, Sapporo (in Japanese).

——, ——, FUJITA, T. & EHARA, S. 1975 *Komagatake, its Volcanic Geology, History of Eruption, Present State of Activity and Prevention of Disasters.* Committee for Prevention of the Natural Disasters of Hokkaido, Sapporo (in Japanese).

——, ——, OKADA, H. & TAKAGI, H., 1982. *Shiretoko-Iwozan, its Volcanic Geology, History of Eruption, Present State of Activity and Prevention of Disasters.* Committee for Prevention of the Natural Disasters of Hokkaido, Sapporo (in Japanese).

——, ——, —— & TSUBO, T., 1983. *Esan, its Volcanic Geology, History of Eruption, Present State of Activity and Prevention of Disasters.* Committee for Prevention of the Natural Disasters of Hokkaido, Sapporo (in Japanese).

LIPMAN, P. W. 1976. Caldera-collapse breccias in the western San Juan Mountains, Colorado. *Geological Society of America Bulletin,* **87**, 1397–1410.

MIYAJI, N., SUMITA, M., YOSHIDA, M., KONDO, Y., YAMAZAKI, T., KOUYAMA, K. & SONE, T., 1990. Tephra-stratigraphical study of the 1988–1989 eruptions of Tokachi-dake Volcano, Central Hokkaido. *Bulletin of the Volcanology Society of Japan, Ser. 2,* **35**, 131–145.

NIIDA, K. *ET AL.*, 1980 The 1977–1978 eruption of Usu Volcano. *Journal of the Faculty of Science, Hokkaido University, Ser. 4,* **19**, 357–394.

RODOLFO, K. S. 1989. Origin and early evolution of lahar channel at Mabinit, Mayon Volcano, Philippines. *Geological Society of America Bulletin,* **101**, 414–426.

SCOTT, K. M., 1988. *Origins, behavior, and sedimentology of lahars and lahar-runout flows in the Toutle-Cowlitz River System*. US Geological Survey Professional Paper, **1447-A**.

SMITH, G. A. 1986. Coarse-grained nonmarine volcaniclastic sediment: Terminology and depositional process. *Geological Society of America Bulletin*, **97**, 1–10.

—— & LOWE, D. R. 1991. Lahar: volcano-hydrologic events and deposition in the debris flow-hyperconcentrated flow continuum. *In*: FISHER, R. V. & SMITH, G. A. (eds) *Sedimentation in Volcanic Settings*. Society for Sedimentary Geology, Special Publication, No. **45**, 59–70.

SOYA, T., KATSUI, Y., NIIDA, K. & SAKAI, K. 1981. *Geological map of Usu Volcano, scale 1 : 25 000*. Geological Survey of Japan.

UI, T. 1985 Debris avalanche deposits associated with volcanic activity. *Proceedings of the IVth International Conference and Field Workshop on Landslides*. Tokyo, 405–410.

WRIGHT, J. V., SMITH, A L. & SELF, S. 1980. A working terminology of pyroclastic deposits. *Journal of Volcanology and Geothermal Research*, **8**, 315–336.

YAMAGISHI, H. 1977. Pyroclastic Flow Deposits from the Shikaribetsu Volcanoes, Hokkaido, Japan. *Report of the Geological Survey of Hokkaido*, **49**, 37–48 (in Japanese with English abstract).

——1993. Giant Collapses in Hokkaido. *Report of the Geological Survey of Hokkaido*, **65**, 85–96 (in Japanese with English abstract).

—— & FEEBREY, C. 1994. Ballistic ejecta from the 1988–1989 andesitic Vulcanian eruptions of Tokachidake volcano, Japan: morphological features and genesis. *Journal of Volcanology and Geothermal Research*, **59**, 269–278.

——, MIYAMOTO, K., OKAMURA, T., AKITA, F. & OKAZAKI, N. 1991. Debris flows generated in August, 1989, on the western slope of the Tokachi-dake Volcano. *Shinsabo*, **44**(4), 30–35 (in Japanese with English abstract).

——, MORIYA, I. & MATSUI, K. 1982. Deformation, erosion and debris transportation in Usu Volcano since the 1977 eruptions. *Earth Science (Chikyu Kagaku)*, **36**, 307–320 (in Japanese with English abstract).

YOKOYAMA, I., KATSUI, Y., OBA, Y. & EHARA, S., 1973. *Usu-zan, its Volcanic Geology, History of Eruption, Present State of Activity and Prevention of Disasters*. Commitee for Prevention of Disasters of Hokkaido, Sapporo (in Japanese).

Turbidites from slope failure on Hawaiian volcanoes

MICHAEL O. GARCIA

*Hawaii Center for Volcanology, Geology and Geophysics Department,
University of Hawaii, Honolulu, HI 96822, USA*

Abstract: Turbidites are common in the sediments surrounding the Hawaiian Islands. Cores were taken during leg 136 of the Ocean Drilling Program 320 km west of the island of Hawaii on the outer side of the arch that surrounds the southern end of the Hawaiian chain. They contain Pleistocene to late Oligocene graded volcanic sand layers with fresh glass (or its alteration products) and mineral fragments (olivine, plagioclase, and clinopyroxene). Some layers have mixed assemblages of Pleistocene to Eocene radiolarians or Eocene and Cretaceous ichthyoliths. The glass fragments are weakly vesicular and blocky to platy in shape. The glass fragments from individual Pleistocene to Pliocene layers have large compositional ranges (i.e. larger than expected for a single eruption). These features indicate that the turbidites probably were deposited from turbidity currents that originated on the flanks of Hawaiian volcanoes. The low to moderate sulfur content of the sand glasses indicates that they were derived from partially degassed lavas that were erupted under shallow marine to subaerial conditions. The turbidity currents ran over the *c.* 500 m high Hawaiian Arch, which indicates that the currents were at least 325 m thick. Similar turbidite deposits are located 930 km south of the Hawaiian Islands. Thus, debris avalanche from Hawaiian volcanoes can generate enormous turbidity currents that transport sediments long distances from their source. This phenomenon is an alternative explanation to Antarctic bottom waters for generating mixed assemblages of Pleistocene and Eocene radiolarians in deep-sea sediments.

The rapid growth (<1 Ma) and enormous size of Hawaiian volcanoes (up to 8.5 km of relief) causes them to be gravitationally unstable and to generate some of the largest landslides on Earth (up to 200 km in length and 5000 km³ in volume; Moore *et al.* 1989). Dozens of major landslides have been recognized on the submarine flanks of the Hawaiian Ridge (Moore *et al.* 1994) and Hawaii has become the type-example for this phenomenon. As detailed bathymetry and side-scan sonar images become available for other oceanic islands, large-scale landslides are being identified on the flanks of these islands, including Reunion (Lenat *et al.* 1989), Marquesas (Borgia & Treves 1992) and the Canaries (Holcomb & Searle 1991). Thus, giant landslides are apparently a common feature of oceanic islands.

Some giant Hawaiian landslides produced large debris avalanches (up to 2 km thick and 230 km long; Moore *et al.* 1994). Recently, it has been recognized that turbidites are associated with these debris avalanches (Garcia 1993). The turbidity currents were able to cross the moat surrounding the Hawaiian Islands and run up and over the 500 m high arch that parallels the moat. This paper focuses on the turbidites that are associated with these giant landslides and summarizes the results from several studies of the volcanic sands in cores recovered from two holes on the outer side of the Hawaiian Arch during leg 136 of the Ocean Drilling Program (ODP). Garcia & Hull (1994) presented a condensed version of their results from the ODP cores. This paper builds on that paper by presenting new data on disseminated sands within the cores and new ideas on the mechanics of the turbidity currents generated by debris avalanches from Hawaiian volcanoes.

These giant landslide-related turbidites may be of importance beyond Hawaii and other oceanic islands. Traditionally, it has been thought that Antarctic-derived bottom currents are responsible for the mixed radiolarian assemblages (typically Eocene and Pleistocene) that are observed in Pacific deep-sea cores (e.g. Reidel & Funnel 1964; Beiersdorf 1987), including those from around the Hawaiian Islands (e.g. DSDP sites 67 and 68; Winterer *et al.* 1971; Tracey *et al.* 1971). However, at least some of these mixed assemblages are found in volcanic sand layers, which are interpreted as products of turbidity currents (Schreiber 1969). This paper examines the consequence of these landslide-related turbidites for deep-sea sedimentation, which could be particularly important for the western Pacific, where large seamounts and islands are relatively abundant.

Geological setting

The Hawaiian Islands were formed by the most active hotspot on Earth (Sleep 1990). A typical Hawaiian shield volcano produces about

From McGuire, W. J., Jones, A. P. & Neuberg, J. (eds) 1996, *Volcano Instability on the Earth and Other Planets*, Geological Society Special Publication No. 110, pp. 281–294.

100 million m³ of lava per year (Tilling & Dvorak 1993) and is completely formed within 1 Ma (Frey *et al.* 1990). Mauna Loa, which is still active (its last eruption was in 1984), has obtained a maximum thickness of about 13 km, which includes over 5 km of subsidence as a result of the rapid loading of the lithosphere (Moore 1987). The total volume of Mauna Loa is over 80 000 km³ (Garcia *et al.* 1995). This rapid loading has created a depression (the Hawaiian Deep) around the volcanoes that is *c.* 140 km from the axis of the Hawaiian chain (Fig. 1). Outward from the deep, about 250 km from the volcanic chain, is a *c.* 500 m high arch that parallels it. Together these features form a substantial barrier to restrict distribution of sediment derived from the Hawaiian Islands. The topographical expression of the Hawaiian Arch and Deep diminishes with the age of the adjacent Hawaiian volcano as a consequence of sediment deposition. North of the island of Oahu, the deep contains about 2 km of debris,

most of which was derived from a landslide off the north flank of the island (Rees *et al.* 1993). The total sediment volume in the deep around the Hawaiian Islands is estimated to be 90 000 km³ (Rees *et al.* 1993).

Hawaiian volcanoes grow by relatively quiescent eruption of lavas from fissures and central vents. When active lava flows enter the ocean they produce huge volumes of fragmental debris as the hot lava and ocean water react with each other. This debris is redistributed by longshore currents and eventually is transported down the submarine flanks of the volcanoes (e.g. Fisher 1984). Explosive volcanism is rare on Hawaiian volcanoes. It generally occurs during the final stages of shield volcanism or during the post-erosional stage of volcanism, although Kilauea Volcano has erupted explosively twice in the last two centuries (Walker 1990). Nevertheless, the contribution of Hawaiian explosive volcanism to the sedimentary record is probably minor.

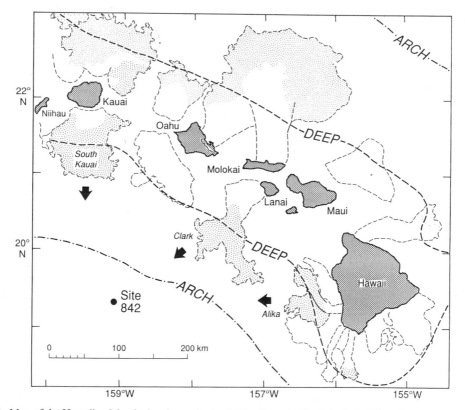

Fig. 1. Map of the Hawaiian Islands showing major landslides (bounded by light dashed lines; Moore *et al.* 1989). The debris avalanches are shown by the stippled pattern. The avalanches that travelled toward ODP site 842 (solid circle) are the Alika Slide from Mauna Loa Volcano, Clark Slide from Lanai, and the South Kauai Slide from Kauai. The axis of the Hawaiian Deep is shown by the heavy dashed line; the Hawaiian arch axis is shown by the heavy dashed-dotted line.

Landslides form during any stage of growth of Hawaiian volcanoes. They are common on the youngest Hawaiian volcano, Loihi seamount (Fornari *et al.* 1988), which is in the preshield stage. They have formed during the early (Kilauea; Fornari *et al.* 1979) and late stages of shield volcanism (e.g. Mauna Loa; Lipman *et al.* 1988) and may have formed during the post-shield stage (Waianae; Presley 1994). The largest landslides probably occur during the late stages of shield volcanism when the volcano is near its maximum size and is still seismically active (Moore *et al.* 1994). Some of the largest Hawaiian earthquakes, such as the magnitude 7 and greater events in 1868, 1951 and 1975, are thought to have been the results of episodic movement on some of these slides (Moore & Mark 1992).

Hawaiian landslides have been subdivided into two types, slumps and debris avalanches, based on their morphology and degree of dislocation, although both types may occur in the same landslide (Moore *et al.* 1994). Slumps are deeply rooted into the volcanic edifice and are up to 10 km thick and 110 km long. Portions of the slumps may collapse to produce debris avalanches. Debris avalanches are thinner (0.05–2 km), longer (230 km) and have more gentle slopes (<3°) than do slumps (Moore *et al.* 1994). Some of the young Mauna Loa's debris avalanches can be traced back to huge amphitheatres whose heads are just below or somewhat above sea level (Lipman *et al.* 1988). Debris avalanches are thought to have formed during catastrophic events because they are relatively thin, long and were able to travel across the Hawaiian Deep and up onto the Hawaiian Arch (Moore *et al.* 1989). Such catastrophic events probably evolve into turbidity currents at the distal margins of the debris avalanches. Turbidites have been reported around the Hawaiian islands for decades (e.g. Schreiber 1969; Edsall 1975). Is it possible to discriminate turbidite deposits associated with debris avalanches from those related to other types of turbidity currents? In the discussion below, this question will be examined using the cores obtained during ODP leg 136 at site 842 where two holes were drilled near to each other (*c.* 10 m apart). This site was drilled on the backside of the Hawaiian Arch, which should restrict or prohibit most turbidity currents from reaching this site.

Stratigraphy and age

Volcanic sand is probably the best indicator of turbidites in the site 842 core. It occurs as a minor to major component in the clay-rich portion of the site 842 core above *c.* 36 m below the sea floor (bsf); this sediment is Pleistocene to late Oligocene in age and overlies massive chert (Shipboard Scientific Party 1992). The clay-rich part of the core has been subdivided into two units: an upper unit (0–21.4 m bsf), which is Pleistocene to late middle Miocene in age and is distinctive in containing common mineral fragments (especially augite) and no clinoptilolite (a diagenetic mineral); and a lower unit (21.4–*c.* 36 m bsf), which is middle Miocene to late Oligocene in age and contains rare mineral fragments but abundant zeolite (Tribble *et al.* 1993). The upper 10 m of the upper unit contains fresh glass, which is suitable for microprobe analysis. Below that level, any glass that was present has been partially or completely replaced by zeolite or clay minerals (Tribble *et al.* 1993).

Volcanic sand occurs as disseminated grains with pelagic sediment and in discrete layers. The layers are dark grey in colour and have sharp basal contacts. The glass grain size fines upward from the base into the overlying brown clay-rich sediment. There are four distinct sand layers in core from hole 842A (Fig. 2). The core from hole 842B contains three sand layers between 13 and 14 m bsf, and 11 between 29.8 and 34.8 m bsf (Shipboard Scientific Party 1992). These layers range in preservation from soupy and poorly preserved (layer 1 in hole 842A) to indurated zones 1–3 cm thick in the lower portion of the clay-rich core from hole 842B. Most of the sandy layers are 1–2 cm thick and continuous across the width of the core. A few of the layers consist of multiple, closely spaced sandy horizons with sharp bases and gradational tops. Layer 2 in the core from hole 842A consists of an 11 cm thick zone with four sand-rich zones (0.5 to 2 cm thick) overlain by finer-grained sediments 1–3 cm thick (Fig. 3).

The site 842 core also contains many remnants of sand-rich horizons that are now disrupted into round to elongate globules 2–4 mm wide, which are distributed over zones 10 to 45 cm thick. This disruption is probably a result of bioturbation. Much of the rest of both cores contains finely disseminated volcanic glass mixed with clay that gives the core a light greyish-brown colour. However, there are zones 5 to 65 cm thick that are tan and contain pelagic sediment with little or no volcanic glass (Naka *et al.* 1993). Three of these zones occur just below sand layers (see Fig. 2).

The age of the volcanic sand layers can be constrained by palaeomagnetic data (using the new time scale of McDougall *et al.* 1992) and biostratigraphy. Layer 1 at *c.* 25 cm bsf is from a

Hole 842A

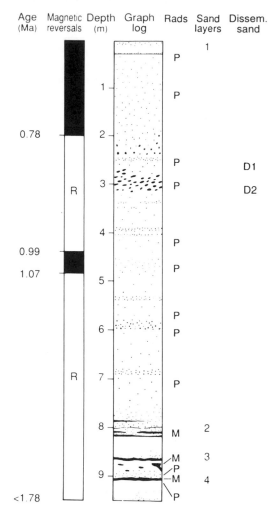

| Age (Ma) | Magnetic reversals | Depth (m) | Graph log | Rads | Sand layers | Dissem. sand |

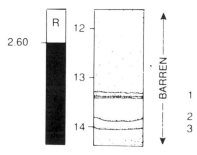

Hole 842B

normally polarized, 200 cm thick section of sediment (Fig. 2). It may be *c.* 100 ± 20 ka, assuming a constant sedimentation rate at the site and no erosion associated with deposition of the sand. This age is consistent with the absence of the radiolarian species *Axoprunum angelium* in a sample taken 3 cm below the sand layer. This species is common in the core from hole 842A below 1.2 m bsf; it last occurred about 0.36 ± 0.02 Ma (Hull 1993). Two zones of disseminated sand were examined: the one at 2.88 m bsf (D1) is medium grey and has coarser sand than the light grey sand from 3.17 m bsf (D2). Both are from near the middle of a reversely magnetized section (Shipboard Scientific Party 1992) that was probably deposited between 0.80 and 0.85 Ma.

The lower three sand layers from hole 842A are from near the bottom of a reversely magnetized section (Matuyama; 1.07 and 1.78 Ma; Shipboard Scientific Party 1992). They are probably 1.4 to 1.6 Ma based on estimates of sedimentation rates from palaeomagnetic data. This is consistent with the presence of nanofossils assignable to the lower part of Quaternary Zone NN19 in a sample taken between the bottom two sand layers in this hole (Hull 1993). In particular, the presence of *Calcidiscus macintyrei*, whose last occurrence was at 1.3 Ma (Hull 1993), in sediment between sand layers 3 and 4 (see Fig. 2) places a minimum age for these sands. These sand layers also contain an assemblage of poorly to moderately preserved, early to middle Eocene radiolarians (Hull 1993). Eocene radiolarians are not present in sediment above or below the sand layers. Hull (1993) interpreted the presence of both Pleistocene and Eocene radiolarians in the same sand layers to be the result of reworking.

The three volcanic glass sand layers in hole 842B at 13 to 14 m bsf are in a reversely magnetized section (Fig. 2), which was inferred to have been deposited 2.75 to 3.0 Ma (Garcia

Fig. 2. Summary logs of the sand distribution in and magnetic polarity of Pliocene to Pleistocene sediments for a composite section form holes 842A and 842B. The magnetic polarity determinations are from Shipboard Scientific Party (1992); polarity ages are from McDougall *et al.* (1992). Locations where samples were taken for palaeontological examination are noted under the Rad column. Samples with only Pleistocene radiolarian are noted by P; samples with mixed Pleistocene and Eocene radiolarian are noted by M (see Hull (1993) for details). The locations of the sand layers and disseminated sand horizons that were analysed geochemically are noted.

1993). Unfortunately, this zone is barren for microfossils (Hull 1993). The age of the older sand layers from hole 842B is early Miocene to late Oligocene based on ichthyolith (shark teeth)

biostratigraphy (Firth & Hull 1993). Reworked Eocene to late Cretaceous ichthyolith taxa were also found in these cores near some of these deeper volcanic sand horizons (Firth & Hull 1993).

Hole 842A-Layer 2

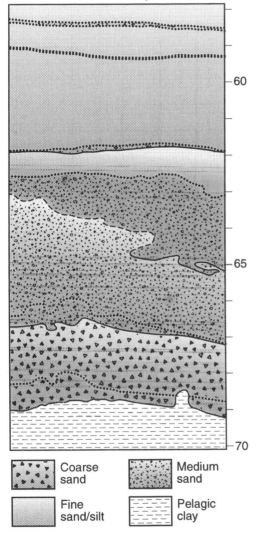

	Coarse sand		Medium sand
	Fine sand/silt		Pelagic clay

Fig. 3. Sketch of the multi-horizon sand layer 2 from hole 842A. The shade of grey indicates the relative amount of volcanic material. Solid lines indicate sharp discontinuities; these lines are dashed where the contact is unclear. The dotted lines mark the beginning of zones where the percentage of volcanic material decreases upward, except the two, thin upper zones which are parallel laminations. The coarseness of the symbol is related to the grain size, except the bottom unit which is pelagic clay. The units on the side of the drawing are in centimetres.

Petrography

The volcanic sand layers are lithologically heterogeneous. Their main components are glass and rock fragments (50–70 vol%), clay (<10 to 40 vol%), biogenic material (radiolarian and diatom tests and sponge spicules (<1 to 5 vol%), and mineral fragments (olivine <1 to 5 vol%, plagioclase <1 to 10 vol%, and clinopyroxene <1 to 4 vol%). Glass and mineral fragments range from 0.01 to 0.42 mm in length and are anhedral. Virtually all (>99%) of the glass fragments are blocky or platy. Some are strongly elongate (aspect ratios up to 1 to 8). Bubble-wall forms are uncommon (<10%). The glass fragments range in appearance from fresh to completely altered. The fresh glass is tan to light brown in colour. Equal proportions of the glass fragments are cloudy to opaque and dark grey in thin section under plain light. Altered glass is yellowish to reddish and, in the extreme cases, has completely altered to clay or zeolites. Altered glass is rare (<1 vol%) in the upper part of the cores (<10 m bsf), but is ubiquitous in the deeper samples in hole 842B.

The mineral fragments are fresh throughout the upper unit of the core but are altered to varying degrees in the lower unit. Olivine fragments are generally larger than plagioclase and clinopyroxene fragments. This is consistent with the observation that olivine is the dominant and, in many cases, the only phenocryst phase in Hawaiian basalts (Macdonald & Katsura 1964; Wright 1971).

The zones of disseminated sands contain a diverse assortment of particles but a greater portion of fine silt and clay (Naka *et al.* 1993; Tribble *et al.* 1993). The sand is finer in these zones than in the sand layers and they lack sponge spicules. Otherwise, these zones are quite similar in lithology to the sand layers.

Geochemistry

Methods

The University of Hawaii, five-spectrometer electron microprobe was used to determine the composition of glass fragments in the core. Beam conditions for glass analyses were 15 kV with a 10 nA sample current and a 15–20 μm beam diameter. Peak counting times were 50 s for most elements, except Mn and P (90 s). Na was analysed first in each analysis to minimize the possibility of its loss during analysis. The Smithsonian glass standards VG-2 and A99 (Jarosewich *et al.* 1979) were used for calibration and to monitor calibration drift. Precision for major elements is 1% to 2% relative; for minor elements, it is 5% to 10% relative. For glass sulphur analyses, a troilite standard was employed and counting times of 200 to 400 s were used. Precision for S analyses is estimated to be 5% to 10% relative based on repeated analyses of a glass standard, VG-2. For olivine analyses, a focused beam at 15 kV with a sample current of 15 nA was used. Peak counting times were 30 s. Precision for olivine analyses is estimated to be <0.5% forsterite based on repeated analyses of an olivine standard, San Carlos. A ZAF correction scheme was employed to obtain the final analyses.

Glass

Analyses were made of at least 20 glass fragments per sample. All the different morphologies present within a sample were analysed. The totals for most of the major element analyses are >99.0 wt% (see Table 1 for representative analyses or Garcia (1993) for a more complete listing of the analyses), which indicates that the glasses are fresh and may contain relatively low volatile contents. A study of Hawaiian tholeiitic submarine glasses collected in water depths between 1 and 4 km showed that they contain total volatile contents between 0.3 and 0.9 wt% (Garcia *et al.* 1989).

To gain a better estimate of the volatile content of the leg 136 volcanic glass sands, microprobe analyses were made for S on ten or more grains per sample. Glasses from the sand layers have low S contents (<0.02 wt%; see Fig. 4A); glasses from the disseminated sand zone have higher S contents (0.04–0.09 wt%). Typical Hawaiian submarine tholeiitic glasses have S contents >0.04 wt%; subaerially erupted tholeiitic glasses have S contents <0.015 wt% (see Fig. 4A). Thus, the glasses from the sand layers were probably erupted under shallow marine to subaerial conditions that allowed extensive degassing of S before the lava solidified. The disseminated glasses probably were derived from submarine eruptions on the flanks of the volcanoes.

All of the glasses are tholeiitic (Fig. 4B) and are similar in composition to Hawaiian tholeiites

compared to other types of tholeiites (e.g. >0.30 wt% K_2O; see Table 1). The glasses from the sand layers show wide compositional variations; they span larger ranges than the current data base for any individual Hawaiian tholeiitic volcano (Fig. 4B). The sand compositional variability may indicate that the glasses in these layers are from a larger portion of Hawaiian volcanoes than has been sampled subaerially and from dredging its submarine flanks. Two of the samples from hole 842A (layer 1 and D2) have glasses with high MgO contents (11.7 and 11.0 wt%), which are higher than any glass reported from any Hawaiian lava. Similar, high MgO content (up to 14.7 wt%) glasses have been reported from sands taken in a box core at 5.5 km water depth to the east of Kilauea Volcano (Clague *et al.* 1991). It is ironic that the Hawaiian glasses with the highest MgO contents have been found in turbidite sands.

Within individual sand layers, there are also wide ranges in TiO_2 at a given MgO content (Fig. 4C). These wide ranges are well beyond those that could be caused by crystal fractionation of the observed minerals (olivine, clinopyroxene, and plagioclase). This is especially true for the more mafic glasses (>7.0 wt% MgO; so-called olivine-controlled Hawaiian lavas; Wright 1971). For comparison, the field for lavas from the current long-lived (13+ year) Puu Oo eruption of Kilauea Volcano is relatively narrow despite the complex history of crystal fractionation of olivine, clinopyroxene, and plagioclase and magma mixing that these lavas have experienced (Garcia *et al.* 1992). Thus, the wide range in the glass compositions from individual sand layers must reflect lavas that were derived from many compositionally distinct parental magmas. In contrast, the glasses from each of the disseminated sand horizons have narrow compositional ranges and are similar to lavas from the Puu Oo eruption (Fig. 4C).

Olivine

The olivine fragments in the volcanic sands have a large and heterogeneous range in composition (Fig. 5). The range for individual layers is nearly as large as that observed for olivines in a large suite of submarine basalts from the east rift zone of Kilauea Volcano (e.g. layer 1 in hole 842B; forsterite 90.8 to 79.4 vs. 90.3 to 77.8; Clague *et al.* in press). However, the range for the layers also is similar in magnitude to that observed for the long-lived, current eruption (1983 to present) of Kilauea (forsterite 88 to 73; Garcia *et al.*

Table 1. *Microprobe analyses of glass sands from ODP site 842*

SiO$_2$	TiO$_2$	Al$_2$O$_3$	FeO	MnO	MgO	CaO	Na$_2$O	K$_2$O	P$_2$O$_2$	Sum
842A – Layer 1										
51.00	1.87	12.30	10.42	0.17	11.74	9.14	2.07	0.31	0.16	99.18
50.77	2.29	12.82	10.70	0.17	9.46	10.38	2.41	0.45	0.25	99.70
51.75	1.97	14.47	9.68	0.19	7.65	11.29	2.27	0.29	0.13	99.69
53.74	1.83	13.94	9.40	0.16	7.43	10.50	2.36	0.25	0.12	99.73
51.95	2.32	13.99	10.12	0.18	7.23	11.14	2.25	0.34	0.19	99.71
52.85	2.10	14.15	9.90	0.15	7.01	10.93	2.26	0.31	0.13	99.79
51.70	2.36	14.10	10.07	0.21	6.53	11.19	2.32	0.38	0.20	99.06
842A – Disseminated Glass (D1)										
51.05	2.33	13.10	11.20	0.15	9.08	10.32	1.96	0.37	0.15	99.71
51.06	2.50	13.31	10.73	0.20	8.20	10.27	2.19	0.37	0.18	99.01
50.99	2.35	13.47	11.08	0.20	8.00	10.74	2.17	0.38	0.22	99.60
50.94	2.49	13.54	10.72	0.15	7.78	10.76	2.21	0.40	0.27	99.26
51.43	2.63	13.70	10.54	0.15	7.10	11.26	2.21	0.36	0.19	99.57
51.47	2.49	13.68	10.78	0.19	6.96	10.79	2.27	0.38	0.20	99.21
842A – Disseminated Glass (D2)										
49.82	2.16	12.35	11.64	0.16	11.05	10.10	2.00	0.33	0.18	99.85
50.17	2.18	12.67	11.45	0.16	10.06	10.26	2.00	0.34	0.20	99.49
50.33	2.22	12.87	11.14	0.15	9.38	10.47	2.09	0.34	0.19	99.18
50.52	2.24	13.06	11.52	0.16	8.97	10.87	2.05	0.35	0.18	99.92
50.95	2.37	13.33	10.75	0.16	8.19	11.08	2.10	0.39	0.21	99.53
50.62	2.51	13.50	11.28	0.18	7.54	11.32	2.16	0.38	0.22	99.71
842A – Layer 2										
51.71	2.10	13.65	10.98	0.14	8.15	10.42	2.20	0.26	0.16	99.77
53.07	2.44	13.51	10.06	0.14	8.08	10.50	1.76	0.16	0.18	99.90
52.41	2.01	13.95	10.48	0.16	7.08	10.67	2.20	0.25	0.16	99.37
52.86	2.06	14.43	9.92	0.17	6.81	10.30	2.36	0.31	0.19	99.41
53.01	2.15	13.90	10.80	0.17	6.55	10.90	2.20	0.31	0.14	100.13
52.39	2.51	13.82	11.07	0.20	6.39	10.86	2.39	0.35	0.22	100.20
842A – Layer 3										
52.77	1.93	13.82	10.45	0.18	7.55	10.08	2.40	0.35	0.24	99.77
53.57	1.99	14.01	9.73	0.15	7.24	10.35	2.28	0.30	0.20	99.82
52.13	2.46	13.71	10.76	0.17	7.06	11.17	2.08	0.34	0.25	100.13
53.80	1.79	14.05	10.25	0.17	7.05	10.22	2.39	0.32	0.18	100.22
52.05	2.14	13.93	10.95	0.14	6.89	10.52	2.28	0.34	0.22	99.46
52.63	2.45	13.50	10.67	0.15	6.38	10.27	2.39	0.44	0.24	99.12
842A – Layer 4										
52.15	2.33	13.85	10.42	0.18	7.67	10.57	2.19	0.32	0.21	99.89
53.35	2.20	14.07	9.33	0.16	7.43	10.33	2.40	0.36	0.21	99.84
52.02	2.42	14.28	10.04	0.17	7.05	10.46	2.44	0.38	0.23	99.49
54.54	1.70	14.65	8.85	0.19	7.00	9.39	2.78	0.24	0.18	99.52
50.97	2.57	14.17	10.53	0.17	6.77	10.85	2.44	0.45	0.18	99.10
54.87	1.84	14.33	8.60	0.14	6.36	9.49	2.73	0.40	0.23	98.99
842B – Layer 1										
50.59	2.20	13.30	10.97	0.19	9.26	10.55	2.20	0.40	0.19	99.85
51.40	2.28	13.85	10.62	0.20	7.86	10.97	2.22	0.37	0.21	99.98
51.37	2.17	14.38	9.86	0.16	7.61	11.27	2.31	0.49	0.18	99.80
50.60	2.67	14.27	9.92	0.20	7.10	11.34	2.36	0.48	0.23	99.17
53.29	2.21	14.18	9.53	0.21	6.73	10.56	2.40	0.35	0.20	99.66
52.66	2.26	14.51	9.79	0.20	6.65	10.62	2.46	0.37	0.22	99.74

1992). Thus, olivine composition is apparently not a useful discriminant for evaluating the time period represented by individual sand layers because Hawaiian shield lavas display a somewhat restricted range in major element composition, and single eruptive events can produce as much compositional variation in olivine as observed on a regional scale. The high forsterite content of some olivines from layer 1 in hole 842B supports the hypothesis that Hawaiian magmas are derived from high MgO parental magmas (e.g. >16 wt% MgO; Clague *et al.* 1995; Garcia *et al.* 1995)

Multiple analyses were made on the larger grains to determine if they are compositionally zoned. All are homogeneous (i.e. forsterite content varies by less than 1%). However, the original rims on these grains, where compositional zoning is most likely to have been present, were probably removed during transport.

Origin of the volcanic sand layers

The Pliocene to Pleistocene sand layers from site 842 have sharp basal contacts, graded bedding and several have a mixed assemblage of Pleistocene and Eocene radiolarians. Glasses within the layers are heterogeneous in composition, platy to blocky in shape, and have low vesicularity. These features are inconsistent with a pyroclastic origin, which has been suggested for other sand layers with similar features that were derived from the Hawaiian Islands (e.g. Edsall 1975; Rehm & Halbach 1982). These sand layers are better explained by erosion and sedimentation from turbidity currents. What was the source for the turbidity flows? Although there are several Cretaceous seamounts near site 842, the fresh nature of most of the glass frag-ments and the similarity of the glass compositions to Hawaiian lavas (Figs 4B and 4C) indicate that the source of the sands was the Hawaiian Islands. Thus, the turbidites travelled at least

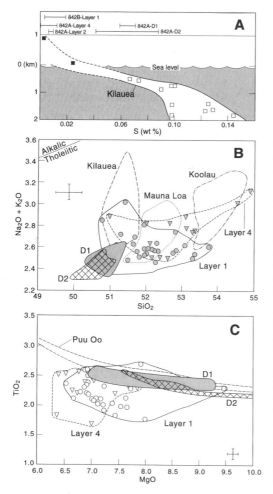

Fig. 4. (**A**) Sulphur content of some site 842 glasses. The brackets show the range of sulfur contents for 10 to 15 glass fragments per sample. The variation of S content in Kilauea volcanic glasses vs. depth (above and below sea level) is shown for comparison. The low S content of the glasses from the sand layers indicates that they were nearly degassed at the time of quenching. The disseminated sands have higher S contents indicating less degassing and possible shallow marine eruption. For comparison, data are shown for Kilauea subaerial-erupted samples (solid boxes) and submarine-erupted glasses (open boxes); data from Byers *et al.* (1985), Dixon *et al.* (1991), and D. Muenow (unpublished data). (**B**) SiO_2 vs. total alkalis ($Na_2O + K_2O$) diagram for glasses from two hole 842A sand layers and two disseminated sand horizons and several Hawaiian shield volcanoes (MgO > 6.35 wt%). Note the large range in SiO_2 for glasses from the sand layers compared to glasses from some well-studied Hawaiian volcanoes, and the even smaller fields for the glasses from the disseminated sand horizons. The field boundary for Hawaiian tholeiitic and alkalic lavas is from Macdonald & Katsura (1964). Data for Hawaiian glasses are from Garcia *et al.* (1989) for Kilauea and Mauna Loa; and unpublished data (Garcia) for Koolau. (**C**) MgO vs. TiO_2 variation diagram for site 842 glasses. The dashed field shows the lava compositions for the 11 year old Puu Oo eruption of Kilauea Volcano (data from Garcia *et al.* 1992). The data for ODP samples are from Garcia (1993) and this study. Note the wide range in TiO_2 content at a given MgO content for glasses from the sand layers compared to the Puu Oo lavas, which have experienced both magma mixing and crystal fractionation (Garcia *et al.* 1992). In contrast, the glasses from the disseminated sand horizons define narrow compositional ranges.

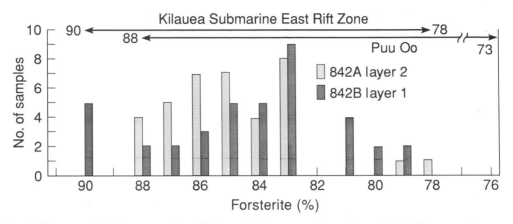

Fig. 5. Histogram of olivine compositions (% forsterite) in two sand layers from site 842. For comparison, the olivine compositions for lavas from the long-lived Puu Oo eruption of Kilauea Volcano (Garcia *et al.* 1992) and pillow lavas from the submarine portion of Kilauea's east rift zone (Clague *et al.* 1995) are shown.

240 km from the nearest island (Oahu) and up and over the gently sloping (<1°) Hawaiian Arch, which has about 500 m of relief near the drill site.

What was the nature of the turbidity flows? The presence of reworked Eocene radiolarians in the sand layers (Hull 1993) indicates that the turbidites may be related to major erosional events. The flanks of Hawaiian volcanoes have been the source for some of the largest landslides on Earth (Moore *et al.* 1989). These landslides provided the energy to drive debris avalanches that could have substantially eroded unconsolidated deep-sea Tertiary sediments near the islands. The minimum height of the turbidity flows that deposited the sandy layers at site 842 can be estimated using the maximum run-up elevation that the flow encountered, which is approximately 500 m. Since the height of the turbidity flow must be at least 65% of the bathymetric obstruction to be able to crest the feature (Muck & Underwood 1990), the turbidity flows that deposited the sand layers at site 842 must have been at least 325 m thick. Similar-sized or larger turbidity flows have been interpreted to have formed from landslides off the northeast flank of South America (Dolan *et al.* 1989). A cartoon illustrating a landslide model for producing the sand layers at site 842 is shown in Figure 6.

Several of the layers consist of multiple horizons of graded sediment (e.g. Fig. 3). These horizons may have been deposited in quick succession and be part of one catastrophic event. Allen (1991) used experimental data and theoretical arguments to suggest that full turbidite sequences (*c.* 27 cm thick) may be deposited in a few tens of minutes, assuming the sediment is quartz. The site 842 sand layers are thinner (1 to 11 cm) and generally contain few parallel laminations and no ripple structures (divisions B and C of the Bouma sequence). Thus, they contain only the lower part of a typical turbidite sequence (see Allen 1991) and could have been deposited quickly, except for the platy glass grains. In the case of layer 2 from hole 842A (Fig. 3), the basal layer was disrupted by a second turbidity current before deposition of parallel laminations. This second layer was disrupted by a third turbidity current. Thus, some of the landslides probably involved multiple but closely spaced turbidity currents that may have been derived from successive debris avalanches such as apparently occurred during the Alika slide off the west flank of Mauna Loa (Lipman *et al.* 1988).

The source of the early Miocene to late Oligocene volcanic sand layers is problematic because of their high level of alteration. They may have been derived from the nearby Cretaceous seamounts but their deposition would have been long after formation of these seamounts (>50 Ma) unlike the turbidites from the Hawaiian Ridge. Alternatively, these older turbidites may have been derived from the Hawaiian Ridge. During this time period, site 842 would have been located approximately 900 km south of its current position. Pleistocene sand layers up to 30 cm thick have been reported 930 km south of Hawaii but are interpreted to be airfall deposits from explosive eruptions of the island of Maui (Rehm & Halbach 1982). An alternative origin is presented in the final section of this paper.

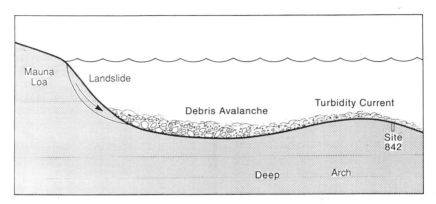

Fig. 6. Cartoon illustrating the proposed relationship of landslides on the flanks of Hawaiian volcanoes to debris avalanches and turbidity flows that might have deposited sand layers at site 842.

Origin of the disseminated sand zones

Are the zones of disseminated sand remnants of turbidites from debris avalanches that were disturbed by bioturbation? The sands in these zones are finer grained, have limited compositional variation (they could have been derived from a single eruption like the Puu Oo eruption; see Fig. 4C), and lack mixed assemblages of Pleistocene–Eocene radiolarian (Hull 1993). Thus, it is unlikely they were derived from the same type of catastrophic events that produced the sand layers. Instead, they are probably related to slope failure during or following a shallow submarine eruption such as the 1877 eruption of Mauna Loa (Moore *et al.* 1985).

Formation of the volcanic sand

The relative scarcity of vesicles in the site 842 glass grains precludes a pyroclastic cause for their origin (see Heiken & Wohletz 1985). The platy to blocky shape and low vesicularity of the site 842 glass grains are identical to glasses formed by hydroclastic eruptions (e.g. Fisher 1968; Batiza *et al.* 1984). However, the sulphur content of the glass in the sand layers is low, indicating that they were erupted near or above sea level (Fig. 4A). Large volumes of glass sand are produced during Hawaiian eruptions when lava enters the ocean for weeks to years as the volcano extends its coastline seaward (e.g. Moore *et al.* 1973). A preliminary examination of glasses formed as lava entered the ocean from the current Puu Oo eruption of Kilauea Volcano showed that they are moderately vesicular (K. Okano, pers. comm. 1993) unlike the site 842 glasses. However, these glasses were collected from beaches, which may sample only the

littoral component of this process. Granulation and thermal spallation in deeper water, especially on the steep submarine slopes of Hawaiian volcanoes, may produce less vesicular glasses. Such hydroclasts have been reported from lavas that have undergone internal explosions (e.g. implosions; Fisher 1984; Fisher & Smith 1991). More work is needed to characterize the glass fragments produced during eruption of lava into shallow water because they may constitute a significant component of the sediments around Hawaiian volcanoes.

The landslide model for the origin of the site 842 sand layers proves an additional mechanism for forming glass grains. During a landslide event, it is likely that glassy lavas are brecciated. The glassy margins of lava flows would have served as zones of weakness along which fragmentation could occur (see Fisher (1984) for a more complete description of this process).

Correlation of sand layers with specific Hawaiian landslides

The age and petrology of the sand layers can be used to correlate them with specific Hawaiian landslides. Only three Hawaiian landslides formed debris flows that are directed toward site 842 (Fig. 1). The youngest debris flow directed toward site 842 is the Alika Slide from Mauna Loa. It is thought to be *c.* 105 ka (Moore *et al.* 1989). The next youngest debris flow pointed towards site 842 is probably the Clark Slide from Lanai. The age of the slide is not known but subaerial lavas from the island have been dated by K–Ar at about 1.2 to 1.5 Ma (Bonhommet *et al.* 1977), which serves as a maximum age for the Clark Slide. The other major slide directed toward site 842 is from Kauai. The age of the South Kauai Slide is also unknown, but the age of shield-building volcanism on the island has been dated at about 3.9 to 5.8 Ma (McDougall 1979; Clague & Dalrymple 1988).

The sand layers in the cores that might correlate with these slides are layer 1 from hole 842A with Mauna Loa; layers 2, 3 and 4 from hole 842A with Lanai; and layers 1, 2 and 3 from hole 842B with Kauai. The palaeomagnetic ages for the sand layers are consistent with these

correlations (i.e. they are not older than the slides or volcanoes).

Comparison of glass compositions for the sand layers with glasses from these volcanoes is problematic for Lanai and Kauai, because there were no published glass data for either volcano prior to this study (although a few unpublished glass analyses are available for Lanai). A visit was made to Kauai to collect glass from dyke margins. Seventeen glassy dykes were sampled but only 13 yielded glass suitable for microprobe

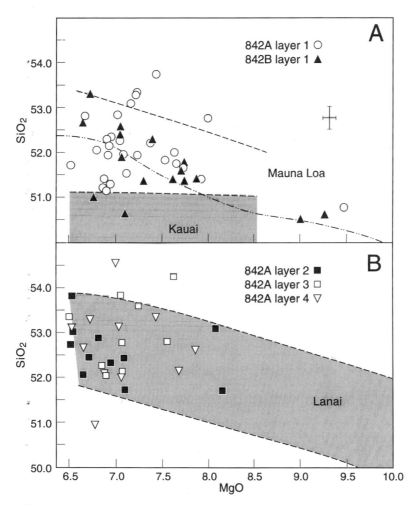

Fig. 7. Comparison of SiO$_2$ vs. MgO trends for glasses from individual site 842 sand layers with Hawaiian glasses (Mauna Loa and Lanai) and/or whole-rock (Lanai and Kauai) data (shown by dashed lines). Data sources: Mauna Loa (Garcia *et al.* 1989); Lanai (Garcia (unpublished) for glass; West *et al.* (1992) for whole rock); Kauai (Garcia (1993) for glasses; Macdonald & Katsura (1964) for whole rocks); ODP glasses (Garcia 1993). Two sigma error bar shown for reference. The larger range in glass composition for each of the sand layers compared to individual Hawaiian volcanoes indicates that each layer has sampled a larger portion of a volcano than represented by our data base for these volcanoes.

analysis. Seven of these glasses have MgO contents >6.4 wt% but all are <7.2 wt% (see Garcia (1993) for analyses). If glass compositions (and whole-rock compositions for Lanai and Kauai) are used to define the fields for individual Hawaiian volcanoes, there is general agreement between the composition of the sand layers and those of the correlated volcano (Fig. 7) except for Kauai, which has a small data base. The correlations with Lanai and Kauai lavas need to be checked against pillow rim glasses from those volcanoes, because they may be different than the younger glasses that were sampled from the subaerial portions of those volcanoes.

Importance of turbidity currents to Pacific deep-sea sedimentation

Mixed radiolarian assemblages (typically Eocene and Pleistocene) have been reported in cores taken around the Hawaiian Islands (e.g. DSDP sites 67 and 68; Winterer *et al.* 1971; Tracey *et al.* 1971). Early workers and many since have attributed the mixed assemblages to bottom currents from Antarctica (e.g. Reidel & Funnel 1964; Beiersdorf 1987). However, one early study noted that mixed assemblages were commonly associated with volcanic sand layers, which were interpreted as products of turbidity currents but assumed to be of only local significance (i.e. within the Hawaiian Arch; Schreiber 1969). Similar deposits were found 930 km south of the Hawaiian Islands in cores taken near the Clarion Fracture Zone (Rehm & Halbach 1982). The volcanic glass sand layers in these cores are up to 30 cm thick, tholeiitic in composition, and 1 to 2 Ma in age (Rehm & Halbach 1982). It was thought that the sands originated from the island of Maui but could not have been deposited from turbidity currents because a 400 m deep trough is located 20 km north of the coring sites, which was considered an insurmountable barrier for any turbidity current (Rehm & Halbach 1982). Instead, they proposed an aeolian origin for the sand layers. This explanation is dubious given the low to non-vesicular nature of the glass sand, the substantial thickness of the sandy layers (up to 30 cm thickness), the site's remoteness from the Hawaiian Islands, and its location at a right angle to the prevailing northeasterly trade winds from the Hawaiian Islands. These sands are probably products of turbidity currents associated with the catastrophic slope failures on the flanks of the Hawaiian Islands. Certainly the deposits are identical to those from site 842, and the 500 m high Hawaiian Arch was not a deterrent to the turbidity currents from the islands. If the sands from south of the Clarion Fracture Zone are from giant Hawaiian turbidity currents, then these currents travel vast distances (1000+ km), transporting debris far from their source and could disrupt sedimentation in the abyssal regions of the ocean floor. Similar far-travelled turbidites have been reported near Barbados and are interpreted to have been derived from the South American continental margin (Dolan *et al.* 1989). These giant turbidity currents provide an alternative mechanism for creating mixed radiolarian assemblages in deep-sea sediments.

Conclusions

The ODP site 842 core contains abundant volcanic sand as disseminated grains within pelagic sediment and as distinct layers. The sand layers were probably deposited by turbidity currents derived from debris flows that originated on the flanks of Hawaiian volcanoes. Palaeomagnetic, biostratigraphical and glass composition data are consistent with the sources of these sand layers being Mauna Loa, Lanai, and possibly Kauai volcanoes. The turbidity currents associated with these landslides may have travelled great distances (up to 1000 km) and travelled over significant bathymetric highs and lows. Thus, they may have been enormous in size and energy. Because theoretical modelling and small-scale experiments of turbidity currents have severe limitations for revealing the complex hydraulic phenomena associated with large-scale catastrophic events (Middleton 1993), it is essential that we examine sediment cores taken at various distances from an identifiable landslide source to understand the dynamics of turbidity currents generated by giant landslides. As Varnes (1975) said 'It is well to remember that the largest of all slope movements on Earth appear to have occurred on the bottom of the sea...'. Since Hawaiian volcanoes are some of the tallest features on the planet (up to 8.5 km of relief), we should expect them to generate some of the Earth's largest debris avalanches and turbidity currents.

I thank D. Hull and J. Resig for help on biostratigraphical questions, T. Hulsebosch for maintaining the U.H. microprobe in superb working order, K. Okano for access to her unpublished data on Puu Oo hydroclasts, Nancy Hulbirt for drafting the final figures for this paper and R. V. Fisher, W. Normark, M. Underwood and P. Lipman for their comments on an early version of this manuscript. This research was supported by NSF grant ODP-TamRF 20505. SOEST contribution No. 4011.

References

ALLEN, J. R. L. 1991. The Bouma division A and the possible duration of turbidity currents. *Journal of Sedimentary Petrology*, **61**, 291–295.

BATIZA, R., FORNARI, D. J., VANKO, D. A. & LONSDALE, P. 1984. Craters, calderas, and hyaloclastites on young Pacific seamounts. *Journal of Geophysical Research*, **89**, 8371–8390.

BEIERSDORF, H. 1987. Interpretation of seafloor relief and acoustic facies in the Clarion-Clipperton block southeast of Hawaii. *Geologisches Jahrbuch Reiche D*, **87**, 27–69.

BONHOMMET, N., BEESON, M. H. & DALRYMPLE, G. B. 1977. A contribution to the geochronology and petrology of the island of Lanai, Hawaii. *Geological Society of America Bulletin*, **88**, 1282–1286.

BORGIA, A. & TREVES, B. 1992. Volcanic plates overriding the oceanic crust: structure and dynamics of Hawaiian volcanoes. *In*: PARSON, L. H., MURTON, B. J. & BROWNING, P. (eds) *Ophiolites and their Modern Oceanic Analogues*. Geological Society of London Special Publication, **60**, 277–299.

BYERS, C. D., GARCIA, M. O. & MUENOW, D. W. 1985. Volatiles in pillow rim glasses from Loihi and Kilauea volcanoes, Hawaii. *Geochimica Cosmochimica Acta*, **49**, 1887–1896.

CLAGUE, D. A. & DALRYMPLE, G. B. 1988. Age and petrology of alkalic post-shield and rejuvenated-stage lava from Kauai, Hawaii. *Contributions to Mineralogy and Petrology*, **99**, 202–218.

——, MOORE, J. G., DIXON, J. E. & FRIESEN, W. B. 1995. The mineral chemistry and petrogenesis of submarine lavas from Kilauea's east rift zone. *Journal of Petrology*, **36**, 299–349.

——, WEBER, W. S. & DIXON, J. E. 1991. Picritic glasses from Hawaii. *Nature*, **353**, 553–556.

DIXON, J. E., CLAGUE, D. A. & STOLPER, E. M. 1991. Degassing history of water, sulfur, and carbon in submarine lavas from Kilauea volcano, Hawaii. *Journal of Geology*, **99**, 371–394.

DOLAN, J. F., BECK, C. & OGAWA, Y. 1989. Upslope deposition of extremely distal turbidites: an example from the Tiburon Rise, west-central Atlantic. *Geology*, **17**, 990–994.

EDSALL, D. G. 1975. *Submarine Geology of Volcanic Ash Deposits: Age, and Magmatic Composition of Hawaiian and Aleutian Tephra; Eocene to Recent*. PhD thesis, Columbia University.

FIRTH, J. V. & HULL, D. M. 1993. Ichthyolith biostratigraphy of deep-sea clays from the southwestern Hawaiian arch. *In*: DZIEWONSKI, A., WILKENS, R., FIRTH, J. & BENDER, J. *ET AL.* (eds) *Proceedings of the Ocean Drilling Program, Scientific Results*, **136**. College Station, Texas, 27–43.

FISHER, R. V. 1968. Puu Hou littoral cones, Hawaii. *Geologische Rundschau*, **57**, 837–864.

——1984. Submarine volcaniclastic rocks. *In*: KOKELAAR, B. P. & HOWELLS, M. F. (eds) *Marginal Basin Geology*. Geological Society, London, Special Publication, **16**, 5–27.

—— & SMITH, G. A. 1991. Volcanism, tectonics and sedimentation. *In*: FISHER, R. V. & SMITH, G. (eds) *Sedimentation in Volcanic Settings*. Society of Economic Paleontologists and Mineralogists Special Publication, **45**, 1–5.

FORNARI, D. J., GARCIA, M. O., TYCE, R. & GALLO, D. 1988. Morphology and structure of Loihi Seamount based on Seabeam sonar mapping. *Journal of Geophysical Research*, **93**, 15 227–15 238.

——, MALAHOFF, A. & HEEZEN, B. C. 1979. Submarine slope micromorphology and volcanic substructure of the island of Hawaii inferred from visual observations made from U.S. Navy deepsubmergence vehicle (DSV) 'Sea Cliff'. *Marine Geology*, **32**, 1–20.

FREY, F. A., WISE, W. S., GARCIA, M. O., WEST, H. B., KWON, S.-T. & KENNEDY, A. 1990. Evolution of Mauna Kea volcano, Hawaii: Petrologic and geochemical constraints on postshield volcanism. *Journal of Geophysical Resarch*, **95**, 1271–1300.

GARCIA, M. 1993. Plio-Pleistocene volcanic sand layers from site 842: Products of giant landslides. *In*: DZIEWONSKI, A., WILKENS, R., FIRTH, J. & BENDER, J. *ET AL.* (eds) *Proceedings of the Ocean Drilling Program, Science Results*, **136**. College Station, Texas, 53–63.

—— & HULL, D. M. 1994. Turbidites from giant Hawaiian landslides: results from Ocean Drilling Program Site 842. *Geology*, **22**, 159–162.

——, HULSEBOSCH, T. P., & RHODES, J. M. 1995. Glass and mineral chemistry of olivine-rich basalts, Southwest rift zone, Mauna Loa Volcano: implications for magmatic processes. *Mauna Loa Revealed*. Geophysical Monograph, American Geophysical Union, **92**, 219–239.

——, MUENOW, D. W., AGGREY, K. E. & O'NEIL, J. R. 1989. Major element, volatile, and stable isotope geochemistry of Hawaiian submarine tholeiitic glasses. *Journal of Geophysical Research*, **94**, 10 525–10 538.

——, RHODES, J. M., WOLFE, E. W., ULRICH, G. E. & HO, R. A. 1992. Petrology of lavas from Episodes 2–47 of the Puu Oo eruption of Kilauea volcano, Hawaii: Evaluation of magmatic processes. *Bulletin of Volcanology*, **55**, 1–12.

HEIKEN, G. & WOHLETZ, K. 1985. *Ash*. University of California Press, Berkeley.

HOLCOMB, R. T. & SEARLE, R. C. 1991. Large landslides from oceanic volcanoes. *Marine Geotechnology*, **10**, 19–32.

HULL, D. M. 1993. Quaternary, Eocene and Cretaceous radiolaria from the Hawaiian Arch, Northern Equatorial Pacific. *In*: DZIEWONSKI, A., WILKENS, R., FIRTH, J. & BENDER, J. *ET AL.* (eds) *Proceedings of the Ocean Drilling Program, Sci-entific Results*, **136**. College Station, Texas, 3–25.

JAROSEWICH, E., PARKES, A. S. & WIGGINS, L. B. 1979. Microprobe analyses of four natural glasses and one mineral: an interlaboratory study of precision and accuracy. *Smithsonian Contribution to Earth Sciences*, **22**, 53–67.

LENAT, J.-F., VINCENT, P. & BACHELAERY, P. 1989. The offshore continuation of an active basaltic volcano: Piton de la Fournaise. *Journal of Volcanology and Geothermal Research*, **36**, 1–36.

LIPMAN, P. W., NORMARK, W. R., MOORE, J. G., WILSON, J. B. & BUTMACHER, C. E. 1988. The giant submarine Alika debris slide, Mauna Loa, Hawaii. *Journal of Geophysical Research*, **93**, 4279–4299.

MACDONALD, G. A. & KATSURA, T. 1964. Chemical composition of Hawaiian lavas. *Journal of Petrology*, **5**, 82–133.

MCDOUGALL, I. 1979. Age of shield-building volcanism of Kauai and linear migration of volcanism in the Hawaiian island chain. *Earth and Planetary Science Letters*, **46**, 31–42.

——, BROWN, F. H., CERLING, T. E. & HILLHOUSE, J. W. 1992. A reappraisal of the geomagnetic polarity time scale to 4 Ma using data from the Turkana Basin, East Africa. *Geophysical Research Letters*, **19**, 2349–2352.

MIDDLETON, G. V. 1993. Sediment deposition from turbidity currents. *Annual Review of Earth and Planetary Sciences*, **21**, 89–114.

MOORE, J. G. 1987. Subsidence of the Hawaiian Ridge. *In*: DECKER, R., WRIGHT, T. & STAUFFER, P. (eds) *Volcanism in Hawaii*. United States Geological Survey Professional Paper, **1350**, 85–110.

—— & MARK, R. K. 1992. Morphology of the island of Hawaii. *Geological Society of America Today*, **2**, 257–259.

——, CLAGUE, D. A., HOLCOMB, R. T., LIPMAN, P. W., NORMARK, W. R. & TORRESAN, M. E. 1989. Prodigious submarine landslides on the Hawaiian ridge. *Journal of Geophysical Research*, **94**, 17465–17484.

——, FORNARI, D. J. & CLAGUE, D. A. 1985. The 1877 submarine eruption of Mauna Loa, Hawaii. *United States Geological Survey Bulletin*, **1663**, 1–11.

——, NORMARK, W. R. & HOLCOMB, R. T. 1994. Giant Hawaiian landslides. *Annual Review of Earth and Planetary Sciences*, **22**, 119–144.

——, PHILLIPS, R. L., GRIGGS, R. W., PETERSON, D. W. & SWANSON, D. A. 1973. Flow of lava into the sea, 1969–1971, Kilauea Volcano, Hawaii. *Geological Society of America Bulletin*, **84**, 537–546.

MUCK, M. T. & UNDERWOOD, M. B. 1990. Upslope flow of turbidity currents: a comparison among field observations, theory, and laboratory models. *Geology*, **18**, 54–57.

NAKA, J., TSUGARU, R., DANHARA, T., TANAKA, T. & FUJIOKA, K. 1993. Sedimentary processes of volcaniclastic sediments, Leg 136. *In*: DZIEWONSKI, A., WILKENS, R., FIRTH, J. & BENDER, J. *ET AL.* (eds) *Proceedings of the Ocean Drilling Program, Scientific Results*, **136**. College Station, Texas, 85–95.

PRESLEY, T. 1994. *Geology of the Southern Waianae Range, Oahu, Hawaii*. MS Thesis, University of Hawaii.

REES, B. A., DETRICK, R. S. & COAKLEY, B. J. 1993. Seismic stratigraphy of the Hawaiian flexural moat. *Geological Society of America Bulletin*, **105**, 189–205.

REHM, E. & HALBACH, P. 1982. Hawaiian-derived volcanic ash layers in equatorial northeastern Pacific sediments. *Marine Geology*, **50**, 25–40.

RIEDEL, W. R. & FUNNEL, B. M. 1964. Tertiary sediment cores and microfossils from the Pacific Ocean floor. *Jounal of the Geological Society, London*, **120**, 305–368.

SCHREIBER, B. C. 1969. New evidence concerning the age of the Hawaiian Ridge. *Geological Society of America Bulletin*, **80**, 2601–2604.

SHIPBOARD SCIENTIFIC PARTY, 1992. Site 842. *In*: DZIEWONSKI, A., WILKENS, R., FIRTH, J. *ET AL.* (eds) *Proceedings of the Ocean Drilling Program; Initial Reports*, **136**. College Station, Texas, 65–99.

SLEEP, N. H. 1990. Hotspots and mantle plumes: some phenomenology. *Journal of Geophysical Research*, **95**, 6715–6736.

TILLING, R. I. & DVORAK, J. J. 1993. Anatomy of a basaltic volcano. *Nature*, **363**, 125–133.

TRACEY, J. I. & SUTTON, G. H. *ET AL.* 1971. *Initial Reports of the Deep Sea Drilling Progam*, **8**. United States Government Printing Office, Washington, DC .

TRIBBLE, J. S, WILKINS, R., ARVIDSON, R. S. & BUSING, C., 1993. Sediments of the Hawaiian arch: x-ray mineralogy and microfabric. *In*: DZIEWONSKI, A., WILKENS, R., FIRTH, J. & BENDER, J. *ET AL.* (eds) *Proceedings of the Ocean Drilling Program, Scientific Results*, **136**. College Station, Texas, 65–76.

VARNES, D. J. 1975. Slope movements in the western United States. *In*: YATSU, E., WARD, A. J. & ADAMS, F. (eds) *Mass Wasting, 4th Guelph Symposium on Geomorphology*. 1–17.

WALKER, G. P. L. 1990. Geology and volcanology of the Hawaiian islands. *Pacific Science*, **44**, 315–347.

WEST, H. B., GARCIA, M. O., GERLACH, D. C. & ROMANO, J. 1992. Geochemistry of tholeiites from Lanai, Hawaii. *Contributions to Mineralogy and Petrology*, **112**, 520–542.

WINTERER, E. L. & RIEDEL, W. R. *ET AL.* 1971. *Initial Reports of the Deep Sea Drilling Program*, **7**. United States Government Printing Office, Washington.

WRIGHT, T. L. 1971. *Chemistry of Kilauea and Mauna Loa lava in space and time*. United States Geological Survey Professional Paper **735**. United States Government Printing Office, Washington, 1–39.

Recurrent landslides events on the submarine flank of Piton de la Fournaise volcano (Reunion Island)

PHILIPPE LABAZUY

Centre de Recherches Volcanologiques, Université Blaise Pascal, URA 10 CNRS,
5 rue Kessler, 63038 Clermont-Ferrand Cedex, France

Abstract: New studies confirm the existence of large landslide events related to both the Piton des Neiges and the Piton de la Fournaise volcanic systems. Like many other island basaltic shield volcanoes, Réunion Island has had a complex evolution combining construction processes and recurrent destructive events. Landslide deposits probably form an important part of its internal structure. Sliding events and related tsunamis are one of the major hazards of this kind of volcanic activity, in an intraplate oceanic context.

The submarine flank of Piton de la Fournaise has been extensively studied using Seabeam bathymetry and high resolution side-scan sonar images. The eastern submarine flank is entirely covered by 550 km^3 of landslide deposits, which are mainly subaerially erupted basaltic lavas, transported and fractured in large-scale mass wasting. Volumetric considerations imply recurrent partial destruction of the edifice, by landsliding, during its construction. For each sector collapse the fundamental process is the sliding of large blocks, up to several kilometres in length. Fractions of the slide blocks break up and evolve into debris avalanches.

Analogue experiments have been carried out to tentatively explain the geometry of these periodic large landslides of the unbuttressed flank. The morphology and the deformation in the landslides of the model are compared to the natural system of Piton de la Fournaise.

The witnessed failure of the northern flank of Mount St Helens on 18 May 1980 certainly led to a new understanding of the instability processes on volcanic edifices (Voight *et al.* 1981, 1983). Following this event, typical features of past flank landslides, in particular horseshoe-shaped craters and hummocky deposits of volcanic debris, have been most commonly recognized on many volcanoes (Siebert 1984). However, most large flank landslides have been recognized on andesitic stratovolcanoes. Among factors favouring flank failure are the steep slopes (exceeding 20–30°) and presence of pyroclastic material with weak cohesion (unconsolidated or hydrothermally altered pyroclastic deposits).

Until recently, flank landslides on basaltic shield volcanoes had received less attention. Probably due to their lower slope angles (5–12°) and more homogeneous internal structure, they were regarded as virtually stable edifices. However, recent systematic mapping of the Hawaiian Chain (Lipman *et al.* 1988; Moore *et al.* 1989) and around other oceanic islands (Holcomb 1990) has revealed the presence of numerous huge landslides on their flanks. Oceanic island landslides are the largest observed on Earth. Moore *et al.* (1989) have identified two general types of landslides on the flank of the Hawaii islands: slumps and debris avalanches. Similar huge landslides are present on the flanks of Reunion Island (Fig. 1). The eastern submarine flank of Piton de la Fournaise has been extensively studied during two cruises, using Seabeam bathymetry, gravity, magnetics, high resolution side-scan sonar images, bottom cameras, dredging and coring. Combined, these data shows that the submarine flank is almost entirely covered by landslide deposits. The aim of this paper is to report the main observations on the eastern flank of Piton de la Fournaise volcano and to propose a general model that involves recurrent landsliding. An associated paper by Ollier *et al.* (in press) is focused on the surficial sedimentary deposits and analyses the sedimentary processes leading to the transport and the deposition in a submarine fan of epiclastic material produced by a shield volcano.

Geological setting

Reunion island is elliptical in shape (50 km × 70 km) with a NW–SE elongation (Fig. 1). It rises above a nearly flat ocean floor at a depth of more than 4000 m. At the level of the surrounding sea floor, its basal dimensions are 200 km × 240 km. The island comprises of two volcanoes, Piton des Neiges, a dormant volcano that occupies the northwestern two-thirds of the island and Piton de la Fournaise, which began to erupt more than 500 ka ago (McDougall 1971; Gillot & Nativel 1989) and is one of the Earth s most active volcanoes.

The Enclos Fouqué structure (Fig. 2), located in the central part of Piton de la Fournaise, is

From McGuire, W. J., Jones, A. P. & Neuberg, J. (eds) 1996, *Volcano Instability on the Earth and Other Planets*, Geological Society Special Publication No. 110, pp. 295–306.

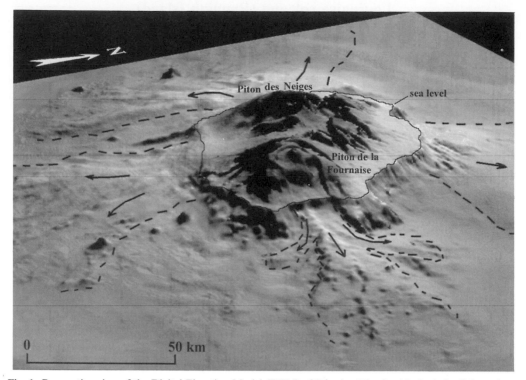

Fig. 1. Perspective view of the Digital Elevation Model (DEM) of Réunion Island, with shaded-relief overlay; looking from the SE. Three times vertical exaggeration. Piton de la Fournaise is in the foreground and Piton des Neiges in the background. The DEM is a compilation of several sets of data (see text). Dashed lines define the limits of inferred landslides on the submarine flanks of Réunion Island.

breached in the east, where it merges with the Grand Brûlé depression (Figs 1 and 2). The north and south boundaries of this depression are two subvertical 100–300 m high ramparts, limited to the west by a steeply dipping area extensively draped by recent lava flows, called the Grandes Pentes (Steep Slopes). While the Grand Brûlé trough is interpreted as a slide (Vincent & Kieffer 1978), the Grandes Pentes area is interpreted as a zone of headwall fault scarps. The flank is composed of several sequences of subaerial and submarine flows, as observed by drilling in the Grand Brûlé area (Rançon *et al.* 1989). The presence of subaerial flows down to 718 m below sea level should indicate large subsidence of the area. This downward movement can be alternatively explained by seaward sliding of the eastern flank of the volcano (Labazuy 1991).

Data

A digital terrain model has been created encompassing the subaerial and submarine

parts of the island. Offshore from the southern and eastern parts of the island the bathymetry is based on mulitbeam data. Nearshore bathymetry was completed with detailed 'conventional' bathymetric data, provided by the Service Hydrographique and Océanographique de la Marine, and the other parts of the study area from a general bathymetric map (Averous 1983). The 100 m contours of the resulting compilation were digitized and a grid of regularly spaced data was then calculated (square mesh of 250 m) for automatic contouring, graphic representations and volume calculations.

Sonar images were obtained with the deep-towed sonar SAR (Système Acoustique Remorqué) of IFREMER (Institut Français de Recherche pour l'Exploitation de la Mer). The SAR sonar generates sonographic images of 700 to 750 m on each side of the ship track and has a nominal resolution of 0.30 m. The sonar profiles (a total of 950 km) were digitally mosaicked to produce a map of the area under investigation. Profiles of 3.5 kHz were simultaneously recorded with the SAR system and provide useful microbathymetric information.

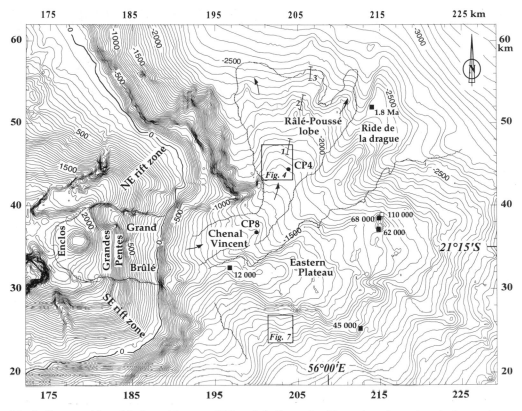

Fig. 2. Topographic and bathymetric map of Piton de la Fournaise. Names have been given to the most prominent features of the undersea domain. Available dates of dredged samples are given: black squares (K/Ar method; P.-Y. Gillot, pers. comm. 1989) and open squares (U/Th method; C. Deniel, pers. comm. 1989). The dashed lines show the limits of the submarine landslide deposits (Râlé-Poussé lobe and eastern Plateau; see Fig. 3 for detailed interpretation). The shiptracks corresponding to the three profiles of Fig. 5 are shown by numbered solid lines, in the Râlé-Poussé area. Bottom cameras sites (CP) are shown by black circles.

K/Ar datings (P.-Y. Gillot, pers. comm. 1989) and U/Th datings (C. Deniel, pers. comm. 1989) were obtained on some dredged samples, almost located on the surface of the Eastern Plateau (Fig. 2).

Summary of the main submarine observations

The main submarine topographic features were described by Lénat *et al.* (1989, 1990) based on bathymetric, magnetic and gravity data (Rousset *et al.* 1987), from the first cruise 'Fournaise 1'. Although these earlier data indicated that most of the surveyed submarine area records extensive mass wasting, the most crucial data were obtained from high resolution sonar images, bottom pictures and samples collected during the second cruise 'Fournaise 2'. Except the nearshore part of the rift zones and a remnant

flank portion of an older inferred volcano (Labazuy 1991; J.-F. Lénat, pers. comm. 1995), called 'Ride de la Drague' (Fig. 2), virtually all the dredged and cored material of the seafloor has been identified as subaerial lavas, lava breccias and sediments. Dated samples from the eastern landslide deposits exhibit ages from a few ka up to 110 ka (Fig. 2). Although these few dates may be far from representative, their location on the Eastern Plateau suggest a relationship between the rock age and the distance from the seashore (see below).

Following the study of Moore *et al.* (1989), the data indicate that two general types of landslide can be identified: debris avalanches and slumps.

Debris avalanche deposits

The fan-shaped Râlé-Poussé area (Lénat *et al.* 1989) corresponds to a downslope-widening lobe of avalanche material, that was emplaced on the northern part of the flank, downward from the Chenal Vincent depression (Figs 2 and 3). The Chenal Vincent valley is the submarine counterpart of the subaerial Grand Brûlé trough. Another debris avalanche deposit has been emplaced in the southern valley, called Pente Citrons Galets (Figs 2 and 3). These two submarine valleys follow the northern and the southern edges of the Eastern Plateau and influenced the sliding and the flowing of the debris avalanches.

The Ralé-Poussé lobe corresponds to the bulk of the main depositional area and is largely made up of decametric to hectometric blocks over a surface area of about $200 \, km^2$ (Fig. 4). Debris avalanche deposits have an average thickness of about 100 m and a total volume of about $30 \, km^3$, for both Ralé-Poussé and Chenal Vincent areas. The characteristic hummocky topography of the lobe is common to many debris avalanches (Glicken 1982), and has been described from both subaerial equivalents (Voight *et al.* 1981; Ui 1983; Siebert 1984; Ui

et al. 1986; Francis & Wells 1988), and submarine environments (Lipman *et al.* 1988; Von Huene *et al.* 1989).

The lobe records the superposition of several avalanches. Three distinct stacked units were recognized on side-scan sonar images and on 3.5 kHz profiles (Figs 4 and 5), suggesting the existence of several landslides. They are respectively called unit I (the oldest), unit II and unit III (the youngest). Criteria for recognition on the sonar images and on 3.5 kHz profiles are the characteristic hummocky morphology, the average sizes of the hummocks and the steep fronts of each deposits. The 3.5 kHz records shows the abrupt upslope limits of the three units, with 40 to 100 m high walls (Fig. 5). Average block heights and sizes decrease from unit I (from 100 to more than 500 m in diameter) to unit III (from 10 to 50 m in diameter). The distribution of the hummocks is also more homogeneous within unit III. The volume of each debris avalanche unit has been estimated using a Digital Elevation Model (DEM): $15 \, km^3$ for unit I $10 \, km^3$ for unit II and $6 \, km^3$ for unit III. H/L ratios of the debris

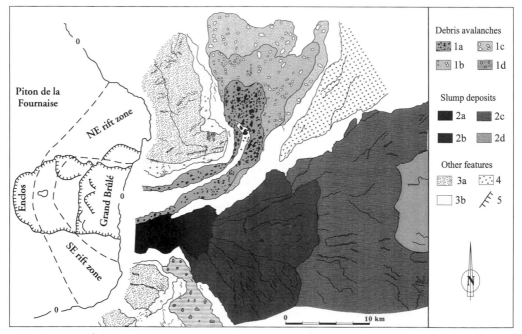

Fig. 3. Map showing the main features of the off-shore part of Piton de la Fournaise, based on acoustic data. Slide complex: (1) Debris avalanches deposits. (1a, 1b, 1c) Superposition of three successive events (respectively U III, U II, U I), identified as debris avalanches, within the Râlé-Poussé lobe; (1d) southern debris avalanche deposit. (2) Submarine Plateau of the eastern flank (slump deposits). (2a) Coherent block in proximal zone; (2b) blocks in median zone of the Plateau, disturbed by numerous fractures; (2c) disorganized set of blocks in distal zone showing a chaotic surface; (2d) terminal front of the Plateau, described as highly chaotic formations. Other features: (3) Volcanic rift zones. (3a) Undisturbed formations, could be affected by intense channeling on the flanks; (3b) Rock fall accumulations, at the base of the structures. (4) Ride de la Drague: older unit, partially recovered by the formations described above; formation more or less disturbed, possibly in situ. (5) Faults and scarps.

55°55.3'   55°58'
                                                                    —21°08'

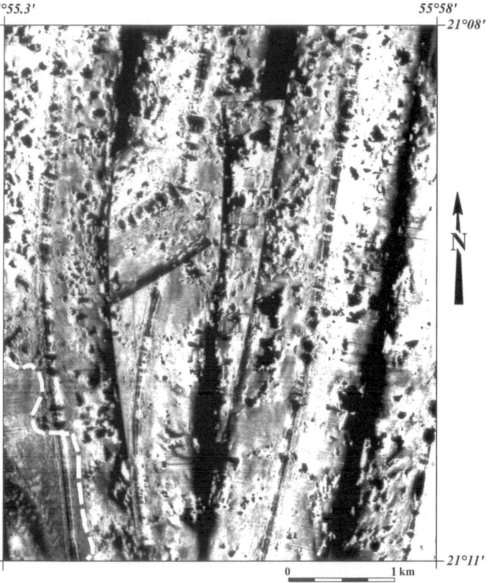

N

0   1 km

Fig. 4. Mosaic sample of acoustic images offshore Piton de la Fournaise, in the Râlé-Poussé area. The swaths are about 1200 m wide. Light shades designate regions of greater acoustic backscatter. Dark areas behind blocks are acoustic shadows. The displayed area corresponds to a portion of a debris avalanche, with blocks (several tens of meters wide and high) protruding from the matrix. Location shown in Fig. 2.

avalanches of the Râlé-Poussé (Ui 1983), equivalent to the apparent coefficient of friction defined by Hsü (1975), range from 0.10 to 0.11, which are classical values for the range of debris avalanche deposit volumes observed (Ui *et al.* 1986; Siebert *et al.* 1987).

Two different morphological features are found within the youngest phase. In the proximal zone, within the Chenal Vincent depression, the deposit is characterized by two marginal levees, marking the lateral limit of the event, separated by a depression about 3.5 km wide (Fig. 3). The levees are very narrow and promi-nent, between 700 and 1200 m waterdepth, before widening out to form less well defined structures. Similar levees are described for Phase 2 of the Alika

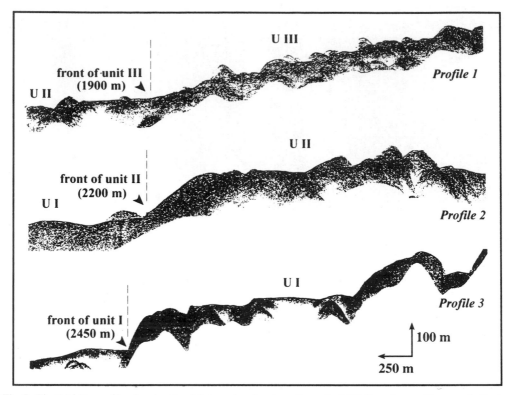

Fig. 5. The 3.5 kHz profiles showing the debris avalanches deposits on the Râlé-Poussé area. The records display a typical hummocky surface and the abrupt front of each unit, between 40 to 120 m high. Note the decreasing hummock heights from U I to U III. The location of each record is shown in Fig. 2.

slide complex, within a channel 40 km in length and 10 km wide (Moore & Normark 1990). Photographs from station CP8 (Fig. 6a, see location on Fig. 2), from one of the marginal levees show rounded outcrops of breccia facies made up of massive decimetric blocks embedded within a finer matrix. The transition to the second morphological facies, in the Râlé-Poussé area, at 1700 m waterdepth, is marked by the disappearance of the marginal levees and of the central depression (Fig. 3), filled up by a proximal sedimentary delta (Ollier *et al.* in press). These morphological variations are the direct result of the changes in flow dynamics during the outflow of the deposits. They correspond to the slope changes at the base of the nearshore wall (from 16° between 0 and 700 m waterdepth to 6° below 700 m and about 3° below 1500 m) and to the 90° turn of the debris avalanche in a northern direction, downward from the Chenal Vincent depression (Figs 2 and 3). These two factors imply a significant decrease of the energy and velocity of the flow during the transit of the debris avalanche, therefore inducing the deposition of the main

bulk of products in the Râlé-Poussé area, over the two older avalanche deposits.

Below 1700 m, the lateral extension of the upper debris avalanche deposit increases (from 1 km wide to 5 km over a distance of 4 km). The surface of Phase III presents a field of decametric hummocks (10 to 30 m high, and up to 100 m in diameter), homogeneously distributed over the entire area covered by the deposits (Fig. 4). Their distribution, in average one block for a square of 250 m in width, does not indicate preferential block accumulation or segregation. Bottom photographs (Fig. 6b, site CP4) show that the debris avalanche surface has disjointed blocks, with blunt angles, incorporated in a fine beige matrix.

The Eastern Plateau

The Eastern Plateau forms the most prominent structure in the studied area (Fig. 2). The Plateau formations are characterized by their high and fine texture on the sonar images, related to the roughness of their surface (Fig. 7). The main

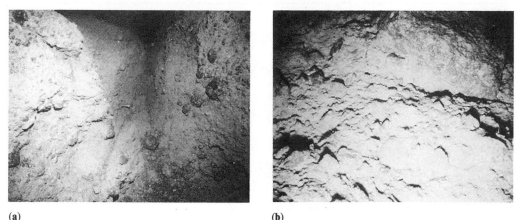

(a)   (b)

Fig. 6. Photographs from the surface of debris avalanche deposits (location shown in Fig. 2). (**a**) CP8 site (Chenal Vincent depression): typical hummocky morphology showing rounded outcrops of breccia facies. The deposit is made up of decimetric blocks sealed within a matrix. Photocoverage: about 5×7 m. (**b**) CP4 site (zone of Râlé-Poussé), showing blocks which are caught in a matrix composed of fine particles. The block in the background is about 50 cm wide.

bulge has a triangular shape and occupies the central part of the studied area. It is a few kilometres wide in the proximal zone, widening downslope to over 60 km, at a depth of 3000 m (Figs 2 and 3). Its volume is about 500 km³, for an estimated maximum thickness of 850 m in the central part.

Dredged samples and bottom photgraphs taken on the Eastern Plateau show that virtually all the material sampled on its surface consists of subaerially erupted, fragmented lavas, down to 2500 m waterdepth and up to 30 km from the seashore. Dredged or cored subaerial basalt fragments have a chemical composition similar to that of the subaerial basalts studied on Piton de la Fournaise volcano (P. Boivin, pers. comm. 1989).

The triangular-shaped bulk is cut by three families of more or less sinuous faults and scarps. One set has a general S–N orientation, whereas the two others are trending respectively, at about 040° in the northern half of the Plateau and about 130° in its southern half (Fig. 7). In fact, there is more or less a continuum between the last two families, forming a fan of faults and scarps open toward the east (Fig. 3). The existence of several distinct blocks is confirmed by the analysis of the sonar data and of the 3.5 kHz profiles. The blocks which are distinguished on Figs 3 and 8 are thought to result from a succession of slumps. The accretion of the blocks has formed the Plateau, and the boundaries of the blocks are marked by faults or scarps up to 150 m high (Figs 3 and 8; Labazuy 1991). In this scheme, the age of the blocks

increases from the west to the east. This hypothesis is in agreement with (1) the distribution of the available datings and (2) the observed structures of the blocks.

Indeed, although there are only a limited number of dredged samples dated on the Plateau, there is a clear increase in ages, from less than 10 ka in the proximal block to about 110 ka in the distal part. The evolution of the structure of the blocks, from west to east, is also conspicuous. The blocks become progressively more fragmented or chaotic eastward. The front of the Plateau (at the east) exhibits a blend of scarps and chaotic terrains which is inferred to mark a zone of compression (Fig. 8).

The interpretation of this body is the following:

– the recognized blocks derived from a succession of block-slumps (at least three main episodes);
– the blocks have collided and accreted to form the Plateau;
– the oldest blocks have been increasingly fragmented;
– the front of the Plateau is characterized by thrusts corresponding to the displacement of the blocks over their basement;
– those processes have been acting since at least 110 ka.

Small-scale model experiments

Experiments have been carried out on small-scale models to study some of the landslide processes on the flanks of shield volcanoes in the

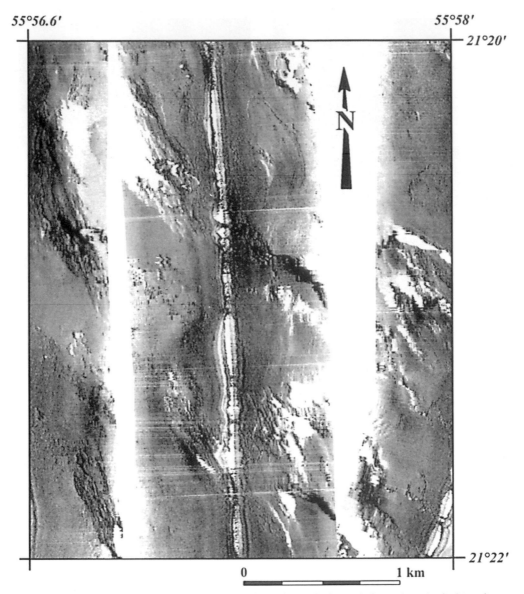

Fig. 7. Sample of the sonar mosaic, on the Plateau's formations. The image is focused on the faults and scarps system found in the southern part of the Plateau, trending about 130°. The scars appear as dark areas. The location of the image is shown in Fig. 2.

presence of a superficial glide surface (Fig. 9). The models and the scaling of the experiments were mainly tailored to the characteristics of Piton de la Fournaise, revealed by the submarine studies. The morphology and the deformation of the slides in the models are studied and compared to the natural system of Piton de la Fournaise. However, the results can probably be extended beyond the case of Piton de la Fournaise, to analogue gravitational instabilities on similar volcanoes.

All the models in our experiments are composed of a cone resting on a plane. The cone is buttressed on its west side to mimic the morphological pattern of Piton de la Fournaise buttressed on the rest of the island. The plane may be horizontal or tilted toward the east. The bulk of the cone is made of dry sand which has a

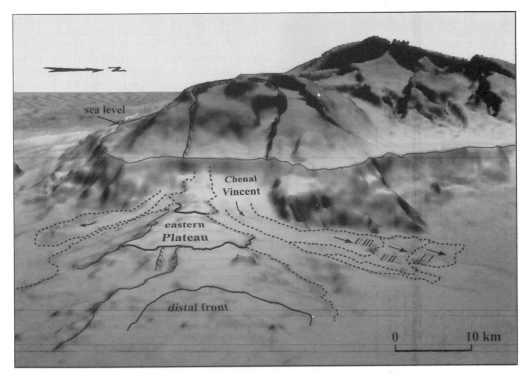

Fig. 8. Three-dimensional representation of the DEM of Piton de la Fournaise, with shaded-relief overlay, showing the main structural features of the eastern flank. Vertical exaggeration: 3. The view is toward the west. The limits of the landslide deposits are shown by dashed lines. The three units are distinguished within the Râlé-Poussé lobe. The three main blocks and the distal front of the eastern Plateau are delimited by thick black lines. They correspond to the S–N set of faults. Some obvious scarps are also shown by thin black lines.

brittle behaviour. A layer of viscous silicone (ductile behaviour) is interbedded within a sector of the cone to simulate the inferred glide plane (Fig. 9). The plane that surrounds the propagation of the displacement outside of the cone (discussions of the scaling problems in small-scale models using sand and silicone can be found in Ramberg (1981), for example).

In these types of models, the cone will spontaneously slide over the interbedded silicone layer. To simulate the recurrence of sliding events, the flank of the cone was repeatedly reloaded with sand of different colours. At the end of the experiments, the structures of the slides were studied both in plan-view, for the surface features, and in sections, for the internal distribution of the material and of the fault geometry.

Some general results can be derived from the experiments (Fig. 10):

– The fault systems that developed within the lobate slide, at the base of the cone, are transverse faults coupled to the glide planes. They are oblique to the main extensional direction.

– These transverse faults generated the apparition of horsts (slide blocks) and graben, forming a major blocky structure, as observed in natural systems.

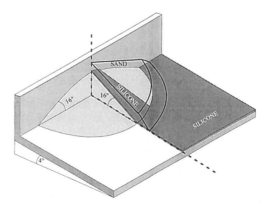

Fig. 9. Experimental apparatus used for simulating superficial landslides on the flanks of volcanoes.

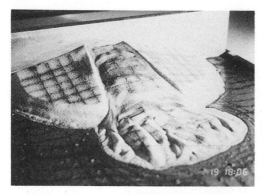

Fig. 10. Oblique view of a small-scale experiment, at the final state of deformation. The reference grid drawn on the surface has a square mesh of 2 cm. One can observe the obvious morphological similarities with the DEM of Piton de la Fournaise (Fig. 8). At the base of the horseshoe-shaped crater, the lobate deposits exhibit host and graben structures resulting from the generation of transverse faults during the sliding processes. They form a fan of faults open toward the front. The front of the lobe corresponds clearly to a compressive zone, between the slumped blocks and the basal silicone layer.

– The front of the slide deposits corresponds to a well-marked compressive zone, at the contact with the basement.

One can note the obvious similarities between the morphologies of the small-scale models and the natural system (Figs 8 and 10). In addition, the comparison between the fault pattern of the natural system and of the experimental one (Figs 3 and 10) strongly support the hypothesis of slides over a superficial plane (1–2 km in depth) at Piton de la Fournaise.

Discussion

The existence of slide deposits on the submarine part of Piton de la Fournaise volcano had already been proposed by Lénat *et al.* (1989, 1990). However, the key result of the present study, based on a more complete data set, is that almost all the material involved in the landslides is composed of subaerially erupted basaltic lavas. Thus, the giant landslide complex observed on the eastern submarine flank of Piton de la Fournaise has to be linked with episodes of destruction of large parts of the subaerial edifice.

The existence of a succession of slides is based on several arguments. The first one stems from volume considerations. The use of a DEM allows several types of calculations. On the one

hand, the volume of the submarine bulge may be estimated to be 550 km3 (difference between the actual topography and that of a regular submarine slope based on submarine topography outside of the bulge). On the other hand, the volume of the present edifice depression (i.e. the Grand-Brûlé graben and the Enclos) is nearly one order of magnitude less (about 60 to 80 km^3). It is therefore evident that the whole of the slide material cannot originate from the present scars of the edifice, even if we admit that it has been partially filled by the eruption products. Recurrent cycles of construction by volcanic activity and destruction by sector collapses have to be taken into account. For reference, one can recall that 550 km^3 would represent the total magma production of Piton de la Fournaise in about 50 ka, if we refer to the data from Lénat & Bachèlery (1988) based on historic records. Since only part of the edifice is destroyed by the eastward slides, the succession of slide events must span a longer period of time. The work by Bachèlery & Mairine (1990) provides some elements to try to appraise the history of the landslides at Piton de la Fournaise. They propose that a major flank collapse occurred 150 ka ago and was accompanied by the displacement of the active centre towards the east and therefore to its present location. Two other volcano-tectonic events have been recognized at about 60 ka and 4.2 ka (Bachèlery & Mairine 1990). The first corresponds to the collapse of the Plaine des Sables rim whilst the younger is responsible for the formation of the Enclos depression and of the Grand Brûlé trough. Although they had been previously associated with caldera formations (Chevallier & Bachèlery 1981), their interpretation as flank landslides has to be considered seriously in the light of the study on the submarine flank (this latter interpretation being favoured by the author). There would thus be three major inferred landslide events during the last 150 ka. If the succession of landslides was restricted to the last 150 ka, then about one-third of the edifice constructed during this period would have been destroyed by flank collapse.

From the interpretation of the submarine data, it seems reasonable to propose that both the younger debris avalanche unit of the Râlé-Poussé and the coherent block of the proximal zone of the Eastern Plateau result from the 4.2 ka flank collapse. Similarly, the older debris avalanches and the other blocks of the Plateau could be associated with two others volcano-tectonic events at about 150 ka and 60 ka.

Those recurrent sector collapses can be understood if the presence of a gliding-plane is assumed. We think that the geological section from the deep Grand-Brûlé drill-hole provides proof of the existence of such a zone, between 200 m and 700 m below the sea level (Rançon et al. 1989; Labazuy 1991). The results of the small-scale model experiments carried out show that the morphological and tectonic relationships observed on the eastern flank of Piton de la Fournaise are well explained by slides over a rather superficial sliding plane. Therefore, in this case, the landslides appear to be intra-edifice processes and not deep seated ones (contact between the edifice and the sediments of the oceanic floor) as has been proposed for other sites (Borgia et al. 1990).

The present study demonstrates the importance of cyclic landslide processes in the evolution of the volcano. The eastern flank comprises a giant landslide complex, involving both slow slumping and more rapid events (debris avalanches). The spatial association of huge fractured slumped blocks and debris avalanche deposits has been described from the Hawaiian volcanoes (Moore et al. 1989), and seems to be characteristic of landslides occurring on the flanks of oceanic island volcanoes.

Questions remain concerning the amplitude and the nature of the driving forces responsible for huge slope failures during the evolution of basaltic volcanoes. It seems that stress changes related to magma chamber inflation and associated intrusions have the capability to generate or trigger flank instabilities (Elsworth & Voight 1995). In this context, summit inflation due to the emplacement of intrusions could play a major role in the gravitational instability of the eastern flank of Piton de la Fournaise. According to the deformation observations over a period of about 15 years, it appears that the dyke intrusions during volcanic crises can give rise to an asymmetric inflation of the central zone of several tens of metres per century (Lénat & Bachèlery 1990), thus increasing slopes on the east flank. In addition, the edifice of Piton de la Fournaise also grows by the accumulation of volcanic products (lava flows mostly) which accumulate preferentially on the eastern flank for topographic reasons. Thus the east flank will tend to acquire steeper slopes and hence be more rapidly loaded than the other areas. We think that the mechanical stresses induced by these phenomena are periodically relaxed by the displacement of the eastern flank and associated seismicity, as observed on the southern flank of Kilauea volcano (Swanson et al. 1976; Lipman et al. 1985). Large landslides are thus periodically triggered (Labazuy & Lénat 1990; Lénat & Labazuy 1990; Lipman 1990). These processes are continuous over a long period of time and, therefore, new landslides can be anticipated in the future. Because they represent one of the major hazards from volcanic activity in an intraplate oceanic context, it comes as a challenge to understand better these phenomena by studying past events as well as by long-term monitoring of the seaward flanks.

The author is indebted to D. G. Masson and an anonymous reviewer for their valuable comments which have substantially improved the manuscript. Many thanks also must go to J.-F. Lénat and M. Davies for their extensive reviews of this paper and all their helpful suggestions.

References

AVEROUS, P. 1983. *Esquisse Géomorphologique des Atterages de l'Île de la Réunion.* Document Terres Australes et Antarctiques Françaises.

BACHÈLERY, P. & MAIRINE, P. 1990. Evolution volcano-structurale du Piton de la Fournaise depuis 053 M.a. *In*: LÉNAT, J.-F.(ed) *Le Volcanisme de La Réunion.* Monographie, Centre de Recherches Volcanologiques, Clermont-Fd, 213–242.

BORGIA, A., BURR, J., MONTERO, W., MORALES, L. D. & ALVARADO, G. E. 1990. Fault propagation folds induced by gravitational failure and slumping of the Central Costa Rica volcanic range: implication for large terrestrial and martian volcanic edifices. *Journal of Geophysical Research*, **95B9**, 14 357–14 382.

CHEVALLIER, L. & BACHÈLERY, P. 1981. Evolution structurale du volcan actif du Piton de la Fournaise,Ile de la Réunion. Océan Indien occidental. *Bulletin Volcanologique*, **44–4**, 723–741.

ELSWORTH, D. & VOIGHT, B. 1995. Dike intrusion as a trigger for large earthquakes and the failure of volcano flanks. *Journal of Geophysical Research*, **100 B4**, 6005–6024.

FRANCIS, P. W. & WELLS, G. L. 1988. Landsat Thematic Mapper of debris avalanche deposits in the Central Andes. *Bulletin of Volcanology*, **50**, 258–278.

GILLOT, P. Y. & NATIVEL, P. 1989. Eruptive history of Piton de la Fournaise volcano, Reunion island, Indian Ocean. *Journal of Volcanological and Geothermal Research*, **36**, 53–65.

GLICKEN, H. 1982. *Criteria for Recognition of Large Volcanic Debris Avalanches.* EOS, **6345**, 1141.

HOLCOMB, R. T. 1990. Effects of giant landslides on the growth and degradation of oceanic shield volcanoes (abstract). *Intraplate Volcanism. The Reunion Hot Spot.* Conference Proceedings. Université de la Réunion, France.

HSÜ, K. J. 1975. Catastrophic debris streams (Sturzstroms) generated by rockfalls. *Geological Society of America Bulletin*, **86**, 129–140.

LABAZUY, P. 1991. *Instabilités au cours de l'évolution d'un édifice volcanique, en domaine intraplaque océanique: Le Piton de la Fournaise (Ile de La Réunion)*. Thèse d'Université, Université Blaise Pascal, Clermont-Fd.

—— & LÉNAT, J.-F. 1990. Recurrent landslides on the east flank of Piton de la Fournaise volcano, Reunion (abstract). *AGU meeting, EOS*, **7143**, 1577.

LÉNAT, J.-F. & BACHÈLERY, P. 1988. Dynamics of magma transfers at Piton de la Fournaise volcano (Réunion Island, Indian Ocean). *Earth Evolution Science*. Special issue *Modeling of Volcanic Processes*, 57–72.

—— & —— 1990. Structure et fonctionnement de la zone centrale du Piton de la Fournaise. *In*: LÉNAT, J.-F.(ed.) *Le Volcanisme de La Réunion. Monographie*. Centre de Recherches Volcanologiques, Clermont-Fd, 257–296.

—— & LABAZUY, P. 1990. Morphologies et structures de La Réunion. *In*: LÉNAT, J.-F.(ed.) *Le Volcanisme de La Réunion. Monographie*. Centre de Re-cherches Volcanologiques, Clermont-Fd, 43–74.

——, ——, BONNEVILLE, A., GALDÉANO, A., LABAZUY, P., ROUSSET, D. & VINCENT, P. 1990. Structure and morphology of the submarine flank of an active basaltic volcano: Piton de la Fournaise (Réunion Island, Indian Ocean). *Oceanologica Acta*, **10**, 211–223.

——, VINCENT, P. M. & BACHÈLERY, P. 1989. The off-shore continuation of an active basaltic volcano: Piton de la Fournaise (Réunion Island, Indian Ocean): structural and geomorphological interpretation from seabeam mapping. *Journal of Volcanological and Geothermal Research*, **36**, 1–36.

LIPMAN, P. W. 1990. Structural evolution of Mauna Loa Volcano, Hawaii: Interactions between growing rift zones and submarine landslides, and comparisons with Piton de la Fournaise (Ile de la Réunion) (abstract). *Intraplate volcanism. The Reunion Hot Spot*. Conference Proceedings. Université de la Réunion, France.

——, LOCKWOOD, J. P., OKAMURA, R. T., SWANSON, D. A. & YAMASHITA, K. M. 1985. *Ground Deformation Associated with the 1975 Magnitude 7.2 Earthquake and Resulting Changes in Activity of Kilauea Volcano*, US Geological Survey Professional Paper, **1276**.

——, NORMARK, W. R., MOORE, J. G., WILSON, J. B. & GUTMACHER, C. E. 1988. The giant submarine Alika debris slide, Mauna Loa, Hawaii. *Journal of Geophysical Research*, **93 B5**, 4279–4299.

MCDOUGALL, I. 1971. The geochronology and evolution of the young volcanic island of Reunion (Indian Ocean). *Geochemical and Cosmochimical Acta*, **35–3**, 261–288.

MOORE, J. G. & NORMARK, W. R. 1990. Giant submarine landslides on Mauna Loa volcano, Hawaii, displayed by multibeam bathymetry (abstract). *Intraplate Volcanism. The Reunion Hot Spot*. Conference Proceedings. Université de la Réunion, France.

——, CLAGUE, D. A., HOLCOMB, R. T., LIPMAN, P. W., NORMARK, W. R. & TORRESAN, M. E. 1989. Prodigious submarine landslides on the Hawaiian Ridge. Journal of Geophysical Research, **94 B12**, 17465–17484.

OLLIER, G., COCHONAT, P., LÉNAT, J.-F. & LABAZUY, P. (in press). Deep-sea volcaniclastic sedimentary systems : example of La Fournaise volcano, Reunion Island, Indian Ocean. *Sedimentology*, in press.

RAMBERG, H. 1981. Gravity, Deformation and the Earth's Crust (2nd edition). Academic Press, London.

RANÇON, J.-P., LEREBOUR, P. & AUGE, T. 1989. The Grand Brûlé exploration drilling: new data on the deep framework of the Piton de la Fournaise Volcano (Reunion Island). Part 1 : Lithostratigraphic units and volcanostructural implications. *Journal of Volcanological and Geothermal Research*, **36**, 113–117.

ROUSSET, D., BONNEVILLE, A. & LÉNAT, J.-F. 1987. Detailed gravity study of the off-shore structure of Piton de la Fournaise volcano, Reunion Island. *Bulletin of Volcanology*, **49**, 713–722.

SIEBERT, L. 1984. Large volcanic debris avalanches: characteristics of source areas, deposits, and associated eruptions. *Journal of Volcanological and Geothermal Research*, **22**, 163–197.

——, GLICKEN, H. & UI, T. 1987. Volcanic hazards from Bezymianny- and Bandai-type eruptions. *Bulletin of Volcanology*, **49**, 435–459.

SWANSON, D. A., DUFFIELD, W. S. & FISKE, R. S. 1976. *Displacement of the South Flank of Kilauea Volcano: the Result of Forceful Intrusion of Magma into the Rift Zones*. US Geological Survey Professional Paper, **963**.

UI, T. 1983. Volcanic dry avalanche deposits-identification and comparison with non volcanic debris stream deposits. *Journal of Volcanological and Geothermal Research*, **18**, 135–150.

——, YAMAMOTO, H. & SUZUKI-KAMATA, K. 1986. Characterization of debris avalanche deposits in Japan. *Journal of Volcanological and Geothermal Research*, **29**, 231–243.

VINCENT, P. M. & KIEFFER, G. 1978. Hypothèse sur la structure et l'évolution du Piton de la Fournaise (Ile de la réunion) après les éruptions de 1977. *6ème Réunion Annuelle des Sciences de la Terre*, Orsay (Soc. Géol. France Ed.), 407.

VOIGHT, B., GLICKEN, H., JANDA, R. J. & DOUGLASS, P. M. 1981. *Catastrophic Rock-slide Avalanche of May 18*. US Geological Survey Professional Paper, 1250, 347–378.

——, JANDA, R. J., GLICKEN, H. & DOUGLASS, P. M. 1983. Nature and mechanics of the Mount St Helens rockslide-avalanche of 18 May 1980. *Géotechnique*, **3**, 243–273.

VON HUENE, R., BOURGEOIS, J., MILLER, J. & PAUTOT, G. 1989. A large tsunamogenic landslide and debris flow along the Peru Trench. *Journal of Geophysical Research*, **94 B2**, 1703–1714.

Calderas on Mars: characteristics, structure, and associated flank deformation

L. S. CRUMPLER, JAMES W. HEAD & JAYNE C. AUBELE

Department of Geological Sciences, Brown University, Providence, RI 02912, USA

Abstract: Calderas and flank structures of martian volcanoes yield insight into general questions of volcano structural evolution and the underlying magma chambers in an environment where erosion is minimal. We have documented, through detailed geological mapping, the structures, associated volcanological features, and the stratigraphical relationships between the flank structures and caldera events during the building of each martian edifice. Two fundamentally different types of calderas are identified on Mars (the Olympus type and the Arsia type) that may represent end member variations in the size and depth of magma chambers.

Many of the flank structures adjacent to caldera rims are consistent with the predicted effects of magma chamber inflation as well as deflation that exert significant influences in the structural development of many volcanoes. Large-scale terracing and steepening of the upper flanks of the larger martian volcanoes may originate from magma chamber inflation and radial thrusting. Thus the endogenous component of volcano growth resulting from accumulated magma chamber growth may be significant.

Many of the deepest calderas are associated with evidence for voluminous eruptions elsewhere on the flanks and along through-going fissures and appear to result largely from evacuation and deflation of magma chambers without extensive precursor inflation. Draining of the magma chamber in these cases may be aided by the lateral propagation of magma in the form of shallow dykes up to several hundred kilometres in length and the associated formation of linear fissures. Nested caldera sequences, related flank pits, large-scale slumping, terracing, and sector structure are frequently arranged in linear patterns and are part of through-going eruptive lines or fissures several hundred kilometres in length that characterize several martian shield volcanoes. Fissures this long are interpreted to be dykes propagated outward from shallow magma chambers that have followed a minimum regional stress orientation. Comparison of the observed shape and orientation of caldera structures with orientation and style of flank deformation, and with the predictions from theory, indicate that regional stresses have probably been an important influence on the caldera and flank structures of martian volcanoes. The minimum regional stress orientation may be controlled largely by regional slopes associated with the Tharsis region and Elysium regions, and, in the case of Tyrrhena Patera, pre-existing radial fractures associated with the Hellas basin.

The flank characteristics of many volcanoes are linked closely with caldera formation due to the large magnitude of the stresses generally associated with caldera development. In order to understand the significance of observed volcano flank structures, it is therefore important to assess the structure and strain history of calderas and their underlying magma chambers. This is especially true for large caldera-volcanic edifice systems such as those on Mars. The excellent preservation of surface faults and related fissures on martian volcanoes offers insight into the poorly understood caldera-formation process in a setting where erosion is minimal and provides a record of the stress field at the surface throughout the development of the underlying magma chambers. By comparing the observed characteristics of faulting with predictions of the ambient stresses from differ-

ent formation models using martian examples, the relative merits of different models for the formation of calderas may be assessed. This paper describes the basic observations that relate to the determination of the stress field(s) associated with calderas and the flanks of each of the known martian volcanoes during its evolution.

The general geological characteristics of the major volcanic edifices and calderas have been previously described in connection with individual studies of volcanoes on Mars (e.g. Hodges & Moore 1994; Plescia 1994; Crown & Greeley 1990, 1993; Mouginis-Mark & Robinson 1992; Mouginis-Mark *et al.* 1990; Crown *et al.* 1987; Mouginis-Mark 1981; Wood 1979; Crumpler & Aubele 1978; Malin 1977), as have some of the morphometric characteristics (Wood 1979; Pike 1978). In this study we first provide an overview

From McGuire, W. J., Jones, A. P. & Neuberg, J. (eds) 1996, *Volcano Instability on the Earth and Other Planets*, Geological Society Special Publication No. 110, pp. 307–348.

of the structural characteristics of all calderas and edifice flanks on Mars and then examine some of the general conclusions that may be drawn from the resulting comparisons.

Several types of structural depressions have been identified on other planets, but the summit depressions on martian volcanoes are consistent with the definition of calderas as 'large volcanic depressions, more or less circular or cirque-like in form, the diameters of which are many times greater than those of the included vent or vents, no matter what the steepness of the walls or form of the floor' (Wood 1984; Williams & McBirney 1968; Williams 1941). The morphology of calderas is characterized by varying degrees of complexity. The consensus of usage defines overlapping calderas as two or more adjacent calderas that form serially such that the geometric centre of the subsequent caldera(s) lies outside the circumference of the earlier caldera(s). Nested calderas are those in which the geometric centre of later collapse calderas lies within the circumference of an earlier caldera; nested calderas may also be concentric. In addition, several fundamental types of caldera are identified and include collapse, explosion and erosional. These are divided on the basis of differing depth to width ratios, rim or wall steepness, nature of the responsible eruption, degree of modification, and structure of the subsided interior and margins. Williams & McBirney (1979) identified two fundamental types of collapse caldera formation on the basis of whether the collapse was accompanied by voluminous eruptions of ash and pumice or effusive lava flows. In either case, the content of a subsurface reservoir is partially erupted to the surface. Although it is useful to identify the differences in explosivity as they relate to characteristic petrologic associations, the primary characteristics of shape, depth, and catastrophic formation (Simkin & Howard 1970) all seem to be similar among calderas of different sizes regardless of magmatic composition or eruption style.

Unresolved questions concerning caldera formation

The exact mechanism leading to collapse in caldera formation has been a volcanologic controversy for more than 100 years (McBirney 1990). Volume changes associated with magma movement are the general origin of surface subsidence in caldera formation, but disagreement has arisen over whether the evacuation of the magma causes caldera collapse or whether caldera collapse initiates magma eruption. The relative roles of eruption versus lateral dyke propagation are also poorly understood. In all cases, it is the dynamic history of the subsurface volume beneath the caldera that is responsible for the surface deformation. Based on the record of geological events preceding and post-dating collapse at historic calderas on Earth, three fundamental types of magma chamber or subsurface behaviour have been proposed as initiators of caldera collapse: (1) magma chamber deflation (Williams & McBirney 1968); (2) magma chamber inflation (McBirney 1990; Gudmundsson 1988; Cullen *et al.* 1987); and (3) intrusive loading (Walker 1988).

The primary difficulty in determining which mechanism is responsible for individual calderas results from the inability to resolve the relative contributions on the overall strain history of inflation versus deflation. Part of the difficulty arises from the lack of information on the initial state of deformation prior to the collapse event or knowledge of the precise sequence of eruptive events before and during collapse. Thus it is a problem of the dynamics of caldera formation. Over the past century evidence has accumulated for the importance of caldera collapse as an initiator of eruptions, rather than a consequence of eruptions (McBirney 1990). In contrast to the obvious inference that collapse is caused by evacuation of an underlying magma chamber, in many calderas it can be demonstrated that the evacuation is a response to the initial collapse (McCall 1963) and that the volume of magma erupted or laterally intruded is less than the collapsed volume. The volume that subsides is accommodated by means other than eruption of the magma chamber contents onto the surface around the caldera. One solution is that caldera collapse may reflect magma chamber growth in these cases (Gudmundsson 1988), rather than magma chamber evacuation, in which the overlying elastic crust is upwardly expanded until the tensile failure limit is reached. Consideration of the stress field predicted in association with a shallow disc or lens-shaped magma chamber shows that the radial and circumferential stresses are greatest above the margins of the magma chamber rather than its centre and that caldera ring fracture formation is likely to occur with a diameter that is directly related to the size of the underlying chamber. More important, Gudmundsson (1988) showed that the initiation of this type of faulting occurs only for certain shallow depths of the chamber with respect to its diameter (width to depth ratio greater than or equal to 2.5). This model explains the apparent concentration of caldera boundary faults, formation of steep-sided margins, and relatively coherent and unde-formed form of the caldera floors. If the magma chamber is spherical rather than sill or lens-shaped, then the inflation results in a surface tensile stress that is at a maximum directly over the centre of the magma chamber and faulting patterns are typically predicted to be less coherent, radial, or 'polygonal'. There-fore, many calderas with well-defined caldera walls, but relatively coherent floors and interiors that have subsided as piston-like plugs, appear to be best explained by expansion of shallow and relatively thin but large-diameter magma chambers.

In many calderas, the evacuation or depres-surization of the magma chamber can be shown to be responsible for the current surface deformation (Williams & McBirney 1968). This model appears to apply particularly for smaller calderas such as Kilauea (Ryan *et al.* 1983) where it can be demonstrated that the magma chamber is relatively spherical and where lateral evacuation of magma takes place to form eruptions at sites removed from the area of subsidence. The efficacy of this mechanism has been shown with simple experiments (Komuro 1987), and its validity is the basis for the models of caldera formation that assume magma evacuation to be the cause of subsidence. More recently, finite element models predict that the deflation of a magma chamber beneath the calderas of Olympus Mons can explain most of the surface deformation in that caldera (Zuber & Mouginis-Mark 1992). As the deflationary models predict relatively high compressive stresses at the surface over the centre of the deflated magma chamber, contractional struc-tures (thrust faults and mare-type wrinkle ridges) are predicted to occur on the floor of the subsiding block as is observed in many cases. The inverse of the analytical model used by Gudmundsson (1988), a contraction in a shal-low, tabular or sill-like magma chamber, also predicts that the caldera interior will be char-acterized by structures related to compression.

An additional complication in interpreting the strain history results from the observation that both inflation and deflation may be re-sponsible for structures seen in a single caldera. Thus the inflation and deflation history of the magma chamber may be important. In a series of experiments Marti *et al.* (1994) found that when tumescence occurs prior to deflation of the magma chamber, uplift of the region immediately overlying and surrounding the chamber is accommodated along a series of concentric inward-dipping reverse faults and radial network of irregular fractures closer to the centre of the tumescence. The reverse faults are subsequently converted to normal faults during collapse associated with later deflation of the magma chamber; and the region inside these faults tends to subside in a flat funnel shape. In contrast, deflation of a magma chamber without prior tumescence results in a steep-walled depression in which the floor subsides coherently to form a flat floor.

Summit subsidence of large shield volcanoes need not reflect inflation or deflation cycles of a shallow magma chamber alone. As postulated by Walker (1988), gravitational loading of the interior due to dense intrusions is a viable mechanism for certain types of broad summit subsidence. This mechanism for subsidence has not been adequately modelled as yet, although it can explain many of the internal structural characteristics of the Hawaiian shield volcanoes as a whole. Because the dynamics of intrusive loading are similar to those of models of magma chamber deflation, in the sense that a negative pressure is exerted at the surface, it is likely that this mechanism would result in compressive stresses in a zone overlying the subsiding interior and would thus bear many of the characteristics of the deflated magma chamber model. How-ever, the compressive stresses might be expected to be somewhat more broadly distributed because the subsiding intrusions may lie con-siderably deeper than active magma chambers (Walker 1988).

There are notably fewer large calderas on Earth as compared with those on Mars (Pike 1978) and Venus (Head *et al.* 1992). One reason for this difference may be that large caldera-like depressions of a scale similar to those on Mars and Venus may be present on Earth but are as yet poorly recognized or studied. In addition to calderas, large magmatic centres on Venus, consisting primarily of complex circular pat-terns of ridges and grooves and called corona (plural, coronae) and arachnoids may represent a class of feature obliterated on Earth by erosion. Some of the circular structural patterns surrounding volcanic centres on Mars have been previously compared to coronae on Venus (Watters *et al.* 1993; Barlow & Zimbelman 1988). The similarity of calderas to coronae and arachnoids may be understood from the perspective that all three of these features represent patterns of surface deformation asso-ciated with subsurface volume changes, and are broadly circular to ovoid in shape. Certain large subsidences associated with large eruptions may produce broad and bowl-shaped sags with relatively minor, but large-scale, apparent fracturing and faulting of the surface. These include the 'downsag' calderas of Walker (1984). Even larger structures of potentially related nature occur in association with major volcanic provinces (Erlich 1989; Heiken 1976), all of which may be less easily identified due to the combination of their great size, low relief, obscuration by erosion, and complex interaction with regional stress patterns and corresponding tectonic structure. Or it may be a partial consequence of the relatively mobile plate tectonic style on Earth wherein large volcanic centres and corresponding large subsurface intrusive magma bodies are unable to grow due to the lateral instability of the lithosphere with respect to sublithospheric sources. An additional factor is the relation of planetary environmental conditions in the formation and evolution of volcanoes (Head 1996). On the Moon, there are no large calderas because of the lack of shallow reservoirs due to the great depth of neutral buoyancy zones at the base of the crust (Head & Wilson 1992, 1993). On Venus, the style and distribution of edifices and calderas is related to variations in atmospheric pressure as a function of altitude, and to the depth of shallow magma reservoirs (Grosfils & Head 1994; Head & Wilson 1992). On Mars, low atmospheric pressure enhances gas exsolution and thus favours low density substrate and abundant shallow reservoirs (Wilson & Head 1994).

Geology and structure of the calderas and flanks of martian volcanoes

Calderas are associated with all of the major volcanic centres on Mars and are consequently widely, but unevenly, distributed on the surface (Fig. 1) and throughout the planet's geological history. Although there is a great range in morphology and dimensions of calderas on Mars, there are three common themes in the geology of the larger calderas: (1) apparent long-lived development; (2) structural complexity; and (3) extreme changes in style of deformation throughout their development. Tables 1 and 2 list some summary characteristics of martian calderas drawn from previous reports (Crumpler *et al.* 1990, 1994; Hodges & Moore 1994; Plescia 1994; Crown & Greeley 1993; Mouginis-Mark & Robinson 1992; Zimbelman & Edgett 1992; Zuber & Mouginis-Mark 1992; Greeley & Crown 1990; Robinson 1990; Watters & Chadwick 1990; Thomas *et al.* 1989; Crumpler & Aubele 1978, 1989; Wood 1984; Francis & Wadge 1983; Schaber, 1982; Mouginis-Mark 1981; Malin 1977; Carr *et al.* 1977) and from the results of our mapping in this study. The dimensions of calderas refer to the topographic rims outlining the region of negative relief. Structural rims, the fault margins along which most of the subsidence has occurred, are generally somewhat smaller than

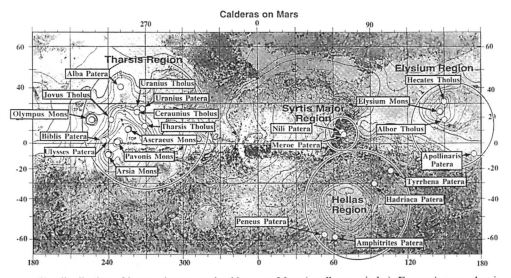

Fig. 1. The distribution of large volcanoes and calderas on Mars (small open circles). Four primary volcanic regions are recognized: the Tharsis region, Elysium region, Hellas region and Syrtis Major region (large, open circles). Mercator projection on shaded relief base; 1 km contour intervals relative to planetary datum (mean 6 mb level).

Table 1. *General characteristics and dimensions of calderas on Mars*

Caldera	Latitude	Longitude	Diameter (km)	Depth (km)	Volcano diameter (km)	Elastic lithosphere sphere thickness (km)	Image numbers	General reference
Alba Patera	40.6	110	55 (120)(12)	0.15	2700; 1200	25 – 50	MTM40107 & 40112; 253S1	Catermole (1989)
Albor Tholus	18.6	209.8	35 (8)	–	130	–	846A21	Malin (1977)
Amphitrites Patera	−59	299	145 (75)	–	–	–	361S01,02; 94A75	Greeley & Spudis (1978)
Apollinaris Patera	−8.6	185.7	86	0.8	180 × 280	–	635A57; 372S56	Robinson et al. (1993)
Arsia Mons	−9.5	121.2	115	0.6	390; 700	25 – 50	090A03–08; 641A83,85	Crumpler & Aubele (1978)
Ascraeus Mons	11.1	104.2	45 × 33 (24)(20)(18)	2.5	435; 123 × 700	40 ± 15	892A11,32; 401B14–24; 90A50	Crumpler & Aubele (1978)
Biblis Patera	2.3	123.8	52	3	86	–	044B48,50	Plescia (1994)
Ceraunius Tholus	24.1	97	24	1	90.00 × 130	–	516A22,24	Robinson et al. (1993)
Elysium Mons	24.5	213.3	14	1	196; 415	50 ± 10	541A46; 106A85,86; DAS13496083	Malin (1977)
Hadriaca Patera	−30.5	267	77	–	300 × 500	–	410S02,04	Crown & Greeley (1993)
Hecates Tholus	31.5	210	8.5 (8)(4.5)(4.5)	0.47	188	–	651A19; 625A16,17,18	Mouginis-Mark et al. (1982)
Jovus Tholus	18.5	117.5	26	2	54	–	041B17,19	Plescia (1994)
Meroe Patera	7.2	291.5	40	0.5	–	>100	375S32; 496A48	Schaber (1982)
Nili Patera	9.3	293	70	0.5	–	>100	375S13; 496A48	Schaber (1982)
Olympus Mons	18.3	133.2	64 (50)(35)(24)(22)	1.7–3.3 (2.5)	800	>150	890A68; 641A52	Mouginis-Mark & Robinson (1992)
Pavonis Mons	1.1	112.6	80 (50)	5	380; 460	30 ± 10	643A25,27,54; 210A33	Crumpler & Aubele (1978)
Peneus patera	−58	307.5	100	–	–	–	361S02; 578B01	Wood (1984)
Tharsis Tholus	13.5	90.9	30 × 50	2.4	120 × 150	–	858A23	Robinson & Rowland (1994)
Tyrrhena Patera	−21.3	253.5	45	0.5–1.0	160	–	445A53–56; 480A48	Greeley & Crown (1990)
Ulysses Patera	2.8	121.4	55	2.3	100	–	049B85; 461A32	Plescia (1994)
Uranius Patera	26.5	92.8	100	2.2	230 × 275	–	516A21,22,24; 857A43	Plescia (1994)
Uranius Tholus	26.4	97.2	21	0.2	60	–	516A23	Plescia (1994)

Caldera and volcano diameter measured for this study or from other sources. Caldera diameters in parentheses are the small caldera in caldera complexes. Caldera depths from various sources: Hodges & Moore (1994), Robinson (1990), Bibring et al. (1990), Wu et al. (1984), Mouginis-Mark (1981). Estimated elastic lithosphere from Comer et al. (1985).

Table 2. *Comparison of the principal observed geological characteristics of martian calderas*

	Caldera topographic margins well-defined	Terraced caldera margins	Furrowed caldera margins	Nested sequence of calderas	Over-lapping sequence of calderas	Circum-ferential fracture patterns	Circum-ferential ridge patterns	Radial fracture/ridge patterns
Alba Patera	×			×	×	×		×
Albor Tholus	×				×	×		
Amphitrites Patera							×	×
Apollinaris Patera	×	×		×	×	×		
Arsia Mons	×					×		×
Ascraeus Mons	×	×	×	×	×	×		
Biblis Patera	×	×				×		
Ceraunius Tholus	×		×		×			×
Elysium Mons	×					×		×
Hadriaca Patera						×	×	×
Hecates Patera	×	×		×	×	×		
Jovus Tholus	×			×	×			
Meroe Patera								
Nili Patera								
Olympus Mons	×	×	×	×	×	×		×
Pavonis Mons	×		×		×	×		×
Peneus Patera								
Tharsis Tholus	×	×	×	×	×			
Tyrrhena Patera					×			
Ulysses Patera	×		×					
Uranius Patera	×			×	×	×		
Uranius Tholus								

	Linear fissue eruptions	Arcuate fissue eruptions	Parasitic cones	Radial flank patterns	Fan-shaped flank patterns	Flank pits/rilles	Flank terraces	Sector structure
Alba Patera						×		
Albor Tholus						×		
Amphitrites Patera				×				
Apollinaris Patera					×			×
Arsia Mons	×	×		×	×	×	×	(×)
Ascraeus Mons	×	×			×	×	×	(×)
Biblis Patera						×		
Ceraunius Tholus				×	×	×		×
Elysium Mons						×		
Hadriaca Patera				×	×	×		(×)
Hecates Patera								
Jovus Tholus								
Meroe Patera								
Nili Patera								
Olympus Mons						×	×	
Pavonis Mons	×	×	×	×	×	×	×	(×)
Peneus Patera								
Tharsis Tholus								×
Tyrrhena Patera								
Ulysses Patera				×				
Uranius Patera		×	×			×		
Uranius Tholus								

Note: Parentheses indicate transitional morphology present.

the topographic rims, particularly where pronounced terracing is evident. However, in a few cases, particularly those calderas that are relatively shallow as compared with their diameters and where the caldera walls are relatively simple and unterraced, the structural and topographic rims coincide. Although the primary purpose here is to document the structural characteristics of calderas, many adjacent flank structures are revealing as regards the state of stress at the time of caldera formation and for this reason we include discussions of potentially relevant structures on the flanks. For a few volcanoes, the descriptions in this paper will be reviews of previous work, with some additional new observations and interpretations; others have not been studied in detail prior to this paper.

Some specialized nomenclature exists for Mars that should be clarified. Most of the calderas occur on volcanic edifices with noticeable relief, and the names used here for the calderas are those of the host volcano, as is common practice on Earth. A few of the highland volcanoes are so low in relief that the caldera is more pronounced than the topographic volcano on which it occurs, as, for example, is the case for ash-flow calderas on Earth. Although there is no strict correlation, in general, a low volcano with a large summit caldera on Mars is referred to as a 'patera' (plural 'paterae'). The formal definition of patera accepted by the International Astronomical Union is 'a large, flat-floored depression with irregular margins', a reference mainly to the caldera of Alba Patera, the type example; and Greeley et al. (1978) classified paterae into four types based on morphology. But the term, as currently used, is applied to volcanoes of very low relief with large calderas regardless of the circularity of the caldera. Volcanoes of large basal diameter, characterized by gentle lower flanks and steeper upper flanks, and interpreted to be shield-type volcanoes, are called 'mons' (plural 'montes'). Volcanoes with a more domical (convex upward) form are referred to as 'tholus' (plural 'tholi'). The steeper slopes of tholi may be a function of more viscous lava, lower eruption rates, or higher pyroclast content; however, some of the tholi may simply be the upper flanks of large buried shield volcanoes (Cattermole 1989). With regard to stratigraphical terminology, martian stratigraphy is divided into three time-stratigraphical systems: Noachian (oldest), Hesperian, and Amazonian (youngest) which are correlated with specific impact crater abundances (Tanaka et al. 1988; Neukum & Hiller 1981). Most of the volcanism on Mars responsible for identifiable central volcanoes and calderas is confined to the Hesperian and Amazonian.

We have individually processed the images shown from raw image data to enhance detail through contrast stretch, reseau mark removal, and blending of mosaicking contrasts. These Viking images together with selected Mariner 9 B-frames were then used for preparing structural maps of each of the calderas, combining our results where possible with the results of previous maps or discussions. Following standard photogeological practice, structural characteristics on martian volcanoes are identified on the basis of their surface morphological expression, examples of which are illustrated in Fig. 2. Some structural characteristics contribute to distinctive surface characteristics over broad areas and are thus mappable as distinct geological units. Thus many of the maps are a combination of both structural and geological units.

For the purposes of organization we have divided the discussion of caldera occurrences into several physiographic provinces corresponding generally to accepted divisions in the location, age, and style of martian central volcanism: Tharsis, Elysium, Hellas, and Syrtis. There are other possible divisions according to age or morphology (Hodges & Moore 1994), but this arrangement suffices for the purposes here and no particular inference is implied by the divisions chosen.

Tharsis region

The youngest volcanism (Tanaka et al. 1988; Scott & Tanaka 1986; Hiller et al. 1982; Neukum & Hiller 1981; Plescia & Saunders 1979) and largest volcanic centres identified on Mars occur within the Tharsis region. Of the 22 individual volcanoes that are identified on Mars, 12 occur in the Tharsis region. The complete spectrum of morphologies of calderas seen on Mars also occurs in this group as well as some more unusual characteristics not seen elsewhere. The combination of great size and morphologically fresher appearance makes the Tharsis volcanoes of particular interest in understanding the complexity of caldera formation processes.

Olympus Mons. The relatively young age and great size of the summit caldera of Olympus Mons (Fig. 3) makes it particularly useful as a source of information about several elements of

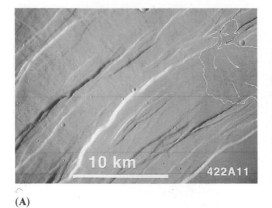

(A)

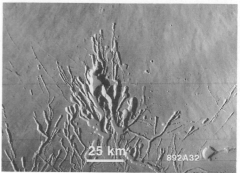

(B)

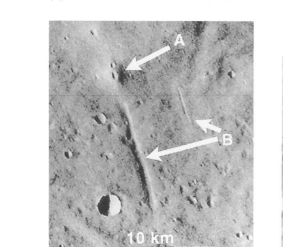

(C)

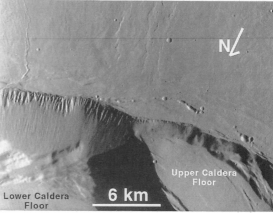

(D)

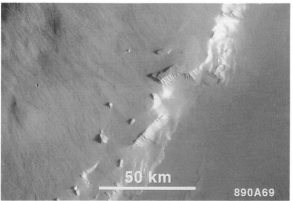

(E)

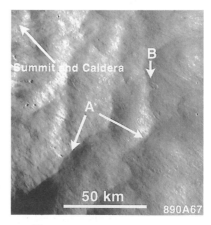

(F)

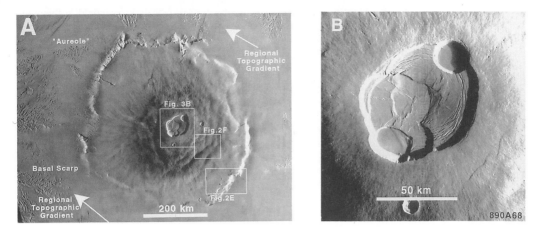

Fig. 3. The summit caldera complex of Olympus Mons. Several smaller calderas are nested, the largest of which is characterized by complex circumferential graben and interior wrinkle ridges. Deformation of the caldera floor appears to have occurred subsequent to all but the smaller and latest two calderas in the sequence and may represent late subsidence of the caldera region above the primary magma chamber. The overall shape of the complex is elongate in a northeast–southwest orientation as is the short scarp on the summit immediately to the southeast. Viking Orbiter image 890A68.

the structural style, sequence of formation, and overall geometry associated with simple calderas on Mars. Few impact craters disturb the myriad digitate lava flows radiating from the summit and the flanks because Olympus Mons is among the youngest surfaces (late Amazonian) on Mars (Hiller *et al.* 1982; Plescia & Saunders 1979). Many of the details of sequence and apparent mode of deformation associated with the nested caldera collapse complex on the summit have been worked out previously on the basis of a combination of photogeological (Mouginis-Mark & Robinson 1992; Mouginis-Mark 1981) and numerical analysis of predicted stress patterns (Zuber & Mouginis-Mark 1992). The interior of the largest and oldest caldera in the nested caldera complex is characterized by dominantly circumferential scarps and graben indicative of tensional strain in radial directions, radially oriented ridges indicative of circumferentially directed contractional strain, and

smaller, but morphologically similar, circumferentially oriented ridges indicative of radially directed contractional strain (Mouginis-Mark & Robinson 1992; Watters & Chadwick 1990). Compressional features characterize the inner area of the caldera, and extensional features the outer parts of the caldera. Although the superposition relationships between ridges and graben are difficult to distinguish clearly in many cases, the relative timing inferred for these distinct strain patterns indicates that the circumferential contraction pre-dates both the radial contraction and extension features.

Given the large size and mass of Olympus Mons, gravitational body forces of large magnitude and corresponding failure of its slopes might be expected. Several structural characteristics on or near the flanks of Olympus Mons have been attributed to deformation-associated local and regional slope failure and gravity sliding. Observed structures may be

Fig. 2. Examples of the morphology of some basic structural features together with their geological interpretation and significance. (**a**) Parallel scarps interpreted as caldera boundary faults, locally forming graben; some are the source of fisssure eruptions and local flows (outlined in upper right of image); (**b**) pits, pit chains, and flank channels interpreted as flank vents and lava channels; (**c**) small cones interpreted as fissure eruptions (arrow A) aligned with local graben (arrows B); (**d**) spur and gulley walls on the summit caldera of Ascraeus Mons interpreted as modification of caldera walls through slumping and debris flows off the upper walls; (**e**) scarp at the base of Olympus Mons interpreted to represent the results of large-scale slumping of the lower flanks; and (**f**) distinct changes in slope or 'terraces' (arrow A) on the upper flank of Olympus Mons interpreted to represent deformation of the surface due to radially directed thrust faulting; arrow B indicates a lava flow lobe that has widened on encountering a terrace surface. Viking Orbiter image numbers 210A32, 892A32, 857A46, 401B18, and 222A64.

classified as one of the three following categories: (1) those that deform the lower flanks (Borgia *et al.* 1990; Lopes *et al.* 1982); (2) those that account for deformation of the surroundings (Tanaka 1985; Francis & Wadge 1983; Harris 1977); and (3) those that appear to influence the overall architecture of the shield volcano (McGovern & Solomon 1993).

The first category includes the scarps, with up to several kilometres of relief, that encircle the lower flanks. The scale and nearly continuous presence of these around the base imply that these are the results of slope failure of the distal flanks. In many places lavas have flowed over these scarps and are evidence that the scarps formed contemporaneously with active volcanism. The second category includes the complex deformation of the 'aureole deposit' in the plains to the northwest of the main shield (Morris 1982; Harris 1977; Head 1996). Similar features occur on the west-northwest sides of the Tharsis Montes (Zimbelman & Edgett 1992). These have been generally interpreted as being due to basal detachment phenomena and large-scale thrusting of the substrate to the northwest associated with gravity sliding of the immense mass of Olympus Mons on the regional slopes of the Tharsis region. Evidence for the third category of structural characteristics suggests regional control on the orientation of large-scale patterns of strain in Olympus Mons. The calderas are clustered along an axis oriented northeast–southwest and the nested and overlapping caldera complex is slightly elongated in this direction. The caldera complex and the topographic summit are not symmetrically centred with respect to the base of the main shield volcano, but are slightly offset to the southeast. A short arcuate caldera-facing scarp to the immediate southeast of the caldera complex in the summit region accentuates the impression of a pronounced northwest–southeast least-principal stress orientation. The pronounced regional stress field arising from the northwesterly slope of the Tharsis region appears to have acted to impart a small component of axisymmetric northwest–southeast minimum compressive stress within the main body of the shield volcano through gravitational stresses at its base (McGovern & Solomon 1993). This subtle influence may have controlled magma ascent within the main shield and correspondingly influenced the growth of magma chambers associated with calderas along a northeast–southwest zone. Similar arrangements are noted for a few of the other large volcanoes situated on regional slopes, as will be noted below, and suggest that regional slopes may be an important

element of the overall stress field influencing patterns of volcano growth and deformation on Mars.

A series of arcuate, outward-facing terraces or ridges occur around the summit region and on the upper flanks (Fig. 2F). These are interpreted as folds over blind inward-dipping thrust faults. Although they may result from large-scale flexure of the lithosphere under the load of the edifice and corresponding compression of the upper flanks, in the light of the experiments of Marti *et al.* (1994) described previously, they are also likely to reflect reverse faults originating during tumescence of the summit during inflation of the magma chamber associated with later caldera formation.

Arsia Mons. Three volcanoes comprise the group known as the 'Tharsis Montes' (Arsia Mons, Pavonis Mons, and Ascraeus Mons). They are all slightly older on average than Olympus Mons based on crater counts from their flanks and from their latest eruption deposits (Hodges & Moore 1994; Neukum & Hiller 1981; Plescia & Saunders 1979; Crumpler & Aubele 1978). All three volcanoes are aligned in a N40°E direction, suggesting strong regional

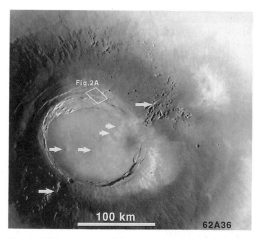

Fig. 4. Oblique view of the summit caldera of Arsia Mons, the largest caldera on Mars associated with an edifice. A though-going rift transects the entire volcano and consists of a row of small vents on the caldera floor and coalesced pits and channels (arrows) on the northeast and southwest flanks. The caldera floor and the extensive fan of lava flows on the northeast and southwest flanks are equivalent in age, or slightly younger, than the caldera collapse event. Extensive circumferential graben are best developed on the west flank. Viking Orbiter image 62A36.

structural control on their initiation and development, yet the summit calderas appear little influenced by this trend. Although they are characterized by some of the most obvious expressions of through-going linear structure, these linear structures are not simply oriented along the trend of alignment of the three volcanoes, but are instead arranged en echelon implying that the alignment of the volcanoes is not merely a single linear fissure. Several previous studies have discussed the characteristics of these volcanoes, particularly as they relate to the overall pattern of faulting or flank characteristics (McGovern & Solomon 1993; Zimbelman & Edgett 1992; Mouginis-Mark 1981; Crumpler & Aubele 1978).

The 110–115 km diameter summit caldera of Arsia Mons (Fig. 4) is the largest circular caldera on Mars, associated with an edifice, and is a rich source of information about the structure and relative timing of volcanic features associated with caldera collapse. Topographic relief across the boundary of the caldera is non-uniform, such that the margins form an amphitheatre-shaped depression that opens to the northeast onto the flanks of the volcano. Boundary fractures and graben are more numerous on the west and southwest walls of the caldera, and disappear on the northeast rim where the floor opens on to the flank; lavas inundating the caldera floor appear to spill out across pre-existing margin fractures in this area and thus bury many caldera margin faults. High resolution image data of the margins and floor show that some of the normal faults forming the circumferential fractures on the western rim acted as fissures for eruption of post-caldera lava flows; some of these flows can be seen to cascade over the fault blocks onto the caldera floor (Mouginis-Mark 1981). Further outward and on to the flanks, circumferential graben occur with decreasing frequency, particularly on the east flank. At or near the base of the main shield the circumferential pattern of faulting bends to the north and south forming an axisymmetric pattern of graben parallel to the through-going fracture trends. Most of the faults that occur off the flanks can be explained as arising from strain of the lithosphere under the load imposed by the volcano (Comer *et al.* 1985) whereas those closer to the rim of the caldera are more likely to be a result of strain associated with caldera formation.

A through-going structural trend or fissure occurs in Arsia Mons. It is characterized by distinct pits that coalesce to form large embayments in the northeast and southwest flanks (Crumpler & Aubele 1978; Carr et al. 1977) and a linear arrangement of small vents on the caldera floor. These form a distinct row of small, low relief, cone-shaped features interpreted to be small shield volcanoes occurring along the connecting trend across the caldera floor. These features are further characterized in high resolution image data by small summit pits and arrays of radial textures interpreted to represent lava patterns around central vents. The pits on the northeast and southwest flanks are sources for copious amounts of lava flows that inundate the north and south flanks in aprons of lava at least midway up the flanks forming secondary or parasitic shields on the flank of the main shield (Crumpler & Aubele 1978). Together with the flank fissure, the row of small shield volcanoes is strong evidence for linear fissure volcanism in martian volcanic edifices. Similar through-going fissures occur in the other two Tharsis Montes and are described below. Curiously, the linear fissure line in the caldera of Arsia Mons is slightly offset to the east from the centre point of the caldera. It may be significant that many more of the circumferential graben and faults occur to the west of the fissure line than to the east. This may indicate a preferential strain toward the west, perhaps due to body forces associated with the regional topography (McGovern & Solomon 1993), which resulted in preferential growth of the caldera margins to the west and away from a centre of volcanism located along the fissure trend line. These same body forces may be responsible for the anomalous arcuate patterns characterized as possible flank slumping (Zimbelman & Edgett 1992) on the lower west flank. There is thus evidence that regional extensional stress patterns may have interacted with the caldera-related stress patterns in controlling the overall arrangement of faults and fissures. For this reason Crumpler & Aubele (1978) originally suggested that Arsia Mons is more comparable to the Galápagos shield volcanoes of Earth (Rowland & Munro 1992; Munro & Rowland 1994; Chadwick & Howard 1991) than to the Hawaiian shield volcanoes. A similar pattern of through-going extension and fissure eruption also characterizes the Nyiragongo volcano of the west arm of the East African rift system (Pottier 1978).

The through-trending fissure, flank pits, and caldera margin fissure eruptions on Arsia Mons are evidence for on-going and voluminous volcanism subsequent to caldera collapse. Thus the collapse event itself was not a terminal event in the history of the volcano, nor was it a result of simple thermal contraction of a potentially cooling and sinking sub-volcano lithosphere

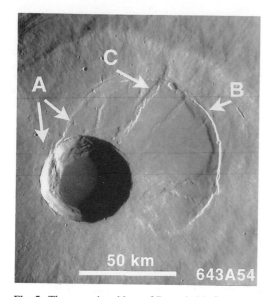

Fig. 5. The summit caldera of Pavonis Mons consists of a broad sag-like depression and a later deep (5 km) circular caldera with complexly terraced walls. Small cones appear to occur on circumferential fractures (A). The sag-like depression is bounded by a high ridge (B) on the east. Radial wrinkle-ridges (C) are evidence for compressive deformation of the surface within the interior of the sag-like depression during collapse. Viking Orbiter image 643A57.

after magma generation and replenishment of the magma chamber had ceased. Instead, volcanic eruptions continued to occur long after caldera collapse, an observation that implies that the collapse was a consequence of the continued growth of a large magma reservoir. Clear differences in the crater abundance of the early shield and latest eruption have been observed (Crumpler & Aubele 1978). These differences in apparent age are important as they establish a lower limit on the time span over which central volcanism was active in this locality. Depending on the cratering rate scale used, the observed crater abundances imply an age difference in these surfaces between 100 and 700 Ma. The lower limit of this age range is comparable to that known to occur on Earth in association with intraplate volcanism, so volcanism from a single source over this scale of time is plausible. High-resolution images of the caldera floor, acquired subsequent to the crater counts of Crumpler & Aubele (1978), confirm that there are in fact very few impact craters on this surface. Thus it must be among the youngest lava flow surfaces on Mars. Given the great age range of volcanism calculated from

previous crater counts, it seems possible that some of the flows on the caldera floor of Arsia Mons were emplaced in the geologically very recent past.

Pavonis Mons. The summit region of Pavonis Mons (Fig. 5) is unusual in that two distinct styles and scales of subsidence have occurred, both of which are relatively simple in structure. The larger of the two is defined by a circular 80 km diameter ridge around most of the periphery enclosing a broad concave summit depression. Radial mare-type ridges within the depression clearly indicate that the subsidence resulted in circumferential contraction of the surface. Exterior to the circular ridge enclosing the apparent depression there are a few arcuate summit-facing scarps that merge with the 80 km ridge on the south and west. Assuming that this summit depression is the result of subsidence of the type interpreted by Zuber & Mouginis-Mark (1992) to have occurred in the larger summit caldera of Olympus Mons, then the abrupt outward transition from circumferential compression to radial extension implied by the ridges and the circumferential scarps provides constraints on the geometry of the depressurized or evacuated source region responsible for the collapse.

A steep-walled, circular caldera 45–50 km in diameter with furrowed and terraced walls occurs on the southeastern interior of the large summit depression. This caldera is among the deepest identified on Mars. Imaging spectrometer data from the Phobos 2 mission ISM instrument have been interpreted to imply a depth of 5 km ± 0.3 km (Bibring *et al.* 1990). This depth is particularly remarkable when one considers the great circularity and the steep slopes of the caldera walls. A subsidence of this magnitude with few exterior patterns of extension is unlikely to have formed from a single deep magma chamber, as the stress associated with deflation would have encompassed a much greater area. Multiple cycles of collapse over a relatively small, laterally stable magma chamber might account for the great accumulated amount of subsidence. Several small volcanoes, interpreted to be small pyroclastic cones (Wood 1979; Edgett 1990; Zimbelman & Edgett 1992) or small lava cones, occur near the caldera on the southwest margin in association with nearby scarps. These small volcanoes are evidence that at least some of the extensional faults here were the source of small fissure eruptions, although the timing with respect to the caldera is not known. No impact craters appear to occur on the caldera floor, which is relatively featureless.

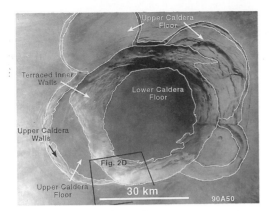

Fig. 6. The overlapping caldera complex on Ascraeus Mons consists of several shallow-floored calderas superseded by a single deep caldera with steep margins and complexly terraced walls. The entire complex is slightly elongated along the direction of the through-going rift trend of the volcano as a whole.

Either the floor is obscured by a dust mantle or the surface is geologically recent. Detailed observations provide stratigraphical evidence for the following sequence of events: (1) formation of the large summit depression; (2) lava flows and channels emanated from a source area in the centre of the depression and buried part of the south margin of the circumferential ridge surrounding the depression; and (3) the small caldera formed, obliterating the source area of the small lava flows and channels.

Arcuate and circumferential graben occur on the lower flanks, as with Arsia Mons, but appear more uniformly distributed between both east and west flanks. As with Arsia Mons, some of these are the sources of circular-headed channels that extend for several kilometres and thus appear to have been sites of small fissure-fed eruptions lower on the flanks. Also similar to Arsia, numerous pits that are sources for short channels and voluminous late-stage lava flows occur on the northeast and southwest flanks, locally coalescing to form distinct embayments into the main shield volcano.

Ascraeus Mons. The summit caldera complex of Ascraeus Mons (Fig. 6) consists of overlapping, and steep-sided calderas (Zimbelman & Edgett 1992; Zimbelman 1984; Mouginis-Mark 1981; Crumpler & Aubele 1978). At least four separate collapse events are recorded in the sequence. Three shallower calderas in the sequence occurred prior to the last and deepest central caldera.

The inner walls of the central caldera are complexly terraced on the northeast and southwest sides resulting in an elongated outline of the upper rim. The floor is, however, circular and relatively smooth. Stereo image data indicate that the terracing on the northeast side has developed in the floor of a previous higher-standing caldera, the floor of which has slumped inward along large re-entrants toward the central caldera. The circularity, steep walls, and great depth and diameter of this last caldera in the complex are similar to that of the late-stage circular caldera of Pavonis. Apparently, conditions during the final activity at the summits of both of these volcanoes were in some manner especially favourable to the formation of unusually deep and circular collapse structures.

A distinct mare-type wrinkle ridge occurs on the flanks immediately south of the summit region and is oriented approximately circumferentially with respect to the summit. This structure may be comparable to the circumferential ridge of the larger summit depression of Pavonis Mons. If so, this is evidence that the summit region of Ascraeus has subsided somewhat in an analogous manner, and to some extent implies that broad subsidence of the summit region has occurred on all three of the Tharsis Montes. Alternatively, it may represent deformation associated with a compressional stress regime predicted (McGovern & Solomon 1993) to occur in the upper flanks of large volcanoes on Mars as a consequence of lithospheric loading or simple reverse faulting accompanying tumescence of the summit during magma chamber inflation cycles as alluded to with the arcuate 'terraces' of Olympus Mons.

As with the other Tharsis Montes, circumferential graben also occur on the lower flanks, although they are much less complex and abundant, and numerous pits, channels (Fig. 2B), and eruptions of voluminous lava flows occur on the northeast and southwest flanks. The volume of lavas erupted from these late-stage flank vents is considerably less than that seen at Pavonis Mons and Arsia Mons.

Alba Patera. Arguably the largest volcano in the solar system in terms of diameter (2700 km), Alba Patera is also unique on Mars in terms of its characteristic radiating pattern of wide and thick lava flows, very low profile, and diverse flank characteristics (Mouginis-Mark *et al.* 1988; Greeley & Spudis 1981; Greeley *et al.* 1978). Lava flows forming Alba Patera are Hesperian to early Amazonian in age and span

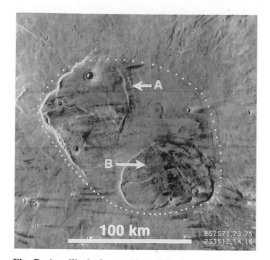

Fig. 7. An elliptical area (dotted line) consisting of several irregular shaped calderas and encircling graben and scarps results in an unusually shallow and irregular summit caldera complex on Alba Patera. Lavas from a circular vent region near the centre of the complex appear to have inundated the east rim of the larger of the two enclosed calderas (arrow A). The floor of the elongate and latest caldera (B) appears complex and includes several small cones on the southern interior. Mosaic of Viking Orbiter images 255S13–17.

source region in the eastern half of the caldera, from a point now characterized by a flat-topped, circular ridge enclosing a small circular depression. Subsequently, an irregular-shaped caldera between 50 and 60 km in diameter formed on the south-southeastern margin of the 120 km diameter summit depression. This caldera is partially encircled by arcuate graben on the west and distinct topographic scarp-like walls of scalloped shape on the south. Scalloping of scarps generally reflects episodic overlap of arcuate to circular collapse areas. Several episodes of caldera collapse are required for this shape to develop. This caldera also appears to be the centre of radiating patterns of small lobate lava flows characterizing the summit. Irregular topographic ridges and depressions across the floor, including at least two cones, suggest that the style of volcanism responsible for some of the latest volcanic activity was extremely diverse. Mare-type ridges appear to be accentuated in the caldera floor and terminate at the inner caldera walls, although ridges of similar orientation and amplitude occur further out on the flanks of the main shield volcano.

a considerable period from about the time of some of the oldest lava flows in the Tharsis region to the time of late-stage flows on the younger Tharsis shield volcanoes (Cattermole 1986, 1989).

The summit caldera of Alba Patera (Fig. 7) consists of a nested sequence of at least three to five distinct depressions, two of which are irregular-shaped, and flat-floored calderas clearly transecting lobate lava flows of the summit region. The caldera is situated in a northeast–southwest oriented rise bounded by some of the numerous graben that form a radial fracture set about the Tharsis region as a whole. The largest caldera is irregular in shape and in apparent topographic profile. The western margin of this caldera consists of a scalloped series of terraced scarps that decrease in height at both the northern and southern extremities. This scarp forms the western segment of a circle of faults, scarps and graben continued on the east by arcuate graben, and on the south by extremely small-scale fractures that together define a roughly circular pattern 120 km across. This asymmetry may originate in part from the eruption of voluminous lava flows from a small

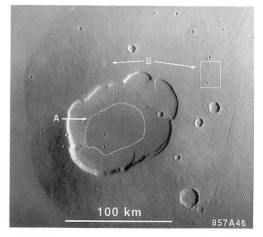

Fig. 8. The irregular outline of the summit caldera complex of Uranius Patera appears to have formed from an overlapping series of smaller calderas. A broad, inward-sloping bench and wrinkle ridges (A) around the outer caldera floor are evidence for concave sagging and compressive deformation of the interior prior to inundation of the interior by late lava flows. The latter form a broad surface with little relief filling the interior and overlapping the sloping bench (outlined area). Circumferential fractures on the flanks surround the complex and are the site of several small fissure eruption cones (B). Box outlines small fissure and cone shown in Fig. 2C. Viking Orbiter Image 857A46.

Uranius Patera. Uranius Patera is a low shield volcano of Amazonian age located in the northern part of the Tharsis region. The summit caldera (Fig. 8) is 100×75 km in diameter and elongate in a northwest direction parallel to the regional trend of fractures (Ceraunius Fossae), one of the many groups of fractures and graben that are approximately radial to the Tharsis region. Thus the orientation of the caldera may reflect the influence of a pronounced regional stress field on magma emplacement.

Uranius Patera differs in several respects from many of the other calderas on Mars. The margins are steep and well-defined, and characterized by relatively minor terracing, but the caldera is scalloped in map plan indicating that it is the result of the coalescence of many smaller collapse events. In addition, the caldera floor does not appear to be a uniformly flat surface like that in many other calderas, but instead is characterized by evidence for a broad bench adjacent to the foot of the caldera walls that slopes gently toward the caldera centre. Segments of pre-existing small-diameter caldera margins, probably responsible for the scalloped form of the overall caldera, are preserved locally on this sloping bench. The slope of this bench is steep enough that locally it forms ramps that reach to the rim of the caldera. Mare-type ridges, particularly on the northwest slopes of the bench, attest to compressional deformation that accompanied the collapse and in many ways is similar to that seen in the calderas of Olympus Mons and elsewhere. These observations imply an evolution in which an arrangement of nested small-diameter calderas subsided centrally during a late phase of evolution of Uranius Patera and resulted in the formation of the single larger caldera that now occupies the summit. However, the central part of the floor is relatively flat over a region with a diameter of 50 km. This area is characterized by a well-defined contact with the sloping margins and this is evidence for subsequent flooding and burial of the interior over small central portions of the sloping interior. Therefore, caldera collapse appears to have been accompanied by relatively small volumes of lava flows responsible for partially flooding the central interior.

Exterior to the caldera rim are several encircling graben, scarps and fissures that mark the extent of extensional deformation exterior to the central collapsed region. Low cones with distinct summit pits arranged on the outermost circumferential graben to the northwest and northeast are evidence that these circumferential fractures were the site of late fissure eruptions,

perhaps contemporaneous with the eruptions that inundated the central portion of the caldera floor.

Ceraunius Tholus. Ceraunius Tholus is unique among the Amazonian age Tharsis volcanoes in that its flanks are characterized by numerous radial channels (Gulick & Baker 1990) instead of distinct lava flows. In this respect, it is similar to Hecates Tholus in the Elysium region and the much older highland paterae of the southern hemisphere. In addition, Ceraunius Tholus is characterized by a distinctive sector structure in which the western margin of the simple, circular, 24 km diameter caldera flares outward onto a sector of the flank that is both smoother and lower than the adjacent radially channelled slopes. The caldera (Fig. 9) is steep-walled with maximum relief occurring on the east and a small segment of a pre-existing caldera on the north rim. The west wall of the caldera is considerably lower and formed in part in the smooth materials of the western flank.

We interpret the smooth flanks on the west side as late deposition of large volumes of material, perhaps pyroclastic deposits, associated with the final caldera-forming eruptions.

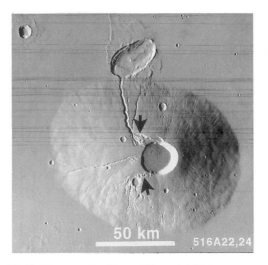

Fig. 9. The summit caldera of Ceraunius Patera opens to the west onto a smoother flank, a possible consequence of slumping of the western caldera wall and runout of pyroclastic material to the west. Arrows indicate amphitheatre-like north and south walls opening the caldera rim to the west. Numerous small valleys radiate from the summit, the largest of which appears to post-date the smooth material of the western flank and serves as a channel for deposition of a material fan on the floor of an adjacent impact crater. Viking Orbiter images 516A22 and 516A24.

There is a variety of evidence from many
martian volcanoes, as well as theoretical arguments, to support this interpretation (Wilson &
Head 1981, 1982, 1994; Crown & Greeley 1990;
Mouginis-Mark *et al.* 1982, 1988; Greeley &
Spudis 1978). Large-volume ash eruptions are
not common on shield-shaped basaltic shield
volcanoes of this dimension on Earth. The
edifices produced by ash-flow calderas on
Earth are shield-shaped and may be analogous,
but they are generally silicic in composition,
rather than basaltic (Francis & Wood 1982).
However, the greater ease of volatile disruption
of basaltic magmas on Mars (Wilson & Head
1994) may make voluminous basaltic ash
eruptions more common.

The floor of the caldera appears locally rough
and numerous pits occur along the floor near the
base of the eastern wall. More concentrated pits
occur in the northern half of the floor that are
similar in some respects to the pits occurring on
the floors of the calderas at Hecates Tholus and
Elysium Mons. A small cone-like mound at the
base of the northern wall may be a small
pyroclastic cone which developed on caldera
margin fractures or a rounded slump block from
the northern caldera wall. The sequence of
formation of the Ceraunius Tholus caldera can
be determined from the existing relationships:
(1) formation of early, relatively small diameter
summit caldera(s); (2) sector-like collapse of the
western summit resulting in an amphitheatre-
shaped summit; (3) deposition of the smooth
materials of the western flank; and (4) final
collapse of a circular central region, perhaps in
association with the deposition of materials on
the smooth western flank. Ceraunius Tholus is
slightly elongate in basal outline in an east–west
direction. The occurrence of the sector-like west
flank along the axial symmetry of elongation
may be related to this fact, although the longer
and presumably shallower slope in the western
direction would seem to be more stable against
collapse than the relatively steeper north or
south flanks. Alternatively, the sector-like
structure may be unrelated to gravita-tional
stability and may have originated through an
underlying cause such as an elongate magma
chamber or interaction of a larger fissure-like
structure with the caldera and the flanks.

Contemporaneous with or subsequent to the
final caldera collapse, a wide channel formed on
the north that is headed in a series of smaller
tributary channels near the caldera. Materials,
either lava or pyroclastic, appear to have flowed
down this channel where they were subsequently
deposited in a delta on the floor of an obliquely
formed impact crater in the plains at the base of

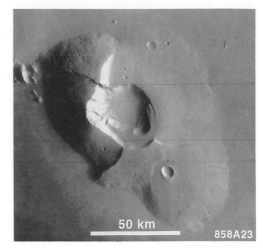

Fig. 10. Several arcuate scarps intersect on the flanks
of Tharsis Tholus and may represent a complex form
of sector collapse involving most of the visible flanks.
Most of the lower flanks of this volcano appear buried
beneath surrounding plains-lava flows. Viking Orbiter
image 858A23.

the volcano. This crater has been cited as a
candidate (Mouginis-Mark *et al.* 1992) for the
impact believed to be responsible for the SNC
meteorites, which are thought to be of martian
origin (Wood & Ashwal 1981); although
Treiman (1994) has cited evidence for more than
one source crater. The surrounding lava plains
have partially buried the lower flanks.

Tharsis Tholus. Tharsis Tholus is a relatively
small volcano in the northeastern part of the
Tharsis region. Its primary distinction from
the other smaller Tharsis volcanoes discussed
below is the unusual number of arcuate scarps
distributed over its flanks and summit. These are
either segments of partially preserved caldera
margins or large sector-type (Robinson &
Rowland 1994) fault patterns. The summit
caldera (Fig. 10) is relatively deep and irregular
in shape with maximum relief occurring on the
western wall. The latest caldera (approximately
30 km in diameter) abuts the head wall of a
broad arcuate and scalloped sector-type scarp
that cuts the north and east flanks and the
summit. As a result, the summit caldera shares
one (western) wall with this scarp and the total
relief is accordingly greater on that side of
the caldera. High-resolution image data of the
caldera show that the walls are fluted on the
western slopes, terraced on the south margin,
and appear modified by erosion.

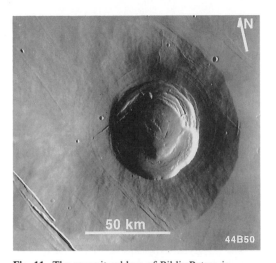

Fig. 11. The summit caldera of Biblis Patera is unusual because of the circularity of both the central collapse and its circumferential fractures. Broad inner terraces and wrinkle-ridge style floor deformation characterize the caldera interior. Nearly circular circumferential graben on the flanks of the shield volcano attest to relatively uniform radial stress associated with caldera formation. Note that the main flanks are buried by surrounding plains-forming lava flows that have flowed down the regional gradient (lower right to upper left). Viking Orbiter image 44B50.

The part of the flank included within the sector structure is somewhat smoother than the adjacent and apparently older parts of the flanks. Additional scarps of a similar form cut the western flank such that the north and south flanks are now higher standing than the rest of the volcano. These higher standing remnants are rougher in appearance. The whole volcano is surrounded by younger plains lavas which appear to bury the lower flanks. Thus any details of the lower flanks that might yield clues to the sector-like structure of the summit region are obscured. A cluster of knobs and ridges occurs off the western flank and is isolated from the main volcano by these plains. The origin of the knobs is unclear, but their chaotic arrangement suggests that they are remnants of large slumps from the main shield. Tharsis Tholus presents the appearance of a volcano that has undergone extensive sector-type collapse of its flanks.

Biblis Patera. Although it is one of the smaller of the volcanoes in the Tharsis region, Biblis Patera is interesting because its 52 km diameter summit caldera (Fig. 11) is unusually circular yet complexly terraced. Whereas many of the calderas on Mars, particularly the more circular ones, have relatively smooth floors, a chaotic arrangement of ridges occurs on the floor of the Biblis Patera caldera. Many of the ridges are parallel to the caldera margins and appear to be slumped segments of the terraced caldera walls that have spread out across the caldera floor (Plescia 1994). A series of circumferential graben form nearly complete circles around the caldera rim out to a radius of 40 to 50 km from the caldera centre. Whereas many of the calderas on Mars appear to have an axial symmetry, apparently in response to the interaction of caldera faulting with regional extensional stress fields, the circular form of the faulting around the summit caldera of Biblis Patera has been suggested to represent an example of a caldera that has formed in a homogeneous stress environment (Crumpler & Aubele 1989). Later graben strike northwesterly across the flanks and indicate that at a later time, after formation of Biblis, a pronounced regional extensional stress field existed.

Ulysses Patera, Uranius Tholus, Jovus Tholus. These are the smallest of the Tharsis volcanoes and have been described recently by Plescia (1994). They are also among the older of the Tharsis volcanoes and are all heavily modified by impact craters on their flanks and inundation of their lower flanks by later plains-forming lavas. The summit calderas (Fig. 12A, B, C) are relatively simple and circular, although that of Jovus Tholus is somewhat scalloped in plan form, and that of Uranius Tholus consists of a smaller caldera nested within a larger one. All are characterized by steep margins, minor terracing and relatively few structural characteristics exterior to the caldera rims.

Elysium region

The Elysium region (Fig. 1) includes the second most topographically prominent and youngest (Greeley & Guest 1987; Neukum & Hiller 1981; Plescia & Saunders 1979) edifices after those of the Tharsis region. Calderas in the Elysium region occur in association with three volcanoes, Hecates Tholus, Elysium Mons, and Albor Tholus. Each is morphologically different and records a differing geological development. We also include in this discussion Apollinaris Patera (Fig. 1), even though it is not part of the same regional geological setting, as it lies near Elysium and is in many ways distinctive from highland paterae identified elsewhere on Mars.

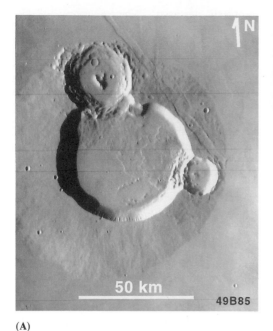

(A)

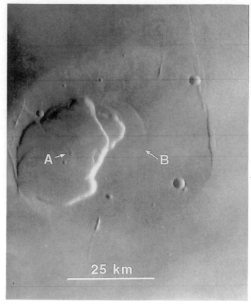

(C)

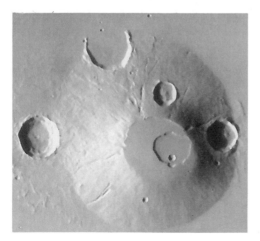

(B)

Fig. 12. Summit calderas of the smaller Tharsis volcanoes. **(A)** A large fraction of the visible flanks and caldera floor of Ulysses Patera is modified by superimposed impact craters, but the existing caldera appears relatively circular and structurally simple. **(B)** The nested caldera sequence of Uranius Tholus includes a large caldera that has been nearly filled by later lavas. **(C)** Although the volcano appears relatively small and low in overall relief, the summit caldera of Jovus Tholus is characterized by overlapping caldera relations and a single large irregular caldera with a nested sequence of depressions and smaller pits (arrow A) in the interior. Scarp at arrow B appears to be the site of an early caldera margin. Viking Orbiter images 49B85, 516A23, and 49B19.

Albor Tholus. The summit caldera of Albor Tholus (Fig. 13) is relatively small (35 km) and simple compared with many of the calderas on Mars. Image data are insufficient to establish the details of the interior walls or floor but, based on illumination and shadow patterns, the caldera appears relatively deep in relation to its width. The rim is sharply defined and slightly scalloped suggesting that the current size of the caldera represents the accumulation of at least two and perhaps three caldera events. Malin (1977) noted on the basis of lower resolution, but more

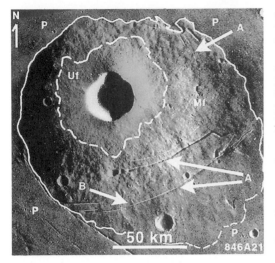

Fig. 13. The summit caldera of Albor Tholus consists of at least two overlapping calderas. A region extending out to approximately one caldera radius (unit Uf) is relatively featureless compared with the lower flanks (unit Mf) and may represent areas mantled by ash deposits. Two sets of circumferential fractures occur on the lower flanks (A). Individual lava flows (B) may also be identified. Surrounding plains lavas (P) inundate the lower flanks. Viking Orbiter image 846A21.

favourably illuminated, Mariner 9 image data that the scalloped or indented northern rim of the main caldera can be attributed to a smaller 8 km diameter caldera in the interior.

The flank of Albor Tholus immediately exterior to the summit caldera is unusually devoid of detail and implies that the caldera margins may be blanketed by ash or related late eruption deposits. Circumferential graben occur further down the slope of the southern and eastern flanks. Locally, lava flows are visible on the south flank and it is inferred that most of the volcano is constructed of lava flows. The relatively simple form of the caldera, with the evidence for possible pyroclastic materials in the near summit surrounding the caldera rim, suggest that the caldera formed with related pyroclastic activity.

Apollinaris Patera. The caldera of Apollinaris Patera (Fig. 14) is relatively complex and demonstrates that the detailed geological characteristics of individual calderas can frequently reflect pre-collapse surface characteristics. The margins of the Apollinaris caldera are relatively distinct and correspond to a topographic rim separating the interior of the caldera from the surrounding radially channelled flanks. Additional details of the topography and flanks are described by Robinson *et al.* (1993) and Robinson (1990); and Apollinaris Patera was classified as a uniquely 'shield volcano-type' patera by Greeley *et al.* (1978). The caldera margins truncate and obliterate the upper portions of prominent channels occurring throughout the upper flanks of the main shield volcano. We suggest that the caldera collapse occurred subsequent to the development of these channels. The interior of the caldera consists of several terraces or benches, with concentric scarps and small arcuate graben throughout the inner benches, surrounding a flat floor of irregular outline. Some of these terraces and benches may be flat-lying deposits filling the caldera; but others are clearly structurally formed.

The caldera appears to be the result of piecemeal collapse, partially of sag-like form,

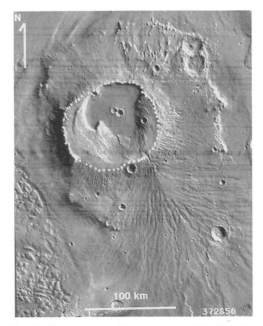

Fig. 14. The summit caldera complex of Apollinaris Patera (dotted outline) consists of a broad circular central region along which radial valleys on the flanks are truncated, and a complex inner region characterized by multiple benches and scarps. The low northern floor appears to have elongated and widened along an arc at the base of the north wall and largely post-dates caldera collapse. The large fan-shaped deposit on the south flank radiates from a narrow channel on the southeast rim of the caldera complex and may be related to the events leading to collapse. Viking Orbiter image 372S56.

throughout the interior and concentric about a point near the south-central interior. The flat-floored segments on the north end of the caldera floor appear to reflect subsequent enlargement of a central depression along ring graben and bench fractures. The timing of caldera formation in relation to the extensive fan-shaped deposit on the south flank of Apollinaris Patera is not clearly resolved. Near its apex the fan-like deposit appears to have emerged from a channel cutting the caldera rim. The apparent apex of the fan deposit, near the current margin of the summit caldera, may relate mainly to the abrupt change in slope of the flanks on which the erupted flows (either ash or lava) of the fan spread out over the lower flanks as a terminal distributary apron. Part of the channel is within the caldera margins, and abruptly terminates toward the interior at a short arcuate scarp segment bounding an interior depression. Linear to arcuate traces of the channel may continue toward the interior of the current flat floor where the channel is truncated. This is interpreted to mean that part of the terraced inner slope of the caldera preserves the surface characteristics of the volcano flanks prior to caldera collapse and that collapse of the summit region was broadly distributed. This interpretation also implies that

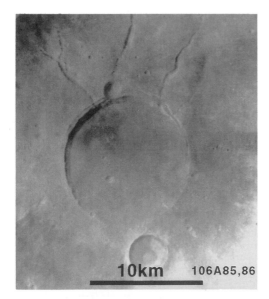

Fig. 15. The summit caldera of Elysium Mons is relatively smooth-floored and extremely circular compared with other calderas on Mars. The northern wall consists of at least two terraces which post-date some of the deep radial valleys. Viking Orbiter image 106A85 and 106A86.

the prominent fan-shaped deposit on the southern flank may represent an eruption initiated by early stages of caldera collapse.

Elysium Mons. Compared with other calderas occurring on the summit of large volcanoes on Mars, the caldera of Elysium Mons (Fig. 15) is particularly circular in plan form. In detail the margins are characterized by two concentric escarpments approximately 200 m apart. In this respect the rim terracing is both narrow and relatively simple in faulting geometry, implying a relatively simple collapse sequence or single collapse event. The floor of the caldera is pocked with several craters of undetermined origin and possible escarpments of irregular outline.

Sinuous channels breach the northern rim of the outer caldera and originate in circular depressions near the caldera rim or on the inner terrace. These channels taper downslope and line up with pit chains farther down the northeast and southwest slopes. Malin (1977), in an analysis of Elysium based on Mariner 9 B-frame data (which are slightly better resolution than Viking image data for this caldera), noted that this orientation is parallel to regional trends of mare-type ridges and related structures, suggesting that the channels are in part structurally controlled and resulted from fracturing and collapse of the flanks at the time of caldera collapse. As the regional topographic slope is down to the northwest, the through-going structural trend might also reflect regional stresses associated with the topographic gradient, similar to that noted above for Olympus Mons.

Hecates Tholus. The most prominent summit caldera of Hecates Tholus (Fig. 16A, B) is small (10 km) in diameter, and records four to five caldera collapse events (Mouginis-Mark *et al.* 1982) in a series of closely nested moderately circular calderas ranging from 4 km to 10 km in diameter and decreasing in size with time. The overall nested complex is somewhat elongated in a northeast–southwest orientation and the sequence of caldera formation appears to progress roughly from north to south. The caldera walls are sharply defined topographic scarps and relatively unscalloped. A few pits may be distinguished on the inner three caldera floors. The floor of the third highest caldera is anomalously dark, pitted and topographically rough-appearing compared with those of the adjacent calderas. Subtle ridge-like features traverse the lowest caldera level and the third highest caldera floor. Resolution is insufficient to determine if these are actually ridges associated

(A) (B)

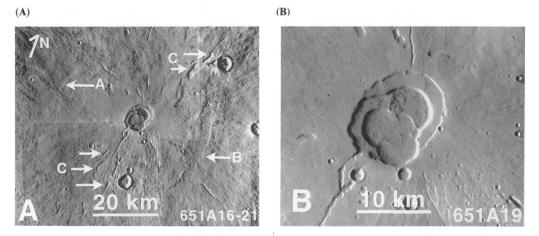

Fig. 16. (A) The summit region and caldera of Hecates Tholus. A nested caldera complex is enclosed by an arcuate wrinkle ridge (arrow A) to the northwest and a wrinkle ridge/graben pair on the southeast (arrow B). The similarity to ridges and circumferential fractures around the summit of Pavonis Mons suggests that a central 40 km diameter region has subsided. Note that the abundance of pits and channels (arrow C) is greatest on the northeast and southwest flanks along the strike of the overall axial elongation of the nested central caldera complex. Mosaic of Viking Orbiter images 651A16–651A21. (B) Enlargement of the nested summit caldera. Each successive caldera collapse event in this complex is smaller and deeper. Unless flooded by later lavas, repeated nested caldera formation can lead to anomalously deep caldera complexes. Viking Orbiter image 651A19.

with slumping of the inner caldera walls or if they are analogous to mare-type ridges seen in other martian calderas, such as those mapped in the floor of the Olympus Mons caldera (Mouginis-Mark & Robinson 1992; Mouginis-Mark *et al.* 1990). If they are mare-type wrinkle ridges, they are evidence for late-stage compressional deformation possibly associated with late subsidence. Alternatively they may be part of a through-going ridge system that traverses the flanks and intercepts the summit caldera.

At a larger scale the nested sequence of summit calderas is encircled partially by arcuate structures to the northwest and southeast forming a subtle summit ring fracture 70 km in diameter. The ring consists of a series of low ridges to the west and northwest, and a 5 km wide arcuate graben arrangement to the southeast. The northeast and southwest segments of the circle are absent, and the overall impression is that the summit region is enclosed by ring fractures that define a slightly elongate summit depression with the same sense of azimuthal orientation as the nested caldera complex. As with Elysium Mons, channels are common on the northeast and southwest summit flanks and further down the flanks give way to aligned pit chains. These characteristics, together with the elongation of the summit caldera complex and a regional slope to the northwest, imply that the structure of the summit region, as with Elysium Mons and Olympus Mons, may be influenced by

regional slopes on which the main shield volcanoes have been built.

Hellas region

Volcanism in the Hellas region is largely mid- to late-Hesperian in age (Crown & Greeley 1990; Greeley & Crown 1990; Greeley & Guest 1987) and includes some of the oldest recognizable volcanic centres on Mars (Fig. 1). A variety of evidence has been interpreted to suggest that highland paterae of the Hellas region consist of a combination of lava flows and ash deposits. Because of the possibility that the crust was enriched in water or ice in the earlier history of Mars, the eruptions responsible for these volcanoes could have been hydromagmatic with non-juvenile volatiles driving the pyroclastic eruptions (Wilson & Head 1994; Crown & Greeley 1993). The record of calderas associated with highland paterae is important as they may be indirect evidence for the characteristics and dimensions of magma chambers occurring at this early period of martian geological history.

Amphitrites Patera. The caldera of Amphitrites Patera (Fig. 17) is characterized by a 150 km diameter circular pattern of arcuate scarps and ridges with associated radial lineations. The latter are interpreted to be erosionally modified lava flows and few unequivocal radial

Fig. 17. The caldera of Amphitrites Patera consists of a collection of radial and concentric ridges centred around a topographic depression. The morphology of Amphitrites Patera bears some resemblance to that of features on Venus known as 'arachnoids'. Mosaic of Viking Orbiter images 361S01,02 and 94A75.

fractures appear to be present. With the exception of a few arcuate scarps on the margins of a 40 km central depression, that may be interpreted as normal faults, structural features associated with tensile stress at the surface are relatively absent. Both circumferential ridges and radial ridges are more common. Some of these may be similar to mare-type ridges which are generally believed to be associated with compressional or thrusting modes of surface failure.

The prominent 150 km ring consists of discontinuous knobs and ridges that appear to form the boundary between the radial flank patterns and a smoother summit region. Several flank ridges terminate abruptly at the caldera rim. On the southeast segment the ring is defined by two parallel, opposite-facing scarps suggesting that the ring is part of a circumferential graben system. Details on the caldera floor, apart from the central 40 km depression, include mare-type ridges, bench-like regions of subdued radial ridges between the outer and inner rings and short circumferential ridge segments. Numerous pedestal craters provide evidence for regional aeolian stripping of the surface. This underscores the need for caution in interpreting the detailed structure, as several of the smaller features may be a consequence of topographic inversion.

Amphitrites differs from most other martian calderas in that it serves as the locus for prominent local mare-type ridges, many of which appear to be oriented radially to the

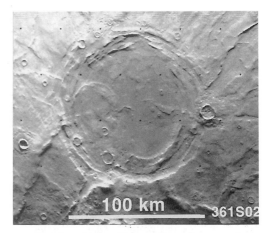

Fig. 18. The caldera of Peneus Patera is extremely circular and bears some of the characteristics of an impact crater but is interpreted to be volcanic because of the presence of circumferential graben and an associated regional pattern of digitate lava flows. In addition to a primary magmatic origin, it is also possible that 'opportunistic' magmas ascended, filled, and modified the site of an initial impact basin. Viking Orbiter image 361S02.

central caldera region. In this respect Amphitrites bears many of the characteristics of magmatic centres on Venus known as 'arachnoids' (Head *et al. 1992*).

Peneus Patera. Whereas topographic edifices, or evidence for exterior radial slopes, character- ize all other martian calderas, the 100 km diameter caldera of Peneus Patera (Fig. 18) has no apparent associated edifice. Whether Peneus Patera is volcanic at all is unclear, and its classification as a caldera is not universally accepted. An alternative interpretation is that it is an impact crater that is partially inundated by lava plains and modified by erosion (Wood 1984). The relatively great circularity, and absence of distinctive radial structure indicative of an edifice of associated lava flows, are the primary arguments against a volcanic origin. However, despite its unusual circularity, it bears some similarity to other calderas on Mars that are less equivocal. In addition, the continuity of

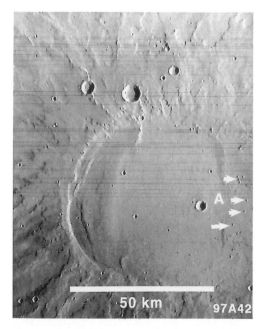

Fig. 19. The circular summit caldera of Hadriaca Patera is relatively shallow and truncates a radial pattern of ridges and valleys. The northeastern rim appears to be partially buried by later volcanic materials perhaps associated with a series of small cones (arrows) located on the eastern caldera margin. The cones together with the relatively featureless and apparently lava-flooded caldera floor are evidence for post-collapse filling and smoothing of the caldera floor by later volcanism. Viking Orbiter image 97A42.

the circumferential graben, proximity to known volcanic centres, and local radially ˙oriented striations, particularly on the northeast margins and exterior which are interpreted to represent degraded lava flows, provide arguments for a volcanic origin. In detail the margins are defined on the basis of discontinuous arcuate scarps, both inward- and outward-facing, and arcuate graben surrounding a relatively flat and feature- less floor.

Hadriaca Patera. Hadriaca Patera (Fig. 19) has been recently mapped as part of the Mars geological 1:500 000 scale mapping programme (Crown & Greeley 1995). Its caldera has been discussed previously by Crown & Greeley (1993) who noted that it is a relatively circular depression (77 km diameter) at the summit of a distinct radially patterned edifice in many ways similar to Tyrrhena Patera. They attribute the relatively indistinct north and eastern rims to partial burial by volcanic materials. The pre- sence of small domes or cones on the site of the indistinct margin also suggests that local erup- tions, perhaps from ring fractures in this region, may have resulted in local burial of the caldera rim. Distinct radially furrowed scarps occur on the west side of the caldera.

Extremely fine scarps on the west flank suggest that the caldera may be elongate in an east–west direction. If so, most of the subsidence and later filling with volcanic materials occurred in a circular region defining the western interior. Alternatively the caldera collapse may have occurred in at least two stages with a more or less circular caldera of similar overall diameter forming first to the east, and being partially overlapped by another caldera during later stages of activity. The caldera floor is relatively featureless compared with many other martian calderas, although faint scarps and arcuate patterns in the southeast floor define a circular area *c.* 30 km in diameter that may be evidence for other sites of earlier caldera formation, now nearly buried by the latest volcanic materials associated with later caldera activity.

Tyrrhena Patera. Tyrrhena Patera is currently being mapped as part of the Mars geological 1:500 000 scale mapping programme. It was the focus of a study by Greeley & Crown (1990) who described the general characteristics of the volcano as a whole; it was previously classified as a class II patera characterized by deeply incised radial channels (Greeley *et al.* 1978). Here we focus our discussion on the detailed

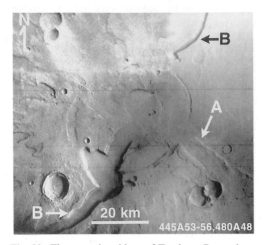

Fig. 20. The summit caldera of Tyrrhena Patera is relatively complex and consists of a series of irregular and elongate calderas nested within a much larger circumferential fracture pattern. In addition to graben and arcuate pits, circumferential ridges occur to the east. Mare-type wrinkle ridges (arrow A) striking northwest–southeast appear to be transected by the inner ring fracture. Pit-headed valleys (arrows B) are arranged along a trend from southwest to northeast. Mosaic of Viking Oribiter images 445A53–445A56 and 480A48.

geological characteristics of the summit region. The caldera of Tyrrhena Patera (Fig. 20) is more complex than that of most of the highland patera-type volcanoes and appears to record a more complex sequence of development. Also, unlike the other highland paterae, there does not appear to be a single distinct caldera. Instead, several arcuate graben and clustered depressions occur within a concentrated region near the centre of a pattern of prominent radial ridges. If one takes as a boundary the ring of graben forming the most complete arc of a circle, the summit caldera is 45 km in diameter, but includes a circular depression 13 km in diameter which is connected by a wide rill-like valley to a depression on the southwest flank. The 45 km ring fracture corresponds to the up-flank terminus of most of the radial ridges and valleys, and in this respect is comparable to the pattern seen at Amphitrites.

At least three narrow valleys oriented radially with respect to the summit terminate at caldera margins. Deep and narrow valleys on the southwest and northeast flanks originate in elongate depressions that developed along the main caldera ring structure. The depression which forms the source for the valley on the southwest margin is at least as large as the

centrally located summit depression. Provided that the valleys are the results of volcanic processes and not simply valleys formed by later erosion, this is evidence that the ring fracture formation pre-dated the last volcanic activity. The depression, the sources for the two most prominent valleys, and several smaller summit pits are all oriented along a northeast–southwest trend suggesting possible alignment. Although it may be fortuitous, this orientation is radial to the Hellas basin suggesting the possibility that the volcanic centre is situated at the intersection between radial and circumferentially arranged basin fractures that have favoured preferential magma ascent pathways and corresponding central edifice development. A prominent mare-type ridge transects the summit from south to northwest on a trend parallel to the local orientation of proposed basin ring fractures and may be the surface manifestation of structural deformation along a basin ring. Age relations between the ridge and structural elements of the volcano are difficult to establish but, based on the absence of any expression of the mare-type ridge in the central flat-floored depression, the latest volcanic activity appears to post-date the formation of the mare-type ridge.

Additional faint scarps, ridges and aligned pits form arcuate patterns on the flanks as much as 50 km from the summit. A series of broader, flat-floored arcuate depressions, approximately concentric to the summit, occur more than 100 km to the north in more flat-lying units. The overall impression is that, although most of the caldera collapse is associated with near-summit processes, the radial stress field associated with the volcanic centre exerted an influence on the distal flanks as well (Crumpler & Aubele 1989).

Syrtis Major region

Two relatively simple calderas (Nili Patera and Meroe Patera) occur in the Syrtis Major region, in association with extensive ridged Hesperian age lava plains that form a broad plateau on the west margin of the Isidis Planitia basin. Schaber (1982) originally described these calderas and, as revealed by radar-derived topographic profiles, suggested that they occur near the centre of a broad low-relief shield volcano that extends over much of Syrtis Major. In addition to these calderas, Schaber also cited evidence that both calderas lie within a much broader depression, 280 km in diameter. Based on crater counts the surrounding plains are estimated to be similar in

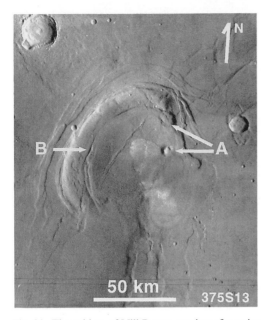

Fig. 21. The caldera of Nili Patera consists of a series of arcuate fractures and graben that open to the southeast onto the plains of Syrtis Major. Two cones with summit pits (A) are situated on the inner ring fracture, which is locally ridge-like (B). Immediately exterior to the inner fracture is a low bench with a hummocky surface of unknown origin. In high-resolution image data the whitish areas are shown to be small dune fields apparently formed by trapping of aeolian mantle materials in the caldera floor. Viking Orbiter image 375513.

and normal faults that form the western margin of an asymmetrical depression opening onto ridged plains to the east. The outer fractures appear to merge to the northeast and southwest with a regional NNE to SSW pattern of mare-type ridges and local graben. A single, nearly linear, graben traverses the caldera floor from NNE to SSW, parallel to the general sense of elongation of the caldera, and regional structural trends. The innermost (40 km) ring encircles a relatively flat floor, the surface geological unit of which is indistinguishable from the surrounding plains. A small breached cone occurs along the continuation of the inner fracture ring on the east and three low, coalesced cratered cones occur along the northeast segment of the inner fracture. Although detailed stratigraphical relationships among the smaller features within the caldera cannot be determined, it is likely that these cones represent sources for lavas and possible pyroclastic material during the late stages of the eruptions. The overall impression is that Nili Patera marked the location of significant fissure eruptions which fed the plains forming Syrtis Major, and the prolonged eruption from this source led to the development of a local magma

age to other highland paterae (mid- to late-Hesperian in age). The mineralogy of this region, determined from the Imaging Spectrometer on board the Soviet Phobos 2 spacecraft, is interpreted to be best fit by a basaltic lithology characterized by moderate iron and two pyroxenes, probably augite and pigeonite (Mustard & Sunshine 1995; Mustard *et al.* 1993), in keeping with the relatively unevolved and monotonous morphologic appearance of most of the plateau which suggests the presence of extensive sheets of low-viscosity basalt flows. This mineralogy is also consistent with some of the SNC meteorites, Shergotty, Zagami, EETA79001 and ALHA77005 (Mustard & Sunshine 1995).

Nili Patera. Nili Patera (Fig. 21) is the more northerly of the two Syrtis calderas and is elongate along the margin of the proposed 280 km diameter Syrtis Major summit depression. It is characterized by a 40 to 70 km diameter 'C'-shaped pattern of parallel graben

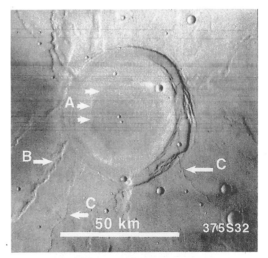

Fig. 22. The caldera of Meroe Patera is circular and characterized by a nearly continuous inner terrace surrounding a flat floor. In high-resolution image data the inner floor consists of a hummocky deposit with a distinct contact (A) that is interpreted to represent late lavas filling an inner depression. Several mare-type wrinkle ridges are truncated at the caldera margin (B) and thus pre-date caldera collapse. Lava channels (C) appear to radiate from the caldera on the southeast and southwest. Viking Orbiter image 375S32.

chamber elongate along the local fissure trend ultimately responsible for the caldera formation.

Meroe Patera. Meroe Patera (Fig. 22) is smaller (40 km) and more circular in outline than Nili Patera. The outermost scarp defining the caldera margin is nearly continuous, in contrast to that seen in many calderas on Mars, and encircles a terraced bench 2 to 5 km wide. The inner ring is also defined by a scarp but appears discontinuous on the west side. A single rounded knob or cone occurs just interior to the inner scarp on the eastern floor and may be either a pyroclastic or lava cone.

The central 10 to 15 km of the floor is characterized by an unusual castellated texture of ridges and may represent the surface of a late-stage lava lake. Alternatively, the ridges could simply represent aeolian materials trapped in the local depression formed by Meroe Patera, as numerous wind streaks throughout Syrtis Major attest to an abundant supply of fines. Although mare-type ridges appear to occur on the terraced margins of the caldera, they are absent on the caldera floor. This implies that either the latest stage of subsidence post-dated the formation of mare-type ridges in the region or that the ridges were unable to propagate across the caldera floor due to the unfavourable mechanical characteristics of the caldera floor materials.

Classification and interpretation of calderas

Caldera sizes

Observed caldera sizes on Mars range from less than 10 km to 145 km, and fit an exponential distribution (Fig. 23). The slight downturn in abundance of smaller calderas on the cumulative curve may reflect selective destruction of small calderas during late-stage large-scale subsidence. No apparent relationship exists between individual caldera dimensions or their geological characteristics and variations in local estimated thickness (Comer *et al.* 1985) of the elastic lithosphere.

Information on caldera diameter distributions as measured on Earth is limited to morphologically well-preserved Quaternary calderas since many deeply eroded calderas are either unrecognized or their original topographic rims are no longer available for comparison. With few exceptions Quaternary calderas on Earth are less than about 20 km in diameter, and calderas larger than 60 km are unknown (Walker 1984). While the three-fold greater size range of calderas on Mars may, in principle, reflect the fact that the thickness of the lithosphere and crust of Mars are two to three times the terrestrial values, an even greater size distribution is observed in calderas on Venus where the elastic lithosphere is thought to be considerably

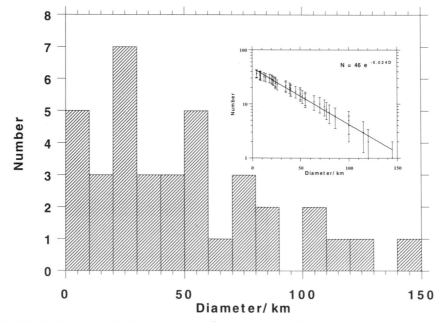

Fig. 23. Relative frequency of caldera diameters. The cumulative size distribution (inset) follows an exponential distribution ($N = 46e^{-0.024D}$).

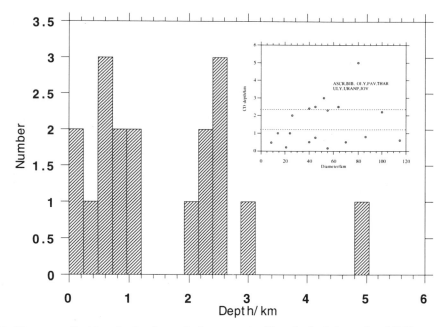

Fig. 24. Histogram of caldera depths. A paucity in apparent caldera depths between 1 and 2.4 km may be an artifact of the measurement techniques, but it is clear that many calderas are shallow whereas a few, such as the summit caldera of Pavonis Mons, are anomalously deep. Inset: Shallow calderas occur throughout the diameter range, but deep calderas tend to be large. Calderas greater than 2 km in depth are Ascraeus, Biblis, Olympus, Pavoris, Tharsis, Ulysses, Uranius Patera and Jovus.

thinner. Factors other than lithospheric characteristics alone must be important in the disparity in caldera sizes. The relative mobility of the surface of Earth due to plate tectonics, which does not favour the formation of large magma chambers, may be a factor. However, on the basis of the current record it must be concluded that larger calderas on Earth may occur, but due to their relatively rarer occurrences, few have accumulated in the geological record in the time interval available within the Quaternary which comprises only 0.0002 of 1% of Earth geologic history.

The topographic relief, geological, and structural characteristics of martian calderas are variable, and suggest that different styles of deformation may occur depending on the magnitude of the caldera relief and the overall caldera diameter. Caldera depths (Fig. 24) appear to be slightly bimodal and calderas may be divided into those less than or equal to 1 km and those greater than or equal to 2 km in depth. Calderas greater than 2 km in depth include large and intermediate diameters. Calderas less than 1 km in depth occur throughout the observed diameter range (Fig. 24, inset). Two calderas of similar diameters can vary in depth, implying that there is a more complex

situation than a simple linear relationship between diameter and depth.

Whereas steep, terraced or furrowed caldera walls and irregular or scalloped margins are common among calderas less than 80 km in diameter, more gently sloping margins and circumferential fractures characterize those 80 km in diameter or larger. Large calderas (110 km or greater) are rarely overlapping, are characterized by fewer interior subsidiary or nested calderas, and their floors are less complex. Within the diameter range 80 to 110 km, a few calderas exhibit some characteristics of both end members. These observations imply a transition in martian caldera morphology and structure at approximately 100 km in diameter from steep-walled and nested or overlapping caldera arrangements to gently sloping, circular and circumferentially fractured caldera styles.

Two types of caldera

On the basis of a comparison of the characteristics of all calderas on Mars (Fig. 25), two fundamental types of caldera are identified (Crumpler et al. 1990, 1994): (1) simple single scarp-bounded

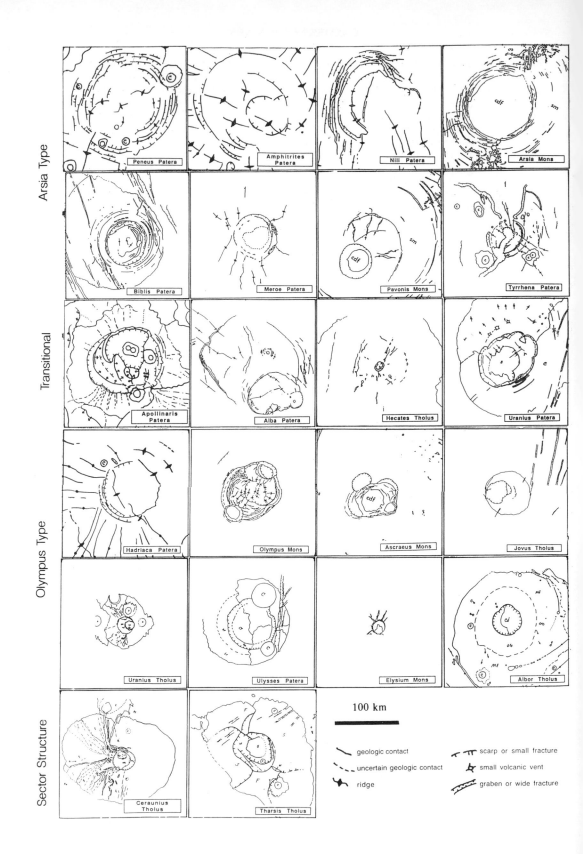

Arsia Type

Transitional

Olympus Type

Sector Structure

Peneus Patera	Amphitrites Patera	Nili Patera	Arsia Mons
Biblis Patera	Meroe Patera	Pavonis Mons	Tyrrhena Patera
Apollinaris Patera	Alba Patera	Hecates Tholus	Uranius Patera
Hadriaca Patera	Olympus Mons	Ascraeus Mons	Jovus Tholus
Uranius Tholus	Ulysses Patera	Elysium Mons	Albor Tholus
Ceraunius Tholus	Tharsis Tholus		

100 km

⟋ geologic contact

⟋ uncertain geologic contact

⟋ ridge

⟞⟙ scarp or small fracture

⟡ small volcanic vent

⟋⟍ graben or wide fracture

volcanic depressions, often with nested or overlapping sets of collapse craters (type example, Olympus Mons); and (2) large-scale concave volcanic depressions or sags with multiple scarps defining their margins (type example, Arsia Mons). Both types occur on the large and relatively young shield volcanoes as well as on the older highland patera-type volcanoes.

Olympus-type. This type includes the calderas of most of the smaller Tharsis and the Elysium shield volcanoes. The overall characteristics of the Olympus type are similar in morphology and apparent structural development to calderas typically associated with central shield volcanism (Macdonald 1965) over a variety of compositions and replenishment rate regimes on Earth. Calderas of this type are characterized by distinct fault-related boundary walls, and often occur in nested and overlapping sets of individual collapse craters, each of generally circular plan shape. The Olympus-type calderas on many volcanoes are contemporaneous with flows which erupted after formation of the main shield. Four sub-types of the Olympus-type caldera may be defined on the basis of the cluster patterns and the overlapping shape of the calderas contributing to the complex: (a) overlapping, (b) nested, (c) irregular, and (d) circular.

The summit caldera complex of Ascraeus Mons is an example of the 'overlapping' type, in which one or more of the smaller calderas lies on the margin of the largest caldera in the sequence. The summit caldera complex of Hecates Tholus is the clearest example of the 'nested' type, in which several smaller calderas all occur within a single much larger summit caldera or depression. The calderas of Uranius Patera and Uranius Tholus, and to some extent Tyrrhena Patera and Apollinaris Patera, may be defined as nested in this sense. The summit caldera of Olympus Mons consists of both nested and overlapping morphologies. Individual calderas of this type on Earth (Walker 1984; Williams & McBirney 1979) as well as Mars (Wood 1984) are generally no more than a few tens of kilometres in diameter. The presence of either nested or overlapping calderas is an indication that magma has been emplaced at

shallow depths with repetitive cycles, the interval of time between caldera collapse events reflecting the relative rates of accumulation in the magma chamber in comparison to the rates of eruption at the surface; that is, accumulation is long and eruptions are short in duration by comparison.

The 'irregular' type is defined on the basis of scalloped and irregular margins. These may represent a further evolution of the complex in which former nested calderas have become subsequently flooded. The calderas of Uranius Patera, Jovus Tholus, and Tharsis Tholus are irregular.

The 'circular' sub-type is often a single caldera or a caldera complex with one or more very small calderas associated with a much larger caldera of extremely circular planform. This sub-type includes Albor Tholus, Ulysses Patera, Elysium Mons, Hadriaca Patera and Ceraunius Tholus. The summit caldera of Elysium Mons is the best example of this type and ranks as one of the most circular compared with the typical shape of small calderas. Because the circularity is comparable to that of many impact craters, the volcanic origin might be suspect, and perhaps unrecognized, were the caldera not located at the summit of one of the major volcanoes.

Arsia-type. The second type of caldera is exemplified by the broadly concave depression on the summit of Arsia Mons. The Arsia-type has gently sloping (sag-like) margins rather than the abrupt bounding escarpments characteristic of the Olympus type, occurs characteristically as a single caldera, is generally more circular, and is larger in diameter than the simple Olympus-type calderas. The smoothly arcuate or circular outline, rather than scalloped and irregular margins, suggests that the Arsia type is not formed through simple flooding of the interior of an Olympus-type caldera complex. The Arsia type has no directly recognizable counterpart on Earth, although some depressions surrounding broad volcanic regions (Erlich 1989; Heiken 1976) and sag-type calderas (Walker 1984) may be comparable in some respects. The broad summit depressions of Pavonis Mons, Alba Patera, and some highland paterae may be

Fig. 25. Structural maps of all calderas on Mars shown at the same scale. Many calderas (Arsia type) appear to be surrounded by ring fractures, arcuate graben and arcuate ridges and are generally shallow in relation to their diameters. Others consist of complex overlapping and nested groups of shallow to relatively deep smaller calderas (Olympus type). At least two volcanoes (Ceraunius Tholus and Tharsis Tholus) appear to have a large-scale sector structure.

included in this category. Relatively shallow relief, as compared with diameter, also characterizes some of these larger calderas as exemplified by the larger circular Arsia-type summit caldera structure of Pavonis Mons.

The occurrence of two of the examples of this type (Arsia and Pavonis) in association with major outflows of lava from the lower flanks of the volcanoes on which they occur is the strongest evidence that at least a significant component of their deformation is related to draining of a large underlying magma reservoir, perhaps over extended periods of time. The Arsia type may alternatively form by thermal contraction and lithospheric loading of a deep intrusive mass. The formations of several calderas of the Arsia type are characteristically late events, in contrast to the contemporaneous timing of the Olympus type with the main period of edifice growth, and reflect a major rejuvenation or re-activation after a significant (by crater counts) period of quiescence (Crumpler & Aubele 1978). On this basis it seems more plausible that the Arsia type result from incremental growth over the lifetime of the associated magmatic systems, a process that may reflect a balance between continued magma chamber growth and long-term subsidence through intrusive loading. Calderas of the Arsia type might represent the end result of unusually long-lived shallow magma chambers that continue to grow laterally with time and in which a significantly large fraction of the magmatism contributes to intrusion rather than edifice building. The mid-life development of this type of caldera on Arsia Mons and Pavonis Mons, prior to and during later major flank eruptions, implies that conditions were unfavourable for the emplacement of vertical dykes from the magma chambers in these two cases until the magma chambers were exceptionally large in diameter, at which point lateral dyke propagation resulting from continued growth of the magma chamber in conjunction with a regional biaxial stress field was sufficient to open fissures of relatively great length.

Additional evidence for caldera collapse prior to termination of eruptions occurs at Tyrrhena Patera and Apollinaris Patera. In both cases significant enlargement along post-collapse ring fractures has occurred, apparently in association with continued eruptions along the ring fractures. Small cones on the low margin of the summit caldera of Hadriaca Patera and fissure-aligned cones on the outer circumferential graben of Uranius Patera are also evidence for volcanism following formation of the major caldera structure.

Origin of two caldera types. The division of calderas into either the Olympus type or Arsia type appears generally, but not entirely, dependent on diameter, as there is a tendency for transitional morphology combining both characteristics in the diameter range between 80 to 100 km. The fundamentally different morphologies of the Olympus-type and Arsia-type calderas could arise from differences in the aspect ratio of the magma chambers, such that the Olympus type occurs in association with a spherical magma chamber and the Arsia type is associated with a tabular chamber. Alternatively, the two types may result from differences in the interaction between stress fields around large magma chambers and the surface, particularly if differences in the depth of the magma chamber are small in relation to variations in the diameter of the chamber. In addition, longer-lived development and incremental, rather than catastrophic, formation may account for the different patterns of deformation around magma chambers of the Arsia type.

Interpretation of caldera/magma chamber-related deformation

The patterns of deformation on the surface within calderas may provide evidence for the orientation of the regional stress field, the mechanism of caldera formation, and the origin and sign of strains affecting the exterior flanks of the associated volcano. Many calderas on Mars exhibit relatively flat, featureless, or smooth floors, but others are characterized by complex deformation that has accompanied or followed collapse. Examples with flat, featureless, or smooth floors include the calderas of Alba Patera, Peneus Patera, Ascraeus Mons, Biblis Patera, the smaller Tharsis volcanoes (Jovus Tholus, Tharsis Tholus, Ulysses Patera), the smaller calderas of Pavonis Mons and Hecates Tholus, Elysium Mons, Albor Tholus, and Ceraunius Tholus.

Calderas in which complex structure occurs on the caldera floor are exemplified by the interior of the larger caldera on Olympus Mons. In this example both circumferential and radial mare-type wrinkle ridges indicative of contraction occur within an annulus of circumferential graben and scarps. Together these represent evidence for an inner zone of compression and an exterior zone of extension. Zuber & Mouginis-Mark (1992) have compared the predictions from finite element models of magma chamber evolution with the observed tectonic patterns in the larger Olympus Mons caldera and find that the observed pattern of deformation may be explained by subsidence over a deflated magma chamber. This agrees with general baseline results determined from models of the deformation of an elastic plate over an expanding or contracting source at depth that predict the formation of concentric extensional faulting and interior compression in calderas associated with magma chamber deflation. On this basis Zuber & Mouginis-Mark (1992) explored the depth and relative magnitude of subsidence necessary to generate the observed characteristics. A key to these results is the transition from radial contraction to radial extension, as this is sensitive to the depth and lateral size of any magma chamber. They found that deflation of a relatively flat magma chamber at a depth equivalent to the base of the volcanic pile was capable of generating the observed latest deformation within the summit caldera.

Similar evidence for compressional deformation in caldera interiors occurs in the summit calderas of Pavonis Mons, Uranius Patera, Amphitrites Patera, and Apollinaris Patera. This type of deformation seems to have occurred in the larger calderas, particularly where the relief across the caldera floor is concave. On this basis it might be predicted that the floors of Arsia Mons, Nili Patera and Meroe Patera are characterized by similar deformation. However, evidence for contractional structures is not present in these cases, possibly in part because these caldera floors appear buried by late lava flows. On the basis of high-resolution image data it can be shown that small mare-type ridges occur on the floor of the Ascraeus Mons caldera (Mouginis-Mark 1981) that are otherwise unobservable at low resolutions. Thus, many of the apparently smooth-floored calderas may also be characterized by this type of deformation that cannot be readily identified with available data. The absence of uniformly high-resolution data for all of the calderas on Mars limits the ability to compare their strain characteristics. The applicability of these types of observations to understanding caldera formation and evolution would be greatly facilitated by uniform and high resolution data from each volcano.

Simple physical models of deformation associated with magma chamber expansion (Marti et al. 1994), predict entirely different patterns of deformation than that of the magma chamber deflation discussed above. Magma chamber inflation for a broad range of likely magma chamber geometries is expected to result in extensional deformation at the surface near the

centre of the associated caldera and peripheral compressional deformation on the flanks. In addition accumulated strain associated with the period of magma chamber growth is likely to be accommodated through thrusting along concentric faults in the upper flanks and directed outward from the caldera. Considering that the long-term effects of magma chamber inflation and continued growth may be cumulative, a significant endogenous component of edifice volume growth and flank deformation might be expected. These effects will be more pronounced for shallow magma chambers residing above the base of the edifice, a condition that is to be expected on Mars due to the tendency for intrusions and magma chambers to stall at neutral buoyancy zones located within the larger edifices (Wilson & Head 1994). The long-term consequences of the thrusting associated with the growth stage of magma chambers may be significant, and directly influence the large-scale characteristics of the flanks of many volcanic edifices. For example, the relatively steeper upper flanks of Olympus Mons and the presence there of unusual arcuate terraces may originate in part from the accumulated effects of magma chamber growth. A somewhat similar interpretation has been suggested for the unusually steep flanks of the Galapagos shield volcanoes (McBirney & Williams 1969). An endogenous component of growth may be important in many large edifices on Earth and Mars and could have significant influence on adjacent flank slope and structural characteristics.

Characteristics, classification, and interpretation of flank structure

A recurring theme in many of the calderas and flank structures on martian volcanoes is the presence of through-going fissures and linear fault trends that extend through the summit and flanks. Several of the calderas and caldera complexes are elongate in directions that parallel these through-going tectonic patterns. Similar patterns occur on many terrestrial volcanoes and are characterized by an apparently high degree of influence and interaction with regional stress fields (Nakamura 1977, 1984). Nakamura proposed that the pattern of dykes and fissures associated with many volcanoes may be used as a guide to evaluating the orientation of regional stress fields because the emplacement of dykes and fissures is sensitive to the orientation of the regional minimum compressive stress orientation.

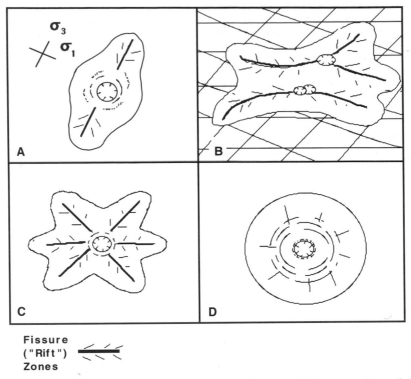

Fissure ("Rift") Zones

Fig. 26. Summary of four fundamental patterns of caldera and flank structural features seen in martian volcanoes and the interpretation of their significance according to the apparent influence of regional stress fields in the overall pattern of summit and flank fractures and caldera alignments: (**A**) strong, (**B**) intermediate, (**C**) weak, and (**D**) no interaction with regional stress field. Cross-hatched lines in (**B**) represents orientations of pre-existing regional 'structural fabrics'.

These characteristics, together with structural features on the flanks, may be used to infer the long-term patterns of deformation. Many of the observed largest scale structural characteristics of martian volcanoes may be attributed to gravitational instabilities of one type or another.

Four types of flank structure pattern

We identify four simple categories of flank structure (Fig. 26) in terms of the apparent degree of interaction with regional or exterior stress fields: (A) strong, (B) moderate, (C) weak, and (D) none. These divisions are based on a comparison of our structural maps of all large volcanoes on Mars with predictions from the theory of stress control on dyke and fissure orientation (Muller & Pollard 1977) and the Nakamura (1977, 1984) interpretation of stress patterns in volcanoes.

Type (A) (strong influence of regional stress) is characterized by vent locations and feature alignments that follow the same linear pattern both on a regional and a local scale. If a pre-existing structural fabric consisting of several orientations is present, only one orientation is well-developed in this type. This may apply to central volcanoes as well as isolated areal volcanic fields on Earth. Where developed in association with a central volcano, a single fissure trend usually dominates which bisects the central vent, caldera, or nested caldera (Fig. 26A). This type of pattern is well-developed in the larger Galápagos shield volcanoes where concentric faulting and eruptive fissures are common near the summit and less dominant radial fissures occur at greater distances, usually on the lower flanks (Rowland & Munro 1992; McBirney & Williams 1969). Additional examples of this morphology on Earth, where through-going fissure trends are prominent, include Nyiragongo, in the West African Rift, and Hekla in Iceland. Examples of this type on Mars include Arsia Mons, Pavonis Mons, Ascraeus Mons and Apollinaris Patera.

Type (B) (moderate influence of regional stress) is characterized by structures influenced by both regional and local tectonic stress sources. In this type, there may be some tendency for vents, rifts, and faulting to follow regional stress orientations, but there is also a tendency for vents, fissures, and rifts to follow pre-existing structural fabric orientations (Fiske & Jackson 1972) and local tectonic or gravitational stresses (McTigue & Mei 1981). The resulting pattern of volcanic fissures and vents reflects the sum of tectonic and body stresses, and local structural fabrics oriented in differing directions and varying in local intensity, often with time, as the volcano or its nearest neighbours grow and interact (Fig. 26B). The latter effects are largely a consequence of the so-called 'edifice effects' and are a result of the gravitational body stresses in the flanks in response to the shape of the volcano (Lipman 1980), magmatic inflation and deflation, the presence of a weak substrate, and the presence or absence of a buttressing effect by adjacent volcanoes (Dieterich 1988; Lipman 1980; Fiske & Jackson 1972). On Earth the young Hawaiian volcanoes are the best known example of this type of complex interaction between tectonic and local stress fields. Other volcanoes known to exhibit some of these characteristics include many oceanic islands, such as Reunion (Duffield *et al.* 1982). Examples of the influence of moderate regional stresses on Mars include Hecates Tholus, Olympus Mons, Elysium Mons, and Tyrrhena Patera.

Type (C) (weak interaction with a regional stress field) is characterized by little apparent regional tectonic influence on the orientation of eruptive fissures and vents, and gravitational or body stresses may dominate (Fig. 26C). In addition to a few oceanic volcanoes, many continental central (composite) volcanoes are dominated by potential gravitational stress influences on the orientation of flank structures. Examples of this type of independent development in the absence of a strong regional stress pattern are the Geisha seamounts (Rubin & Pollard 1987; Vogt & Smoot 1984). On Mars, Tharsis Tholus, Alba Patera and Uranius Patera appear to have formed in the absence of a strong regional stress regime..

Type (D) (no apparent interaction with a regional stress field) is not identified on Earth in large volcanoes, although it may occur in small vents such as plains-type shield volcanoes and cinder cones. In the absence of any regional gradients in the stress field or local gravitational body stresses, the stresses in the near field associated with the inflation and deflation of the magma chamber are likely to dominate (Fig. 26D), and simple radial and circumferential patterns of strain develop. Examples of this type on Mars include Biblis Patera, in particular, plus Uranius Tholus, Ceraunius Tholus, Jovus Tholus, Ulysses Patera and Albor Tholus.

These categorizations are tentative, particularly for types (C) and (D), and require more detailed analysis. But it is clear that regional tectonic stresses are more strongly expressed in the evolution and structure of the larger martian calderas, an indication that size may be important in accentuating the role of regional stresses.

Rift zones and axial symmetry

Rifts and linear fissure patterns occur on martian volcanoes, and are similar to some fissure patterns occurring on volcanoes on Earth. On Earth at least three distinct overall geometries of rifting are identified: (1) fissures that trend through the main shield (e.g. Galápagos, Hekla, Nyiragongo); (2) fissures and small vents associated with circumferential fracture patterns about caldera margins (e.g. Galápagos) and (3) arcuate, ridge-like fissures ('rift zones') that are concave, in plan view, away from adjacent volcanic centres (e.g. Piton de la Fournaise, Hawaii). Through-going or axial fissure trends, linear vent and pit alignments, and eruptions from circumferential fractures are the dominant form of fissure on martian volcanoes. Linear styles of rifts (Arsia Mons, Pavonis Mons, Ascraeus Mons), through-trending linear structures (Elysium Mons, Hecates Tholus), and elongate caldera sequences (Olympus Mons, Uranius Patera) on martian volcanoes are oriented roughly tangentially to regional slopes. This suggests that asymmetric gravitational stresses arising from regional slopes on which the martian volcanoes are situated may be the primary cause of the axial eruptive patterns rather than gravitational stresses on the flanks of each edifice. The rifts in martian volcanoes are in this respect more analogous to the Galápagos, Hekla, and Nyiragongo, which occur in locations where there is a regionally uniform orientation of the minimum principal stress, than to the rifts of Hawaiian volcanoes.

Strong orientations of flank stress in Hawaii appear to arise from the continual lateral translation of new centres of volcanism associated with plate movement over the Hawaiian hot spot such that each new shield volcano must build on the flanks of existing edifices (Lipman & Moore 1994; Lipman 1980; Fiske & Jackson 1972). As each new volcano grows to dimensions large enough for gravitational spreading to become significant, the buttressing effect of adjacent older volcanoes acts to confine spreading, and spreading of the new volcano occurs in a uniform direction. An arcuate detachment style of deformation dominates, analogous to break-away zones on major landslides which provide convenient access for magmas. As a result, magmas utilizing the fissures in Hawaiian shield volcanoes tend to be arcuate such that the concave side faces away from an adjacent older edifice.

The long-term stability of the lithosphere with respect to deep magma source regions has enabled single large volcanic centres to accumulate on Mars rather than the overlapping, multiple edifices as in Hawaii. Each volcano has grown relatively unconfined from a single source such that the tendency for gravitational spreading in the larger martian volcanoes is radially symmetric, the lower flanks becoming the principal buttresses against continued spreading with time. Introduction of regional slopes serves to alter the radial strain symmetry and leads to axial symmetry patterns in the long term. The through-going alignment of calderas, pits, and channels in Tyrrhena Patera does not follow this simple pattern of correlation with regional slope, however. Because Tyrrhena Patera lies along a radial line with Hadrica Patera from the centre of the Hellas Basin, it is possible that the axial symmetry in this case developed in response to a radial fracture associated with the Hellas impact basin to the southwest.

Because martian volcano fissure patterns are several hundred kilometres long, the question also arises as to how the fissures form. One interpretation is that the fissures represent the surface expression of extremely large dykes propagated from the magma source region. The difficulty with this model is that the lateral length of dykes ascending from a deep source tends to be slightly less than their vertical length (Maaløe 1987) even under conditions likely to arise in the thick martian lithosphere. Dykes of the observed length would imply source depths in excess of several hundred kilometres for magmas ascending in a single crack. Although the sources are potentially this deep for martian magmas, the elastic lithosphere capable of propagating such dykes is considerably thinner and dykes ascending directly from a great depth will most likely be horizontally shorter than the width of the large martian shield volcanoes.

A plausible alternative for the formation of through-going fissures several hundred kilometres in length is that they result from the lateral propagation of dykes from a magma chamber along the regional minimum stress orientation. Models of the emplacement of lateral dykes from magma chambers at a neutral buoyancy zone under constant driving pressure (Parfitt & Head 1993; Parfitt *et al.* 1993) imply that the dykes can grow very wide and can be propagated over a great distance. The dyke under these conditions can be shown to be directly related to the size of the magma chamber, in as much as the volume that may be erupted from a magma chamber (Blake 1981) to produce a dyke is a fixed percentage of the magma chamber volume. As a result dykes several hundred kilometres long may be easy to propagate from magma chambers associated with the larger martian calderas.

Gravitational flank instability and sector collapse

In addition to influencing the site of vents and fissures, flank instability may result in significant structural deformation of volcanoes. Gravitational instability of the upper flanks of several martian volcanoes (Cave *et al.* 1994; Head 1996; Thomas *et al.* 1989; Crumpler 1980) is likely, considering their great size and the obvious importance of gravitational body forces on volcano flanks on Earth (Lipman & Moore 1994; Duffield *et al.* 1982; Ridley 1971; Moore & Krivoy 1964), and this may have a significant influence on the characteristics of summit calderas.

Flank instabilities. Two fundamental types of flank instability and collapse known to influence eruption characteristics are common on Earth: (1) catastrophic and (2) incremental. The first type is common among large silicic composite volcanoes with steep slopes and appears to result from oversteepening of the flanks during inflation of a shallow magma chamber. Catastrophic flank collapse is now typified by the historic collapses of Mount St. Helens and Bezymianny (Belousov 1994). Other examples of this type of volcano flank collapse and its importance in the ensuing eruptions have been recognized in other volcanoes on Earth (Boudon & Semet 1994). Large-scale sector structure resulting from incremental flank sector sliding or collapse was recognized to occur on some terrestrial volcanoes (Ridley 1971) with implications for large martian shield volcanoes (Crumpler 1980).

Incremental flank collapse has been interpreted to reflect long-term gravity spreading associated with large flank and regional slopes, and appears to be characteristic of large shield-type volcanoes in certain environments (Nakamura 1982) such as Hawaii (Swanson *et al.* 1976; Moore & Krivoy 1964), Mount Etna (McGuire & Pullen 1989), Piton de la Fournaise (Duffield *et al.* 1982), and other large volcano complexes (Borgia *et al.* 1990). The importance of internal body stresses within volcanic edifices on the location of vents and internal magma ascent pathways is less frequently discussed, but potentially significant in large volcanoes on Earth (Shteynberg & Solov'yev 1976; Francis & Abbot 1973). A complete assessment of the influence of body forces on the location of flank vents within the larger volcanoes on Earth and Mars has not yet been made.

Several scales and styles of gravity-induced flank structure on martian volcanoes have been identified, and are summarized in Fig. 27. These may be divided into stresses related to (1) the relief of individual volcanoes, (2) the regional slopes on which individual volcanoes have been constructed, and (3) the loading of the lithosphere by the mass of the volcanoes. Many of these are best characterized by the structure of Olympus Mons, but are present to some extent in many of the larger shield volcanoes.

Several previously proposed models suggest that gravitational body forces in Olympus Mons arise from the relief associated with the main shield (Thomas *et al.* 1989; Crumpler 1980). Several variations on this model have been used to account for differing characteristics throughout Olympus Mons, its flanks, and its surroundings (Borgia *et al.* 1990; Tanaka 1985; Francis & Wadge 1983; Lopes *et al.* 1980, 1982; Harris 1977). Although Hawaiian-type listric slumping instabilities do not appear to play a part in the large-scale structure of the summits of martian volcanoes, some aspects of the lower flank morphology of the larger Tharsis volcanoes have been interpreted as reflecting body stresses in the edifice (Borgia *et al.* 1990; Thomas *et al.* 1989; Francis & Wadge 1983). These include the scarp-like lower flanks of Olympus Mons. The collapse process responsible for the scarps must be similar to the catastrophic landslides on the lower slopes of Hawaiian volcanoes (Moore 1964). But whereas the plate motion eventually brings the distal flanks of Hawaiian volcanoes over the centre of the hot spot source of ascending magmas, the martian lithosphere is stable and the collapse on the lower flanks is perpetually isolated far from the centre of eruption. Accordingly, there is little chance that

stresses operating on the distal flanks can interact with centralized magma bodies near the vent. As on Hawaii, the collapse probably occurs because the lower flanks are unbuttressed. But as there were no adjacent volcanoes, radial instability of the edifice occurred at great distance from the magma source and did not produce the uniquely Hawaiian-style fissure system.

At a much larger scale, gravity sliding of the whole volcano on a regional topographic slope can occur (McGovern & Solomon 1993; Harris 1977). Tensile strain of the whole volcano under these conditions can account for the prevalent biaxial symmetry in the larger volcanoes of Tharsis, and the unusual tectonic deformation described as 'aureoles' that occurs down the regional topographic gradient and far beyond the flanks of Olympus Mons (Borgia *et al.* 1990; Tanaka 1985; Francis & Wadge 1983; Lopes *et al.* 1980, 1982; Harris 1977) and the Tharsis Montes (Zimbelman & Edgett 1992). Variously described as landslides, landslips, and gravity slides, the scale and magnitude are more like that associated with regional gravity sliding in which the allocthonous mass moves more or less coherently. Landslides generally refer to situations in which the coherence is lost and the allochthonous mass is a jumble of disconnected materials shed from steep slopes. The landslip model bears some resemblance to the situation with Kilauea in that the whole volcano, or significant portions of the volcano, is interpreted to be sliding on a substrate comprising of the pre-existing seafloor and the flanks of Mauna Loa. In the case of Olympus Mons, the buttressing slope is not another volcano, but the regional slope of the Tharsis province. Long-term gravity sliding, even on slopes as shallow as that of the Tharsis region, may be possible given the potential lubrication of the underlying pre-volcanic crust with water ice (Tanaka 1985).

Lithospheric loading by the large mass of martian volcanoes (McGovern & Solomon 1993; Comer *et al.* 1985) is an additional source of deformation potentially capable of influencing the near-field stresses at calderas on their summits as well as the tectonic characteristics of their flanks. Analysis of the bending stresses predicts that extensional deformation will occur on the outer flanks, with compressional deformation on the main body of the volcanoes. The unusual arcuate terraces (Olympus Mons and Ascraeus Mons) and mare-type wrinkle ridges (Ascraeus Mons) on the upper flanks of the larger Tharsis volcanoes may arise in part through this type of deformation. Alternatively, as discussed above, under certain conditions of magma chamber expansion, uplift of the

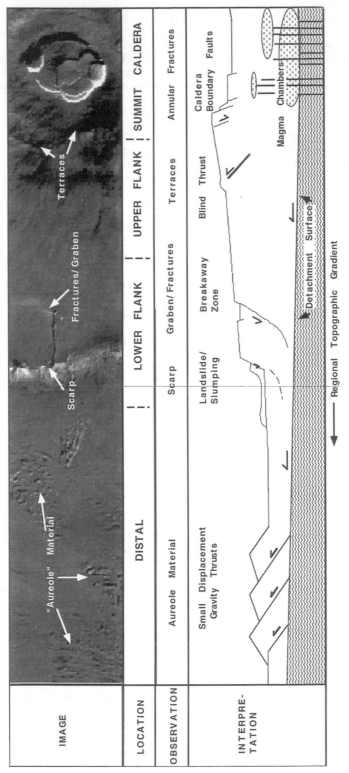

Fig. 27. Differing styles of flank structures and their interpretation as shown by the northwest flank of Olympus Mons. Many of the regional patterns of strain in and around the flanks and calderas of martian shield volcanoes suggest orientation of the regional minimum stress direction at right angles to regional slopes on which the volcanoes are built. In the diagram the regional topographic gradient is down from right to left; however, due to loading of the surface by the mass of the shield volcano, the base of the volcano may be depressed as shown here. The regional topographic gradient, in combination with the topographic relief of the volcano flanks, may thus enhance gravity stress on the down-gradient side of the edifice. This suggests that in addition to gravitational body stresses associated with topographic edifices of the larger volcanoes, tectonic stresses arising from the surrounding regional slopes may have influenced the patterns of deformation in many individual volcanoes in the Tharsis and Elysium regions.

overlying material is expected to occur along inward-dipping reverse faults (Marti *et al.* 1994). The terraces may represent the upward termination of blind thrust faults accommodating magma chamber expansion. In this case, the terraces represent a response of the flanks to endogenous (intrusive) growth of the shield volcano possibly aided by loading stresses associated with the edifice as a whole.

Sector structure. Potentially related to all of the above styles of deformation are sector structures. Sector structure, similar to that seen in many volcanoes on Earth, is present on some smaller martian volcanoes in which a significant fraction of the volcano flank undergoes either catastrophic or incremental collapse. Tharsis Tholus represents the best example of sector structure (Robinson & Rowland 1994). The summit caldera lies at the head of several arcuate scarps that cut through the flanks and summit region, and the summit caldera is elongate along the intersecting trends of the scarps. The large-scale faulting and slumping appears best developed on the northeast and southwest flanks. The lower flanks are covered by later regional plains-forming lava flows, so that the details of the lower flanks and the nature of the deformation associated with the summit collapse are obscured. Although the slopes of Tharsis Tholus are locally somewhat steeper than those of typical martian volcanoes (Robinson & Rowland 1994), this is probably not the origin of the sector structure. It may be significant that Tharsis Tholus, like Olympus Mons, is situated on the regional topographic gradient of the Tharsis region and this may have controlled the orientation of large-scale gravity sliding in a manner similar to that seen in other, but larger, volcanoes of the Tharsis region.

Another style of sector structure occurs at Ceraunius Tholus and is completely different. A circular summit caldera opens westward onto the deeply channelled flanks of the main shield. The lower flanks are obscured by later plains-forming lavas. But there is no evidence for the influence of either regional topographic slopes or regional tectonic stresses, as the volcano flanks and the sector structure are oriented at right angles to these potential influences. Because the sector structure is oriented along the axis of elongation of the volcano as a whole, it is more likely that the emplacement of magmas was asymmetric and resulted in an off-axis stress in the summit region and subsequent collapse on the west flank. The channelled and furrowed flanks are atypical of large shield volcanoes in the Tharsis region and appear to be analogous to highland paterae that are thought to be dominantly pyroclastic in origin. This, together with the absence of significant apparent flank deformation and the rather smooth west flanks, suggests that sector collapse in this case may have been similar to the type seen in silicic volcanoes on Earth and associated with catastrophic rather than incremental collapse.

Discussion and conclusions

On Earth erosion and vegetation both obscure many of the important relationships necessary to assess the evolving stress patterns associated with volcano evolution. Because of the excellent preservation of structure on martian volcanoes and the corresponding ability to determine the timing of deformation associated with caldera development, the influence of magma chambers on edifice flanks may be examined in ways that are not easily assessed on terrestrial calderas.

The stress environment associated with the two basic and opposing scenarios for caldera formation (inflation versus deflation) predicts very different initial structural patterns that have important implications for the surrounding edifice flanks. On the basis of the general characteristics preserved in martian calderas, inflation, deflation and loading can each account for different elements of the deformation seen at individual calderas. Some characteristics predicted from all three models occur in the more complex and larger calderas because the collapse process itself leads to an entirely different stress regime and the corresponding strain pattern is overprinted on the initial patterns. For many of the structurally simpler calderas, the observed structures are consistent with the following sequence of events (with martian caldera examples annotated for relevant events): (1) magma chamber overpressurization and expansion or propagation of large dykes laterally to form linear eruption lines or fissures, (2) failure of the elastic overburden under radial tension over the corresponding uplift, and initiation of caldera collapse, (3) eruption of the magma and continued collapse and subsidence of the overlying crust, continued tensile fracturing of the margins (Nili Patera, Peneus Patera, Amphitrites Patera, Meroe Patera, Biblis Patera, Hecates Tholus, Elysium Mons, upper calderas of Ascraeus Mons, Jovus Tholus, Albor Tholus, Uranius Tholus, Ulysses Patera, Ceraunius Tholus), (4) onset of compressive stress and strains in the subsiding block (Olympus Mons,

Pavonis Mons, Ascraeus Mons), and (5) possible long-term sagging of the dense, cooling intrusives beneath the caldera as new intrusions of magma continue during the late stages in the evolution of the magmatic system. Tharsis Tholus appears to represent an additional case where sector-type collapse has been particularly important in the structure. In a few of the more complex and larger calderas, post-collapse extension along the margins of the caldera appears to be the site of subsequent fissure vents (Arsia Mons, Pavonis Mons, Hadriaca Patera, Tyrrhena Patera, Uranius Patera, Apollinaris Patera, Alba Patera). The deepest calderas are associated with evidence for voluminous eruptions elsewhere on the flanks, and in these cases appear to form largely from evacuation and deflation of magma chambers with or without extensive precursor inflation (Arsia Mons, Pavonis Mons, Ascraeus Mons, Olympus Mons). Draining of the magma chamber in these cases appears to be aided by the development of flank vents and linear fissures.

The prevalence of horizontal axial symmetry and through-going rifts in many of the martian volcanic edifices is interpreted to represent the influence of regional topographic slope in controlling the regional orientation of the minimum compressive stress and the corresponding propagation of shallow dykes away from the central magma chamber. Propagation of large dykes may also evacuate the shallow magma chambers associated with through-going fissure trends without significant precursor inflation, thus further complicating the interpretation of the preserved structural history.

Because significant strain is expected to occur in association with magma chamber growth, the long-term effects of magma chamber evolution within large volcanoes may have a significant effect on overall volcano volume and shape. In addition, continued deformation of the flanks associated with magma chamber growth between cycles of caldera collapse may contribute to steepening of the upper flanks and local thrust faulting. Steeper flanks and unusual terraces on the upper flanks of the larger martian volcanoes might have arisen from this effect. Similar inflationary influences may be important in volcanoes on Earth, but may be obscured by the long-term effects of erosion during the course of edifice growth.

Research for this paper was supported by grants from the National Aeronautics and Space Administration (NAGW-1873) to J.W.H. Thanks are extended to Peter Neivert for help in preparation of the manuscript. We especially thank Lionel Wilson and Mark Bulmer for their substantive and helpful reviews.

References

BARLOW, N. G. & ZIMBELMAN, J. R. 1988. Venusian coronae: comparisons with Alba Patera, Mars. *Lunar and Planetary Science*, **XIX**, 35–36.

BELOUSOV, A. B. 1994. Large scale sector collapses at Kurile-Kamchatka volcanoes in the 20th century. *Conference on Volcano Instability on Earth and Other Planets*, Geological Society of London, 1–2.

BIBRING, J.-P., COMBES, M., LANGEVIN, Y. *ET AL.* 1990. ISM observations of Mars and Phobos: First results. *Proceedings of the Twentieth Lunar and Planetary Science Conference*, 461–471.

BLAKE, S. 1981. Volcanism and the dynamics of open magma chambers. *Nature*, **289**, 783–785.

BORGIA, A., BURR, J., MONTERO, W., MORALES, L. D. & ALVARADO, G. E. 1990. Fault propagation folds induced by gravitational failure and slumping of the central Costa Rica volcanic range: implications for large terrestrial and martian volcanic edifices. *Journal of Geophysical Research*, **95**, 14 357–14 382.

BOUDON, G. & M. SEMET, G. E. 1994. Repetitive sector collapses at La Grande Decouverte-Soufriere volcano: mechanisms and implications on future activity. *Conference on Volcano Instability on Earth and Other Planets*, Geological Society of London, 3–4.

CARR, M. H., BLASIUS, K. R., GREELEY, R., GUEST, J. E. & MURRAY, J. E. 1977. Observations on some martian volcanic features as viewed from the Viking orbiters. *Journal of Geophysical Research*, **82**, 3985–4015.

CATTERMOLE, P. 1986. Linear volcanic features at Alba Patera, Mars – probable spatter ridges. *Journal of Geophysical Research, Proceedings of the Seventeenth Lunar and Planetary Science Conference*, **91**, E159–E165.

——1989. *Planetary Volcanism: a Study of Volcanic Activity in the Solar System*. Ellis Harwood, Chichester, 285–339.

CAVE, J., GUEST, J. E. & BULMER, M. 1994. Slope instability on Elysium Mons and other martian volcanoes. *Conference on Volcano Instability on Earth and Other Planets*, Geological Society of London, 10–11.

CHADWICK, W. W. & HOWARD, K. A. 1991. The pattern of circumferential and radial eruptive fissures on the volcanoes of Fernandina and Isabela Islands, Galápagos. *Bulletin of Volcanology*, **53**, 257–275.

COMER, R. P., SOLOMON, S. C. & HEAD, J. W. 1985. Mars: Thickness of the lithosphere from the tectonic response to volcanic loads. *Reviews of Geophysics*, **23**, 61–92.

CROWN, D. A. & GREELEY, R. 1990. Styles of volcanism, tectonic associations, and evidence for magma–water interactions in Eastern Hellas, Mars. *Lunar and Planetary Science*, **21**, 250–251.

—— & ——1993. Volcanic geology of Hadriaca Patera and the Eastern Hellas Region of Mars. *Journal of Geophysical Research*, **98**, 3431–3451.

—— & ——1995. *Geologic Map of MTM Quadrangles −30 262 and −30 267, Hadriaca Patera Region of Mars*. United States Geological Survey miscellaneous investigation map series.

——, LESHIN, L. A. & GREELEY, R. 1987. *Explosive volcanic deposits on Mars: Preliminary investigations*. NASA Technical Memorandum, **89810**, 327–329.

CRUMPLER, L. S. 1980. Gravity tectonics and volcanism: implications for the Earth and Mars. *Reports of Planetary Geology and Geophysics Program*, NASA Technical Memorandum, **82385**, 88–89.

—— & AUBELE, J. C. 1978. Structural evolution of Arsia Mons, Pavonis Mons and Ascreus Mons: Tharsis region of Mars. *Icarus*, **34**, 496–511.

—— & ——1989. Influence of tectonic and volcanic stresses on the flank structure of martian volcanoes. *MEVTV Workshop on Tectonic Features on Mars*, Lunar and Planetary Institute-Technical Report, **89-06**, 25–27.

——, —— & HEAD, J. W. 1990. Calderas on Mars: Implications of style and history for subsurface magmatism. *MEVTV Workshop on the Evolution of Magma Bodies on Mars, 27–8*, Lunar and Planetary Institute Technical Report, **90-04**, 27–28.

——, HEAD, J. W. & AUBELE, J. C. 1994. Calderas on Mars: Classification, characteristics, and processses related to mechanisms of formation. *Lunar and Planetary Science*, **25**, 305–306.

CULLEN, A. B., McBIRNEY, A. R. & ROGERS, R. D. 1987. Structural controls on the morphology of Galápagos shields. *Journal of Volcanology and Geothermal Research*, **34**, 143–151.

DIETERICH, J. H. 1988. Growth and persistence of Hawaiian volcanic rift zones. *Journal of Geophysical Research*, **93**, 4258–4270.

DUFFIELD, W. A., STIELTJES, L. & VARET, J. 1982. Huge landslide blocks in the growth of Piton de la Fournaise, La Reunion, and Kilauea volcano, Hawaii. *Journal of Volcanology and Geothermal Research*, **12**, 147–160.

EDGETT, K. S. 1990. Possible cinder cones near the summit of Pavonis Mons, Mars. *Lunar and Planetary Science*, **XXI**, 311–312.

ERLICH, E. I. 1989. Specific type of volcano-tectonic depression surrounding great groups of volcanoes. *IAVCEI Abstracts, Continental Magmatism*, New Mexico Bureau of Mines and Mineral Resources, Bulletin **131**, 83.

FISKE, R. S. & JACKSON, E. D. 1972. Orientation and growth of Hawaiian volcanic rifts: the effects of regional structure and gravitational stresses. *Proceedings of the Royal Society*, **A329**, 299–326.

FRANCIS, P. W. & ABBOTT. 1973. Sizes of conical volcanoes. *Nature*, **244**, 22–23.

—— & WADGE, G. 1983. The Olympus Mons aureole: formation by gravitational spreading. *Journal of Geophysical Research*, **88**, 8333–8344.

—— & WOOD, C. A. 1982. Absence of silicic volcanism on Mars: Implications for crustal composition and volatile abundance. *Journal of Geophysical Research*, **87**, 9881–9889.

GREELEY, R. & CROWN, D. A. 1990. Volcanic geology of Tyrrhena Patera, Mars. *Journal of Geophysical Research*, **95**, 7133–7149.

—— & GUEST, J. E. 1987. *Geologic Map of the Eastern Equatorial Region of Mars*. United States Geological Survey, Miscellaneous Investigation Series, 1:15 000 000-scale, Map I-1802B.

—— & SPUDIS, P. D. 1978. Volcanism in the cratered terrain hemisphere of Mars. *Geophysical Research Letters*, **5**, 453–455.

—— & ——1981. Volcanism on Mars. *Reviews of Geophysics and Space Physics*, **19**, 13–41.

——, —— & WOMER, M. B. 1978. The patera of Mars – a unique syle of planetary volcanism. *EOS Transactions of the American Geophysical Union*, **59**, 310.

GROSFILS, E. B. & HEAD, J. W. 1994. The global distribution of giant radiating dike swarms on Venus: Implications for the global stress state. *Geophysical Research Letters*, **21**, 701–704.

GUDMUNDSSON, A. 1986. Formation of crustal magma chambers in Iceland. *Geology*, **14**, 164–166

—— 1988. Formation of collapse calderas. *Geology*, **16**, 808–810.

GULICK, V. C. & BAKER, V. R. 1990. Origin and evolution of valleys on martian volcanoes. *Journal of Geophysical Research*, **95**, 14 325–14 344.

HARRIS, S. A. 1977. The aureole of Olympus Mons, Mars. *Journal of Geophysical Research*, **82**, 3099–3107.

HEAD, J. W. 1996. Volcano instability development: A planetary perspective. *This volume*.

—— & WILSON, L. 1992. Magma reservoirs and neutral buoyancy zones on Venus: implications for the formation and evolution of volcanic landforms. *Journal of Geophysical Research*, **97**, 3877–3903

—— & ——1993. Lunar graben formation due to near-surface deformation accompanying dike emplacement. *Planetary and Space Sciences*, **10**, 719–727.

——, CRUMPLER, L. S., AUBELE, J. C., GUEST, J. E. & SAUNDERS, R. S. 1992. Venus volcanism: Classifications of volcanic features and structures, associations and global distribution from Magellan data. *Journal of Geophysical Research*, **97**, 13 153–13 198.

HEIKEN, G. 1976. Depressions surrounding volcanic fields: a reflection of underlying batholiths? *Geology*, **4**, 568–573.

HILLER, K. H., JANLE, P., NEUKUM, G., GUEST, J. E. & LOPES, R. 1982. Mars: Stratigraphy and gravimetry of Olympus Mons and its aureole. *Journal of Geophysical Research*, **87**, 9905–9911.

HODGES, C. A. & MOORE, H. J. 1994. *Atlas of Volcanic Landforms on Mars*. United States Geological Survey Professional Paper, **1534**.

KOMURO, H. 1987. Experiments on cauldron formation: polygonal cauldron and ring fractures. *Journal of Volcanology and Geothermal Research*, **31**, 139–149

LIPMAN, P. W. 1980. The southwest rift zone of Mauna Loa: Implications for structural evolution of Hawaiian volcanoes. *American Journal of Science*, **280**, 752–776.

—— & MOORE, J. G. 1994. Interplay between volcanic growth, subsidence, and landsliding at Mauna Loa, Hawaii. *Conference on Volcano Instability on Earth and Other Planets*, Geological Society of London, 32–33.

LOPES, R. M. C., GUEST, J. E. & WILSON, C. J. 1980. The origin of the Olympus Mons aureole and perimeter scarp. *Moon and Planets*, **22**, 221–234.

——, ——, HILLER, K. & NEUKUM, G. 1982. Further evidence for mass movement origin of the Olympus Mons aureole. *Journal of Geophysical Research*, **87**, 9917–9928.

MCBIRNEY, A. R. 1990. An historical note on the origin of calderas. *Journal of Volcanology and Geothermal Research*, **42**, 303–306.

—— & WILLIAMS, H. 1969. Geology and petrology of the Galápagos Islands. *Geological Society of America Memoir*, **118**, 21–100.

MCCALL, G. J. H. 1963. Classification of calderas: Krakatoan and Glencoe types. *Nature*, **197**, 136–138.

MACDONALD, G. A. 1965. Hawaiian calderas. *Pacific Science*, **19**, 320–334.

MCGOVERN, P. J. & SOLOMON, S. C. 1993. State of stress, faulting, and eruption characteristics of large volcanoes on Mars. *Journal of Geophysical Research*, **98**, 23 553–23 579.

MCGUIRE, W. J. & PULLEN, A. D. 1989. Locations and orientation of eruptive fissures and feeder-dikes at Mount Etna: influence of gravitational and regional tectonic stress regimes. *Journal of Volcanology and Geothermal Research*, **38**, 325–344.

MCTIGUE, D. F. & MEI, C. C. 1981. Gravity-induced stresses near topography of small slope. *Journal of Geophysical Research*, **86**, 9268–9278.

MAALØE, S. 1987. The generation and shape of feeder dikes from mantle sources. *Contributions to Mineraleralogy and Petrology*, **96**, 47–55.

MALIN, M. C. 1977. Comparison of volcanic feaures of Elysium (Mars) and Tibesti (Earth). *Geological Society of America Bulletin*, **88**, 908–919.

MARTI, J., ABLAY, G. J., REDSAW, L. T., & SPARKS, R. S. 1994. Experimental studies of collapse calderas. *Journal of the Geological Society, London*, **151**, 919–929.

MOORE, J. G. 1964. Giant submarine landslides on the Hawaiian ridge. *Geological Survey Research*, Chapter D. United States Geological Survey Professional Paper, **501-D**, D95–D98.

—— & KRIVOY, H. L. 1964. The 1962 flank eruption of Kilauea volcano and structure of the east rift zone, *Journal of Geophysical Research*, **69**, 2033–2045.

MORRIS, E. C. 1982. Aureole deposit of the martian volcano Olympus Mons. *Journal of Geophysical Research*, **87**, 1164–1178.

MOUGINIS-MARK, P. J. 1981. Late stage summit activity of martian shield volcanoes. *Proceedings of the Twelfth Lunar and Planetary Science Conference*, 1431–1447.

—— & ROBINSON, M. S. 1992. Evolution of the Olympus Mons Caldera, Mars. *Bulletin of Volcanology*, **54**, 347–360.

——, MCCOY, T. J., TAYLOR, G. J. & KEIL, K. 1992. Martian parent craters for the SNC meteorites. *Journal of Geophysical Research*, **97**, 10 213–10 336.

——, ROBINSON, M. S. & ZUBER, M. T. 1990. Evolution of the Olympus Mons Caldera, Mars. *Lunar and Planetary Science*, **XXI**, 815–816.

——, WILSON, L. & HEAD, J. W. 1982. Explosive volcanism of Hecates Tholus, Mars: Investigation of eruption conditons. *Journal of Geophysical Research*, **87**, 9890–9904.

——, ——, & ZIMBELMAN, J. R. 1988. Polygenetic eruptions on Alba Patera, Mars. *Bulletin of Volcanology*, **50**, 361–379.

MULLER, O. H. & POLLARD, D. D. 1977. The stress state near Spanish Peaks, Colorado, determined from a dike pattern. *Pure and Applied Geophysics*, **115**, 69–86.

MUNRO, D. C. & ROWLAND, S. K. 1994. Implications of patterns of caldera instability in the Western Galápagos Islands for mechanisms of caldera formation on the terrestrial planets. *Conference on Volcano Instability on Earth and Other Planets*, Geological Society of London, 39–40.

MUSTARD, J. F. & SUNSHINE, J. M. 1995. Seeing through the dust: Martian crustal heterogeneity and links to the SNC meteorites. *Science*, **267**, 1623–1626.

——, ERARD, S., BIBRING, J.-P. *ET AL*. 1993. The surface of Syrtis Major: composition of the volcanic substrate and mixing with altered dust and soil. *Journal of Geophysical Research*, **98**, 3387–3400.

NAKAMURA, K. 1977. Volcanoes as possible indicators of tectonic stress orientation: Principle and proposal. *Journal of Volcanology and Geothermal Research*, **2**, 1–16.

——1982. Why do long rift zones develop better in Hawaiian volcanoes – a possible role of thick oceanic sediments. *Bulletin of the Volcanological Society of Japan*, **25**, 255–267.

——1984. Distribution of flank craters of Miyake-jima volcano and the nature of the ambient crustal stress field. *Bulletin of the Earthquake Research Institute*, **29**, S17-S23.

NEUKUM, G. & HILLER, K. 1981. Martian ages. *Journal of Geophysical Research*, **86**, 3097–3121.

PARFITT, E. A. & HEAD, J. W. 1993. Buffered and unbuffered dike emplacement on Earth and Venus: implications for magma reservoir size, depth, and rate of magma replenishment. *Earth, Moon, and Planets*, **61**, 249–281.

——, WILSON, L., & HEAD, J. W. 1993. Basaltic magma reservoirs: factors controlling their rupture characteristics and evolution. *Journal of Volcanology and Geothermal Research*, **55**, 1–14.

PIKE, R. J. 1978. Volcanoes on the inner planets: Some preliminary comparisons of gross topography, *Proceedings of the Ninth Lunar and Planetary Science Conference*, 3239–3273.

PLESCIA, J. B. 1994. Geology of the small Tharsis volcanoes: Jovus Tholus, Ulysses Patera, Biblis Patera, Mars. *Icarus*, **111**, 246–269.

—— & SAUNDERS, R. S. 1979. The chronology of the martian volcanoes. *Proceedings of the Tenth Lunar and Planetary Conference*, 2841–2859.

POTTIER, Y. 1978. Première eruption historique du Nyiragongo et manifestation adventives simultanées du Volcan Nyamulagira. *Musée Royal de l'Afrique Centrale, Rapport Annual du Départment de Géologie et de Minéralogie*, 157–175.

RIDLEY, W. I. 1971. The origin of some collapse structures in the Canary Islands. *Geological Magazine*, **108**, 477–484.

ROBINSON, M. S. 1990. Precise topographic measurements of Apollinaris and Tyrrhena Patera, Mars. *Lunar and Planetary Science*, **21**, 1027–1028.

—— & ROWLAND, S. 1994. Evidence for large scale sector collapse at Tharsis Tholus. *Conference on Volcano Instability on Earth and Other Planets*, Geological Society of London, 44.

——, MOUGINIS-MARK, P. J., ZIMBELMAN, J. R. & WU, S. S. C. 1993. Chronology, eruption duration, and atmospheric contribution of Apollinaris Patera, Mars. *Lunar and Planetary Science*, **24**, 1209–1210.

ROWLAND, S. K. & MUNRO, D. C. 1992. The caldera of Volcan Fernandina: a remote sensing study of its structure and recent activity. *Bulletin of Volcanology*, **55**, 97–109.

RUBIN, A. M. & POLLARD, D. D. 1987. Origins of blade-like dikes in volcanic rift zones. *In*: DECKER, R. W., WRIGHT, T. L. & STAUFFER, P. H. (eds) *Volcanism in Hawaii*. United States Geological Survey Professional Paper, **1350**, 1449–1470.

RYAN, M. P., BLEVINS, J. K., OKAMURA, A. T. & KOYANAGI, R. Y. 1983. Magma reservoir subsidence mechanics: Theoretical summary and application of Kilauea Volcano, Hawaii. *Journal of Geophysical Research*, **88**, 4147–4181.

SCHABER, G. G. 1982. Syrtis Major: a low relief volcanic shield. *Journal of Geophysical Research*, **87**, 9852–9866.

SCOTT, D. H. & TANAKA, K. L. 1986. *Geologic Map of the Western Hemisphere of Mars*. United States Geological Survey Miscellaneous Investigations Series, Map I-1802A.

SHTEYNBERG, G. S. & SOLOV'YEV, T. V. 1976. The shape of volcanoes and the position of subordinate vents. *Izvestiya Earth Physics*, **12**, 83–84.

SIMKIN, T. & HOWARD, K. 1970. Caldera collapse in the Galápagos Islands. 1968. *Science*, **196**, 429–437.

SWANSON, D. A., DUFFIELD, W. A. & FISKE, R. S. 1976. *Displacement of the South Flank of Kilauea Volcano: the Result of Forceful Intrusion of Magma into the Rift Zones*. United States Geological Survey Professional Paper, **963**.

TANAKA, K. L. 1985. Ice-lubricated gravity spreading of Olympus Mons aureole deposits. *Icarus*, **62**, 191–206.

——, ISBELL, N. K., SCOTT, D. H., GREELEY, R. & GUEST, J. E. 1988. The resurfacing history of Mars: a synthesis of digitized, Viking-based geology. *Proceedings of the Eighteenth Lunar and Planetary Conference*, 665–678.

THOMAS, P. J., SQUYRES, S. W. & CARR, M. H. 1989. Flank tectonics of martian volcanoes. *Journal of Geophysical Research*, **95**, 14 345–14 355.

TREIMAN, A. H. 1994. Two source areas for the SNC meteorites: petrologic, chemical and chronologic evidence. *Lunar and Planetary Science*, **25**, 1413–1414.

VOGT, P. R. & SMOOT, N. C. 1984. The Geisha Guyots: Multibeam bathymetry and morphometric interpretation. *Journal of Geophysical Research*, **89**, 11 085–11 107.

WALKER, G. P. L. 1984. Downsag calderas, ring faults, caldera sizes, and incremental caldera growth. *Journal of Geophysical Research*, **84**, 8407–8415.

——1988. Three Hawaiian calderas: origin through loading by shallow intrusion? *Journal of Geophysical Research*, **93**, 14 773–14 784.

WATTERS, T. R. & CHADWICK, D. J. 1990. Distribution of strain in the floor of the Olympus Mons caldera. *Lunar and Planetary Science Conference*, **21**, 1310–1311.

——, ZIMBELMAN, J. R. & SCOTT, D. H. 1993. Arcuate and circular structures in the Tharsis Region: evidence of coronae on Mars. *Lunar and Planetary Science*, **24**, 1495–1496.

WILLIAMS, H. 1941. Calderas and their origin. *Bulletin of the Department of Geological Sciences, University of California*, **25**, 239–346.

—— & MCBIRNEY, A. R. 1968. *An Investigation of Volcanic Depressions. Part I: Geologic and Geophysical Characteristics of Calderas*. Progress Report on NASA Grant NGR-38-033-012, University of Oregon.

—— & ——1979. *Volcanology*. Freeman, Cooper, and Company, San Francisco, Chapter 9.

WILSON, L. & HEAD, J. W. 1981. Ascent and eruption of magma on Earth and Moon. *Journal of Geophysical Research*, **86**, 2971–3001.

—— & ——1982. A comparison of volcanic eruption processes on Earth, Moon, Mars, Io and Venus. *Nature*, **302**, 663–669.

—— & ——1994. Mars: Review and analysis of volcanic eruption theory and relationships to observed landforms. *Reviews of Geophysics*, **32**, 221–264.

WOOD, C. A. 1979. Monogenetic volcanoes of the terrestrial planets. *Proceedings of the Tenth Lunar and Planetary Science Conference*, 2815–2840.

——1984. Calderas: a planetary perspective. *Journal of Geophysical Research*, **89**, 8391–8406.

—— & ASHWAL, L. D. 1981. SNC meteorites: igneous rocks from Mars? *Proceedings of the Twelfth Lunar and Planetary Science Conference*, 1359–1375.

WU, S. S. C., GARCIA, P. A., JORDAN, R., SCHAFER, F. J. & SKIFF, B. A. 1984. Topography of the shield volcano, Olympus Mons on Mars. *Nature*, **309**, 432–435.

ZIMBLEMAN, J. R. 1984. *Geologic Interpretation of Remote Sensing Data for the Martian Volcano Ascreus Mons*. PhD Dissertation, Arizona State University, in *Advances in Planetary Geology*, NASA Technical Memorandum **88784**, 1, 271–572.

—— & EDGETT, K. S. 1992. The Tharsis Montes, Mars: comparison of volcanic and modified landforms. *Proceedings of Lunar and Planetary Science*, **22**, 31–44.

ZUBER, M. T. & MOUGINIS-MARK, P. J. 1992. Caldera subsidence and magma chamber depth of the Olympus Mons volcano, Mars. *Journal of Geophysical Research*, **97**, 18 295–18 307.

Modified volcanic domes and associated debris aprons on Venus

M. H. BULMER[1] & J. E. GUEST

University of London Observatory, University College London, 33/35 Daws Lane,
Mill Hill, London NW7 4SD, UK
[1] *Present address: Centre for Earth and Planetary Studies, National Air and Space Museum,*
Smithsonian Institution, Washington DC L0560, USA

Abstract: The Magellan SAR images show that volcanic domes occur on the surface of Venus. Edifices with scalloped margins are similar to volcanic domes and fall within a spectrum ranging from unmodified to remnant forms. Over 320 domes have been located of which more than 80% have modified morphologies. Broadly, the modified domes can be described by five sub-categories which are related to three unmodified dome sub-categories. Many modified domes have deposits associated with them that possess characteristics indicative of their having been formed from mass movements. Evidence for slope failure is not seen on volcanic shields on Venus due to them having shallow flanks. Several steep-sided cones show some evidence of slope failure but on a much smaller scale than failures associated with domes. Slope failures on venusian domes appear to have been triggered by non-explosive and explosive events. Collapse on the edges of domes, either as a result of explosive events of oversteepening, is common on Earth but the collapses on Venus are on a scale that is more in common with major sector collapses of volcanoes on Earth. Four morphological sub-groups of debris deposit have been recognized. The deposits in groups one and two are analogous to terrestrial volcanic debris avalanche deposits and the deposits in group three are analogous to pyroclastic flows on Earth. The characteristics of the fourth group of deposits are similar to those resulting from deep-seated slides on Earth.

During the early stages of the Magellan mission a volcanic edifice with scalloped margins whose origin was enigmatic was found to the north of Alpha Regio (18.1°S, 5.5°E). As the mission progressed, other edifices with scalloped margins were identified. The radar characteristics and morphologies of many of these edifices are similar to volcanic domes and form a spectrum ranging from unmodified to remnant forms. Based on the characteristic margins, the edifices were termed scalloped margin domes, or SMDs (Guest *et al.* 1992a, b). Many of the domes are an order of magnitude larger than terrestrial domes. Debris aprons associated with modified domes possess a range of radar and morphologic characteristics indicative of mass movement deposits (Guest *et al.* 1991, 1992a, b; Bulmer *et al.* 1992, 1993). Large arcuate backscarps on the flanks of some domes indicate that large-scale collapses have occurred. There is an absence of debris aprons around some domes, which may be explained in some cases by burial by younger material. Elsewhere the deposits may form only a thin unconsolidated mantle that was penetrated by the radar or have the same radar backscatter as the surrounding plains.

Using the Magellan dataset an extensive database was compiled from a global survey of volcanic domes on Venus (Bulmer 1994). It incorporates information on the morphological and morphometrical aspects of domes and large debris aprons associated with them. Over 300 modified domes were identified during the survey indicating that if SMDs are modified volcanic domes, then domes are more common than suggested in previous work (Head *et al.* 1992; Pavri *et al.* 1992). A greater number of modified domes were identified than unmodified domes.

A range of morphological characteristics of modified domes was recognized from the survey but they can broadly be divided into five categories labelled MD1 to MD5. It is proposed that modified domes are derived from the different dome sub-categories D_1 to D_2 discussed in Guest *et al.* (1992a). As part of the global survey of modified domes, details of debris aprons associated with volcanic domes were compiled. Over 100 debris aprons were identified. The database includes information on the morphological and morphometric aspects of mass movement deposits. A descriptive classification using the headscarp–debris apron relationship, the surface texture and the plan view, was devised that allowed the deposits to be placed into one of four categories, labelled G1 to G4. These four different morphological groups exhibit distinctive radar characteristics and morphometrical trends. The data obtained from the survey were designed to build upon an extensive database of large landslides on

From McGuire, W. J., Jones, A. P. & Neuberg, J. (eds) 1996, *Volcano Instability on the Earth and Other Planets,*
Geological Society Special Publication No. 110, pp. 349–371.

Table 1. *Morphological and morphometric characteristics of unmodified (D) and modified domes (MD)*

Type	Plan view	Profile	Diameter (km)	Height (m)	Slope (°)	Crater	Radar characteristics
D_1	Circular	Steep convex margins, relatively flat top	2–5	?	?	?	Radar-bright backscatter on foreslope
D_2	Circular	Steep convex slopes, raised rim	10	311	15	Single, central	Radar-bright backscatter, steep margins, steep rampart
D_3	Circular	Steep convex margins, rounded top	20–30	618	20	Single, often central	Radar-bright backscatter, steep margins
D_4	Near circular	Steep perimeter, concave inner surface	20	?	?	Surface downsagged	Radar-bright backscatter, steep margins. constant backscatter, inner surface
MD1	Circular	Steep slopes, conical	15–28	1500	27.4	Single, central	Radar-bright backscatter, steep slopes, often show lay-over
MD2	Circular	Steep sided with breaks of slope, convex summit area	17–32	1700	27.1	Single, central	Radar-bright backscatter, steep slopes, often show lay-over
MD3	Near circular	Flat upper surface, steep flanks	13–48	1200	28.2	Small pits	Radar-bright backscatter, steep slopes, often show lay-over on foreslopes
MD4	Circular	Steep sided, flat upper surface	23–50	1500	22.4	No pit craters identified	Radar-bright backscatter, steep slopes, often show lay-over
MD5	Circular	Steep slopes, concave inner surface	13–57	800	26.2	Large central downsag	Radar-bright backscatter, steep margins

Mars, the Moon and the Earth compiled by Shaller (1991), incorporating information on morphologic and morphometric aspects of large landslide phenomena.

Morphological characteristics of modified domes

When domes that have undergone only limited modification on the flanks are compared with the four dome categories D_1–D_4 (Guest *et al.* 1992*a*) morphological similarities are evident (Table 1). A sequence of progressively modified domes can be constructed that encompasses the different morphologies seen in the images. Domes have a range of planimetric forms, from those that have not been modified, to those that are nearly circular with small scallops, through to those that have irregular forms with little of the original edifice remaining. The majority of domes that are modified are greater than 10 km in diameter. The five sub-categories of modified domes represent only three categories of unmodified domes (Fig. 1).

The first group of modified domes (MD1) have steep flanks that rise to large central craters 5 km in diameter (Fig. 1). Some crater walls

show evidence of slope failure and several of the edifices have flanks with distinct backscarps which are associated with debris aprons. Diffuse radar backscatter materials around the base of the majority of domes in this group are interpreted to be talus. Examples of domes in this group include a dome in Helen Planitia (31.7°S 260.2°E), that has steep flanks rising to a near-circular central crater. The northern flank of the dome has radial protuberances producing a stellate plan-form (Fig. 2). The central crater of another dome with the characteristics of this group situated in Ut Rupes (64.4°N, 306.6°E), is cross-cut by fractures which may have formed as a result of slope failure forming several small terraces (Fig. 3).

Modified domes in group two (MD2) are near-circular in plan-form, have gently convex upper surfaces and steep flanks with multiple breaks of slope (Fig. 1). The breaks in slope may have resulted from different eruptive pulses or phases. Several domes in this group have small summit craters a few kilometres in diameter. Diffuse radar backscatter materials interpreted to be talus are also observed around the base of the domes. Examples of domes in this group include a dome to the south of Atla Regio (16.2°S, 211.8°E) which has several breaks in

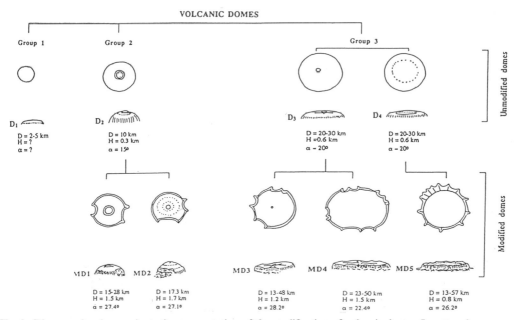

Fig. 1. Diagram showing a schematic representation of the modification of volcanic domes. In group 1 no modified forms related to D_1 were identified. In group 2 modified dome MD1 and MD2 are related to the unmodified dome sub-category D_2. In the third group of modified domes, MD3 and MD4 are related to unmodified domes in sub-category D_3. The modified dome MD5 is related to the unmodified sub-category D_4.

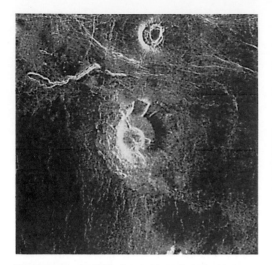

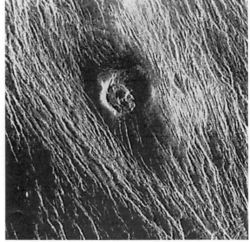

Fig. 2. Dome (md244) situated in Helen Planitia (31°S, 260.2°E). The dome has a diameter of *c.* 15 km and the characteristics of sub-category MD1. The upper surface of the dome is cross-cut by north to south trending fractures that do not extend into the surrounding plains. This indicates that the fractures were buried by younger lavas which may also have buried any debris aprons. The dome is situated in the floor of a volcano-tectonic structure. Magellan image C1 MIDR 30S261;1. Radar illumination is from the left.

Fig. 3. Dome (md14) situated in Ut Rupes (64.4°N, 306.5°E). The dome is *c.* 15 km in diameter, is coded as i,a,2 and has the characteristics of sub-category MD1. The central crater has several terraces which may have formed from slope failure. The dome is superimposed on lavas that embay a northwest to southeast trending fracture set. Fractures trending north to south cross-cut the dome indicating they are younger than the dome. Magellan image C1 MIDR 60N319;1. Radar illumination is from the left.

slope (Fig. 4). The southern flank of the dome has several distinct backscarps that extend from the lower slopes to the summit.

The third group of modified domes (MD3) have slope angles of approximately 30° that rise to a flat upper surface (Fig. 1). Small central depressions and pits are common on the upper surfaces. The central depressions are likely to be the result of magma withdrawal at the end of the eruptive episode. The pits may have formed as a result of minor explosive events. Examples of the range of morphologies possessed by domes in this group include a little-modified dome situated in Tinatin Planitia (12.1°N, 8.9°E). Numerous small pit craters are present on the upper surface of the dome, but the margins are largely unmodified (Fig. 5). A more degraded dome to the north of Mokosha Mons (61.5°N, 248°E) has radial protuberances on the flanks and numerous small pit craters as well as fractures on the upper surface (Fig. 6). An example of a remnant dome occurs to the west of Phoebe Regio (7.6°S, 256°E). Little of the original dome remains and debris aprons occur at the base of individual scallops (Fig. 7).

Modified domes in group four (MD4) typically have near-circular or elongated plan-forms and have large diameter to height ratios with steep flanks (>20 km) that rise to extensive flat upper surfaces (Fig. 1). Several of these large-volume domes have downsags. An example of one such downsagged dome (Fig. 8), is situated on the summit region of a shield volcano in Navka Planitia (8.8°S, 305.3°E). Domes with the characteristics of this group that are situated on ridge-belts are often heavily modified, such as one in Bereghinya Planitia (48.9°N, 16°E). The dome is heavily modified by younger cross-cutting fractures (Fig. 9).

Modified domes in the fifth group (MD5), have concave upper surfaces with relatively uniform radar backscatter cross-sections (Fig. 1). The downsagged surfaces on several of the domes in the group are bounded by complex sets of terraces possibly resulting from several stages of caldera collapse. Radar-dark backscatter materials seen on the floor of some calderas may be congealed lavas. The majority of the domes in this group have near-circular plan-forms with stellate perimeters produced by coalesced backscarps. Some of the backscarps have radar-bright talus slopes at their bases and extensive mass movement deposits associated with them. One of the best examples of this

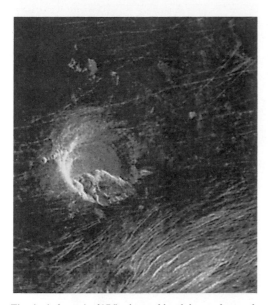

Fig. 4. A dome (md176), situated in plains to the south of Atla Regio (16.2°S, 211.7°E). The gently convex upper surface and steep slopes are characteristic of dome sub-category MD2. The dome has a diameter of 26 km, and an average slope angle of 24.3° and a calculated height of 2.8 km. The south flank has undergone a number of mass movements. The debris aprons are younger than the plains since the fractures do not cross-cut them. Magellan image C1 MIDR 15S215;1. Radar illumination is from the left.

dome morphology is situated on the northern margin of Alpha Regio (18.1°S, 5.5°E). The dome has a distinctive stellate plan-form with numerous radial protuberances and a concave interior which may have formed as a result of a breach to the west (Fig. 10).

Morphometrical characteristics of modified domes

The diameters of modified domes range from <10 km to 120 km with the majority ranging between 10 km and 35 km (Fig. 11). Domes with diameters greater than 70 km tend to consist of several superimposed or coalesced domes whose margins are often indistinguishable (4°N, 19°E). Over 300 modified domes are identified on the surface of Venus compared with a total of 154 domes found in a previous study (Pavri *et al.* 1992). The reason for the difference in numbers is, we believe, that a spectrum exists from unmodified to highly modified domes. This allowed remnant volcanic edifices to be examined and their likely original forms determined.

Only a limited number of dome heights were obtained from the altimetry data owing to the resolution of the data. The majority of heights were calculated using the symmetry of the volcano seen in the SAR images. The calculated heights of modified domes range from 0.4 km to 3.8 km (Fig. 12). The mean height is 1.3 km which is four times the mean for terrestrial sub-aerial domes. However, the mean height values can be used only as a guide since the calculation of height using radar clinometry required domes to have near-circular plan-forms and includes inaccuracies in measurements from the digital data of ±150 m. This criterion prevented the heights of many modified domes from being obtained. The tendency for domes on Venus to be larger than on Earth is confirmed by a plot of the relationship between height and diameter (Fig. 13). Domes on Venus are, in many instances, an order of magnitude larger in diameter than terrestrial sub-aerial domes. The altitudinal range in the distribution of domes is from 1.4 km below datum to 2.9 km above datum. The majority are located between 6051.0 km and 6052.0 km mean planetary radius, very close to the mean planetary radius of 6051.8 km.

Morphological characteristics of debris deposits associated with modified domes

Four different morphological groups of debris aprons can be recognized from the 105 debris aprons identified from the global survey (Bulmer 1994). Each groups has distinctive radar characteristics and morphometric trends. Deposits in the first group (G1) cover large areas (>100 km²), have long travel distances (>20 km) and are characterized by hummocky topography. The surface textures of the deposits are rough on a coarse scale, consisting of large hummocks (>1 km), surrounded by a matrix of material. In plan view, the deposits are often fan-shaped or lobate. Some large debris aprons extend from the base of a dome, while other deposits are discontinuous with the base, lying beyond the margins of a dome.

An example of deposits in group one (G1) is in Helen Planitia (at 29.5°S, 183.6°E). It consists of massive hummocks and has fan-shaped plan form with well-defined lobate margins (Fig. 14). The deposit is discontinuous with the base of the dome. Another dome, in eastern Mokosha Mons (55°N, 266°E) has a large sector detached on the east flank (Fig. 15). The large hummocks at the base of the dome and the extensive deposits that extend outwards across plains, may have formed from the failed sector having

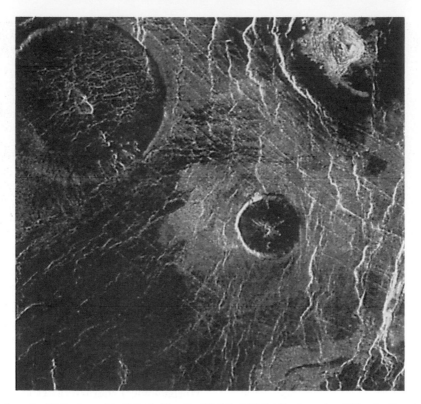

Fig. 5. A dome (md111) situated in Tinatin Planitia (12.1°N, 8.9°E). The dome is *c*. 20 km in diameter and has the characteristics of sub-category MD3. The dome has undergone little modification but numerous small pits occur on the upper surface. The dome is situated on the margin of concentric fractures that define a volcano-tectonic structure. Magellan image C1 MIDR 15N009;1. Radar illumination is from the left.

moved initially as a coherent mass before it collapsed catastrophically. It seems likely that the failure occurred after the eruption had ceased and the dome had become solid. This then explains the massive nature of the deposits and why the mass initially underwent only limited disintegration during motion. A dome in Guinevere Planitia (14°N, 229°E) has a large detached debris apron made up of large hummocks which form the margin of the fan-shaped deposit (Fig. 16). The origin of the debris is enigmatic. The absence of debris towards the base of the dome may be explained if the collapsed mass moved away from the dome as a coherent mass prior to disintegrating. If the debris apron formed as a result of one massive failure, a clear debris–headscarp relationship would be expected. However, no such relation-ship is observed. One possibility is that the failure occurred on a previous dome which was de-stroyed, and that a new dome has been emplaced subsequently. Alternatively, after the initial massive failure, subsequent smaller

volume slope failures, that formed the small embayments on the west flank, may have buried large hummocks close to the base of the dome.

Only a few examples of deposits in the second group (G2) have been identified. The debris aprons are often detached from the base of the dome and have narrow proximal zones that spread laterally towards the distal zone. The deposits have a lower radar backscatter coeffi-cient than the deposits in group one, owing to smoother surface textures made up of smaller dispersed radar-bright hummocks (≤1 km). In plan view, the deposits have irregular lateral and distal margins.

One dome in Navka Planitia (26°S, 296.7°S) has at least five debris aprons with the characteristics of subcategory G2 (Fig. 17). The proximal zones of the debris aprons are situated some distance from the base of the slopes from where they originated. The aprons of debris are made up of dispersed radar-bright hummocks. The long and narrow plan-forms of the deposits are characteristic of debris masses

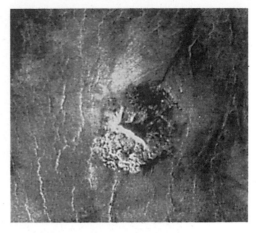

Fig. 6. A dome (md17) situated north of Mokosha Mons (61.5°N, 248°E), with the characteristics of subcategory MD3. The dome has a 50 km diameter and an average slope angle of 24°. The calculated height of the dome is 5.8 km. The radar-bright lavas that surround the dome appear to mantle the underlying fractured plains. The fractures on the dome can no longer be traced on the plains as they have been buried by subsequent lavas indicating the dome is an old feature. These younger lavas may have buried any debris aprons. Magellan image C1 MIDR 60N236;1. Radar illumination is from the left.

Fig. 7. Dome (md159) situated west of Phoebe Regio (7.6°S, 256°E). The diameter of the remnant dome is *c.* 25 km and the calculated height is 1.6 km. The dome has the characteristics of sub-category MD3. The margin of the dome is heavily scalloped and debris aprons occur around the base. Only a small part of the horizontal upper surface remains due to the central crater having undergone several stages of collapse. The debris aprons mantle the surrounding fractured plains. Magellan image C1 MIDR 00N249. Radar illumination is from the left.

that travelled away from the dome at relatively high velocity, thereby influencing their form and accounting for location of the proximal zones. The presence of large hummocks in the deposits indicates that the source was solid and the debris mass underwent only limited disintegration during runout. The lack of well-defined boundaries around the deposits and the lower radar backscatter coefficient than deposits in group one may also reflect the influence of post-deposition reworking processes. For example, younger material may have mantled deposits partly burying them. In addition, chemical and physical erosion could have subdued the surface textures causing lower backscatter coefficients by reducing roughness.

The deposits in group three (G3) tend to be narrow and typically have debris aprons attached to the lower slopes of domes. They have shorter runout distances (≤20 km) than deposits in groups one and two. Some of the deposits can be traced up into embayments or to backscarps. The debris aprons spread laterally once they were no longer confined to the troughs

down which they travelled. Often the material embays the local topography surrounding a dome. The uniform radar-dark backscatter of the material indicates that the surficial textures are relatively smooth composed of small fragments >4 mm. In plan view the deposits have irregular lateral and distal margins.

Two domes on the summit of the shield volcano Sapas Mons (8.5°N, 188.2°E), have deposits with the characteristics of group three (Fig. 18). Radar-dark deposits around these domes can be traced back up into the heads of scallops suggesting they originated near the top of dome margins. The collapsed materials appear to have been confined as they descended down existing troughs on the flanks of the domes, spreading out once they reached the base of the slope. Some of the deposits were controlled by, and now embay, local topography.

Large failures with broad steep scarps characterize deposits in the fourth group (G4). They are the most common category of deposits. The deposits have travel distances <20 km and

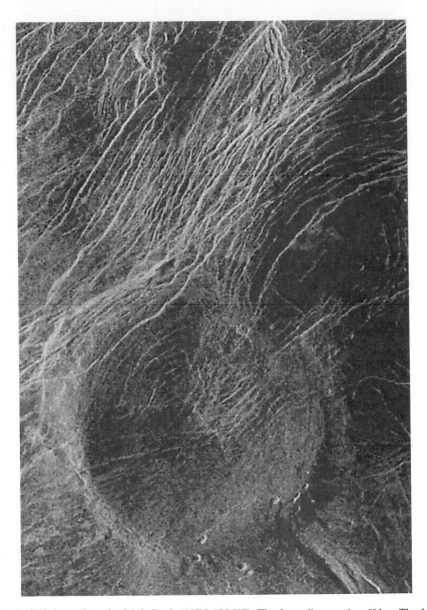

Fig. 8. Dome (md90) situated north of Atla Regio (18°N, 195.9°E). The dome diameter is *c.* 60 km. The dome has the characteristics of sub-category MD4. The concave upper surface may have resulted from magma withdrawl or degassing. Pit craters can be seen on the southern margin. The dome is superimposed on lavas associated with a volcanic centre to the south. The NE–SW trending fractures are younger than the dome since they cross-cut the upper surface and may have been influenced by the downsag. Magellan image C1 MIDR 15N197;1. Radar illumination is from the left.

the proximal zone is at the foot of the slope from which they originated. The surface textures of the deposits in this group appear to be related to the size of failure and distance they travelled. Large blocks tend to have relatively smooth gross textures, whereas disintegrated debris has a rough gross texture. In plan-form the deposits are either blunt with near-parallel lateral and distal margins, or lobate with convex lateral and distal margins.

Domes with the characteristics of group four such as one in Niobe Planitia (27.5°N, 134.8°E)

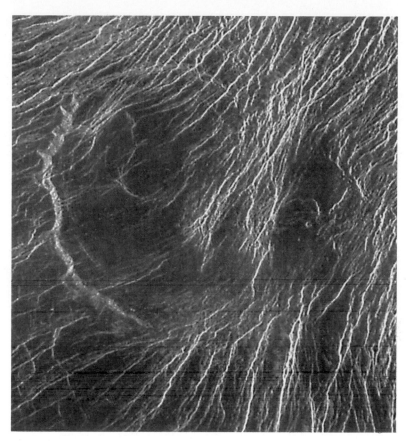

Fig. 9. An example of a dome (md29) in sub-category MD4, situated in Bereghinya Planitia (48.9°N, 16°E). The dome has a diameter of 50 km. The fractures trending northeast to southwest are younger than the dome. Magellan image C1 MIDR 45N011;1. Radar illumination is from the left.

have a large sector collapse (Fig. 19). The failed sector has remained largely intact and shows no evidence of back-tilting suggestive of a rotational component, indicating that the failure was planar. The lack of break-up of the failed sector may be explained, in part, by the short travel distance of the mass. The failure of the dome margin appears to have occurred after the eruptive activity had ceased and the dome had become rigid. Another dome in Navka Planitia (25.4°S, 308°E) has two deposits composed of large blocks that travelled away from the base of the dome (Fig. 20). One debris apron travelled to the northwest and the other moved to the northeast. The collapse to the northwest removed a large sector of the dome slope leaving a steep backscarp. The nature of the backscarp suggests that the slope failure was deep-seated. The large steep-sided block forming the proximal portion of the slide indicates that part of the slide remained coherent and may

have moved with a rotational component. The distal zone shows a well-defined steep lobate margin. This may be explained if the failed rock mass underwent little disintegration and came to rest as several large blocks. If the failure was essentially rotational, the distal region would formerly have been the base of the dome slope that may have undergone severe distortion and fracturing. Once the base failed, the upper part of the slope would have pushed the collapsed material outwards as it back-tilted during rotation. The deposit to the northeast of the dome appears to have been shallower than the one to the northwest and the deposits are less coherent containing smaller blocks. Both failures are thought to have occurred after the eruption had ceased and the dome had become rigid.

Another dome to the south of Atla Regio (16.2°S, 211.7°E), has a series of well-defined arcuate backscarps that may have formed as a

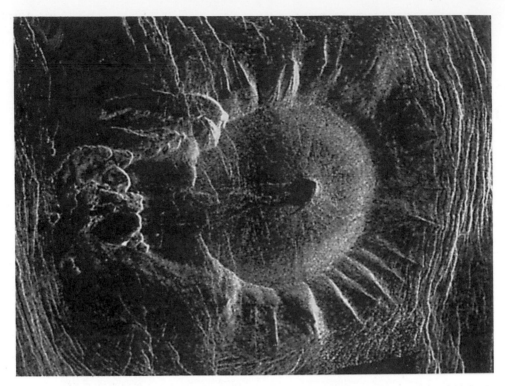

Fig. 10. An example of a dome (md184) in sub-category MD5, situated on the northern margin of Alpha Regio (18.1°S, 5.5°E). The dome has a diameter of *c.* 50 km, an average slope angle of 26.2° and a calculated height of 1 km. A central crater is visible and it appears the dome was breached on the west flank. Magellan image C1 MIDR 15S009;1. Radar illumination is from the left.

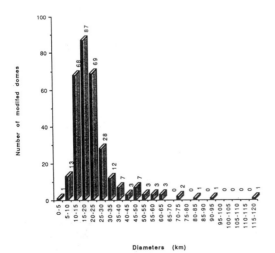

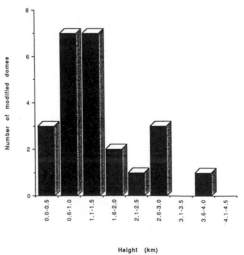

Fig. 11. Histogram showing the range of diameters of modified domes from a global population of 306.

Fig. 12. Histogram showing the height of modified domes from a global population of 24.

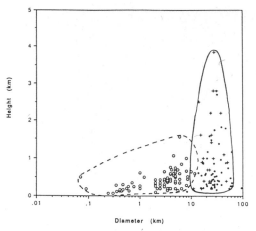

Fig. 13. Diagram showing the trend of domes on Earth and domes on Venus plotted as height vs. diameter. The open circles (○) show data for terrestrial sub-aerial domes, the dots (●) show data for unmodified domes on Venus (from Pavri *et al.* 1992), and the crosses (+) show data for modified domes on Venus.

Fig. 14. A dome (md223) with the morphological characteristics of sub-category MD5, situated in Helen Planitia (29°S, 183.6°E). The dome has a diameter of *c.* 15 km and a height of 0.9 km. The debris apron has characteristics of group one (G1). The debris apron extends *c.* 40 km, contains large blocks and has a lobate plan-form. The proximal zone is detached from the dome's lower slopes. Fractures trending east to west cross-cut the debris apron. Magellan image C1 MIDR 30S189;1. Radar illumination is from the left.

series of slides during a single phase. Alternatively, successive slope failures may have occurred after an initial slide had destabilized the slope (Fig. 21). The failures are deep-seated and a large section of the dome has collapsed. In spite of the size of slope failures, deposits travelled only short distances. This can be explained by the slope breaking into large coherent blocks which then moved as a series of failures, each on a curved surface.

Morphometric characteristics of debris deposits

Twenty domes in the global survey have more than one associated deposit, but the majority have only one large debris deposit (Fig. 22). Despite many of the larger debris aprons being detached from the base of the dome, the travel distance of a deposit was measured in this survey from the toe of the debris mass to the base of the dome. It was not measured from the toe to the uppermost point of the headscarp because of problems in distinguishing headscarps on many slopes, due to distortions in the images. The horizontal lengths travelled by the debris range from 2.1 km to 81.6 km, with a mean length of 22.7 km. The majority of debris travelled <10 km from the base of the dome (Fig. 23). Within the different morphological groups, those in the first (G1) have travel distances that range between *c.* 20 km and *c.* 80 km with a mean of *c.* 40 km (Table 2). The lengths of deposits in the second group (G2) are similar to those in group one and range between *c.* 15 km and *c.* 70 km with a mean of *c.* 45 km. Deposits in group three (G3) have smaller run-out lengths ranging between *c.* 10 km and *c.* 20 km with a mean of *c.* 15 km. The distances travelled by deposits in group four (G4) range between *c.* 0 km and *c.* 20 km with a mean of *c.* 10 km.

For all the debris deposits associated with domes, the horizontal distance across the widest section of the deposits, ranges from 0.5 km to 62.5 km with a mean of 17.2 km (Fig. 24). The deposits in group one have the greatest widths ranging between 4.2 km and 62.5 km with a mean of *c.* 30 km (Table 2). The widths of deposits in group two range between 6.8 km and 26.1 km with a mean of *c.* 15 km. Deposits in group three have smaller widths that range from 2.1 km to 12.8 km with a mean of *c.* 3 km. The widths of deposits in group four are greater than in group three, ranging from 0.5 km to 26.7 km.

The area covered by a debris apron was calculated by mapping a boundary around the toe of a deposit to the top of the headscarp

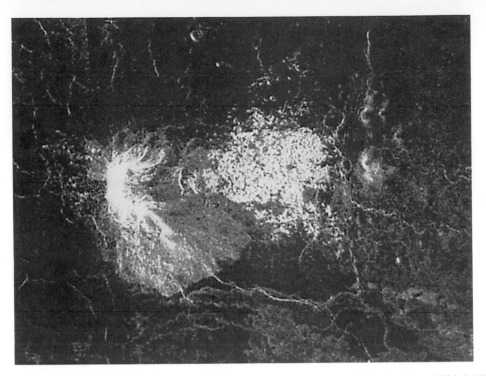

Fig. 15. An example of a dome (md21), sub-category MD3 situated in eastern Mokosha Mons (55°N, 266°E). The dome has a diameter of *c.* 20 km. The apron to the east has the characteristics of deposits in group one (G1). The proximal zone of the apron is situated on the lower slopes of the dome. The deposits are superimposed on the surrounding fractured plains. Magellan image C1 MIDR 60N097;1. Radar illumination is from the left.

or the top of the dome slope. For detached debris aprons, a minimum area measurement was made which included only the material visible in the SAR images. Debris apron areas range from 11.1 km^2 to 2138.8 km^2, with a mean of 349.5 km^2. The most common range in areas is <100 km^2 (Fig. 25). Within the different groups, deposits in group one cover areas ranging from *c.* 150 km^2 to *c.* 2150 km^2 with a mean of *c.* 800 km^2 (Table 2). Deposits in group two have similar characteristics ranging from *c.* 150 km^2 to 1450 km^2 with a mean of *c.* 600 km^2. The areas covered by deposits in group three are smaller than those in the previous groups ranging from *c.* 10 km^2 to *c.* 200 km^2. The areas of deposits in group four range between *c.* 10 km^2 and *c.* 300 km^2 with a mean of *c.* 70 km^2.

Attempts to measure the volume of deposits were restricted by the resolution of the data. It was not possible to determine whether a debris mass had been modified by secondary processes, or what the pre-event topography had been. The absence of headscarps in many instances also

hindered attempts to approximate pre-event dome slopes. Crude estimates of the volume of a deposit (assuming a uniform thickness), were possible using the product of the debris apron area and marginal thickness. However, thickness estimates were only possible on debris masses that contained large hummocks, and were dependent upon the orientation of the deposits relative to the SAR look direction and incidence angle. Due to the limited number of volume estimates obtained, deposits are compared by their respective areas, rather than by volume.

The fall height of the majority of mass movements could not be determined from the data. Therefore the total vertical distance from the top of a dome to the base was used as a substitute in calculations of the ratio of height to length (H/L). The H/L ratio gave the angle of a line connecting the uppermost point of a dome with the toe of a deposit. The calculation of H/L is based on the equation used by Heim (1932), which used the uppermost point of a headscarp and the lowest point along the toe of a deposit. The H/L ratio was used to compare the travel

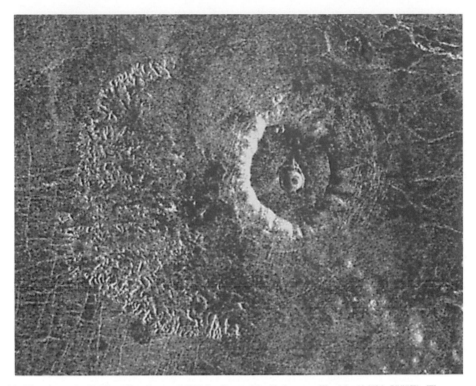

Fig. 16. The dome (md101), sub-category MD3 is situated in Guinevere Planitia (14°N, 299°E). The mass movement to the west has the morphological characteristics of group one (G1). The detached debris apron has a very rough surface texture and fan-shaped plan-form. No large backscar exists that may have been the source of the deposits. The dome is surrounded by circumferential fractures and the deposits appear to mantle the fractured plains. Several east to west trending fractures cross-cut the dome and the deposits. Magellan image C1 MIDR 15N300;1. Radar illumination is from the left.

distance of debris aprons when it was not possible to determine an average coefficient of friction. Shaller (1991) expressed caution in using the H/L ratio to compare the travel distances of large landslides since the value of the ratio coincides with the true coefficient of friction only for those mass movement deposits whose centres of gravity lie close to the toe. However, the calculations of the height to length ratio remain a convenient approximation of true friction for comparing the behaviour of large debris masses since it underestimates the friction coefficient. The H/L ratios for debris aprons on Venus ranges from 0.001 to 0.4 with a mean of 0.06 (Table 2). The deposits in group one have a range in H/L values between 0.001 and 0.01 with a mean of 0.02. The ratios for the other groups of deposits are higher ranging between 0.04 and 0.1 with a mean of 0.08 for group two, between 0.04 and 0.1 with a mean of 0.04 for group three, and between 0.02 and 0.4 with a mean of 0.13 for deposits in group four.

Destructive geomorphic processes modifying domes

Destructive geomorphic processes on volcanic domes on Earth can occur during or after emplacement, exhibiting a broad range of complexity, diversity and magnitude. During dome emplacement slope failure of the edifice margin under gravity may occur as a result of oversteepening (Neumann van Padang 1933; van Bemmelen 1949; Francis *et al.* 1974; Ui 1983; Siebert 1984), and this in turn can lead to decompression of the magma which will cause an explosion (Fink & Kieffer 1993; Gorshkov 1959; Voight *et al.* 1981; Fisher *et al.* 1987). Such an explosion can result in pyroclastic flows and surges (Walker & McBroome 1983; Cas & Wright 1987; Sato *et al.* 1992; Nakada & Fujii 1993). After an eruption has ceased, further destructive processes are mainly the result of gravitationally induced slope failure, for example caused by seismic activity. These geomorphic

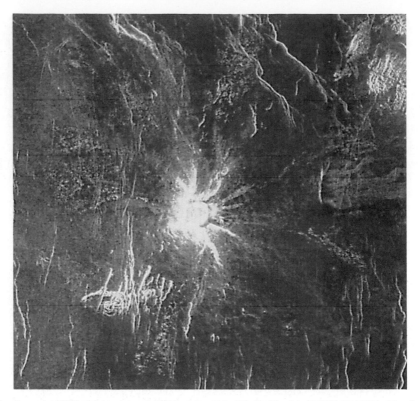

Fig. 17. The dome (md210), sub-category MD3 is situated in Navka Planitia (260°S, 296.7°E). The dome has a diameter of *c*. 15 km and a calculated height of 2.5 km. The mass movements have the characteristics of group two (G2). The detached debris aprons have long, narrow and irregular plan-forms that spread towards the distal margins. The deposits are cross-cut by north to south trending fractures and grabens. Magellan image C1 MIDR 30S297;1. Radar illumination is from the left.

processes, which can be divided into either explosive or non-explosive events, are now examined to determine which could have operated on domes on Venus.

The high atmospheric pressures on Venus (95 bar at 6051.8 km mpr), will inhibit the expansion of exsolved bubbles in magmas and consequently the stress in bubble walls, and in turn, the energy available to drive an eruption. The reduced atmospheric pressure at the summit of large volcanoes will allow for greater expansion of exsolved bubbles in magmas rising in conduits. Explosive activity will be limited to cases in which large bubbles are produced by coalescence, or where the magma initially had a high volatile content. Pyroclastic eruptions involving continuous magma disruption by gas bubble growth can only occur if the exsolved magma volatile contents exceed several weight per cent. Calculated minimum volatile contents on Venus required to cause disruption

are high compared with Earth; for CO_2, a value of 5% is required in the lowlands, and 2% in the highlands (Head & Wilson 1986). The high atmospheric pressures and temperatures will also suppress the rise of a convective plume and consequently limit the area of dispersal of entrained material. The development of a high convecting plume requires an unlikely combination of high volatile contents, high initial temperatures, and high altitude eruptions (Thornhill 1993). If pyroclastic events do occur on Venus, explosively ejected material is likely to have low fragment velocities and undergo rapid clast cooling by convective heat loss. Ground-hugging pyroclastic flows are therefore the most likely product of explosive eruptions on Venus. Debris deposits in group three (G3) that are composed of relatively uniformly sized smooth material could be derived from explosive activity, which may explain why the upper surfaces of the two domes on the summit of

Fig. 18. Two domes (md122, md126), sub-category MD3, situated on the summit of the shield volcano Sapas Mons (8.5°N, 188.2°E). The northern dome is *c.* 20 km in diameter. Both domes have deposits with the characteristics of group three (G3), have long, narrow and irregular plan-forms. The debris travelled down narrow canyons and spread out once away from the base of the dome. The deposits are superimposed on the surrounding lava flows. C1 MIDR 15N188;1. Radar illumination is from the left.

Sapas Mons (8.8°N, 188.2°E) are mantled in radar-dark, smooth material ranging in size from 5 mm to 20 mm (Fig. 18). The domes occur at an elevation of 6054.3 km mpr where volatile exsolution would be easier than on the plains. The morphology of the deposits indicates that localized events occurred and that flows travelled down valleys and spread out over plains forming flat or sub-horizontal upper surfaces. They could have formed from block-and-ash flows or from scoria-flow deposits triggered by the collapse of blocks on the dome margins. These events would have

required only localized volatile concentrations, making them far more likely than a large explosive eruption. The existence of small pit craters on many domes on Venus, which may have resulted from small explosive events, suggests that localized volatile concentrations have occurred in some domes.

Non-explosive mass movement can result from gravitational collapse of the front of a lava dome. In this case, initial velocities are determined solely by the conversion of potential energy into kinetic energy as fragments fall. All slope-forming materials have a tendency to

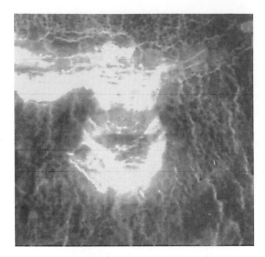

Fig. 19. A dome (md65), sub-category MD3, situated in Niobe Planitia (27.5°N, 134.8°E). The dome is *c.* 20 km in diameter. The debris deposit to the northwest has the characteristics of group four. It is 8.8 km wide and extends 15.2 km. The deposits mantle the fractured plains which surround the dome. C1 MIDR 30N135;1. Radar illumination is from the left.

move downwards under the influence of gravity, which is counteracted by a shearing resis-tance. For a given slope, if stress exceeds resistance then failure occurs and the slope will move to a new position of equilibrium (Brunsden 1979). Slope failures can be triggered either by internal changes of shearing resistance or by external factors that produce an increase in shear stress. No change in the shearing resistance of the

Fig. 21. The dome (md176), sub-category MD2 is situated to the south of Atla Regio (16.2°S, 211.7°E). The dome is *c.* 25 km in diameter and 2.8 km high. The deposits on the southern part of the dome have the characteristics of group four (G4). The surface textures of the deposits are rough and the plan-forms blunt. Several arcuate backscarps have deposits at their base. The deposits are superimposed on east–west trending fractures. Magellan image C1 MIDR 15S215;1. Radar illumination is from the left.

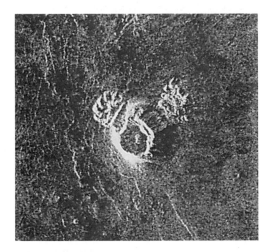

Fig. 20. The dome (md206), sub-category MD1, is situated in Navka Planitia (25.4°S, 308°E). The dome is *c.* 10 km in diameter. The debris aprons to the northwest and northeast have the characteristics of group four (G4). The deposit to the northeast has a rough surface texture and irregular plan-form. The deposit to the northwest has a steep backscarp and a lobate plan-form. The debris aprons are superimposed on the surrounding plains. Magellan image C1 MIDR 30S315;1. Radar illumination is from the left.

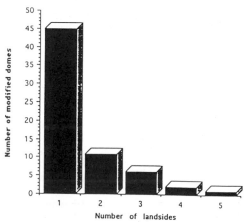

Fig. 22. Histogram showing the number of debris aprons per dome. Population 105.

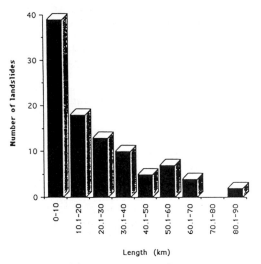

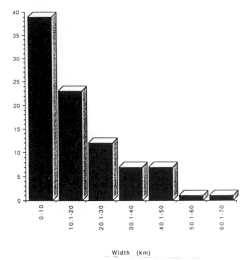

Fig. 23. A plot of the frequency of mass movement travel distances. Population 105.

Fig. 24. Histogram showing the width of debris deposits associated with domes. Population 105.

slope-forming materials is necessary for failure to occur (Terzaghi 1960).

Internal causes of slope failure during emplacement of domes (Williams 1932; Swanson *et al.* 1987; Beget & Kienle 1992; Nakada & Fujii 1993) arise from overloading of a slope by lavas, excess weight of lavas at the top of a slope, and from rapid emplacement leading to oversteepening of a flow front (Siebert 1984; Guest *et al.* 1984). On Venus, as on Earth, the eruption style, rate, rheology and local topography are likely to have determined the internal stresses experienced during the growth of domes. Failure of a dome as a result of overloading of a slope by lavas, will depend on the mode of emplacement. If a dome's growth is endogenous and a crust forms on the margin, then lateral advance can occur only as a result of stresses imposed by newer lavas. If the stress exceeds the strength of

the crust, then slope failure will occur and the flow front advances. If a dome is exogenous then new lavas erupting onto the surface of the dome can cause slope failure due to the weight of lavas exceeding the strength of the slope.

The morphology of venusian domes suggests that growth was endogenous. On terrestrial domes (e.g. Lassen Peak, California; Mount Pelée, Martinique; Metcalf dome, Alaska (MacDonald 1972)), talus occurs around the margins. Many domes on Venus have radar-bright margins that may be interpreted as rough talus. On terrestrial domes, talus results from fracturing of the crust as the dome grows, and the stresses set up in the rock as it contracts during cooling. The resulting angular blocks are moved by the growing dome and those on the margin topple down to the base. Three mono-lithological landslides have occurred in the

Table 2. *Morphometric characteristics of the different groups (G1–G4) of debris aprons associated with modified domes*

Group	Area (km²)	Length (km)	Width (km)	Height (km)	H/L	Total
Ranges						
G1	148–2138.8	21.8–80.7	4.2–62.5	0.2–1.4	0.001–0.01	32
G2	171.1–1459.7	14.4–68.8	6.8–26.1	2.2–2.8	0.04–0.1	11
G3	9–202.5	10.7–21.8	2.1–12.8	0.9–1.2	0.04–0.1	7
G4	11.1–315.6	2–18.7	0.5–26.7	2.8–0.2	0.02–0.4	54
Means						
G1	805.4	41.5	31.6	0.6	0.02	32
G2	626.7	44.1	14.6	2.5	0.08	11
G3	62.6	15.9	3.2	0.7	0.04	54
G4	77.8	8.04	9.5	1.3	0.13	54

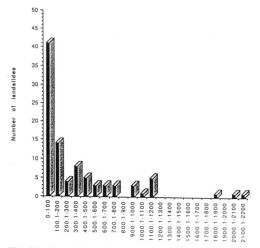

Fig. 25. Graph showing the areas covered by debris aprons associated with domes. Population 105.

Chaos Crags region of Lassen Peak, California. These were formed at different periods during the growth of the same dacite dome as a result of construction of gravitationally unstable jointed rock masses (Eppler *et al.* 1987). Progressive failure of jointed rock slopes occurs along joints and other discontinuities, along which strength is a product of friction between the rock faces (Terzaghi 1960, 1962). The total effective cohesion or resistance of jointed rock slopes is equal to the combined strength of blocks plus the friction between the joint planes. If stress increases slowly, fracturing occurs progressively, resulting in stress increasingly being concentrated on the remaining intact rock. Once the reduction in strength reaches a point where the average shear resistance is equal to the average shear stress, the slope will fail to a stable angle which is dependent on the jointing pattern and the orientation of the discontinuities relative to the slope.

An external cause of mass movement on volcanic edifices on Earth is seismicity. This can produce structural alteration of the constituent parts of a slope (by disturbing intergranular bonds, and by decreasing cohesion and internal friction), dislodgement of otherwise stable slopes, and horizontal and vertical fault movements resulting in increased slope angles. Other external causes of slope failure include weathering and erosion. In the absence of any meaningful seismic data for Venus, the existence of seismic events is inferred from the evidence of extensive faulting and deformation seen in the images. Slope failure triggered by seismicity

appears possible, given the existence of large fractures around many domes and the interrelationship between many domes and circumferential fractures. A strong association has also been recognized on Earth between seismicity and the sub-surface movements of magma. Studies of earthquake-triggered slope failures (Keefer 1984; Wilson & Keefer 1985; Cotecchia 1989; Crozier 1991; Perrin & Hancox 1992) have shown that rockfalls and rockslides are some of the most abundant types of failure. Seismic events are inferred to have triggered slope failures on volcanic edifices at Socompa, Chile (Francis & Self 1987), on the flanks of Mauna Loa, Hawaii (Lipman *et al.* 1988), and on Vesuvius, Italy (Hazlett *et al.* 1991). It therefore seems reasonable to suggest that some slope failures on Venus may have been seismically triggered.

Categories of debris deposits that show no evidence of having been triggered by explosive events include deposits in groups one (G1), two (G2) and four (G4). The characteristics of the debris deposits in groups one (G1) and two (G2) are morphologically similar to terrestrial volcanic debris avalanche deposits. In plan view, the deposits in these two groups often have long travel distances relative to widths, and are fan-shaped with lobate or irregular lateral and distal margins (Fig. 26). Terrestrial debris avalanche deposits result from the downward movement of newly detached fragments of bedrock moving on bedding, joint or fault surfaces or any other plane or separation (Sharpe 1938). The failure of a rockmass is followed by rapid and extensive movements of debris as slide blocks disintegrate and move away from the source. Debris avalanche deposits consist of a poorly sorted mixture of brecciated debris, the dominant constituent being lithic material of the source volcano, and are generally more poorly sorted than pyroclastic flow deposits, and typically have coarser textures. Hummocky surfaces have been noted as typical topographic features of volcanic debris avalanche deposits (Siebert 1984; Ui 1983). Each hummock consists of one or a few megablocks composed of a former portion of the volcanic edifice transported by the avalanche. Hummocks may have been formed by horst and graben formation during lateral spreading (Voight *et al.* 1981; Glicken *et al.* 1981). Hummocky surfaces, characteristic of deposits in groups one and two, are similar to those in the Pungarehu formation at Egmont, New Zealand (Neall 1979). If the surfaces of venusian domes are composed of angular blocks, they will be susceptible to failure along planes of weakness especially where blocks dip

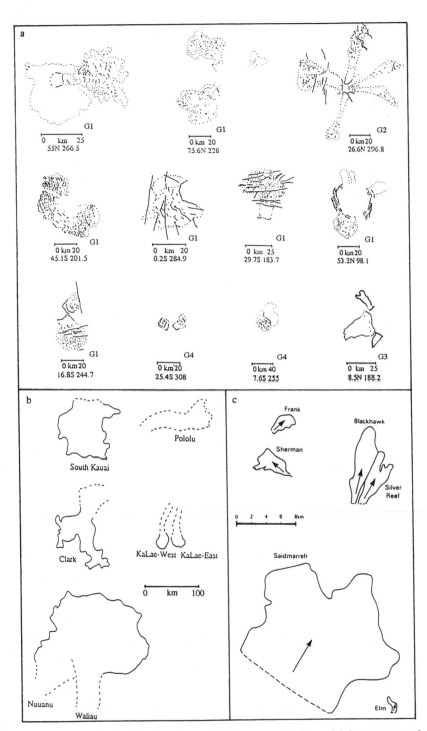

Fig. 26. Schematic diagram showing the plan-forms of debris aprons; (**a**) shows debris aprons associated with domes on Venus, (**b**) and (**c**) show sub-marine (adapted from Moore *et al.* 1989) and sub-aerial (adapted from Shreve 1968) debris aprons on Earth.

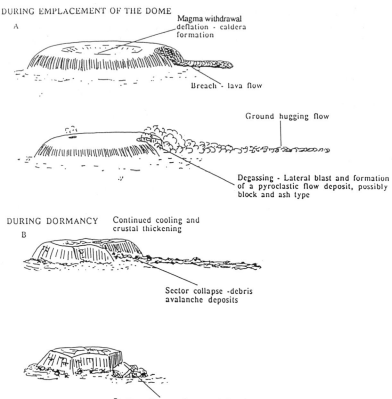

Fig. 27. Schematic representation of destructive processes responsible for the modification of domes during emplacement and after dormancy: (**A**) shows the upper surface domes being modifed by magma withdrawal, caldera formation or deflation. During dome growth oversteepening of the margins may result in a breach. Mass movements producing deposits with the characteristics of G3 may be caused by explosions; (**B**) shows modification of domes by slope failure after the dome has ceased to grow. Slope failures on the margins of rigid domes may result in deposits with the characteristics of G1, G2 and G4.

at angles close to the angles of friction on those surfaces. Large rock masses that have failed may disintegrate as they move away from the dome forming brecciated debris.

Some of the deposits in groups one and two are also similar to terrestrial non-volcanic landslides, such as Blackhawk and Silver Reef, California (Shreve 1968), Loma Redonda, Loma de la Aspereza, Avalancha del Zarzo 1 and Avalancha del Zarzo 2, Argentina (Foque & Strecker 1988), as well as seven landslides on Mars (Shaller 1991). In plan, the Blackhawk landslide forms a narrow, symmetrical lobe that is distally raised (Fig. 26). The deposit has an overall length of 8 km and an average width of 2.4 km. The depth of the deposit increases uniformly from the proximal to distal zone and the surface of the slide consists of low, rounded hills and small, closed basins. Several large volcanic sub-marine deposits off the Hawaiian

coast also have similar morphological characteristics to venusian deposits in groups one and two (Fig. 26). These have well-developed backscarps, and large blocks in their mid-sections that terminate in aprons of hummocky terrain (Lipman *et al.* 1988; Moore *et al.* 1989).

The characteristics of the deposits in group four are similar to non-explosively triggered deep-seated slides on Earth. These slides typically occur along lines of weakness such as joints, faults or possible bedding planes. Slides that include a planar element exhibit severe distortions and fracturing of the mass. Those slides that occur on curved failure surfaces have been termed 'rotational' slides and can be single, multiple or successive (Hutchinson 1968). The main part of the failure surface is controlled by shear and tension cracks that often form in the upper parts of the slope during the initial phases of movement. These cracks close as the mass back-tilts during rotation. Several domes such as those in Niobe Planitia (27.5°N, 134.8°E), and in Navka Planitia (25.4°S, 308°E), have slope morphologies characteristic of having formed as a result of a single rotational slide. Multiple rotational slides occur as a retrogressive series of slips, each on a curved surface that is linked tangentially to a common failure line (Brunsden 1979). In plan-form such deposits often show a sequence of arcuate blocks arranged one behind another. The complex of scarps on the dome south of Atla Regio (16.2°S, 211.7°E) has the characteristics of having formed from multiple rotational slides.

It appears from analysis of the image data, that destructive processes that modify domes can be divided into those that are accompanied by an explosive component, and those that are non-explosive. Given the constraints imposed on explosive activity by atmospheric conditions, and the high magma volatile concentrations needed to cause disruption, the most likely internal causes of slope failure on venusian domes are the result of localized volatile accumulations and the oversteepening of slopes during dome growth (Fig. 27). The formation of a chilled carapace composed of angular blocks during the growth of venusian domes, will produce slopes predisposed to progressive failure along joints and other discontinuities. The internal stresses within a growing dome, combined with external factors such as the nature of the local topography will control the magnitude and frequency of slope failures. The majority of slope failures appear to have occurred after domes had cooled, and were solid. Some large slope failures were probably seismically triggered. The characteristics of deposits suggest that different forms of mass movement have occurred. The deposits in G1 and G2 have characteristics similar to those of terrestrial volcanic debris avalanche deposits, while those in G3 are similar to terrestrial pyroclastic flow deposits. The characteristics of G4 are analogous to deep-seated slides on Earth.

Conclusion

A range of modified dome morphologies occurs on Venus. The majority of domes on Venus are an order of magnitude larger in diameter than sub-aerial domes on Earth. Five sub-categories of modified domes can be recognized that have the common characteristic of scalloped margins. Domes are more common on Venus than has previously been proposed. Mass movement deposits associated with domes on Venus can

be divided into four distinct morphologies. Each morphological group possesses unique surface textures and plan-forms, and has distinctive morphometric characteristics. The deposits in groups one and two have average travel distances greater than 40 km and the lowest coefficients of friction of the four groups, while deposits in group four have the smallest average travel distances and highest coefficients of friction.

Slope failures on venusian domes appear to have been triggered by explosive and non-explosive events. The conditions on Venus will inhibit the sub-surface exsolution of volatiles, so for pyroclastic events to occur, magma volatile contents must exceed 5% in the lowlands. Unless the volatile content and initial eruption temperatures are high, then the formation of a convective plume will be unlikely and the dense atmosphere will favour the production of ground-hugging flows. Domes with large downsags indicate that volatiles were released through non-explosive degassing, though small pit craters are likely to have formed by explosion resulting from localized volatile concentrations. The smooth surface textures and confined plan-forms of deposits in group three are similar to terrestrial pyroclastic flows. These are thought to have occurred during the emplacement of a dome from the collapse of blocks on the dome margins, or through localized volatile enhancement building stresses greater than the tensile strength of the local rock resulting in an explosively directed blast. The surface textures and plan-forms of the deposits in groups one and two are similar to volcanic debris avalanche deposits on Earth. These have long travel distances, low coefficients of friction and cover large areas. The characteristics of the fourth group of deposits are similar to those resulting from deep-seated slides on Earth. The largest of these removed substantial volumes of material. The blocky nature of deposits indicates that those in groups one, two and four were emplaced after the dome had cooled following the cessation of an eruption. Slope failures are likely to have occurred along structural discontinuities. The characteristics of domes and their associated deposits suggest they are composed of a relatively homogeneous rock.

References

BEGET, J. E., & KIENLE, J. 1992. Cyclic formation of debris avalanches at Mount St Augustine volcano. *Nature*, **356**, 701–704

BRUNSDEN, D. 1979. Mass movements. *In*: EMBLETON, C. & THORNES, J. B. (eds) *Process in Geomorphology*. Arnold, London.

BULMER, M. H. 1994. *An examination of small volcanoes in the plains of Venus; with particular reference to the evolution of domes.* PhD Thesis, University of London, Senate House, England.

——, ——, BERATAN, K., MICHAELS, G. & SAUNDERS, S. 1992a. Debris avalanches and slumps on the margins of volcanic domes on Venus: characteristics of deposits (abstract). *International Colloquium on Venus.* Lunar & Planetary Institute Contribution, **789**, 14–15.

——, ——, MICHAELS, G. & SAUNDERS, S. 1993. Scalloped margins domes: What are the processes responsible and how do they operate? (abstract). *Lunar and Planetary Science*, **24**, 215–216.

——, —— & STOFAN, E. R. 1992b. Calderas on Venus (abstract). *Lunar Planetary Science*, **23**, Part 1, 177–178.

CAS, R. A. F. & WRIGHT, J. V. 1987. *Volcanic Successions.* Allen and Unwin, Winchester, Mass.

COTECCHIA, V. 1989. Earthquake-prone environments. *In*: ANDERSON, M. G. & RICHARDS, K. S. (eds) *Slope stability.* Geotechnical Engineering and Geomorphology, J. Wiley & Sons, Chichester, 287–330.

CROZIER, M. J. 1991. Determinatin of palaeoseismicity from landslides. *In*: BELL (ed.) *Landslides.* Balkema, Rotterdam.

EPPLER, D. B., FINK, J. & FLETCHER, R. 1987. Rheologic properties and kinematics of emplacement of the Chaos Jumbles rockfall avalanche, Lassen volcanic National Park, California. *Journal of Geophysical Research*, **92**(B5), 3623–3633.

FINK, J. H. & KIEFFER, S. W. 1993. Estimate of pyroclastic flow velocities resulting from explosive decompression of lava domes. *Nature*, **363**, 612–615.

FISHER, R. V., GLICKEN, H. X. & HOBLITT, R. P. 1987. May 18, 1980. Mount St. Helens deposits in South Coldwater Creek, Washington. *Journal of Geophysical Research*, **92**, 10 267–10 283.

FOQUE, L. & STRECKER, M. R. 1988. Large rock avalanche deposits (Sturzstrome, sturzstroms) at Sierra Aconquija, northern Sierras Pameanas, Argentina. *Eclogae Geolicae Helvetiquw*, **81**(3), 579–592.

FRANCIS, P. W. & SELF, S. 1987. Collapsing volcanoes. *Scientific American*, **256**, 90–97.

——, ROOBOL, M. J., WALKER, G. P. L., COBOLD, P. R. & COWARD, M. P. 1974. The San Pedro and San Pablo volcanoes of North Chile and their hot avalanche deposits. *Geologische Rundschau*, **63**, 357–388.

GLICKEN, H., VOIGHT, B. & JANDA, R. J. 1981. Rock-slide debris avalanche of May 18, 1980, Mount St. Helens volcano (abstract). *IAVCEI Symposium on Arc Volcanism, Tokyo and Hakone*, **22**, 109–110.

GORSHKOV, G. S. 1959. Gigantic eruption of the volcano Bezymianny. *Bulletin of Vulcanology*, **20**, 77–112.

GUEST, J. E., BULMER, M. H., AUBELE, J. *ET AL.* 1992a. Small volcanic edifices and volcanism in the plains of Venus. *Journal of Geophysical Research*, **97**(E8), part 2 15 949–15 966.

——, ——, BERATAN, K., MICHAELS, G., DESMARIS, K. & WEITZ, C. 1991. Slope failure of the margins of volcanic domes on Venus (abstract). *EOS Transactions American Geophysical Union*, **72**, 278–279.

——, ——, ——, —— & SAUNDERS, S. 1992b. Gravitational collapse of the margins of volcanic domes on Venus (abstract). *Lunar and Planetary Science*, **23**, Part 1, 461–462.

——, CHESTER, D. K. & DUNCAN, A. M. 1984. The Valle Del Bove, Mount Etna: its origin and relation to the stratigraphy and structure of the volcano. *Journal of Volcanology and Geothermal Research*, **21**, 1–23.

HAZLETT, R. W., SCANDONE, R. & BUESCH, D. 1991. Unusual slope failures and related deposits of the 1944 eruption of Mount Vesuvius, Italy. *Journal of Volcanology and Geothermal Research*, **47**, 249–264.

HEAD, J. W. & WILSON, L. 1986. Volcanic processes and landforms on Venus: Theory, predictions, and observations. *Journal of Geophysical Research*, **91**, 9407–9446.

——, CRUMPLER, L. S., AUBLELE, J. C., GUEST, J. E. & SAUNDERS, R. S. 1992. Classification of volcanic features and structures, associations, and global distribution from Magellan data. *Journal of Geophysical Research*, **97**(E8), 13 153–13 198.

HEIM, A. 1932. *Bergsturz und Menschenleben.* Fretz und Wasmuth, Zurich.

HUTCHINSON, J. N. 1968. Mass movement. *In*: FAIRBRIDGE, R. W. (ed.) *Encyclopedia of Earth Sciences.* Reinhold, New York, 688–695.

KEEFER, D. K. 1984. Landslides caused by earthquakes. *Geological Society of America Bulletin*, **95**, 406–421.

LIPMAN, P. W., BANKS, N. G. & RHODES, J. M. 1985. Gas-release induced crystallization of 1984 Mauna Loa magma, Hawaii, and effects on lava rheology. *Nature*, **317**, 604–607.

——, NORMARK, W. R., MOORE, J. G., WILSON, J. & GUTMACHER, C. E. 1988. The giant submarine Alika debris slide, Mauna Loa, Hawaii. *Journal of Geophysical Research*, **93**, 4279–4299.

MACDONALD, G. A. 1972. *Volcanoes.* Prentice-Hall, Englewood Cliffs, New Jersey.

MOORE, J. G., CLAGUE, D. A., HOLCOMB, R. T., LIPMAN, P. W., NORMARK, W. R. & TORRESAN, M. E. 1989. Prodigious submarine landslides on the Hawaiian Ridge. *Journal of Geophysical Research*, **94**, 17 465–17 484.

NAKADA, S. & FUJII, T. 1993. Preliminary report on the activity at Unzen Volcano (Japan), November 1990–November 1991: Dacite lava domes and pyroclastic flows. *Journal of Volcanology and Geothermal Research*, **54**, 319–333.

NEALL, V. E. 1979. *Sheets P19, P20 and P21, New Plymouth, Egmont, and Manaia* (1st edn). Geological map of New Zealand 1 : 500 000, three maps and notes. NZ Dept. Sci. Ind. Res., Wellington.

NEUMANN VAN PADANG, M. 1933. De uitbarsting van den Merapi (Midden Java). *In*: *de jaren 1930–31. Ned. Indes. Dienst Mijnbouwk. Vulkan. Seism. Mededel.*, 12.

PAVRI, B., HEAD, J. W., KLOSE, K. B. & WILSON, L. 1992. Steep sided domes on Venus: Characteristics, geological setting, and eruption conditions from Magellan data. *Journal of Geophysical Research*, **97**(E8), 13 445–13 478.

PERRIN, N. D. & HANCOX, G. T. 1992. Landslide-dammed lakes in New Zealand – preliminary studies on their distribution, causes and effects. *Proceedings of Sixth Internatational Symposium on Landslides, Christchurch*. 1–10.

SATO, H., FUJII, T. & NAKADA, S. 1992. Crumbling of dacite dome lava and generation of pyroclastic flows at Unzen volcano. *Nature*, **360**, 664–666.

SHALLER, P. J. 1991. *Analysis and Implications of Large Martian and Terrestrial Landslides*. PhD Thesis. California Institute of Technology.

SHARPE, C. F. S. 1938. *Landslides and Related Phenomena*. Columbia University Press, New York.

SHREVE, R. L. 1968. *The Blackhawk Landslide*. Geological Society of America, Special Paper, **108**, 47.

SIEBERT, L. 1984. Large volcanic debris avalanches: Characteristics of source areas, deposits, and associated eruptions. *Journal of Volcanology and Geothermal Research*, **22**, 163–197.

SPARKS, R. J. S. 1978. The dynamics of bubble formation and growth in magmas: a review and analysis. *Journal of Volcanology and Geothermal Research*, **3**, 1–37.

SWANSON, D. A., DZURISIN, D., HOLCOMB, R. T. ET AL. 1987. Growth of the lava dome at Mount St Helens, Washington. *In*: FINK, J. H. (ed.) *The Emplacement of Silicic Domes and Lava Flows*. Geological Society of America, Special Paper, **212**, 1–16.

TERZAGHI, K. 1960. Mechanism of landslides. *In*: *Application of Geology to Engineering practice*. Berkeley volume, Geological Society of America, 83–123.

——1962. Stability of steep slopes on hard unweathered rock. *Geotechnique*, **12**, 251–270.

THORNHILL, G. D. 1993. Theoretical modelling of eruption plumes on Venus. *Journal of Volcanology and Geothermal Research*, **98**(E5), 9107–9111.

UI, T. 1983. Volcanic dry avalanche deposits – identification and comparison with nonvolcanic debris stream deposits. *Journal of Volcanology and Geothermal Research*, **18**, 135–150.

VAN BEMMELEN, R. W. 1949. *The geology of Indonesia and adjacent archipelago*. The Hague: Government Printing Office.

VOIGHT, B., GLICKEN, H., JANDA, R. J. & DOUGLASS, P. M. 1981. Catastrophic rockslide avalanche on May 18. *In*: LIPMAN, P. W. & MULLINEAUX, D. R. (eds) *The 1980 Eruption of Mount St. Helens, Washington*. US Geological Survey Professional Paper, **1250**, 347–378.

WALKER, G. P. L. & MCBROOME, L. A. 1983. Mount St. Helens 1980 and Mount Pelee 1902 – flow or surge? *Geology*, **11**, 571–574.

WILLIAMS, H. 1932. *The History and Character of Volcanic Domes*. University of California Berkeley, Bulletin of the Department of Geological Science, **21**.

WILSON, R. C. & KEEFER, D. K. 1985. Predicting areal limits of earthquake-induced landsliding. *In*: ZIONY, J. I. (ed.) *Evaluating Earthquake Hazards in the Los Angeles Region – An Earth-Science Perspective*. US Geological Survey Professional Paper, **136**, 317–345.

Spectral analysis of volcanic tremor associated with the 1993 paroxysmal events at Stromboli

ROBERTO CARNIEL, SIRO CASOLO & FRANCO IACOP

Dipartimento di Georisorse e Territorio - Università di Udine,
Via Cotonificio, 114, 33100 Udine, Italy

Abstract: The year 1993 was characterized by three paroxysmal phases at Stromboli: two (February and October) consisted of a series of violent explosions, the third (May) of strong Strombolian activity, accompanied by a small lava flow. Here we investigate the characteristics of the tremor before, during and after these paroxysmal phases. One evident feature is that the three phases analysed are significant expressions of the Strombolian activity. In fact, they mark a considerable change in the dynamics of the volcano. The energy content, both in terms of volcanic tremor and of number of events drops to very low values after the periods of intense activity. Concerning the evolution of the spectral content of the tremor before the paroxysmal phases, there seems to be a concentration of energy in the low frequency range (below 5 Hz for the crisis in May; below 3 Hz for the February and October events), with clearly identifiable peaks in some cases, while after the crisis the spectrum becomes again much more scattered. This transition, especially in the case of the strong explosions of February and October, happens abruptly. A continuous monitoring of the spectral content of volcanic tremor on Stromboli can therefore be a useful tool to identify the beginning of an instability which may lead to a paroxysmal phase.

Stromboli volcano, one of the Aeolian islands, is located north of Sicily and exhibits a permanent activity which has been reported for thousands of years. This activity results, from the seismic point of view, in a considerable number of explosion-quakes (several per hour) and in persistent volcanic tremor.

One of the most interesting features of Stromboli is the well-known persistence of its craters (Washington 1917) which remained practically unchanged through a number of strong eruptive episodes, despite their relatively small size. Also the seismicity shows a considerable stability and long-term monitoring of its behaviour is essential in order to understand the dynamics of the volcano, and therefore to determine its actual risk (Schick & Müller 1985). There are a number of waveforms that appear again and again in the explosion-quakes (Peterschmitt & Tazieff 1962; Fadeli 1984; Beinat *et al.* 1988; Falsaperla *et al.* 1989). Although each of these 'morpho-types' can be linked to a particular crater, the problem of the automatic association of the explosion-quakes to the crater of origin remains quite difficult, particularly because not all the external explosions produce appreciable seismic waves (Carniel & Iacop 1994). New results in this sense come from broad-band recordings, obtained using seismometers with a much wider response in the long period range (Neuberg *et al.* 1994; Dreier *et al.* 1994). In any case, the tagging of the activity to the different vents would be a useful tool for de-veloping a model for Stromboli and therefore permitting

prediction of its behaviour (Settle & McGetchin 1980). Other features are associated with the explosions, such as air-waves (Braun & Ripepe 1993) and characteristic dynamics of the emission of ejecta at the different craters (Ripepe *et al.* 1993). Many of these phenomena suggest, in terms of stability, independent and long conduits for the different craters, connection of which is assumed to be quite deep in the basement (Riuscetti 1994).

With regard to tremor near the time of a paroxysmal phase, a description of the June–October 1990 crisis, which ended with a small lava flow, is presented in Riuscetti (1992), where the presence of a spectral line just below 4 Hz is highlighted in the tremor samples before eruption and a decrease of the amplitude of the tremor after the eruption is observed, with spectra appearing to be due to a source of radiating waves with a 'coloured Gaussian distribution' (Schick & Riuscetti 1973).

The station and the data

A one-component seismic station (Beinat *et al.* 1989) was installed by our department near the summit of Stromboli volcano in October 1989, mainly in order to monitor the ground motion connected with the explosion-quakes. The hardware was upgraded in 1992 to a full three-component station (Beinat *et al.* 1994) which is now recording, besides the triggered events caused by the explosions, regular samplings of

From McGuire, W. J., Jones, A. P. & Neuberg, J. (eds) 1996, *Volcano Instability on the Earth and Other Planets,* Geological Society Special Publication No. 110, pp. 373–381.

the persistent tremor, which surely contains as much information as the stronger quakes.

The year 1993 was characterized by three paroxysmal phases. Two of these, on 10 February and 16 October, consisted of a series of violent explosions which ejected a considerable amount of pyroclastic material towards the path leading to 'Pizzo sopra la Fossa', a popular tourist place. The other, which developed during the course of May, was characterized by a small lava flow in the 'usual' direction of 'Sciara del Fuoco'. Here we investigate the characteristics of the seismicity before, during and after these paroxysmal phases.

The data analysed in this work were recorded by the three-component seismic station, sited at 800 m a.m.s.l., approximately 300 m from the craters area (see Fig. 1). The sensors are three Willmore MK III tuned to a natural period of 2 seconds, placed on a concrete basement. Seismic data are transmitted analogically to a receiving site (see Fig. 1) located in the village of Stromboli, where the analogue-to-digital conversion is accomplished by a 80386 PC with a Keithley DAS8 board, with 12 bit resolution and a dynamic range of 68 dB at a sampling frequency of 80 Hz, after an anti-alias filtering at 25 Hz.

The trigger for discriminating explosion-quakes is based on the verification of two distinct conditions which are checked on consecutive 1 second windows. The first condition uses a combined amplitude–frequency threshold, while the second is based on the classical STA/LTA algorithm (Allen 1982), i.e. on the ratio between the integral of the wave within the time window and the integral of a tremor sample.

While the explosion-quake acquisition is triggered, the volcanic tremor is sampled regularly; samplings are 60 seconds long, corresponding to 4800 points, and are recorded every 60 minutes.

Summary of 1993 activity

The seismic station is permanently recording explosion-quakes and volcanic tremor, offering a unique opportunity to study the long-term behaviour of the dynamics of the volcano. Reports on the seismic activity are regularly published in the *Bulletin of the Global Volcanism Network of the Smithsonian Institution*.

Figure 2 summarizes the seismic activity of 1993. In the plot, the line indicates daily tremor intensity, the shaded bars show the number of recorded events per day, and the solid bars the number of saturating explosion-quakes (i.e. those characterized by ground velocities exceeding 100 μm/s). The gaps in the plot indicate periods when the seismic station was not acquiring data, mainly due to power problems during the winter (actually, this is a result of a compromise between solar cell efficiency and security against vandalism). It is worth stressing that all the features of the recording system, e.g. the amplification gain and the trigger algorithm, have remained constant throughout the year. At first sight, one can immediately notice how the general behaviour is characterized by three main discontinuities, in February, May, and October respectively, which seem to be exceptional events for the normal Strombolian activity.

The most evident feature is that the daily average of tremor amplitude drops to very low values after the examined periods. In particular, this is very abrupt after the explosions of February and October. It is also interesting to note that the February crisis happened when the tremor level was practically stable. The May lava flow followed a period of increasing activity, while the October explosions interrupted a period in which the tremor level was characterized by a slowly decreasing trend. This observation leads to the conclusion that the trend in the mean tremor amplitude recorded by our 2 second instrument is by itself not suitable to forecast possible paroxysmal phases.

As previously mentioned, besides mean tremor level, we also monitor the long-term behaviour of other parameters, such as the total number of explosion-quakes recorded by the

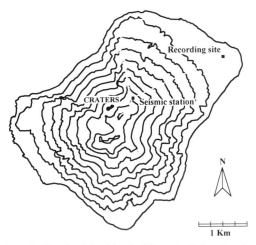

Fig. 1. Sketch of the island of Stromboli showing the position of the seismic station, where the seismometer is located, and of the recording site, where the analogue to digital conversion, triggering, and recording take place.

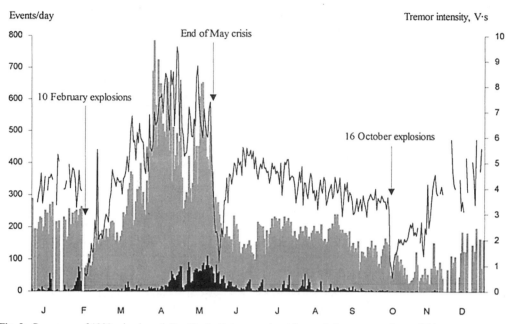

Fig. 2. Summary of 1993 seismic activity. Shaded bars: number of recorded events per day; solid bars: events with ground velocities exceeding 100 μm/s. The curve is a measure of the daily tremor intensity, obtained by integrating the absolute value of the signal over the 60 second samples and then averaging over each day. The gaps in the plot indicate periods when the seismic station was not acquiring data, mainly due to power problems during the winter.

seismic station, and the number of stronger events that saturate the acquisition system. These two quantities also drop to quite low values after the three 1993 crises, suggesting that seismic activity as a whole decreases after the paroxysmal phases.

Spectral analysis

In order to understand how seismic energy is spread across the frequency spectrum during the periods before and after the paroxysmal phases, a mixed radix Fourier transform (Elliott & Rao 1982) was carried out on the 60 second tremor samples recorded every hour. After removing possible DC offsets, the samples were multiplied by a Hanning window in order to avoid the leakage effect generated by the discontinuities at the edges. In order to smooth the results of the amplitude spectra, and at the same time reduce the effect of short-lived spectral peaks, a daily average was computed on the resulting hourly spectra. Three-dimensional plots of the daily spectra were then constructed, including several days before and after each paroxysmal phase (see Figs. 3–5).

The February crisis

The first crisis of 1993 consisted of a short series of violent explosions which occurred from the summit craters on 10 February at 16.10 GMT, ejecting a large tephra column. Lithic blocks and lava fragments fell 1 km from the summit and heavy ashfall occurred at the village of Ginostra, about 2 km SW of the summit (GVN 1993a). The seismic activity showed a very abrupt decrease after the explosions. This is also confirmed by records made at other seismic stations in the island (GVN 1993a).

In order to investigate the change in the spectral content, 15 daily spectra were computed for several days ranging from 15 December 1992 to the day of the explosions, and seven more spectra belonging to the period from the explosions to 1 April 1993. The spectral analysis shows that for all three components of the ground motion there is, during the period leading to the strong explosions, a trend towards the concentration of seismic energy at frequencies below 3 Hz. This concentration suddenly disappears after the crisis, when the spectra become much more scattered over the whole frequency range and much more similar

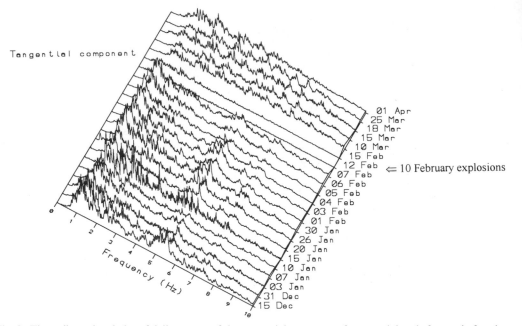

Fig. 3. Three-dimensional plot of daily spectra of the tangential component for several days before and after the paroxysmal phase of February 1993. Note the concentration of the seismic energy at frequencies below 3 Hz and the appearance of a peak at around 1.25 Hz before the crisis. The spectrum again becomes much more scattered over the whole frequency range after the explosions of 10 February.

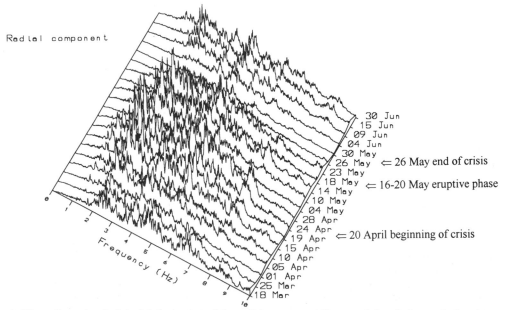

Fig. 4. Three-dimensional plot of daily spectra of the radial component for several days before and after the paroxysmal phase of May 1993. Note the concentration of the seismic energy at frequencies below 6.5 Hz and the appearance and disappearance of a peak at around 7.8 Hz before the crisis. The spectrum again becomes much more scattered over the whole frequency range after the crisis.

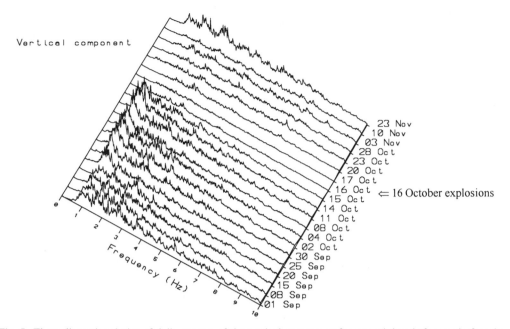

Fig. 5. Three-dimensional plot of daily spectra of the vertical component for several days before and after the paroxysmal phase of October 1993. Note the similarity with the crisis in February: concentration of the seismic energy at frequencies below 3 Hz and appearance of a peak at around 1 Hz before the crisis. The spectrum again becomes much more scattered over the whole frequency range after the explosions of 16 October.

to the spectra computed during the period long before the paroxysmal phase.

In particular, the vertical and the tangential components show relevant peaks which build up during the period preceding the crisis and suddenly disappear after the explosions. This behaviour is evident for a peak centred at about 1 Hz for the vertical component, while the frequency at which the major tangential component peak is centred is slightly greater, about 1.25 Hz (see Fig. 3). The distribution of the radial component spectrum is a bit wider, with most of the energy concentrated around 2 Hz.

The May crisis

It is not as easy to delimit in time the May crisis as it is for the one in February. In fact, there was a period of very high Strombolian activity which ranged approximately from 20 April to 26 May 1993. This activity culminated in a small lava flow which issued from the base of a cone in the NE crater. During the night the flow travelled about 30 m down the slope, reaching the feeding fissure of the 1985 eruption before stopping. The flow then resumed on 18 May, covering about

60 m of 1985 lava NE towards the very steep slope called the 'Sciara del Fuoco' (GVN 1993b).

The end of the crisis was characterized by a slow decay of the tremor intensity, which lasted five or six days, and was accompanied by a similar decay of the number of recorded shocks; the difference with respect to the end of the February crisis was mainly due to the rate of this decay. For the spectral analysis of the crisis, seven daily spectra were computed ranging from 18 March to 19 April, i.e. before the beginning of the period of high Strombolian activity. Although there are not such evident peaks in the low frequency range (below 2 Hz) as for the February crisis, the spectra seem to evolve from scattered to more concentrated over the whole low frequency range (less than about 5 Hz for the vertical component, and 6.5 for the horizontal ones). This trend continues in the eight daily spectra corresponding to the days of high Strombolian activity, i.e. from 24 April to 26 May. Moreover, during this period higher frequency peaks appear in the vertical (about 8.7 Hz) and in the radial (about 7.8 Hz, see Fig. 4) component. These peaks are less evident during the days just before the lava flow, then reappear, and finally disappear again after the end of the crisis. No significant peaks appear in the frequency range above 6.5 Hz in the tangential component. In fact, the five daily spectra shown for the period following the paroxysmal phase (from 30 May to 30 June) indicate a trend towards a much more scattered spectral content, which at the end becomes quite similar to that recorded in March.

The October crisis

The last crisis of 1993 happened in October. Two strong explosions felt at 1.10 GMT on 16 October destroyed the small spatter cone that was built during the October 1990 eruption. Large blocks and spatter up to 2 m in diameter were ejected as far as 500 m from the crater, and

reddish ash fell on the NW slope of the volcano along the Sciara del Fuoco. One woman was injured by hot ashes near the crater area and some bushes caught fire along the slopes (GVN 1993c).

This crisis seems to be very similar to the one in February. The spectral analysis was carried out by computing 12 daily spectra in the period before the crisis, i.e. from 1 September to 15 October. Here the same behaviour described for the February crisis was observed; in the vertical (see Fig. 5) and in the tangential component a clear organization of a peak can be seen, centred at frequencies which are the same as in the February crisis, i.e. about 1 Hz for the vertical, 1.25 Hz for the tangential component. Moreover, the distribution of the radial component spectrum is again characterized by a concentration around 2 Hz, with no evident peaks. The

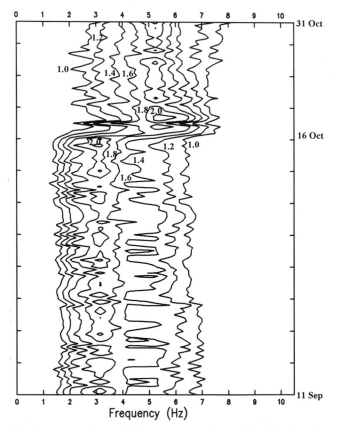

Fig. 6. Contour plot of hourly spectra of the radial component before and after the October crisis. The data are mean values S_j of 1 Hz wide sectors normalized by the mean value S_{tot} computed over the whole range. Time averages of ten samples were then taken in order to smooth the plot. Note the construction of a peak at the 3 Hz sector, which disappears immediately after the explosions of 16 October, 1.10 GMT to give birth to another one, centred at about 5 Hz.

other peaks which were present between 1 and 4 Hz before the February explosion, especially in the vertical component, are not evident in the period before the October crisis, although a general concentration of the spectral content towards the low frequency range (below 3 Hz) can be recognized.

Just as happened after the February explosions, an abrupt decay of all features of the seismic activity, i.e. tremor intensity and number of recorded explosion-quakes, follows the explosions of 16 October. The decrease is so abrupt that only one hour after the explosions the tremor level is almost at the detection limit of the instruments. The spectral content once again becomes much more spread over the whole examined frequency range. The eight daily tremor spectra shown for the following days (from 16 October to 23 November) indicate a slow return of the spectral content towards the state which existed prior to the October crisis.

Another type of analysis was conducted for the October crisis, in order to better investigate both the build up of the spectral content before the explosions, and the abrupt change after them. This was suggested by the fact that peaks evident during the paroxysmal phases could be simply masked by the low tremor level after the crisis. All hourly sampled tremor data recorded by the summit seismic station from 11 September to 31 October were analysed individually. After the usual DC offset removal and Hanning windowing, the amplitude spectra were computed. The frequency ranging from 0.5 to 10.5 Hz was then divided into ten 1 Hz wide sectors, and the mean value S_j of the amplitude in each sector was computed. Additionally, the mean value S_{tot} over the whole range 0.5–10.5 Hz was evaluated; this was used to normalize the sector mean value in order to determine the relative weight S_j/S_{tot} of each sector with respect to the global mean value. Finally, a contour plot of the time evolution of this ratio was prepared for each component after smoothing irregularities by averaging ten consecutive hourly values in order to reduce instant effects.

The plots relative to the vertical and to the tangential component again show a peak which is growing in correspondence to the sector centred at 1 Hz. After the strong explosions of 16 October, this peak suddenly disappears, thus confirming that the sparseness of the spectrum after the crisis is not a consequence of the difficulty in identifying patterns in low level tremor. The analysis of the plot relative to the radial component (see Fig. 6) shows a feature less evident from the previous daily non-normalized analysis, i.e. the construction of a

peak at the sector centred at 3 Hz, which very abruptly disappears after the explosions to give birth to another one, centred at about 5 Hz. Of course the normalization has to be taken into consideration when trying to explain such behaviour.

Conclusions

In this work we have analysed the three Stromboli paroxysmal phases of 1993. Both from the analysis of the general seismic behaviour throughout the year and from the spectral analysis of volcanic tremor recorded before and after the crises, we conclude that these three episodes constitute singularities in the dynamics of the volcano. Major changes can be observed immediately after these episodes. First of all, the tremor level decreases considerably, at a rate which is very high for the February and October crises and more moderate for the one in May. Secondly, the number of recorded explosion-quakes decreases, thus confirming a general reduction of the seismic activity. Moreover, the spectral analysis shows a drastic change in the spectral content, which becomes much more spread after the paroxysmal phases. This is evident both from the analysis of non-normalized daily averaged spectra and from hourly sector-divided normalized ones.

With regard to the periods preceding the paroxysmal phases, which are the most important as they permit the search for precursors of these phases, previous works have suggested the analysis of time and amplitude distribution of explosion-quakes (Schick & Müller 1985; Falsaperla & Neri 1986); however, no marked modification of seismicity preceded the 1985 eruption, when only slight variations were observed in microearthquakes such as modifications in the amplitude distribution (Ishimoto–Iida law) due to the reduced presence of the smaller explosion-quakes (Falsaperla & Neri 1986). From analysis of the three crises of 1993, a trend towards the concentration of tremor energy in the low frequency range (below 5 Hz) can be generally observed, and in some cases the building up of clear peaks can be recognized which disappear quite abruptly after the crises. This confirms the importance of the spectral analysis of the tremor made clear by the study of the June–October 1990 crisis (Riuscetti 1992), where the transition from a spectrum distribution characterized by a marked multimodality to one dominated by a sharp spectral line below 4 Hz is shown. It is worthwhile stressing that a previous analysis of the amplitude and spectral composition of the tremor before 'normal' eruptions gave different results: 'no precursors of any kind could be found in the composition of the tremor' (Schick & Müller 1985). This might suggest that the change in the spectral content is a forerunner for more energetic explosions.

With regard to interpreting this change in the spectral content, i.e less narrow peaks which are centred at slightly different frequencies for the different components, the simple explanation of a resonance effect cannot be supported. Alternatively, we propose a hypothesis within which such peaks are associated with different types of seismic waves, which may originate from different sources.

From a dynamic point of view, the volcano appears to evolve from a 'stable' situation to a critical 'unstable' one via a slow modification which is highlighted by the change in the frequency content. The critical state is then abandoned to return to another stable state by means of a rapid transition accompanied by paroxysmal external activity. Moreover, the behaviour we observe in the seismic activity, i.e. an abrupt fall after the paroxysmal phases followed by a slower re-establishment of a 'normal' level of activity which then evolves towards a new crisis, can be considered distinctive of the Strombolian activity with respect to seismic energy radiation.

The results presented here are not in themselves sufficient to demonstrate that a change in the frequency content of the tremor is a precursor of a crisis. They do suggest, however, that continuous monitoring of the spectral content of Stromboli volcanic tremor provides a useful tool for 'pattern recognition' which may permit identification of the onset of instability which may lead to a paroxysmal phase.

The authors wish to thank Jürgen Neuberg and an anonymous referee for critically reviewing the manuscript. This work was carried out with the financial support of the Gruppo Nazionale di Vulcanologia – CNR, Italy.

References

ALLEN, R., 1982. Automatic phase pickers: their present use and future prospects. *Bulletin of the Seismology Society of America*, **72**(6), S225–S242.

BEINAT, A., CARNIEL, R. & IACOP, F. 1994. Seismic station of Stromboli: 3-component data acquisition system. *ESC Workshop, Dynamical Behaviour of Strombolian Activity*, Stromboli, Italy, 13–18 May 1992. *Acta Vulcanologica*, **5**, 221–222.

——, IACOP, F., RIUSCETTI, M. & SALEMI, G. 1988. Caratterizzazione statistica dell'attività sismica di Stromboli. Atti VII Conv. Gr. Naz. Geofisica Terra Solida CNR, 1471–1482

——, ——, & ——1989. Studio della sismicità legata all'attività esplosiva di Stromboli. *Bollettino Gruppo Nazionale Vulcanologia CNR*, **I**, 47–53

BRAUN, T. & RIPEPE, M. 1993. Interaction of seismic and air waves recorded at Stromboli volcano. *Geophysical Research Letters*, **20**, 65–68

CARNIEL, R. & IACOP, F. 1994. On the persistency of crater assignment criteria for Stromboli explosion-quakes. *ESC Workshop, Seismic Signals on Active Volcanoes: Possible Precursors of Volcanic Eruptions*, Nicolosi, Italy, 21–25 September 1994 and *Annali di Geofisica*, in press.

DREIER, R., WIDMER, R., SCHICK, R. & ZURN, W. 1994. Stacking of broad-band seismograms of shocks at Stromboli. *Acta Vulcanologica* **5**, 165–172.

ELLIOTT, D. F. & RAO, K. R. 1982. *Fast Transforms: Algorithms, Analyses, Applications*. Academic Press, Orlando.

FADELI, A. 1984. *A Study on the Eruption Mechanism of Volcano Stromboli (Italy)*. Institute of Geophysics, University of Stuttgart, **213**.

FALSAPERLA, S. & NERI, G. 1986. Seismic monitoring of volcanoes: Stromboli (Southern Italy). *Mineralogy*, **55**, 153–163

——, MONTALTO, A. & SPAMPINATO, S. 1989. Analysis of seismic data concerning explosive sequences on Stromboli volcano in 1989. *Bollettino Gruppo Nazionale di Vulcanologia CNR*, **5**, 249–258

GVN 1993a. Stromboli volcanic activity report. *Smithsonian Institution, Bulletin of the Global Volcanism Network*, **18**, 1.

GVN 1993b. Stromboli volcanic activity report. *Smithsonian Institution, Bulletin of the Global Volcanism Network*, **18**, 4.

GVN 1993c. Stromboli volcanic activity report. *Smithsonian Institution, Bulletin Global Volcanism Network*, **18**, 9.

NEUBERG, J., LUCKETT, R., RIPEPE, M. & BRAUN, T. 1994. Highlights from a seismic broadband array on Stromboli volcano. *Geophysical Research Letters*, **21**, 747–752.

PETERSCHMITT, E. & TAZIEFF, H. 1962. Sur un noveau type de secousse volcanique enregistrée au Stromboli. *Comptes Rendus del Academie des Sciences, Paris*, **255**, 1971–1973

RIPEPE, M., ROSSI, M. & SACCOROTTI, G. 1993. Image processing of explosive activity at Stromboli, *Journal of Volcanology and Geothermal Research*, **54**, 335–351.

RIUSCETTI, M. 1994. Seismic activity as monitored by the summit station. *ESC Workshop, Dynamical Behaviour of Strombolian Activity*, Stromboli, Italy, 13–18 May 1992. *Acta Vulcanologica*, **5**, 207–210.

SCHICK, R. & MÜLLER, W. 1985. Volcanic activity and eruption sequences at Stromboli during 1983–1984. *In*: KING, C. & SCARPA, R. (eds) *Modeling of Volcanic Processes*. Friedr. Vieweg & Sohn, Wiesbaden.

—— & RIUSCETTI, M. 1973. An analysis of volcanic tremors at South Italian volcanoes. *Zeitschrift für Geophysik*, **39**, 247–262.

SETTLE, M. & MCGETCHIN, T. R. 1980. Statistical analysis of persistent explosive activity at Stromboli, 1971: implications for eruption prediction, *Journal of Volcanology and Geothermal Research*, **8**, 45–58.

WASHINGTON, H. S. 1917. Persistence of vents at Stromboli and its bearing on volcanic mechanism, *Bulletin of the Geological Society of America*, **26**, 249–275.

Index

DUE DATE